Pocket PC Network Programming

Pocket PC Network Programming

Steve Makofsky

✦ Addison-Wesley

Boston • San Francisco • New York • Toronto • Montreal
London • Munich • Paris • Madrid
Cape Town • Sydney • Tokyo • Singapore • Mexico City

Many of the designations used by manufacturers and sellers to distinguish their products are claimed as trademarks. Where those designations appear in this book, and Addison-Wesley was aware of a trademark claim, the designations have been printed with initial capital letters or in all capitals.

The author and publisher have taken care in the preparation of this book, but make no expressed or implied warranty of any kind and assume no responsibility for errors or omissions. No liability is assumed for incidental or consequential damages in connection with or arising out of the use of the information or programs contained herein.

The publisher offers discounts on this book when ordered in quantity for bulk purchases and special sales. For more information, please contact:

U.S. Corporate and Government Sales
(800) 382-3419
corpsales@pearsontechgroup.com

For sales outside of the U.S., please contact:

International Sales
(317) 581-3793
international@pearsontechgroup.com

Visit Addison-Wesley on the Web: www.awprofessional.com

Library of Congress Cataloging-in-Publication Data

Makofsky, Steve.
    Pocket PC network programming / Steve Makofsky.
       p.   cm.
    ISBN 0-321-13352-8 (alk. paper)
    1. Pocket computers—Programming.   2. Computer networks.   I. Title.
    QA76.5.M19145 2003
    005.2'762—dc21   2003048067

ISBN 0-321-13352-8
Text printed on recycled paper
1 2 3 4 5 6 7 8 9 10—CRS—0706050403
First printing, July 2003

To Liz, my wife and soul mate.
You are my best friend and the love of my life.

Contents

Chapter 8   **Pocket PC Phone Edition** **267**

Chapter 9   **Desktop Syncrhonization** **335**

Figures

Preface

Get busy living, or get busy dying.

—*Andy Dufresne*, The Shawshank Redemption

Every once in a while, new technologies emerge that profoundly change the way we conduct our daily lives. A recent example is the "invasion" of the cellular phone. Once thought to be just a "toy for the rich," cell phones are now an essential (and some would say bothersome) part of everyday life—in fact, I know several people who have replaced their home phones exclusively with cell phones. Over the last few years, Personal Digital Assistants (PDAs) have been slowly changing the way people manage their personal information and the way they communicate.

When Microsoft originally launched the Windows CE operating system in 1996 with the Handheld PC, people were not quite sure what to make of these "mini-computers," and questioned whether they would actually replace notebooks and paper organizers. Over the last few years, they have slowly made their way through the back doors of companies as people begin to realize the potential, convenience, and power of having ultraportable computing devices in their pocket, regardless of the strange looks from co-workers. Combined with its capability to communicate on a network with both other devices and the Internet, the mobile device is now recognized as a revolutionary technology.

With the recent advent of higher-speed wireless connections, the true power of the Pocket PC platform can finally be exploited by developers and the users of their applications. Wireless communication is often called the PDA "killer application," and the demand for applications that are networked has skyrocketed.

The mobile device revolution is upon us.

About This Book

This book is both a tutorial and reference guide for writing network applications on Pocket PC 2002 and Pocket PC Phone Edition devices. The term *network application* does not limit the scope of this book only to programs that use the Internet, however. It refers to any type of application that needs to communicate with another device or computer over some form of communications link. Topics such as device synchronization, network protocols and programming, and even writing applications with the new .NET Compact Framework are covered. If you are writing any type of software that falls into those categories, you will likely want this book as part of your reference library.

Although the complexity of the material in this book ranges from beginner to advanced, it is written in a fashion that will enable developers to jump around to whatever topics are of particular interest to them. The book includes a handy "frequently asked questions" list, located on the inside covers of the book, which will help you locate the answers to common questions).

Intended Audience for This Book

Pocket PC Network Programming is written for software developers who understand the basics of writing Pocket PC applications in C/C++ and have written software for these devices before. If you have developed programs with Visual Basic for Windows CE, or have done any type of programming on the Windows platform, you should feel fairly comfortable with the material in this book. This book is *not* intended as an introduction to Pocket PC programming or the basics of Windows CE, but if you have previously written any type of application, you should be able to follow along without much difficulty. In addition, the final chapter covers topics specific to the future of networking applications using C# and the .NET Compact Framework for the Pocket PC.

System Requirements

In order to write software for the Pocket PC 2002 platform, you need to have installed Embedded Visual C++ version 3.0, along with the Pocket PC 2002 Platform SDK. The toolkit and SDK are currently available for free download from http://www.microsoft.com/mobile/developer/downloads.

To work with the .NET Compact Framework (described in Chapter 12), you need to use Visual Studio.NET 2003, which is also available from Microsoft.

Organization of This Book

This book is organized as follows:

- Chapters 1 through 3 focus on writing applications that use the Internet to communicate. This includes the basics of Winsock, WinInet, and the IPHelper APIs, and includes information about popular Internet protocols such as HTTP and FTP.
- Chapter 4 looks at using a Pocket PC device with a Windows-based network, including using network resources such as shared drives and printers.
- Chapter 5 covers aspects of working with both serial and infrared communications.
- Chapters 6 and 7 focus on using the remote access capabilities of the Pocket PC. This includes creating, establishing, and controlling dial-up network connections, as well as detailed information about integrating your application with the Pocket PC Connection Manager.
- Chapter 8 deals exclusively with the Pocket PC Phone Edition and covers topics such as SMS Messaging, GSM, and interacting with the Subscriber Identity Module.
- Chapter 9 describes how to build applications that are designed for synchronization with a desktop computer. Everything from remote control of a device from a desktop to building an ActiveSync synchronization provider is covered here.
- Chapter 10 dives into the Pocket Outlook Object Model and explains how to build applications that seamlessly integrate with contact, application, and task data.
- Chapter 11 describes the Mail API. Everything you ever would want to know about writing e-mail-enabled applications is in this chapter.
- Chapter 12 examines using the new .NET Compact Framework with regard to network applications, .NET Web Services, and interoperating with unmanaged Pocket PC functions.

For Updated Information

Although every effort was made to ensure that this book is accurate and contains no errors, sometimes things do slip through the cracks. If you do find any errors, please check the errata on my Web site at http://www.furrygoat.com. There you will find the most recent changes, source code for the book, as well as my contact information if you have any questions or suggestions.

Acknowledgments

There are so many people to thank for making a project such as this come to life.

The first person that I need to thank is my wife, Liz. Without her support, I simply would not have been able to write this book. She kept me going on the days when I wanted to toss the whole thing in the garbage, and motivated me with her smile to keep on writing. Liz, I love you.

This book would have contained a considerable amount of typos and goofs if it weren't for the diligence of the numerous reviewers who provided invaluable feedback: Jeremy Kercheval, Randy Santossio, Jay Loney, Rick Kingslan, and Kirk Radeck.

A very special thanks is also due to the fantastic staff at Addison-Wesley with whom I worked over the course of the project, including Jessica Goldstein, Emily Frey, Karen Gettman, Curt Johnson, Patrick Cash-Peterson, and Stephane Thomas. My copy editor, Luann Rouff, also deserves a special round of applause—without her, my words would just be a jumbled mess.

I would like to thank my family for all the encouragement and support that they have always given me. Perhaps now that this project is completed, I can find more time to fix your computer problems.

Finally, in no specific order, I would like to thank the following people for just being who you are: Diane Allerdice, Lisa Baratta, Rob and Laura Blanch, Dan and Libby Braband, J. and Denise Broad, Lynn and Bruce Byerly, Lou-Anne Leune, Stacy and Brett Heinemann, Kerensa Long, Tim Lubrano, Rhonell Kercheval, Jennifer and Korby Parnell, Kevin and Maria Perveiler, Chris and Jake Petersen, Shellie Pierce, Stacy and Matthew Ployhar, Nicole Riggs, Fred Ring, Ginger Staffanson, Emily Stevenson, Samantha and Sam Sudore, and Paula Tomlinson.

CHAPTER 1

Winsock

Flying through wormholes ain't like dusting crops, Farm Boy.

—*John Crichton,* Farscape

Welcome to the world of communications and network programming using a Pocket PC device. You probably already know that these devices can perform a wide variety of useful functions—from scheduling to playing MP3s. However, one of the Pocket PC's least utilized features has been its capability to communicate with other devices and consume available services on the Internet.

In the past, getting access to a network usually involved plugging a modem or network card into your device, which typically is not the most portable means of communications. Today, with the advent of wide area wireless networking (using some cellular connection) and home/office wireless (using 802.11b or Bluetooth), connectivity issues have become a thing of the past. From the workplace to the home to the cafe, the Internet is now available everywhere.

As with most technologies, network programming is comprised of a set of building blocks—one piece built on top of another, providing more specific functionality the closer you get to the application level. **Windows Sockets** (also called *Winsock*) is a network application programming interface (API) that simplifies access to the network services of various protocols on your Pocket PC device. On Windows CE, it specifically provides an interface to the Transmission Control Protocol/Internet Protocol (TCP/IP), the network protocol for communications over the Internet; and for infrared communication (IrDA, which is covered in Chapter 5). You can think of TCP/IP as what talks to your network hardware, and Winsock as what your application uses to talk to TCP/IP.

Although most of the core Internet "applications," such as the Web (**Hypertext Transfer Protocol, HTTP**), e-mail (**Simple Mail**

Transfer Protocol, SMTP) and FTP (**File Transfer Protocol**) provide a simplified API using WinInet (see Chapter 2), APIs such as WinInet are *all built on top of Winsock and TCP/IP*. Therefore, it is important to understand how the underlying functionality works in order to build efficient and compelling network applications.

A Quick Look at TCP/IP

To better understand how Winsock works on Pocket PC, it is important to understand how TCP/IP itself is constructed. As mentioned previously, TCP/IP stands for Transmission Control Protocol/Internet Protocol, which typically represents the **Internet Protocol Suite**. The TCP/IP protocol suite is actually a collection of several protocols that form the basis of Internet communications. Table 1.1 describes the TCP/IP protocol suite.

Table 1.1 The TCP/IP Protocol Suite

Protocol	Usage
IP	The **Internet Protocol** is responsible for the addressing, routing and packetization of data. It basically moves data between computers.
TCP	The **Transport Control Protocol** is a reliable connection–based data transport.
UDP	The **User Datagram Protocol** is a connectionless-based data transport that does not guarantee packets will arrive at their destination.
ICMP	The **Internet Control Message Protocol** handles error and control messages.
ARP	The **Address Resolution Protocol** performs IP address to hardware address translation for outgoing packets.

Developing applications that use Winsock on a Pocket PC device will require you to work with and understand the various TCP/IP protocols in order to effectively use networking in your application.

A Breakdown of TCP/IP

When you look at the various parts of TCP/IP, it is typically represented in the **International Standards Organization/Open Systems Interconnect** (ISO/OSI) network model, which divides networks into various layers depending on individual functionality (see Figure 1.1). The combination of each layer provides what is commonly known as the *TCP/IP protocol stack*. Note that the data-link layer and the physical

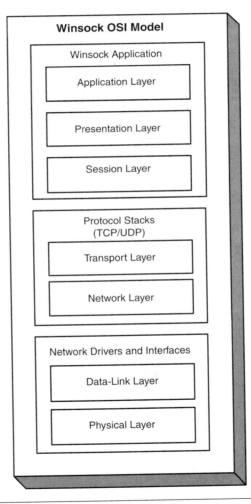

Figure 1.1 The ISO/OSI model

layer are *not* technically part of the Internet Protocol Suite; this is what enables TCP/IP to talk over a variety of network types and mediums.

Let's take a quick look at each of the layers:

Physical: The physical layer is essentially the network hardware. This layer talks directly to the media (wireless, twisted pair cable, and so on) that is carrying the network data.

Data Link: The data-link layer (which is sometimes also called the network driver layer) manages requests to the network interface, and transfers data between the physical and network layers. Most importantly, it also hides the network's physical implementation from the network layer. This ensures that the protocol (in our case, TCP/IP) doesn't care about the specifics of what network technology is being used (such as Ethernet versus WiFi)—it simply passes data back and forth.

Network: The network layer is the core of TCP/IP. It is responsible for the addressing, routing, and packetization of data that it has received from the transport layer over the **Internet Protocol** (**IP**), and for passing it to the data-link layer. The network layer also provides the mapping of IP addresses to hardware addresses via the **Address Resolution Protocol** (**ARP**); the processing of error and control messages through the **Internet Control Message Protocol** (**ICMP**); and the control of multicast communications through the **Internet Group Membership Protocol** (**IGMP**).

Transport: The transport layer is what applications will typically talk to when running Winsock applications, and is sometimes called a **low-level connection**. It provides the transfer of data between a source and destination on the network. Pocket PC supports two transfer protocols: the **Transfer Control Protocol** (**TCP**) and the **User Datagram Protocol** (**UDP**). TCP is a connection-based protocol that reliably streams data from source to destination, whereas UDP is an unreliable, connectionless protocol that uses packets to send data from point A to point B.

Session: The session layer essentially creates a connection, controls it, and then finally closes the communications session. It is also sometimes referred to as a **high-level connection,** and it starts the **upper layer** of the OSI model. A session is usually defined by a specific application protocol, such as Telnet, for establishing and maintaining a connection between a client and a server.

Presentation: The presentation layer basically handles the formatting of data that two applications will use during the course of a session. Transfer protocols, such as FTP, SMTP, and HTTP, are considered part of the presentation layer.

Application: The application layer is what interacts with the user. It is the user interface for your application.

TCP/IP Addresses

In order for a device to talk on a TCP/IP network, it needs a valid network "address." TCP/IP on Pocket PC currently supports IP version 4 (IPv4), whereby network addresses are represented as a 32-bit number, which can be broken down into a **host address** and a **subnet address**. Typically, a user can recognize an IPv4 address by what's more commonly known as **dotted notation**, such as 192.168.0.1.

You should be aware of the following address types:

- **Unicast Address:** A unicast address is typically what is assigned to your device, either through a hard-coded IP address, or one that is assigned to you via a DHCP server. This is the unique address that is used to identify your device on a network.

- **Broadcast Address:** While not recommended, if you need to broadcast data to every device on a local network, you can send data to the address 255.255.255.255. Sending data here is considered a **limited broadcast** because most routers will never forward packets sent to this address. A **directed broadcast** address can also be used to send data to all devices on a specific subnet, such as 192.168.0.x, by sending data to 192.168.0.255. In order send data packets over a broadcast address, you need to set a socket option to accept broadcast communications, as well as use the UDP protocol as described later in the section "Connectionless (UDP) Sockets."

- **Loopback Address:** Any network address that begins with the number 127 is considered a **loopback** address for the device. Typically, the address 127.0.0.1 is used to communicate with itself.

- **Multicast Address:** The best way to think of a multicast address is to think of a "group" address. When you are a part of a multicast group, all of the devices that have joined that group will receive data that is sent to the group address. Multicast groups use a reserved address range from 224.0.0.0 through 239.255.255.255.

Whenever a Winsock function requires a TCP/IP address, it is specified by using the `SOCKADDR_IN` structure, which is defined as follows:

```
struct sockaddr_in {
    short       sin_family;
    u_short     sin_port;
    struct      in_addr sin_addr;
    char        sin_zero[8];
};
```

The `sin_family` parameter represents the address family, and must be set to `AF_INET` to use IP addressing (`AF_IRDA` is available for infrared, which is covered in Chapter 5). The next parameter, `sin_port`, specifies the communications port that you want your protocol, whether TCP or UDP, to talk on. The port typically represents a well-known service, such as HTTP or FTP. The `sin_addr` parameter specifies the IP address and can be either a local address or a remote address, depending on how the field is being used by the Winsock operation. The last parameter, `sin_zero`, is unused and serves as padding for the standard `SOCKADDR` structure.

Ports

As mentioned above, a TCP/IP port represents a specific communications port used by an application protocol to identify a service, such as HTTP or FTP. While you can certainly use any port for your own application, take care not to use the ones that are already defined by the Internet Assigned Numbers Authority (IANA), which are known as **well-known ports** (see Table 1.2).

Table 1.2 Well-Known Ports

Protocol	Port
File Transfer Protocol (FTP)	21
Telnet Protocol	23
Simple Mail Transfer Protocol (SMTP)	25
Trivial File Transfer Protocol (TFTP)	69
Gopher Protocol	70
Finger Protocol	79
Hypertext Transfer Protocol (HTTP)	80
Post Office Protocol (POP3)	110

A list of up-to-date assigned port numbers is available at http://www. iana.org/assignments/port-numbers.
Ports are divided into three basic categories:

- **Well-known ports (0–1023):** These are controlled by the IANA and are reserved for well-known ports.
- **Registered ports (1024–49151):** These ports are listed and controlled by IANA, but they can also be used for normal applications.
- **Dynamic or private ports (49152–65535):** The IANA does not track any applications that use ports in this range.

Therefore, for example, if you are writing an application that needs to read data from a Web server, you will use the well-known port 80. If you need to develop a custom application, it is safe for you to use any port in the range of 1024–49151.

If you are interested in more in-depth details about TCP/IP, IP addressing, and TCP/IP ports, I highly recommend that you read RFC 1180, "A TCP/IP Tutorial," and RFC 1122, "Requirements for Internet Hosts—Communication Layers."

Winsock Basics

Now that we have covered the basics of TCP/IP, let's look at actual Winsock APIs that your application will use to communicate over the network with. To use the Winsock functions in your applications, make sure you include `winsock.h` in your source, and that you link with the `winsock.lib` library.

Initializing and Cleaning Up

The first thing to do in order to use Winsock is to make sure that the correct version of winsock.dll is loaded into memory. Even though Pocket PC currently supports only a subset of Winsock version 1.1, it still needs to be initialized in the same way as its desktop counterpart before it is used. This is done by calling the `WSAStartup()` function, which is defined as follows:

```
int WSAStartup(WORD wVersionRequired, LPWSADATA lpWSAData);
```

The `wVersionRequired` parameter specifies which version of Winsock you want to load. For Pocket PC, this value needs to be version 1.1, which can be created by using the `MAKEWORD(1,1)` macro. The `lpWSAData` parameter is a pointer to a `WSAData` structure that `WSAStartup()` will fill in with information about the version of Winsock that is loaded:

```
typedef struct WSAData {
    WORD       wVersion;
    WORD       wHighVersion;
    char       szDescription[WSADESCRIPTION_LEN+1];
    char       szSystemStatus[WSASYS_STATUS_LEN+1];
    unsigned short iMaxSockets;
    unsigned short iMaxUdpDg;
    char FAR *lpVendorInfo;
} WSADATA;
```

Both the `wVersion` and `wHighVersion` parameters will return the current version of Winsock that is actually loaded into memory, which will be `0x0101`, as only 1.1 is supported. The `szDescription` and `szSystemStatus` parameters are not used on Pocket PC and are `NULL`. The `iMaxSockets` parameter indicates the recommended maximum number of sockets that an application can actually open. There is no guarantee that your application will be able to open this many sockets. The `iMaxUdpDg` parameter specifies the largest size of a UDP datagram packet. If this value is 0, there is no limit in this Winsock version. Finally, the `lpVendorInfo` parameter has a pointer to optional vendor-specific information.

`WSAStartup()` will return 0 if it succeeds; otherwise, it will return an error code.

Before your application closes, you should call the function `WSACleanup()`, which is defined as follows:

```
int WSACleanup(void);
```

However, note that this function doesn't actually do anything, and is there only to maintain compatibility with desktop applications that have been ported to Windows CE.

Winsock Errors

If an error occurs when calling a Winsock function (except `WSAStartup()`, which will return an error code), most functions will return the standard Winsock `SOCKET_ERROR` (defined in `winsock.h` as -1).

To obtain more information about the error that occurred, you can call the function `WSAGetLastError()` to find out why the function failed:

```
int WSAGetLastError (void);
```

The return value will be the error code for the last network error that occurred. If you need to set the last error for any reason (or to set it to 0), you can use the function `WSASetLastError()`:

```
void WSASetLastError (int iError);
```

The parameter `iError` specifies the new error code.

You can find definitions for the individual Winsock error codes in the `winsock.h` header file.

Differences between Windows and Pocket PC Winsock Implementations

Besides the fact that Pocket PC supports only a subset of Winsock version 1.1, note a few other minor differences compared to the desktop implementation:

- **There are no asynchronous socket calls.** There is no support in Pocket PC for desktop function calls such as `WSAAsync Select()` for notification of socket events.
- **There are no service name APIs.** The desktop functions `getservbyname()` and `getservbyport()` are not supported on Pocket PC.
- **There are no protocol name APIs.** The desktop functions `getprotobyname()` and `getprotobynumber()` are not supported on Pocket PC.
- **Unicode and ASCII.** Although data that you send over TCP (and UDP messages) can be Unicode or ASCII (Winsock doesn't care, as long as corresponding support exists on both ends and everything is handled properly), most of the Winsock support functions support ASCII parameters only. You need to convert the Unicode strings to ASCII to use them.
- **Blocking versus nonblocking.** Sockets are in blocking mode by default. You can set a socket to nonblocking mode by setting the correct socket option, as described in the section "Socket Options."
- **Several socket options are not supported.** `IP_MULTICAST_ LOOP`, `SO_ACCEPTCONN`, `SO_RCVLOWAT`, `SO_SNDLOWAT`, `SO_`

`SNDTIMEO`, and the `SO_TYPE` socket options are not supported on Pocket PC.

- **IrDA supports only TCP stream sockets.** Infrared communication via Winsock (covered in Chapter 5) supports using TCP sockets only.
- **Applications can drop UDP packets.** The internal UDP queue buffer size is set to 2. This is a known bug and is documented in Microsoft KB article Q290206.
- **No raw socket support.** There currently is no way to create a raw socket. However, you can use the ICMP support functions described in the section "Internet Control Message Protocol (ICMP)" to send ping data.

Finally, note that Windows CE.NET (Windows CE v4.x) now supports Winsock v2.0.

TCP/IP, ActiveSync, and Pocket PC Emulation Issues

While TCP/IP communications are a great way of enabling a Pocket PC device to network with a desktop, a server, or another Pocket PC device, accessing incoming TCP/IP connections can sometimes be a bit tricky if you are not using a network card or a wireless connection. This is typically true during development stages, when devices are often cradled to a desktop and you use the emulation environment.

Neither the emulator nor the device should have any problems establishing connections to a TCP/IP server (in essence, when the device/emulation is acting as a client or initiating a connection), but external resources will not be able to find the device when the device/emulation itself is waiting for incoming connections (i.e., it's acting as a server).

These problems are caused by the way IP addresses are assigned. The emulator uses a private IP address, and ActiveSync uses a Network Address Table (NAT) for cradled communications. Both render it unreachable from the outside world. You can, however, use the "localhost" address on the device itself to establish a connection within the device. For example, if you are writing an application to respond to HTTP requests, and the application is running in the emulation environment, you could use Pocket Internet Explorer inside the emulator to go to http://localhost to access your server.

This should not affect your device when using a dial-up connection, a wireless connection, or a network card.

Streaming (TCP) Sockets

Streaming (or connection-oriented) sockets are probably the most commonly used type of communication transport protocol over TCP/IP that you will use. TCP sockets provide you with a reliable, nearly error-free data pipe between two endpoints, both of which can send and receive streams of bytes back and forth, without data being lost or duplicated. A good analogy would be to compare a TCP socket connection to a telephone call between devices—one calls another (the phone number being the server device's IP address, and its phone extension being the server device's IP port). Once the other device picks up, a conversation can proceed between the two devices, with both transmitting and receiving data. Finally, the call is completed, and both sides hang up. The connection thus made is known as a communications **session** (this is the same session described previously in the OSI model).

This type of connection between devices is also sometimes referred to as a **client/server model**. One device, known as the client, creates a socket, connects to the server, and then begins sending and receiving data. On the other side, the server creates a socket and listens for an incoming connection from the client. Once a connection is initiated, the server accepts the connection, and then starts to send and receive data to and from the incoming client. The data that the client and server send back and forth is completely up to you; however, several well-known communication protocols have already been established, such as HTTP or FTP.

Figure 1.2 shows the process for creating both client and server TCP socket connections and how data flows between both network endpoints.

Creating a Socket

The first step in establishing a network connection via Winsock is to create a *socket*. A socket is a data type, similar to a file handle, that identifies a unique descriptor that allows access to your network object. What the actual descriptor identifies is not specifically detailed in the Winsock specification; rather, it is determined by the specific Winsock implementation, so we don't really know what that value means. For our purposes, the actual contents of the descriptor are not important. What is important is the understanding that a socket is what you use to access your network connection.

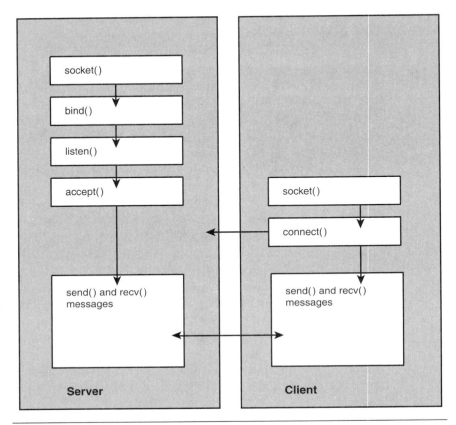

Figure 1.2 Socket process for connection-oriented clients and servers

To create a socket, you use the `socket()` function, which is defined as follows:

```
SOCKET socket (int af, int type, int protocol);
```

The `af` parameter specifies the protocol's address family, which determines what type of socket will be created. Pocket PC supports either the `AF_INET` or `AF_IRDA` socket types. If you wanted to create a socket for infrared communications, you would use `AF_IRDA` (see Chapter 5); otherwise, for normal TCP/IP usage, you would use `AF_INET`. The `type` parameter is the protocol's communication type, and can be either `SOCK_STREAM` or `SOCK_DGRAM`. To create a TCP connection-oriented socket, use `SOCK_STREAM`. When creating a connectionless UDP socket, use `SOCK_DGRAM` (see the section "Connectionless (UDP)

Sockets"). You must use SOCK_STREAM if you are creating a socket to be used for infrared communications. The final parameter, protocol, specifies which protocol to use with the socket. If you want to specify the TCP protocol, you use the value IPPROTO_TCP. Conversely, IPPROTO_UDP specifies the UDP protocol.

When the function returns, you will receive either a new socket handle or the error INVALID_SOCKET. If you want to find out why you could not create a socket, use the WSAGetLastError() function described previously.

The following code shows how to create a connection-oriented socket:

```
// Create a connection-oriented socket
SOCKET s = socket(AF_INET, SOCK_STREAM, IPPROTO_TCP);


// Check to see if we have a valid socket
if(s == INVALID_SOCKET) {
    int iSocketError = WSAGetLastError();
    return FALSE;
}
```

Connecting to a Server (from the Client)

Once you have created a socket, you can use it to establish a connection to a server. This is done by using the connect() function call:

```
int connect (SOCKET s, const struct sockaddr *name, int namelen);
```

The first parameter, s, specifies the socket descriptor that was returned from the socket function. The name parameter is the socket address structure, SOCKADDR_IN, which identifies the server to which we are attempting to connect (see "TCP/IP Addresses"). The namelen parameter is the length of the buffer used for the name parameter.

If you are successful in establishing a connection to the server specified by the name parameter, the function will return a 0; otherwise, a SOCKET_ERROR will occur. To find out more information about why a connection could not be established, call WSAGetLastError(). Remember that you cannot call connect() on a socket that is already connected.

Once a connection has been established, the socket is ready to send and receive data. Note that if a connection is broken during the course of

communications between client and server, your application will need
to discard the old socket and create a new one if it needs to reestablish
communications.

The following example shows how to connect with a server:

```
// First, get the host information
HOSTENT *hostServer = gethostbyname("www.microsoft.com");
if(hostServer == NULL) {
    int iSocketError = WSAGetLastError();
    return FALSE;
}


// Set up the target device address structure
SOCKADDR_IN sinServer;
memset(&sinServer, 0, sizeof(SOCKADDR_IN));
sinServer.sin_family = AF_INET;
sinServer.sin_port = htons(80);
sinServer.sin_addr = *((IN_ADDR *)hostServer>h_addr_list[0]);


// Connect with a valid socket
if(connect(s, (SOCKADDR *)&sinServer, sizeof(sinServer)) ==
    SOCKET_ERROR) {
    int iSocketError = WSAGetLastError();
    return FALSE;
}


// Do something with the socket

closesocket(s);
```

Sending and Receiving Data

Now that we have established a connection to a server, we are ready to
send and receive data between the two network endpoints. On a connection-oriented socket, data can be transmitted in either direction, so both
client and server can use the same methods to communicate data over
the wire.

To transmit data on a connected socket, you use the send() function, which is defined as follows:

```
int send (SOCKET s, const char *buf, int len, int flags);
```

The s parameter is the same socket handle that we previously used with the connect function, and was originally created using the socket() function. The buf parameter is a pointer to a buffer that contains the data we want to send, and its length is specified in the len parameter. The final parameter, flags, is used to affect the way the data is sent, and can be 0 or MSG_DONTROUTE, which specifies that the data should not be routed. Typically, this parameter will be set to 0, as MSG_DONTROUTE is used only for testing or routing messages.

When the send function returns, it will return the number of actual bytes that were sent over the network, or a SOCKET_ERROR if there was some problem in transmitting the data.

To receive data on a socket, you use the recv() function:

```
int recv (SOCKET s, char *buf, int len, int flags);
```

Again, s indicates the socket on which we want to receive data. The second parameter, buf, is the buffer that will receive the data; and its size is specified by the len parameter. Finally, the flags parameter must be set to 0.

The return value for the recv() function is either the number of bytes received or 0, if the connection has been closed. You may also get a SOCKET_ERROR if an error has occurred.

Note that both the send() and recv() functions do not always read or write the exact amount of data you have requested. This is because TCP/IP allocates a limited amount of buffer space for both the outgoing and incoming data queues, and it typically fills up rather quickly. For example, if you request a 10MB file from a Web site, your incoming data queue will **block** (see the section "Socket Options") until you have read the data from the queue (using the recv() function). The same applies when transmitting, so you need to manually ensure that all your outgoing data has been sent. For example, to send a buffer over TCP:

```
// Send a request to the server
char cBuffer[1024] = "";
int nBytesSent = 0;
int nBytesIndex = 0;

// Set up the buffer to send
sprintf(cBuffer, "GET / HTTP/1.0\r\n\r\n");
int nBytesLeft = strlen(cBuffer);
```

```
// Send the entire buffer
while(nBytesLeft > 0) {
   nBytesSent = send(s, &cBuffer[nBytesIndex], nBytesLeft, 0);
   if(nBytesSent == SOCKET_ERROR)
      break;

   // See how many bytes are left. If we still need to send, loop
   nBytesLeft -= nBytesSent;
   nBytesIndex += nBytesSent;
}
```

The following example shows how to use TCP sockets to create a basic client that will connect to a Web page, send a command, and receive the Web site's default HTML page. When it has completed, it will display its contents in a message box. The actual buffer that is returned from the request is shown in Figure 1.3.

Figure 1.3 HTTP response from our request

```
// Initialize Winsock
WSADATA wsaData;

memset(&wsaData, 0, sizeof(WSADATA));
if(WSAStartup(MAKEWORD(1,1), &wsaData) != 0)
    return FALSE;

// Create a connection-oriented socket
SOCKET s = socket(AF_INET, SOCK_STREAM, IPPROTO_TCP);

// Check to see if we have a valid socket
if(s == INVALID_SOCKET) {
    int iSocketError = WSAGetLastError();
    return FALSE;
}

// Get the host information
HOSTENT *hostServer = gethostbyname("www.microsoft.com");
if(hostServer == NULL) {
    int iSocketError = WSAGetLastError();
    return FALSE;
}

// Set up the target device address structure
SOCKADDR_IN sinServer;
memset(&sinServer, 0, sizeof(SOCKADDR_IN));

sinServer.sin_family = AF_INET;
sinServer.sin_port = htons(80);
sinServer.sin_addr =
    *((IN_ADDR *)hostServer>h_addr_list[0]);

// Connect
if(connect(s, (SOCKADDR *)&sinServer, sizeof(sinServer)) ==
    SOCKET_ERROR) {
    int iSocketError = WSAGetLastError();
    return FALSE;
}

// Send a request to the server
char cBuffer[1024] = "";
int nBytesSent = 0;
int nBytesIndex = 0;
```

```
// Set up the buffer to send
sprintf(cBuffer, "GET / HTTP/1.0\r\n\r\n");
int nBytesLeft = strlen(cBuffer);

// Send the entire buffer
while(nBytesLeft > 0) {
   nBytesSent = send(s, &cBuffer[nBytesIndex], nBytesLeft, 0);
   if(nBytesSent == SOCKET_ERROR)
      break;

   // See how many bytes are left. If we still need to send, loop
   nBytesLeft -= nBytesSent;
   nBytesIndex += nBytesSent;
}

// Get the response
TCHAR tchResponseBuffer[1024] = TEXT("\0");
char cResponseBuffer[1024] = "";
BOOL fBreak = FALSE;
int nBytesReceived = 0;

while(!fBreak) {
   nBytesReceived = recv(s, &cResponseBuffer[0], 1024, 0);
   if(nBytesReceived == SOCKET_ERROR)
      break;

   // Convert the data from ANSI to Unicode
   mbstowcs(tchResponseBuffer, cResponseBuffer, nBytesReceived);

   // Show the MessageBox
   MessageBox(NULL, tchResponseBuffer, TEXT("Web Output"), MB_OK);

   // Check to see if this is the end of the HTTP response by
   // looking for \r\n\r\n
   if(_tcsstr(tchResponseBuffer, TEXT("\r\n\r\n")))
      fBreak = TRUE;

   // Clear the buffers
   memset(tchResponseBuffer, 0, 1024);
   memset(cResponseBuffer, 0, 1024);
}

closesocket(s);
WSACleanup();
```

Receiving an Incoming Connection (Server)

The only real difference between transferring data between a client and a server stream connection is how the connection is established (a client makes the connection, a server listens for the connection). Otherwise, both use `send()` and `recv()` to transfer data between the two. Now that we have looked at the client, let's examine how we can create an application that services incoming connection requests (made by a client's call to the `connect()` function). The first thing we need to do is create a socket, in the same way you would a client, by calling the `socket()` function.

Once we have created a socket, instead of connecting to a server, we need to put our new socket into a state in which it can listen for incoming connections. To do this, we need to **bind** the newly created socket with a local address. Create this association by using the `bind()` function:

```
int bind (SOCKET s, const struct sockaddr *addr, int namelen);
```

The first parameter, `s`, is the handle to a new socket created by the `socket()` function, which will be the socket on which you want to wait for connections. The `addr` parameter is a pointer to an address buffer, which is determined by the protocol you want to use, and specifies protocol-specific address information. If you want to use the standard TCP/IP protocol, then you will want to use a `SOCKADDR_IN` buffer (see the section "TCP/IP Addresses"). If you are using infrared, you will use `SOCKADDR_IRDA` instead (see Chapter 5). Finally, `namelen` is the size of the address structure being passed in the `addr` parameter.

If there are no errors, `bind()` will return 0; otherwise, a `SOCKET_ERROR` will occur.

For example, the following binds a TCP connection on port 80 to a socket for all IP addresses on the device:

```
SOCKADDR_IN sListener;
memset(&sListener, 0, sizeof(SOCKADDR_IN));

// Set up the port to bind on
sListener.sin_family = AF_INET;
sListener.sin_port = htons(80);
sListener.sin_addr.s_addr = htonl(INADDR_ANY);
```

```
// Create a TCP socket
SOCKET s = socket(AF_INET, SOCK_STREAM, IPPROTO_TCP);
if(s == INVALID_SOCKET)
   return FALSE;

// Bind to the socket
if(bind(s, (SOCKADDR *)&sListener, sizeof(sListener)) ==
  SOCKET_ERROR) {
   int iSocketError = WSAGetLastError();
   return FALSE;
}
```

You may notice that I used the IP address INADDR_ANY instead of a specific adapter's IP address. Using INADDR_ANY enables us to bind our socket to all available IP addresses on our device, so that incoming connections on any interface will be accepted by our socket.

Once the socket has been bound to some address (or addresses), we need to put the socket into listening mode. This will actually enable the socket to wait for incoming connections:

```
int listen (SOCKET s, int backlog);
```

The parameter s is the bound socket. The backlog parameter specifies the size of the queue for pending incoming connections, and typically is set to SOMAXCONN (on Pocket PC, this is currently limited to two connections). The backlog queue is used when there are several simultaneous incoming connections. When the queue is full, all other requests will be refused until a connection request is removed from the queue by the accept() function.

If there is an error, the listen() function will return SOCKET_ERROR; otherwise, it will return 0.

Finally, to get the socket of the incoming connection, we need to call the accept() function, which is defined as follows:

```
SOCKET accept (SOCKET s, struct sockaddr *addr, int *addrlen);
```

The first parameter is the socket that we have previously placed into listening mode. The next parameter, addr, is a buffer that receives either a SOCKADDR_IN or SOCKADDR_IRDA structure, depending on the protocol used by the socket, which contains information about the incoming connection. The last parameter, addrlen, indicates the size of the structure addr.

You might notice that the accept() function does not return imme-diately. This is because accept() is a *blocking function,* which means that it won't return until a client makes a connection or the listening socket is destroyed (you can also set a socket option to put it into non-blocking mode, which is discussed in the section "Socket Options"). When accept() finally returns, it will return either a new socket handle for the incoming client, or a SOCKET_ERROR. All further communica-tions with the client should be done using this new socket handle, while the original socket continues to listen for more incoming connections.

The following example listens for incoming TCP server connections for a client that is requesting a Web page using HTTP, and returns a basic response to the request:

```
// Initialize Winsock
WSADATA wsaData;

memset(&wsaData, 0, sizeof(WSADATA));
if(WSAStartup(MAKEWORD(1,1), &wsaData) != 0)
   return FALSE;

// Create a connection-oriented socket
SOCKET s = socket(AF_INET, SOCK_STREAM, IPPROTO_TCP);

// Check to see if we have a valid socket
if(s == INVALID_SOCKET) {
   int iSocketError = WSAGetLastError();
   return FALSE;
}

SOCKADDR_IN sListener;
memset(&sListener, 0, sizeof(SOCKADDR_IN));

// Setup the port to bind on
sListener.sin_family = AF_INET;
sListener.sin_port = htons(80);
sListener.sin_addr.s_addr = htonl(INADDR_ANY);

// Bind to the socket
if(bind(s, (SOCKADDR *)&sListener, sizeof(sListener)) ==
   SOCKET_ERROR) {
   int iSocketError = WSAGetLastError();
   return FALSE;
}
```

```
// Listen for incoming connections
if(listen(s, SOMAXCONN) == SOCKET_ERROR) {
   int iSocketError = WSAGetLastError();
   return FALSE;
}

// Wait for a connection
SOCKADDR_IN sIncomingAddr;
memset(&sIncomingAddr, 0, sizeof(SOCKADDR_IN));
int iAddrLen = sizeof(SOCKADDR_IN);

SOCKET sIncomingSocket = accept(s, (SOCKADDR *)
  &sIncomingAddr, &iAddrLen);
if(sIncomingSocket == SOCKET_ERROR) {
   int iSocketError = WSAGetLastError();
   return FALSE;
}

// We have an incoming socket request
char cResponseBuffer[1024] = "";
int nBytesReceived = 0;

// Get a basic request. In reality, we would want to check
// the HTTP request to see if it's valid, but let's just
// send a simple response.
nBytesReceived = recv(sIncomingSocket, &cResponseBuffer[0],
  1024, 0);

if(nBytesReceived == SOCKET_ERROR) {
   int iSocketError = WSAGetLastError();
   return FALSE;
}

// Send out a response
char cBuffer[1024] = "";
int nBytesSent = 0;
int nBytesIndex = 0;

// Setup the buffer to send
sprintf(cBuffer, "HTTP/1.0 200 OK\r\n\r\nTest
  Response\r\n\r\n");
int nBytesLeft = strlen(cBuffer);
```

```
// Send the entire buffer
while(nBytesLeft > 0) {
    nBytesSent = send(sIncomingSocket, &cBuffer[nBytesIndex],
        nBytesLeft, 0);
    if(nBytesSent == SOCKET_ERROR)
        break;

    // See how many bytes are left. If we still need to send, loop
    nBytesLeft -= nBytesSent;
    nBytesIndex += nBytesSent;
}


// Close the sockets
closesocket(sIncomingSocket);
closesocket(s);
WSACleanup();
```

Closing a Socket

Once you are finished using a socket, whether you are on a server or a client, you must release the device resources that are associated with that socket.

Before you actually close the socket, you should call the shut down() function. You can destroy a socket by directly closing it, but you are better off calling shutdown() first because it ensures that all data in the TCP/IP transfer queue is sent or received before the socket is closed:

```
int shutdown (SOCKET s, int how);
```

The handle to the socket, s, is the first parameter we pass in to this function. The how parameter specifies how subsequent socket functions are processed on this socket, and can be set to SD_RECEIVE, SD_SEND, or SD_BOTH. Setting this to SD_RECEIVE will prevent any further recv function calls from being completed, and SD_SEND will prevent any further send calls. Obviously, SD_BOTH will stop sending and receiving for the socket (however, all data already queued will be processed).

If there are no errors, shutdown() will return 0. Once a socket has been `shutdown()`, you cannot use it again, except to close it with the `closesocket()` function:

```
int closesocket (SOCKET s);
```

The only parameter that `closesocket()` takes is the handle to the socket descriptor you want to close.

Connectionless (UDP) Sockets

Connectionless sockets (the User Datagram Protocol, or UDP) are your other option for transferring data between two networked devices. These are typically used in applications that require little overhead and that want to achieve higher network throughput, such as multimedia streaming protocols. Another advantage in using UDP is that it is capable of transmitting data to multiple endpoints simultaneously because a connection is not bound to a single address. Because UDP transfers **datagrams** (message packets) instead of a connected stream, these connections are considered unreliable and connectionless. However, don't mistake the term *unreliable* for low quality—unreliable in this context means only that the protocol does not guarantee that your data packets will ever arrive at your destination. Moreover, there is no sequenced order in which they are guaranteed to arrive, nor any notification if a packet never arrives.

You can compare using UDP datagrams to checking in several pieces of luggage (your packets) at the airport at the same time. Even though they boarded the plane in some order (the packets going out over the network), you're pretty sure that they'll arrive at their destination. Once you get off the plane and attempt to claim your luggage, you're not exactly sure what order they'll be unloaded in (packets arriving at the endpoint), but you can be relatively certain that they'll get there in one piece. Unfortunately, once in a while, something does get lost and never is seen again.

If you are planning to use UDP as your method to send data, it's probably a good idea to have your application either send some sort of acknowledgment that it received a datagram, or provide some way to reassemble packets in a predetermined order by using some sort of sequence—such as a packet number or timestamp—in your datagram message. This can ensure some amount of reliability with the protocol.

Figure 1.4 shows the process for creating both client and server UDP socket connections and how data flows between both network endpoints.

Before you can send or receive UDP packets, whether you are the client or the server, you need to create a socket to talk to using the `socket()` function, and pass the `SOCK_DGRAM` and `IPPROTO_IDP` parameters:

```
SOCKET sUDPSocket = socket(AF_INET, SOCK_DGRAM, IPPROTO_UDP);
```

Once you have created your sockets, you also need to `bind()` the socket to the interface on which you want to receive data. This is done exactly the same way as using a TCP connection.

Now that we have our sockets ready, let's take a look at what is required to both send and receive datagram packets. Remember that

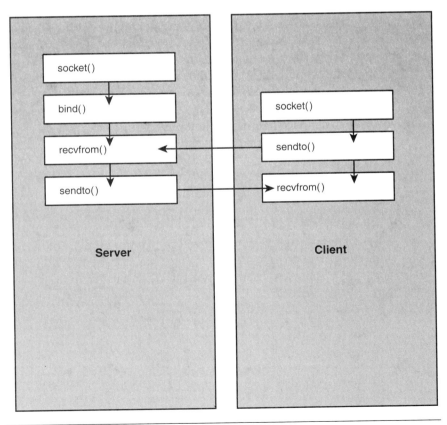

Figure 1.4 Socket process for connectionless clients and servers

even though we have bound the socket, we don't need to call the `listen()` or `accept()` functions, as we are going to be operating in a connectionless manner, which enables us to send or receive packets to any device on the network.

Sending a UDP Datagram

Once you have created your sockets, sending a packet over UDP is fairly straightforward. To send a message, you need to call the `sendto()` function, which is defined as follows:

```
int sendto (SOCKET s, const char *buf, int len, int flags,
   const struct sockaddr *to, int tolen);
```

You might notice that the parameters are similar to the `send()` function.

The `s` parameter is the socket on which we want to send data, which was created using the `socket()` function. The `buf` parameter is a pointer to a buffer that contains the data we want to send, and its length is specified in the `len` parameter. The `flags` parameter is used to affect the way the data is sent, and can be 0 or `MSG_DONTROUTE`, which specifies that the data should not be routed. Typically, this parameter will be set to 0. The `to` parameter contains a pointer to a `SOCKADDR_IN` address structure with the packet's destination address. You can also construct a broadcast packet (sending it to every machine on the network, which is usually not advised), and you can use the address `INADDR_BROADCAST` if you have set the socket option to broadcast mode (see the section "Socket Options"). Finally, the `tolen` parameter specifies the length of the `to` address.

The `sendto()` function will return the number of bytes it has transferred, or a `SOCKET_ERROR` if there was a problem sending the datagram.

The following example sends a UDP datagram:

```
// Create a connectionless socket
SOCKET sUDPSocket = socket(AF_INET, SOCK_DGRAM, IPPROTO_UDP);

// Check to see if we have a valid socket
if(sUDPSocket == INVALID_SOCKET) {
   int iSocketError = WSAGetLastError();
   return FALSE;
}
```

```
// Set up the target device address. For this sample,
// we are assuming it is a machine at 192.168.0.1, and on
// port 40040
SOCKADDR_IN sTargetDevice;
memset(&sTargetDevice, 0, sizeof(SOCKADDR_IN));

sTargetDevice.sin_family = AF_INET;
sTargetDevice.sin_port = htons(40040);
sTargetDevice.sin_addr.s_addr = inet_addr("192.168.0.1");

// Send a datagram to the target device
char cBuffer[1024] = "Test Buffer";
int nBytesSent = 0;
int nBufSize = strlen(cBuffer);

nBytesSent = sendto(sUDPSocket, cBuffer, nBufSize, 0,
    (SOCKADDR *) &sTargetDevice,
    sizeof(SOCKADDR_IN));

// Close the socket
closesocket(sUDPSocket);
```

Receiving a UDP Datagram

To have your application receive a UDP packet, you need to call the
recvfrom() function, which will block until data has arrived from a
client (or it can return immediately if in nonblocking mode; see "Socket
Options"):

```
int recvfrom (SOCKET s, char *buf, int len, int flags,
    struct sockaddr *from, int *fromlen);
```

Notice that the parameters are very similar to those described for
the recv() function. The first parameter, s, is the socket on which
we want to receive data. Next, buf is a pointer to a buffer for the incoming data, and its size is specified by the len parameter. The flags
parameter must be set to 0. Finally, the from parameter contains a
pointer to the SOCKADDR_IN structure, which contains information
about the device that sent the data. A pointer to its length is in the
fromlen field.

If the packet is received successfully, recvfrom() will return a 0;
otherwise, a SOCKET_ERROR will occur.

The following example shows how to receive a UDP datagram packet:

```
// Create a connectionless socket
SOCKET sUDPSocket = socket(AF_INET, SOCK_DGRAM, IPPROTO_UDP);

// Check to see if we have a valid socket
if(sUDPSocket == INVALID_SOCKET) {
   int iSocketError = WSAGetLastError();
   return FALSE;
}


// Setup a bind on the socket, telling us what port and
// adapter to receive datagrams on. Assume we are listening
// on port 40040
SOCKADDR_IN sReceiveFromAddr;
memset(&sReceiveFromAddr, 0, sizeof(SOCKADDR_IN));

sReceiveFromAddr.sin_family = AF_INET;
sReceiveFromAddr.sin_port = htons(40040);
sReceiveFromAddr.sin_addr.s_addr = htonl(INADDR_ANY);

if(bind(sUDPSocket, (SOCKADDR *)&sReceiveFromAddr,
   sizeof(SOCKADDR_IN)) ==
    SOCKET_ERROR) {
    int iSocketError = WSAGetLastError();
    return FALSE;
}


// Receive a datagram from another device
char cBuffer[1024] = "";
int nBytesRecv = 0;
int nBufSize = strlen(cBuffer);
int nReceiveAddrSize = 0;

// Get the datagram
nBytesRecv = recvfrom(sUDPSocket, cBuffer, nBufSize, 0,
   (SOCKADDR *) &sReceiveFromAddr,
   &nReceiveAddrSize);

// Close the socket
closesocket(sUDPSocket);
WSACleanup();
```

One final note regarding the sending and receiving of UDP data: You can also transfer data by using the `connect()`, `send()`, and `recv()` functions. Transmitting UDP data this way is considered a somewhat "directed" connectionless transfer, and should be used only if you plan to communicate with one other device during a session (i.e., all packets are sent to the same address). To do this, after your UDP socket has been created, call the `connect()` function with `SOCKADDR_IN` set to the machine you want to establish a session with. No real connection will be established, but you can use the `send()` and `recv()` functions to transfer data with the associated address.

TCP versus UDP: What Should Your App Use?

Deciding which transport protocol to use can be the hardest part of developing TCP/IP-based applications. The general rule of thumb is to use TCP unless your specific application calls for bandwidth sensitivity or congestion control, which can be relevant issues on Pocket PC devices now that wireless connections are becoming more accessible. UDP should be used in the following situations: when writing applications that require the capability to broadcast data to multiple devices (IP Multicast however, is much less bandwidth-intensive); when writing real-time multimedia applications that can afford to drop packets when congestion occurs; or for extremely small transmissions that require acknowledgment only.

TCP (stream)-based applications are considered much more reliable, and TCP's guarantee of message delivery combined with relatively low overhead makes it an extremely flexible and robust protocol. My best advice is to consider carefully the type of data that you will be sending, as well as your available bandwidth and network conditions, before making your decision.

Internet Control Message Protocol (ICMP)

The **Internet Control Message Protocol** (**ICMP**) is a "support" protocol that is used for sending informational, control, and error messages between network endpoints. It was originally designed to give network routers a way to deliver errors to the network layer of the OSI model so it could decide how to handle the error. ICMP uses a form of IP datagrams known as **raw sockets** to send information between hosts and servers. Pocket PC, however, does not allow you to explicitly create raw sockets; rather, it uses a set of functions that enable you to send limited ICMP ping messages.

ICMP pinging can be extremely useful when performing functions such as network diagnostics, as it can be used to test network connections, routing, and your TCP/IP stack. To use the ICMP functions, you should include the files `icmpapi.h`, `ipexport.h`, and `winsock.h` in your project's source, as well as link with both the `icmplib.lib` and `winsock.lib` libraries.

In order to send an ICMP message, you must first obtain an ICMP handle by calling the following function:

```
HANDLE IcmpCreateFile (void);
```

No parameters are required, and an ICMP handle will be returned. If an error has occurred, you will receive an `INVALID_HANDLE_VALUE` and you can use the `GetLastError()` function to obtain more information about why it failed.

Once you have a valid ICMP handle, you can send your ICMP request by calling the `IcmpSendEcho()` function:

```
DWORD IcmpSendEcho (HANDLE IcmpHandle,
    IPAddr DestinationAddress,
    LPVOID RequestData, WORD RequestSize,
    PIP_OPTION_INFORMATION RequestOptions,
    LPVOID ReplyBuffer,
    DWORD ReplySize, DWORD Timeout);
```

For the first parameter, we pass in the handle to the newly created ICMP packet. The `DestinationAddress` parameter is an `unsigned long` value specifying the target IP address. You can get this by using one of the IP support functions, such as `inet_addr()`, described in the section "Name Resolution," later in this chapter. If you want to pass any *additional* data along with the ICMP message, you can pass a pointer to your buffer using the `RequestData` parameter, and set its size with the `RequestSize` field. You will also want to make sure that you don't try to stuff large messages into this buffer, as there is a limit of 8KB on most systems.

The next parameter, `RequestOptions`, is a pointer to an `IP_OPTION_INFORMATION` structure:

```
struct ip_option_information {
    unsigned char Ttl;
```

```
    unsigned char Tos;
    unsigned char Flags;
    unsigned char OptionsSize;
    unsigned char FAR *OptionsData;
};
```

The `IP_OPTION_INFORMATION` structure is used to configure your echo request. The `Ttl` (time to live) parameter determines the amount of time that the packet will be around before it expires. Next, the `Tos` field specifies the type of service for the ICMP packet, which should be set to 0. The only option that the `Flags` parameter supports on Pocket PC is `IP_FLAG_DF`, which instructs ICMP not to fragment the message. Finally, `OptionsSize` is set to the size of the `OptionsData` parameter, which is a pointer to any additional options. Currently, Pocket PC supports only `IP_OPT_RR`, which records the record route; and `IP_OPT_TS`, which records the timestamp.

The next parameters in `IcmpSendEcho()` are `ReplyBuffer` and `ReplySize`. The `ReplyBuffer` is a pointer to an array of `ICMP_ECHO_REPLY` structures that contains responses to our ICMP echo message from each machine to which our request was sent. It is important to ensure that the buffer you have allocated to receive the reply is set to be the size of `ICMP_ECHO_REPLY` plus eight additional bytes, which are used for any additional error information. The last parameter is `Timeout`, which is the amount of time `IcmpSendEcho()` will wait in milliseconds before failing.

`IcmpSendEcho()` will return the number of packets that are waiting in the `ReplyBuffer` if it is successful; otherwise, it will return 0. The `ICMP_ECHO_REPLY` response structure is defined as follows:

```
struct icmp_echo_reply {
    IPAddr Address;
    unsigned long Status;
    unsigned long RoundTripTime;
    unsigned short DataSize;
    unsigned short Reserved;
    void FAR *Data;
    struct ip_option_information Options;
};
```

Each network node with which we communicated during our echo request will respond with an `ICMP_ECHO_REPLY` package. The first field contains the `Address` of the machine that responded. The `Status` field should return `IP_SUCCESS` if successful; otherwise, it will contain an error code (defined in `ipexport.h`). Next, `RoundTripTime` contains the amount of time in milliseconds that it took for our request to get there. The `DataSize` field contains the size of the data, returned to us in the `Data` field. The last field, `Options`, is an `IP_OPTIONS_STRUCTURE` containing any options of the returning packet.

Finally, when you are finished sending your echo requests, you can close and clean up your ICMP packets by calling into the `IcmpClose Handle()` function, which is defined as follows:

```
BOOL IcmpCloseHandle(HANDLE IcmpHandle);
```

The only parameter, `IcmpHandle`, is the ICMP session handle that you have been using. If ICMP closes successfully, this function will return `TRUE`. `FALSE` will be returned to you if an error has occurred.

The following example shows how we can use the ICMP functions to ping another network endpoint to determine whether our Internet connection is active (similar to the desktop ping utility):

```
// Initialize Winsock
WSADATA wsaData;

memset(&wsaData, 0, sizeof(WSADATA));
if(WSAStartup(MAKEWORD(1,1), &wsaData) != 0)
   return FALSE;

// Create a new ICMP message session
HANDLE hIcmpSession = IcmpCreateFile();
if(hIcmpSession == INVALID_HANDLE_VALUE)
   return FALSE;

// Convert the target address to a network address
HOSTENT *hostServer = gethostbyname("www.furrygoat.com");
if(hostServer == NULL) {
   int dwError = WSAGetLastError();
   return FALSE;
}

DWORD dwTargetAddress = *((u_long*)hostServer>h_addr_list[0]);

// Setup the option_information structure
IP_OPTION_INFORMATION ipOptions;
memset(&ipOptions, 0, sizeof(IP_OPTION_INFORMATION));
```

```
ipOptions.Ttl = 32;
ipOptions.Flags = IP_FLAG_DF;

// Send our request
BYTE bOutPacket[32];
BYTE bInPacket[1024];

int nTrace = IcmpSendEcho(hIcmpSession, dwTargetAddress, bOutPacket,
    sizeof(bOutPacket), &ipOptions, bInPacket,  1024, 5000);
if(nTrace == 0) {
    DWORD dwError = GetLastError();
    IcmpCloseHandle(hIcmpSession);
    return 0;
}

ICMP_ECHO_REPLY *pER = (PICMP_ECHO_REPLY)bInPacket;
for(int i =0;i<nTrace;i++) {
    TCHAR tchOutput[512] = TEXT("\0");
    struct in_addr sReplyAddr;
    sReplyAddr.S_un.S_addr = (IPAddr)pER->Address;

    wsprintf(tchOutput, TEXT("Reply from %hs"),
        inet_ntoa(sReplyAddr));
    MessageBox(NULL, tchOutput, TEXT("Ping"), MB_OK);
    pER++;
}

IcmpCloseHandle(hIcmpSession);
```

Socket Options

You can set several socket options to further control the behavior of an individual socket. Some of these attributes are used to query information about a socket, such as its current state, while other options are used to change how a socket interacts with the network. For example, if you wanted to send a UDP datagram that is broadcast to the entire network, you would enable the SO_BROADCAST socket option on that particular socket.

Socket options can affect either the socket itself or the protocol that it is using. For example, the option TCP_NODELAY is designed to toggle the Nagle algorithm when using the TCP protocol, and will produce an error on a socket that is currently UDP-based. Note that options that begin with SO_ are generic items for the socket layer, whereas those that begin with TCP_ or IP_ are for the underlying protocol. In addition, you need to verify that some of the generic socket options, such as SO_BROADCAST, are supported by the underlying socket protocol for your socket. In other words, if you try to create a broadcast socket on one that was created to use the TCP protocol, it will also fail.

The function that you use to get socket options is getsockopt() and is defined as follows:

```
int getsockopt (SOCKET s, int level, int optname, char *optval,
    int *optlen);
```

To set socket options, you use the setsockopt() function:

```
int setsockopt (SOCKET s, int level, int optname, const
    char *optval, int optlen);
```

Both take almost the exact same parameters. The s parameter is the socket for which you want to get or set an option. The next parameter, level, defines what level in the OSI model the option will affect. On Pocket PC, this can be SOL_SOCKET, IPPROTO_TCP, or IPPROTO_IP. The available socket options described in Table 1.3 will help you determine the proper level for the option you want to manipulate. The optname field identifies the option you want to get or set. The last two parameters work a bit differently depending on whether you are getting or setting a socket option value. If you are using getsockopt(), the optval parameter points to the value of the option, and optlen is a pointer to the size of the buffer to which optval points. When setting values using setsockopt(), optval points to the new value you want to set, and optlen is the size of the optval buffer.

The SO_LINGER option is somewhat related to the SO_DONTLINGER option in that when it is disabled, SO_DONTLINGER is enabled. Both of the "linger" options determine how the socket should react when the closesocket() function call is made and there is

Table 1.3 Socket Options

Level	Option Name	Type	Get/Set	Description
SOL_SOCKET	SO_ACCEPTCONN	BOOL	Get	Is the socket listening?
	SO_BROADCAST	BOOL	Both	Allows broadcast messages on the socket
	SO_DONTLINGER	BOOL	Both	Enables or disables immediate return from `closesocket()`
	SO_KEEPALIVE	BOOL	Both	Sends keep-alive messages
	SO_LINGER	struct linger	Both	Enables or disables immediate return from `closesocket()`
	SO_OOBINLINE	BOOL	Get	Out-of-band data is in the normal data stream
	SO_REUSEADDR	BOOL	Both	Enables or disables the reuse of a bound socket
	SO_SECURE	DWORD	Both	Enables or disables SSL encryption on the socket
	SO_SNDBUF	int	Both	Size of the buffer allocated for sending data
	SO_TYPE	int	Get	Socket type
IPPROTO_TCP	TCP_NODELAY	BOOL	Both	Turns on/off the Nagle algorithm
IPPROTO_IP	IP_MULTICAST _TTL	int	Both	Time to live for a multicast packet
	IP_MULTICAST _IF	unsigned long	Both	Address of the outgoing multicast interface
	IP_ADD_ MEMBERSHIP	struct ip_mreg	Set	Adds socket to a multicast group
	IP_DROP_ MEMBERSHIP	struct ip_mreg	Set	Removes socket from a multicast group

additional data in the TCP send buffer. SO_LINGER uses a LINGER structure to set its state, which is defined as follows:

```
struct linger {
   u_short l_onoff;
   u_short l_linger;
}
```

The l_onoff parameter determines if linger is currently on or off. When SO_DONTLINGER is set to TRUE, l_onoff is 0 (i.e., don't linger). When l_onoff is enabled and set to 1, the l_linger field specifies the time to wait, in seconds, before the socket is closed.

Broadcast Sockets

Use the SO_BROADCAST socket option with care. It is generally considered bad practice to flood a network with data, especially when using a device such as a Pocket PC for which bandwidth and network resources are crucial. It does have some practical uses, such as discovering devices on a subnet, or sending information to a wide group of devices at once, so there can be some benefit to using broadcast sockets.

Broadcasting is only available for sockets that are on UDP, as TCP sockets are not capable of transmitting broadcast messages. It is important to ensure that your broadcast packets are small enough that datagram fragmentation doesn't occur, which means you should not exceed 512 bytes for your message. When setting up your SOCKADDR_IN structure, both the client using recvfrom() and the sender using sendto() should configure their functions to send/receive from the same port, and they can use the address INADDR_BROADCAST to designate the target address as a broadcast message.

Secure Sockets

Pocket PC devices also support the capability to use the device's built-in security to create secure sockets using SSL 2.0 and 3.0. When using the SO_SOSECURE socket option, set the DWORD value you are passing in for the optval parameter to SO_SEC_SLL.

Blocking and Nonblocking Sockets

When a socket is initially created, it is in *blocking mode,* which means that your program will not return from a blocking function until it has completed its operation. For example, when using a TCP socket, if you call the `accept()` function, your program will appear to "hang" until an incoming connection has arrived. Another example would be the `connect()` function, which will not return until either it has connected to its destination or an error has occurred. This can be rather unnerving on a device such as Pocket PC, as it will appear as if the device has "locked up" until it returns from the blocking function.

On a Windows-based system, this is solved by using the asynchronous Winsock functions, which provide Windows notification messages when a socket event has occurred. Unfortunately, these are not available on Pocket PC devices; instead, you need to put the sockets into nonblocking mode if you want them to return immediately. When a socket is set to nonblocking mode, any call to a blocking function will *immediately* return to you with a `SOCKET_ERROR` result. Calling `WSAGetLastError()` will return the error code `WSAWOULDBLOCK`, which means that you will need to check the socket again at some point to see whether the operation has completed. This can be done by using the `select()` function, rather than repeatedly calling into the nonblocking function to see whether it has completed.

To change the blocking mode of a socket, you can call the following function:

```
int ioctlsocket (SOCKET s, long cmd, u_long *argp);
```

The first parameter is the socket for which you want to change the mode. The `cmd` parameter is used to specify what operation you want to perform on the socket, and can be either `FIONBIO` or `FIONREAD`. Setting `cmd` to `FIONBIO` will set the socket's blocking mode to nonblocking if `argp` is set to 0; otherwise, setting `argp` to a positive value will put the socket into blocking mode. The `FIONREAD` command will return the number of bytes that are currently in the receive queue for the socket to the pointer passed in for the `argp` parameter.

For example, you could use the following if you wanted to change a socket from blocking to nonblocking:

```
// Create a connection-oriented socket
SOCKET s = socket(AF_INET, SOCK_STREAM, IPPROTO_TCP);

// Check to see if we have a valid socket
if(s == INVALID_SOCKET) {
   int iSocketError = WSAGetLastError();
   return FALSE;
}
```

```
// Make it non-blocking
DWORD dwNonBlocking = 0;
if(ioctlsocket(s, FIONBIO, &dwNonBlocking) != 0) {
    int iSocketError = WSAGetLastError();
    return FALSE;
}
```

Once you have placed the socket into nonblocking mode, you can use the `select()` function to see if any data is available on the socket. It is *extremely* important that you use this method of notification on your nonblocking sockets to determine their completion, as continuously polling the socket is a major drain of device resources.

The `select()` function is defined as follows:

```
int select (int nfds, fd_set *readfds, fd_set *writefds,
   fd_set *exceptfds, const struct timeval *timeout);
```

The first parameter, `nfds`, is ignored. The next three parameters, `readfds`, `writefds`, and `exceptfds`, are pointers to a collection of socket sets (`FD_SET`), which are used for determining whether it can be read or written to, and whether there is out-of-band data. An `FD_SET` collection is an internal structure that is used to maintain a collection of sockets that you want `select` to monitor. Winsock provides several macros for adding and removing sockets from an `FD_SET` collection:

- `FD_ZERO(*set)`—Initializes the set to `NULL`
- `FD_CLR(s, *set)`—Removes the socket s from the set
- `FD_ISSET(s, *set)`—Determines whether socket s is a part of the set, and returns `TRUE` if so
- `FD_SET(s, *set)`—Adds socket s to the set

For example, if you want to monitor a socket to determine when it is safe to write to it, you can simply add your socket to the `writefds` set by calling the `FD_SET` macro.

Finally, the `timeout` parameter of the `select()` function is a pointer to a `timeval` structure (defined in `winsock.h`):

```
struct timeval {
    long tv_sec;
    long tv_usec;
};
```

The `tv_sec` field specifies how long the `select()` function will wait in seconds, and the `tv_usec` field indicates the number of milliseconds. If these two fields are set to 0, `select()` will return immediately. If the pointer `timeout` is NULL, it will wait indefinitely; otherwise, `select()` will wait the specified number of seconds and milliseconds defined in this structure.

Select will return 0 if a timeout has occurred, or a SOCKET_ERROR if there is an error. Otherwise, the select function won't return until a specific socket event has happened, and the return value will be the number of sockets on which the event has occurred.

Sockets in the `readfds` set will be identified under the following conditions:

- There is data in the receive queue.
- The connection has been lost, closed, or reset.
- The socket is in `listen()` mode and a client is attempting to connect. This will allow `accept()` to succeed.

Sockets in the `writefds` set will be identified under these circumstances:

- There is data to be sent on the socket.
- A `connect()` has been accepted by a server.

Finally, sockets that are included in the `exceptfds` set are identified under the following conditions:

- A `connect()` has failed from the server.
- Out-of-band data is available for reading.

Support Functions

Several extremely useful Winsock support functions can help you get information about peers, make DNS queries, and convert between various data formats that are supported with Winsock.

Connected Peer Functions

To get address information for a connection that a socket is currently connected with, you can use the `getpeername()` function:

```
int getpeername (SOCKET s, struct sockaddr *name, int *namelen);
```

The first parameter is the socket for which you want information, the `name` parameter is a pointer to a SOCKADDR structure (which will be a SOCKADDR_IN for TCP/IP), and `namelen` is a pointer to its length.

To retrieve address information for the local interface of a connected socket, the following function is defined:

```
int getsockname (SOCKET s, struct sockaddr *name, int *namelen);
```

The `getsockname()` function takes the same parameters as the `getpeername()` function, except that the `name` parameter will return local address information, rather than the remote connection.

Host Names

To get your device's host name, you can call the aptly named `gethostname()` function:

```
int gethostname (char *name, int namelen);
```

The `name` parameter is a pointer to a character buffer that will receive the name, and `namelen` is the length of the name buffer specified.

To set the device's host name, use the `sethostname()` function, which is defined as follows:

```
int sethostname(char *pName, int cName);
```

This function takes two parameters. The first is a pointer to a buffer that contains the new host name, and the second is the `cName` parameter, which specifies the buffer's length.

Name Resolution

The `inet_addr` function is used to convert an IP "dot" address (e.g., 192.158.0.0) into an `unsigned long` value:

```
unsigned long inet_addr (const char *cp);
```

It takes a single parameter, a pointer to a character buffer `cp` containing the IP "dot" address string.

If you want to perform the inverse function, use `inet_ntoa()`, which will convert an address to a string:

```
char * inet_ntoa (struct in_addr in);
```

Here, you pass in an address structure; typically, a `SOCKADDR_IN` that defines the address you want to convert.

The next set of support functions we will look at deals with host name resolution. All Winsock functions dealing with host addresses and names use a `HOSTENT` data structure. This structure contains all the available information about an individual host. It is defined as follows:

```
struct hostent {
    char *h_name;
    char **h_aliases;
    short h_addrtype;
    short h_length;
    char **h_addr_list;
};
```

The `h_name` field contains the official name of the host. The `h_aliases` field points to an array of alternative host name string pointers that are terminated by a `NULL` pointer value. The `h_addrtype` field is the type of address being returned, and will be either `AF_INET` or `AF_IRDA`. The `h_length` field is the length in bytes of each address in the `h_addr_list` array. The `h_addr_list` array is a null-terminated array of network addresses in network byte order.

To get host information for a network device by name, use the following:

```
struct hostent *gethostbyname(const char *name);
```

The only parameter needed is the name of the host for which you want information.

Use the following to get information about a host by address:

```
struct hostent *gethostbyaddr(const char *addr, int len, int type);
```

Here, you need to pass in a bit more information about the host. The first parameter is the address structure, with information about the host you want to query. This will typically be the value that is returned from calling the `inet_addr()` function. The `len` parameter is the length in bytes of the address, and the `type` parameter is the type of address—either `AF_INET` or `AF_IDRA`.

Byte Order

The final set of support functions deals with converting values from host byte order to network byte order.

To convert a long value to/from host byte order to network byte order, use the following functions:

```
u_long htonl (u_long hostlong);
u_long ntohl (u_long netlong);
```

Convert a short value to/from host byte order to network byte order as follows:

```
u_short htons (u_short hostshort);
u_short ntohs (u_short netshort);
```

IP Multicasting

Using multicast provides a form of "limited" broadcast support for Pocket PC devices. When you send a traditional broadcast message (a UDP datagram that has the `SO_BROADCAST` option turned on), it is sent to every machine on a particular subnet. This is typically frowned upon, as sending broadcast messages can cause an extreme amount of network congestion, involve a lot of overhead, and use an enormous amount of bandwidth. The best way to think of multicast is as a "point-to-multipoint" broadcast message, in which a multicast message is sent only to devices that are interested in receiving the message.

This is accomplished by having the target devices join what is known as a **multicast group**. For example, if ten devices need to be able to communicate with one another, each one joins the same group address. Any messages sent to that group address are replicated to each member, including the device that sent the original message. A **multicast address** is a class D IP address in the range of 224.0.0.0 through 239.255.255.255 (except for 224.0.0.0 and 224.0.0.1, which are reserved by the IANA). You should be aware that while any device can send multicast datagrams, the only way to receive them is to join a multicast group. Finally, only routers that are capable of using the Internet Group Management Protocol (IGMP) will allow multicast data to traverse them.

IP Multicast Groups

To join or leave an IP Multicast group, you need to use the `setsock opt()` function to change the membership state of a socket. Both options use a special multicast data structure that is defined as follows:

```
struct ip_mreq {
    struct in_addr imr_multiaddr;
    struct in_addr imr_interface;
};
```

The `imr_multiaddr` field is the address of the multicast host group to join, and the `imr_interface` field specifies the IP address of the local network interface on which you want to receive multicast datagrams. You can typically set this to `INADDR_ANY`, which will specify the default interface.

In order to join a multicast group, you should create a UDP datagram socket using the `socket` function, and then call the `setsockopt()` function with the option `IP_ADD_MEMBERSHIP`. Remember that you do not have to join a multicast group to send multicast datagrams to the group, and your socket can be a member of up to 20 different multicast groups. In addition, if you want multiple sockets in your application to join the same group on the same port, you need to call the `setsock opt()` function with the `SO_REUSEADDR` option enabled.

If you want to leave a group, you can call `setsockopt()` and use the `IP_DROP_MEMBERSHIP` option.

Sending and Receiving Multicast Data

To send and receive data from a multicast group, you can use the standard UDP `sendto()` and `recvfrom()` messages. Make sure your datagram messages are sent to the multicast group address, rather than an individual host's address.

If you want to send multicast packets beyond the local network, you need to change the IP time-to-live (or TTL) value for the socket. This is typically set to 1, but you can change it using `setsockopt()` with the `IP_MULTICAST_TTL` option. Note that to send packets beyond the local network, all the routers between you and your target device must be multicast-capable.

CHAPTER 2

WinInet

The avalanche has started; it is too late for the pebbles to vote.

—*Kosh*, Babylon 5

This chapter describes how you can greatly facilitate developing your Internet applications by using the Internet support libraries on Pocket PC, instead of pure socket interfaces. Although sockets do offer you the lowest level of control over a TCP/IP connection, interacting with standard Internet protocols that communicate over TCP/IP can be a bit cumbersome and time-consuming.

The **Windows Internet Services** library, also known as **WinInet**, is used primarily for writing client Internet applications, as it handles all the communications between your program and the socket level. For example, suppose you need to write an application that transfers data over an HTTP connection. You could easily spend time researching the HTTP protocol (RFC 1945) and writing socket code that handles all the functions to connect, read and write data, maintain a session, and so on. WinInet *simplifies* this by handling all these functions for you, enabling you to concentrate on the specifics of your application, rather than the details of the protocol. On Pocket PC, WinInet supports both HTTP and FTP protocols, as well as basic Internet connections.

Windows Internet Overview (WinInet)

As previously mentioned, WinInet is a set of helper API functions that eases the creation of Internet client applications that use the more popular Internet protocols such as HTTP and FTP. What this basically means is that WinInet enables you to write programs over these protocols without having to worry about the underlying socket details. Just for the record, WinInet sits on top of Winsock.

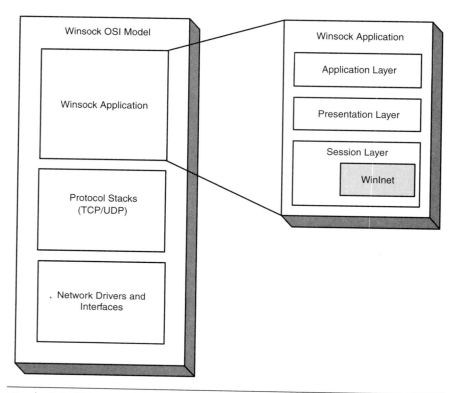

Figure 2.1 WinInet and the TCP/IP OSI layers

To get a better idea of how WinInet interacts with Winsock, Figure 2.1 shows how it fits into the TCP/IP OSI model described in Chapter 1.

You can see that WinInet resides in the session layer of the protocol stack, talking directly with the transport layer to send information. Instead of working with TCP directly and creating sockets to read and write over a particular protocol, your application uses a WinInet session. HTTP and FTP sessions created with WinInet have a special kind of handle type, `HINTERNET`, which is synchronized and can be shared among multiple threads.

To use the WinInet library with your application, you need to include the header `wininet.h`, and link with the `wininet.lib` library.

Handling WinInet Errors

To get the last error from any WinInet API call, you can use the standard system `GetLastError()` function to return the error code for the last function that failed. More specific error definitions are located in `wininet.h` if you want to look up more information about an error code. If you require a more "human friendly" description of an error, or extended error information, you can simply call the `InternetGet LastResponseInfo()` function:

```
BOOL InternetGetLastResponseInfo(LPDWORD lpdwError,
  LPTSTR lpszBuffer, LPDWORD lpdwBufferLength);
```

The `lpdwError` parameter is a pointer to a variable that will contain the error code of the last function. The `lpszBuffer` and `lpdwBuffer Length` parameters are used to describe the buffer that will contain the error text. When calling `InternetGetLastResponseInfo()`, set `lpdwBufferLength` to the size of `lpszBuffer`. If the buffer is too small, the function will return `FALSE`, with an error code of `ERROR_ INSUFFICIENT_BUFFER`. The size of the buffer that is required will then be stored in `lpdwBufferLength`. If the function succeeds, it will return `TRUE` and the error description will be in the buffer pointed to by `lpszBuffer`.

If you are using the HTTP protocol over WinInet, Pocket PC also supports displaying a system error dialog box into which a user can enter data (such as a username or password) if an HTTP request fails. Table 2.1

Table 2.1 Errors Supported by `InternetErrorDlg()`

Error Name	Dialog Box Displayed
`ERROR_INTERNET_HTTP_TO_HTTPS_ON_REDIR`	Notification that the user is crossing secure/nonsecure zones
`ERROR_INTERNET_INCORRECT_PASSWORD`	User/Password dialog box
`ERROR_INTERNET_INVALID_CA`	Notification of an invalid security certificate authority
`ERROR_INTERNET_POST_IS_NON_SECURE`	Notification about passing data through a nonsecure connection
`ERROR_INTERNET_SEC_CERT_CN_INVALID`	Notification that the SSL Common Name is invalid
`ERROR_INTERNET_SEC_CERT_DATE_INVALID`	Notification that the SSL certificate has expired

shows the HTTP errors that are returned from `GetLastError()` by using the `InternetErrorDlg()` function.

The function is defined as follows:

```
DWORD InternetErrorDlg(HWND hWnd, HINTERNET hRequest,
  DWORD dwError, DWORD wFlags, LPVOID *lppvData);
```

The `hWnd` parameter is the handle to a parent window for the dialog box and can be `NULL`. The next parameter, `hRequest`, is a `HINTERNET` handle to the Internet connection that was used to make the `Http SendRequest()` that failed, and `dwError` is the error code that was returned from the `GetLastErrror()` function. The `wFlags` parameter specifies the action that the function should take (and can be one or a combination of the following values):

- `FLAGS_ERROR_UI_FILTER_FOR_ERRORS` examines the HTTP header for additional errors.
- `FLAGS_ERROR_UI_FLAGS_CHANGE_OPTIONS` saves the results of the dialog box in the `HINTERNET` handle that was passed in.
- `FLAGS_ERROR_UI_FLAGS_GENERATE_DATA` inspects the `hRequest` handle for any additional information for the error.
- `FLAGS_ERROR_UI_SERIALIZE_DIALOGS` enables the serialization of multiple password requests.

Finally, `lppvData` contains any additional data that is returned from the error dialog box. Using the `FLAGS_ERROR_UI_FLAGS_GENERATE_DATA` flag will cause `lppvData` to be filled with error-specific data, such as invalid certificates, and `FLAGS_ERROR_UI_SERIALIZE_DIALOGS` will return an `INTERNET_AUTH_NOTIFY_DATA` structure with user/password data.

The `InternetErrorDlg()` function's return value will tell you how the user interacted with the dialog box. If the function was successful, it will return `ERROR_SUCCESS`; if the user decided to cancel the dialog box, an `ERROR_CANCELLED` result is returned. If the function needs to retry any part of the original request (such as rechecking a password), you would then be returned the value `ERROR_INTERNET_FORCE_RETRY`.

Internet Connections and Proxies

In order to use WinInet (and Winsock, for that matter), you first need an active Internet connection. Because Pocket PC does *not* support the desktop `InternetAutodial()` function, which would automatically establish a connection if you were not online already, you have to use the Pocket PC Connection Manager to establish an Internet connection (see Chapter 7).

Proxy servers are also supported by the WinInet APIs. A proxy server is typically used as both a speed enhancement and a security measure for internal networks. While a proxy prevents your network from unauthorized access, a user/password combination is usually required when making Internet requests over the proxy server. To specify that you want to use a proxy server for a current Internet session, you need to set the `INTERNET_OPEN_TYPE_PROXY` flag when you use `InternetOpen()` to start your Internet session. You can then use the `InternetSet Option()` function (see the section "Internet Options") with the flags `INTERNET_OPTION_PROXY_USERNAME` and `INTERNET_OPTION_ PROXY_PASSWORD` to set your authorization; otherwise, Pocket PC will attempt to use your default server login information instead. If you receive an error when accessing proxy resources, you can use the `InternetErrorDlg()` function to have users re-enter their username and password.

Currently, WinInet supports the CERN and SOCKS proxies for HTTP and TIS gateway proxies for FTP requests. You can also use a CERN proxy for FTP requests as long as the request is converted to an HTTP address or made by opening a connection with a URL.

Uniform Resource Locators (URLs)

If you have ever used a Web browser (and I'm sure you have or you would not be reading this), then you have already seen and used **Uniform Resource Locators**, otherwise known as **URLs**. A URL is a string that represents the location of a particular resource (a file, a directory, and so on) that is somewhere on the Internet. The accepted syntax for a well-formed URL address is as follows:

```
[protocol]://[username:password]@[servername]:[port]/[resource]
```

For example, a well-formed URL could be something as simple as http://www.microsoft.com, or it might appear as something more complicated, such as the following:

```
ftp://anonymous:anonymous@ftpsite.com:21/files/somefile.wav
```

If you look at the individual parts of a URL, you can see that the address contains all the information you need to create an application for working with this resource. Normally, if you want to parse the address, you need to perform a great deal of string manipulation for all of the possible combinations.

Fortunately, WinInet provides functions that enable you to create, parse, combine, and convert (also called **canonicalize**) URL addresses.

Because a URL can contain numerous "parts," both of the functions that create and break up a URL address use the URL_COMPONENTS structure. Before examining the specific WinInet URL functions, let's examine this structure:

```
typedef struct {
    DWORD dwStructSize;
    LPWSTR lpszScheme;
    DWORD dwSchemeLength;
    INTERNET_SCHEME nScheme;
    LPWSTR lpszHostName;
    DWORD dwHostNameLength;
    INTERNET_PORT nPort;
    LPWSTR lpszUserName;
    DWORD dwUserNameLength;
    LPWSTR lpszPassword;
    DWORD dwPasswordLength;
    LPWSTR lpszUrlPath;
    DWORD dwUrlPathLength;
    LPWSTR lpszExtraInfo;
    DWORD dwExtraInfoLength;
} URL_COMPONENTS, * LPURL_COMPONENTS;
```

The URL_COMPONENTS structure contains all the individual pieces of a URL:

- dwStructSize is the size of the URL_COMPONENTS structure.
- lpszScheme and dwSchemeLength are the address and length, respectively, of the string buffer containing the scheme (or

protocol) name. `nScheme` is the value of an `INTERNET_SCHEME` enumeration that specifies the protocol scheme.

- `lpszHostName` and `dwHostNameLength` are the address and length, respectively, of the string buffer containing the host address.
- `nPort` is the server port.
- `lpszUserName` and `dwUserNameLength` are the address and length, respectively, of the string buffer containing the user name.
- `lpszPassword` and `dwPasswordLength` are the address and length, respectively, of the string buffer containing the password.
- `lpszUrlPath` and `dwUrlPathLength` are the address and length, respectively, of the string buffer containing the URL path.
- `lpszExtraInfo` and `dwExtraInfoLength` are the address and length, respectively, of the string buffer containing any extra URL information, such as additional anchor links (e.g., #anchor).

The `nScheme` member uses the `INTERNET_SCHEME` enumerator to determine the appropriate value for the protocol specified in the URL address. The enumerator is defined as follows:

```
typedef enum {
    INTERNET_SCHEME_PARTIAL = -2,
    INTERNET_SCHEME_UNKNOWN = -1,
    INTERNET_SCHEME_DEFAULT = 0,
    INTERNET_SCHEME_FTP,
    INTERNET_SCHEME_GOPHER,
    INTERNET_SCHEME_HTTP,
    INTERNET_SCHEME_HTTPS,
    INTERNET_SCHEME_FILE,
    INTERNET_SCHEME_NEWS,
    INTERNET_SCHEME_MAILTO,
    INTERNET_SCHEME_SOCKS,
    INTERNET_SCHEME_JAVASCRIPT,
    INTERNET_SCHEME_VBSCRIPT,
    INTERNET_SCHEME_FIRST = INTERNET_SCHEME_FTP,
    INTERNET_SCHEME_LAST = INTERNET_SCHEME_VBSCRIPT
} INTERNET_SCHEME, *LPINTERNET_SCHEME;
```

Now that you have defined all of the components of a URL address, let's take a look at what is required to create and parse this string.

To create a new URL string, you call the following function:

```
BOOL InternetCreateUrl(LPURL_COMPONENTS lpUrlComponents,
    DWORD dwFlags, LPWSTR lpszUrl, LPDWORD lpdwUrlLength);
```

The function takes the passed-in pointer to a URL_COMPONENTS structure, the lpUrlComponents parameter, and constructs a new URL that is placed in the string buffer to which lpszUrl points. The dwFlags parameter controls certain aspects of the URL's creation, and can be a combination of the flags found in Table 2.2.

Table 2.2 InternetCreateUrl() Flags

Flag	Description
ICU_ESCAPE	Converts all escape sequences into characters
ICU_USERNAME	Uses the default system username

Finally, the lpdwUrlLength parameter contains a pointer to a DWORD value, which is the size of the lpszUrl buffer. If the function successfully returns, lpdwUrlLength will contain the size of the new URL address string; otherwise, it will contain the required size of the buffer if it is too small. Finally, if you don't require a particular component piece, just make that member of URL_COMPONENTS a NULL value.

You can create a URL with the following:

```
URL_COMPONENTS url;
TCHAR tchURL[1024] = TEXT("\0");
DWORD dwLength = 1024;
BOOL fSuccess = FALSE;

// Setup the URL_COMPONENTS structure
memset(&url, 0, sizeof(URL_COMPONENTS));
url.dwStructSize = sizeof(URL_COMPONENTS);
url.lpszScheme = TEXT("http");
url.lpszHostName = TEXT("www.microsoft.com");
url.nScheme = INTERNET_SCHEME_HTTP;
url.nPort = 80;
url.lpszUrlPath = TEXT("index.htm");
```

```
// Create the URL
fSuccess = InternetCreateUrl(&url, ICU_ESCAPE, tchURL,
  &dwLength);
```

The corresponding output URL (the value of `tchURL`) from the preceding code would look as follows:

```
http://www.microsoft.com/index.htm
```

Now that you've seen what's required to assemble a URL, you can use the `InternetCrackUrl()` function to perform the inverse operation—that is, take a string and parse it into a URL_COMPONENTS structure:

```
BOOL InternetCrackUrl(LPCWSTR lpszUrl, DWORD dwUrlLength,
  DWORD dwFlags, LPURL_COMPONENTS lpUrlComponents);
```

When using `InternetCrackUrl()`, you first need to prepare the URL_COMPONENTS structure that will receive the parts of the string you pass in. Make sure that you initialize the structure's `dwStructSize` parameter to the size of URL_COMPONENTS, and that you set the corresponding length member value of the part you want to parse to a nonzero value, as shown in the following example:

```
URL_COMPONENTS urlCracked;
memset(&urlCracked, 0, sizeof(URL_COMPONENTS));
urlCracked.dwStructSize = sizeof(URL_COMPONENTS);

// Set which parts of URL_COMPONENTS we want to have
// returned
urlCracked.dwHostNameLength = 1;
urlCracked.dwSchemeLength = 1;
urlCracked.dwUrlPathLength = 1;
```

Once the structure has been set up, you can call `InternetCrack Url()`. Set the `lpszUrl` parameter to the string of the URL, and its length in the `dwUrlLength` parameter. The `dwFlags` parameter can be one of the values shown in Table 2.3.

Finally, `lpUrlComponents` is a pointer to your URL_COMPONENTS structure.

Table 2.3 `InternetCrackUrl()` Flags

Flag	Description
`ICU_DECODE`	Converts all encoded characters into their normal form
`ICU_ESCAPE`	Converts all escape sequences into their corresponding characters

You can crack the previously created URL in the following way:

```
fSuccess = InternetCrackUrl(tchURL, lstrlen(tchURL)*sizeof(TCHAR),
    0, &urlCracked);
```

When the function returns, the `urlCracked` structure will contain all the parts of the passed-in URL parameter.

To combine two separate URL parts, such as a base URL and a relative URL, into one string, you can use the `InternetCombineUrl()` function:

```
BOOL InternetCombineUrl(LPCWSTR lpszBaseUrl, LPCWSTR
  lpszRelativeUrl, LPWSTR lpszBuffer, LPDWORD lpdwBufferLength,
  DWORD dwFlags);
```

The first two parameters are the URLs you want to combine—first the base URL, followed by the relative URL. The `lpszBuffer` parameter is a pointer to a string buffer that will hold your new URL, and `lpdwBufferLength` contains a pointer to the buffer size. If the buffer is too small, the required size will be in `lpszBufferLength` when the function fails. Finally, the `dwFlags` parameter can be one of the following:

- `ICU_BROWSER_MODE` prevents the encoding or decoding of any characters following the # or ? characters.
- `ICU_DECODE` coverts all escape sequences to characters.
- `ICU_ENCODE_SPACES_ONLY` encodes spaces. Spaces are encoded as %20.
- `ICU_NO_ENCODE` prevents the conversion of any unsafe characters.
- `ICU_NO_META` prevents the removal of any meta-sequences from your URLs.

If the function succeeds, it will return TRUE.

Finally, to canonicalize a URL (which converts the URL into a "safe" form), you can use the "InternetCanonicalizeUrl" function:

```
BOOL InternetCanonicalizeUrl(LPCWSTR lpszUrl, LPWSTR lpszBuffer,
    LPDWORD lpdwBufferLength,  DWORD dwFlags);
```

The lpszUrl parameter is the URL you want to convert. The lpszBuffer points to a string buffer that will hold the converted URL and its length, as specified by lpdwBufferLength. If the function fails because the buffer is too small, lpdwBufferLength will point to the length of the required buffer size. The last parameter, dwFlags, is the same as that in the InternetCombineUrl() function.

Internet Cache (Temporary Internet Files)

The temporary Internet cache is a storage area on your device that captures all data received over the network via WinInet transactions. Web pages downloaded with Pocket Internet Explorer, as well as files downloaded via FTP or HTTP, are stored here. When a request is made to download an Internet resource, WinInet first checks the cache to see if it already exists. If it does, then the data is retrieved from the cache instead, enabling an overall faster transfer (it's already on your device), and providing you with the capability to access resources when you are not connected to the network. All WinInet functions will store data (for both FTP and HTTP sessions) in the cache, unless you specify the INTERNET_FLAG_NO_CACHE_WRITE flag when downloading data.

WinInet's APIs enable you to enumerate items in the cache, set cached item data, and delete cache entries. Most of the functions use an INTERNET_CACHE_ENTRY_INFO structure to represent a cached item's information:

```
typedef struct _INTERNET_CACHE_ENTRY_INFO {
    DWORD dwStructSize;
    LPWSTR  lpszSourceUrlName;
    LPWSTR  lpszLocalFileName;
    DWORD CacheEntryType;
    DWORD dwUseCount;
    DWORD dwHitRate;
    DWORD dwSizeLow;
    DWORD dwSizeHigh;
```

```
FILETIME LastModifiedTime;
FILETIME ExpireTime;
FILETIME LastAccessTime;
FILETIME LastSyncTime;
LPBYTE lpHeaderInfo;
DWORD dwHeaderInfoSize;
LPWSTR  lpszFileExtension;
union {
    DWORD dwReserved;
    DWORD dwExemptDelta;
  };
} INTERNET_CACHE_ENTRY_INFO, * LPINTERNET_CACHE_ENTRY_INFO;
```

Table 2.4 describes the members of INTERNET_CACHE_ENTRY_ INFO.

Table 2.4 INTERNET_CACHE_ENTRY_INFO Members

Member	Description
dwStructSize	Specifies the size of the INTERNET_CACHE_ENTRY_INFO structure.
lpszSourceUrlName	Specifies the URL name of the file.
lpszLocalFileName	Specifies the local filename.
CacheEntryType	Specifies the type of cache entry. If the file was downloaded from the Internet, the value is 0. If the file is a cookie or history entry, it is a combination of EDITED_CACHE_ENTRY, NORMAL_CACHE_ENTRY, and STICKY_CACHE_ENTRY.
dwUseCount	Specifies the user count of the cache entry.
dwHitRate	Specifies how many times the cache entry was used.
dwSizeLow	Specifies the low order of the cache file size.
dwSizeHigh	Specifies the high order of the cache file size.
LastModifiedTime	Specifies when the file was last modified in GMT format.
ExpireTime	Specifies when this cache file will expire in GMT format.
LastAccessTime	Specifies when the cache file was last accessed.
LastSyncTime	Specifies when the cache file was last synchronized.
lpHeaderInfo	Points to a buffer that contains the header information for the cached file.
dwHeaderInfoSize	Specifies the size of the buffer used in lpHeaderInfo.
lpszFileExtension	Points to a buffer that contains the cached file's extension.
dwReserved	Must be 0.
dwExemptDelta	Specifies the exemption time from the last accessed time, in seconds.

For cache entries that are history or cookie files, the `CacheEntry Type` member can be a combination of two values. The `EDITED_ CACHE_ENTRY` value is used for entries that have been changed since the entry was originally downloaded, the `NORMAL_CACHE_ENTRY` value is for normal entries, and the `STICKY_CACHE_ENTRY` value is used for entries that are persistent and ignore the `dwExemptDelta` member.

Finding Out What's in the Cache

Enumerating entries that are in the local Internet cache is similar to the `FindFirstFile()` and `FindNextFile()` APIs that are used on local files. To "walk" through the cache and receive an `INTERNET_CACHE_ ENTRY_INFO` structure for each entry, you'll use the `FindFirstUrl CacheEntry()` and `FindNextUrlCacheEntry()` functions:

```
HANDLE FindFirstUrlCacheEntry(LPCWSTR lpszUrlSearchPattern,
    LPINTERNET_CACHE_ENTRY_INFO lpFirstCacheEntryInfo,
    LPDWORD lpdwFirstCacheEntryInfoBufferSize);

BOOL FindNextUrlCacheEntry(HANDLE hEnumHandle,
    LPINTERNET_CACHE_ENTRY_INFO lpNextCacheEntryInfo,
    LPDWORD lpdwNextCacheEntryInfoBufferSize);
```

To walk the cache files, you first call `FindFirstUrlCache Entry()`. The `lpszUrlSearchPattern` parameter can be set to `NULL` (to return all entries), `"visited:"` (to return only URLs), or `"cookie:"` (to return only Web site cookie information). Next, the `lpFirstCacheEntryInfo` entry should point to an initialized `INTERNET_CACHE_ENTRY_INFO` structure. Make sure you set the structure's `dwStructSize` member variable to the size of `INTERNET_ CACHE_ENTRY_INFO` before calling the function. The last parameter, `lpdwFirstCacheEntryInfoBufferSize`, should point to a `DWORD` that is the size of the `lpFirstCacheEntryInfo` parameter.

After calling `FindFirstUrlCacheEntry()`, the function should return a valid handle that you can use to walk through the rest of the cache files by passing it into the first parameter of the `FindNextUrl CacheEntry()` function. If it fails, you will be returned a `NULL` value.

To continue enumerating through the Internet cache, you repeatedly call `FindNextUrlCacheEntry()` to get each cached item until it returns `FALSE`. Once it does, you can close your enumerator by calling the following:

```
BOOL FindCloseUrlCache(HANDLE hEnumHandle);
```

Therefore, to walk through all the cache files, you can simply do the following:

```
INTERNET_CACHE_ENTRY_INFO *piCacheInfo = NULL;
HANDLE hCacheHandle = NULL;
DWORD dwCacheInfoSize = 1024;
BOOL fSuccess = FALSE;

// Create a buffer, which will be of 1024 bytes for the
// INTERNET_CACHE_ENTRY_INFO structure. This is larger than
// the normal size (80 bytes), to make sure it's large
// enough for most cache data.
piCacheInfo = (INTERNET_CACHE_ENTRY_INFO *)LocalAlloc(LPTR,
   dwCacheInfoSize);
if(!piCacheInfo)
   return FALSE;

piCacheInfo->dwStructSize = dwCacheInfoSize;
hCacheHandle = FindFirstUrlCacheEntry(NULL, piCacheInfo,
  &dwCacheInfoSize);

if(!hCacheHandle) {
   if(GetLastError() == ERROR_INSUFFICIENT_BUFFER) {
      // Under normal circumstances, we would have to reallocate
      // a larger buffer, and try to make the call again.
      return FALSE;
   }
   return FALSE;
}

// By this point, we should have a good handle, so let's
// start enumerating
do {
   dwCacheInfoSize = 1024;
   memset(piCacheInfo, 0, dwCacheInfoSize);
   piCacheInfo->dwStructSize = dwCacheInfoSize;

   // Walk through to the next entry
   fSuccess = FindNextUrlCacheEntry(hCacheHandle,
     piCacheInfo, &dwCacheInfoSize);
   if(!fSuccess) {
      if(GetLastError() == ERROR_INSUFFICIENT_BUFFER) {
```

```
        // Under normal circumstances, we would have to
        // reallocate a larger buffer and try to make
        // the call again.
      }
      break;
  }
} while(fSuccess);

LocalFree(piCacheInfo);
FindCloseUrlCache(hCacheHandle);
return 0;
```

While walking through all of the files in the cache is interesting, it's typically more useful to directly interact with a cache entry for a particular URL:

```
BOOL GetUrlCacheEntryInfo(LPCWSTR lpszUrlName,
    LPINTERNET_CACHE_ENTRY_INFO lpCacheEntryInfo,
    LPDWORD lpdwCacheEntryInfoBufferSize);
```

The `lpszUrlName` parameter specifies the URL for which you want to retrieve information from the local cache, and the rest of the parameters are the same as the `FindFirstUrlCacheEntry()` function.

Once you have found a particular cache entry you are interested in, you need to lock the cache file in order to do anything with it. To do so, you can call `RetrieveUrlCacheEntryFile()`:

```
BOOL RetrieveUrlCacheEntryFile(LPCWSTR lpszUrlName,
    LPINTERNET_CACHE_ENTRY_INFO lpCacheEntryInfo,
    LPDWORD lpdwCacheEntryInfoBufferSize, DWORD dwReserved);
```

The parameters are the same as for `GetUrlCacheEntryInfo()`. If the function is successful, your cached data file is now locked, and will not be removed by other processes. You can now do whatever you want with the file, but remember to unlock it before the cache manager can access it again.

To unlock a cache file, use the `UnlockUrlCacheEntryFile()` function, which is defined as follows:

```
BOOL UnlockUrlCacheEntryFile(LPCWSTR lpszUrlName, DWORD dwReserved);
```

The `lpszUrlName` parameter is the URL of the cache file, and `dwReserved` must be set to 0.

Creating a Cached File

Although using the WinInet functions to download files through HTTP and FTP will automatically add files to the cache, you may sometimes need to manually add a new file. Doing so is basically a two-step process: You need to first specify where to store the entry in the cache:

```
BOOL CreateUrlCacheEntry(LPCWSTR lpszUrlName, DWORD
    dwExpectedFileSize, LPCWSTR lpszFileExtension,
    LPWSTR lpszFileName, DWORD dwReserved);
```

The first parameter, `lpszUrlName`, is the URL for the file you want to put in the cache. The `dwExpectedFileSize` parameter is the size of the file, or 0 if you don't currently know it. You will also pass in the `lpszFileExtension` parameter, which is a buffer containing the extension of the file you are storing. The `lpszFileName` parameter should point to a buffer that is at least the length of MAX_PATH. This parameter will receive the cache path and name for your file when the function returns. Finally, `dwReserved` is set to 0.

Now that you have a cache file path (returned in `lpszFileName`), you can get the file you want to put in the cache using whatever method you want. Once you have the entire file, all you need to do to store it in the cache is call the following:

```
BOOL CommitUrlCacheEntry(LPCWSTR lpszUrlName, LPCWSTR
    lpszLocalFileName, FILETIME ExpireTime, FILETIME
    LastModifiedTime, DWORD CacheEntryType, LPWSTR
    lpHeaderInfo, DWORD dwHeaderSize, LPCWSTR
    lpszFileExtension, DWORD dwReserved);
```

As you've seen before, the `lpszUrlName` parameter is the URL of the file you are sending to the cache. The `lpszLocalFileName` parameter should be the set to the same name that you received from calling the `CreateUrlCacheEntry()` function, which was set in its `lpszFileName` parameter. The `ExpireTime` and `LastModified Time` parameters are time values for the newly cached file. `Cache EntryType` can be set to STICKY_CACHE_ENTRY if you want to make this file persistent in the cache; otherwise, set it to 0. The `lpHeader Info` and `dwHeaderSize` parameters can be used to set any additional header information for your file. Finally, the `lpszFileExtension` parameter should point to a buffer specifying the current file's extension; and `dwReserved` can be set to 0.

Deleting Cache Entries

Deleting an entry in the cache is as simple as calling the `DeleteUrl CacheEntry()` function:

```
BOOL DeleteUrlCacheEntry(LPCWSTR lpszUrlName);
```

The only parameter, `lpszUrlName`, represents the URL for the cached file you want to delete.

Cache Groups

The final topic to cover regarding caching is **cache groups**. Basically, a cache group is a set of several cache entries that relate to one another and are represented by a group identifier. For example, suppose you have an application that reads data from multiple Web sites—you might want to use a cache group to identify all of the entries from one particular site. Later, when your program is offline, you could easily retrieve any entries you are interested in for that site from the cache group, rather than enumerating all of the cache entries.

Before you can add cache entries to a group, you must first create a new cache group identifier by using the function `CreateUrlCacheGroup()`, which is defined as follows:

```
GROUPID CreateUrlCacheGroup(DWORD dwFlags, LPVOID lpReserved);
```

The only option that you can use with the `dwFlags` parameter is `CACHEGROUP_FLAG_GIDONLY`, which creates a unique group identifier, rather than the actual group. Most of the time, you can pass in 0 here. The second parameter, `lpReserved`, must be set to `NULL`.

If it is successful, the function will return a new group identifier that you can use to add cache entries to the group. `CreateUrlCacheGroup()` will return `FALSE` if it fails.

Now that you have a group ID, you can add and remove cache entries to and from the new group. This is done by using the function `SetUrl CacheEntryGroup()`:

```
BOOL SetUrlCacheEntryGroup(LPCWSTR lpszUrlName, DWORD
    dwFlags, GROUPID GroupId, LPBYTE pbGroupAttributes,
    DWORD cbGroupAttributes, LPVOID lpReserved);
```

The first parameter is the familiar `lpszUrlName`, which is the URL for the cache entry. The `dwFlags` parameter specifies whether you are adding or removing an entry from the group. Use the flag `INTERNET_CACHE_GROUP_ADD` to add a file, and `INTERNET_CACHE_ GROUP_REMOVE` to remove it. The `GroupId` parameter should be set to the group ID for which you want to add or remove the file. The last three parameters must all be set to NULL.

If you need to delete the cache group, you can call the following:

```
BOOL DeleteUrlCacheGroup(GROUPID GroupId, DWORD dwFlags,
    LPVOID lpReserved);
```

Finally, if you want to enumerate all the files in a particular group, you can use the `FindFirstUrlCacheEntryEx()` and `FindNextUrl CacheEntryEx()` functions. These work the same as the `FindFirst UrlCacheEntry()` and `FindNextUrlCacheEntry()` functions, with the addition of a few new parameters. When you are finished enumerating, you must call `FindCloseUrlCache()`:

```
HANDLE FindFirstUrlCacheEntryEx(LPCWSTR lpszUrlSearchPattern,
    DWORD dwFlags, DWORD dwFilter, GROUPID GroupId,
    LPINTERNET_CACHE_ENTRY_INFO lpFirstCacheEntryInfo,
    LPDWORD lpdwFirstCacheEntryInfoBufferSize,
    LPVOID lpGroupAttributes, LPDWORD pcbGroupAttributes,
    LPVOID lpReserved);
```

```
BOOL FindNextUrlCacheEntryEx(HANDLE hEnumHandle,
    LPINTERNET_CACHE_ENTRY_INFO lpFirstCacheEntryInfo,
    LPDWORD lpdwFirstCacheEntryInfoBufferSize, LPVOID
    lpGroupAttributes, LPDWORD pcbGroupAttributes,
    LPVOID lpReserved);
```

The parameters are basically the same as what you previously defined for `FindFirstUrlCacheEntry()` and `FindNextUrlCacheEntry()`. The only real addition is the `GroupId` parameter, which specifies the group for which you want to enumerate the entries. `lpGroup Attributes`, `pcbGroupAttributes`, and `lpReserved` should all be set to NULL.

Internet Options

Although you can set several available options for an Internet session, you need only two functions to manipulate them: `InternetSetOption()` and `InternetQueryOption()`. Let's look at their definitions:

```
BOOL InternetSetOption(HINTERNET hInternet, DWORD dwOption,
    LPVOID lpBuffer, DWORD dwBufferLength);
```

```
BOOL InternetQueryOption(HINTERNET hInternet, DWORD
    dwOption, LPVOID lpBuffer, LPDWORD lpdwBufferLength);
```

When working with Internet session options, the first parameter always specifies the Internet handle; the second parameter, `dwOption`, specifies what option you will be working with (see Table 2.5). The last two parameters depend on whether you're getting or setting an option

Table 2.5 Pocket PC Internet Options

Option Name	Get/Set	Description
INTERNET_OPTION_ CALLBACK	Get	The address of the callback for this handle, specified as a DWORD
INTERNET_OPTION_ CONTEXT_VALUE	Both	The context value associated with this handle, specified as a DWORD pointer
INTERNET_OPTION_ CONNECT_TIMEOUT	Both	The timeout value, in milliseconds, before a connection request is cancelled, specified as an unsigned long
INTERNET_OPTION_ CONNECT_RETRIES	Both	The number of times a request will attempt to resolve and connect before failing, specified as an unsigned long
INTERNET_OPTION_ SEND_TIMEOUT	Both	The timeout value, in milliseconds, before a send request is cancelled, specified as an unsigned long

(continued)

Table 2.5 Pocket PC Internet Options (*continued*)

Option Name	Get/Set	Description
INTERNET_OPTION_ RECEIVE_TIMEOUT	Both	The timeout value, in milliseconds, before a receive request is cancelled, specified as an unsigned long
INTERNET_OPTION_ READ_BUFFER_SIZE	Both	The size, in bytes, of the read buffer, specified as an unsigned long
INTERNET_OPTION_ WRITE_BUFFER_SIZE	Both	The size, in bytes, of the write buffer, specified as an unsigned long
INTERNET_OPTION_ USERNAME	Both	The username associated with the session handle, specified as a LPWSTR
INTERNET_OPTION_ PASSWORD	Both	The password associated with the session handle, specified as a LPWSTR
INTERNET_OPTION_ PROXY	Both	Information about the current proxy associated with the session handle, specified as an INTERNET_PROXY_INFO structure
INTERNET_OPTION_ PROXY_PASSWORD	Both	The current proxy password, specified as a LPWSTR
INTERNET_OPTION_ PROXY_USERNAME	Both	The current proxy username, specified as a LPWSTR
INTERNET_OPTION_ USER_AGENT	Both	The User-Agent header that is used for HTTP requests, specified as a LPWSTR
INTERNET_OPTION_ SETTINGS_CHANGED	Both	Notifies the system that an option value has changed, which will force Pocket PC to reload values from the registry
INTERNET_OPTION_ HANDLE_TYPE	Get	The type of Internet connection associated with the session handle (FTP, HTTP, HTTPS), specified as an unsigned long
INTERNET_OPTION_ PARENT_HANDLE	Get	The parent handle to this handle as a HINTERNET

value. If you are setting an option value, lpBuffer will be a pointer to a buffer that contains the option setting, and dwBufferLength will specify its size. When getting option values, lpBuffer will be a pointer to a buffer that receives the option data, and lpdwBufferLength will be a pointer to a variable that contains the length of lpBuffer. When the function returns, if the buffer wasn't large enough, you will get the error ERROR_INSUFFICIENT_BUFFER, and lpdwBufferLength will contain the size, in bytes, that you need to get the option data.

Both functions will return TRUE if they succeed, or FALSE if they fail.

The INTERNET_OPTION_PROXY option uses an INTERNET_PROXY_ INFO structure that specifies the current proxy settings for an Internet session handle:

```
typedef struct {
    DWORD dwAccessType;
    LPCWSTR lpszProxy;
    LPCWSTR lpszProxyBypass;
} INTERNET_PROXY_INFO, *LPINTERNET_PROXY_INFO;
```

The dwAccessType member contains the current access method for the handle, which is the same as what was defined previously for the InternetOpen() function. The lpszProxy field will contain the name of the proxy sever associated with the session handle, and lpsz ProxyBypass will be NULL.

Differences between Windows and Pocket PC WinInet

Note several minor differences between the desktop version of WinInet and what is currently supported on Pocket PC devices:

- There is no direct support for autodialing an Internet connection. The InternetAutodial(), InternetAutodialHangup(), InternetGetConnectedState(), InternetHangup(), and InternetGoOnline() functions are not currently supported on Pocket PC.
- The gopher protocol is not supported on Windows CE.
- Windows CE does not support multiple proxy servers. You can specify only a single proxy server when establishing an Internet connection.
- Several Internet options are not supported on Pocket PC. Consult Table 2.5 for the Internet options currently supported on Pocket PC.
- InternetGetCookie() does not support "named" cookie values.
- The FtpCommand() function is not supported on Pocket PC.
- The FtpGetFile() and FtpPutFile() functions always return the ERROR_INVALID_PARAMETER error. This is a known bug and is documented in Microsoft KB article Q312039 (found at http://support.microsoft.com/).
- Windows CE does not support proxy bypass lists.

Using WinInet

Recall that in order to start a new Internet session through WinInet, you must first get an Internet handle. Note that `HINTERNET` handles are not the same as file system handles, and cannot be used with other functions outside of the WinInet API.

There are basically four steps in performing any operation through WinInet:

1. Open a new Internet session by using the `InternetOpen()` function. A `HINTERNET` connection handle for your current session is returned if successful.
2. Connect to a server using the `InternetOpenUrl()` or `InternetConnect()` functions. You will be returned a connection `HINTERNET` handle for your new connection if successful.
3. Perform the necessary protocol-specific operations to send and receive data (see the sections "Hypertext Transfer Protocol (HTTP and HTTPS)" and "File Transfer Protocol (FTP)").
4. Close your `HINTERNET` handles in reverse order. This is important because Internet handles are hierarchical—you must close your connection `HINTERNET` handle (which was derived from `InternetOpenUrl()` or `InternetConnect()`) before you call `InternetCloseHandle()` on your main Internet session.

To create a new Internet session, you must call the `InternetOpen()` function:

```
HINTERNET InternetOpen(LPCWSTR lpszAgent, DWORD dwAccessType,
    LPCWSTR lpszProxy, LPCWSTR lpszProxyBypass, DWORD dwFlags);
```

When you call this function, the `lpszAgent` parameter is a string that contains the name of the application creating the session, and will be sent as the `User-Agent` header value on HTTP requests. The next parameter describes how your connection will be established with the server. The `dwAccessType` parameter can be set to one of the following:

- `INTERNET_OPEN_TYPE_DIRECT` if you are making a direct connection to the server.

- INTERNET_OPEN_TYPE_PROXY if you are going to be using a proxy server to connect to a server.
- INTERNET_OPEN_TYPE_PRECONFIG to get the configuration information from the registry. This will use the information that the user has configured in Pocket Internet Explorer for his or her Internet connection.

To set the name of the proxy server, use the lpszProxy parameter. This value can be NULL if there is no proxy server. The next parameter, lpszProxyBypass, is ignored by Pocket PC and should be set to NULL. Finally, the dwFlags parameter can be set to INTERNET_FLAG_ASYNC to enable asynchronous (nonblocking) mode on the InternetReadFile() and InternetQueryDataAvailable() functions when a callback is configured with the InternetSetStatusCallback() function. If everything works correctly, InternetOpen() should return a valid HINTERNET handle for your session.

In order to receive data asynchronously (if you used the INTERNET_FLAG_ASYNC flag), you must also set up a callback routine:

```
INTERNET_STATUS_CALLBACK InternetSetStatusCallback
   (HINTERNET hInternet, INTERNET_STATUS_CALLBACK
   lpfnInternetCallback);
```

The first parameter is the handle to the Internet session you just created, and lpfnInternetCallback is a pointer to the address of an INTERNET_STATUS_CALLBACK function, which you write using the following prototype:

```
void CALLBACK INTERNET_STATUS_CALLBACK(HINTERNET hInternet,
   DWORD dwContext, DWORD dwInternetStatus, LPVOID
   lpvStatusInformation, DWORD dwStatusInformationLength);
```

When this function is called, you are passed the handle of the Internet session calling the callback, as well as an application-defined context value in the dwContext parameter (which you set when calling InternetConnect() or InternetOpenUrl()). The next parameter, dwInternetStatus, is the most important one, as it contains the status code for which the callback is being called (and is defined in wininet.h). The final two parameters, lpvStatus Information and dwStatusInformationLength, contain the size and buffer for any additional callback information. The return value is

INTERNET_INVALID_STATUS_CALLBACK if the callback could not be created.

Now that you have completed setting up your Internet session, let's open a connection to a server. This can be accomplished by using the InternetConnect() and InternetOpenUrl() functions. Which function you use depends on what information you have about the server with which you are trying to connect. If you have all the connection information for your server in a well-formed URL address, use Internet OpenUrl(); otherwise, InternetConnect() is probably your better option.

The InternetConnect() function is defined as follows:

```
HINTERNET InternetConnect(HINTERNET hInternet, LPCWSTR
    lpszServerName, INTERNET_PORT nServerPort, LPCWSTR lpszUserName,
    LPCWSTR lpszPassword, DWORD dwService, DWORD wFlags, DWORD
    dwContext);
```

The first parameter is the handle to your Internet session, followed by lpszServerName, which is a null-terminated string containing the host name of the server with which you want to connect. This can also be an address in dotted notation, such as 10.0.5.50. The next parameter, nServerPort, is the server port with which you want to connect. It can be any IANA port or one of the defaults for a specific protocol: INTERNET_DEFAULT_FTP_PORT (port 21), INTERNET_ DEFAULT_HTTP_PORT (port 80), INTERNET_DEFAULT_HTTPS_PORT (port 443), or INTERNET_DEFAULT_SOCKS_PORT (port 1080). The next two parameters, lpszUserName and lpszPassword, are null-terminated strings that set up authorization on the server and that InternetConnect() will use to log on with. If both the username and password parameters are NULL, it will use the system default of "Anonymous" for the username, and the client's e-mail address for the password. The dwService parameter specifies the protocol you want to use, and can be either INTERNET_SERVICE_FTP or INTERNET_SERVICE_HTTP. If you want an FTP connection in passive mode, you need to set the wFlags parameter to INTERNET_ FLAG_PASSIVE; otherwise, it can be set to 0. Finally, to associate an application-defined context value with the connection handle, use the dwContext parameter. If everything proceeds smoothly, you will be returned a HINTERNET handle once a connection is opened; otherwise, a NULL will indicate failure.

If you already have the server information in URL format, it's a lot easier to use the `InternetOpenUrl()` function to create a connection. `InternetOpenUrl()` will parse the address, protocol, username, and password from the URL for you; it is defined as follows:

```
HINTERNET InternetOpenUrl(HINTERNET hInternet, LPCWSTR
    lpszUrl, LPCWSTR lpszHeaders, DWORD dwHeadersLength, DWORD
    dwFlags, DWORD dwContext);
```

The first parameter is the handle to your Internet session, followed by `lpszUrl`, which is a null-terminated string containing the server URL. Pocket PC supports only URLs that point to FTP, HTTP, or HTTPS addresses. If you are using HTTP, the next parameter, `lpszHeaders`, is used if you want to add any additional header strings to the HTTP connection. Use `dwHeadersLength` to specify the size of any added headers. The `dwFlags` parameter contains any additional option flags for the request, and it can be set to `INTERNET_FLAG_RAW_DATA`, `INTERNET_FLAG_RELOAD`, or `INTERNET_FLAG_SECURE`.

The `INTERNET_FLAG_RAW_DATA` option is only for FTP requests. If set, directory data will be returned to a `WIN32_FILE_DATA` structure (the same that is used with `FindFirstFile()`), instead of an HTML representation of the directory. `INTERNET_FLAG_RELOAD` forces the request to get information over the Internet without looking at the local cache. Finally, you can use `INTERNET_FLAG_SECURE` if you want to establish an HTTPS connection. The final parameter, `dwContext`, works the same as in the `InternetConnect()` function. Once a connection is opened, you will be returned an `HINTERNET` handle for the connection, or `NULL` if the connection failed.

Once you are finished with an Internet connection or session, you can close any `HINTERNET` handle by using the `InternetCloseHandle()` function:

```
BOOL InternetCloseHandle(HINTERNET hInternet);
```

Remember that `HINTERNET` handles derive from their parent, so you will want to close the handles returned to you from `InternetConnect()` and `InternetOpenUrl()` before closing the main Internet session handle that was returned from `InternetOpen()`.

Let's look at a short example of how you can set up a basic WinInet session to connect to Microsoft's Web site using `InternetConnect()` and `InternetOpenUrl()`:

```
HINTERNET hInternet = NULL, hIConnect = NULL, hIUrlConnect =
  NULL;

// First, open the Internet connection
hInternet = InternetOpen(TEXT("Sample Application"),
  INTERNET_OPEN_TYPE_DIRECT, NULL, NULL, 0);

// Make sure there are no errors
if(!hInternet)
   return FALSE;

// Next, connect to the Internet via InternetConnect
hIConnect = InternetConnect(hInternet, TEXT("www.
   microsoft.com"), INTERNET_DEFAULT_HTTP_PORT, NULL, NULL,
   INTERNET_SERVICE_HTTP, 0, 0);

// Here would go your functions to download data

// Finally, close the handle
InternetCloseHandle(hIConnect);

// -OR- Connect to the Internet via InternetOpenUrl
hIUrlConnect = InternetOpenUrl(hInternet, TEXT("http://www.
  microsoft.com"), NULL, 0, 0, 0);

// Here would go your functions to download data

// Finally, close the handle
InternetCloseHandle(hIUrlConnect);

// Remember to close the main Internet open handle when you
// are complete.
InternetCloseHandle(hInternet);
```

One last note: If your application needs to make multiple Internet requests, you can typically make a single call to `InternetOpen()`, and continuously reuse the `HINTERNET` session handle for various `Internet`

`Connect()` and `InternetOpenUrl()` connections. Naturally, if your basic connection type (i.e., your proxy connection) needs to change between each connection, you can always call `InternetOpen()` again to get a new session handle.

Hypertext Transfer Protocol (HTTP and HTTPS)

As with any piece of software that communicates over TCP/IP, a protocol is needed to delegate how information is transferred between a client and its server, as well as to define its "session." In the case of the Web, the protocol that is used is the Hypertext Transfer Protocol, also known as HTTP (or HTTPS when referring to "secure" transactions). HTTP is an extremely flexible protocol—it is relatively simple to use, it can make resource requests over firewalls (as most have been designed to allow traffic over port 80), and it can be adapted for numerous types of information transfer between applications other than Web browsers (such as .NET Web Services, SOAP, and so on). In fact, so many applications and technologies are making use of HTTP, it has been referred to as "the cockroach of Internet protocols."

The HTTP Protocol

There are two major versions of HTTP on the Internet today: HTTP/1.0 and HTTP/1.1 (for more detailed information about the protocol commands and extensions, you should check out RFC 1945 and RFC 2068). While they both can make requests in the same basic fashion, HTTP/1.1 adds some additional functionality to the core protocol, such as sessions that stay active between requests, and block transfers.

The HTTP protocol itself is known as a **stateless** protocol. It does not keep track of things that other session-based protocols do, such as connection time, idle time, and so on. Rather, it is intended to be simple: connect, make a request, get a response, and disconnect.

In its most simplistic form, the whole process looks something like what is shown in Figure 2.2.

Although a complete description of the HTTP protocol is beyond the scope of this book, it is important to understand a few basic concepts about what HTTP requests and responses look like. While WinInet will provide you with plenty of support functions and APIs to manipulate the

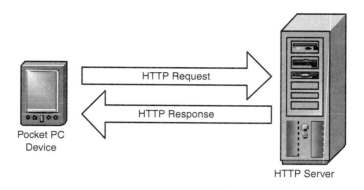

Figure 2.2 HTTP protocol

protocol and download information, the following sections provide basic information about how extendable and useful HTTP can be.

HTTP Requests

When you query an HTTP server for a particular resource (e.g., file, Web page, and so on), the request is accomplished by first making a connection to the server (usually on the well-known HTTP port 80) and then sending an HTTP request message. An HTTP request is typically made up of three parts: the request line, the HTTP header, and an optional HTTP body.

An example of a request line could look something like the following:

```
GET /Index.html HTTP/1.1\r\n
```

The general format is an HTTP command, followed by the resource to download, and the HTTP version that the client can support. In the preceding example, you are instructing the server to GET the /Index.html file using version 1.1 of the HTTP protocol.

The next block of information needed by the server is the actual HTTP header. An HTTP header contains instructions about the request itself, along with information about the client that might be useful to the server, such as the browser type, or connection information. A server can use this information to dynamically create customized content (with an ASP server, such as IIS).

An HTTP request header could look like the following:

```
Connection: Keep-Alive\r\n
Accept: */*\r\n
User-Agent: Sample Application\r\n
Host: www.microsoft.com\r\n\r\n
```

As you can see, the header is comprised of several lines that are formed by a description and a value. For example, the `Accept` line of this request states that the client can receive any data type (designated by the `*/*` value). A blank line is used at the end of the header to indicate that the header is complete.

The final part of an HTTP request is the HTTP body. Typically, the body is left blank unless you are passing specific data to a server (such as form data using the `POST` command).

Therefore, you could construct an entire HTTP request as follows:

```
GET /Index.html HTTP/1.1\r\n
Connection: Keep-Alive\r\n
Accept: */*\r\n
User-Agent: Sample Application\r\n
Host: www.microsoft.com\r\n\r\n
```

HTTP Responses

Once the server receives an HTTP request, it will process it and return an HTTP response to the client (which can be an application, a browser, and so on). An HTTP response contains almost the same type of data as the HTTP request. It will be made up of the response line, the HTTP header, and an HTTP body.

An HTTP response line contains the status of the request (e.g., if it failed, succeeded, needs authorization, and so on):

```
HTTP/1.1 200 OK
```

You can see here that the first piece of a response is the HTTP version that the server is using to communicate with you, followed by an HTTP status code. In this case, the code 200 indicates that the request was successful.

Next, the HTTP response header is returned. This is similar to the request header that was originally sent to the server, as the HTTP response header is comprised of several lines of information, which are formed with a description and a value. It can contain very useful information about the server, response data, and so on, as shown in the following example:

```
Server: Microsoft-IIS/5.0\r\n
Content-Location: http://www.microsoft.com/default.htm\r\n
Date: Tue, 25 Jun 2002 19:33:18 GMT\r\n
Content-Type: text/html\r\n
Accept-Ranges: bytes\r\n
Last-Modified: Mon, 24 Jun 2002 20:27:23 GMT\r\n
Content-Length: 26812\r\n
```

Finally, if the HTTP request was successful, the HTTP response body will then contain the data you requested (which can be binary, HTML, and so on). Once the response body has been transmitted, the HTTP server (if not using HTTP/1.1 Keep-Alive requests) will then disconnect.

Putting the entire process together provides a clearer view of a request and response, as shown in Figure 2.3.

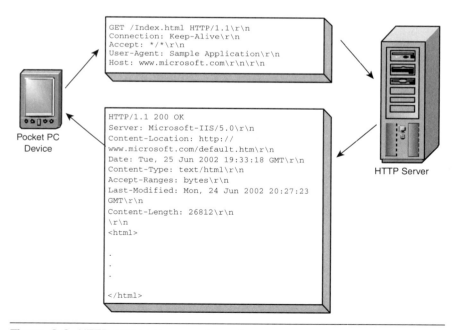

Figure 2.3 HTTP protocol requests and responses

Cookies

A **cookie** is a standardized method by which a server creates user-specific information that is stored on a client device—information such as preferences, passwords, or other types of data. When a client makes an HTTP request to the server that originally created the cookie, it will also transfer the data contained in the cookie. For example, if a Web site has a way to customize its look and feel based on user preferences, those preferences could be stored on a device in the form of a cookie. When the client device accesses that Web site, the browser sends the preference information along with the HTTP request so that the server knows how to customize it.

The actual data that is stored inside a cookie is a set of properties in the form of `name=value` pairs that are separated by commas, with the parameter separated with a semicolon. For example, a cookie might look like the following:

```
username=emily,dogsname=stout,coffee=starbucks;expires=Sat,
   01-Jan-2007 00:00:00 GMT;
```

Table 2.6 lists a few of the reserved value names used with cookies:

Table 2.6 Cookie Reserved Value Names

Name	Description
expires	The date that the cookie expires in GMT. If no expiration date is set, the cookie will expire as soon as the process creating the cookie ends.
domain	The domain for which the cookie is valid.
path	The path part of a URL for which the cookie is valid.
secure	No value is associated with the secure flag. It only indicates that the cookie is safe for sending to HTTPS server requests (`name=value;secure`).

Even though cookies are typically used for Web-based applications, there is no reason why you couldn't use the WinInet cookie functions to store client-specific information for your own applications. You can use two functions on Pocket PC to create and read cookie information: `InternetSetCookie()` and `InternetGetCookie()`.

To create a new cookie, you can use the following:

```
BOOL InternetSetCookie(LPCWSTR lpszUrl, LPCWSTR
  lpszCookieName, LPCWSTR lpszCookieData);
```

The first parameter, `lpszUrl`, is the URL for which the cookie is valid. The `lpszCookieName` parameter can be used to set the name of a cookie, but it also can be set to `NULL` if it is not needed. Finally, `lpszCookieData` should point to the buffer that contains the actual cookie value.

A simple example for creating a cookie would look like the following:

```
TCHAR tchURL[64] = TEXT("http://myweb.com");
TCHAR tchCookieName[64] = TEXT("MyCookie");
TCHAR tchCookieData[128] =
TEXT("username=emily,dogsname=stout,coffee=starbucks;
   expires=Sat, 01-Jan-2007 00:00:00 GMT;");

BOOL fSucceeded = InternetSetCookie(tchURL, tchCookieName,
   tchCookieData);
```

To read cookie information, you use the `InternetGetCookie()` function:

```
BOOL InternetGetCookie(LPCWSTR lpszUrl, LPCWSTR lpszCookieName,
   LPWSTR lpCookieData, LPDWORD lpdwSize);
```

`InternetGetCookie()`'s parameters are similar to those of `InternetSetCookie()`. As before, the `lpszUrl` parameter specifies the URL for which you want to get the cookie, and `lpszCookieName` should be set to `NULL`, as searching for named cookies is not implemented on Pocket PC. When the function returns, the buffer that `lpCookieData` points to will contain the actual cookie information. Finally, `lpdwSize` should point to a `DWORD` value that specifies the size of the `lpCookieData` buffer; otherwise, it will set this to the number of bytes that are needed if the buffer is too small.

Therefore, to read a cookie, you could do the following:

```
TCHAR tchURL[64] = TEXT("http://myweb.com");
TCHAR tchCookieBuffer[128] = TEXT("\0");
DWORD dwSize = 128;
```

```
BOOL fSucceeded = InternetGetCookie(tchURL, NULL, tchCookieBuffer,
   &dwSize);
```

Making an HTTP Request

Using HTTP to request resources is a relatively easy process regardless of which HTTP version you are using (as discussed earlier, the basic protocol works the same for HTTP/1.0 and HTTP/1.1). There are typically four steps for creating an HTTP transaction:

1. Create a connection to an HTTP server on a specified port (typically, port 80).
2. Create a request and send it to the server. A request typically consists of a command and a set of request headers.
3. Read the response from the server. Usually, you should inspect the response header for additional information (such as the size of the response).
4. Close the session. If you are using HTTP/1.1, you can use the `Keep-Alive` header to keep your connection to the server open. Requesting additional URL resources in this situation would only require you to repeat this process from Step 2. Otherwise, the server will automatically close its connection when the transfer is complete.

The first thing you need to do is create a connection to an HTTP server and send it a request for a URL. You can accomplish this by using the `HttpOpenRequest()` function to create a new Internet handle for your request session, followed by `HttpSendRequest()` to build and send the actual request. When using these functions, an actual connection to the server is not made until you call `HttpSendRequest()`:

```
HINTERNET HttpOpenRequest(HINTERNET hConnect, LPCWSTR
   lpszVerb, LPCWSTR lpszObjectName, LPCWSTR lpszVersion, LPCWSTR
   lpszReferrer, LPCWSTR FAR *lplpszAcceptTypes, DWORD dwFlags,
   DWORD dwContext);
```

The first parameter you need to pass in is the handle to the open Internet session returned from previously calling the `InternetOpen()` function. The next three parameters are used to build the actual HTTP request. The HTTP action, such as `GET` or `POST`, is set by using the `lpszVerb` parameter. If you set this to `NULL`, it will default to the `GET` action. Next, `lpszObjectName` should point to a string that has the name of the resource you want to target, and the `lpszVersion` parameter specifies the HTTP version to use for the transfer. If this is set to `NULL`, it will default to HTTP/1.1.

The next set of parameters is used to build the HTTP request header. Use the `lpszReferrer` parameter to specify the URL address of the location making the request (setting the `Http-Referrer` header field), and use `lplpszAcceptTypes` to indicate which MIME content types are accepted by the client. If you set this to `NULL`, no types are accepted (this sets the `Content-Type` header field).

The `dwFlags` parameter is used to control any of the specifics of the actual request, and can be one or more of the flags described in Table 2.7.

The final parameter, `dwContext`, enables you to attach an application-specific value to the session handle. If you receive a `NULL` value when the function returns, an error has occurred. Otherwise, at this point, you should have a valid HTTP request handle (remember that you will need to call `InternetCloseHandle()` on this handle once you have finished using it).

Now that you have a request handle, you can send the request to the server for processing. This is accomplished by using the `HttpSend Request()` function, which is defined as follows:

```
BOOL HttpSendRequest(HINTERNET hRequest, LPCWSTR
   lpszHeaders, DWORD dwHeadersLength, LPVOID lpOptional,
   DWORD dwOptionalLength);
```

The `hRequest` parameter is the request handle returned from `HttpOpenRequest()`. If you have any additional headers to add to this request, you can use the `lpszHeaders` and `dwHeadersLength` parameters to specify the buffer and the size of them (or, you can specify the size to be `-1L` if you want the function to automatically calculate the length of the additional headers). If you have no headers to add, just set both of these to a `NULL` value. The `lpOptional` parameter is used to point to any additional data that you need to send after the headers if you are doing a `POST` operation; otherwise, this too can be set to `NULL`. Finally, `dwOptional Length` is the size of the buffer used for `lpOptional`.

If the function succeeds, it will then contact your server and send the following: the HTTP request, any HTTP headers that are determined

Table 2.7 `HttpOpenRequest()` Flags

Flag	Description
`INTERNET_FLAG_CACHE_ IF_NET_FAIL`	If the network or resource is inaccessible, return the data from the cache.
`INTERNET_FLAG_DONT_ CACHE`	Do not cache any data.
`INTERNET_FLAG_ HYPERLINK`	Force a reload of the data.
`INTERNET_FLAG_IGNORE_ CERT_CN_INVALID`	Disable SSL certificate checking.
`INTERNET_FLAG_IGNORE_ CERT_DATE_INVALID`	Disable SSL certificate date checking.
`INTERNET_FLAG_IGNORE_ REDIRECT_TO_HTTP`	Transparently allow redirection from HTTP to HTTPS locations.
`INTERNET_FLAG_IGNORE_ REDIRECT_TO_HTTPS`	Transparently allow redirection from HTTPS to HTTP locations.
`INTERNET_FLAG_KEEP_ CONNECTION`	Use Keep-Alive for HTTP/1.1 transactions.
`INTERNET_FLAG_MAKE_ PERSISTENT`	Make this item persistent in the cache.
`INTERNET_FLAG_MUST_ CACHE_REQUEST`	Create a temporary file if the file cannot be cached.
`INTERNET_FLAG_NEED_ FILE`	Same as `INTERNET_FLAG_MUST_CACHE_ REQUEST`.
`INTERNET_FLAG_NO_AUTH`	Do not attempt automatic authentication.
`INTERNET_FLAG_NO_ AUTO_REDIRECT`	Do not automatically handle redirection.
`INTERNET_FLAG_NO_ CACHE_WRITE`	Same as `INTERNET_FLAG_DONT_CACHE`.
`INTERNET_FLAG_NO_ COOKIES`	Do not automatically add cookie headers to any requests.
`INTERNET_FLAG_NO_UI`	Disable the cookie UI dialog box.
`INTERNET_FLAG_PRAGMA_ NOCACHE`	Force a request to be handled by the server regardless of whether there is cache data.
`INTERNET_FLAG_RELOAD`	Reload data from the wire.
`INTERNET_FLAG_ RESYNCHRONIZE`	Reload HTTP data if the resource was modified since the last time it was requested.
`INTERNET_FLAG_SECURE`	Use SSL for secure transactions.

by the flags you set, and any additional headers you've specified in `HttpSendRequest()`, followed by the optional data. Be aware that if you use the `lpOptional` parameters, you will need to start your buffer using "/r/n" to ensure that your buffer is properly separated from the HTTP header.

Sending a basic request to get the root Web page would be as simple as the following:

```
// Make an HTTP-style request to a server
// hIConnect is the handle returned to us from a previous call to
// InternetConnect

HINTERNET hIRequest = HttpOpenRequest(hIConnect,
  TEXT("GET"), TEXT("/"), NULL,
  NULL, NULL, 0, 0);


// Send the request
BOOL fSuccess = HttpSendRequest(hIRequest, NULL, 0, NULL, 0);
```

If you examined the HTTP header for what was just sent to the server, it would look like the following:

```
GET / HTTP/1.1\r\n
User-Agent: Sample Application\r\n
Host: www.microsoft.com\r\n\r\n
```

In some instances—especially if you are using HTTP to transfer data for some custom information, rather than a Web site—you might need to add additional headers for your HTTP request. While you can also do this with the `HttpSendRequest()` function, you can get more control of the HTTP headers by using `HttpAddRequestHeaders()`, as you have the capability to add, remove, or replace header commands:

```
BOOL HttpAddRequestHeaders(HINTERNET hRequest, LPCWSTR
  lpszHeaders, DWORD dwHeadersLength, DWORD dwModifiers);
```

As with `HttpSendRequest()`, the `hRequest` parameter is the current request handle returned from `HttpOpenRequest()`. The `lpszHeaders` parameter is a pointer to a buffer of carriage return/ linefeed (or "\r\n") terminated headers that you want to add to your request, and the size is specified by the dwHeadersLength parameter. If you would like HttpAddRequestHeaders() to automatically calculate the length, set dwHeadersLength to –1L. The last parameter, dwModifiers, specifies how the new request headers should be added to the current request. It can be one or more of the following listed in Table 2.8.

Table 2.8 HTTP Request Modifier Flags

Modifier	Description
HTTP_ADDREQ_FLAG_ADD	Add the header if it does not exist.
HTTP_ADDREQ_FLAG_ADD_IF_NEW	Add the header only if it does not exist.
HTTP_ADDREQ_FLAG_COALESCE	Append to the header of the same name.
HTTP_ADDREQ_FLAG_COALESCE_ WITH_COMMA	Append to the header of the same name, with a comma.
HTTP_ADDREQ_FLAG_COALESCE_ WITH_SEMICOLON	Append to the header of the same name, with a semicolon.
HTTP_ADDREQ_FLAG_REPLACE	Replace or remove the header. If the header value is empty, the header is removed; otherwise, it is replaced.

Note that if you are trying to replace or remove a header, you can only modify a single header entry at a time; otherwise, you can use HttpAddRequestHeader() to modify multiple entries.

Now that you have completed modifying the headers, you can then proceed to call HttpSendRequest() to submit your HTTP request. Let's take a look at the previous example now that some of the HTTP headers have been modified:

```
HINTERNET hIRequest = HttpOpenRequest(hIConnect,
    TEXT("GET"), TEXT("/"), NULL, NULL, NULL, 0, 0);

// Modify some headers
TCHAR tchNewHeaders[256] = TEXT("MyHeader:
    TestHeader\r\nCoffee-Order: Double Tall Mocha\r\n");
BOOL fSuccess = HttpAddRequestHeaders(hIRequest,
    tchNewHeaders, -1, HTTP_ADDREQ_FLAG_ADD);
```

```
// Send the request
fSuccess = HttpSendRequest(hIRequest, NULL, 0, NULL, 0);
```

The preceding code would result in a new HTTP header that looked like the following:

```
GET / HTTP/1.1\r\n
MyHeader: TestHeader\r\n
Coffee-Order: Double Tall Mocha\r\n
User-Agent: Sample Application\r\n
Host: www.microsoft.com\r\n\r\n
```

Getting Information from the HTTP Headers

Before we look at retrieving the actual result data from the request, we should take a quick look at how to get information from your HTTP session headers. Both the HTTP request and the HTTP response headers can provide us with a lot of interesting and useful information about the state of your HTTP session. Fortunately, there is an easier method using the HttpQueryInfo() function.

The prototype for HttpQueryInfo() is as follows:

```
BOOL HttpQueryInfo(HINTERNET hRequest, DWORD dwInfoLevel,
  LPVOID lpBuffer, LPDWORD lpdwBufferLength, LPDWORD lpdwIndex);
```

Once again, the hRequest parameter needs to be the HTTP request handle that was previously created with the call to either HttpOpen Request() or InternetOpenUrl(). Next, the dwInfoLevel parameter specifies what information you want to get from the headers that will be placed inside the return buffer to which lpBuffer points. This buffer can be a variety of different types: a string, a SYSTEMTIME value, or a DWORD, depending on what information you are requesting with the dwInfoLevel parameter. For example, if you want to find out the size of the content returned on the request (Content-Length), you use a DWORD value. The lpdwBufferLength parameter is a pointer to the size of your buffer. If the function fails, this will contain the size of bytes you actually need if your buffer is too small. Finally, the lpdwIndex parameter is used if you have multiple headers with the same name—you pass in a pointer to the index of the header to use.

Table 2.9 describes the possible values for the dwInfoLevel parameter.

Table 2.9 Possible Values for `dwInfoLevel`

Value	Description
`HTTP_QUERY_ACCEPT`	Get the accepted media types.
`HTTP_QUERY_ACCEPT_CHARSET`	Get the accepted character sets.
`HTTP_QUERY_ACCEPT_ENCODING`	Get the accepted encoding values.
`HTTP_QUERY_ACCEPT_LANGUAGE`	Get the accepted language name.
`HTTP_QUERY_ACCEPT_RANGES`	Get the range request.
`HTTP_QUERY_AGE`	Get the age value.
`HTTP_QUERY_ALLOW`	Get the supported methods on the server.
`HTTP_QUERY_AUTHORIZATION`	Get the username/password for the request.
`HTTP_QUERY_CACHE_CONTROL`	Get cache control directives.
`HTTP_QUERY_CONNECTION`	Get connection-specific directives.
`HTTP_QUERY_COOKIE`	Get any cookies for the request.
`HTTP_QUERY_CONTENT_BASE`	Get the base URL of the request.
`HTTP_QUERY_CONTENT_ENCODING`	Get any additional response encodings.
`HTTP_QUERY_CONTENT_ID`	Get the identification of the content.
`HTTP_QUERY_CONTENT_LANGUAGE`	Get the language of the content.
`HTTP_QUERY_CONTENT_LENGTH`	Get the length of the content in bytes.
`HTTP_QUERY_CONTENT_LOCATION`	Get the location of the content in the message.
`HTTP_QUERY_CONTENT_MD5`	Get the MD5 digest of the content body.
`HTTP_QUERY_CONTENT_RANGE`	Get the location in the content where the partial data begins.
`HTTP_QUERY_CONTENT_ TRANSFER_ENCODING`	Get any additional content encoding.
`HTTP_QUERY_CONTENT_TYPE`	Get the MIME content type.
`HTTP_QUERY_DATE`	Get the date and time the content was created.
`HTTP_QUERY_ETAG`	Get the entity tag for the content.
`HTTP_QUERY_EXPIRES`	Get the date and time that the content expires.
`HTTP_QUERY_FROM`	Get the e-mail address of the requestor of the content.
`HTTP_QUERY_HOST`	Get the host name and port of the resource request.
`HTTP_QUERY_IF_MATCH`	Get the `If-Match` header field.
`HTTP_QUERY_IF_MODIFIED_ SINCE`	Get the `If-Modified-Since` header field.
`HTTP_QUERY_IF_NONE_MATCH`	Get the `If-None-Match` header field.
`HTTP_QUERY_IF_RANGE`	Get the `If-Range` header field.
`HTTP_QUERY_IF_UNMODIFIED_ SINCE`	Get the `If-Unmodified-Since` header field.

(continued)

Table 2.9 Possible Values for `dwInfoLevel` (*continued*)

Value	Description
`HTTP_QUERY_LAST_MODIFIED`	Get the date and time that the resource was last modified.
`HTTP_QUERY_LOCATION`	Get the URL from the response header.
`HTTP_QUERY_MAX`	Get the maximum value of an `HTTP_QUERY` value.
`HTTP_QUERY_MAX_FORWARDS`	Get the maximum number of forwards for the request.
`HTTP_QUERY_MIME_VERSION`	Get the MIME version of the request.
`HTTP_QUERY_PRAGMA`	Get any application-specific commands.
`HTTP_QUERY_PROXY_ AUTHENTICATE`	Get the authentication request from the proxy server.
`HTTP_QUERY_PROXY_ AUTHORIZATION`	Get the authorization information from the proxy server.
`HTTP_QUERY_PUBLIC`	Get the supported methods on the server.
`HTTP_QUERY_RANGE`	Get the byte range for the content.
`HTTP_QUERY_RAW_HEADERS`	Get all the headers from the server response. Each header value is null-terminated.
`HTTP_QUERY_RAW_HEADERS_CRLF`	Get all the headers from the server response. Each header value is terminated by a carriage return/linefeed (\r\n).
`HTTP_QUERY_REFERER`	Get the URL from which the request originated.
`HTTP_QUERY_REQUEST_METHOD`	Get the action type for the current request.
`HTTP_QUERY_RETRY_AFTER`	Get the amount of time between request retries.
`HTTP_QUERY_SERVER`	Get the name of the server software.
`HTTP_QUERY_SET_COOKIE`	Get the value information to set a cookie on the request.
`HTTP_QUERY_STATUS_CODE`	Get the return status code for the request.
`HTTP_QUERY_STATUS_TEXT`	Get the return status text for the request.
`HTTP_QUERY_TRANSFER_ENCODING`	Get the transfer encoding information.
`HTTP_QUERY_UPGRADE`	Get information about any additional protocols supported on the server.
`HTTP_QUERY_URI`	Get the URL information for the request.
`HTTP_QUERY_USER_AGENT`	Get the `User-Agent` header for the request.
`HTTP_QUERY_VARY`	Get the header information for multiple-version responses.

Value	Description
HTTP_QUERY_VERSION	Get the version information from the server response.
HTTP_QUERY_VIA	Get information on any intermediate protocols between the client and server.
HTTP_QUERY_WARNING	Get the return status information for the request.
HTTP_QUERY_WWW_AUTHENTICATE	Get the authentication scheme of the server.

In addition, you can combine any of the queries with the modifiers described in Table 2.10.

Table 2.10 HTTP Query Modifiers

Modifier	Description
HTTP_QUERY_CUSTOM	Search the header for a name that is specified in `lpBuffer`, and store the value in the same buffer when returning.
HTTP_QUERY_FLAG_NUMBER	Return the header value as a DWORD.
HTTP_QUERY_FLAG_REQUEST_HEADERS	Return header values only for the request headers.
HTTP_QUERY_FLAG_SYSTEMTIME	Return the header value as a SYSTEMTIME.

As you can see by the variety of flags, `HttpQueryInfo()` enables you to inspect any part of the header information that is part of an HTTP request or its response. For example, if you wanted to look at the outgoing HTTP header for the previous example, you could simply do something like this:

```
HINTERNET hIRequest = HttpOpenRequest(hIConnect,
  TEXT("GET"), TEXT("/"), NULL, NULL, NULL, 0, 0);

DWORD dwHeaderSize = 1024;
TCHAR tchHeader[1024] = TEXT("\0");
```

```
// Send the request
BOOL fSuccess = HttpSendRequest(hIRequest, NULL, 0, NULL, 0);

// Inspect the send headers
fSuccess = HttpQueryInfo(hIRequest,
   HTTP_QUERY_FLAG_REQUEST_HEADERS|HTTP_QUERY_RAW_HEADERS_
   CRLF, tchHeader, &dwHeaderSize, 0);
```

The preceding example creates a text buffer to capture the entire outgoing request header. After `HttpQueryInfo()` returns, `tchHeader` will look like the following:

```
GET / HTTP/1.1\r\n
User-Agent: Sample Application\r\n
Host: www.microsoft.com\r\n\r\n
```

If you were interested only in the `User-Agent` field, you could modify the request as follows:

```
fSuccess = HttpQueryInfo(hIRequest,
   HTTP_QUERY_USER_AGENT|HTTP_QUERY_FLAG_REQUEST_HEADERS,
   tchHeader, &dwHeaderSize, 0);
```

After this executes, the `tchHeader` buffer will contain only your `User-Agent` string:

```
Sample Application\r\n
```

Finally, if you need to convert the response information (which is by default stored as a string) into a different data type, such as a number, you can use the `HTTP_QUERY_FLAG_NUMBER` or `HTTP_QUERY_FLAG_SYSTEMTIME` modifiers. For example, if you wanted to find out the length of the content that was returned to you after you made your request, it would be easier to do something with that information if it were in a number format. You could simply call `HttpQueryInfo()` as follows:

```
DWORD dwLength = 0;
DWORD dwLengthSize = sizeof(DWORD);
```

```
// Get the content length
fSuccess = HttpQueryInfo(hIRequest, HTTP_QUERY_CONTENT_LENGTH|
    HTTP_QUERY_FLAG_NUMBER, &dwLength, &dwLengthSize, 0);
```

Your `DWORD` variable, `dwLength`, now will contain the size of the data you received from the server.

Reading HTTP Results

Now that you have learned how to make a request and inspect the response information, you have everything you need to read the actual contents. You can download data from your request using the `Internet ReadFile()` function. Be aware that both HTTP and FTP use this function the same way, and WinInet will determine the protocol it is using by the request handle you pass into it.

Here's what the prototype for `InternetReadFile()` looks like:

```
BOOL InternetReadFile(HINTERNET hFile, LPVOID lpBuffer,
    DWORD dwNumberOfBytesToRead, LPDWORD lpdwNumberOfBytesRead);
```

The `hFile` parameter is the handle to your HTTP request, which you make with either `InternetOpenUrl()` or `HttpOpenRequest()`. Next, `lpBuffer` is a pointer to a buffer that will receive the downloaded content, and `dwNumberOfBytesToRead` is the number of bytes you are attempting to read from the request. The last parameter, `lpdwNumber OfBytesRead`, points to the actual number of bytes that are downloaded into `lpBuffer`. If the function succeeds, the return value for `InternetReadFile()` will be `TRUE`. Be aware that `InternetRead File()` works in a similar fashion to a file handle—if there is no more data to be read, the function will still return `TRUE`, but the `lpdwNumber OfBytesRead` parameter will be 0.

Here's an example of how to read the response from a request:

```
// Download the file
LPVOID lpBuffer = NULL;
DWORD dwRead = 0;
BOOL bActive = TRUE;

lpBuffer = (LPVOID)LocalAlloc(LPTR, 4096);
```

```
if(!lpBuffer) {
    // An error has occurred, so close the handles
    InternetCloseHandle(hIRequest);
    InternetCloseHandle(hIConnect);
    InternetCloseHandle(hInternet);
    return FALSE;
}

do{
    fSuccess = InternetReadFile(hIRequest, lpBuffer, 4096,
        &dwRead);

    if(!fSuccess || dwRead == 0) {
        bActive = FALSE;
        break;
    }

    // Do something with the buffer, and get more data

    memset(lpBuffer, 0, 4096);
    dwRead = 0;
} while(bActive);

LocalFree(lpBuffer);

// Ok, we got our data; make sure to close the handles!
InternetCloseHandle(hIRequest);
InternetCloseHandle(hIConnect);
InternetCloseHandle(hInternet);
```

TIP: Because the data you are receiving is being transmitted over a network, the safest way to ensure that you receive all your content is to first query your request handle for the actual content size (using `HttpQueryInfo()`), before you start reading data. Once you know the size of the content the server is sending, you can compare it with what you have received to make sure you have the entire amount of data.

Once you have completed downloading all of your data, be sure to close all the handles you used to make the request in reverse order (close the request, then the session, then the main Internet handle) using the `InternetCloseHandle()` function.

Additional WinInet HTTP Functions

Several other available WinInet API functions will enable you to have more precise control over an HTTP request (or will just make your life easier). For the sake of completeness, I have included them here.

Time Conversion

HTTP requests use a standardized format for displaying date/time information, which is defined by RFC 1123. The text-based format is in GMT, and can be easily converted from/to a SYSTEMTIME value using the following functions:

```
BOOL InternetTimeFromSystemTime(CONST SYSTEMTIME *pst,
   DWORD dwRFC, LPWSTR lpszTime, DWORD cbTime);

BOOL InternetTimeToSystemTime(LPCWSTR lpszTime,
   SYSTEMTIME *pst, DWORD dwReserved);
```

To convert a SYSTEMTIME structure to a GMT format, use the InternetTimeFromSystemTime() function. The first parameter is the time value to convert, and dwRFC specifies the format. Pocket PC supports only INTERNET_RFC1123_FORMAT for this parameter. Finally, the cbTime and lpszTime parameters point to a text buffer and its size, respectively. This will be used to store the string containing the converted time format.

For example, the following converts the current time to a valid RFC 1123 Internet time:

```
SYSTEMTIME sysTime;
TCHAR tchInternetTime[256] = TEXT("\0");
GetLocalTime(&sysTime);

InternetTimeFromSystemTime(&sysTime, INTERNET_RFC1123_FORMAT,
   tchInternetTime, 256);
```

This would cause the tchInternetTime buffer to be set as follows:

```
Tue, 18 Jun 2002 09:52:40 GMT
```

To do the reverse conversion (from an Internet time to a `SYSTEM TIME`), you can use the `InternetTimeToSystemTime()` function. The only parameter it needs is `lpszTime`, which is a buffer in GMT format, and `pst`, which points to a `SYSTEMTIME` variable to receive the converted data. The `dwReserved` parameter is not used and should be set to 0.

Advanced HTTP File Operations

The `InternetSetFilePointer()` function enables you to set the position in the remote file where you would like the file pointer to be set for future calls to `InternetReadFile()`. This function can be used only when the target file is already in the local Internet cache, or the HTTP server you are talking with supports random access reading of files, specifically to be used with the HTTP/1.1 protocol. Here's the definition of `InternetSetFilePointer()`:

```
DWORD InternetSetFilePointer(HINTERNET hFile, LONG
    lDistanceToMove, PVOID pReserved, DWORD dwMoveMethod,
    DWORD dwContext);
```

As usual, the `hFile` parameter is the Internet handle that was returned from either the `InternetOpenUrl()` or `HttpOpenRequest()` functions. The `lDistanceToMove` parameter is the number of bytes (positive or negative) that the file pointer should move, and the `pReserved` parameter should be set to `NULL`. As with the file-based `SetFile Pointer()` function, the `dwMoveMethod` parameter can be `FILE_BEGIN`, `FILE_CURRENT`, or `FILE_END`, depending on where you want to start the move from. The final parameter, `dwContext`, is not used and should be set to `NULL`.

Another function to mention is `InternetQueryDataAvailable()`. This function provides you with an easy way to query the amount of data, in bytes, that is currently available in the receive buffer for a particular request handle (that was created by using the `InternetOpenUrl()` or `HttpOpenRequest()` functions). You can use this as an alternative to checking the result header information along with the return values to the `InternetReadFile()` function. Here's what the function looks like:

```
BOOLAPI InternetQueryDataAvailable(HINTERNET hFile,
    LPDWORD lpdwNumberOfBytesAvailable, DWORD dwFlags,
    DWORD dwContext);
```

The first parameter will be the handle for your request, which is followed by `lpdwNumberOfBytesAvailable`, a pointer to a `DWORD` value, which will return the number of bytes that are ready for you to read with the next call to `InternetReadFile()`. The last two parameters should be set to 0.

Locking Cached Data

Because you are on a portable device, your applications need to perform both on and off the network, as you might go offline frequently. In this operating mode, it is important to frequently update your Internet-cached files so that your application can perform properly even when the network is not available. If you ever need to lock a file that is in the Internet cache, you can use the functions `InternetLockRequestFile()` and `InternetUnlockRequestFile()`. Once a file is locked, if your application attempts to download data from the data Internet location as specified in the cache, Pocket PC will protect the file until you call the unlock function. Here's how the functions are prototyped:

```
BOOL InternetLockRequestFile(HINTERNET hInternet,
    HANDLE *lphLockRequestInfo);


BOOL InternetUnlockRequestFile(HANDLE hLockRequestInfo);
```

The `InternetLockRequestFile()` function is fairly simple: Pass in a `HINTERNET` request handle from `InternetOpenUrl()` or `HttpOpenRequest()` and you will be passed back a pointer to a lock request handle. The `InternetUnlockRequestFile()` function needs this handle to unlock the file.

File Transfer Protocol (FTP)

Another popular method for transferring files over the Internet is the **File Transfer Protocol** (**FTP**). Unlike HTTP, an application that uses FTP will typically connect to a server and remain connected while it transfers multiple files back and forth. Even though the last few years have seen a significant number of file transfer operations moving toward using HTTP and GET requests, FTP still remains a popular protocol, as it provides good access control and a reliable file transfer mechanism. Pocket PC supports FTP through many of the same WinInet API functions you have already seen (such as `InternetReadFile()`), with the addition of a few FTP-specific commands.

WARNING: Be aware of a bug that currently exists in Pocket PC regarding FTP connections and user authorization. Currently, WinInet's FTP support *always* uses "anonymous" for the username and password, regardless of what you set them to, making FTP unusable on servers that require authorization. This problem has been fixed in the latest service pack to Pocket PC. Please visit http://www.microsoft.com/pocketpc for more information.

The FTP Protocol

Before we dive into how you can use WinInet to perform FTP-based transfers, let's take a quick look at the FTP protocol itself (see Figure 2.4).

FTP is unlike other protocols we've seen so far in that it actually uses *two* TCP connections to communicate to the server and transfer files. The first connection, which is known as the *control* connection, is established when a client connects to an FTP server (its well-known port is 21). Once you have connected, the client application uses the control connection to communicate back and forth with the FTP server, sending commands and receiving responses much in the same way HTTP does. This may include operations such as navigating directories and removing files.

Once the client finds a file to transfer, you need to establish your second connection, which is known as the *data* connection. The data connection is unlike others you've seen so far—the server initiates the connection

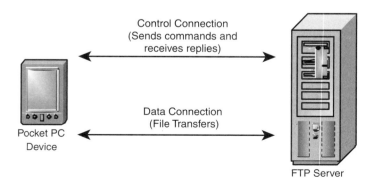

Figure 2.4 FTP protocol

by contacting the client on a specified port. This happens when a client sends the server the `PORT` command (which contains the client's IP address and an available port), which is followed by the actual file request (using the `RETR` command). Once a connection from the server to the client has been accepted, the server transfers the file to the client. Once the transfer is complete, the data connection is closed; however, the control connection remains active throughout the process until you disconnect from the FTP server or a timeout occurs.

If you are concerned about security, or are running your device inside a firewall or NAT server, the FTP protocol also supports the concept of a passive (or `PASV`) data connection. Instead of sending the server a port that is currently available on the client to host the data connection, FTP can request a transfer that instructs the server to open an additional port for it to listen on. Using a passive FTP transfer still requires two connections; however, both are initiated from the client. You can specify that you want to be in passive mode by using the `INTERNET_FLAG_PASSIVE` flag when creating a new Internet connection handle.

While FTP might initially seem more complicated than HTTP, you will find that WinInet handles most of the complexities associated with the protocol for you. More detailed information about the actual FTP protocol commands can be found in RFC 959.

Establishing an FTP Connection

Before you can perform any specific WinInet FTP command, you need to have a `HINTERNET` handle for an active connection to your target FTP server. This can be accomplished in the same way you created a connection for HTTP. First, initiate an Internet connection using the `InternetOpen()` function, and then establish a connection to the FTP server using either the `InternetConnect()` or `InternetOpenUrl()` functions:

```
HINTERNET hInternet = NULL, hIConnect = NULL, hIUrlConnect =
   NULL;

// First, open the Internet connection
hInternet = InternetOpen(TEXT("Sample Application"),
   INTERNET_OPEN_TYPE_DIRECT, NULL, NULL, 0);

// Make sure there are no errors
if(!hInternet)
   return FALSE;
```

```
// Next, connect to the Internet via InternetConnect
hIConnect = InternetConnect(hInternet,
   TEXT("ftp.microsoft.com"), INTERNET_DEFAULT_FTP_PORT,
   NULL, NULL, INTERNET_SERVICE_FTP, INTERNET_FLAG_PASSIVE, 0);

// Finally, close the handles
InternetCloseHandle(hIConnect);

// -OR- Connect to the Internet via InternetOpenUrl
hIUrlConnect = InternetOpenUrl(hInternet,
   TEXT("ftp://ftp.microsoft.com/"), NULL, 0, INTERNET_FLAG_PASSIVE, 0);

// Finally, close the handles
InternetCloseHandle(hIUrlConnect);
InternetCloseHandle(hInternet);
```

As with HTTP, any HINTERNET handle that you have opened must be closed using the `InternetCloseHandle()` function. Notice that in both instances of connecting to an FTP server, you use the INTERNET_FLAG_PASSIVE flag to create a passive FTP session.

After you have established a connection to the FTP server, you can proceed to navigate around and transfer files using the WinInet FTP APIs.

FTP Navigation and Manipulation

Because the files located on an FTP server are stored in a directory structure (similar to the Pocket PC object store or the Win32 file system), several available functions will simplify finding files, navigating directories, and deleting files.

Once you have established an FTP connection, you can enumerate the files that are located in a remote FTP directory by using the `FtpFindFirstFile()` and `InternetFindNext()` file functions. The `FtpFindFirstFile()` function is similar to the other enumeration functions we've already examined, such as `FindFirstUrlCache Entry()` or `FindFirstFile()`, which enable you to "walk" the files in a particular directory that match a specific pattern. After calling the first function, you receive a handle that you can keep calling to get additional file information until there are no more to enumerate.

Here is the definition for `FtpFindFirstFile()`:

```
HINTERNET FtpFindFirstFile(HINTERNET hConnect, LPCWSTR
  lpszSearchFile, LPWIN32_FIND_DATA lpFindFileData, DWORD dwFlags,
    DWORD dwContext);
```

The first parameter is the handle to your active FTP connection, followed by a string that contains the filename or path you want to search. You can always pass a `NULL` value into `lpszSearchFile` if you want to return all files in the current directory. The next parameter, `lpFindFileData`, is a pointer to the standard Windows `WIN32_FIND_DATA` structure, which will receive information about the file. The `dwFlags` parameter is used to control how data is received from the server, and can be one of the flags in Table 2.11.

Table 2.11 FTP Control Flags

Flag	Description
INTERNET_FLAG_DONT_CACHE	Do not cache any data.
INTERNET_FLAG_HYPERLINK	Force a reload of the data.
INTERNET_FLAG_MUST_CACHE_ REQUEST	Create a temporary file if the file cannot be cached.
INTERNET_FLAG_NEED_FILE	Same as INTERNET_FLAG_MUST_ CACHE_REQUEST.
INTERNET_FLAG_RELOAD	Reload data from the wire.
INTERNET_FLAG_RESYNCHRONIZE	Reload FTP data if the resource was modified since the last time it was requested.

The final parameter, `dwContext`, is an application-defined value that you can use to send your callback routine if you created one using the `InternetSetStatusCallback()` function. You cannot create multiple file enumerations at the same time over FTP. Once you call `FtpFindFirstFile()`, you must close the enumerator with `InternetCloseHandle()` before you can create a new instance of `FtpFindFirstFile()`, or else the function will fail.

Now that you have created your enumerator, you can list additional files that match the pattern specified by calling the `InternetFind NextFile()` function:

```
BOOL InternetFindNextFile(HINTERNET hFind, LPVOID lpvFindData);
```

This function takes only two parameters: `hFind`, which is the handle you were returned from `FtpFindFirstFile()`, and a pointer to a `WIN32_FIND_DATA` structure to receive additional file information.

Once you have finished with your enumeration, you need to call `InternetCloseHandle()` to properly close it. For example, if you wanted to output all of the files located in the root directory of an FTP site, you could simply do the following:

```
HINTERNET hInternetFind = NULL;
WIN32_FIND_DATA w32FindData;
BOOL fContinue = TRUE;
memset(&w32FindData, 0, sizeof(WIN32_FIND_DATA));

hInternetFind = FtpFindFirstFile(hIConnect, NULL,
  &w32FindData, 0, 0);

do {
   // Do something with the file information here

   // Get the next file
   memset(&w32FindData, 0, sizeof(WIN32_FIND_DATA));
   fContinue = InternetFindNextFile(hInternetFind,
      &w32FindData);
} while(fContinue);

// Close the find enumerator
InternetCloseHandle(hInternetFind);
```

If you need to directly navigate to a directory or want to find out where you are in the FTP directory tree, you can simply use the `FtpSetCurrentDirectory()` and `FtpGetCurrentDirectory()` functions to set or retrieve information about the current path:

```
BOOL FtpSetCurrentDirectory(HINTERNET hConnect, LPCWSTR
  lpszDirectory);
```

```
BOOL FtpGetCurrentDirectory(HINTERNET hConnect,
  LPWSTR lpszCurrentDirectory, LPDWORD lpdwCurrentDirectory);
```

The `FtpSetCurrentDirectory()` function simply takes the current FTP connection handle as the first parameter, followed by the directory to which you want to switch.

To use the `FtpGetCurrentDirectory()` function, pass the connection handle along with a buffer to receive the directory name. The last parameter, `lpdwCurrentDirectory`, will receive a pointer to the size of the buffer that was copied into `lpszCurrentDirectory`.

Finally, using FTP also enables you to manipulate directories by either creating or removing them (as long as your current authorization level permits it). To remove a directory, call the `FtpRemoveDirectory()` function:

```
BOOL FtpRemoveDirectory(HINTERNET hConnect, LPCWSTR lpszDirectory);
```

Once again, you will pass in the active FTP connection handle as the first parameter, followed by a buffer containing the name of the directory you want to delete. Conversely, if you want to create a new directory, just call `FtpCreateDirectory()`, which is defined as follows:

```
BOOL FtpCreateDirectory (HINTERNET hConnect, LPCWSTR lpszDirectory);
```

The `FtpCreateDirectory()` function takes the same parameters as `FtpRemoveDirectory()`.

Working with Files

Now that you've learned how to explore what is on an FTP server, as well as navigate around, let's take a look at what FTP is designed to do—transfer files.

Downloading a file from an FTP server is similar to what you saw with HTTP—you first need to open the file, and then use the `Internet ReadFile()` function to read the data for the transfer. To open an FTP file request, you can use the `FtpOpenFile()` function:

```
HINTERNET WINAPI FtpOpenFile(HINTERNET hConnect, LPCWSTR
  lpszFileName, DWORD dwAccess, DWORD dwFlags, DWORD dwContext);
```

After passing in the handle to your active FTP connection, you use the `lpszFileName` parameter to pass in the name of the file you want to download. The next parameter, `dwAccess`, specifies how you are accessing the remote file, and can be set to either the `GENERIC_READ` or `GENERIC_WRITE` flag. The `dwFlags` parameter is used to set specifics of the file download, and can be a combination of the flags in Table 2.12.

Table 2.12 FTP File Download Flags

Flag	Description
FTP_TRANSFER_TYPE_ASCII	Transfer the file as an ASCII file.
FTP_TRANSFER_TYPE_BINARY	Transfer the file as a binary file (default).
FTP_TRANSFER_TYPE_UNKNOWN	Same as FTP_TRANSFER_TYPE_BINARY.
INTERNET_FLAG_TRANSFER_ASCII	Same as FTP_TRANSFER_TYPE_ASCII.
INTERNET_FLAG_TRANSFER_BINARY	Same as FTP_TRANSFER_TYPE_BINARY.
INTERNET_FLAG_DONT_CACHE	Do not cache any data.
INTERNET_FLAG_HYPERLINK	Force a reload of the data.
INTERNET_FLAG_MUST_CACHE_REQUEST	Create a temporary file if the file cannot be cached.
INTERNET_FLAG_NEED_FILE	Same as INTERNET_FLAG_MUST_CACHE_REQUEST.
INTERNET_FLAG_RELOAD	Reload data from the wire.
INTERNET_FLAG_RESYNCHRONIZE	Reload FTP data if the resource was modified since the last time it was requested.

The final parameter, `dwContext`, can be set to a `DWORD` value that will be passed to a callback function if you have set one up using the `InternetSetStatusCallback()` API. Be aware that once `FtpOpenFile()` has been called, all other FTP functions that use the same FTP connection handle will fail until you have called `InternetCloseHandle()` on the file handle returned from the original call to `FtpOpenFile()`.

The following example downloads a file using the connection previously established:

```
// Download a file
HINTERNET hTransfer = NULL;
```

```
LPVOID lpBuffer = NULL;
DWORD dwRead = 0, dwBytesAvailable = 0;
BOOL bActive = TRUE, fSuccess = FALSE;
HANDLE hFileDownload = NULL;
TCHAR tchName[MAX_PATH] = TEXT("\\MISC\\INDEX.TXT");

// Open the transfer
hTransfer = FtpOpenFile(hIConnect, tchName, GENERIC_READ,
   FTP_TRANSFER_TYPE_ASCII, 0);

// Ok, the file transfer is active. Create a new file to write to
hFileDownload = CreateFile(TEXT("\\index.txt"), GENERIC_WRITE, 0,
   NULL, CREATE_ALWAYS, FILE_ATTRIBUTE_NORMAL, NULL);
lpBuffer = (LPVOID)LocalAlloc(LPTR, 4096);

if(!lpBuffer) {
   // Close the handles
   InternetCloseHandle(hTransfer);
   InternetCloseHandle(hIConnect);
   InternetCloseHandle(hInternet);
   return FALSE;
}

// Looks like everything's ok, so use InternetReadFile to download
// the file
do{
   fSuccess = InternetReadFile(hTransfer, lpBuffer, 4096,
      &dwRead);

   if(!fSuccess || dwRead == 0) {
      bActive = FALSE;
      break;
   }

   // Write out the buffer, and get more data
   DWORD dwWritten = 0;
   WriteFile(hFileDownload, lpBuffer, dwRead, &dwWritten, NULL);

   // Clear the buffer
   memset(lpBuffer, 0, 4096);
   dwRead = 0;
} while(bActive);
```

```
LocalFree(lpBuffer);
CloseHandle(hFileDownload);
InternetCloseHandle(hTransfer);
```

Sending a file to an FTP server is essentially the same operation as downloading a file: First open a file connection handle using `FtpOpenFile()`, and then write the data in "blocks" to the server using the `InternetWriteFile()` function. When you call `FtpOpenFile()` to send a file, be sure to specify `GENERIC_WRITE` for the `dwAccess` parameter. `InternetWriteFile()` is defined as follows:

```
BOOL InternetWriteFile(HINTERNET hFile, LPCVOID lpBuffer,
   DWORD dwNumberOfBytesToWrite, LPDWORD lpdwNumberOfBytesWritten);
```

To use `InternetWriteFile()`, you will need to pass in the `HINTERNET` handle you received from the original call to `FtpOpenFile()` in the `hFile` parameter. The `lpBuffer` parameter contains a pointer to the buffer of data that you want to send to the server, whose size is specified by a `DWORD` that you place in `dwNumberOfBytesToWrite`. Finally, `lpdwNumberOfBytesWritten` returns a pointer to a `DWORD` value that specifies the number of bytes that were sent to the server.

Sending a file to an FTP server then would look something like the following:

```
// Upload a file
HINTERNET hTransfer = NULL;
LPVOID lpBuffer = NULL;
DWORD dwRead = 0, dwBytesAvailable = 0;
BOOL bActive = TRUE, fSuccess = FALSE;
DWORD HANDLE hFileUpload = NULL;
TCHAR tchName[MAX_PATH] = TEXT("\\Misc\\UploadName.txt");

// Open the transfer
hTransfer = FtpOpenFile(hIConnect, tchName, GENERIC_WRITE,
   FTP_TRANSFER_TYPE_ASCII, 0);

// Ok, the file transfer is active. Open the local file
hFileUpload = CreateFile(TEXT("\\UploadName.txt"),
   GENERIC_READ, 0, NULL, OPEN_EXISTING, FILE_ATTRIBUTE_NORMAL,
      NULL);
lpBuffer = (LPVOID)LocalAlloc(LPTR, 4096);
```

```
if(!lpBuffer) {
    // Close the handles
    InternetCloseHandle(hTransfer);
    InternetCloseHandle(hIConnect);
    InternetCloseHandle(hInternet);
    return FALSE;
}


// Looks like everything's ok, so use InternetWriteFile to upload
// the file
do{
    DWORD dwWritten = 0;

    // Read into the buffer from the local file
    ReadFile(hFileUpload, lpBuffer, 4096, &dwRead, NULL);

    // Send the buffer
    fSuccess = InternetWriteFile(hTransfer, lpBuffer, dwRead,
        &dwWritten);

    if(!fSuccess || dwRead == 0) {
        bActive = FALSE;
        break;
    }

    memset(lpBuffer, 0, 4096);
    dwRead = 0;
} while(bActive);


LocalFree(lpBuffer);

CloseHandle(hFileUpload);
InternetCloseHandle(hTransfer);
```

Finally, the last piece of functionality to examine is the ability to rename and delete files on the server. To delete a file, you use the FtpDeleteFile() function:

```
BOOL FtpDeleteFile(HINTERNET hConnect, LPCWSTR
    lpszFileName);
```

The first parameter, hConnect, is the typical FTP connection handle, and lpszFileName is the name and path of the file you want to delete on the remote server. If the file is successfully deleted, the function will return TRUE; otherwise, it will return FALSE.

Finally, if you want to rename a file, you can use the following function:

```
BOOL FtpRenameFile(HINTERNET hConnect, LPCWSTR lpszExisting,
    LPCWSTR lpszNew);
```

The FtpRenameFile() function also requires an active FTP connection handle. This is followed by the lpszExisting parameter, which specifies the current filename, and the lpszNew parameter, which contains a string buffer for the new name for the file.

Remember that both the FtpDeleteFile() and FtpRename File() functions will fail if you do not have sufficient access on the FTP server.

CHAPTER 3

Internet Protocol Helper APIs

The details of my life are quite inconsequential.

—*Dr. Evil*, Austin Powers: International Man of Mystery

This chapter explores the **Internet Protocol Helper** (**IPHelper**) library. The IPHelper APIs provide you with several functions that enable your application to programmatically interact with the various layers of the TCP/IP protocol stack (described in Chapter 1). You can use IPHelper to reconfigure your network connections, query various protocol statistics, manage individual network adapters, and modify the current network route tables. In addition, the IPHelper event notification APIs are used to signal your application when certain network configuration properties change on the device. Bottom line: IPHelper is a great tool if you want to explore the nitty-gritty details of what's going on with any part of TCP/IP on your device.

Looking at Figure 3.1, you can see how IPHelper communicates with the various levels of the TCP/IP stack to provide information about the current network configuration, network adapters, and various protocol statistics.

To use the IPHelper library with your application, you need to include the `iphlpapi.h` and `iptypes.h` header files and link with the `iphlpapi.lib` library.

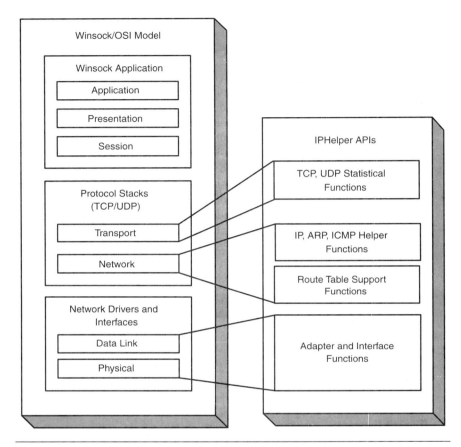

Figure 3.1 The IPHelper library and TCP/IP OSI layers

Network Adapters and Configuration

To find out some basic information about the device's overall network configuration, such as its host name or the DNS servers that are currently being used, you can use the GetNetworkParams() function:

```
DWORD GetNetworkParams(FIXED_INFO *pFixedInfo, ULONG *pOutBufLen);
```

The first parameter, pFixedInfo, is a pointer to a FIXED_INFO structure that will receive the current configuration information; it is followed by pOutBufLen, a pointer to a ULONG that specifies the size of the pFixedInfo structure. If the function succeeds, it will return a value of ERROR_SUCCESS. If the function returns with a value of ERROR_BUFFER_OVERFLOW, the size of the variable you passed in for pFixedInfo was not large enough, and the pOutBufLen pointer will contain the actual size that you need, as shown in the following example:

```
FIXED_INFO *pFixedInfo = NULL;
DWORD dwSize = 0;

// Call into GetNetworkParams to get the size we need for
// FIXED_INFO
if(GetNetworkParams(NULL, &dwSize) != ERROR_BUFFER_OVERFLOW)
   return FALSE;

// Allocate a buffer
pFixedInfo = (FIXED_INFO *)LocalAlloc(LPTR, dwSize);
if(!pFixedInfo)
   return FALSE;

// Get the network information
if(GetNetworkParams(pFixedInfo, &dwSize) != NO_ERROR) {
   LocalFree(pFixedInfo);
   return FALSE;
}

// Do something with pFixedInfo here

// Remember to free the buffer when done with it
LocalFree(pFixedInfo);
```

The FIXED_INFO structure used with GetNetworkParams() is defined as follows:

```
typedef struct {
   char HostName[MAX_HOSTNAME_LEN+4];
   char DomainName[MAX_DOMAIN_NAME_LEN+4];
   PIP_ADDR_STRING CurrentDnsServer;
   IP_ADDR_STRING DnsServerList;
   UINT NodeType;
   char ScopeId[MAX_SCOPE_ID_LEN+4];
   UINT EnableRouting;
   UINT EnableProxy;
   UINT EnableDns;
} FIXED_INFO, *PFIXED_INFO;
```

The first field, `HostName`, is the name of your device as defined by DNS, and is followed by the current DNS domain in the `DomainName` field. The next two fields, `CurrentDnsServer` and `DnsServerList`, contain information about the DNS servers that the device is currently using. `CurrentDnsServer` points to the primary domain server, and `DnsServerList` is an `IP_ADDR_STRING` list of servers. The `IP_ADDR_STRING` structure is used frequently in the IPHelper APIs for enumerating lists of IP addresses. It is defined as follows:

```
typedef struct _IP_ADDR_STRING {
    struct _IP_ADDR_STRING* Next;
    IP_ADDRESS_STRING IpAddress;
    IP_MASK_STRING IpMask;
    DWORD Context;
} IP_ADDR_STRING, *PIP_ADDR_STRING;
```

Because the `IP_ADDR_STRING` structure is used as a linked list, the `Next` field points to the next `IP_ADDR_STRING` in the list. If there are no further addresses to be enumerated, this will be a `NULL` value. It is followed by `IpAddress`, a character string (not Unicode) containing the dotted decimal representation of an IP Address (e.g., 192.168.0.1). This is followed by its corresponding subnet mask in the `IpMask` field. These values can be converted from dotted notation to `IPAddr` format using the `inet_addr()` and `inet_ntoa()` functions described in Chapter 1. Finally, the `Context` field specifies a network table entry (NTE), which is used when adding and deleting IP addresses.

If we continue to look at `FIXED_INFO`, the next fields—`NodeType` and `ScopeId`—specify whether we're using a DHCP connection, and are followed by our current scope name if DHCP is enabled. The final three fields, `EnableRouting`, `EnableProxy`, and `EnableDns` indicate whether routing, ARP proxy services, and DNS are enabled on the local device, respectively.

Adapter Management

Now that we've taken a look at retrieving the overall device network settings, let's look at how you can get more detailed information regarding the individual network adapters. This can be accomplish by using the `GetAdaptersInfo()` function, which will return a linked list of `IP_ADAPTER_INFO` structures—each of which contains information unique to the network adapter, such as its MAC address or DHCP lease information. The `GetAdaptersInfo()` function is defined as follows:

```
DWORD GetAdaptersInfo(IP_ADAPTER_INFO *pAdapterInfo,
    ULONG *pOutBufLen);
```

The `pAdapterInfo` parameter is a pointer to a buffer that will receive the linked list of `IP_ADAPTER_INFO` structures when the function returns. The `pOutBufLen` parameter is also a pointer and should point to a `ULONG` buffer that contains the size of the buffer passed into the `pAdapterInfo` structure. Similar to the `GetNetworkParams()` function, if the buffer is not large enough to hold the adapter data, the function will return with an `ERROR_BUFFER_OVERFLOW` return value and `pOutBufLen` will contain the required buffer size to contain the data.

Here's what the `IP_ADAPTER_INFO` looks like:

```
typedef struct _IP_ADAPTER_INFO {
    struct _IP_ADAPTER_INFO* Next;
    DWORD ComboIndex;
    char AdapterName[MAX_ADAPTER_NAME_LENGTH+4];
    char Description[MAX_ADAPTER_DESCRIPTION_LENGTH+4];
    UINT AddressLength;
    BYTE Address[MAX_ADAPTER_ADDRESS_LENGTH];
    DWORD Index;
    UINT Type;
    UINT DhcpEnabled;
    PIP_ADDR_STRING CurrentIpAddress;
    IP_ADDR_STRING IpAddressList;
    IP_ADDR_STRING GatewayList;
    IP_ADDR_STRING DhcpServer;
    BOOL HaveWins;
    IP_ADDR_STRING PrimaryWinsServer;
    IP_ADDR_STRING SecondaryWinsServer;
    time_t LeaseObtained;
    time_t LeaseExpires;
} IP_ADAPTER_INFO, *PIP_ADAPTER_INFO;
```

Table 3.1 describes the fields of the `IP_ADAPTER_INFO` structure.

If you need more specific information about an individual adapter's configuration, such as the DNS address list, you can use the `GetPer AdapterInfo()` function. To use it, however, you must already know

Table 3.1 `IP_ADAPTER_INFO` Field Descriptions

Field	Description
`Next`	Pointer to the next `IP_ADAPTER_INFO` structure. `NULL` if there are no further adapters
`ComboIndex`	Unused
`AdapterName`	The name of the adapter
`Description`	The description of the adapter
`AddressLength`	The length of the `Address` field
`Address`	The hardware MAC address of the adapter
`Index`	The adapter index
`Type`	The adapter type
`DhcpEnabled`	Specifies if DHCP is enabled on the device
`CurrentIpAddress`	Pointer to the current IP address
`IpAddressList`	A linked list of `IP_ADDR_STRING` structures specifying the IP addresses associated with the adapter
`GatewayList`	An `IP_ADDR_STRING` structure specifying the default gateway associated with the adapter
`DhcpServer`	An `IP_ADDR_STRING` structure specifying the default DHCP server associated with the adapter
`HaveWins`	Specifies if WINS is enabled
`PrimaryWinsServer`	An `IP_ADDR_STRING` structure specifying the primary WINS server associated with the adapter
`SecondaryWinsServer`	An `IP_ADDR_STRING` structure specifying the secondary WINS server associated with the adapter
`LeaseObtained`	The date/time information specifying when the current DHCP lease was obtained
`LeaseExpires`	The date/time information specifying when the current DHCP lease will expire

the `Index` of the particular adapter you want to query. This can be obtained either from the `IP_ADAPTER_INFO` structure's `Index` field or by using the `GetAdapterIndex()` function:

```
DWORD GetAdapterIndex(LPWSTR AdapterName, ULONG *pIfIndex);
```

The `AdapterName` parameter is a buffer containing the name of the adapter, followed by `pIfIndex`, which is a pointer to a `ULONG` variable that will receive the adapter index if the function returns successfully.

Once you have the obtained the adapter index, you can use the following function:

```
DWORD GetPerAdapterInfo(LONG IfIndex, IP_PER_ADAPTER_INFO
   *pPerAdapterInfo,
   ULONG *pOutBufLen);
```

The first parameter, `IfIndex`, is the index of the adapter, and is followed by a pointer to an `IP_PER_ADAPTER_INFO` structure that will receive the adapter information. The final parameter, `pOutBufLen`, is a pointer to the size of the buffer specified by the `pPerAdapterInfo` parameter.

The `IP_PER_ADAPTER_INFO` structure is defined as follows:

```
typedef struct _IP_PER_ADAPTER_INFO {
   UINT AutoconfigEnabled;
   UINT AutoconfigActive;
   PIP_ADDR_STRING CurrentDnsServer;
   IP_ADDR_STRING DnsServerList;
} IP_PER_ADAPTER_INFO, *PIP_PER_ADAPTER_INFO;
```

The first two fields of `IP_PER_ADAPTER_INFO` deal with the auto-configuration status of an adapter. If it is enabled, the `Autoconfig Enabled` field will be set to 1; and if it is currently active, the `AutoconfigActive` field will also be set to 1. The last two parameters contain information about the adapter's DNS servers. The `Current DnsServer` field points to the IP address of the primary DNS server for the device, and is followed by the `DnsServerList` field, a linked list of `IP_ADDR_STRING` structures containing additional DNS servers.

The following example shows how you could get the DHCP lease information for a network adapter:

```
void GetDHCPExpireTime() {
   // Get the adapter information
   IP_ADAPTER_INFO *pIpAdapterInfo = NULL;
   DWORD dwAdapterSize = 0;
   TCHAR tchDHCPTime[128] = TEXT("\0");
   TCHAR tchDate[64] = TEXT("\0");
   TCHAR tchTime[64] = TEXT("\0");
   TCHAR tchOutputString[256] = TEXT("\0");
   SYSTEMTIME sysTime;

   // Find out the size of the adapter info table, allocate,
   // and call again
   if(GetAdaptersInfo(NULL, &dwAdapterSize) !=
      ERROR_  BUFFER_OVERFLOW)
      return FALSE;
```

```
        pIpAdapterInfo = (IP_ADAPTER_INFO *)LocalAlloc(LPTR,
           dwAdapterSize);
        if(!pIpAdapterInfo)
           return FALSE;

        if(GetAdaptersInfo(pIpAdapterInfo, &dwAdapterSize) !=
           NO_ERROR) {
           LocalFree(pIpAdapterInfo);
           return FALSE;
        }

        // The DHCP lease time is in time_t format let's convert
        // it to SYSTEMTIME
        TimeToSystemTime(pIpAdapterInfo->LeaseObtained,
           &sysTime);

        GetDateFormat(NULL, NULL, &sysTime, TEXT("ddd, MM/dd/
           yyyy "), tchDate, sizeof(tchDate));
        GetTimeFormat(NULL, NULL, &sysTime, TEXT("hh:mm:ss tt"),
           tchTime, sizeof(tchTime));
        _tcscpy(tchDHCPTime, tchDate);
        _tcscat(tchDHCPTime, tchTime);

        // Put together our output string
        wsprintf(tchDHCPTime, TEXT("%s Lease Expires: %s"),
           pIpAdapterInfo->AdapterName, tchDHCPTime);

        // Free it when we're done
        LocalFree(pIpAdapterInfo);
    }

    void TimeToSystemTime(time_t t, SYSTEMTIME *pSysTime)
    {
        // This function will convert a LONG time_t value to
        // a SYSTEM_TIME structure
        FILETIME ft, ftLocal;

        if(!pSysTime)
           return;

        // Convert to File Time
        LONGLONG ll = Int32x32To64(t, 10000000) + 116444736000000000;
```

```
ft.dwLowDateTime = (DWORD) ll;
ft.dwHighDateTime = (DWORD) (ll >>32);

// Convert to Local System Time
FileTimeToLocalFileTime(&ft, &ftLocal);
FileTimeToSystemTime(&ftLocal, pSysTime);
return;
}
```

The last type of information specific to a particular adapter involves **unidirectional** network adapters, which can only receive UDP datagram packets. The `GetUniDirectionalAdapterInfo()` function is defined as follows:

```
DWORD GetUniDirectionalAdapterInfo(
    IP_UNIDIRECTIONAL_ADAPTER_ADDRESS *pIPIfInfo,
    ULONG *pdwOutBufLen);
```

The `pIPIfInfo` parameter is a pointer to a buffer that will receive an array of unidirectional adapters that are specified by an `IP_UNIDIRECTIONAL_ADAPTER_ADDRESS` structure. Here's what the structure looks like:

```
typedef struct _IP_UNIDIRECTIONAL_ADAPTER_ADDRESS {
    ULONG NumAdapters;
    IPAddr Address[1];
} IP_UNIDIRECTIONAL_ADAPTER_ADDRESS,
    *PIP_UNIDIRECTIONAL_ADAPTER_ADDRESS;
```

The structure contains two fields: `NumAdapters`, which is the number of unidirectional adapters on the devices, followed by `IPAddr`, an array containing actual IP addresses of those adapters.

The final parameter of the `GetUniDirectionalAdapterInfo()` function is `pdwOutBufLen`, which is a pointer to a variable that contains the size of the buffer specified in the `pIPIfInfo` parameter.

Network Interfaces

The network adapter functions just described work directly with the data-link layer of the TCP/IP stack. To get detailed protocol information, you have to move up on the TCP/IP stack to talk directly with the network layer. Fortunately, the IPHelper APIs have functions that do just that.

To determine exactly how many interfaces are currently available on the device, you can call the GetNumberOfInterfaces() function:

```
DWORD GetNumberOfInterfaces(DWORD *pdwNumIf);
```

The function simply takes a single parameter, a pointer to a DWORD variable that will receive the number of interfaces. If it is successful, the function will return NO_ERROR.

Internally, each interface adapter is stored as an IP_ADAPTER_INDEX_MAP structure. Most of the functions that map to an adapter's interface use this structure, which is defined as follows:

```
typedef struct _IP_ADAPTER_INDEX_MAP {
    ULONG Index;
    WCHAR Name[MAX_ADAPTER_NAME];
}IP_ADAPTER_INDEX_MAP, *PIP_ADAPTER_INDEX_MAP;
```

The structure contains only two fields: Index, an internal index of the network interface, and the Name of the adapter. To fully enumerate the available network interfaces and their corresponding adapters, simply call the following function:

```
DWORD GetInterfaceInfo(IP_INTERFACE_INFO *pIfTable, ULONG
    *pdwOutBufLen);
```

The first parameter, pIfTable, is a pointer to an IP_INTERFACE_INFO structure. This structure will contain the array of network interfaces. The other parameter, pdwOutBufLen, is a pointer to a ULONG variable that contains the size of the pIfTable parameter, in bytes.

The IP_INTERFACE_INFO structure looks like the following:

```
typedef struct _IP_INTERFACE_INFO {
    LONG NumAdapters;
    IP_ADAPTER_INDEX_MAP Adapter[1];
} IP_INTERFACE_INFO,*PIP_INTERFACE_INFO;
```

This structure also contains only two fields: NumAdapters, which indicates how many network interface adapters are on the device, followed by the array of IP_ADAPTER_INDEX_MAP structures for each interface.

For example, if you want to enumerate the names of all network interface adapters on your device, you can do the following:

```
// Interface name enumeration
IP_INTERFACE_INFO *pIpInterface = NULL;
DWORD dwInterfaceSize = 0;

// Find out the size of the interface table
if(GetInterfaceInfo(NULL, &dwInterfaceSize) !=
  ERROR_INSUFFICIENT_BUFFER)
    return FALSE;

pIpInterface = (IP_INTERFACE_INFO *)LocalAlloc(LPTR,
  dwInterfaceSize);
if(!pIpInterface)
    return FALSE;

if(GetInterfaceInfo(pIpInterface, &dwInterfaceSize) !=
  NO_ERROR) {
    LocalFree(pIpInterface);
    return FALSE;
}

// Walk through the available interfaces
TCHAR tchInterfaceBuffer[256] = TEXT("\0");
for(int nInterface = 0; nInterface < pIpInterface->
  NumAdapters; nInterface++) {
    IP_ADAPTER_INDEX_MAP *pIpAdapterMapEntry = NULL;

    pIpAdapterMapEntry =
        (IP_ADAPTER_INDEX_MAP *)&pIpInterface->
        Adapter[nInterface];
    wsprintf(tchInterfaceBuffer, TEXT("Interface Name: %s
        Interface Index: %d"),pIpAdapterMapEntry->Name,
        pIpAdapterMapEntry->Index);
}
```

As you walk through the loop, the `tchInterfaceBuffer` text buffer will receive the name and interface index for each available network interface.

Now that you know a particular interface adapter's index, you can use the `GetIfEntry()` function to retrieve the full statistics and

configuration information about the interface. The GetIfEntry()
function is defined as follows:

```
DWORD GetIfEntry(MIB_IFROW *pIfRow);
```

The only parameter you need to pass in is a pointer to a MIB_IFROW
structure. Before calling the function, this structure should have its
dwIndex field filled in with the index of the network interface for which
you want to receive information, as shown in the following example:

```
MIB_IFROW mibInterface;
memset(&mibInterface, 0, sizeof(MIB_IFROW));

// To get a specific interface entry, just set the dwIndex
// field before calling the GetIfEntry function
mibInterface.dwIndex = pIpAdapterMapEntry->Index;
if(GetIfEntry(&mibInterface) != NO_ERROR)
   return FALSE;
```

The MIB_IFROW structure contains a great deal of interesting information about a particular network interface:

```
typedef struct _MIB_IFROW
{
   WCHAR wszName[MAX_INTERFACE_NAME_LEN];
   DWORD dwIndex;
   DWORD dwType;
   DWORD dwMtu;
   DWORD dwSpeed;
   DWORD dwPhysAddrLen;
   BYTE bPhysAddr[MAXLEN_PHYSADDR];
   DWORD dwAdminStatus;
   DWORD dwOperStatus;
   DWORD dwLastChange;
   DWORD dwInOctets;
   DWORD dwInUcastPkts;
   DWORD dwInNUcastPkts;
   DWORD dwInDiscards;
   DWORD dwInErrors;
   DWORD dwInUnknownProtos;
   DWORD dwOutOctets;
   DWORD dwOutUcastPkts;
   DWORD dwOutNUcastPkts;
   DWORD dwOutDiscards;
```

```
        DWORD dwOutErrors;
        DWORD dwOutQLen;
        DWORD dwDescrLen;
        BYTE bDescr[MAXLEN_IFDESCR];
    } MIB_IFROW,*PMIB_IFROW;
```

Table 3.2 describes the individual fields of the MIB_IFROW structure:

Table 3.2 MIB_IFROW Structure Fields

Member	Description
wszName	Name of the interface
dwIndex	Index that identifies the interface
dwType	Type of interface
dwMtu	Maximum Transmission Unit for the interface
dwSpeed	Speed of the interface, in bits per second
dwPhysAddrLen	The length, in bytes, of bPhysAddr
bPhysAddr	The physical MAC address of the interface
dwAdminStatus	Specifies if the interface is administratively up or not
dwOperStatus	Specifies the operational status of the interface
dwLastChange	Specifies the last time that dwOperStatus changed
dwInOctets	The number of octets received by this interface
dwInUcastPkts	The number of unicast packets received by this interface
dwInNUcastPkts	The number of non-unicast packets received by this interface
dwInDiscards	The number of incoming packets that were discarded by this interface
dwInErrors	The number of incoming packets that were discarded because of errors by this interface
dwInUnknownProtos	The number of incoming packets that were discarded because of an unknown protocol error by this interface
dwOutOctets	The number of octets sent by this interface
dwOutUcastPkts	The number of unicast packets sent by this interface
dwOutNUcastPkts	The number of non-unicast packets sent by this interface
dwOutDiscards	The number of outgoing packets that were discarded by this interface
dwOutErrors	The number of outgoing packets that were discarded because of errors by this interface
dwOutQLen	The length of the output queue
dwDescrLen	The length, in bytes, of bDescr
bDescr	The description of the interface

If you want to change the administrative status for a particular interface, you can call the `SetIfEntry()` function:

```
DWORD SetIfEntry(MIB_IFROW *pIfRow);
```

The function simply takes a pointer to a `MIB_IFROW` structure with two populated fields: `dwIndex`, to specify the adapter whose status you want to change, and the `dwAdminStatus` field. This can be set to either `MIB_IF_ADMIN_STATUS_UP` (if the interface is enabled) or `MIB_IF_ADMIN_STATUS_DOWN` (if it is disabled).

To retrieve all the of the current interface information for all of the adapters, instead of repeatedly calling `GetIfEntry()`, you can use the `GetIfTable()` function, which is defined as follows:

```
DWORD GetIfTable(MIB_IFTABLE *pIfTable, ULONG *pdwSize,
   BOOL bOrder);
```

The `pIfTable` parameter should point to a `MIB_IFTABLE` structure that will receive the array of `MIB_IF_ROW` information for the adapters. The next parameter, `pdwSize`, needs to point to a variable that contains the size, in bytes, of the `pIfTable` structure (if the buffer size is too small, the function will fail and put the proper size in `pdwSize`). The final parameter, `bOrder`, specifies whether or not the function should sort the adapters by interface index.

Because there is no obvious way to know how large the `pIfTable` buffer should be for all of the interfaces, you will probably be better off by first calling `GetIfTable()` with a `NULL` value for the `pIfTable` parameter. The function call will fail, but the `pdwSize` pointer will tell you how large of a buffer to allocate. You can then proceed to allocate your buffer and call `GetIfTable()` again with the correct size.

The `MIB_IFTABLE` structure that you are returned from `GetIfTable()` looks like the following:

```
typedef struct _MIB_IFTABLE {
   DWORD dwNumEntries;
   MIB_IFROW table[ANY_SIZE];
} MIB_IFTABLE, *PMIB_IFTABLE;
```

The structure returned is straightforward: The `dwNumEntries` field indicates the number of `MIB_IFROW` interfaces that are located in the `table` array.

IP Addresses

In order for an application to communicate with another host over TCP/IP, the device must have a valid IP address. Network interfaces and adapters on Pocket PC devices always have a unique IP address associated with them. You can use the IP Helper APIs to add and remove them, as well as to release or renew DHCP-assigned addresses.

You can retrieve the IP addresses that are currently assigned on your device by using the `GetIpAddrTable()` function:

```
DWORD GetIpAddrTable(MIB_IPADDRTABLE *pIpAddrTable, ULONG *pdwSize,
    BOOL bOrder);
```

The first parameter, `pIpAddrTable`, is a pointer to a buffer that will receive a `MIB_IPADDRTABLE` structure, which outlines the entire interface to IP address mappings on the device. The `pdwSize` parameter should point to an `unsigned long` that specifies the size of the `pIpAddrTable` buffer. If you want to have the IP address table sorted, you should set the last parameter, `bOrder`, to `TRUE`.

The `MIB_IPADDRTABLE` structure is defined as follows:

```
typedef struct _MIB_IPADDRTABLE {
    DWORD dwNumEntries;
    MIB_IPADDRROW table[ANY_SIZE];
} MIB_IPADDRTABLE, *PMIB_IPADDRTABLE;
```

The structure contains two fields. The first, `dwNumEntries`, is the number of `MIB_IPADDRROW` structures in the `table` field. The `table` field contains the actual array of `MIB_IPADDRROW` structures that contain the IP address information. Each `MIB_IPADDRROW` structure is defined as follows:

```
typedef struct _MIB_IPADDRROW {
    DWORD dwAddr;
    DWORD dwIndex;
    DWORD dwMask;
    DWORD dwBCastAddr;
    DWORD dwReasmSize;
    unsigned short unused1;
```

```
      unsigned short unused2;
} MIB_IPADDRROW, *PMIB_IPADDRROW;
```

- The dwAddr field specifies the IP address.
- The dwIndex field specifies the index of the interface associated with the dwAddr field.
- The dwMask field specifies the subnet mask.
- The dwBCastAddr field specifies the broadcast address for this IP address.
- The dwReasmSize field specifies the datagram reassembly size.
- The final two parameters, unused1 and unused2, are not currently used.

The following example shows how you can enumerate the IP address table:

```
// IP address table list
MIB_IPADDRTABLE *pIpAddressTable = NULL;
DWORD dwIPTableSize = 0;

// Find out the size of the IP table
if(GetIpAddrTable(NULL, &dwIPTableSize, FALSE) !=
   ERROR_INSUFFICIENT_BUFFER)
   return FALSE;

pIpAddressTable = (MIB_IPADDRTABLE *)LocalAlloc(LPTR,
  dwIPTableSize);
if(!pIpAddressTable)
   return FALSE;

// Get the IP table
if(GetIpAddrTable(pIpAddressTable, &dwIPTableSize, TRUE) !=
  NO_ERROR) {
   LocalFree(pIpAddressTable);
   return FALSE;
}

// Enumerate the IP addresses. Convert the IP address
// from a DWORD to a string using inet_ntoa
TCHAR tchIPTableEntry[256] = TEXT("\0");
for(DWORD dwIP = 0; dwIP < pIpAddressTable->dwNumEntries; dwIP++) {
```

```
    MIB_IPADDRROW *pIpAddrRow = NULL;
    struct in_addr sAddr;

    pIpAddrRow = (MIB_IPADDRROW *)&pIpAddressTable->table[dwIP];
    sAddr.S_un.S_addr = (IPAddr)pIpAddrRow->dwAddr;

    wsprintf(tchIPTableEntry, TEXT("IP Address: %hs"),
        inet_ntoa(sAddr));
}


LocalFree(pIpAddressTable);
```

TIP: You cannot modify the value of an existing IP address—you have to delete it and then add a new entry with the corrected value.

To add an IP address to an adapter, call the `AddIPAddress()` function:

```
DWORD AddIPAddress(IPAddr Address, IPMask IpMask, DWORD IfIndex,
    ULONG *NTEContext, ULONG *NTEInstance);
```

The first two parameters, `Address` and `IPMask`, specify the adapter's new IP address and subnet mask values, respectively. The `IfIndex` parameter is the adapter index to which you want to add the address, followed by a pointer to a `ULONG` variable that will receive the context value associated with the new address. The final parameter, `NTEInstance`, is returned an instance value for the IP address.

To delete an individual IP address, you can use the `DeleteIP Address()` function:

```
DWORD DeleteIPAddress(ULONG NTEContext);
```

The only parameter that `DeleteIPAddress()` needs is a network table entry (NTE) context value that describes the address you want to delete. You can get the context value from a previous call to the `Get AdaptersInfo()` function and by looking at the `IP_ADDR_STRING` structure.

DHCP-Assigned IP Addresses

Finally, we will look at two functions that specifically deal with IP addresses that are created when your device uses a DHCP server. When you use a DHCP server to request an IP address for a network adapter, you are given what is known as a **lease** on that particular address. The address assigned to your device from a DHCP server is typically taken from a pool of addresses that are defined and distributed by the server. A DHCP lease specifies the fixed amount of time for which you have rights to use that assigned IP address. You can find out more information about when the lease was obtained and when it expires by using the `GetAdaptersInfo()` function.

Devices that obtain their IP address through a DHCP server usually need to either *renew* or *release* their addresses. Renewing an IP address lets the server know that you still need to use the IP address, and that you are requesting that its expiration time be extended. Conversely, releasing the address lets the server know that you no longer need it so that it can be returned to the pool of available addresses that the DHCP server can assign.

Both tasks can be accomplished by using either the `IpRelease Address()` or `IpRenewAddress()` function:

```
DWORD IpReleaseAddress(IP_ADAPTER_INDEX_MAP *AdapterInfo);

DWORD IpRenewAddress(IP_ADAPTER_INDEX_MAP *AdapterInfo);
```

The `AdapterInfo` parameter is a pointer to an `IP_ADAPTER_INDEX_MAP` structure that you can get from calling the `GetInterface Info()` function.

For example, the following releases the primary IP address from its DHCP lease:

```
if(GetInterfaceInfo(pIpInterface, &dwInterfaceSize) !=
  NO_ERROR) {
  LocalFree(pIpInterface);
  return FALSE;
}

IP_ADAPTER_INDEX_MAP *pIpAdapterMapEntry = (IP_ADAPTER_INDEX_MAP *)
  &pIpInterface->Adapter[0];
IpReleaseAddress(pIpAdapterMapEntry);
```

Address Resolution Protocol Information (ARP)

Every network adapter has a unique hardware address burned into its ROM. When data is sent over the network, the **media access control** (**MAC**) header in an Ethernet frame will contain both the source and destination hardware addresses (also known as MAC addresses) for the packet. TCP/IP then uses **address resolution** to map a network interface's IP address to its physical hardware address.

The **Address Resolution Protocol** (**ARP**) is a *support protocol* and is part of the network layer of the TCP/IP OSI stack. ARP is responsible not only for performing the IP address to hardware mapping, but also for making requests and forwarding packets to the default gateway on the network.

The ARP Table

Pocket PC devices use an internal cache to store information about the mapping of IP addresses to physical MAC addresses. This cache is known as the **ARP Map Table**, and can be examined using the IPHelper API functions. To do so, you can use the following:

```
DWORD GetIpNetTable(MIB_IPNETTABLE *pIpNetTable, ULONG *pdwSize,
   BOOL bOrder);
```

The first parameter, `pIpNetTable`, is a pointer to a buffer that will contain the map table when the function returns. The `pdwSize` parameter is used to specify a pointer to a variable that contains the size of the buffer `pIpNetTable`. If the buffer is too small, the function will return an error and put the proper size into this variable. Finally, the `bOrder` parameter should be set to `TRUE` if you want the map table to be sorted in ascending order of IP addresses.

The map table returned from `GetIpNetTable()` is in the format of a `MIB_IPNETTABLE` structure. This structure contains the total number of IP address mappings, along with an array of `MIB_IPNETROW` structures that contain the actual ARP map information per address. The `MIB_IPNETTABLE` structure is defined as follows:

```
typedef struct _MIB_IPNETTABLE {
   DWORD dwNumEntries;
   MIB_IPNETROW table[ANY_SIZE];
} MIB_IPNETTABLE, *PMIB_IPNETTABLE;
```

Each mapping entry is in the format of a `MIB_IPNETROW` structure:

```
typedef struct _MIB_IPNETROW {
    DWORD dwIndex;
    DWORD dwPhysAddrLen;
    BYTE bPhysAddr[MAXLEN_PHYSADDR];
    DWORD dwAddr;
    DWORD dwType;
} MIB_IPNETROW, *PMIB_IPNETROW;
```

The first field, `dwIndex`, specifies the index of the network adapter. The next two fields define the hardware MAC address—`dwPhysAddr Len` specifies the length, in bytes, of `bPhysAddr`, which contains the actual physical address. This is followed by the `dwAddr` field, which contains the IP address to which the hardware is mapped. Finally, `dwType` specifies the type of ARP address entry; it can be one of the values listed in Table 3.3.

Table 3.3 IP Address-Entry Types

Type	Description
MIB_IPNET_TYPE_OTHER	Other entry
MIB_IPNET_TYPE_INVALID	Invalid entry
MIB_IPNET_TYPE_DYNAMIC	Dynamic entry
MIB_IPNET_TYPE_STATIC	Static entry

If you want to delete all of the IP address mappings from your local ARP map table cache, you can simply call the `FlushIpNetTable()` function, which is defined as follows:

```
DWORD FlushIpNetTable(DWORD dwIfIndex);
```

The only parameter `FlushIpNetTable()` needs is the index to the network interface for which you wish to delete all mappings. If the cache is successfully flushed, the function will return a value of `NO_ERROR`.

ARP Table Entries

The IPHelper API functions also enable you to create, delete, or modify an ARP table mapping.

To create a new entry in the ARP table, you must first completely populate a `MIB_IPNETROW` structure with the mapping information, and then call the `CreateIpNetEntry()` function:

```
DWORD CreateIpNetEntry(MIB_IPNETROW *pArpEntry);
```

If the creation of the ARP entry was successful, `CreateIpNet Entry()` will return a `NO_ERROR` value.

To modify an existing entry, you can use the `SetIpNetEntry()` function, which is defined as follows:

```
DWORD SetIpNetEntry(MIB_IPNETROW *pArpEntry);
```

The only parameter that `SetIpNetEntry()` needs is a pointer to a `MIB_IPNETROW` structure containing the information you want to modify in the mapping.

Finally, to delete an entry, use the following:

```
DWORD DeleteIpNetEntry(MIB_IPNETROW *pArpEntry);
```

Once again, the parameter `pArpEntry` is a pointer to a `MIB_IPNETROW` structure. The structure only needs to have its `dwIndex` and `dwAddr` fields completed to successfully delete an entry.

Sending an ARP Message

To determine the physical address of another device on the network, all you need to do is send that device an ARP request message using the `SendARP()` function, which is defined as follows:

```
DWORD SendARP(IPAddr DestIP, IPAddr SrcIP, ULONG *pMacAddr,
    ULONG *PhyAddrLen);
```

The first parameter, `DestIP`, is the address of the host from which you want to get the MAC address. The next parameter, `SrcIP`, is your own device's IP address. Because this is an optional parameter, it can be set to 0. The last two parameters point to buffers that contain the MAC address and the size of the destination IP when the function returns.

ARP Proxy Entries

ARP proxies, while rarely used on a handheld device, can be useful when you have multiple network interfaces and need the capability to route packets between two separate subnets. Essentially, using an ARP proxy (PARP) is a way to trick IP into correctly routing packets over multiple subnets.

For example, when a device needs to send a packet of data to a destination, it will first transmit an ARP request (using SendARP()) on the same subnet as itself. The request basically asks, "Who has the IP address x.x.x.x mapped to its hardware?" The device that has mapped the requested IP address will then respond with a message containing its MAC address. From this point forward, all packets to that IP address are sent to the MAC address of the device that responded.

Setting up an ARP proxy enables your adapter to respond and forward those requests. To create an ARP proxy, you can call the CreateProxy ArpEntry() function, which is defined as follows:

```
DWORD CreateProxyArpEntry(DWORD dwAddress, DWORD dwMask,
  DWORD dwIfIndex);
```

The first parameter is the IP address that you want to act as an ARP proxy. Next, dwMask is the subnet mask for the IP address specified by dwAddress. The last parameter, dwIfIndex, is the index of the interface you want to proxy.

If the function successfully creates the proxy, it will return a value of NO_ERROR.

To delete an ARP proxy entry, you need to call the following function. Notice that the DeleteProxyArpEntry() function takes exactly the same parameters as your initial call to CreateProxyArpEntry(). The function is defined as follows:

```
DWORD DeleteProxyArpEntry(DWORD dwAddress, DWORD dwMask,
  DWORD dwIfIndex);
```

Network Layer Protocol Statistics

The network layer of the TCP/IP stack, as you have already seen in Chapter 1, is responsible for the packetization, addressing, and routing of data. By using the IPHelper library, you can query both the ICMP and IP protocols for statistical information regarding the data packets and messages that the network adapter has received.

Internet Control Message Protocol (ICMP)

Because ICMP is a "support" protocol, it is generally used for sending informational, control, and error messages between two network endpoints. To find out more information about the ICMP messages that a device is sending and receiving, you can use the `GetIcmpStatistics()` function:

```
DWORD GetIcmpStatistics(MIB_ICMP *pStats);
```

When you call this function, it will return to you a `MIB_ICMP` structure in the variable that you pointed to using the `pStats` parameter. The structure is defined as follows:

```
typedef struct _MIB_ICMP {
   MIBICMPINFO stats;
} MIB_ICMP,*PMIB_ICMP;
```

The `MIB_ICMP` structure simply contains another structure that is defined as follows:

```
typedef       struct _MIBICMPINFO {
   MIBICMPSTATS icmpInStats;
   MIBICMPSTATS icmpOutStats;
} MIBICMPINFO;
```

The `MIBICMPINFO` structure contains two additional `MIBICMP` `STATS` structures containing the statistical data for ICMP. The first field, `icmpInStats`, contains information about incoming messages, whereas the `icmpOutStats` field is for outgoing messages. The `MIBICMPSTATS` structure is defined as follows:

```
typedef struct _MIBICMPSTATS {
   DWORD dwMsgs;
   DWORD dwErrors;
   DWORD dwDestUnreachs;
   DWORD dwTimeExcds;
   DWORD dwParmProbs;
   DWORD dwSrcQuenchs;
   DWORD dwRedirects;
   DWORD dwEchos;
   DWORD dwEchoReps;
```

```
        DWORD dwTimestamps;
        DWORD dwTimestampReps;
        DWORD dwAddrMasks;
        DWORD dwAddrMaskReps;
    } MIBICMPSTATS;
```

Table 3.4 describes the fields of the `MIBICMPSTATS` structure.

Table 3.4 `MIBICMPSTATS` Field Descriptions

Member	Description
dwMsgs	The number of messages sent or received.
dwErrors	The number of errors sent or received.
dwDestUnreachs	The number of messages that were marked as destination-unreachable.
dwTimeExcds	The number of TTL-exceeded messages that were sent or received. See the `SetIpTTL()` function for more information.
dwParmProbs	The number of parameter problem messages sent or received.
dwSrcQuenchs	The number of source "quench" messages sent or received.
dwRedirects	The number of redirect messages sent or received.
dwEchos	The number of echo request messages sent or received.
dwEchoReps	The number of echo reply messages sent or received.
dwTimestamps	The number of timestamp request messages sent or received.
dwTimestampReps	The number of timestamp reply messages sent or received.
dwAddrMasks	The number of address mask request messages sent or received.
dwAddrMaskReps	The number of address mask reply messages sent or received.

Internet Protocol (IP)

The Internet Protocol (IP) is the hardware-independent method that TCP/IP uses for the fragmentation and reassembly of data packets (known as *datagrams*). You can use IPHelper to find out more information about the current IP status by calling `GetIpStatistics()`:

```
DWORD GetIpStatistics(MIB_IPSTATS *pStats);
```

The only parameter you need to pass in, `pStats`, is a pointer to a `MIB_IPSTATS` structure that will receive the statistical data when the function returns. The `MIB_IPSTATS` structure is defined as follows:

```
typedef struct _MIB_IPSTATS {
    DWORD dwForwarding;
    DWORD dwDefaultTTL;
    DWORD dwInReceives;
    DWORD dwInHdrErrors;
    DWORD dwInAddrErrors;
    DWORD dwForwDatagrams;
    DWORD dwInUnknownProtos;
    DWORD dwInDiscards;
    DWORD dwInDelivers;
    DWORD dwOutRequests;
    DWORD dwRoutingDiscards;
    DWORD dwOutDiscards;
    DWORD dwOutNoRoutes;
    DWORD dwReasmTimeout;
    DWORD dwReasmReqds;
    DWORD dwReasmOks;
    DWORD dwReasmFails;
    DWORD dwFragOks;
    DWORD dwFragFails;
    DWORD dwFragCreates;
    DWORD dwNumIf;
    DWORD dwNumAddr;
    DWORD dwNumRoutes;
} MIB_IPSTATS, *PMIB_IPSTATS;
```

MIB_IPSTATS provides a lot of interesting information regarding incoming and outgoing datagrams. Table 3.5 describes the fields of MIB_IPSTATS.

The dwDefaultTTL value for a datagram defines how long an IP packet can "live" on the network. As a packet travels across the Internet, TCP/IP requires each router it crosses to decrement the TTL field of the datagram's header. If the TTL field reaches 0 before it gets to its destination address, TCP/IP destroys the packet and notifies the sending host through an ICMP message.

To turn IP forwarding (also known as *routing*) on or off, or to change the default time to live (TTL) for a datagram, you can use the SetIpStatistics() function:

```
DWORD SetIpStatistics(MIB_IPSTATS *pIpStats);
```

The pIpStats parameter is a pointer to a MIB_IPSTATS structure that has either the dwForwarding or the dwDefaultTTL field

Table 3.5 MIB_IPSTATS Field Descriptions

Member	Description
dwForwarding	Specifies whether IP forwarding is enabled or not.
dwDefaultTTL	Specifies the time to live (TTL) for datagrams that are sent from the device. This value can be changed using the SetIpTTL function.
dwInReceives	The number of datagrams received.
dwInHdrErrors	The number of datagrams that have header errors.
dwInAddrErrors	The number of datagrams that have been received with address errors.
dwForwDatagrams	The number of datagrams forwarded.
dwInUnknownProtos	The number of datagrams received with an unknown protocol.
dwInDiscards	The number of datagrams received that were discarded.
dwInDelivers	The number of datagrams received that were delivered.
dwOutRequests	The number of datagrams that IP has been requested to transmit. This does not include forwarded datagrams.
dwRoutingDiscards	The number of outgoing datagrams that were discarded.
dwOutDiscards	The number of datagrams sent that were discarded.
dwOutNoRoutes	The number of datagrams that did not have a routing destination.
dwReasmTimeout	The maximum amount of time that a fragmented datagram needs to arrive.
dwReasmReqds	The number of datagrams that require reassembly.
dwReasmOks	The number of datagrams that were successfully reassembled.
dwReasmFails	The number of datagrams that could not be reassembled.
dwFragOks	The number of datagrams that were successfully fragmented.
dwFragFails	The number of datagrams that could not be fragmented.
dwFragCreates	The number of datagram fragments created.
dwNumIf	The number of IP interfaces on the device.
dwNumAddr	The number of IP addresses on the device.
dwNumRoutes	The number of routes in the IP routing table.

completed. If you want to preserve the default value for either, you set the field to either MIB_USE_CURRENT_TTL or MIB_USE_CURRENT_ FORWARDING.

If you only need to configure IP's TTL value, you can also call SetIpTTL():

```
DWORD SetIpTTL(UINT nTTL);
```

The only parameter, `nTTL`, is the new time-to-live value for datagrams on the device.

Transport Layer Protocol Statistics

The next layer of the TCP/IP stack for which you can use IPHelper to get statistical information is the transport layer. This layer, as described in Chapter 1, is used to transfer data between a source and a destination on the network through two protocols: TCP and UDP.

Transmission Control Protocol (TCP)

TCP is a connection-oriented protocol that provides you with a reliable, error-free data pipe between two endpoints that can send and receive streams of bytes back and forth, without data being lost or duplicated.

You can query the TCP protocol using IPHelper APIs for two different types of information: details about the currently connected TCP connections, and their transfer states. To do so, you retrieve the current TCP table by calling the following:

```
DWORD GetTcpTable(MIB_TCPTABLE *pTcpTable, DWORD *pdwSize,
    BOOL bOrder);
```

The first parameter is a pointer to a `MIB_TCPTABLE` buffer that contains the TCP connection details. This is followed by the pointer `pdwSize`, which points to the size, in bytes, of the buffer that was allocated for `pTcpTable`. If this buffer is too small, `GetTcpTable()` will set this to the size it needs. The final parameter, `bOrder`, should be set to `TRUE` if you want the returned array to be sorted by local IP address.

The `MIB_TCPTABLE` structure contains the number of entries in the TCP table, along with a `MIB_TCPROW` array for each TCP connection. It is defined as follows:

```
typedef struct _MIB_TCPTABLE {
    DWORD dwNumEntries;
    MIB_TCPROW table[ANY_SIZE];
} MIB_TCPTABLE, *PMIB_TCPTABLE;
```

Finally, let's look at the actual TCP connection table structure, `MIB_TCPROW`:

```
typedef struct _MIB_TCPROW {
    DWORD dwState;
    DWORD dwLocalAddr;
    DWORD dwLocalPort;
    DWORD dwRemoteAddr;
    DWORD dwRemotePort;
} MIB_TCPROW, *PMIB_TCPROW;
```

The first field, `dwState`, specifies the current state of the connection. It can be one of the states specified in Table 3.6.

Table 3.6 TCP Connection State Values

State	Description
MIB_TCP_STATE_CLOSED	The TCP connection is closed.
MIB_TCP_STATE_LISTEN	The TCP connection is waiting for a remote connection.
MIB_TCP_STATE_SYN_SENT	The TCP connection is waiting for a connection request.
MIB_TCP_STATE_SYN_RCVD	The TCP connection is waiting for a confirmation request acknowledgment after a connection request has been established.
MIB_TCP_STATE_ESTAB	The TCP connection is open.
MIB_TCP_STATE_FIN_WAIT1	The TCP connection is waiting for a connection termination request, or acknowledgment of a previously transmitted termination request.
MIB_TCP_STATE_FIN_WAIT2	The TCP connection is waiting for a connection termination request.
MIB_TCP_STATE_CLOSE_WAIT	The TCP connection is waiting for a termination request from the local connection.
MIB_TCP_STATE_CLOSING	The TCP connection is waiting for a termination request acknowledgment from the remote connection.
MIB_TCP_STATE_LAST_ACK	The TCP connection is waiting for a previously sent termination request.
MIB_TCP_STATE_TIME_WAIT	The TCP connection is waiting to make sure that the remote connection has received acknowledgment of its termination request.
MIB_TCP_STATE_DELETE_TCP	The TCP connection is marked for deletion.

The next two fields, dwLocalAddr and dwLocalPort, define the local IP address and the local port for the connection. The last two fields, dwRemoteAddr and dwRemotePort, define the remote IP address and port, respectively.

You can also manually mark a TCP connection for deletion by using the SetTcpEntry() function:

```
DWORD SetTcpEntry(MIB_TCPROW *pTcpRow);
```

To use SetTcpEntry(), you must set the pTcpRow parameter to point to a MIB_TCPROW structure for the connection you want to delete. All the member fields of MIB_TCPROW should be populated, using the MIB_TCP_STATE_DELETE_TCP flag for the dwState parameter.

In addition to getting information about the active TCP connections, you can also use IPHelper to get general statistical information about the TCP protocol itself. To do so, call the GetTcpStatistics() function:

```
DWORD GetTcpStatistics(MIB_TCPSTATS *pStats);
```

The parameter pStats should point to a MIB_TCPSTATS structure, which is defined as follows:

```
typedef struct _MIB_TCPSTATS {
    DWORD dwRtoAlgorithm;
    DWORD dwRtoMin;
    DWORD dwRtoMax;
    DWORD dwMaxConn;
    DWORD dwActiveOpens;
    DWORD dwPassiveOpens;
    DWORD dwAttemptFails;
    DWORD dwEstabResets;
    DWORD dwCurrEstab;
    DWORD dwInSegs;
    DWORD dwOutSegs;
    DWORD dwRetransSegs;
    DWORD dwInErrs;
    DWORD dwOutRsts;
    DWORD dwNumConns;
} MIB_TCPSTATS, *PMIB_TCPSTATS;
```

Table 3.7 describes the fields of the MIB_TCPSTATS structure.

Table 3.7 `MIB_TCPSTATS` Field Descriptions

Member	Description
dwRtoAlgorithm	The current timeout algorithm being used. This can be `MIB_TCP_RTO_CONSTANT`, `MIB_TCP_RTO_RSRE`, `MIB_TCP_RTO_VANJ`, or `MIB_TCP_RTO_OTHER`.
dwRtoMin	The minimum retransmission timeout value in milliseconds.
dwRtoMax	The maximum retransmission timeout value in milliseconds.
dwMaxConn	The maximum number of TCP connections allowed on the device. This can also be set to -1 if a variable number of connections is allowed.
dwActiveOpens	The number of TCP connections opening connections to a server.
dwPassiveOpens	The number of TCP connections that are listening.
dwAttemptFails	The number of TCP connection attempts that have failed.
dwEstabResets	The number of TCP connections that have been reset after being established.
dwCurrEstab	The number of TCP connections that are currently active and established.
dwInSegs	The number of segments received.
dwOutSegs	The number of segments transmitted.
dwRetransSegs	The number of segments that have been retransmitted.
dwInErrs	The number of errors received.
dwOutRsts	The number of segments transmitted that were marked as "reset."
dwNumConns	The total number of connections.

By using the `GetTcpStatistics()` function, you can easily get some general information on TCP:

```
MIB_TCPSTATS mibTcpStats;

memset(&mibTcpStats, 0, sizeof(MIB_TCPSTATS));
GetTcpStatistics(&mibTcpStats);
```

User Datagram Protocol (UDP)

In addition to TCP, the TCP/IP stack also supports connectionless data transfer through the UDP protocol. To look at the table of UDP sockets the device is currently using to listen for incoming UDP packets, you can use the `GetUdpTable()` function:

```
DWORD GetUdpTable(MIB_UDPTABLE *pUdpTable, DWORD *pdwSize,
  BOOL bOrder);
```

The first parameter, pUdpTable, points to a structure that will be populated with a MIB_UDPTABLE structure when the function returns. Next, pdwSize points to a DWORD value that specifies the size of the buffer allocated for pUdpTable. If the buffer is not large enough, GetUdpTable() will fill this in with the correct size needed when it returns. Finally, if you want to sort the array of UDP connections by IP address, you can set the bOrder parameter to TRUE.

The MIB_UDPTABLE structure looks like the following:

```
typedef struct _MIB_UDPTABLE {
   DWORD dwNumEntries;
   MIB_UDPROW table[ANY_SIZE];
} MIB_UDPTABLE, *PMIB_UDPTABLE;
```

The structure contains the number of entries in the table, dwNum Entries, which is followed by an array of MIB_UDPROW structures that define the UDP connection table. The MIB_UDPROW structure is defined as follows:

```
typedef struct _MIB_UDPROW {
   DWORD dwLocalAddr;
   DWORD dwLocalPort;
} MIB_UDPROW, *PMIB_UDPROW;
```

As you can see, each MIB_UDPROW structure simply contains the local address and local port for each UDP connection currently active on the device.

Finally, if you want to get more general statistical information about UDP itself, you can call the following function:

```
DWORD GetUdpStatistics(MIB_UDPSTATS *pStats);
```

The GetUdpStatistics() function takes a single parameter, pStats, which is a pointer to a MIB_UDPSTATS structure. The structure receives the current UDP statistics for the device, and looks like the following:

```
typedef struct _MIB_UDPSTATS {
   DWORD dwInDatagrams;
   DWORD dwNoPorts;
```

```
   DWORD dwInErrors;
   DWORD dwOutDatagrams;
   DWORD dwNumAddrs;
} MIB_UDPSTATS,*PMIB_UDPSTATS;
```

The `dwInDatagrams` field specifies the total number of UDP datagrams that the device has received. This is followed by `dwNoPorts`, which is the total number of datagrams that UDP has discarded because the port number was bad. It is followed by the total number of erroneous datagrams that were received in the `dwInErrors` field. The `dwOutDatagrams` field indicates the total number of datagrams transmitted, and is followed by the total number of UDP entries in the table that can be retrieved using the `GetUdpTable()` function.

Route Tables

The basis for delivering data packets over the Internet Protocol (IP) is the route table. The IP route table contains addresses for various destinations on the network, and enables the stack to search the table for the best way to reach a specific host on the Internet. For more detailed information about how TCP/IP routing works and is managed, I recommend that you read RFC 1354, "IP Forwarding Table MIB."

To look at a device's IP route table, you simply need to call the `GetIpForwardTable()` function:

```
DWORD GetIpForwardTable(MIB_IPFORWARDTABLE *pIpForwardTable,
   ULONG *pdwSize, BOOL bOrder);
```

The first parameter, `pIpForwardTable`, is a pointer to a buffer that receives the route table when the function returns. The `pdwSize` parameter should point to a `ULONG` variable that specifies the size, in bytes, of the `pIpForwardTable` buffer. Finally, if you want to sort the route table by destination IP address, set the `bOrder` flag to `TRUE`.

The route table is defined by the `MIB_IPFORWARDTABLE` structure, and looks like the following:

```
typedef struct _MIB_IPFORWARDTABLE {
   DWORD dwNumEntries;
   MIB_IPFORWARDROW table[ANY_SIZE];
}MIB_IPFORWARDTABLE, *PMIB_IPFORWARDTABLE;
```

The `MIB_IPFORWARDTABLE` structure contains some basic information about the route table. The first field, `dwNumEntries`, indicates the total number of `MIB_IPFORWARDROW` items in the route table array. The actual routing entry information is stored in the `table` parameter.

Each route table entry is specified by a `MIB_IPFORWARDROW` structure:

```
typedef struct _MIB_IPFORWARDROW {
    DWORD dwForwardDest;
    DWORD dwForwardMask;
    DWORD dwForwardPolicy;
    DWORD dwForwardNextHop;
    DWORD dwForwardIfIndex;
    DWORD dwForwardType;
    DWORD dwForwardProto;
    DWORD dwForwardAge;
    DWORD dwForwardNextHopAS;
    DWORD dwForwardMetric1;
    DWORD dwForwardMetric2;
    DWORD dwForwardMetric3;
    DWORD dwForwardMetric4;
    DWORD dwForwardMetric5;
}MIB_IPFORWARDROW, *PMIB_IPFORWARDROW;
```

Table 3.8 describes the fields of the `MIB_IPFORWARDROW` structure.

Table 3.8 `MIB_IPFORWARDROW` Field Descriptions

Member	Description
dwForwardDest	The IP address of the destination.
dwForwardMask	The subnet mask of the destination address.
dwForwardPolicy	Unused.
dwForwardNextHop	The IP address of the next hop in the route.
dwForwardIfIndex	The index of the interface for this route.
dwForwardType	The route type, which can be one of the following: MIB_IPROUTE_TYPE_INDIRECT, MIB_IPROUTE_TYPE_DIRECT, MIB_IPROUTE_TYPE_INVALID, or MIB_IPROUTE_TYPE_OTHER.
dwForwardProto	The protocol that generated the route (see Table 3.9).
dwForwardAge	The age of the route, in seconds.

(continued)

Table 3.8 `MIB_IPFORWARDROW` Field Descriptions (*continued*)

Member	Description
dwForwardNextHopAS	The autonomous system number of the net hop.
dwForwardMetric1	A routing-protocol-specific metric value. See RFC 1354 for more information.
dwForwardMetric2	A routing-protocol-specific metric value. See RFC 1354 for more information.
dwForwardMetric3	A routing-protocol-specific metric value. See RFC 1354 for more information.
dwForwardMetric4	A routing-protocol-specific metric value. See RFC 1354 for more information.
dwForwardMetric5	A routing-protocol-specific metric value. See RFC 1354 for more information.

Table 3.9 IP Route Forwarding Protocols

Protocol	Description
MIB_IPPROTO_OTHER	Protocol not specified
MIB_IPPROTO_LOCAL	Local interface
MIB_IPPROTO_NETMGMT	Static route
MIB_IPPROTO_ICMP	Result of an ICMP redirect
MIB_IPPROTO_EGP	Exterior Gateway Protocol
MIB_IPPROTO_GGP	Gateway-Gateway Protocol
MIB_IPPROTO_HELLO	FuzzBall HelloSpeak protocol
MIB_IPPROTO_RIP	Berkeley RIP or RIP-II protocol
MIB_IPPROTO_IS_IS	Dual IS-IS protocol
MIB_IPPROTO_ES_IS	ISO 9542 protocol
MIB_IPPROTO_CISCO	Cisco IGRP protocol
MIB_IPPROTO_BBN	BBN SPF IGP protocol
MIB_IPPROTO_OSPF	Open Shortest Path First protocol
MIB_IPPROTO_BGP	Border Gateway Protocol
MIB_IPPROTO_NT_AUTOSTATIC	Routes that were originally added by a routing protocol and are not static
MIB_IPPROTO_NT_STATIC	Static routes
MIB_IPPROTO_NT_STATIC_NON_DOD	Static routes that do not cause Dial on Demand

Route Table Entries

The IPHelper API functions also give you the capability to create, delete, or modify route table entries.

To create a new entry in the route table, you must first completely fill out a `MIB_IPFORWARDROW` structure. In order to successfully create a route, you must also specify that the new route will use the `PROTO_IP_NETMGMT` route protocol, by setting it in the `dwForwardProto` field before calling `CreateIpForwardEntry()`:

```
DWORD CreateIpForwardEntry(MIB_IPFORWARDROW *pRoute);
```

The only parameter required is a pointer to the new route structure.

If you want to modify an existing route entry, call `SetIpForwardEntry()`:

```
DWORD SetIpForwardEntry(MIB_IPFORWARDROW *pRoute);
```

Once again, this function needs only a pointer to a `MIB_IPFORWARDROW` structure passed in for its `pRoute` parameter. You must also specify the `dwForwardIndex`, `dwForwardDest`, `dwForwardMask`, and `dwForwardNextHop` parameters. In addition, you must use `PROTO_IP_NETMGMT` for the `dwForwardProto` member.

To delete a route entry, call `DeleteIpForwardEntry()`:

```
DWORD DeleteIpForwardEntry(MIB_IPFORWARDROW *pRoute);
```

The only parameter that the function needs to successfully delete a route entry is a pointer to a `IPFORWARDROW` structure. The structure should be configured in the same manner as you configured the `SetIpForwardEntry()` function.

Route Support Functions

In addition to manipulating and reading the route table, some router management functions enable you to get more information about how data packets are routed over the network. To find out the route table entry that describes the best route to a specific IP address, call the `GetBestRoute()` function:

```
DWORD GetBestRoute(DWORD dwDestAddr, DWORD dwSourceAddr,
   MIB_IPFORWARDROW *pBestRoute);
```

The `dwDestAddr` and `dwSourceAddr` parameters specify the source and destination IP addresses. When the function returns, the `MIB_IPFORWARDROW` buffer that is pointed to by the `pBestRoute` parameter is filled in with details about the best route from the source to the destination addresses.

Finding out the best interface for the route to a particular address is accomplished with the `GetBestInterface()` function:

```
DWORD GetBestInterface(IPAddr dwDestAddr, DWORD *pdwBestIfIndex);
```

Here, you pass in the `dwDestAttr` parameter, which is the destination IP address and a pointer to a `DWORD` buffer. When the function returns, it will place the index of the best route interface in the `pdwBestIfIndex` buffer.

The last piece of information you can get from the route functions is the total round trip time (RTT) and hop count to a particular destination address. You can determine this information by calling the following:

```
BOOL GetRTTAndHopCount(IPAddr DestIpAddress, ULONG *HopCount,
    ULONG MaxHops, ULONG *RTT);
```

The `DestIpAddress` parameter tells the route table the destination address for which it needs to calculate the RTT and hop count. `HopCount` points to a `ULONG` variable that contains the hop count when the function returns. This is followed by `MaxHops`, which you should specify the maximum number of hops to search. Finally, the `RTT` parameter is a pointer to a `ULONG` buffer that will get the round trip time, in milliseconds, when the function completes.

Network Event Notification

The IPHelper library can also notify you when something changes in regard to your device's TCP/IP configuration for either IP address or the IP route table. However, be aware that these notifications *do not* tell you exactly what has changed, only that something has. To find out more details about the changes, you'll need to reexamine the tables by calling either `GetIpAddrTable()` or `GetIpForwardTable()`.

To be notified of any changes that occur in the IP address table, use the following:

```
DWORD NotifyAddrChange(HANDLE *Handle, LPOVERLAPPED overlapped);
```

The first parameter, `Handle`, is a pointer to a handle that you want to be signaled when something has changed in the address table. If you set this to `NULL`, the function will block until a change has occurred. The second parameter, `overlapped`, is not used on Pocket PC.

To be notified of any changes to the IP routing table, you can use the `NotifyRouteChange()` function:

```
DWORD NotifyRouteChange(HANDLE *Handle, LPOVERLAPPED
  overlapped);
```

The parameters for `NotifyRouteChange()` are the same as for `NotifyAddrChange()`.

CHAPTER 4

Network Redirector

*It's about who controls the information. What we see and hear,
how we work, what we think; it's all about the information!*

—*Cosmo,* Sneakers

The first three chapters described how you can use a Pocket PC device to communicate over the Internet, and how the TCP/IP stack is implemented in the Windows CE operating system. We looked at developing applications using both the low-level socket interface, as well as writing robust HTTP and FTP protocol-based software using the WinInet API. This chapter examines the final topic to cover regarding network programming on a Pocket PC device—the **Common Internet File System** (**CIFS**) network redirector.

The Pocket PC network redirector is a subset of the desktop-based **WNet API**. On desktop platforms such as Windows XP, the WNet APIs are a set of network-independent functions that enable you to use shared network resources without having to focus on the specifics of a provider or the actual network infrastructure. Because the Pocket PC contains a limited implementation of WNet, the Microsoft Windows Network protocol (using the Windows NT LM 0.12 dialect) is the only supported network. By using the WNet APIs, an application can communicate with a variety of network resources, including remote file systems, network shares, and printers. Figure 4.1 shows a Pocket PC browsing some of the available network resources.

As mentioned previously, the Pocket PC's network redirector is based on the Common Internet File System protocol. The primary responsibility of CIFS is the management of network connections and the processing of remote file system requests in a way that is compatible with accessing local resources. Once a request is made, CIFS packages and transmits this request to the remote host for processing, and waits for the results to be returned to the device. What this means is that functions designed to work on the Pocket PC object store, such as `CopyFile()`,

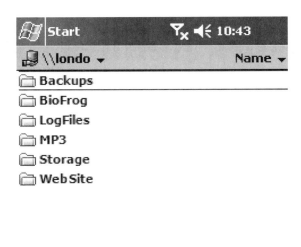

Figure 4.1 Viewing available network resources

can be used on a remote resource once a network connection has been established.

As you might have already guessed by its name, CIFS is implemented on top of TCP/IP, and is situated across the presentation and session layers of the TCP/IP OSI model (see Figure 4.2).

Since the introduction of Pocket PC 2002, most devices now ship with the network redirector as part of the system's ROM. To ensure that the redirector is installed, both the `redir.dll` and `netbios.dll` libraries should be located in the `\Windows` folder. If they are not present, your application will receive an `ERROR_NO_NETWORK` result when using any of the WNet API functions.

To use the WNet network redirector functions with your application, you need to include the header `winnetwk.h`, and link with the `coredll.lib` library in your project.

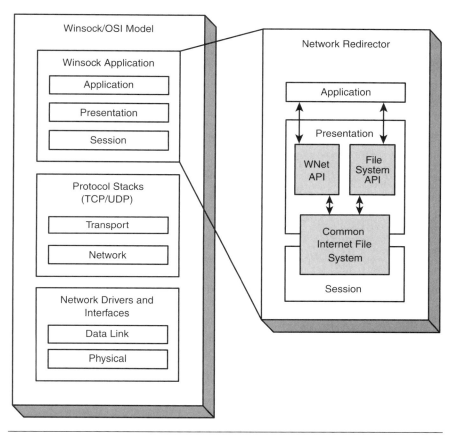

Figure 4.2 Pocket PC network redirector and the TCP/IP OSI model

Pocket PC and Windows Networking

Using the Pocket PC network redirector, you can enable your device to browse, add, cancel, and enumerate network connections anywhere on a Windows network. Accessing an actual network resource can be done in two different ways on the Pocket PC. The first is by mapping the network resource to a name that is placed in the \Network folder, which will appear to the file system as a local folder. The other method is by directly calling the resource by using its **Universal Naming Convention** (**UNC**) name.

Network Names

To successfully use a Windows Network resource, you first must make sure that your device has a unique name on the network. This is typically done by configuring it in the network control panel applet, or by setting the registry value `HKEY_LOCAL_MACHINE\Ident\Name` to a unique device name. If you attempt to access a network resource without a valid name, the network redirector will fail and return an error. Be aware that when a network connection is accessed for the first time, Pocket PC will attempt to register the name on the network. This means that the first operation on a network can take up to 15 seconds longer while it completes the initial registration.

Device network names can be up to 15 characters long, and may contain any characters from A to Z, 0 through 9, or a hyphen. Invalid characters, such as the # or * will not register correctly on the network.

Pocket PC also uses the network login information that you have entered in the control panel for authentication when accessing a network resource. If you connected to the network via a RAS connection instead of a network card, whatever username and password you used for the dial-up connection will be sent when accessing a resource on that network. If an error occurs, a dialog box will prompt you for information.

Universal Naming Convention

One method for accessing network resources is to call any function that requires a filename and path, such as `CreateFile()` or `CopyFile()`. Instead of passing in a file path that is located in the Pocket PC object store, you can instead use a UNC path.

A UNC path is a standard, case-insensitive naming convention that contains the server name, the share name, and a filename (much like a URL does for an HTTP resource). Here is an example of a UNC path:

```
\\MyServer\MyShare\SomeDirectory\SomeFile.txt
```

A UNC path *always* begins with double backslashes and is followed by the server name. In this example, the server name for the resource is `MyServer`, and is followed by the network share name `MyShare`. In this example, we are explicitly looking at the file `SomeFile.txt` located in a directory named `SomeDirectory`.

The `\Network` Folder

The other method for using a network resource is to directly map it to a local path that will be placed underneath the `\Network` folder. Because Pocket PC does not support drive letters like the desktop, you can only make a network resource appear as a directory in the local object store.

For example, suppose you have a server named `\\Copper` that has a directory that is shared with the name `StacyH`. If you mapped the share to the device with a local name `BrettH`, you could then access all the files and directories in the `\\Copper\StacyH` share by accessing the local path `\Network\BrettH`.

TIP: By default, Pocket PC does not expose network drive mappings in the `\Network` folder to the common system dialogs (such as `GetSaveFileName()`) or the local folder browsers. To expose your network mappings to the local system, just set the `DWORD` value `RegisterFSRoot`, which is located under the `HKEY_LOCAL_MACHINE\Comm\Redir` key, to a nonzero value. When the device is reset, the `\Network` folder will be visible.

Once a resource has been mapped to the local device, you can then use any of the standard file system functions, such as `CreateFile()` and `WriteFile()`, to work with files and directories located in the share. However, be aware that the only operations you can perform at the *root* level of the `\Network` folder are adding connections using the `WNetAddConnection3()` function, removing connections with the `WNetCancelConnection2()` function, and enumerating share names using `FindFirstFile()` and `FindNextFile()`. Because `\Network` contains only virtual folders, it is not considered a real object in the file system, and standard operations other than enumeration will fail.

Handling Network Errors

If an error occurs when using any of the network redirector functions, use the standard `GetLastError()` function to get details about the failure. Because only one network is supported, the desktop-based `WNetGetLastError()` function is not implemented on Pocket PC devices.

For example, if you wanted to get further information about an error that occurred when querying for the local device name, you could use the following:

```
if(dwReturn != ERROR_SUCCESS) {
    // The function has failed, get standard error code
    DWORD dwError = GetLastError();

    // Let's get the full error text as well
    LPVOID lpErrorText = NULL;
    FormatMessage(FORMAT_MESSAGE_ALLOCATE_BUFFER|
        FORMAT_MESSAGE_FROM_SYSTEM|FORMAT_MESSAGE_IGNORE_INSERTS,
        NULL, dwError, 0, (LPTSTR) &lpErrorText, 0, NULL);

    // Format and pop a message box with the error number and
    // message
    TCHAR tchErrorString[1024] = TEXT("\0");
    wsprintf(tchErrorString, TEXT("Error Number: %d\r\nError
        Message: %s"), dwError, lpErrorText);

    MessageBox(NULL, tchErrorString, TEXT("Network Error"),
        MB_OK|MB_ICONERROR);
    return FALSE;
}
```

Typically, when calling `GetLastError()` for a WNet error, one of the values described in Table 4.1 will be returned.

Table 4.1 Network Errors Returned by `GetLastError()`

Error Code	Description
ERROR_ACCESS_DENIED	Access is denied to the network resource.
ERROR_ALREADY_ASSIGNED	The local name has already been connected.
ERROR_BAD_DEVICE	The local name is invalid.
ERROR_BAD_NET_NAME	The remote name is not valid or cannot be found.
ERROR_BUSY	The network was busy and could not connect to the resource.
ERROR_CANCELLED	The connection attempt was cancelled.
ERROR_DEVICE_ALREADY_ REMEMBERED	The local name has already been defined for another resource.
ERROR_INVALID_PASSWORD	The network password is invalid.
ERROR_NO_NET_OR_BAD_PATH	The network could not be started.
ERROR_NO_NETWORK	There is no network installed or available.

Differences between Windows and Pocket PC Network APIs

Besides the fact that Pocket PC supports only a subset of the WNet APIs, note a few other minor differences compared to desktop implementations:

- **Pocket PC has no support for drive letters.** Network resources should be mapped to local folders under the `\Network` directory, or can be accessed directly via UNC.
- **No NetBIOS function support.** Although parts of NetBIOS are present in CIFS, there is no direct access to NetBIOS outside of the WNet APIs.
- **The only network supported is the Microsoft Windows Network.**
- **Connections are not restored over a device warm reboot.** The only way to reestablish a connection over a reboot is to mark the connection as persistent.
- **Pocket PC does not support network mail slots or named pipes.**
- **The `WNetGetLastError()` function is not supported.** Use the `GetLastError()` function to retrieve network error messages.
- **There is no concept of network context on Pocket PC.**

Mapping Network Resources

As previously mentioned, you cannot directly add or remove folders in the \Network folder by using traditional file system functions such as CreateFile(). This is because the \Network folder is really a virtual representation of mapped network resources that have been mounted on the device. In order to connect or disconnect a network resource to this folder, you must use the WNet network APIs.

Connecting to the Network

To map a network resource to your Pocket PC device, you can use the WNetAddConnection3() function, which is defined as follows:

```
DWORD WNetAddConnection3(HWND hwndOwner, LPNETRESOURCE
    lpNetResource, LPCWSTR lpPassword, LPCWSTR lpUserName,
    DWORD dwFlags);
```

The first time you call into this function, the system attempts to validate the device name on the network, so it might take a few seconds to return (in fact, it can take up to 15 seconds).

The first parameter that WNetAddConnection3() expects is a handle to a window that the redirector can use as the parent for any dialog boxes that it might need to display. It can be set to a NULL value if you don't need to have an owner window. The next parameter, lpNet Resource, is a pointer to a NETRESOURCE structure that defines some information about the resource to which you are trying to connect. This is followed by two null-terminated strings: lpPassword and lpUser Name, which are used for authentication on the resource. If these values are set to NULL, Pocket PC will try to use the default username and password that were configured in the network control panel. If no defaults have been defined, a dialog box requesting the authentication details will be displayed. Lastly, the dwFlags parameter can be set to either 0 or CONNECT_UPDATE_PROFILE. Using the CONNECT_UPDATE_ PROFILE flag will mark the new connection as persistent, and the device will store the network mapping in the registry and automatically attempt to reconnect it if the connection is lost. Note that Pocket PC cannot make a connection persistent if the connection is invalid or does not have a name.

The NETRESOURCE structure you pass in to the lpNetResource parameters is used for both the enumeration and connection of a network resource, and is defined as follows:

```
typedef struct _NETRESOURCE {
    DWORD dwScope;
    DWORD dwType;
    DWORD dwDisplayType;
    DWORD dwUsage;
    LPWSTR lpLocalName;
    LPWSTR lpRemoteName;
    LPWSTR lpComment;
    LPWSTR lpProvider;
} NETRESOURCE, *LPNETRESOURCE;
```

The first three fields (dwScope, dwType, and dwDisplayType) are used when enumerating network resources only. When you use the NETRESOURCE structure with the WNetAddConnection3() function, you can set them all to 0.

The first field, dwScope, defines the scope of the network resource, and can be one of the flags in Table 4.2.

Table 4.2 Network Resource Scope Flags

Flag	Description
RESOURCE_CONNECTED	Return the currently connected resources
RESOURCE_GLOBALNET	Return all resources on the network
RESOURCE_REMEMBERED	Return network connections that have been marked as persistent

The next field, dwType, can be one of the network resource types listed in Table 4.3.

Table 4.3 Network Resource Types

Flag	Description
RESOURCETYPE_ANY	Any network resource
RESOURCETYPE_DISK	Drive and disk resource
RESOURCETYPE_PRINT	Printer resources

The `dwDisplayType` field can be used to obtain more specific information about the resource. It can be one of the types in Table 4.4.

Table 4.4 Network Resource Display Types

Flag	Description
RESOURCEDISPLAYTYPE_DOMAIN	The resource is a domain controller.
RESOURCEDISPLAYTYPE_GENERIC	The resource type does not matter.
RESOURCEDISPLAYTYPE_SERVER	The resource is a server.
RESOURCEDISPLAYTYPE_SHARE	The resource is a drive share.

The next field, `dwUsage`, is used only if the `dwScope` member is set to `RESOURCE_GLOBALNET`; otherwise, this should be set to `NULL`. This field further defines the scope during enumeration (see Table 4.5).

Table 4.5 Network Resource Usage Types

Flag	Description
RESOURCEUSAGE_CONNECTABLE	The resource is connectable, such as a drive share or printer.
RESOURCEUSAGE_CONTAINER	The resource is a container, such as a server or domain.

The `lpLocalName` field is a pointer to a null-terminated string that represents the local name of the connection. If you set this to `NULL`, a connection will still be established, but there will be no local name in the `\Network` folder. This is followed by the `lpRemoteName` field, which points to a null-terminated string that is the UNC name of the remote resource with which you want to connect. Be aware that the local name is limited to 99 characters, and the remote name is limited to 64.

Next is the `lpComment` field, which is an optional null-terminated string that contains information provided by some servers. The last field, `lpProvider`, should be set to `NULL`, as it is currently unused.

After calling `WNetAddConnection3()`, you will be returned an `ERROR_SUCCESS` value if the connection was successfully established and mapped to the device. Otherwise, you can use the `GetLast Error()` function or look at the return value to determine what the error message is.

For example, if you wanted to connect to a network share named `Backups` that was located on the server `\\LONDO`, you would do the following:

```
NETRESOURCE netResource;

memset(&netResource, 0, sizeof(NETRESOURCE));
netResource.lpLocalName = TEXT("NetBackup");
netResource.lpRemoteName = TEXT("\\\\LONDO\\Backups");
DWORD dwReturn = WNetAddConnection3(NULL, &netResource,
   NULL, NULL, CONNECT_UPDATE_PROFILE);
```

Figure 4.3 shows the files contained in the new network mapping, which has been added to the `\Network` folder on the device.

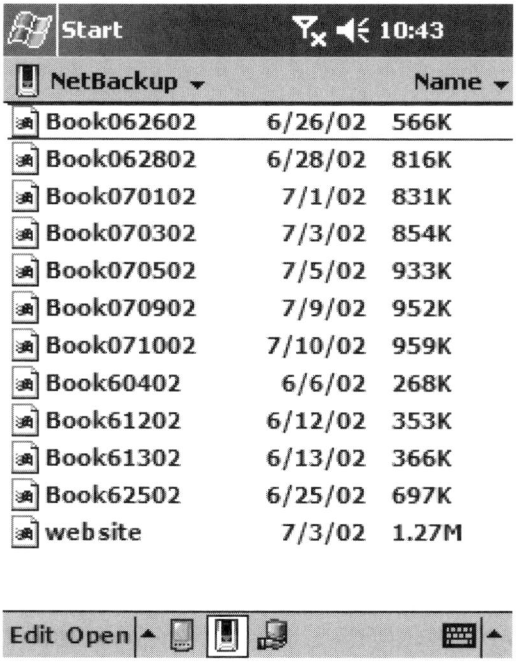

Figure 4.3 The `\Network` folder

Disconnecting a Network Connection

Once you have established a network mapping and are finished using it, you can remove it as follows:

```
DWORD WNetCancelConnection2(LPCWSTR lpName, DWORD dwFlags,
  BOOL fForce);
```

The first parameter points to a null-terminated string that contains either the local or the remote resource name from which you want to disconnect. This is followed by dwFlags, which can be set to either 0 or CONNECT_UPDATE_PROFILE. If you use the CONNECT_UPDATE_ PROFILE flag, the device will no longer consider it a persistent connection. The last parameter, fForce, should be set to TRUE if you want the connection disconnect to occur even if there are open files or jobs on the connection. If it is set to FALSE, it will fail if a resource is in use.

If the WNetCancelConnection2() function returns successfully, you will receive an ERROR_SUCCESS result. Otherwise, you can use the GetLastError() function to find out what went wrong.

To disconnect from the share created in the last example, you could disconnect with a function that looks like the following:

```
DWORD dwReturn = WNetCancelConnection2(TEXT("NetBackup"),
  CONNECT_UPDATE_PROFILE, TRUE);
```

Using the Network Connections Dialog Box

Another way to add and remove network connections is to use the built-in network connection dialogs. Users are presented with a dialog box that asks them for the remote resource location as well as the local name. To add a connection, you can call the WNetConnectionDialog1() function, which is defined as follows:

```
DWORD WNetConnectionDialog1(LPCONNECTDLGSTRUCT
  lpConnDlgStruct);
```

The function takes a single parameter, which is a pointer to a CONNECTDLGSTRUCT structure. This structure is prototyped as shown here:

```
typedef struct _CONNECTDLGSTRUCT{
    DWORD cbStructure;
    HWND hwndOwner;
    LPNETRESOURCE lpConnRes;
```

```
    DWORD dwFlags;
    DWORD dwDevNum;
} CONNECTDLGSTRUCT, FAR *LPCONNECTDLGSTRUCT;
```

The first field, `cbStructure`, should be set to the size, in bytes, of the structure. Next, `hwndOwner` should be set to the handle of the window that owns the dialog. The `lpConnRes` field should point to a `NETRESOURCE` structure that contains information about the remote resource with which you want to connect. If you want to have the dialog automatically insert a remote name, you can fill in the `lpRemoteName` field of the `NETRESOURCE` structure; otherwise, set it to `NULL`. The rest of the `NETRESOURCE` structure can be set to 0.

If you have set the `lpRemoteName` field of the `NETRESOURCE` structure to a remote name, and you want this value to be read only in the dialog, you can set the `dwFlags` parameter to `CONNDLG_RO_PATH`; otherwise, set it to 0.

The last field, `dwDevNum`, is not used and should be set to 0.

When the dialog box closes, it will return an `ERROR_SUCCESS` value if the connection was established. If the user cancelled the dialog, you will be returned a value of `0xFFFFFFFF`; otherwise, you can use the `GetLastError()` function to find out what went wrong.

Figure 4.4 shows the dialog box that is displayed with the following example:

```
CONNECTDLGSTRUCT connectDlg;
NETRESOURCE netResource;

memset(&connectDlg, 0, sizeof(CONNECTDLGSTRUCT));
memset(&netResource, 0, sizeof(NETRESOURCE));

connectDlg.cbStructure = sizeof(CONNECTDLGSTRUCT);
connectDlg.lpConnRes = &netResource;
DWORD dwReturn = WNetConnectionDialog1(&connectDlg);
```

Two different dialog boxes can be used to disconnect a network mapped resource. The first function, `WNetDisconnectDialog()`, displays a dialog box that lists all the currently connected and persistent connections, and allows the user to select which one to remove. The function looks like the following:

```
DWORD WNetDisconnectDialog(HWND hwnd, DWORD dwType);
```

The first parameter, `hwnd`, is the handle to the window that owns the dialog. The `dwType` parameter is not used and should be set to 0.

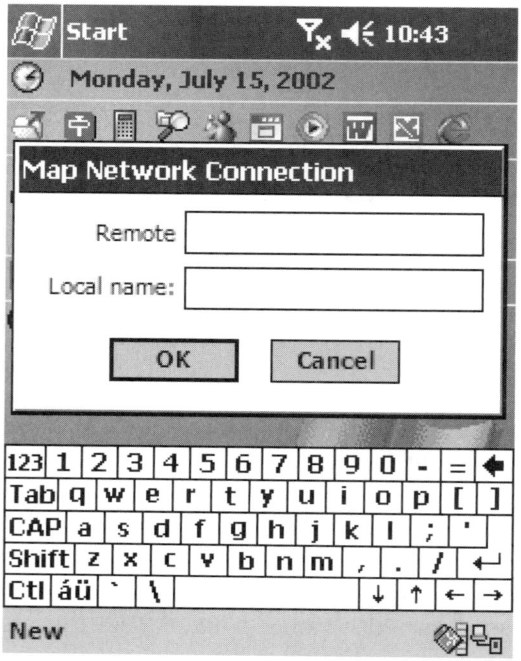

Figure 4.4 The `WNetConnectionDialog1` dialog box

The other function to disconnect a mapped network resource is
`WNetDisconnectDialog1()`. This function will attempt to disconnect the resources specified by the structure you pass in. If there is any
current activity, such as an open file, on the network, the user is
prompted for confirmation. The function looks like the following:

```
DWORD WNetDisconnectDialog1(LPDISCDLGSTRUCT
  lpConnDlgStruct);
```

The only parameter that is passed in is a pointer to a `DISCDLG`
`STRUCT` structure, which is prototyped as follows:

```
typedef struct _DISCDLGSTRUCTW{
    DWORD cbStructure;
    HWND hwndOwner;
    LPWSTR lpLocalName;
    LPWSTR lpRemoteName;
```

```
    DWORD dwFlags;
} DISCDLGSTRUCTW, FAR *LPDISCDLGSTRUCTW;
```

The `cbStructure` field should contain the size of the structure, in bytes. This is followed by `hwndOwner`, which is the handle to the window that owns the dialog (if it pops up). The `lpLocalName` field points to a null-terminated string that specifies the local name to disconnect, and is followed by `lpRemoteName`. If the `lpLocalName` field contains a value, you can then set `lpRemoteName` to `NULL`; otherwise, it should point to a string that specifies the remote resource name. The last field, `dwFlags`, can be set to 0, or you can use the `DISC_NO_FORCE` flag if you do not want the dialog to appear.

To disconnect a network mapping using the `WNetDisconnect Dialog1()` function, you can do the following:

```
DISCDLGSTRUCT disconnectDlg;

memset(&disconnectDlg, 0, sizeof(DISCDLGSTRUCT));
disconnectDlg.cbStructure = sizeof(DISCDLGSTRUCT);
disconnectDlg.lpLocalName = TEXT("NetBackup");

DWORD dwReturn = WNetDisconnectDialog1(&disconnectDlg);
```

Using Network Resources

The preceding section explained how to connect and disconnect from a network resource. However, it can be somewhat difficult to establish a connection to a resource without explicit knowledge of its location, or what is currently available. Fortunately, the WNet APIs provide several functions that enable you to enumerate network resources, as well as to query them for additional information.

Enumerating Network Resources

Enumerating available network resources is similar to enumerating files or Internet cache entries—you must first open the enumeration and get a handle, "walk" each item of the enumeration, and finish by closing the enumeration handle.

The first step in enumerating either available network resources or items that you have already mapped to your device is accomplished by calling the `WNetOpenEnum()` function:

```
DWORD WNetOpenEnum(DWORD dwScope, DWORD dwType, DWORD
   dwUsage, LPNETRESOURCEW lpNetResource, LPHANDLE lphEnum);
```

The first parameter, `dwScope`, defines the scope of network-connected resources you want to enumerate, and can be one of the values in Table 4.6.

Table 4.6 Network Resource Scope Flags

Flag	Description
RESOURCE_CONNECTED	Return only the currently connected resources
RESOURCE_GLOBALNET	Return all resources on the network
RESOURCE_REMEMBERED	Return network connections that have been marked as persistent whether they are connected or not

The `dwType` parameter specifies what types of network resources you want to view in your enumeration (see Table 4.7).

Table 4.7 Network Resource Types

Flag	Description
RESOURCETYPE_ANY	Enumerate all network resources
RESOURCETYPE_DISK	Enumerate disk resources
RESOURCETYPE_PRINT	Enumerate print resources

The next parameter, `dwUsage`, further defines the enumeration scope by how it is being used. If the dwScope parameter is not set to `RESOURCE_GLOBALNET`, then this parameter must be set to 0; otherwise, it can be one of the flags listed in Table 4.8.

Table 4.8 Network Resource Usage Types

Flag	Description
0	All resources
RESOURCEUSAGE_CONNECTABLE	All connectable resources (such as shares)
RESOURCEUSAGE_CONTAINER	All server resources

The `lpNetResource` parameter is used to define the starting point for an enumeration. It should contain a pointer to a NETRESOURCE structure, as long as the `dwScope` parameter is set to RESOURCE_GLOBALNET; otherwise, it should be set to NULL. To correctly start an enumeration, you must also set the NETRESOURCE structure's `lpRemoteName` field to the root of the server you want to enumerate, and set its `dwUsage` member to RESOURCEUSAGE_CONTAINER:

```
NETRESOURCE netResource;

memset(&netResource, 0, sizeof(NETRESOURCE));
netResource.lpRemoteName = TEXT("\\\\LONDO");
netResource.dwUsage = RESOURCEUSAGE_CONTAINER;
netResource.dwScope = RESOURCE_GLOBALNET;
```

The last parameter, `lphEnum`, is a pointer to a handle for your enumeration. If your call to `WNetOpenEnum()` is successful, then the function will return an ERROR_SUCCESS return value.

Once you have successfully returned an enumeration handle, you can begin the actual enumeration of network resources by using the `WNetEnumResource()` function, which is defined as follows:

```
DWORD WNetEnumResource(HANDLE hEnum, LPDWORD lpcCount,
    LPVOID lpBuffer, LPDWORD lpBufferSize);
```

The first parameter you use with `WNetEnumResource()` is the handle to the enumeration that you received from your previous call to `WNetOpenEnum()`. Next, `lpcCount` is a pointer to a DWORD value that specifies the number of items you are requesting. To get as many items as possible, you can set this to 0xFFFFFFFF. When the function returns, the variable to which `lpcCount` is pointing will contain the actual number of items that were returned. Next, the `lpBuffer` parameter should point to a buffer that contains the array of NETRESOURCE structures for each returned resource. The final parameter, `lpBufferSize`, should point to a `DWORD` value specifying the size, in bytes, of the buffer you pointed to with the `lpBuffer` parameter.

When the function returns, if you were able to successfully enumerate the network resources, you will receive an `ERROR_SUCCESS` return value. Your application should keep calling the `WNetOpenEnum()` function until you get `ERROR_NO_MORE_ITEMS` as a return value, which specifies that there are no more resources to enumerate. An error of `ERROR_MORE_DATA` indicates that there is still additional enumeration information.

You can use three different techniques to enumerate network resources:

1. **Specify a large buffer and attempt to get all the network enumerations in as a single call.** You can allocate a large buffer (around 16KB), and pass `0xFFFFFFFF` as the `lpcCount` value. Setting the `lpcCount` to this results in an attempt to get all of the network resources at once:

```
DWORD dwReturn = WNetOpenEnum(RESOURCE_GLOBALNET, RESOURCETYPE_ANY,
   0, &netResource, &hNetEnum);

// Allocate a large buffer, and get the resources in one shot
DWORD dwNumEnum = 0xFFFFFFFF;
NETRESOURCE netResources[15];
DWORD dwBufferSize = sizeof(NETRESOURCE)*15;

// Make the enum call
dwReturn = WNetEnumResource(hNetEnum, &dwNumEnum,
   &netResources, &dwBufferSize);

if(dwReturn == ERROR_SUCCESS) {
   for(DWORD dwEnum = 0; dwEnum < dwNumEnum; dwEnum++) {
      // Walk through the enumerated resources
      MessageBox(NULL, netResources[dwEnum].lpRemoteName,
         TEXT("Resource"), MB_OK);
   }
}

WNetCloseEnum(hNetEnum);
```

2. **Call WNetEnumResource() multiple times**. The second option is to call WNetEnumResource() and pass in a relatively small buffer for the NETRESOURCE array. When the function returns, you need to create a loop until you receive a return code of ERROR_NO_MORE_ITEMS:

```
DWORD dwNumEnum = 1;
NETRESOURCE *pNetResource = NULL;

// Allocate a small buffer
pNetResource = (NETRESOURCE *)LocalAlloc(LPTR, sizeof(NETRESOURCE));
DWORD dwBufferSize = sizeof(NETRESOURCE);
BOOL fContinue = TRUE;

do {
    // Make the enum call
    DWORD dwReturn = WNetEnumResource(hNetEnum, &dwNumEnum,
        pNetResource, &dwBufferSize);

    // Was the buffer large enough?
    if(dwReturn == ERROR_MORE_DATA) {
        LocalFree(pNetResource);
        pNetResource = (NETRESOURCE *)LocalAlloc(LPTR, dwBufferSize);

        // Call again
        dwReturn = WNetEnumResource(hNetEnum, &dwNumEnum,
            pNetResource, &dwBufferSize);
    }

    if(dwReturn == ERROR_SUCCESS)
        MessageBox(NULL, pNetResource->lpRemoteName,
            TEXT("Resource"), MB_OK);
    if(dwReturn == ERROR_NO_MORE_ITEMS)
        fContinue = FALSE;
} while(fContinue);

LocalFree(pNetResource);
WNetCloseEnum(hNetEnum);
```

3. **Determine the size of the network resource buffer, and then call WNetEnumResource() again to get the actual**

data. Another option is to call the `WNetEnumResource()` function and pass a `NULL` value for the `lpBuffer` parameter. When the function returns, the size required for the resource array will be placed in the `lpBufferSize` parameter.

To end the resource enumeration, just call the `WNetCloseEnum()` function:

```
DWORD WNetCloseEnum(HANDLE hEnum);
```

`WNetCloseEnum()` takes a single parameter, which is the handle to the enumeration that you received in your initial call to `WNetOpen Enum()`.

Getting Network Resource Information

In addition to the network enumeration functions, the WNet API also has some functions for obtaining information about network connections.

To find out the UNC path of a mapped drive that is currently connected, you can call the following function:

```
DWORD WNetGetConnection(LPCWSTR lpLocalName, LPWSTR
   lpRemoteName, LPDWORD lpnLength);
```

The first parameter, `lpLocalName`, is a pointer to a null-terminated string that contains the local name of the mapped network resource. The next parameter, `lpRemoteName`, points to a buffer that will get the UNC network path for the locally mapped resource. Finally, `lpn Length` points to a `DWORD` value that specifies the size of the buffer pointed to with the `lpRemoteName` parameter. If the buffer is not large enough, the required size will be stored here, as shown in the following example:

```
TCHAR tchRemoteName[1024] = TEXT("\0");
DWORD dwBufferSize = 1024;

dwReturn = WNetGetConnection(TEXT("NetBackup"),
  tchRemoteName, &dwBufferSize);
```

The `WNetGetUniversalName()` function gets the full UNC path (i.e., `\\ServerName\Sharename`) to any mapped resource, regardless of its current connection status. The parameters you pass in will determine the UNC format that is returned.

The `WNetGetUniversalName()` function is prototyped as follows:

```
DWORD WNetGetUniversalName(LPCWSTR lpLocalPath, DWORD
    dwInfoLevel, LPVOID lpBuffer, LPDWORD lpBufferSize);
```

You first need to pass in the full path as a null-terminated string for a network resource that is mapped into the `\Network` folder. The next parameter, `dwInfoLevel`, determines the type of buffer returned from the function, and can be set to either UNIVERSAL_NAME_INFO_LEVEL or REMOTE_NAME_INFO_LEVEL.

Setting the `dwInfoLevel` flag to UNIVERSAL_NAME_INFO_LEVEL will return a UNIVERSAL_NAME_INFO structure, which looks like the following:

```
typedef struct _UNIVERSAL_NAME_INFO {
    LPWSTR lpUniversalName;
}UNIVERSAL_NAME_INFO, *LPUNIVERSAL_NAME_INFO;
```

The structure simply contains the UNC path to the file that you specified by `lpLocalPath`.

When calling `WNetGetUniversalName()`, if you set the `dwInfoLevel` flag to REMOTE_NAME_INFO_LEVEL (instead of UNIVERSAL_NAME_INFO_LEVEL), you will be returned a REMOTE_NAME_INFO structure. It is defined as follows:

```
typedef struct _REMOTE_NAME_INFO {
    LPWSTR lpUniversalName;
    LPWSTR lpConnectionName;
    LPWSTR lpRemainingPath;
}REMOTE_NAME_INFO, *LPREMOTE_NAME_INFO;
```

The first field, `lpUniversalName`, points to the full UNC path of the file that was specified in `lpLocalPath` (and is the same as the `lpUniversalName` member of the UNIVERSAL_NAME_INFO structure). The next two strings contain a parsed UNC path, which is already divided into the share name and the path of the file. The `lpConnectionName` member contains the share, and `lpRemainingPath` has the UNC name to the file.

The last parameter, `lpBufferSize`, should point to a DWORD value that specifies the size of the buffer passed in the `lpBuffer` parameter.

If the buffer is too small, this value will contain the size that is needed when the function returns.

To get the username that was used to authenticate a remote network resource, WNet provides the `WNetGetUser()` function:

```
DWORD WNetGetUser(LPCWSTR lpName, LPWSTR lpUserName, LPDWORD
   lpnLength);
```

The first parameter is a null-terminated string that contains the local name of the mapped network resource. This is followed by `lpUserName`, which is a buffer that receives the network resource logon name. Finally, `lpnLength` should point to a `DWORD` value that contains the size of the buffer used in the `lpUserName` parameter. If the buffer is too small, it will contain the size needed for the buffer when the function returns.

Working with Files

Working with files that are located on the network is essentially the same as if they were located inside the device's object store. For example, if you wanted to enumerate all of the files on a network-mapped share, you could just use the file system functions `FindFirstFile()` and `FindNextFile()`:

```
HANDLE hFileEnum = NULL;
WIN32_FIND_DATA w32Find;
BOOL fContinue = TRUE;
memset(&w32Find, 0, sizeof(WIN32_FIND_DATA));

SetLastError(0);
hFileEnum = FindFirstFile(TEXT("\\NETWORK\\NetBackup\\*.*"),
   &w32Find);
if(hFileEnum == INVALID_HANDLE_VALUE) {
   DWORD dwError = GetLastError();
   return FALSE;
}

do {
   MessageBox(NULL, w32Find.cFileName, TEXT("File Enum"), MB_OK);

   // Get the next item
   if((FindNextFile(hFileEnum, &w32Find)) != 0) {
      if(GetLastError() == ERROR_NO_MORE_FILES)
```

```
            fContinue = FALSE;
    }
} while(fContinue);

FindClose(hFileEnum);
```

Copying a file to the network is just as easy using the `CopyFile()` function:

```
TCHAR tchSource[MAX_PATH] = TEXT("\\TestFile.txt");
TCHAR tchDest[MAX_PATH] =
   TEXT("\\NETWORK\\NetBackup\\TestFile.txt");
CopyFile(tchSource, tchDest, TRUE);
```

Printing on the Network

Finding and using a printer on the network follows the same process as enumerating or connecting to a drive share. However, you must specify that you are looking for printers when calling the `WNetOpenEnum()` function by setting the `dwType` parameter to `RESOURCETYPE_PRINT`.

For example, if you wanted to enumerate all of the printer resources that were being made available by a particular server (in this case, `"\\\\LONDO"`), you could do the following:

```
HANDLE hNetEnum = NULL;
NETRESOURCE netResource;

memset(&netResource, 0, sizeof(NETRESOURCE));
netResource.lpRemoteName = TEXT("\\\\LONDO");
netResource.dwUsage = RESOURCEUSAGE_CONTAINER;

DWORD dwReturn = WNetOpenEnum(RESOURCE_GLOBALNET,
   RESOURCETYPE_PRINT, 0, &netResource, &hNetEnum);

// Allocate a large buffer, and get the printers in one shot
DWORD dwNumEnum = 0xFFFFFFFF;
NETRESOURCE netResources[3];
DWORD dwBufferSize = sizeof(NETRESOURCE)*3;

// Make the enum call
dwReturn = WNetEnumResource(hNetEnum, &dwNumEnum, &netResources,
   &dwBufferSize);
```

```
if(dwReturn == ERROR_SUCCESS) {
   for(DWORD dwEnum = 0; dwEnum < dwNumEnum; dwEnum++) {
      // Walk through the enumerated resources
      MessageBox(NULL, netResources[dwEnum].lpRemoteName,
   TEXT("Printers"), MB_OK);
   }
}


WNetCloseEnum(hNetEnum);
```

Once you have found a printer you want to use, you have two printing methods from which to choose. One, you can simply call the `Copy File()` function, and pass in the UNC name for the printer as the destination for the file, as shown in the following example:

```
TCHAR tchPrintFile[MAX_PATH] = TEXT("\\My
  Documents\\Channels\\SamplePrint.txt");
TCHAR tchPrinter[MAX_PATH] = TEXT("\\\\LONDO\\Deskjet");

CopyFile(tchPrintFile, tchPrinter, FALSE);
```

Alternately, you can use the `CreateFile()`, `WriteFile()`, and `CloseHandle()` functions. This method gives you more direct control over the buffers that are sent to the printer. Sending a file to the printer in this manner can be accomplished as follows:

```
TCHAR tchPrintFile[MAX_PATH] = TEXT("\\My
  Documents\\Channels\\SamplePrint.txt");
TCHAR tchPrinter[MAX_PATH] = TEXT("\\\\LONDO\\Deskjet");

// Create the print job
HANDLE hPrintJob = NULL;
hPrintJob = CreateFile(tchPrinter, GENERIC_WRITE, 0, NULL,
  CREATE_NEW, FILE_ATTRIBUTE_NORMAL, NULL);

// Open the file
HANDLE hFile = NULL;
LPVOID lpBuffer = NULL;
DWORD dwRead = 0, dwWritten = 0;

hFile = CreateFile(tchPrintFile, GENERIC_READ, 0, NULL,
   OPEN_EXISTING, FILE_ATTRIBUTE_NORMAL, NULL);
lpBuffer = LocalAlloc(LPTR, 1024);
```

```
do {
   ReadFile(hFile, lpBuffer, 1024, &dwRead, NULL);
   if(dwRead > 0) {
      // Send the buffer to the printer
      WriteFile(hPrintJob, lpBuffer, dwRead, &dwWritten, NULL);
   }
} while(dwRead > 0);

CloseHandle(hFile);
CloseHandle(hPrintJob);
LocalFree(lpBuffer);
```

Note that the Pocket PC has no real knowledge of the printer, printer resources, or the printer queue. It is basically sending a raw file dump of data to the network resource, so you are limited to printing only text files in this manner.

CHAPTER 5

Using Serial and Infrared Ports

With insomnia, nothing is real. Everything is far away.
Everything is a copy of a copy of a copy.

—Narrator, Fight Club

Previous chapters have described how you can develop applications on a Pocket PC device to use TCP/IP-based networks in a variety of ways to send and receive data between a client and host. This chapter explores the most basic communication protocol that is supported on these devices—low-level serial input/output. A serial connection is most simply defined as a direct, one-to-one connection between two devices whose data is transferred one bit at a time. Examples of serial connections include those between a Pocket PC device and a modem, printer, or some type of data collection device.

Windows CE supports both serial cable and infrared (IR) communications as a mechanism for establishing a connection between two serial devices. Figure 5.1 shows Pocket PC's built-in capability to receive a file over infrared.

Establishing a connection and transferring data back and forth with another serial device is fairly straightforward—Pocket PC uses the same functions as it does when working with the file system (such as `CreateFile()`, `ReadFile()`, and so on). This is also the same mechanism that is used on the desktop, which makes porting applications from a Windows XP system to a mobile device an easy process.

With regard to where the serial and infrared network APIs sit on the TCP/IP OSI layer, an application that you develop will directly use the serial APIs, which reside in the data-link layer. These functions work with the serial and infrared drivers, which then communicate with the actual serial hardware in the OSI physical layer using the standard RS-232C

Figure 5.1 Using infrared to receive a file

interface. Figure 5.2 shows how both the serial and infrared communication stack fits into the TCP/IP OSI model:

To use the serial or infrared communication functions with your application, you need to include the header `windows.h`, and link with the `coredll.lib` library in your project.

NOTE: Serial-based infrared communications support only *half-duplex* operations. This means that only one device can transmit or receive data over a particular direction at a time.

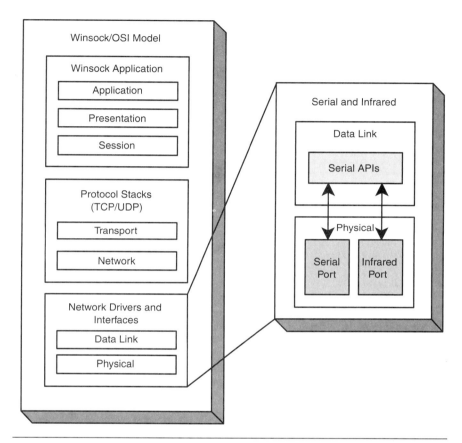

Figure 5.2 Serial and infrared communications and the TCP/IP OSI model

Serial Communications

The device drivers that have been developed on the Pocket PC platform used for serial communications are known as **streaming interfaces**. A streaming interface is simply defined as any device that is attached to the Pocket PC that can provide or use a stream (or flow) of data. It can also be thought of as a "virtual" data source. This concept is similar to how a file is viewed inside the Windows CE object store, which is why talking to a device has been designed in a similar fashion to working with a file.

Just as you need to develop an application in order to open a file for reading or writing, you first need to open a connection with the attached device before you can perform any serial communications. Once you have opened the connection, you are returned a system resource handle to perform any other communication over the serial interface. This handle is similar to other system handles, as it needs to be properly closed when you are finished using it; otherwise, other applications will not be able to access the device.

In addition to reading and writing data, you can also use the device's resource handle to query or modify the serial connection settings, to control the state of the serial line, or even to talk directly to the serial device driver.

Opening a Connection

The first step in working with any serial device is to open the serial port using the `CreateFile()` function, which is defined as follows:

```
HANDLE CreateFile(LPCWSTR lpFileName, DWORD dwDesiredAccess,
    DWORD dwShareMode, LPSECURITY_ATTRIBUTES lpSecurityAttributes,
    DWORD dwCreationDisposition, DWORD dwFlagsAndAttributes,
    HANDLE hTemplateFile);
```

Any serial device you attempt to open uses the same naming scheme for the `lpFileName` parameter: the word COM followed by the specific communications port number to open, and ending with a colon (for example, to open the first serial port, you would use COM1:). The `dwDesiredAccess` parameter defines how the serial device should be accessed, and can be a combination of 0 (for query access), GENERIC_READ (for read access), or GENERIC_WRITE (for write access). The `dwShareMode` parameter *must* be set to 0, because a serial device has to be opened with exclusive access rights; and `lpSecurityAttributes` should be set to NULL.

Because you are accessing a device, rather than a file, `dwCreation Disposition` is always set to OPEN_EXISTING; and `dwFlagsAnd Attributes` is set to FILE_ATTRIBUTE_NORMAL. Finally, `hTemplate File` should be set to NULL.

If the call to `CreateFile()` succeeds, a valid open handle is returned, which you can use for further operations on the serial port. Otherwise, you will receive an INVALID_HANDLE_VALUE return error code.

For example, if you wanted to open the USB serial port (typically, COM9 on Pocket PC), you would do the following:

```
HANDLE hSerialPort = CreateFile(TEXT("COM9:"),
   GENERIC_READ|GENERIC_WRITE, 0, NULL, OPEN_EXISTING,
   FILE_ATTRIBUTE_NORMAL, NULL);
if(hSerialPort == INVALID_HANDLE_VALUE)
   return FALSE;
```

Configuring the Serial Port

Now that you have an open handle to a serial communications device, you can use a few functions to query and configure the opened port.

To set the *recommended* values that the device driver will reserve for the internal buffers used for input and output, call the `SetupComm()` function. Setting the internal buffer size can be useful when a particular protocol that uses the serial port has packets that are larger than the system default of 1,024 bytes.

Be aware, however, that streaming serial device drivers are not required to use your recommended size, and possibly could ignore these values. The `SetupComm()` function is defined as follows:

```
BOOL SetupComm(HANDLE hFile, DWORD dwInQueue, DWORD dwOutQueue);
```

The first parameter is the device handle that you previously opened with the call to `CreateFile()`. This is followed by `dwInQueue` and `dwOutQueue`, which are `DWORD` values for recommended input and output buffer sizes, respectively. The function returns `TRUE` if it successful; otherwise, it returns `FALSE`.

A somewhat more useful function is the `GetCommProperties()` API. This function enables you to examine a serial device to see what features and capabilities are supported on the device. The `GetComm Properties()` function is defined as follows:

```
BOOL GetCommProperties(HANDLE hFile, LPCOMMPROP lpCommProp);
```

The function takes two parameters: the open handle to the device and a pointer to a `COMMPROP` structure containing the device configuration settings when the function returns. If the call is successful, the function returns a `TRUE` value.

The `COMMPROP` structure looks like the following:

```
typedef struct _COMMPROP {
   WORD wPacketLength;
   WORD wPacketVersion;
```

```
    DWORD dwServiceMask;
    DWORD dwReserved1;
    DWORD dwMaxTxQueue;
    DWORD dwMaxRxQueue;
    DWORD dwMaxBaud;
    DWORD dwProvSubType;
    DWORD dwProvCapabilities;
    DWORD dwSettableParams;
    DWORD dwSettableBaud;
    WORD wSettableData;
    WORD wSettableStopParity;
    DWORD dwCurrentTxQueue;
    DWORD dwCurrentRxQueue;
    DWORD dwProvSpec1;
    DWORD dwProvSpec2;
    WCHAR wcProvChar[1];
} COMMPROP,*LPCOMMPROP;
```

The `COMMPROP` structure contains a substantial amount of information about the capabilities of the serial device you are querying:

- `wPacketLength` is the size of the data packet requested, in bytes.
- `wPacketVersion` is the version of the `COMMPROP` structure.
- `dwServiceMask` is the driver type supported by the device. This will always be `SP_SERIALCOMM`.
- `dwReserved1` is not used.
- `dwMaxTxQueue` is the maximum size of the internal output buffer. This will be 0 if there is no maximum size.
- `dwMaxRxQueue` is the maximum size of the internal input buffer. This will be 0 if there is no maximum size.
- `dwMaxBaud` is the maximum possible baud rate of the serial port. It can be any of the values shown in Table 5.1.
- `dwProvSubType` is the communications provider type. It can be any of the values shown in Table 5.2.
- `dwProvCapabilities` specifies the capabilities available on the specific provider type. This parameter can be one of the values shown in Table 5.3.
- `dwSettableParams` are the communications device parameters that can be changed. This parameter can be one of the values shown in Table 5.4.

Table 5.1 Baud Rates

Value	Description
BAUD_075	75 bits per second
BAUD_110	110 bits per second
BAUD_134_5	134.5 bits per second
BAUD_150	150 bits per second
BAUD_300	300 bits per second
BAUD_600	600 bits per second
BAUD_1200	1,200 bits per second
BAUD_1800	1,800 bits per second
BAUD_2400	2,400 bits per second
BAUD_4800	4,800 bits per second
BAUD_7200	7,200 bits per second
BAUD_9600	9,600 bits per second
BAUD_14400	14,400 bits per second
BAUD_19200	19,200 bits per second
BAUD_38400	38,400 bits per second
BAUD_56K	56,000 bits per second
BAUD_57600	57,600 bits per second
BAUD_115200	115,200 bits per second
BAUD_128K	128,000 bits per second
BAUD_USER	Programmable baud rates are available

Table 5.2 Communication Provider Types

Value	Description
PST_RS232	RS-232C serial port
PST_PARALLELPORT	Parallel port
PST_RS422	RS-422 port
PST_RS423	RS-423 port
PST_RS449	RS-449 port
PST_MODEM	Modem device
PST_FAX	Fax device
PST_SCANNER	Scanner device
PST_NETWORK_BRIDGE	Network bridge device
PST_LAT	LAT device
PST_TCPIP_TELNET	TCP/IP Telnet protocol
PST_X25	X.25 standards
PST_UNSPECIFIED	Unspecified device

Table 5.3 Provider Capabilities

Value	Description
PCF_DTRDSR	Data Terminal Ready (DTR) and Data Set Ready (DSR) are supported.
PCF_RTSCTS	Request to Send (RTS) and Clear To Send (CTS) are supported.
PCF_RLSD	Receive Line Signal Detect (RLSD) is supported.
PCF_PARITY_CHECK	Parity checking is supported.
PCF_XONXOFF	Flow control is supported.
PCF_SETXCHAR	Settable XON and XOFF flow control are supported.
PCF_TOTALTIMEOUTS	Total (elapsed) timeouts are supported.
PCF_INTTIMEOUTS	Interval timeouts are supported.
PCF_SPECIALCHARS	Special character support is available.
PCF_16BITMODE	16-bit mode is available.

Table 5.4 Port Parameters

Value	Description
SP_PARITY	Parity can be set on the port.
SP_BAUD	Baud rate can be set on the port.
SP_DATABITS	The number of data bits can be set on the port.
SP_STOPBITS	The number of stop bits can be selected on the port.
SP_HANDSHAKING	Flow control can be set on the port.
SP_PARITY_CHECK	Parity checking can be set on the port.
SP_RLSD	Receive Line Signal Detect can be controlled on the port.

- dwSettableBaud indicates the baud rates that can be used on the device. This will be one of the values specified by dwMaxBaud.
- wSettableData indicates the number of data bits that can be set. This can be set to one of the values shown in Table 5.5.
- wSettableStopParity is the number of stop bits and parity settings that can be selected. This can be set to one of the values shown in Table 5.6.
- dwCurrentTxQueue is the current size of the internal output buffer.
- dwCurrentRxQueue is the current size of the internal input buffer.

Table 5.5 Data Bits

Value	Description
DATABITS_5	5 data bits
DATABITS_6	6 data bits
DATABITS_7	7 data bits
DATABITS_8	8 data bits
DATABITS_16	16 data bits
DATABITS_16X	Wide path data bit

Table 5.6 Stop Bits and Parity

Value	Description
STOPBITS_10	1 stop bit
STOPBITS_15	1.5 stop bits
STOPBITS_20	2 stop bits
PARITY_NONE	No parity
PARITY_ODD	Odd parity
PARITY_EVEN	Even parity
PARITY_MARK	Mark parity
PARITY_SPACE	Space parity

- dwProvSpec1 is used for provider-specific information.
- dwProvSpec2 is used for provider-specific information.
- wcProvChar is used for provider-specific information.

Therefore, to get the properties of the communications port you previously opened, you could do the following:

```
COMMPROP commProp;
memset(&commProp, 0, sizeof(COMMPROP));
GetCommProperties(hSerialPort, &commProp);
```

Finally, to actually configure the communications device that is attached to the serial port, you can use the GetCommState() and SetCommState() functions. The configuration of a serial device is determined by the current settings, which are located in a **device-control-block** (**DCB**) structure. This structure contains all of the relevant settings for the connected device.

To retrieve the current DCB for the port, you can call as follows:

```
BOOL GetCommState(HANDLE hFile, LPDCB lpDCB);
```

Here, the first parameter is the handle to the device that was opened with the initial call to `CreateFile()`. The `lpDCB` parameter is a pointer to a DCB structure. If the function succeeds, it will return a TRUE value.

To set the configuration of a communications device, you can call the `SetCommState()` API, which is defined as follows:

```
BOOL SetCommState(HANDLE hFile, LPDCB lpDCB);
```

The `SetCommState()` function takes the same parameters as `GetCommState()`, and will return TRUE if it successfully configures the serial device.

Be aware of a few things when `SetCommState()` is called. First, using the function will reinitialize all serial hardware and control settings, but it does not actually empty any incoming or outgoing data that is in the device driver's queue. Second, you should ensure that the XonChar and XoffChar members are not set to the same character; otherwise, `SetCommState()` will fail. Finally, when changing settings, it is usually easiest to first call `GetCommState()` to populate the structure for the current port values, modify the DCB structure with any changes you want to make, and then call `SetCommState()` with the same structure.

The device-control-block (DCB) structure looks like the following:

```
typedef struct _DCB {
    DWORD DCBlength;
    DWORD BaudRate;
    DWORD fBinary;
    DWORD fParity;
    DWORD fOutxCtsFlow;
    DWORD fOutxDsrFlow;
    DWORD fDtrControl;
    DWORD fDsrSensitivity;
    DWORD fTXContinueOnXoff;
    DWORD fOutX;
    DWORD fInX;
    DWORD fErrorChar;
    DWORD fNull;
    DWORD fRtsControl;
    DWORD fAbortOnError;
```

```
    DWORD fDummy2;
    WORD wReserved;
    WORD XonLim;
    WORD XoffLim;
    BYTE ByteSize;
    BYTE Parity;
    BYTE StopBits;
    char XonChar;
    char XoffChar;
    char ErrorChar;
    char EofChar;
    char EvtChar;
    WORD wReserved1;
} DCB, *LPDCB;
```

Table 5.7 describes the fields of the DCB structure.

Table 5.7 Device-Control-Block (DCB) Field Descriptions

Value	Description
DCBlength	Size of the DCB structure.
BaudRate	The baud rate at which the device is communicating, which can be one of the following values: CBR_110, CBR_300, CBR_600, CBR_1200, CBR_2400, CBR_4800, CBR_9600, CBR_14400, CBR_19200, CBR_38400, CBR_56000, CBR_57600, CBR_115200, CBR_128000, CBR_256000.
fBinary	Must be set to TRUE.
fParity	TRUE if parity checking is enabled.
fOutxCtsFlow	TRUE if the Clear To Send (CTS) signal is controlled by the serial line for output.
fOutxDsrFlow	TRUE if the Data Set Ready (DSR) signal is controlled by the serial line for output.
fDtrControl	Specifies how the Data Terminal Ready (DTR) signal should be handled. It can be set as follows: DTR_CONTROL_DISABLE to disable it; DTR_CONTROL_ENABLE to enable DTR; or DTR_CONTROL_HANDSHAKE to enable DTR handshaking.
fDsrSensitivity	TRUE if the serial line is aware of any Data Set Ready (DSR) state changes. If set to FALSE, DSR changes will be ignored.

(continued)

Table 5.7 Device-Control-Block (DCB) Field Descriptions (continued)

Value	Description
fTXContinueOnXoff	If set to TRUE, the transmission will stop when the input buffer is full (XoffLim bytes) and the serial driver has sent the XoffChar value to stop receiving bytes. If set to FALSE, the transmission does not continue until the input buffer is empty (XonLim bytes) and the serial driver has sent the XonChar value to resume receiving bytes.
fOutX	TRUE if Xon/Xoff flow control is used when sending data.
fInX	TRUE if Xon/Xoff flow control is used when receiving data.
fErrorChar	Not used.
fNull	TRUE if NULL bytes are thrown away when received.
fRtsControl	Specifies how the Request To Send (RTS) flow control signal should be handled. It can be set as follows: RTS_CONTROL_DISABLE to set the RTS line to a disabled state; RTS_CONTROL_ENABLE to set the RTS line to an enabled state; RTS_CONTROL_HANDSHAKE to specify that the driver should handle the RTS line; RTS_CONTROL_TOGGLE to enable the RTS line if there is data in the output buffer; otherwise, disable it.
fAbortOnError	Not used.
fDummy2	Not used.
wReserved	Reserved.
XonLim	The minimum number of bytes required in the input buffer before the XON signal is sent.
XoffLim	The maximum number of bytes required in the input buffer before the XOFF signal is sent.
ByteSize	The number of bits in the bytes sent or received.
Parity	Specifies the parity scheme to use. It can be set to one of the following: NOPARITY, ODDPARITY, EVENPARITY, MARKPARITY, or SPACEPARITY.
StopBits	Specifies the number of stop bits per byte to be used. It can be set to one of the following: ONESTOPBIT, ONE5STOPBITS, or TWOSTOPBITS.
XonChar	The character to be used for sending and receiving XON.
XoffChar	The character to be used for sending and receiving XOFF.
ErrorChar	Not used.
EofChar	The character to be used for sending and receiving the end-of-data marker.
EvtChar	The character to be used to signal that an event has occurred.
wReserved1	Not used.

For example, the following changes the baud rate on the port previously opened:

```
DCB commDCB;
BOOL fSuccess = FALSE;
memset(&commDCB, 0, sizeof(DCB));

// The current communications port settings
if(GetCommState(hSerialPort, &commDCB)) {
    // Can we change the baud rate? Let's check the commProp
    if(commProp.dwSettableParams && SP_BAUD) {
        commDCB.BaudRate = BAUD_57600;
        fSuccess = SetCommState(hSerialPort, &commDCB);
    }
}

// Were we able to change the baud rate?
if(!fSuccess)
    MessageBox(NULL, TEXT("Could not modify the port's baud
        rate"), TEXT("Error!"), MB_OK);
```

Serial Timeouts

Before we look at how to read and write data from and to a serial device, it is important that your application set the communication timeout values after it opens the port. The timeout values are used to specify the amount of time that the serial driver will wait for data to be transmitted or received from the device. If it is not configured properly, your application could experience serial operations that never complete or that possibly finish before all the data in the queue is transferred.

To get the current timeout values for a serial device, you can call the `GetCommTimeouts()` function, which is defined as follows:

```
BOOL GetCommTimeouts(HANDLE hFile, LPCOMMTIMEOUTS
  lpCommTimeouts);
```

The first parameter, `hFile`, is the handle to the serial port that you originally obtained from calling the `CreateFile()` function. This is followed by a pointer to a `COMMTIMEOUTS` structure. If the function succeeds, it will return `TRUE`.

To set the timeout parameters for a specific serial port, you can use the following function:

```
BOOL SetCommTimeouts(HANDLE hFile, LPCOMMTIMEOUTS
  lpCommTimeouts);
```

The `SetCommTimeouts()` function takes the same parameters as `GetCommTimeouts()`.

Both functions make use of the `COMMTIMEOUTS` structure, which specifies the values that should be used for both the reading and writing timeouts on a serial port. `COMMTIMEOUTS` is defined as follows:

```
typedef struct _COMMTIMEOUTS {
    DWORD ReadIntervalTimeout;
    DWORD ReadTotalTimeoutMultiplier;
    DWORD ReadTotalTimeoutConstant;
    DWORD WriteTotalTimeoutMultiplier;
    DWORD WriteTotalTimeoutConstant;
} COMMTIMEOUTS, *LPCOMMTIMEOUTS;
```

Using the `COMMTIMEOUTS` structure, there are basically three different ways that serial communication timeouts are used:

- **Read Interval Timeouts.** When reading data from the serial line, you can set a timeout to occur when a specific amount of time has elapsed between receiving characters. By setting the `Read IntervalTimeout` value (in milliseconds), a read operation will time out if the amount of time between receiving characters exceeds this value. Setting `ReadIntervalTimeout` to 0 indicates that interval timeouts are not used.

- **Read Byte Timeouts.** To cause a serial read operation timeout after a certain number of bytes have been read, you can use the `ReadTotalTimeoutMultipler` and `ReadTotalTimeout Constant` values. The timeout value is calculated by multiplying the value that you specify in `ReadTotalTimeoutMultipler` (in milliseconds) by the number of bytes you request in your read operation. This total is then added to `ReadTotalTimeout Constant` (also in milliseconds) to determine the total read timeout time. Set both of these values to 0 if you do not want to use byte timeouts for read operations.

- **Write Byte Timeouts.** Calculating the timeout value for serial write operations is similar to read byte timeouts. The value (in milliseconds) specified in `WriteTotalTimeoutMultipler` is multiplied by the number of bytes you request in your write operation.

The total is then added to the `WriteTotalTimeoutConstant` value (in milliseconds) to determine the total write timeout time. Set both of these values to 0 if you do not want to use byte timeouts for write operations.

Note that if you want a read operation to automatically return any data in the input buffer, you can set the `ReadIntervalTimeout` value to `MAXDWORD`, and set `ReadTotalTimeoutConstant` and `ReadTotalTimeoutMultiplier` to 0.

To properly ensure that a read or write operation has timed out, you should look at the number of bytes that you have sent or received after the function returns. If a timeout has occurred and the function returned successfully, then the number of bytes transferred or received will be less than what was requested in the original function call.

For example, if you wanted to set the serial port to return immediately after a read operation (whether or not there was any data in the input queue), you would do the following:

```
COMMTIMEOUTS commTimeOut;
memset(&commTimeOut, 0, sizeof(COMMTIMEOUTS));

// Set the timeouts so that read operations will return
// immediately
commTimeOut.ReadIntervalTimeout = MAXDWORD;
commTimeOut.ReadTotalTimeoutConstant = 0;
commTimeOut.ReadTotalTimeoutMultiplier = 0;

SetCommTimeouts(hSerialPort, &commTimeOut);
```

Controlling Data Flow

In addition to setting the timeout values when reading and writing data over the serial line, you can also control the flow of data, starting and stopping data transmission.

To suspend the transmission of data on a serial port and place it in a *break* state, you can call the following:

```
BOOL SetCommBreak(HANDLE hFile);
```

The function takes a single parameter, the handle to the serial device that was opened with the call to the `CreateFile()` function. To continue transmitting data, you can call the `ClearCommBreak()` function, which is defined as follows:

```
BOOL ClearCommBreak(HANDLE hFile);
```

As with `SetCommBreak()`, the only parameter that `ClearComm Break()` needs is the handle to the open serial port.

To remove any data from the internal read or write buffers of a serial device, call the following:

```
BOOL PurgeComm(HANDLE hFile, DWORD dwFlags);
```

The first parameter is the handle to the open serial device, and is followed by `dwFlags`, which specifies which queue to purge. You can set this to `PURGE_RXCLEAR` to clear the receive buffer, or to `PURGE_TXCLEAR` to purge the transfer buffer. In addition, if you want to ensure that the contents of the transfer buffer are sent before you purge them, you can also call the `FlushFileBuffers()` function (which takes only the handle to the serial device) before using `PurgeComm()`.

To set the specific state of the serial device, you can use the `EscapeCommFunction()` API call. Using this function will send a direct command to the device so it can perform an extended function, such as setting the current break state or a specific signal.

```
BOOL EscapeCommFunction(HANDLE hFile, DWORD dwFunc);
```

The first parameter is a handle to the open serial device, and is followed by the function you want to perform. This can be any of the values shown in Table 5.8.

Reading and Writing Serial Data

Now that you have looked at all of the options for both configuring and using a serial device, it's time to actually send and receive some data. Because Pocket PC does not support overlapped I/O, remember that both reading and writing to the serial port will block until a timeout occurs, an event fires, or the amount of data requested is returned. A good practice to maintain when using the serial port is to perform the data transmission in a separate thread so that the blocking functions do not affect the performance of your application's user interface.

Sending data over a serial port is done in the same manner as writing data to a file using the `WriteFile()` function:

Table 5.8 Serial Port States

Value	Description
SETIR	Set the port to infrared mode.
CLRIR	Set the port to serial mode.
CLRDTR	Clear the Data Terminal Ready (DTR) signal.
CLRRTS	Clear the Request to Send (RTS) signal.
SETDTR	Send the Data Terminal Ready (DTR) signal.
SETRTS	Send the Request to Send (RTS) signal.
SETXOFF	Act as if an XOFF character has been received.
SETXON	Act as if an XON character has been received.
SETBREAK	Identical to the SetCommBreak function, as it will set the line into a break state until ClearCommBreak or EscapeCommFunction is called with the CLRBREAK flag.
CLRBREAK	Identical to the ClearCommBreak function, as it will clear the break state on the serial line.

```
BOOL WriteFile(HANDLE hPort, LPCVOID lpBuffer, DWORD
    nNumberOfBytesToWrite, LPDWORD lpNumberOfBytesWritten,
    LPOVERLAPPED lpOverlapped);
```

The first parameter is a handle to the open serial port. This is followed by lpBuffer, which is a pointer to a buffer containing the data that you want to send, and is followed by nNumberOfBytesToWrite, a DWORD value specifying how many bytes are in the buffer pointed to in the lpBuffer parameter. The next parameter, lpNumberOf BytesWritten, is a pointer to a DWORD value that specifies the total number of bytes that were actually sent with this operation. Finally, lpOverlapped should be set to NULL.

For example, if you wanted to send a small buffer over the serial port to a connected device at 9,600 baud, you could use the following:

```
COMMPROP commProp;
memset(&commProp, 0, sizeof(COMMPROP));
GetCommProperties(hSerialPort, &commProp);

DCB commDCB;
BOOL fSuccess = FALSE;
memset(&commDCB, 0, sizeof(DCB));
```

```
// The the current communication port settings
if(GetCommState(hSerialPort, &commDCB)) {
    // Can we change the settings? Let's check the commProp
    if(commProp.dwSettableParams && SP_BAUD) {
        commDCB.BaudRate = BAUD_9600;
        commDCB.fParity = PARITY_NONE;
        commDCB.StopBits = ONESTOPBIT;
        commDCB.ByteSize = 8;
        fSuccess = SetCommState(hSerialPort, &commDCB);
    }
}

if(!fSuccess)
    MessageBox(NULL, TEXT("Could not modify the port's settings"),
        TEXT("Error!"), MB_OK);

char cBuffer[256] = "\0";
DWORD dwSize = 0, dwWritten = 0;

sprintf(cBuffer, "Hello there");
dwSize = strlen(cBuffer);

WriteFile(hSerialPort, &cBuffer, dwSize, &dwWritten, NULL);
```

Sometimes it is necessary to send a single value, such as an interrupt character (Control-C), at the front of the send queue to alert the device you are talking with. To do so, you should call the `TransmitComm Char()` API function. Once a character has been placed at the front of the transmit queue, the function cannot be called again until the original character has been sent.

The `TransmitCommChar()` function is defined as follows:

```
BOOL TransmitCommChar(HANDLE hFile, char cChar);
```

The function simply takes a handle to the open serial device, followed by the character that you wish to send.

Reading data from the serial port is also comparable to reading data from a file; you use the `ReadFile()` function:

```
BOOL ReadFile(HANDLE hPort, LPVOID lpBuffer, DWORD
    nNumberOfBytesToRead, LPDWORD lpNumberOfBytesRead, LPOVERLAPPED
    lpOverlapped);
```

The first parameter, as with all serial API calls, is the handle to the port. This is followed by the `lpBuffer` parameter, which contains a buffer that receives the incoming data. The `nNumberOfBytesToRead` parameter should specify how many bytes are to be read, and is followed by `lpNumberOfBytesRead`, which contains the actual number of bytes retrieved from the port when the function returns (either when completed or by timeout). Finally, the `lpOverlapped` parameter is not supported, and should be set to `NULL`.

The following example reads 10 characters from the opened serial port:

```
char cBuffer[10] = "\0";
DWORD dwSize = 10, dwRead = 0;

COMMTIMEOUTS commTimeOut;
memset(&commTimeOut, 0, sizeof(COMMTIMEOUTS));
memset(&cBuffer, 0, 10);

// Set the timeouts so that read operations will only
// after our buffer is full (10 characters)
commTimeOut.ReadIntervalTimeout = 0;
commTimeOut.ReadTotalTimeoutConstant = 0;
commTimeOut.ReadTotalTimeoutMultiplier = 0;

SetCommTimeouts(hSerialPort, &commTimeOut);

ReadFile(hSerialPort, &cBuffer, dwSize, &dwRead, NULL);
```

NOTE: To prevent the Pocket PC device from going into suspend mode while a serial operation is in effect, you can call the `System IdleTimerReset()` function while transmitting or receiving data. This function resets the Windows CE internal idle time timer, and will prevent the device from suspending. You should, however, use this function sparingly and with caution, as you can run down your device's battery by continuously calling it.

Retrieving Error and/or Status Information

To get information about an error that has occurred or to get the status of a serial device, you can call the `ClearCommError()` function. This function also clears any error flag that has been set, allowing input and output operations to continue after an error has occurred. The `ClearCommError()` function is defined as follows:

```
BOOL ClearCommError(HANDLE hFile, LPDWORD lpErrors,
  LPCOMSTAT lpStat);
```

As usual, the first parameter is the handle to the open communications port. This is followed by a pointer to a DWORD variable, lpErrors, which will be filled in with the type of error that has occurred. This can be one or more of the conditions described in Table 5.9.

Table 5.9 Communication Errors

Value	Description
CE_BREAK	A break condition has occurred.
CE_FRAME	There was a hardware framing error.
CE_IOE	An I/O error has occurred.
CE_MODE	The communication port requested is invalid.
CE_OVERRUN	A buffer overrun has occurred and data has been lost.
CE_RXOVER	A buffer overrun has occurred on the input buffer.
CE_RXPARITY	A parity error has occurred.
CE_TXFULL	The output buffer is full and cannot transmit any more characters.

The final parameter, lpStat, is a pointer to a COMSTAT structure, which contains the status information for the port. This parameter can be set to NULL if you do not need to get the status information. COMSTAT is defined as follows:

```
typedef struct _COMSTAT {
    DWORD fCtsHold;
    DWORD fDsrHold;
    DWORD fRlsdHold;
    DWORD fXoffHold;
    DWORD fXoffSent;
    DWORD fEof;
    DWORD fTxim;
    DWORD fReserved;
    DWORD cbInQue;
    DWORD cbOutQue;
} COMSTAT, *LPCOMSTAT;
```

Table 5.10 describes the fields of the COMSTAT structure.

Table 5.10 COMSTAT Structure Field Descriptions

Field	Description
fCtsHold	TRUE if the serial device is waiting for a Clear To Send (CTS) signal
fDsrHold	TRUE if the serial device is waiting for a Data Set Ready (DSR) signal
fRlsdHold	TRUE if the serial device is waiting for a Receive Line Signal Detect (RLSD) signal
fXoffHold	TRUE if the serial device is holding since it received a XOFF character
fXoffSent	TRUE if the serial device is waiting for the other serial device to send an XON in response to a transmitted XOFF character
fEof	TRUE if the end of file (EOF) character has been received
fTxim	TRUE if a character has been placed in the front of the transfer queue by the TransmitCommChar() function
fReserved	Reserved
cbInQue	The number of characters currently in the input queue
cbOutQue	The number of characters currently in the output queue

In addition to getting error and status information about the serial line, you can also query the status of any of the modem control signals using the GetCommModemStatus() function:

```
BOOL GetCommModemStatus(HANDLE hFile, LPDWORD lpModemStat);
```

The first parameter is the handle to the serial port you want to query, and is followed by a pointer to a DWORD variable that contains the current state of the modem control-registers. The lpModemStat value can return one or more of the values shown in Table 5.11.

Table 5.11 Modem Status Values

Value	Description
MS_CTS_ON	The Clear To Send (CTS) signal is on.
MS_DSR_ON	The Data Set Ready (DSR) signal is on.
MS_RING_ON	The Ring Indicate (RI) signal is on.
MS_RLSD_ON	The Receive Line Signal Detect (RLSD) signal is on.

Serial Event Notification

A somewhat simple mechanism is in place to determine when specific events occur on a serial connection. Monitoring serial event masks can be useful when you need to perform specific actions if certain conditions exist in a serial data transfer.

To set which events you want to monitor, you use the `SetComm Mask()` API function:

```
BOOL SetCommMask(HANDLE hFile, DWORD dwEvtMask);
```

The first parameter is the handle to the open serial device, and is followed by one or more event masks for which you want to monitor events. Once you have turned on those masks, you can wait for a specific event to occur by calling the `WaitCommEvent()` function. This function will block (so you might want to consider calling it from within a helper thread) until that event occurs. The function is defined as follows:

```
BOOL WaitCommEvent(HANDLE hFile, LPDWORD lpEvtMask,
    LPOVERLAPPED lpOverlapped);
```

`WaitCommEvent()` takes three parameters. The first is the handle to the open serial device, followed by a pointer to a `DWORD` value that receives the event mask when an event occurs. The final parameter, `lpOverlapped`, is not used and should be set to `NULL`.

To query the current event mask for a serial device handle, you can also use the following function:

```
BOOL GetCommMask(HANDLE hFile, LPDWORD lpEvtMask);
```

The `GetCommMask()`, `SetCommMask()`, and `WaitCommEvent()` functions each use the same values for the event mask, which are defined in Table 5.12.

For example, you could use the following to monitor (usually in a separate thread) the serial line for any communication errors that occur:

```
DWORD dwCommMaskRecvd = 0;

// Set the port to watch for errors
SetCommMask(hSerialPort, EV_ERR);

// Wait for the error
if(WaitCommEvent(hSerialPort, &dwCommMaskRecvd, NULL)) {
```

```
if(dwCommMaskRecvd == EV_ERR) {
    MessageBox(NULL, TEXT("An error has occurred"),
        TEXT("Error!"), MB_OK);

    // Handle the error with some code here
    // ...
    }
}
```

Table 5.12 Serial Event Masks

Value	Description
EV_BREAK	A break was detected.
EV_CTS	The Clear To Send (CTS) signal has changed state.
EV_DSR	The Data Set Ready (DSR) signal has changed state.
EV_ERR	An error has occurred. See the `ClearCommError()` function for more information.
EV_RING	A Ring Indicator (RI) was detected.
EV_RLSD	The Receive Line Signal Detect (RLSD) signal has changed state.
EV_RXCHAR	A character was received and is in the input queue.
EV_RXFLAG	An event character (specified by the DCB structure and the `SetCommState()` function) was received and is in the input queue.
EV_TXEMPTY	The output buffer is now empty.

Closing the Connection

Finally, to close an open device handle and free the resource for other processes to use the serial port, you need to call the `CloseHandle()` function:

```
BOOL CloseHandle(HANDLE hObject);
```

The only parameter you need to pass in is the handle to the previously opened port:

```
// Close the serial port
if(hSerialPort)
    CloseHandle(hSerialPort);
```

Differences between Windows and Pocket PC Serial APIs

Be aware of two minor differences between the Windows and Pocket PC implementations of the serial APIs:

1. **Pocket PC does not support overlapped I/O.** Because Pocket PC devices do not support any method for overlapped I/O, you should consider creating a worker thread to handle your serial data transfer. This is necessary because the reading and writing of data operations will block any message processing until they are completed. Creating a helper thread enables your application's primary thread to continue processing messages from your user interface and the operating system while it waits for the serial transfer to complete.
2. **Pocket PC does not support security attributes on serial devices or files.**

Serial Communication Cables

While almost every Pocket PC device that is available today supports RS-232C serial communications, each has its own unique connector (located on the device), which is used for hooking it to another serial device. Typically, most device manufactures provide a cable that enables it to connect it to a standard DB-9 or DB-25 serial connector.

Serial Connectors

Two different classifications of devices use serial connections: **Data Communications Equipment** (**DCE**) devices and **Data Terminal Equipment** (**DTE**) devices. Computers and data terminals are usually classified as DTE devices, whereas DCE devices are typically modems and printers. When a serial connection is established, one typically acts as the DCE, while the other acts as the DTE. For example, a Pocket PC device that is connected to a modem would be considered the DTE; and the modem is considered the DCE.

The RS-232C specification states that serial cables should not be longer than 75 feet at 9,600 bps.

Figure 5.3 shows the standard DB-25 male and female connectors:

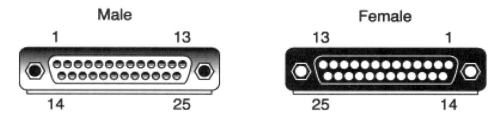

Figure 5.3 25-pin serial connectors

Table 5.13 shows the pin assignments for a standard 25-pin serial connector.

Table 5.13 DB-25 Serial Pinout Assignments

Pin	Description
2	Transmit Data (TD)
3	Receive Data (RD)
4	Request to Send (RTS)
5	Clear to Send (CTS)
6	Data Set Ready (DSR)
7	Signal Ground (SG)
8	Data Carrier Detect (DCD)
20	Data Terminal Ready (DTR)
22	Ring Indicator (Ring)

Because asynchronous serial connections typically use only nine wires, most of the newer serial devices use the DB-9 connector (except modems, which always seem to use DB-25). Figure 5.4 shows two examples of what the DB-9 male and female connectors look like.

Figure 5.4 9-pin serial connectors

Table 5.14 shows the pin assignments for a standard 9-pin serial connector.

Table 5.14 DB-9 Serial Pinout Assignments

Pin	Description
1	Data Carrier Detect (DCD)
2	Receive Data (RD)
3	Transmit Data (TD)
4	Data Terminal Ready (DTR)
5	Signal Ground (SG)
6	Data Set Ready (DSR)
7	Request To Send (RTS)
8	Clear to Send (CTS)
9	Ring Indicator (Ring)

NULL Modems and Cables

When you want to connect two DTE devices (such as two Pocket PC devices or two computers), you need to use what is known as a **crossover cable**, or **null modem cable**. A null modem cable makes the DTE device you are directly connecting to look like a DCE connector by reversing the pin contacts between the two devices.

To make a null connector between two standard DB-25 connectors, you need to cross over the wires as shown in Table 5.15.

To make a null connector between two standard DB-9 connectors, you will need to cross over the wires as shown in Table 5.16.

Table 5.15 DB-25 Null Modem

Pin	Pin	Signal
2	3	Transmit Data
3	2	Receive Data
4	5	Request to Send
5	4	Clear to Send
6, 8	20	Data Set Ready and Data Carrier Detect
7	7	Signal Ground
20	6, 8	Data Terminal Ready

Table 5.16 DB-9 Null Modem

Pin	Pin	Signal
3	2	Transmit Data
2	3	Receive Data
7	8	Request to Send
8	7	Clear to Send
6, 1	4	Data Set Ready and Data Carrier Detect
5	5	Signal Ground
4	6, 1	Data Terminal Ready

Finally, if you need to make a null connector between a DB-25 connector and a DB-9 connector, you can cross over the wires as shown in Table 5.17.

Table 5.17 Null Modem Pinouts (DB-9 to DB-25)

25-Pin	9-Pin	Signal
2	2	Transmit Data
3	3	Receive Data
4	8	Request to Send
5	7	Clear to Send
6, 8	4	Data Set Ready and Data Carrier Detect
7	5	Signal Ground
20	6, 1	Data Terminal Ready

Infrared

Almost every Pocket PC device on the market today has an infrared port. This port is compatible with Infrared Data Association (IrDA) standards (for more information, check out http://www.irda.org) for data communications and protocols over a short-range wireless connection.

Three mechanisms are available for developing applications over the infrared (IR) port on a Pocket PC: **Raw IR**, **IrCOMM**, and **IrSock**. Both Raw IR and IrCOMM treat the infrared connection as a virtual serial port, whereas IrSock uses Winsock to perform its communication tasks, such as handshaking and protocol negotiation.

Raw Infrared (Raw IR)

The most basic way to create an infrared connection between two devices is by using Raw IR. Raw IR mode provides you with nothing more than a simple way to get direct access to the infrared connector on your device—there is no mechanism for handling signal interruptions, data collisions, or any other type of error conditions that can occur. Although Raw IR is not considered IrDA-compliant—as it does not automatically handle handshaking and other protocol tasks—it is considered the best method for taking total control over the IR port. The important thing to remember when developing applications that use Raw IR is that you have to be prepared to handle *everything*, including the management and correction of error conditions.

Before you can use Raw IR, you must first determine what communications port has the IR transceiver attached to it. This can be done by examining the registry key HKEY_LOCAL_MACHINE\Comm\IrDA and looking at the Port sub-key value. This will contain the COM port number to use when opening the infrared connection.

NOTE: On certain Pocket PC devices (such as the iPAQ), the Port sub-key value will not exist. If this is the case, you can check under the Linkage sub-key for the Bind value. You then use the Bind value to determine the port by looking under the HKEY_LOCAL_MACHINE\Comm key (followed by the Bind value), and examine its Parms sub-key for the Raw IR port.

For example, use the following to query a device for its Raw IR port:

```
// Find the Raw IR port to use
DWORD dwRawIRPort = 0;
TCHAR tchRawIRPort[10] = TEXT("\0");


// Step 1. Check under HKEY_LOCAL_MACHINE\Comm\IrDA for it
HKEY hKey = NULL;
DWORD dwValType = 0, dwSize = sizeof(DWORD);
if(RegOpenKeyEx(HKEY_LOCAL_MACHINE, TEXT("Comm\\IrDA"), 0,
    0, &hKey) == ERROR_SUCCESS) {
    if(RegQueryValueEx(hKey, TEXT("Port"), NULL, &dwValType,
        (LPBYTE)&dwRawIRPort, &dwSize) == ERROR_SUCCESS) {
```

```
                    // Ok, we got a port, so set up the buffer so we can call
                    // CreateFile()
                    wsprintf(tchRawIRPort, TEXT("COM%d:"), dwRawIRPort);
            }
    }

    // Step 2. Check under the linkage (if necessary)
    if(dwRawIRPort == 0) {
        TCHAR tchBindKey[256] = TEXT("\0");
        HKEY hSubKey = NULL;
        dwSize = 256;
        dwValType = 0;

        // Step 2a. Get the bind
        if(RegOpenKeyEx(hKey, TEXT("Linkage"), 0, 0, &hSubKey) ==
                ERROR_SUCCESS) {
            if(RegQueryValueEx(hSubKey, TEXT("Bind"), NULL,
                &dwValType, (LPBYTE)&tchBindKey, &dwSize) !=
                ERROR_SUCCESS) {
              RegCloseKey(hSubKey);
              RegCloseKey(hKey);
              return FALSE;
            }
        }

        RegCloseKey(hSubKey);
        RegCloseKey(hKey);

        // Step 2b. Now that we have the bind, open it
        TCHAR tchIRBind[256] = TEXT("\0");
        wsprintf(tchIRBind, TEXT("Comm\\%s\\Parms"), tchBindKey);
        if(RegOpenKeyEx(HKEY_LOCAL_MACHINE, tchIRBind, 0, 0, &hKey) ==
                ERROR_SUCCESS) {
            if(RegQueryValueEx(hKey, TEXT("Port"), NULL, &dwValType,
            (LPBYTE)&dwRawIRPort, &dwSize) == ERROR_SUCCESS) {
                // Ok, we got a port, so set up the buffer so we
                // can call CreateFile
                wsprintf(tchRawIRPort, TEXT("COM%d:"), dwRawIRPort);
            }
        }
    }
```

```
// Step 3. Close up the registry
if(hKey)
    RegCloseKey(hKey);

if(dwRawIRPort == 0)
    return FALSE;
```

On some Pocket PC devices, the serial hardware shares a hardware serial port with the infrared port. If this is the case, your application will need to "switch" the mode of the serial port to infrared mode by calling the `EscapeCommFunction()` described earlier in this chapter:

```
BOOL EscapeCommFunction(HANDLE hFile, DWORD dwFunc);
```

The first parameter is the open device handle to the port for which you want to change to infrared mode. To turn on infrared mode, you can pass the flag `SETIR` for the `dwFunc` parameter. To toggle it back to standard serial mode, you can use the flag `CLRIR`.

Remember a few things when using Raw IR mode: First, you cannot use the serial port at the same time as the Raw IR port if they share the same port number. Second, you have to account for all dropped bytes, and you are responsible for ensuring the data integrity of the information you transfer over the wireless connection. Finally, be aware that your transfers are *half-duplex*, which means you should never have both devices transmitting in the same direction at the same time; otherwise, data corruption will occur.

To send and receive data over Raw IR, you can use the standard serial communications functions, such as `ReadFile()` and `WriteFile()`.

IrCOMM

The easiest way to use a serial infrared connection is by using IrCOMM. IrCOMM is essentially a "virtual" serial port that automatically handles tasks that Raw IR requires you to handle manually. Because IrCOMM is IrDA-compliant, it takes care of issues such as remote device detection, signal collisions, signal interruptions, and the queuing of data. In fact, the infrared connection created with IrCOMM is actually controlled and managed by IrSock internally.

As with Raw IR, there is no direct way to find the IrCOMM port, so you must manually determine the port by examining the registry. To find the actual port number, you need to look at the key HKEY_LOCAL_

MACHINE\Drivers\Builtin\IrCOMM and the value under the Index sub-key.

The following example shows you how to determine the port to use for IrCOMM:

```
// Find the IrCOMM port to use
DWORD dwIrCOMMPort = 0;
TCHAR tchIrCOMMPort[10] = TEXT("\0");

// Step 1. Check under HKEY_LOCAL_MACHINE\Drivers\Builtin\IrCOMM
// for it
HKEY hKey = NULL;
DWORD dwValType = 0, dwSize = sizeof(DWORD);
if(RegOpenKeyEx(HKEY_LOCAL_MACHINE,
    TEXT("Drivers\\Builtin\\IrCOMM"), 0, 0,
    &hKey) == ERROR_SUCCESS) {
    if(RegQueryValueEx(hKey, TEXT("Index"), NULL, &dwValType,
        (LPBYTE)&dwIrCOMMPort, &dwSize) == ERROR_SUCCESS) {
        // Ok, we got a port, so set up the buffer so we can
        // call CreateFile()
        wsprintf(tchIrCOMMPort, TEXT("COM%d:"), dwIrCOMMPort);
    }
}

// Step 2. Close up the registry
if(hKey)
    RegCloseKey(hKey);

if(dwIrCOMMPort == 0)
    return FALSE;
```

Because IrSock manages the infrared port when in IrCOMM mode, you cannot manually configure any of the serial port parameters on the IrCOMM port. If you attempt to call the GetCommState() function on the port, the DCB structure returned will contain all zeros. In addition, be aware that an IrCOMM connection is a direct device-to-device link, and only two devices can be connected at any time.

Infrared Sockets (IrSock)

On Pocket PC devices, Infrared Socket (IrSock) support is what actually implements the abstraction of the IrDA protocol that Windows CE uses. Communicating between devices using IrSock is nearly identical to using the network Winsock API described in Chapter 1, except for a few minor differences:

- You can only use IrSock for connection-oriented TCP sockets; it does not support UDP datagram packets.
- IrSock clients must not call the Winsock function bind().
- You cannot allocate over 80 IrSock sockets simultaneously; otherwise, memory failures will occur.
- IrSock sockets do not support the creation of secure sockets.
- IrSock sockets can browse for available network resources with the range of the device.
- IrSock sockets do not use the Winsock name service functions. Instead, the name service is part of the communication stream.
- The WSAENETDOWN error code is not supported.
- There is no equivalent to INADDR_ANY when using IrSock sockets.
- The address scheme used for IrSock sockets is different from a Winsock network; they use SOCKADDR_IRDA instead.

To use any of the IrSock infrared communication functions with your application, you need to include the header af_irda.h, and link with the winsock.lib library in your project.

Infrared Socket Options and Addressing

Because networking over infrared is very different from a standard network interface, there are several unique options that apply only to an IrSock socket (and, conversely, most of the standard Winsock options don't apply to IrSock sockets). Just like "normal" Winsock, you can use the getsockopt() and setsockopt() functions to query and set your socket options:

```
int getsockopt (SOCKET s, int level, int optname, char *optval,
    int *optlen);

int setsockopt (SOCKET s, int level, int optname, const char
    *optval, int optlen);
```

The parameters that both functions take are identical to those described previously for Winsock, with the exception of the level parameter, which is set to SOL_SOCKET or SOL_IRLMP when used with infrared sockets.

Table 5.18 describes the available socket options for IrSock sockets.

Table 5.18 Infrared Socket Options

Level	Option Name	Type	Get/Set	Description
SOL_SOCKET	SO_DONTLINGER	BOOL	Both	Enables or disables immediate return from closesocket()
	SO_LINGER	struct LINGER	Both	Enables or disables immediate return from closesocket()
SOL_IRLMP	IRLMP_ ENUMDEVICES	*DEVICELIST	Get	Enumerates remote IrDA devices
	IRLMP_IAS_ QUERY	*IAS_QUERY	Get	Queries IAS attributes
	IRLMP_IAS_ SET	*IAS_SET	Set	Sets IAS attributes
	IRLMP_IRLPT_ MODE	BOOL	Set	Sets the IrDA protocol to IrLPT mode
	IRLMP_9WIRE_ MODE	BOOL	Set	Sets the IrDA protocol to standard 9-wire serial mode
	IRLMP_SEND_ PDU_LEN	*int	Get	Gets the maximum size of send packets for IrLPT mode
	IRLMP_SHARP_ MODE	BOOL	Set	Sets the IrDA protocol to Sharp mode

Addressing an IrSock socket is also slightly different from a standard Winsock socket. Whereas a normal TCP/IP network adapter would use the `SOCKADDR_IN` structure for its address, an infrared socket uses `SOCKADDR_IDRA` instead. It is defined as follows:

```
typedef struct _SOCKADDR_IRDA {
    u_short irdaAddressFamily;
    u_char irdaDeviceID[4];
    char irdaServiceName[25];
} SOCKADDR_IRDA,
```

The `irdaAddressFamily` field should be set to `AF_IRDA` (denoting that it is an infrared socket), and is followed by the device identifier `irdaDeviceID`. This is the same identifier that is returned when calling the `getsockopt()` function call with the `SO_IRLMP_ENUMDEVICES` flag. The last parameter is a 25-character, null-terminated string that contains the service name of the application using the socket.

Establishing IrSock Connections

Because IrSock does not use the conventional Winsock name service functions for finding remote hosts, it provides you with the capability to browse other IrDA devices that are nearby and within range. This is easily done by querying the socket options using the `getsockopt()` function with the `IRLMP_ENUMDEVICES` flag. When the function returns, the `DEVICELIST` structure will contain information about the entire list of devices currently in range. The structure is defined as follows:

```
typedef struct _DEVICELIST {
    ULONG numDevice;
    IRDA_DEVICE_INFO Device[1];
} DEVICELIST, *PDEVICELIST;
```

The `numDevice` field specifies the number of `IRDA_DEVICE_INFO` structures in the `Device` array field. Each `IRDA_DEVICE_INFO` structure looks like the following:

```
typedef struct _IRDA_DEVICE_INFO {
    u_char irdaDeviceID[4];
    char irdaDeviceName[22];
```

```
    u_char Reserved[2];
} IRDA_DEVICE_INFO, *PIRDA_DEVICE_INFO;
```

The remote device identifier is stored in the `irdaDeviceID` field, and is followed by the device name. The last field, `Reserved`, is currently unused.

The following example prints a list of all nearby devices:

```
// IrSock Device Locater
SOCKET sIR;

sIR = socket(AF_IRDA, SOCK_STREAM, 0);
if(sIR == INVALID_SOCKET)
   return FALSE;

// Locate all nearby IrDA devices
DEVICELIST *pDevices = NULL;
DWORD dwMaxDevices = 10;
int nSize = dwMaxDevices * sizeof(DEVICELIST);

pDevices = (DEVICELIST *)LocalAlloc(LPTR, nSize);
if(!pDevices) {
   closesocket(sIR);
   return FALSE;
}

// Call getsockopt to find all devices
if(getsockopt(sIR, SOL_IRLMP, IRLMP_ENUMDEVICES,
   (char *)pDevices, &nSize) == SOCKET_ERROR) {
   closesocket(sIR);
   return FALSE;
}

// Walk through the array of nearby devices
for(ulong ulDeviceNum = 0; ulDeviceNum < pDevices-> numDevice;
   ulDeviceNum++) {
   TCHAR tchDevice[256] = TEXT("\0");

   wsprintf(tchDevice, TEXT("IrDA ID: %x:%x:%x:%x"),
      pDevices->Device[ulDeviceNum].irdaDeviceID[0],
      pDevices->Device[ulDeviceNum].irdaDeviceID[1],
      pDevices->Device[ulDeviceNum].irdaDeviceID[2],
      pDevices->Device[ulDeviceNum].irdaDeviceID[3]);
```

```
    MessageBox(NULL, tchDevice, TEXT("IR Device Found"),
        MB_OK);
}

// Cleanup
LocalFree(pDevices);
closesocket(sIR);
```

CHAPTER 6

Remote Access Service

Tell me, Mr. Anderson, what good is a phone call when you are unable to speak?

—*Agent Smith,* The Matrix

Up until this point, we have examined a variety of ways to communicate over a network using TCP/IP and the Windows networking APIs. One topic we have not yet covered is how a device can use a modem (or other type of serial connection) to dial into a network from a remote location and use the available network resources, rather than being local and using a network card. Once a connection is established, you can use WinInet, Winsock, and the other Windows networking functions as if you were directly connected to the LAN. This is known as the **Remote Access Service (RAS)**.

Remote Access Overview

When a Pocket PC device connects to a server over dial-up networking, it is referred to as a **RAS client**. On Windows CE, RAS clients use the **point-to-point protocol (PPP)** to establish a connection, set up communication parameters, and transfer data between the client, the server, and the network. Note that because you are using a dial-up connection, data transmission over RAS is typically much slower than using a network card.

Because PPP is an industry-standard framing and authentication protocol, you can use your Pocket PC device as a remote client of any PPP server, regardless of which operating system the server is running (for example, your device could be a client to either a Windows .NET server or a Unix box that provides a PPP server). Note that although a PPP connection can be established by using a modem, a direct serial connection, or the infrared port, Pocket PC only supports using the TCP/IP protocol over a RAS session.

PPP is generally considered an improvement over the older Serial Line Internet Protocol (SLIP) that was traditionally used for dial-up connections, as PPP supports error correction and is capable of handling either synchronous or asynchronous communications. When a connection is being established, PPP enables both devices that are linking to negotiate various features that will be available to the client, such as the maximum size for datagram packets.

Pocket PC devices support the following standard authentication schemes for a dial-up PPP connection:

- **Password Authentication Protocol (PAP):** A server that requests the username and password is returned a response in an unencrypted form. PAP is generally considered not secure.
- **Challenge Handshake Authentication Protocol (CHAP) using MD5:** When a server requests authentication over CHAP, it sends a challenge and a session ID to the client. The client then uses an MD5 hash to encrypt the challenge, session ID, and client password, and sends the result—with the unhashed username—back to the server for authentication.
- **Microsoft Challenge Handshake Authentication Protocol (Microsoft CHAP):** The Microsoft CHAP authentication scheme sends a challenge string and session ID to the client, similar to the CHAP method. The client must respond with the username, the MD4 hash value of the challenge, the session ID, and a password. The server stores hashed passwords, rather than the clear passwords that standard CHAP uses.
- **Microsoft Challenge Handshake Authentication Protocol (Microsoft CHAP) version 2.0:** Microsoft CHAP 2.0 provides increased security features, including server authentication methods.
- **Extensible Authentication Protocol-Transport Level Security (EAP-TLS):** A series of extensions to PPP that provide authentication with PPP itself through the transport level.

A PPP connection on Pocket PC also supports either 128-bit or 40-bit encryption. You can find more information about how the point-to-point protocol operates in RFC 1134. Be aware that while PPP is the preferred connection protocol for dial-up connections, SLIP is also supported by Pocket PC.

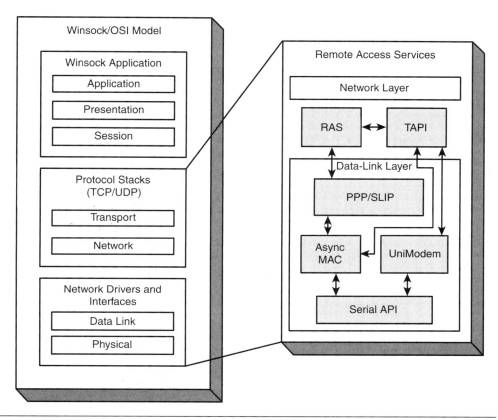

Figure 6.1 Pocket PC Remote Access Service and the TCP/IP OSI model

As you might have guessed, RAS is built on top of TCP/IP. Figure 6.1 shows how the Pocket PC Remote Access client sits within the TCP/IP OSI model.

While establishing a dial-up connection on a Pocket PC device is typically done automatically through the Connection Manager (see Chapter 7) or Remote Network Access dialer (see the section "The Remote Network Access (RNA) Dialer"), it is sometime necessary (or useful) to write applications that programmatically dial and establish a remote connection, and that are capable of manipulating data in the remote access phonebook.

In order to use the Remote Access Service API functions within your application, you need to include the headers `ras.h` and `raserror.h`, and link with the `coredll.lib` library.

Differences between Windows and Pocket PC PPP

You should be aware of the following differences between Pocket PC and desktop implementations of the point-to-point protocol:

- **Pocket PC does not support multilink PPP.**
- **Pocket PC does not support either the NetBEUI or IPX protocols over a dial-up connection.**
- **Pocket PC implements PPP as an NDIS (Network Driver Interface Specification) driver.** PPP communicates through the NDIS layer to the AsyncMAC miniport to perform asynchronous framing, and forwards it to the TAPI device over the serial APIs. If a packet is received over the network, AsyncMAC strips any asynchronous frames from the packet, performs a CRC check, and sends the packet to PPP through NDIS.
- **The RAS phonebook on Pocket PC is stored in the registry, instead of a phonebook file.**
- **`RasDial()` on Pocket PC does not support the `RASDIAL EXTENSIONS` parameter.**
- **Pocket PC does not support multistage connections such as X.25 PAD.**
- **There is no support for changing passwords if they have expired on a Pocket PC device.**

Remote Access Phonebook

Before you can establish a dial-up connection to a remote server, the host you are attempting to connect with must have an entry in the **RAS phonebook**. Just like a regular telephone book, the RAS phonebook contains entries that enable a remote dialer to specify a connection by name. A phonebook entry contains all the necessary information that the device needs to establish a connection to the server, including the phone number to call, the IP address it is assigned once connected (or a flag to get a dynamic IP allocated to it), any user authentication information, and any other connection properties.

The RAS phonebook is stored in the registry under the HKEY_ CURRENT_USER\Comm\RasBook key. Each entry has its own set of values underneath its named key, as shown in Figure 6.2.

The following sections describe how you can create, modify, and delete phonebook entries using the RAS phonebook programming interfaces.

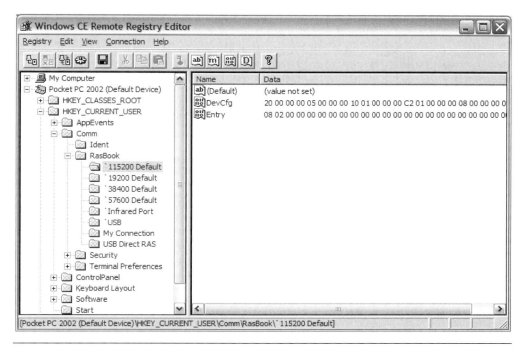

Figure 6.2 The RAS phonebook (as seen by the registry)

Adding a Phonebook Entry

Before you can create a new entry, you must first ensure that the phone-book does not already contain an entry of the same name. In addition, you must verify that an entry contains no illegal characters. To do this, you can call the following function:

```
DWORD RasValidateEntryName(LPWSTR lpszPhonebook, LPWSTR lpszEntry);
```

Because Pocket PC stores its phonebook in the registry, the first parameter, lpszPhonebook, should be set to a NULL value. The second parameter, lpszEntry, must contain a pointer to a null-terminated string that contains the entry name you want to validate. In order to qual-ify as a "good" entry, the name must be 1–20 characters in length, and not contain any of the following: | > < ? * \ / :

The function will return a 0 if successful or ERROR_INVALID_NAME if the name is not valid. If an entry with the same name is already in the phonebook, an ERROR_ALREADY_EXISTS error is returned. This is useful if you are going to modify an entry, as you will see shortly.

Once you have confirmed that the name is valid, you can go ahead and add your new entry using the RasSetEntryProperties() function, which is defined as follows:

```
DWORD RasSetEntryProperties(LPWSTR lpszPhoneBook, LPWSTR szEntry,
    LPRASENTRY lpEntry, DWORD dwEntrySize, LPBYTE lpb, DWORD dwSize);
```

As with all of the phonebook APIs on Pocket PC, the lpszPhone Book parameter should be set to NULL. The szEntry parameter should be set to the name of the new entry, which was previously validated with your call to RasValidateEntryName(). This is followed by lpEntry, a pointer to a RASENTRY structure that contains the actual phonebook entry information. Next, dwEntrySize should specify the size of the lpEntry structure, in bytes. Finally, lpb and dwSize are used to set device-specific configuration information about a Telephone API (TAPI) device. For now, to add new phonebook entries, you can set lpb to NULL and dwSize to 0.

Once the function is called, it will return 0 if the new entry has been successfully added to the phonebook. If the RASENTRY structure passed into lpEntry is invalid, an ERROR_BUFFER_INVALID return code will be returned. If you are returned an ERROR_CANNOT_OPEN_PHONEBOOK result, the phonebook may be corrupted.

The RASENTRY structure that contains a phonebook entry's information looks like the following:

```
typedef struct tagRasEntry {
    DWORD dwSize;
    DWORD dwfOptions;
    DWORD dwCountryID;
    DWORD dwCountryCode;
    TCHAR szAreaCode[RAS_MaxAreaCode+1];
    TCHAR szLocalPhoneNumber[RAS_MaxPhoneNumber+1];
    DWORD dwAlternatesOffset;
    RASIPADDR ipaddr;
    RASIPADDR ipaddrDns;
    RASIPADDR ipaddrDnsAlt;
    RASIPADDR ipaddrWins;
    RASIPADDR ipaddrWinsAlt;
```

```
    DWORD dwFrameSize;
    DWORD dwfNetProtocols;
    DWORD dwFramingProtocol;
    TCHAR szScript[MAX_PATH];
    TCHAR szAutoDialDll[MAX_PATH];
    TCHAR szAutoDialFunc[MAX_PATH];
    TCHAR szDeviceType[RAS_MaxDeviceType+1];
    TCHAR szDeviceName[RAS_MaxDeviceName+1];
    TCHAR szX25PadType[RAS_MaxPadType+1];
    TCHAR szX25Address[RAS_MaxX25Address+1];
    TCHAR szX25Facilities[RAS_MaxFacilities+1];
    TCHAR szX25UserData[RAS_MaxUserData+1];
    DWORD dwChannels;
    DWORD dwReserved1;
    DWORD dwReserved2;
} RASENTRY, *LPRASENTRY;
```

Table 6.1 describes the RASENTRY structure that is used for a phonebook entry.

Table 6.2 describes the options that can be used for the dwf Options field of the RASENTRY structure.

Table 6.1 RASENTRY Field Descriptions

Value	Description
dwSize	Size of the RASENTRY structure.
dwfOptions	Indicates the specific connection options. See Table 6.2 for more information.
dwCountryID	Not used.
dwCountryCode	Country code (valid only if dwfOptions specifies the RASEO_UseCountryAndAreaCodes flag).
szAreaCode	Area code (valid only if dwfOptions specifies the RASEO_UseCountryAndAreaCodes flag).
szLocalPhoneNumber	Phone number of remote host. If dwfOptions specifies the RASEO_UseCountryAndAreaCodes flag, the phone number is combined with dwCountryCode and szAreaCode; otherwise, szLocalPhoneNumber is used as the entire phone number.
dwAlternatesOffset	Alternate phone numbers are not supported on Pocket PC. Not used.

(continued)

Table 6.1 RASENTRY Field Descriptions (*continued*)

Value	Description
ipaddr	IP address to use when connected (valid only if dwfOptions specifies the RASEO_SpecificIpAddr flag).
ipaddrDns	IP address of the primary DNS server (valid only if dwfOptions specifies the RASEO_SpecificNameServers flag).
ipaddrDnsAlt	IP address of the secondary DNS server (valid only if dwfOptions specifies the RASEO_SpecificNameServers flag).
ipaddrWins	IP address of the primary WINS server (valid only if dwfOptions specifies the RASEO_SpecificNameServers flag).
ipaddrWinsAlt	IP address of the secondary WINS server (valid only if dwfOptions specifies the RASEO_SpecificNameServers flag).
dwFrameSize	Network protocol frame size; should be set to 1,006 or 1,500 (valid only if dwFramingProtocol specifies the RASFP_Slip flag).
dwfNetProtocols	Should be set to RASNP_Ip, specifying TCP/IP as the dial-up protocol.
dwFramingProtocol	Specifies the dial-up protocol to use, and can be set to either RASFP_Slip (to use the Serial Line Internet Protocol (SLIP)) or RASFP_Ppp (to use the point-to-point protocol).
szScript	Not supported.
szAutoDialDll	Not supported.
szAutoDialFunc	Not supported.
szDeviceType	Specifies the device type specified by szDeviceName. Can be set to either RASDT_Modem (for a modem) or RASDT_Direct (for a direct serial connection).
szDeviceName	Null-terminated string that specifies the TAPI device to use with the entry.
szX25PadType	Not supported.
szX25Address	Not supported.
szX25Facilities	Not supported.
szX25UserData	Not supported.
dwChannels	Number of channels supported on the device.
dwReserved1	Reserved.
dwReserved2	Reserved.

Table 6.2 RAS Entry Options

Value	Description
RASEO_UseCountryAndAreaCodes	RAS should use the dwCountryCode and szAreaCode members to build the phone number; otherwise, just use szLocalPhoneNumber.
RASEO_SpecificIpAddr	RAS should use the ipaddr member of RASENTRY for the IP address of the dial-up connection; otherwise, request an address via DHCP.
RASEO_SpecificNameServers	RAS should use the ipaddrDns, ipaddrDnsAlt, ipaddrWins, and ipaddrWinsAlt members as the primary and secondary DNS and WINS name servers, respectively.
RASEO_IpHeaderCompression	Use IP header compression to improve performance if it is supported by the dial-up server.
RASEO_RemoteDefaultGateway	Ignored.
RASEO_DisableLcpExtensions	If set, PPP will ignore LCP extensions (RFC 1570); used to maintain compatibility with older PPP implementations.
RASEO_ModemLights	Ignored.
RASEO_SwCompression	If set, software compression (CCP) is negotiated upon establishing a link with the server. This should typically be set for better performance.
RASEO_RequireEncryptedPw	If set, only secure passwords can be used; prevents PPP from using plain-text authentication. This turns on PPP's CHAP authentication scheme.
RASEO_RequireMsEncryptedPW	If set, only Microsoft secure passwords can be used; prevents PPP from using plain-text authentication or MD5 CHAP. This will turn on the Microsoft CHAP authentication scheme.
RASEO_RequireDataEncryption	If set, data encryption must be negotiated between the client and the server; otherwise, the connection is dropped. This is used in conjunction with the RASEO_RequireMsEncryptedPW flag.

(continued)

Table 6.2 RAS Entry Options (*continued*)

Value	Description
RASEO_NetworkLogon	After a connection is established, RAS should log into the network.
RASEO_UseLogonCredentials	RAS should use the username, password, and domain of the current user for logging onto the server.
RASEO_PromoteAlternates	Ignored.
RASEO_DialAsLocalCall	RAS should construct the phone number as a local call.

As you can see, numerous options are available for creating a new phonebook entry. The following example illustrates what's actually involved in creating a new entry called "Work" in the RAS phonebook:

```
// Add an entry to the phonebook
TCHAR tchNewEntry[MAX_PATH+1] = TEXT("\0");
wsprintf(tchNewEntry, TEXT("Work"));

// Validate the entry name
if(RasValidateEntryName(NULL, tchNewEntry) != 0) {
    MessageBox(NULL, TEXT("Invalid Entry Name"), TEXT("RAS
    phonebook Error"), MB_ICONERROR|MB_OK);
    return FALSE;
}

// Set up the RASENTRY structure. Use the country/area codes
RASENTRY rasEntry;
DWORD dwResult = 0;
memset(&rasEntry, 0, sizeof(RASENTRY));

rasEntry.dwSize = sizeof(RASENTRY);
rasEntry.dwfOptions = RASEO_UseCountryAndAreaCodes;
rasEntry.dwCountryCode = 1;
wsprintf(rasEntry.szAreaCode, TEXT("425"));
wsprintf(rasEntry.szLocalPhoneNumber,TEXT("5551212"));

// Create the entry
dwResult = RasSetEntryProperties(NULL, tchNewEntry, &rasEntry,
    sizeof(RASENTRY), NULL, 0);
```

```
// Check for any errors
if(dwResult != 0) {
   TCHAR tchError[256] = TEXT("\0");

   // Print out the error
   wsprintf(tchError, TEXT("Could not create entry -- Error %ld"),
      dwResult);
   MessageBox(NULL, tchError, TEXT("RAS phonebook Error"),
      MB_ICONERROR|MB_OK);
   return FALSE;
}
```

User Credentials

When a RAS entry from the phonebook is dialed, a dialog box appears that enables the user to set up any access credentials (such as a username or password) associated with the session.

To get the current security settings for an entry, you can call the `RasGetEntryDialParams()` function, which is prototyped as follows:

```
DWORD RasGetEntryDialParams(LPWSTR lpszPhoneBook,
   LPRASDIALPARAMS lpRasDialParams, LPBOOL lpfPassword);
```

The first parameter, `lpszPhoneBook`, should be set to `NULL`. Next, `lpRasDialParams` should point to a `RASDIALPARAMS` structure. When retrieving information from the phonebook, you must first set the `dwSize` member of `lpRasDialParams` to the size of the `RASDIAL PARAMS` structure, and set the `szEntryName` parameter to a valid phonebook entry for which you want the data. To test whether the phonebook entry is valid, you can use the `RasValidateEntryName()` function described earlier in this chapter.

The final parameter, `lpfPassword`, should point to a `BOOL` variable that specifies whether the password was returned in the `RASDIAL PARAMS` structure when the function is complete.

If the function returns successfully, it will return 0. If either the `lpRasDialParams` or `lpfPassword` pointers are invalid, it will return `ERROR_BUFFER_INVALID`. If the phonebook entry is not valid, or there are any other issues with the `RASDIALPARAMS` structure (such as the `dwSize` member being set to an invalid value), you will be returned `ERROR_CANNOT_FIND_PHONEBOOK_ENTRY`.

The `RASDIALPARAMS` structure looks like the following:

```
typedef struct tagRASDIALPARAMS {
    DWORD dwSize;
    TCHAR szEntryName[RAS_MaxEntryName+1];
    TCHAR szPhoneNumber[ RAS_MaxPhoneNumber+1];
    TCHAR szCallbackNumber[RAS_MaxCallbackNumber+1];
    TCHAR szUserName[UNLEN+1];
    TCHAR szPassword[PWLEN+1];
    TCHAR szDomain[DNLEN+1];
} RASDIALPARAMS, *LPRASDIALPARAMS;
```

The fields of the structure are defined as follows:

- `dwSize` should be set to the size of the `RASDIALPARAMS` structure.
- `szEntryName` specifies a null-terminated string that contains the phonebook entry name.
- `szPhoneNumber` is not used, and can be set to `NULL`. If you want to retrieve the phone number information, you can use the `RasGetEntryProperties()` function, as described in the section "Modifying Existing Entries."
- `szCallbackNumber` is not used, and can be set to a `NULL` value.
- `szUserName` is a null-terminated string that contains the logon name of the user.
- `szPassword` is a null-terminated string that contains the password of the user.
- `szDomain` is a null-terminated string containing the domain that will be logged into.

For example, if you wanted the user credentials for the phonebook entry called "Work," you would do the following:

```
TCHAR tchRasEntry[MAX_PATH+1] = TEXT("\0");
wsprintf(tchRasEntry, TEXT("Work"));

// Validate the entry name to make sure it exists
if(RasValidateEntryName(NULL, tchRasEntry) !=
    ERROR_ALREADY_EXISTS) {
    MessageBox(NULL, TEXT("Entry does not exist"), TEXT("RAS
    phonebook Error"), MB_ICONERROR|MB_OK);
```

```
      return FALSE;
}

// Get the dial parameters
RASDIALPARAMS rasDialParams;
BOOL fPassword = FALSE;

memset(&rasDialParams, 0, sizeof(RASDIALPARAMS));
rasDialParams.dwSize = sizeof(RASDIALPARAMS);
_tcsncpy(rasDialParams.szEntryName, tchRasEntry,
  RAS_MaxEntryName);

if(RasGetEntryDialParams(NULL, &rasDialParams, &fPassword)
  != 0) {
  MessageBox(NULL, TEXT("Could not get dial parameters"),
  TEXT("RAS phonebook Error"), MB_ICONERROR|MB_OK);
  return FALSE;
}
```

To change the user credentials, you can use the `RasSetEntry`
`DialParams()` function:

```
DWORD RasSetEntryDialParams(LPWSTR lpszPhoneBook,
    LPRASDIALPARAMS lpRasDialParams, BOOL fRemovePassword);
```

The first parameter is not used, and should be set to NULL. Next,
`lpRasDialParams` should point to a structure that contains the
updated `RASDIALPARAMS` information for the connection. Finally,
`fRemovePassword` should be set to `TRUE` if you want to remove the
password associated with this entry.

If the function returns 0, then it was successful. If an ERROR_
CANNOT_FIND_PHONEBOOK_ENTRY error code is returned, then the
buffer you are using to pass into `lpRasDialParams` is invalid.

The following example shows how you could change the user credentials for the entry "Work":

```
// Get the entry as above, then set the values to change
wsprintf(rasDialParams.szUserName, TEXT("The Big Ragu"));
wsprintf(rasDialParams.szDomain, TEXT("CarminesDomain"));

if(RasSetEntryDialParams(NULL, &rasDialParams, FALSE) != 0) {
   MessageBox(NULL, TEXT("Could not modify dial parameters"),
   TEXT("RAS Phonebook Error"), MB_ICONERROR|MB_OK);
```

```
        return FALSE;
}
```

Modifying Existing Entries

Now that you know how to add a new entry to the RAS phonebook, you can easily modify one. Basically, all you need to do is get the current properties for the entry you want to change, modify its RASENTRY structure, and call `RasSetEntryDialParams()` with the newly changed information. Because the `szEntry` name will already exist, Pocket PC will update the entry, rather than create a new one.

To get the current properties for an entry, you can use the `RasGet EntryProperties()` function:

```
DWORD RasGetEntryProperties(LPWSTR lpszPhoneBook, LPWSTR
    szEntry, LPRASENTRY lpEntry, LPDWORD lpdwEntrySize, LPBYTE lpb,
    LPDWORD lpdwSize);
```

As usual for RAS phonebook operations, the first parameter should be set to NULL. The next parameter, `szEntry`, should be set to a valid null-terminated string that represents the entry you want to retrieve. This is followed by a pointer to a RASENTRY structure that will receive the actual data for the entry. You need to make sure that before calling `RasGetEntryProperties()`, the `dwSize` member of the `lpEntry` structure is set to the size of RASENTRY. Next, `lpdwEntrySize` should contain a pointer to a variable that contains the size of the `lpEntry` structure, in bytes. If you do not know the size, you can set `lpEntry` to NULL, and `lpdwEntrySize` will return the number of bytes that are required. Finally, you can set the last two parameters to NULL.

If the function is successful, you will be returned a 0. If you specify an invalid size in the `dwSize` member of the `lpEntry` structure, you will be returned an ERROR_INVALID_SIZE. If the buffer is invalid or too small, you will be returned either ERROR_BUFFER_INVALID or ERROR_ BUFFER_TOO_SMALL, respectively. Finally, an ERROR_CANNOT_FIND_ PHONEBOOK_ENTRY error specifies that the entry is not in the phonebook.

The following example changes the phone number in the entry "Work":

```
// Modify a RAS phonebook entry
TCHAR tchRasEntry[MAX_PATH+1] = TEXT("\0");
wsprintf(tchRasEntry, TEXT("Work"));
```

```
// Validate the entry name to make sure it exists
if(RasValidateEntryName(NULL, tchRasEntry) !=
   ERROR_ALREADY_EXISTS) {
   MessageBox(NULL, TEXT("Entry does not exist"), TEXT("RAS
   phonebook Error"), MB_ICONERROR|MB_OK);
   return FALSE;
}

// Set up the RASENTRY structure to get our entry
RASENTRY rasEntry;
DWORD dwResult = 0;
DWORD dwEntrySize = sizeof(RASENTRY);

memset(&rasEntry, 0, sizeof(RASENTRY));
rasEntry.dwSize = sizeof(RASENTRY);

// Get the entry
dwResult = RasGetEntryProperties(NULL, tchRasEntry,
   &rasEntry, &dwEntrySize, NULL, 0);
if(dwResult != 0) {
   MessageBox(NULL, TEXT("Could not get entry information"),
   TEXT("RAS Phonebook Error"), MB_ICONERROR|MB_OK);
   return FALSE;
}

// Change the phone number of the entry
wsprintf(rasEntry.szLocalPhoneNumber,TEXT("5551234"));

// Save changes
dwResult = RasSetEntryProperties(NULL, tchRasEntry, &rasEntry,
   sizeof(RASENTRY), NULL, 0);
if(dwResult != 0) {
   TCHAR tchError[256] = TEXT("\0");

   // Print out the error
   wsprintf(tchError, TEXT("Could not modify entry -- Error
   %ld"), dwResult);
   MessageBox(NULL, tchError, TEXT("RAS phonebook Error"),
      MB_ICONERROR|MB_OK);
   return FALSE;
}
```

Getting device-specific configuration information is a bit different from a standard desktop Windows platform. With Windows, you would use the `RasGetEntryProperties()` function combined with the last two parameters to return any device information. On Pocket PC, you must use the `RasGetEntryDevConfig()` function instead:

```
DWORD RasGetEntryDevConfig(LPCTSTR szPhonebook, LPCTSTR
   szEntry, LPDWORD pdwDeviceID, LPDWORD pdwSize, LPVARSTRING
   pDeviceConfig);
```

The first parameter is set to `NULL`, which is followed by a valid phonebook entry name. Next, `pdwDeviceID` should be set to a pointer that will retrieve the `DWORD` device ID when the function returns. Finally, `pdwSize` should be set to a pointer that specifies the size of a buffer that will retrieve the device configuration information. The pointer to that buffer should be set at the parameter value for `pDevice Config`.

To set any device configuration information, you can use the `Ras SetEntryDevConfig()` function:

```
DWORD RasSetEntryDevConfig(LPCTSTR szPhonebook, LPCTSTR
   szEntry, DWORD dwDeviceID, LPVARSTRING lpDeviceConfig);
```

The first parameter, `szPhonebook`, should be set to `NULL`. Next, `szEntry` should be set to a valid phonebook entry name, and is followed by setting `dwDeviceID` to the device ID that was returned from a previous call to `RasGetEntryDevConfig()`. Finally, set `lpDevice Config` to a pointer that represents the configuration buffer.

For example, if you wanted to get the device configuration information for the phonebook entry "My Connection", you could do the following:

```
// Get/set device configuration
TCHAR tchRasEntry[MAX_PATH+1] = TEXT("\0");
wsprintf(tchRasEntry, TEXT("My Connection"));

// Validate the entry name to make sure it exists
if(RasValidateEntryName(NULL, tchRasEntry) !=
   ERROR_ALREADY_EXISTS) {
   MessageBox(NULL, TEXT("Entry does not exist"), TEXT("RAS
   phonebook Error"), MB_ICONERROR|MB_OK);
```

```
   return FALSE;
}

// Get the device configuration
DWORD dwDeviceID = 0;
DWORD dwSize = 0;
TCHAR tchDevConfig[256] = TEXT("\0");
LPVARSTRING vsDevConfig;

vsDevConfig = (LPVARSTRING)tchDevConfig;
vsDevConfig->dwTotalSize = sizeof(tchDevConfig);
dwSize = sizeof(tchDevConfig);

DWORD dwError = RasGetEntryDevConfig(NULL, tchRasEntry,
   &dwDeviceID, &dwSize, vsDevConfig);
if(dwError != 0) {
   MessageBox(NULL, TEXT("Could not get device information."),
   TEXT("RAS Phonebook Error"), MB_ICONERROR|MB_OK);
   return FALSE;
}
```

If all you need to do is rename a phonebook entry, you use the `RasRenameEntry()` function:

```
DWORD RasRenameEntry(LPWSTR lpszPhonebook, LPWSTR
   lpszOldEntry, LPWSTR lpszNewEntry);
```

After setting `lpszPhonebook` to NULL, all you need to provide is the valid name of an old entry in the `lpszOldEntry` parameter, which is followed by a valid name to change it to in `lpszNewEntry`.

Finally, if all you need to do is get the current phone number information for a particular entry, you can use the following function:

```
DWORD RasGetDispPhoneNum(LPCWSTR szPhonebook, LPCWSTR
   szEntry, LPWSTR szPhoneNum, DWORD dwPhoneNumLen);
```

As usual, you need to set the `szPhonebook` parameter to NULL, and `szEntry` to a valid phonebook entry name. The `szPhoneNum` parameter should point to a buffer that will contain the phone number of the entry when the function returns. The last parameter, dwPhoneNumLen, should specify, in bytes, the size of the buffer you are using for the szPhoneNum buffer.

Copying Entries

To copy a phonebook entry, you can use a combination of the functions already described:

```
// Copy an entry
TCHAR tchRasEntry[MAX_PATH+1] = TEXT("\0");
TCHAR tchNewRasEntry[MAX_PATH+1] = TEXT("\0");
wsprintf(tchRasEntry, TEXT("Work"));
wsprintf(tchNewRasEntry, TEXT("Copy of Work"));

// Validate the entry name to make sure it exists
if(RasValidateEntryName(NULL, tchRasEntry) !=
   ERROR_ALREADY_EXISTS) {
   MessageBox(NULL, TEXT("Entry does not exist"), TEXT("RAS
   phonebook Error"), MB_ICONERROR|MB_OK);
   return FALSE;
}

// Validate the entry name we're going to copy to
if(RasValidateEntryName(NULL, tchNewRasEntry) != 0) {
   MessageBox(NULL, TEXT("New entry name is not valid"),
   TEXT("RAS phonebook Error"), MB_ICONERROR|MB_OK);
   return FALSE;
}

// Get the data of the source
RASENTRY rasEntry;
RASDIALPARAMS rasDialParams;
BOOL fPassword = FALSE;
DWORD dwResult = 0;
DWORD dwEntrySize = sizeof(RASENTRY);

memset(&rasEntry, 0, sizeof(RASENTRY));
rasEntry.dwSize = sizeof(RASENTRY);
```

```
memset(&rasDialParams, 0, sizeof(RASDIALPARAMS));
rasDialParams.dwSize = sizeof(RASDIALPARAMS);

// Get the source entry
dwResult = RasGetEntryProperties(NULL, tchRasEntry,
   &rasEntry, &dwEntrySize, NULL, 0);
if(dwResult != 0) {
   MessageBox(NULL, TEXT("Could not get source entry information"),
   TEXT("RAS Phonebook Error"), MB_ICONERROR|MB_OK);
   return FALSE;
}

_tcsncpy(rasDialParams.szEntryName, tchRasEntry,
   RAS_MaxEntryName);

if(RasGetEntryDialParams(NULL, &rasDialParams, &fPassword)
   != 0) {
   MessageBox(NULL, TEXT("Could not get source dial parameters"),
   TEXT("RAS Phonebook Error"), MB_ICONERROR|MB_OK);
   return FALSE;
}

// Save changes
dwResult = RasSetEntryProperties(NULL, tchNewRasEntry,
   &rasEntry, sizeof(RASENTRY), NULL, 0);
if(dwResult != 0) {
   TCHAR tchError[256] = TEXT("\0");

   // Print out the error
   wsprintf(tchError, TEXT("Could not copy the entry - Error
   %ld"), dwResult);
   MessageBox(NULL, tchError, TEXT("RAS phonebook Error"),
      MB_ICONERROR|MB_OK);
   return FALSE;
}

if(RasSetEntryDialParams(NULL, &rasDialParams, FALSE) != 0) {
   MessageBox(NULL, TEXT("Could not modify dial
   parameters"), TEXT("RAS Phonebook Error"), MB_ICONERROR|MB_OK);
```

```
      return FALSE;
}
```

Removing Entries

To remove an entry from the RAS phonebook, you can simply call the `RasDeleteEntry()` function:

```
DWORD RasDeleteEntry(LPWSTR lpszPhonebook, LPWSTR
  lpszEntry);
```

The first parameter, `lpszPhonebook`, should be set to NULL. The `lpszEntry` parameter should be set to a null-terminated string that contains the name of the valid RAS entry you want to delete.

If the function returns 0, the entry has been successfully deleted from the phonebook.

The following removes the entry "Work" that was created earlier:

```
if(RasDeleteEntry(NULL, TEXT("Work"))) != 0) {
   MessageBox(NULL, TEXT("Could not remove RAS entry"),
   TEXT("RAS Phonebook Error"), MB_ICONERROR|MB_OK);
   return FALSE;
}
```

Enumerating Entries

When developing an application that uses RAS, it is often useful to display a list of entries in the RAS phonebook. Instead of having to walk through various registry keys, you can use the `RasEnumEntries()` function to return the contents of the phonebook. The function is defined as follows:

```
DWORD RasEnumEntries(LPWSTR Reserved, LPWSTR lpszPhoneBookPath,
   LPRASENTRYNAME lprasentryname, LPDWORD lpcb, LPDWORD lpcEntries);
```

The first two parameters should be set to NULL. This is followed by `lprasentryname`, which points to a buffer that will receive an array of RASENTRYNAME structures—one for each entry in the phonebook. Next, `lpcb` should point to a DWORD value that specifies the size, in bytes, of

the lprasentryname buffer. Finally, lpcEntries should point to a
DWORD value, which will be set with the actual number of entries that
were written to the lprasentryname buffer.

In order to properly use RasEnumEntries(), you must set the
dwSize member of the first RASENTRYNAME structure in the array to
the size of RASENTRYNAME.

If the call to RasEnumEntries is successful, you will be returned
a 0. The lprasentryname array will now point to a list of RASENTRY
NAME structures that contains the phonebook, lpcb will contain the
total number of bytes that lprasentryname uses, and lpcEntries
will contain the number of RASENTRYNAME structures in the array. If the
call fails, you will be returned either an ERROR_BUFFER_TOO_SMALL or
ERROR_NOT_ENOUGH_MEMORY error code.

The RASENTRYNAME structure looks as follows:

```
typedef struct tagRASENTRYNAME {
   DWORD dwSize;
   TCHAR szEntryName[ RAS_MaxEntryName + 1 ];
} RASENTRYNAME, *LPRASENTRYNAME;
```

The first member, dwSize, should be set to the size of RASENTRY
NAME, and szEntryName will contain a null-terminated string for the
phonebook entry name.

Instead of guessing the number of phonebook entries, it can be useful to use the ERROR_BUFFER_TOO_SMALL error to determine the
actual size of the phonebook. To do this, you would first call RasEnum
Entries() to get the size required, and then call it a second time after
you have allocated the proper buffer. For example, to enumerate the
phonebook, you would do the following:

```
// Enumerate the phonebook.
// First, we will call the enum function with no data to get
// the size
DWORD dwReturn = 0;
DWORD dwEntriesSize = 0;
DWORD dwNumEntries = 0;

dwReturn = RasEnumEntries(NULL, NULL, NULL, &dwEntriesSize,
  &dwNumEntries);
if(dwReturn != ERROR_BUFFER_TOO_SMALL) {
  MessageBox(NULL, TEXT("Could not get the size of the RAS
  phonebook"), TEXT("RAS phonebook Error"), MB_ICONERROR|MB_OK);
```

```
      return FALSE;
}


// Allocate a buffer to store the rasentrynames
LPRASENTRYNAME pRasEntries = NULL;


pRasEntries = (LPRASENTRYNAME)LocalAlloc(LPTR, dwEntriesSize);
if(!pRasEntries)
   return FALSE;


pRasEntries->dwSize = sizeof(RASENTRYNAME);

// Get the entries
dwReturn = RasEnumEntries(NULL, NULL, pRasEntries,
   &dwEntriesSize, &dwNumEntries);
if(dwReturn != 0) {
   MessageBox(NULL, TEXT("Could not get the size of the RAS
   phonebook"), TEXT("RAS phonebook Error"), MB_ICONERROR|MB_OK);
   return FALSE;
}


// Print out the entries
for(WORD wEntry = 0; wEntry<dwNumEntries; wEntry++) {
   MessageBox(NULL, (pRasEntries[wEntry]).szEntryName,
   TEXT("RAS phonebook Entry"), MB_OK);
}


// Clean up memory
LocalFree(pRasEntries);
```

Remote Access Devices

Pocket PC supports using either a direct connection or a modem to establish a RAS connection. In order to determine what communication devices are available for dial-up, as well as what type they are, you can use the RasEnumDevices() function:

```
DWORD RasEnumDevices(LPRASDEVINFO lpRasDevInfo, LPDWORD
   lpcb, LPDWORD lpcDevices);
```

The first parameter should point to a buffer that contains an array of
RASDEVINFO structures, one for each RAS device connected. This is followed by lpcb, a pointer to a DWORD value that contains the size of the
lpRasDevInfo buffer. When the function returns, it will contain the
actual number of bytes that were copied into it. Finally, lpcDevices
should point to a DWORD that contains the number of RASDEVINFO
structures that were copied into the array.

Similar to RasEnumEntries(), before you call RasEnumDevices,
you must set the dwSize member of the first RASDEVINFO structure in
the lpRasDevInfo array to the size of RASDEVINFO.

The RASDEVINFO structure is defined as follows:

```
typedef struct tagRasDevInfoW {
   DWORD dwSize;
   WCHAR szDeviceType[RAS_MaxDeviceType+1];
   WCHAR szDeviceName[RAS_MaxDeviceName+1];
} RASDEVINFO;
```

The dwSize member should be set to the size, in bytes, of a RAS
DEVINFO structure. The next two strings are the actual device identifiers.
First is szDeviceType, a null-terminated string that specifies which
type of RAS device is connected. On a Pocket PC, this can be set to either
modem or direct. The last member, szDeviceName, will contain a
null-terminated string with the actual device name.

For example, to enumerate through all of the RAS-capable devices,
you could do the following:

```
// Enumerate available RAS devices
RASDEVINFO rasDevInfo[10];
DWORD dwReturn = 0;
DWORD dwSize = sizeof(RASDEVINFO)*10;
DWORD dwNumDevices = 0;

memset(&rasDevInfo, 0, sizeof(RASDEVINFO)*10);
rasDevInfo[0].dwSize = sizeof(RASDEVINFO);

if(RasEnumDevices((LPRASDEVINFO)&rasDevInfo, &dwSize,
   &dwNumDevices) != 0) {
```

```
   MessageBox(NULL, TEXT("Could not enumerate Ras Devices"),
   TEXT("RAS Error"), MB_ICONERROR|MB_OK);
   return FALSE;
}

// Print out the list of available devices
for(WORD wDevice = 0; wDevice<dwNumDevices; wDevice++) {
   TCHAR tchRasDeviceInfo[256] = TEXT("\0");

   wsprintf(tchRasDeviceInfo, TEXT("Name: %s\r\nType:%s"),
      rasDevInfo[wDevice].szDeviceName,
      rasDevInfo[wDevice].szDeviceType);
   MessageBox(NULL,tchRasDeviceInfo, TEXT("RAS Devices"),
      MB_OK);
}
```

Once you have established which device you are going to use, you may have to configure it for your communications session. To do so, you can manually set it up using the `RasSetEntryDevConfig()` function.

Establishing a RAS Connection

Now that you know how to create new entries in the RAS phonebook, as well as enumerate RAS devices, let's examine how you can actually establish a connection to a remote server.

RAS currently supports two different feedback mechanisms when dialing and connecting to a server. Dialing a host in **synchronous mode** will cause the dial function not to return until it has completed its connection (or an error occurs) with the server. **Asynchronous mode** will return immediately to your control, and enable you to get connection status information while the dialing operation is occurring, via a system notification message.

To dial and connect with a remote server, you use the `RasDial()` function, which has been defined as follows:

```
DWORD RasDial(LPRASDIALEXTENSIONS dialExtensions, LPTSTR
  phoneBookPath, LPRASDIALPARAMS rasDialParam, DWORD NotifierType,
LPVOID notifier, LPHRASCONN pRasConn);
```

The first two parameters should be set to NULL, followed by the `rasDialParam` parameter, which should point to a RASDIALPARAMS structure. This is used to identify any user authentication parameters for the connection. Remember that in order to properly use `RasDial()`, you must set the `dwSize` member of RASDIALPARAMS to the size of the RASDIALPARAMS structure, and the `szPhoneNumber` and `szCall backNumber` members should be set to NULL.

If you want to use `RasDial()` in synchronous mode, then the next two parameters, `NotifierType` and `notifier`, should both be set to NULL.

Using `RasDial()` in asynchronous mode requires you to set the parameters a bit differently. The `NotifierType` parameter should be set to `0xFFFFFFFF`, which specifies that the notification message `WM_RASDIALEVENT` should be sent to a specific window for each `Ras Dial()` event. The `notifier` parameter in this instance should be set to a pointer to the window handle that you want to receive the notification message.

In either case, the last parameter, `pRasConn`, is a pointer to an HRAS CONN connection handle. The variable should be set to NULL prior to calling `RasDial()`, and will contain the handle to the RAS connection once `RasDial()` has completed.

If the function is successful, you will be returned a 0 value; otherwise, a RAS error code will be returned to you. Remember that if the function returns a non-null value in `pRasConn`, you must call `RasHangUp()` (discussed in the section "Closing a Connection") to correctly terminate the connection and free the resources that RAS is using.

One final note: `RasDial()` does *not* display any type of logon dialog box to the user. If you need a user to enter any logon information, then you must manually create the dialog box and get the appropriate information yourself.

Synchronous Mode

As you might have already guessed, using the `RasDial()` function in synchronous mode is the easiest way to establish a remote connection. However, because the function does not return until a connection has been completed (or an error has occurred), you will not receive any notification messages about the connection operations while it is in progress. In order to get further information about the connection once it has been established, you can use the `RasGetConnectStatus()` function, which is described in the section "Connection Management."

Because most applications typically want to inform the user of the pending connection's progress, using `RasDial()` in asynchronous mode is more common.

The following example shows what is required to make a synchronous connection using `RasDial()`:

```
// Dial a RAS entry in synchronous mode
HRASCONN hRasConn = NULL;
RASDIALPARAMS rasDialParams;

// Setup the RASDIALPARAMS structure for the entry we want
// to dial
memset(&rasDialParams, 0, sizeof(RASDIALPARAMS));

rasDialParams.dwSize = sizeof(RASDIALPARAMS);
wsprintf(rasDialParams.szEntryName, TEXT("Work"));
wsprintf(rasDialParams.szUserName, TEXT("BobbieZ"));
wsprintf(rasDialParams.szPassword, TEXT("SomePassword"));
wsprintf(rasDialParams.szDomain, TEXT("SomeDomain"));

if(RasDial(NULL, NULL, &rasDialParams, 0, NULL, &hRasConn)
   != 0) {
   MessageBox(NULL, TEXT("Could not connect w/ server"),
   TEXT("RAS Dial Error"), MB_ICONERROR|MB_OK);
   return FALSE;
}

// Do our communications here ...

// Remember to hang up the connection and free the RAS
// device
if(hRasConn != NULL)
   RasHangUp(hRasConn);
```

Asynchronous Mode

More often than not, you will want to use the asynchronous mode of the `RasDial()` function when establishing a connection with a server. This enables you to obtain dynamic feedback on the connection status, which you can display in your application to the user.

To connect with a server in asynchronous mode, you need to call the `RasDial()` function with the `NotifierType` parameter set to

0xFFFFFFFF. The `notifier` parameter should specify a pointer to a window handle that will receive a notification message when any state changes in the connection operation. Once called, `RasDial()` will return to you immediately, and messages will start being sent to the window that you have specified.

Notification messages are sent to you in the `WM_RASDIALEVENT` message (which is defined as `0xCCCD` in `ras.h`). When you receive the window's message, the `wParam` parameter will indicate the current connection state that the RAS dialer is about to enter, and the `lParam` parameter will contain any errors that have occurred. If you are returned an error state, then you should call `RasHangUp()` to terminate the call and notify the user.

Table 6.3 describes the possible notification constants that you can receive during a RAS dialing event.

Table 6.3 RAS Dialing Notification States

Value	Description
RASCS_OpenPort	Port is about to be opened.
RASCS_PortOpened	Port has been opened successfully.
RASCS_ConnectDevice	A device is about to be connected. Use the `RasGetConnectStatus()` function to find out more information about the device.
RASCS_DeviceConnected	The device has successfully connected. Use the `RasGetConnectStatus()` function to find out more information about the device.
RASCS_AllDevicesConnected	The physical link has been established.
RASCS_Authenticate	The authentication process is starting.
RASCS_AuthNotify	An authentication event has occurred. If the `lParam` value is nonzero, authentication has failed.
RASCS_AuthRetry	The client has requested another attempt at authentication.
RASCS_AuthChangePassword	The client has requested to change the password.
RASCS_AuthProject	The projection phase is starting.
RASCS_AuthLinkSpeed	The link speed is being calculated.
RASCS_AuthAck	The authentication request is being acknowledged.
RASCS_Authenticated	The client has completed authentication successfully.

(continued)

Table 6.3 RAS Dialing Notification States (*continued*)

Value	Description
RASCS_Projected	RAS projection information is available. Use the RasGetProjectionInfo() function to find out more information about the current RAS projection.
RASCS_RetryAuthentication	RasDial() is requesting new user authentication credentials.
RASCS_PasswordExpired	The password has expired.
RASCS_Connected	The connection has been established and is active.
RASCS_Disconnected	The connection has failed or is inactive.

You will stop receiving notification messages once the connection is established (RASCS_Connected), if the connection fails, or if Ras HangUp() has been called on the active connection.

The following example makes a call using RasDial() in asynchronous mode:

```
// Function to dial a RAS entry in asynchronous mode
void Dial(HWND hWnd) {
    HRASCONN hRasConn = NULL;
    RASDIALPARAMS rasDialParams;

    // Set up the RASDIALPARAMS structure for the entry we
    // want to dial
    memset(&rasDialParams, 0, sizeof(RASDIALPARAMS));

    rasDialParams.dwSize = sizeof(RASDIALPARAMS);
    wsprintf(rasDialParams.szEntryName, TEXT("Work"));
    wsprintf(rasDialParams.szUserName, TEXT("RandyZ"));
    wsprintf(rasDialParams.szPassword, TEXT("SomePassword"));
    wsprintf(rasDialParams.szDomain, TEXT("SomeDomain"));

    if(RasDial(NULL, NULL, &rasDialParams, 0xFFFFFFFF, &hWnd,
        &hRasConn)!= 0) {
      MessageBox(NULL, TEXT("Could not connect w/ server"),
        TEXT("RAS Dial Error"), MB_ICONERROR|MB_OK);
      return FALSE;
    }
```

```
    // Continue to process user messages here, since RasDial
    // will return immediately
}

// Inside the window's message loop (specified by hWnd),
// process RAS notification messages
LRESULT CALLBACK WndProc(HWND hWnd, UINT iMessage, WPARAM
    wParam, LPARAM lParam) {
    switch(iMessage)        {
        case WM_RASDIALEVENT: {
            DWORD dwRasNotificationEvent = (DWORD)wParam;
            DWORD dwRasError = (DWORD)lParam;

            // First, let's check to see if any errors have
            // occurred
            if(dwRasError) {
                TCHAR tchRasError[128] = TEXT("\0");

                wsprintf(tchRasError, TEXT("An error has
                    occurred! Error #%d"), dwRasError);
                MessageBox(hWnd, tchRasError, TEXT("RAS Dial
                    Error"), MB_ICONERROR|MB_OK);
                return 0;
            }

            // Check the notification state that we were sent
            TCHAR tchRasNotificationMsg[128] = TEXT("\0");
            switch(dwRasNotificationEvent) {
                case RASCS_OpenPort:
                    wsprintf(tchRasNotificationMsg, TEXT("Opening
                        RAS Port"));
                break;
                case RASCS_Authenticate:
                    wsprintf(tchRasNotificationMsg,
                        TEXT("Starting RAS Authentication"));
                break;
                case RASCS_Projected:
                    wsprintf(tchRasNotificationMsg, TEXT("Remote
                        network projection established"));
```

```
            break;
            case RASCS_Connected:
                wsprintf(tchRasNotificationMsg,
                    TEXT("Connection Established"));
            break;
            case RASCS_Disconnected:
                wsprintf(tchRasNotificationMsg,
                    TEXT("Connection Terminated"));
            break;
        }

        MessageBox(hWnd, tchRasNotificationMsg, TEXT("RAS
            Event"), MB_ICONINFORMATION|MB_OK);
    }
    break;
    default:
        return (DefWindowProc(hWnd, iMessage, wParam,
            lParam));
    }
    return (0L);
}
```

Closing a Connection

Once you have established a connection using `RasDial()`, you can use the `RasHangUp()` function to disconnect and close an active connection handle. The function is defined as follows:

```
DWORD RasHangUp(HRASCONN hSession);
```

The only parameter that `RasHangUp()` needs is `hSession`, which should point to the RAS connection handle that was returned from the earlier call to `RasDial()`. If successful, you will be returned a zero; otherwise, you will get a standard RAS error code. Remember that once you have terminated a connection, the `hSession` handle is no longer valid and cannot be used for further RAS function calls.

TIP: Although you can call `RasHangUp()` at any point, you should ensure that your connection has completely disconnected before attempting to use the same dial-up device again. To do so, you can use the `RasGetConnectStatus()` function to verify that you have received the `RASCD_Disconnected` status from the device.

Connection Management

Once you have created an active RAS connection to a remote server, you can use several functions provided by RAS to find out more information about current connections, device states, and connection properties.

To get information about what state a RAS connection is in, you can use the `RasGetConnectStatus()` function. This function is extremely versatile and can be used in a variety of situations:

- **`RasDial()` connections status.** You can use the `RasGetConnectStatus()` function after `RasDial()` has completed to determine the status of the connection operation (either asynchronous or synchronous).
- **Use as a polling mechanism during synchronous `RasDial()`.** To get the current state of a blocking RAS connection, the `RasGetConnectStatus()` function can be called from a separate thread while a synchronous `RasDial` connection is being established.
- **`RasHangUp()` status.** Use `RasGetConnectStatus()` to ensure that you have received a `RASCD_Disconnected` status message from the RAS device before attempting to use it again.
- **Determine name and device type of an active connection.** The `RasGetConnectStatus()` function can be used to determine the device name and type based on the RAS session handle.

The `RasGetConnectStatus()` function is defined as follows:

```
DWORD RasGetConnectStatus(HRASCONN rasconn,
   LPRASCONNSTATUS lprasconnstatus);
```

The first parameter, `rasconn`, should be the handle for the RAS connection for which you want the current status (which you have from the previous call to `RasDial()` or by using the `RasEnumConnections()` function). This is followed by a pointer to a `RASCONNSTATUS` structure that will receive the current status information. Remember to set the dwSize member of the lprasconnstatus structure to the size of RASCONNSTATUS in order for the function to work properly.

The RASCONNSTATUS structure is defined as follows:

```
typedef struct tagRASCONNSTATUS {
    DWORD dwSize;
    RASCONNSTATE rasconnstate;
    DWORD dwError;
    TCHAR szDeviceType[RAS_MaxDeviceType+1];
    TCHAR szDeviceName[RAS_MaxDeviceName+1];
} RASCONNSTATUS, *LPRASCONNSTATUS;
```

The first member is dwSize, which should be set to the size of the RASCONNSTATUS structure. This is followed by rasconnstate which will specify the current state of the connection process. The possible values for rasconnstate are listed in Table 6.2 (and are the same for asynchronous RasDial()). Next, dwError will contain a nonzero error code if the rasconnstate member has a state that signifies an error condition.

The last two values, szDeviceType and szDeviceName, are null-terminated strings that contain the device name and type.

Enumerating Connections

To get a list of all of the RAS connection handles that are currently active on your device, you can use the RasEnumConnections() function:

```
DWORD RasEnumConnections(LPRASCONN lprasconn, LPDWORD lpcb,
    LPDWORD lpcConnections);
```

The first parameter should point to a buffer that will receive the array of RASCONN structures, one for each active RAS connection. In order to use RasEnumConnections() properly, you must set the dwSize member of the first structure in the buffer to the size of RASCONN. This is followed by lpcb, a pointer to a DWORD value that contains the size, in bytes, of the lprasconn buffer you are passing in. Finally, lpcConnections should point to the actual number of bytes that were written to the lprasconn buffer when it returns.

The RASCONN structure is defined as follows:

```
typedef struct tagRASCONN {
    DWORD dwSize;
    HRASCONN hrasconn;
```

```
    TCHAR szEntryName[RAS_MaxEntryName+1];
} RASCONN, *LPRASCONN;
```

The structure contains three members: the size of the structure in bytes, the active connection handle, and the RAS phonebook entry name that corresponds to the connection handle.

To accurately determine how much memory you need to allocate in order to enumerate all of the active RAS connections, it can be useful to use the ERROR_BUFFER_TOO_SMALL error code. To do this, you would first call RasEnumConnections() to get the size required, and then call it a second time when you have a properly allocated buffer.

Connection Information

To obtain more information about the actual connection, such as the amount of time a RAS connection has been active, or the number of bytes that have been sent or received, you can use the RasGetLinkStatistics() function:

```
DWORD RasGetLinkStatistics(HRASCONN hRasConn, DWORD
    dwSubEntry, RAS_STATS *lpStatistics);
```

The first parameter is a handle to an active RAS connection. This is followed by dwSubEntry and should be set to 0. The last parameter is a pointer to a RAS_STATS structure that will receive the statistical information for the connection. Remember to set the dwSize member of the lpStatistics structure to the size of RAS_STATS before calling RasGetLinkStatistics().

The function will return a 0 value if it is successful, and will fill the lpStatistics buffer with all of the available connection data.

The RAS_STATS structure is defined as follows:

```
typedef struct _RAS_STATS {
    DWORD dwSize;
    DWORD dwBytesXmited;
    DWORD dwBytesRcved;
    DWORD dwFramesXmited;
    DWORD dwFramesRcved;
    DWORD dwCrcErr;
    DWORD dwTimeoutErr;
    DWORD dwAlignmentErr;
```

```
      DWORD dwHardwareOverrunErr;
      DWORD dwFramingErr;
      DWORD dwBufferOverrunErr;
      DWORD dwCompressionRatioIn;
      DWORD dwCompressionRatioOut;
      DWORD dwBps;
      DWORD dwConnectDuration;
} RAS_STATS, *PRAS_STATS;
```

Table 6.4 describes the RAS_STATS structure.

Table 6.4 RAS_STATS Flags

Member	Description
dwSize	Size of the RAS_STATS structure
dwBytesXmited	Number of bytes transmitted
dwBytesRcved	Number of bytes received
dwFramesXmited	Number of frames transmitted
dwFramesRcved	Number of frames received
dwCrcErr	Number of CRC errors that have occurred on this connection
dwTimeoutErr	Number of timeout errors that have occurred on this connection
dwAlignmentErr	Number of alignment errors that have occurred on this connection
dwHardwareOverrunErr	Number of hardware overruns that have occurred on this connection
dwFramingErr	Number of framing errors that have occurred on this connection
dwBufferOverrunErr	Number of buffer overruns that have occurred on this connection
dwCompressionRatioIn	Compression ratio for incoming data
dwCompressionRatioOut	Compression ratio for outgoing data
dwBps	Speed of the connection
dwConnectDuration	Amount of time, in milliseconds, that the connection has been active

NOTE: The dwBps member of RAS_STATS specifies the determined speed of the remote connection that was negotiated upon connection to the remote server. If you want to calculate the actual network throughput of the connection, you can divide the number of bytes that have been

sent over the connection (dwBytesXmited) and received
(dwBytesRcved) by the amount of time that the connection has
been active (dwConnectDuration).

To get any network-protocol-specific information (also known as *net-work projection information*) from a RAS server with which you have
established a connection, you can call the RasGetProjectionInfo()
function. As previously mentioned, Pocket PC supports only SLIP or PPP
as the protocol for remote access connections. This limits the amount of
network projection information that you can query to the IP address that
the server has assigned to the device, as well as any other error informa-tion regarding the protocol. The function is defined as follows:

```
DWORD RasGetProjectionInfo(HRASCONN hRasConn, RASPROJECTION
    rasprojection, LPVOID lpprojection, LPDWORD lpcb);
```

The first parameter should be set to the RAS connection handle
for which you want projection information. This can be the handle that
was originally returned from RasDial(), or one obtained through
the RasEnumConnections() function. Next, you must set the
rasprojection parameter to RASP_PppIp.

The lpprojection parameter is a data structure that will receive
your projection information. The structure, in the case of RASP_PppIP,
is defined as follows:

```
typedef struct tagRASPPPIP {
    DWORD dwSize;
    DWORD dwError;
    TCHAR szIpAddress[RAS_MaxIpAddress+1];
    TCHAR szServerIPAddress[RAS_MaxIPAddress+1];
    DWORD dwOptions;
    DWORD dwServerOptions;
} RASPPPIP, *LPRASPPPIP;
```

The structure contains three basic members: the size of the structure,
any PPP connection negotiation error codes, and the null-terminated
string representing the client's IP address. As usual, you must first set the
dwSize member to the size of RASPPPIP in order for the function to be
called properly.

The final parameter in RasGetProjectionInfo() is a pointer to
a DWORD value that contains the size of the buffer. This also must be set

to the size of RASPPPIP before the function is called in order for it to operate properly.

For example, you could use the following to get the IP address for a newly established IP connection in the notification loop of an asynchronous RasDial() function:

```
case RASCS_Projected: {
   TCHAR tchRasProjectInfo[128] = TEXT("\0");
   DWORD dwReturn = 0;
   DWORD dwSize = 0;
   RASPPPIP rasPPPInfo;

   dwSize = sizeof(RASPPPIP);
   memset(&rasPPPInfo, 0, sizeof(RASPPPIP));
   rasPPPInfo.dwSize = sizeof(RASPPPIP);

   // Get the projection info. Use the global RAS handle
   // from our RasDial (g_hRasConn)
   dwReturn = RasGetProjectionInfo(&g_hRasConn, RASP_PppIp,
      (LPVOID)&rasPPPInfo, &dwSize);
   if(dwReturn != 0) {
      MessageBox(hWnd, TEXT("Couldnt get RAS IP Address"),
         TEXT("RAS Dial Error"), MB_ICONERROR|MB_OK);
      break;
   }

   wsprintf(tchRasProjectInfo, TEXT("IP Address: %s"),
      rasPPPInfo.szIpAddress);
}
break;
```

The Remote Network Access (RNA) Dialer

So far in this chapter, you have learned how to manipulate the RAS phonebook, dial and establish RAS connections, and query the RAS interface to get statistical information about currently active remote sessions. The last thing to cover is how Pocket PC takes advantage of the RAS service to dial, connect to, and maintain a connection with a RAS

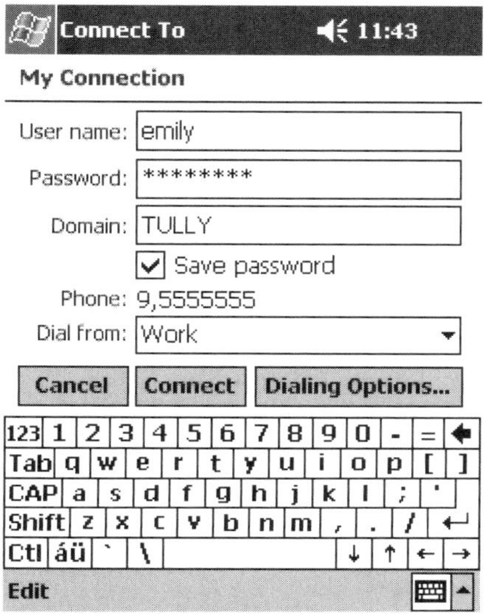

Figure 6.3 The rnaapp.exe Pocket PC dialer

server. The dialer application that is built into Pocket PC is located in the \Windows folder and has the name **rnaapp.exe**. The rnaapp.exe dialer (see Figure 6.3) is nothing more than a wrapper around the RAS functions already discussed.

Besides automating most of the RAS functions, it provides you with a graphical interface for the dialer, which calling RasDial() by itself would not provide. Unless you want to manually provide user feedback and an interface for dialing a RAS connection, you can launch rnaapp.exe to handle your connection.

Creating a RAS Connection with rnaapp.exe

Integrating your application with rnaapp.exe is fairly straightforward. To dial a remote server, you need to launch rnaapp.exe from your application by using the CreateProcess() function. Rnaapp.exe takes the command-line parameters described in Table 6.5.

For example, if you wanted to connect the "Work" RAS entry and use rnaapp.exe to dial it, you could do the following:

```
PROCESS_INFORMATION pi;
```

```
memset(&pi, 0, sizeof(PROCESS_INFORMATION));
CreateProcess(TEXT("\\Windows\\rnaapp.exe"), TEXT("-e\"My
   Connection\" -c00FF"), NULL, NULL, NULL, 0, NULL, NULL, NULL,
   &pi);
```

Once a connection to the server has been established, rnaapp.exe will send a global broadcast message, WM_NETCONNECT, to all of the running applications on your device.

As with any window message, WM_NETCONNECT contains two informational parameters that are sent along with the message. The wParam parameter specifies the connection status of the session. If the value is TRUE, then the connection has been established; otherwise, it will be set to FALSE when the connection has been terminated.

The lParam parameter is a pointer to an RNAAPP_INFO structure. The structure contains information that rnaapp.exe has stored about the particular dial-up session. The RNAAPP_INFO structure is defined as follows:

```
typedef struct tagRNAAppInfo {
    DWORD dwSize;
    DWORD hWndRNAApp;
    DWORD Context;
    DWORD ErrorCode;
    TCHAR RasEntryName[RAS_MaxEntryName+1];
} RNAAPP_INFO, *PRNAAPP_INFO;
```

Table 6.5 rnaapp.exe Command-Line Parameters

Option	Description
-n	Disable all message boxes.
-p	Do not display any user authentication prompts (username/password).
-m	Minimize the connection dialog box.
-cNUM	Set the connection context value in hex (e.g., -c00FF). This value will be used to uniquely identify a RAS connection when sending/receiving messages to the rnaapp.exe dialer.
-eRASPHONEBOOKENTRY	The name of the RAS phonebook entry to dial. If the name contains any spaces, it should be enclosed in quotes.

The RNAAPP_INFO structure contains the following information:

- The dwSize member contains the size of the structure.
- The hWndRNAApp member is the window handle of rnaapp.exe.
- The Context member contains the value that was specified to rnaapp.exe with the -c parameter when the application was run.
- The ErrorCode member specifies the error code of the RAS connection if the wParam value of the WM_NETCONNECT message is FALSE. See raserror.h for more information on RAS errors.
- The RasEntryName member contains a null-terminated string that specifies the RAS phonebook entry name of the connection.

For example, if you wanted to process a WM_NETCONNECT message in your application's main message loop, you would do the following:

```
case WM_NETCONNECT: {
   BOOL fConnected = (BOOL)wParam;
   RNAAPP_INFO *prnaInfo = (RNAAPP_INFO *)lParam;

   // Check to see if we've disconnected
   if(fConnected == FALSE) {
      TCHAR tchRNAError[128] = TEXT("\0");

      wsprintf(tchRNAError, TEXT("RNAError: %d"),
         prnaInfo->ErrorCode);
      MessageBox(NULL, tchRNAError, TEXT("RNA Dial Error"),
         MB_ICONERROR|MB_OK);
      break;
   }

   // Looks like we have an active connection
   MessageBox(NULL, prnaInfo->RasEntryName, TEXT("Connection
      Established"), MB_ICONERROR|MB_OK);
}
break;
```

Working with rnaapp.exe

If you have established a dial-up connection with rnaapp.exe (or want to work with a connection that was created with the Pocket PC Connection Manager), you can use the SendMessage() function to further communicate with the dialer application.

Before you can send a message to rnaapp.exe, however, you must first know the window handle of the connection dialog. This value can be obtained in two ways: by storing the hWndRNAApp handle that was sent as part of the RNAAPP_INFO structure you received when the initial connection was established, or by using the EnumWindow() function.

Because EnumWindow() will enumerate all of the active windows, you need to look at each one for a "magic" number that signifies the dialer. The magic number, RNAAPP_MAGIC_NUM, is defined as 0x006A6D6D, and can be found by calling the GetWindowLong() function on each window handle that is returned when you call EnumWindows().

While this sounds somewhat complicated, it is actually relatively straightforward to find the dialer window:

```
#define RNAAPP_MAGIC_NUM 0x006A6D6D

BOOL RNAEnumFunc(HWND hWnd, LPARAM lParam){
   TCHAR tchClass[128] = TEXT("\0");
   HWND *hRnaWnd = (HWND *)lParam;

   DWORD dwMagicNumber = GetWindowLong(hWnd, DWL_USER);
   if(dwMagicNumber == RNAAPP_MAGIC_NUM) {
      *hRnaWnd = hWnd;
      return FALSE;
   }

   return TRUE;
}


BOOL FindRemoteDialer() {
   HWND hWndRNAWnd = NULL;
   EnumWindows(RNAEnumFunc, (LPARAM)&hWndRNAWnd);

   if(!hWndRNAWnd)
      return FALSE;

   // Send a message here to the dialer

   return TRUE;
}
```

Now that you have the handle to the rnaapp.exe dialer, you can send it an RNA_RASCMD message:

```
SendMessage(hWnd, RNA_RASCMD, wParam, lParam);
```

Table 6.6 describes the three messages that you can send to the rnaapp.exe dialer window.

Table 6.6 Messages sent by rnaapp.exe

wParam	lParam	#define value	Description
RNA_ADDREF	0	1	Add a reference to the current active connection.
RNA_DELREF	0	2	Remove a reference to the active connection. When the reference count hits 0, rnaapp.exe will disconnect the connection.
RNA_GETINFO	Window handle	3	Send a WM_NETCONNECT message to the window handle that is specified in the lParam value.

In other words, if you need to disconnect from a RAS session using the rnaapp.exe dialer, you only need to send it an RNA_DELREF message.

This function is also useful when you want to obtain information about a different dial-up connection that another application has established. Using the RNA_GETINFO message, you could query the dialer for the connection information as follows:

```
#define RNA_GETINFO 3

// Once you have found the RNAAPP.exe window handle, you
// can send it a message
SendMessage(hWndRNAWnd, RNA_RASCMD, (WPARAM)hWnd,
  RNA_GETINFO);
```

CHAPTER 7

Connection Manager

Operator! Give me the number for 911!

—*Homer Simpson,* The Simpsons

The last chapter described how to establish and interact with a connection to a remote server using the Remote Access Service (RAS). Although using the RAS APIs provides you with low-level functions to establish a connection with a server and get status information about it, a variety of aspects about that connection can change, depending on what type of network resource you are accessing. This is especially true on mobile devices such as Pocket PC, for which connectivity and authorization requirements can constantly shift depending on your current environment and what you are requesting.

Consider what happens when you try to access an HTTP resource that is located on the Internet. Whether you are dialed into your Internet service or on a wireless LAN at the local coffee shop, the device merely needs to establish a connection to the Internet to download the request. What happens, however, if you make the same request while you are at work and are connected to the corporate network, which is most likely under a firewall? Without having the user authentication information that is passed to the proxy server, the request will fail. Managing all of the various connection types that a user might have would be a nightmare for every individual application developer.

This is where the **Pocket PC Connection Manager** comes in—it is the best way to manage remote connections (see Figure 7.1).

It is probably easiest to think of the Connection Manger as a centralized location that is used for the configuration of all possible network connections that the device can make. What this accomplishes is a simplified user experience—the user needs to configure what a "Work" connection is only once in order for all networking applications to use it. In addition, the Connection Manager can make some calculations about the cost, latency, and bandwidth required for the request, in an attempt to

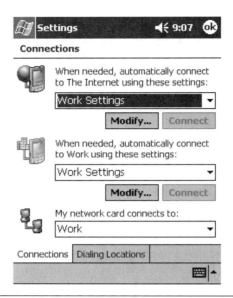

Figure 7.1 Pocket PC Connection Manager

determine the best type of connection to make in order to get the network resource that you've requested.

If you are planning to develop any applications that require network communications, you will most likely want to have them use the Connection Manager to establish and schedule network connections. By doing so, all of the specific details—including dialing parameters, proxy information, VPN authentication, and so on—are handled for you, provided that the user has already configured his or her device. All you need to do is send a request to the Connection Manager to either establish or close a connection.

To use the Connection Manager API functions within your application, you need to include the headers `connmgr.h` and `connmgr_proxy.h`, and link with the `cellcore.lib` library.

Understanding the Connection Manager

You can configure two types of connection settings using the Connection Manager: **Internet** and **Work**. Both maintain connection parameters for the type of resource you are trying to access.

1. The **Internet** connection setting is used for a straightforward dial-up or network connection to the Internet when attempting to access an Internet-style dot-address (such as XX.XX.XX.XX or name.domain.com).
2. The **Work** connection setting offers a variety of connection options, including support for proxy servers, virtual private networks (VPNs), and ActiveSync synchronization. This option also supports the capability to address a WINS network address on a private LAN.

So, what does this mean for you as an application developer? Basically, depending on the type of resource you are requesting, the Connection Manager will choose which connection to use in order to get you access to the network resource. If you are attempting to get something with a fully qualified Internet URL, the Connection Manager will use the Internet setting; otherwise, it will choose Work. Figure 7.2 shows the Work setting configuration dialog box.

It is generally recommended that a user set all three of the Connection Manager's configuration drop-down options (Internet, Work, and Network card) for the Work connection setting. By doing this, the device can easily connect to the Internet, use a VPN connection, synchronize

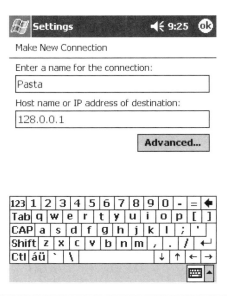

Figure 7.2 Pocket PC VPN settings

with ActiveSync, and use local resources without having to reconfigure Connection Manager whenever the environment changes.

Preparing the Connection Manager

Before you can use the Connection Manager to manage your network communications, you must first make sure that it is available to be used. This is done by simply calling the `ConnMgrApiReadyEvent()` API, which is defined as follows:

```
HANDLE WINAPI ConnMgrApiReadyEvent();
```

The function takes no parameters, but returns a handle to an event that will become signaled when the Connection Manager is ready. Remember that you need to call the `CloseHandle()` function for the event that is returned.

Confirming that the Connection Manager is available is relatively straightforward:

```
// Make sure Connection Manager is ready
HANDLE hConnMgr = NULL;
BOOL bAvailable = FALSE;
hConnMgr = ConnMgrApiReadyEvent();

if(!hConnMgr)
   return FALSE;

// Wait for 1 second to see if Connection Manager has
// signaled the event
DWORD dwResult = WaitForSingleObject(hConnMgr, 1000);

if(dwResult == WAIT_OBJECT_0)
   bAvailable = TRUE;

// Close the event handle
if(hConnMgr)
   CloseHandle(hConnMgr);

// Did it connect ok?
if(!bAvailable)
   return FALSE;

// Do something now that Connection Manager is ready
```

URLs and Network Identifiers

The next thing you need to do before you can make a network request is to determine the globally unique identifier (GUID) for the type of object you are requesting, based on its Uniform Resource Locator (URL). The GUID you are returned has been deemed the best network connection to use for the destination that you passed to the function, based on the connection cost, latency, and so on. You then use the identifier when you eventually establish your connection.

To determine the best network connection to use, you need to call the `ConnMgrMapURL()` function, which is defined as follows:

```
HRESULT WINAPI ConnMgrMapURL(LPCTSTR pwszURL, GUID *pguid,
   DWORD *pdwIndex);
```

The first parameter, `pwszURL`, is the location of the object you are requesting, and should be in standard Internet format (for example, `http://www.furrygoat.com/index.html`). You can also use the URL functions described in Chapter 2, such as `InternetCreate Url()`, to correctly build a resource locator.

The next parameter, `pguid`, is a pointer that receives the GUID of the destination network. Finally, you have `pdwIndex`, which is an optional parameter that serves as a pointer to a `DWORD` index variable. The index is used if there were more than one network mapping for the destination resource. The first time you call the function, you should set the value of the index to 0. If there are additional mappings, then `ConnMgrMapURL()` will increment the index value, which should be passed into each additional call into `ConnMgrMapURL()`.

The following example determines the best network connection to use for a particular URL:

```
// Map a local and remote URL
TCHAR tchLocalUrl[256] = TEXT("\0");
TCHAR tchRemoteUrl[256] = TEXT("\0");
HRESULT hResult = S_OK;

wsprintf(tchLocalUrl, TEXT("http://fifi/report.txt"));
wsprintf(tchRemoteUrl, TEXT("http://fifi.someserver.
  com/report.txt"));

// Map a local URL {a1182988-0d73-439e-87ad-2a5b369f808b}
GUID guidNetworkObject;
DWORD dwIndex = 0;
```

```
if(ConnMgrMapURL(tchLocalUrl, &guidNetworkObject, &dwIndex)
    == E_FAIL) {
  OutputDebugString(TEXT("Could not map a local request to
    a network identifier"));
  return FALSE;
}


// Map a remote URL {436ef144-b4fb-4863-a041-8f905a62c572}
dwIndex = 0;
if(ConnMgrMapURL(tchRemoteUrl, &guidNetworkObject, &dwIndex)
    == E_FAIL) {
  OutputDebugString(TEXT("Could not map a remote request to
    a network identifier"));
  return FALSE;
}
```

Enumerating Network Identifiers

If you want to get more information about a particular network identifier, or just enumerate the available identifiers that are on the device, you can use the ConnMgrEnumDestinations() function, which is defined as follows:

```
HRESULT WINAPI ConnMgrEnumDestinations(int nIndex,
   CONNMGR_DESTINATION_INFO *pDestInfo);
```

The first parameter is the index value of the identifier for which you want to get more information. If you want to enumerate all of the available identifiers, this should be set to 0 the first time the function is called, and incremented for each additional time you call the function. The other parameter, pDestInfo, is a pointer to a CONNMGR_DESTINATION_ INFO structure, which contains the network information for the index specified.

The function will return an S_OK value if it is successful; otherwise, you will be returned an E_FAIL value.

The CONNMGR_DESTINATION_INFO structure looks like the following:

```
typedef struct _CONNMGR_DESTINATION_INFO {
  GUID guid;
```

```
    TCHAR szDescription[CONNMGR_MAX_DESC];
} CONNMGR_DESTINATION_INFO;
```

The structure contains only two pieces of information: the GUID that is associated with the network connection, and a null-terminated string containing the description of the network.

To enumerate all of the available network identifiers, you could do the following:

```
// Enumerate the available network identifiers
DWORD dwEnumIndex = 0;
BOOL fLoop = TRUE;
TCHAR tchNetNameInfo[256] = TEXT("\0");
CONNMGR_DESTINATION_INFO networkDestInfo;

// Walk through the list of Networks
do{
    memset(&networkDestInfo, 0,
        sizeof(CONNMGR_DESTINATION_INFO));

    if(ConnMgrEnumDestinations(dwEnumIndex, &networkDestInfo)
        == E_FAIL) {
        fLoop = FALSE;
        break;
    }

    // If we got a network ID's information, show the
    // description
    wsprintf(tchNetNameInfo, TEXT("Network Name:%s"),
        networkDestInfo.szDescription);
    MessageBox(NULL, tchNetNameInfo, TEXT("Available
        Networks"), MB_OK|MB_ICONINFORMATION);
    dwEnumIndex++;
} while(fLoop);
```

Establishing and Maintaining Connections

Now that you have the proper network identifier to use for the network location from which you are requesting a resource, you can go ahead and tell Connection Manager to make the connection.

The Connection Manager API currently supports two different functions for establishing a connection to the network:

- **Synchronous Mode:** To create a connection request that will not return until the connection either is established or returns an error, you can use the `ConnMgrEstablishConnectionSync()` function.
- **Asynchronous Mode:** To create a connection request that returns immediately, you can use the `ConnMgrEstablish Connection()` function. You need to poll the request handle that you are returned in order to find out the current status of the connection.

Regardless of which method you use to establish your network connection, you need to properly fill out a `CONNMGR_CONNECTIONINFO` structure, which contains the parameters that describe the request. The structure is defined as follows:

```
typedef struct _CONNMGR_CONNECTIONINFO {
    DWORD cbSize;
    DWORD dwParams;
    DWORD dwFlags;
    DWORD dwPriority;
    BOOL bExclusive;
    BOOL bDisabled;
    GUID guidDestNet;
    HWND hWnd;
    UINT uMsg;
    LPARAM lParam;
    ULONG ulMaxCost;
    ULONG ulMinRcvBw;
    ULONG ulMaxConnLatency;
} CONNMGR_CONNECTIONINFO;
```

The `cbSize` member should be set to the size of the `CONNMGR_CONNECTIONINFO` structure.

The `dwParams` member contains a list of optional member fields that are set in the structure, and can be a combination of the values shown in Table 7.1.

The `dwFlags` member defines the list of flags that specify any special properties for establishing the network connection. If no flags are set, the Connection Manager will use a direct IP connection. The `dwFlags` member should be set to one of the values shown in Table 7.2.

Table 7.1 CONNMGR_CONNECTIONINFO Flags

Value	Description
CONNMGR_PARAM_GUIDDESTNET	guidDestNet field is valid
CONNMGR_PARAM_MAXCOST	ulMaxCost field is valid
CONNMGR_PARAM_MINRCVBW	ulMinRcvBw field is valid
CONNMGR_PARAM_MAXCONNLATENCY	ulMaxConnLatency field is valid

Table 7.2 Connection Manager Proxy Flags

Value	Description
CONNMGR_FLAG_PROXY_HTTP	HTTP Proxy supported
CONNMGR_FLAG_PROXY_WAP	WAP gateway proxy supported
CONNMGR_FLAG_PROXY_SOCKS4	SOCKS4 proxy supported
CONNMGR_FLAG_PROXY_SOCKS5	SOCKS5 proxy supported

The dwPriority member specifies the priority level of the connection you are requesting. Remember that the Connection Manager needs to delegate various simultaneous network requests among multiple applications. It gives precedence to those that specify a higher priority value. Table 7.3 describes the priority levels that can be used.

The bExclusive member specifies whether the connection can be shared among multiple applications. If you set this value to FALSE, then other programs will be notified when the connection is available. If you set it to TRUE, then you place the connection in a state in which it cannot be shared. Other applications that request to establish a similar connection will fight for the same resource, with the outcome depending on each connection request's priority.

The bDisabled member prevents the connection request from actually establishing a remote connection if set to TRUE. This can be used to test the availability of a network connection.

The guidDestNet member should contain the GUID for the network identifier that will be used to connect to the network. This is the same identifier returned using the ConnMgrMapURL() or ConnMgr EnumDestinations() functions. A remote connection cannot be established without this identifier.

Table 7.3 Connection Manager Priority Levels

Value	Priority	Description
CONNMGR_PRIORITY_ VOICE	Highest	Voice connection.
CONNMGR_PRIORITY_ USERINTERACTIVE		A user has made this request, and is awaiting the creation of the connection. Use this priority for user-interactive applications.
CONNMGR_PRIORITY_ USERBACKGROUND	High	The application has become idle. You should switch to this priority when the application is not active.
CONNMGR_PRIORITY_ USERIDLE		A user-initiated request has been idle for a length of time. Switching between this and CONNMGR_PRIORITY_ USERINTERACTIVE enables the Connection Manager to optimize shared connections.
CONNMGR_PRIORITY_ HIPRIBKGND		High-priority background.
CONNMGR_PRIORITY_ IDLEBKGND	Low	Idle background task.
CONNMGR_PRIORITY_ EXTERNALINTERACTIVE		A network request has been made from an external application.
CONNMGR_PRIORITY_ LOWBKGND	Lowest	A connection is established only if a higher-priority client is already using the connection.
CONNMGR_PRIORITY_ CACHED	None	Internal caching is being used; no external connection is needed.

To have the Connection Manager send any changes in the connection status to a window handle, you can use the next three members to set that up. The hWnd member is the window handle that you want to receive messages, uMsg should contain the WM_USER message ID that you want to have sent with the status change, and lParam is a DWORD value that will be placed in the lParam parameter of your message. You can set all three of these members to zero if you don't want the Connection Manager to post any messages to your window.

The ulMaxCost member should specify the maximum cost of the connection.

The ulMinRcvBw member specifies the minimum amount of bandwidth that you need in order to accept the connection.

Finally, the ulMaxConnLatency member should specify the maximum acceptable connection latency, in milliseconds, before a connection fails. An acceptable value for the maximum latency would be around 4 seconds, or 4,000 milliseconds.

Establishing Connections

To create a synchronous connection, you can call the following function:

```
HRESULT WINAPI ConnMgrEstablishConnectionSync(
    CONNMGR_CONNECTIONINFO *pConnInfo, HANDLE *phConnection,
    DWORD dwTimeout, DWORD *pdwStatus);
```

The pConnInfo parameter should point to a CONNMGR_CONNECTION INFO structure that contains the instructions for establishing the connection. This is followed by phConnection, a pointer to the connection handle that you are returned from the function. The dwTimeout parameter should be used to set a timeout value, in milliseconds, which the function will return if a connection cannot be established. Finally, the pdwStatus parameter will point to the final status of the connection.

Don't forget that you need to call the ConnMgrRelease Connection() function once you are finished using the connection in order to properly free the connection handle.

The following code establishes a synchronous connection:

```
// Establish a synchronous connection
HANDLE hConnection = NULL;
DWORD dwStatus = 0;
DWORD dwTimeout = 5000;

// Get the network information where we want to establish a
// connection
TCHAR tchRemoteUrl[256] = TEXT("\0");
wsprintf(tchRemoteUrl,
  TEXT("http://www.furrygoat.com/index.html"));
GUID guidNetworkObject;
DWORD dwIndex = 0;

if(ConnMgrMapURL(tchRemoteUrl, &guidNetworkObject, &dwIndex)
    == E_FAIL) {
```

```
    OutputDebugString(TEXT("Could not map the request to a
        network identifier"));
    return FALSE;
}


// Now that we've got the network address, set up the
// connection structure
CONNMGR_CONNECTIONINFO ccInfo;

memset(&ccInfo, 0, sizeof(CONNMGR_CONNECTIONINFO));
ccInfo.cbSize = sizeof(CONNMGR_CONNECTIONINFO);
ccInfo.dwParams = CONNMGR_PARAM_GUIDDESTNET;
ccInfo.dwFlags = CONNMGR_FLAG_PROXY_HTTP;
ccInfo.dwPriority = CONNMGR_PRIORITY_USERINTERACTIVE;
ccInfo.guidDestNet = guidNetworkObject;


// Make the connection request (timeout in 5 seconds)
if(ConnMgrEstablishConnectionSync(&ccInfo, &hConnection,
        dwTimeout, &dwStatus) == E_FAIL) {
    return FALSE;
}


// Connection has been made, continue on...
```

Creating an asynchronous connection is a bit more involved. To make the connection request, you can use the ConnMgrEstablish Connection() function, which is defined as follows:

```
HRESULT WINAPI ConnMgrEstablishConnection(
    CONNMGR_CONNECTIONINFO *pConnInfo, HANDLE *phConnection);
```

The first parameter, pConnInfo, is a pointer to a CONNMGR_ CONNECTIONINFO structure that describes the connection. When the function returns, phConnection will point to a connection handle for the request.

When you are finished using the connection, you must properly free the handle by calling the ConnMgrReleaseConnection() function, as described in the section "Disconnecting from an Active Connection," later in this chapter.

The following code polls the request handle for status changes:

```
// Establish an asynchronous connection
HANDLE hConnection = NULL;
DWORD dwStatus = 0;

// Get the network information where we want to establish a
// connection
TCHAR tchRemoteUrl[256] = TEXT("\0");
wsprintf(tchRemoteUrl, TEXT("http://www.furrygoat.com/index.html"));
GUID guidNetworkObject;
DWORD dwIndex = 0;

if(ConnMgrMapURL(tchRemoteUrl, &guidNetworkObject, &dwIndex)
      == E_FAIL) {
   OutputDebugString(TEXT("Could not map the request to a
      network identifier"));
   return FALSE;
}

// Now that we've got the network address, set up the
// connection structure
CONNMGR_CONNECTIONINFO ccInfo;

memset(&ccInfo, 0, sizeof(CONNMGR_CONNECTIONINFO));
ccInfo.cbSize = sizeof(CONNMGR_CONNECTIONINFO);
ccInfo.dwParams = CONNMGR_PARAM_GUIDDESTNET;
ccInfo.dwPriority = CONNMGR_PRIORITY_USERINTERACTIVE;
ccInfo.guidDestNet = guidNetworkObject;

// Make the connection request
if(ConnMgrEstablishConnection(&ccInfo, &hConnection) ==
      E_FAIL)
   return FALSE;

// Poll to see if the connection has been established
BOOL fLoop = TRUE;
BOOL fConnected = FALSE;

while(fLoop) {
   dwStatus = 0;
   if(FAILED(ConnMgrConnectionStatus(hConnection,
         &dwStatus))) {
      // Do some error processing here
```

```
            fLoop = FALSE;
            break;
        }

        // Got the status, do something with it:
        if(dwStatus & CONNMGR_STATUS_CONNECTED) {
            OutputDebugString(TEXT("Connected!"));
            fLoop = FALSE;
            fConnected = TRUE;
            break;
        }

        if(dwStatus & CONNMGR_STATUS_WAITINGCONNECTION)
            OutputDebugString(TEXT("Establishing a
                connection...."));

        if(dwStatus & CONNMGR_STATUS_DISCONNECTED) {
            OutputDebugString(TEXT("Disconnected from the
                network...."));
            fLoop = FALSE;
        }
    }
}

// Release the handle gracefully
if(!fConnected && hConnection) {
    if(ConnMgrReleaseConnection(hConnection, FALSE) == S_OK)
        hConnection = NULL;
    return FALSE;
}

// Connection has been made, continue on...
```

Getting the Connection Status

To get the status of a Connection Manager connection, you can use the
ConnMgrConnectionStatus() function:

```
HRESULT WINAPI ConnMgrConnectionStatus(HANDLE hConnection,
    DWORD *pdwStatus);
```

The function needs only the handle to a current connection, and will
return the status code for it in the pointer specified by the pdwStatus
parameter.

Table 7.4 shows the possible status values that the Connection Manager can return.

Table 7.4 Connection Manager Status Values

Value	Description
CONNMGR_STATUS_UNKNOWN	Unknown.
CONNMGR_STATUS_CONNECTED	Connected.
CONNMGR_STATUS_DISCONNECTED	Disconnected.
CONNMGR_STATUS_CONNECTIONFAILED	Connection has failed and cannot be reestablished.
CONNMGR_STATUS_CONNECTIONCANCELED	User-aborted connection.
CONNMGR_STATUS_CONNECTIONDISABLED	Connection is ready to connect but disabled.
CONNMGR_STATUS_NOPATHTODESTINATION	No path could be found to the destination.
CONNMGR_STATUS_WAITINGFORPATH	Waiting for a path to the destination.
CONNMGR_STATUS_WAITINGFORPHONE	Voice call is in progress.
CONNMGR_STATUS_WAITINGCONNECTION	Attempting to connect.
CONNMGR_STATUS_WAITINGFORRESOURCE	Resource is in use by another connection.
CONNMGR_STATUS_WAITINGFORNETWORK	No path to the destination could be found.
CONNMGR_STATUS_WAITINGDISCONNECTION	Connection is being brought down.
CONNMGR_STATUS_WAITINGCONNECTIONABORT	Aborting connection attempt.

Connection Priorities

One of the Connection Manager's most useful features is its ability to juggle multiple requests, i.e., from more than one application at the same time. When making a connection request for your application, you are required to set its priority level (the dwPriority member of the CONNMGR_CONNECTIONINFO structure). This enables the Connection Manager to effectively schedule the order in which each request is processed—connection requests that have a higher priority are handled before those with a lower one.

Once a connection has been established, you can manually change its priority at any time by calling the ConnMgrSetConnection Priority() function:

```
HRESULT WINAPI ConnMgrSetConnectionPriority(HANDLE
    hConnection, DWORD dwPriority);
```

The first parameter is the request handle you were returned
from either the ConnMgrEstablishConnection() or ConnMgr
EstablishConnectionSync() function. This is followed by the new
priority level you want to set for the request. The list of possible values is
the same as the list for the dwPriority member of the CONNMGR_
CONNECTIONINFO structure.

A well-behaved application will change its connection priority based
on what the user is currently doing on the device. For example, if
an application is downloading a Web page, you would want to set the
connection to a high-priority level such as CONNMGR_PRIORITY_USER
INTERACTIVE. This provides users with a better experience, because
they expect an immediate response and high-priority requests are
favored by the Connection Manager. However, if a user switches to a
different application or is idle for an extended period of time, you will
want to switch the level to CONNMGR_PRIORITY_USER_IDLE. A lower
priority level enables other processes to more effectively share the connection.

The following code sample shows how to manually change the priority for a connection:

```
if(FAILED(ConnMgrSetConnectionPriority(hConnection,
    CONNMGR_PRIORITY_USERIDLE))) {
    OutputDebugString(TEXT("Could not change connection
        priority.."));
    return FALSE;
}
```

Disconnecting from an Active Connection

To close a connection request, you can simply call the following function:

```
HRESULT WINAPI ConnMgrReleaseConnection(HANDLE hConnection,
  BOOL bCache);
```

The hConnection parameter should be set to the current connection you want to release. If this is the last request handle that the Connection Manager has for the network type with which you are connected,
it will drop the connection; otherwise, it will be left open for any other

active requests. The `bCache` parameter should be set to `TRUE` if you want the Connection Manager to remember the connection in its cache; otherwise, you should set this to `FALSE`.

Connection Service Providers and Proxies

The Connection Manager uses what is known as a **Connection Service Provider** (**CSP**) to talk over a particular network. Each individual provider is a COM object that encapsulates the specifics for an individual network's communications. For example, there are currently CSPs for networking, proxy servers, VPNs, and GRPS connections—each providing specific instructions about how to talk over a network. When you request a network connection, the Connection Manager will determine which CSP to use based on the cost, latency, and bandwidth for the resource you are trying to access.

To exchange information with a CSP object, you can use the `Conn MgrProviderMessage()` API function:

```
HRESULT WINAPI ConnMgrProviderMessage(HANDLE hConnection,
    const GUID *pguidProvider, DWORD *pdwIndex, DWORD dwMsg1,
    DWORD dwMsg2, PBYTE pParams, ULONG cbParamSize);
```

The `hConnection` parameter is optional but can be set to a particular request handle if one is active. The next parameter, `pguid Provider`, should point to the GUID of the CSP to which you want to send a message. If multiple network providers are being used by a single connection, then you can set the `pdwIndex` pointer to the index of the specific provider to which the message should be sent. Both `dwMsg1` and `dwMsg2` are optional and have different meanings depending on the provider and message being sent. The `pParams` parameter should point to a data structure specific to the provider you are talking with, and is followed by `cbParamSize`, which should point to the size of the structure.

By this point, you are probably asking yourself why communicating with the provider interfaces is useful. One of the most common uses for sending a connection service provider a message is to obtain the proxy server configuration options for a particular communications request.

You can get proxy configuration information by passing a `PROXY_ CONFIG` structure to the network provider defined by `IID_ConnPrv_`

`IProxyExtension`. After the `ConnMgrProviderMessage()` function is called, the structure will be filled in with the requested information for the proxy type. The `PROXY_CONFIG` structure is defined as follows:

```
typedef struct _PROXY_CONFIG {
    DWORD dwType;
    DWORD dwEnable;
    TCHAR szProxyServer[CMPROXY_PROXYSERVER_MAXSIZE];
    TCHAR szUsername[CMPROXY_USERNAME_MAXSIZE];
    TCHAR szPassword[CMPROXY_PASSWORD_MAXSIZE];
    TCHAR szProxyOverride[CMPROXY_PROXYOVERRIDE_MAXSIZE];
    TCHAR szExtraInfo[CMPROXY_EXTRAINFO_MAXSIZE];
} PROXY_CONFIG;
```

The `dwType` member specifies the type of proxy server to use. It can be set to the following: `CONNMGR_FLAG_PROXY_HTTP` (for standard HTTP proxies), `CONNMGR_FLAG_PROXY_WAP` (for a WAP gateway), `CONNMGR_FLAG_PROXY_SOCKS4` (for a SOCKS 4.0 server), or `CONNMGR_FLAG_PROXY_SOCKS5` (for a SOCKS 5.0 server). This member should be set before calling the function.

The `dwEnable` member specifies whether the CSP should have the capability to connect to the specified proxy server. The CSP automatically sets this to 1, which enables the proxy server. If you set it to 0, then although the proxy configuration will exist, the CSP will not connect to the server.

The `szProxyServer` member specifies the server and port of the proxy. The correct syntax for setting this should be a null-terminated string that contains the server name, a colon, and the port number (for example, *server:port*).

The `szUsername` and `szPassword` members specify the authorization to be used when communicating with a SOCKS4 or SOCKS5 proxy server.

The `szProxyOverride` and `szExtraInfo` members are not currently used.

The following example shows how you could obtain the proxy information for a standard HTTP request:

```
// Get information on the proxy for an HTTP connection
// request
PROXY_CONFIG proxyConfig;
DWORD dwSize = sizeof(PROXY_CONFIG);
```

```
HRESULT hr = 0;
GUID IID_ConnPrv_IProxyExtension = {0xaf96b0bd, 0xa481,
   0x482c, {0xa0, 0x94, 0xa8, 0x44, 0x87, 0x67, 0xa0, 0xc0}};

memset(&proxyConfig, 0, sizeof(PROXY_CONFIG));
proxyConfig.dwType = CONNMGR_FLAG_PROXY_HTTP;

hr = ConnMgrProviderMessage(NULL, &IID_ConnPrv_IProxyExtension,
    NULL, 0, 0,
    (PBYTE)&proxyConfig, dwSize);

if(FAILED(hr)) {
   OutputDebugString(TEXT("Could not get the proxy
      information"));
   return FALSE;
}
```

Scheduled Connections

The Connection Manager also enables you to configure an event (at a specific time) that will cause the device to wake up (if not already on), establish a connection to a network, and run an application. This can be particularly useful if you want a network operation to do something when the user is not around his or her device. Note that a scheduled event will remain registered until it has run or is deleted. In addition, an event remains scheduled across device reboots.

To set up a scheduled connection, you can use the `ConnMgr RegisterScheduledConnection()` function, which is defined as follows:

```
HRESULT WINAPI ConnMgrRegisterScheduledConnection(
   SCHEDULEDCONNECTIONINFO *pSCI);
```

The only parameter that is needed is a pointer to a SCHEDULED CONNECTIONINFO structure:

```
typedef struct _SCHEDULEDCONNECTIONINFO {
   GUID guidDest;
   UINT64 uiStartTime;
   UINT64 uiEndTime;
```

```
    UINT64 uiPeriod;
    TCHAR szAppName[MAX_PATH];
    TCHAR szCmdLine[MAX_PATH];
    TCHAR szToken[32];
    BOOL bPiggyback;
} SCHEDULEDCONNECTIONINFO;
```

The `guidDest` member specifies the network identifier with which you want to create a connection. The next two members are used to set the start and end times for the connection. These should be set in the same format as the `FILETIME` structure, which specifies the amount of 100-nanosecond intervals since January 1, 1601.

The `uiPeriod` member is the amount of time (in 100-nanosecond units) between each connection attempt. If you set this to 0, the device will not wake up to make your connection.

The `szAppName` and `szCmdLine` members should point to the name of the application to run when the connection is made, and the command line that you want passed to the application, respectively.

The `szToken` member is a unique identifier that you can use to later delete the connection request.

Finally, the `bPiggypack` flag determines how the device should wake up for the event. If `bPiggyback` is set to `TRUE`, then the application specified by the `szAppName` parameter will execute as soon as the network connection to `guidDest` has been established. If it is set to `FALSE`, then the device will wake up only when another application or scheduled event connects to the same network.

The following code shows how you could schedule an application to run, 15 seconds from now. The scheduler will continue to attempt a connection every five minutes for the next hour:

```
// Get the network information where we want to establish a
// connection
GUID guidNetworkObject;
DWORD dwIndex = 0;
TCHAR tchRemoteUrl[256] = TEXT("\0");
wsprintf(tchRemoteUrl, TEXT("http://www.furrygoat.com/index.html"));

if(ConnMgrMapURL(tchRemoteUrl, &guidNetworkObject, &dwIndex)
        == E_FAIL) {
    OutputDebugString(TEXT("Could not map the request to a
        network identifier"));
```

```
      return FALSE;
   }

   // Get the time to launch
   SYSTEMTIME sysTime;
   FILETIME ftCurrent;
   ULARGE_INTEGER ulCurrentTime;

   GetLocalTime(&sysTime);
   SystemTimeToFileTime(&sysTime, &ftCurrent);

   ulCurrentTime.LowPart = ftCurrent.dwLowDateTime;
   ulCurrentTime.HighPart = ftCurrent.dwHighDateTime;

   // Set up the schedule times
   // In 15 seconds, let's try every 5 minutes for an hour
   DWORD dwSecStart = 15;
   DWORD dwSecDuration = 3600;
   DWORD dwSecPeriod = 300;

   // Schedule a connection
   SCHEDULEDCONNECTIONINFO sci;

   memset(&sci, 0, sizeof(SCHEDULEDCONNECTIONINFO));
   sci.uiStartTime =
      ulCurrentTime.QuadPart+(UINT64)(10*1000*1000)*dwSecStart;
   sci.uiEndTime = ulCurrentTime.QuadPart+(UINT64)(10*1000*1000)*
                  (dwSecStart+dwSecDuration);
   sci.uiPeriod = (UINT64)(10*1000*1000)*(dwSecPeriod);
   sci.guidDest = guidNetworkObject;
   sci.bPiggyback = TRUE;

   wsprintf(sci.szAppName, TEXT("\\Windows\\someapp.exe"));
   wsprintf(sci.szCmdLine, TEXT("\\Windows\\someapp.exe"));
   wsprintf(sci.szToken, TEXT("schdToken"));

   HRESULT hr = ConnMgrRegisterScheduledConnection(&sci);

   if(FAILED(hr)) {
      OutputDebugString(TEXT("Could not schedule the connection
         event"));
      return FALSE;
   }
```

To delete a scheduled connection, you can call the following function:

```
HRESULT WINAPI ConnMgrUnregisterScheduledConnection(LPCTSTR
  pwszToken);
```

The only parameter that you need to send is the unique token that identifies the scheduled connection, as shown in the following example:

```
if(SUCCEEDED(ConnMgrUnregisterScheduledConnection(TEXT
        ("schdToken")))) {
   OutputDebugString(TEXT("Scheduled event has been
        cancelled."));
}
```

CHAPTER 8

Pocket PC Phone Edition

Why does Radio Shack ask for your phone number when you buy batteries? I don't know.

—*Kramer*, Seinfeld

The **Pocket PC Phone Edition** is the latest addition to the Windows CE family of mobile devices. Besides providing all of the same applications and a similar user interface as the standard Pocket PC, the Phone Edition adds integrated wireless phone capabilities, as well as some new software (see Figure 8.1) and APIs to support them. Not only does the platform support the capability to make phone calls and perform messaging over the **Short Message Service** (**SMS**), it can also act as an integrated modem that enables users to access data networks whenever the device has cellular coverage. This creates an extremely interesting platform for development, as connectivity becomes more commonplace for the end user.

This chapter describes how to take advantage of the phone and messaging capabilities available on Pocket PC Phone Edition devices. It is divided into three main sections: the Phone API, the SIM Manager, and SMS Messaging.

Because the core platform supports the same networking and dial-up capabilities as the other Pocket PC devices, all of the techniques and APIs described in the previous chapters also work on the Phone Edition. Also recall that it is recommended that any applications you develop should use the Connection Manager APIs (see Chapter 7) to establish a connection to the network. This holds especially true on the Phone Edition because it uses a cellular data network, which is very prone to a variety of changing conditions as the device moves in and out of coverage range.

All of the tools you need to start developing applications for the Pocket PC Phone Edition are already included in the base Pocket PC SDK.

Figure 8.1 Pocket PC Phone Edition dialer

Phone API

Differences between the standard Pocket PC device and the Phone Edition include not only the latter's integrated data capabilities, but its functionality as a cell phone. As the name suggests, the **Phone API** is used to programmatically access the call information logs, call history, and core phone capabilities on a Pocket PC Phone Edition device. These functions enable you to query the statistics associated with both incoming and outgoing calls; make new phone calls; and get statistical information about a particular call, such as whether the call was roaming, the time connected, and caller ID information (see Figure 8.2).

Creating applications that access the Phone API should include the phone.h header file, and link with the phone.lib library.

Call History

Before you can make any queries regarding the device's phone history, you must first get the handle to the call log by using the PhoneOpen CallLog() function. This will also initialize an internal seek pointer for the log to the first entry. The function is defined as follows:

```
HRESULT PhoneOpenCallLog(HANDLE *ph);
```

Figure 8.2 Pocket PC Phone Edition call log

The function takes a single parameter—a pointer that contains the handle to the call log if it is opened and initialized successfully:

```
// Open Phone log
HANDLE hPhoneLog = NULL;
HRESULT hr = S_OK;

hr = PhoneOpenCallLog(&hPhoneLog);
if(FAILED(hr))
   return FALSE;

// Log opened, continue with application
```

Once the call log has successfully been opened, you can either start reading individual call log entries or search for a particular record. In addition, every time you read a log entry, the internal seek pointer is automatically advanced to the next one until it reaches the end of the log. This can be extremely useful when you just need to enumerate all of the calls in the call history, which are organized according to the time the call was started, with the most recent being returned first.

To read the current log entry, the Phone API provides the function `PhoneGetCallLogEntry()`:

```
HRESULT PhoneGetCallLogEntry(HANDLE h, PCALLLOGENTRY pentry);
```

The first parameter is the handle to the call log and is followed by a pointer to a CALLLOGENTRY structure that contains the actual call information. Remember that before you can call PhoneGetCallLog Entry(), you should set the cbSize member to the size of the CALL LOGENTRY structure.

The structure is defined as follows:

```
typedef struct{
    DWORD cbSize;
    FILETIME ftStartTime;
    FILETIME ftEndTime;
    IOM iom;
    BOOL fOutgoing;
    BOOL fConnected;
    BOOL fEnded;
    BOOL fRoam;
    CALLERIDTYPE cidt;
    PTSTR pszNumber;
    PTSTR pszName;
    PTSTR pszNameType;
    PTSTR pszNote;
} CALLLOGENTRY, *PCALLLOGENTRY;
```

The structure's first field, cbSize, must be set to the size of CALLLOGENTRY before calling the function. The next two fields, ftStartTime and ftEndTime, provide the start and end time details for the call. The next field, iom, specifies the type of call, which can be one of the following:

- IOM_MISSED, if the incoming call was not answered
- IOM_INCOMING, if the incoming call was answered
- IOM_OUTGOING, if the call is outgoing

The next four fields of CALLLOGENTRY provide basic call information: fOutgoing will be TRUE if the call is being made instead of received; fConnected will be TRUE if the call went through, or FALSE if there was a busy signal or no answer; fEnded will indicate if the call has ended; and fRoam will be FALSE if the call was made from the home calling area, as opposed to roaming coverage.

The cidt field contains details about caller ID information for the call, and can be one of the following:

- `CALLERIDTYPE_UNAVAILABLE`, if the caller ID information is not available
- `CALLERIDTYPE_BLOCKED`, if the caller ID type information was blocked
- `CALLERIDTYPE_AVAILABLE`, if the caller ID information is available

The last four fields contain contact information related to the call. The `pszNumber` field points to the phone number of the call, `pszName` points to the name associated with the call, `pszNameType` points to a single letter that represents the call type (such as "w" for work or "h" for home), and `pszNote` points to a filename of a note file (if one exists) associated with the call.

One word of caution: Once you have finished using the information that you received from a call to `PhoneGetCallLogEntry()`, you must call the `LocalFree()` function on any strings in the `CALLLOGENTRY` structure that are valid in order to properly release memory.

The following code shows the proper way to enumerate through all of the current phone log entries:

```
// Walk through all Phone log entries
CALLLOGENTRY phoneEntry;
TCHAR tchPhoneEntry[1024] = TEXT("\0");
TCHAR tchIOM[64] = TEXT("\0");
TCHAR tchFrom[128] = TEXT("\0");

do {
   // Clean up the structure
   memset(&phoneEntry, 0, sizeof(CALLLOGENTRY));
   memset(&tchPhoneEntry, 0, 1024);
   memset(&tchIOM, 0, 64);
   phoneEntry.cbSize = sizeof(CALLLOGENTRY);

   // Get the entry
   hr = PhoneGetCallLogEntry(hPhoneLog, &phoneEntry);
   if(FAILED(hr))
      break;

   // Have we reached the end of the log?
   if(hr == S_FALSE)
      break;
```

```
// Look at the phonebook data
switch(phoneEntry.iom) {
   case IOM_MISSED:
      wsprintf(tchIOM, TEXT("Missed Call"));
   break;
   case IOM_INCOMING:
      wsprintf(tchIOM, TEXT("Incoming Call"));
   break;
   case IOM_OUTGOING:
      wsprintf(tchIOM, TEXT("Missed Call"));
   break;
}

if(phoneEntry.pszName != NULL)
   _tcsncpy(tchFrom, phoneEntry.pszName, 128);
else if(phoneEntry.pszNumber != NULL)
   _tcsncpy(tchFrom, phoneEntry.pszNumber, 128);
else
   wsprintf(tchFrom, TEXT("Unknown"));

// Display a MessageBox to the user
SYSTEMTIME sysTime;

FileTimeToSystemTime(&phoneEntry.ftStartTime, &sysTime);
wsprintf(tchPhoneEntry, TEXT("%s from %s on %d-%d-%d"),
   tchIOM, tchFrom, sysTime.wDay, sysTime.wMonth,
   sysTime.wYear);
MessageBox(NULL, tchPhoneEntry, TEXT("Phone Log"), MB_OK |
   MB_ICONINFORMATION);

// Clean up any allocated strings
if(phoneEntry.pszNumber)
   LocalFree(phoneEntry.pszNumber);
if(phoneEntry.pszName)
   LocalFree(phoneEntry.pszName);
if(phoneEntry.pszNameType)
   LocalFree(phoneEntry.pszNameType);
if(phoneEntry.pszNote)
   LocalFree(phoneEntry.pszNote);

} while(1);
```

If you need to search the call log for a particular entry, you can move the current seek pointer to the beginning, end, or a particular log record by using the following API:

```
HRESULT PhoneSeekCallLog(HANDLE hdb, CALLLOGSEEK seek, DWORD
   iRecord, LPDWORD piRecord);
```

The first parameter is the handle to the call log returned from the original call to `PhoneOpenCallLog()`. The next parameter, `seek`, determines where the search should start, and should be set to either `CALLLOGSEEK_BEGINNING` to start from the beginning of the log, or `CALLLOGSEEK_END` to start from the end. The `iRecord` parameter is the zero-based index of the entry to search for, and will begin the search based on the value of the `seek` parameter. The last parameter, `piRecord`, is a pointer that will return the zero-based index value after the search is completed.

The following example moves the seek pointer to the beginning of the log:

```
DWORD dwRecord = 0;
HRESULT hr = PhoneSeekCallLog(hPhoneLog,
  CALLLOGSEEK_BEGINNING, 0, &dwRecord);
```

The next example reads the third entry from the beginning of the log:

```
DWORD dwRecord = 0;
HRESULT hr = PhoneSeekCallLog(hPhoneLog,
  CALLLOGSEEK_BEGINNING, 3, &dwRecord);
```

You can also use the `PhoneSeekCallLog()` function to determine how many entries are in the log by using the following code:

```
DWORD dwCallCount = 0;
HRESULT hr = PhoneSeekCallLog(hPhoneLog, CALLLOGSEEK_END, 0,
   &dwCallCount);
```

When you are finished querying data in the call history, you should release the handle by calling the following function:

```
HRESULT PhoneCloseCallLog(HANDLE h);
```

The only parameter that `PhoneCloseCallLog()` needs is the handle to the call log that was returned from the previous call to `Phone OpenCallLog()`:

```
if(hPhoneLog)
    PhoneCloseCallLog(hPhoneLog);
```

Making a Phone Call

To make a phone call using the Phone APIs, you can simply use the `PhoneMakeCall()` function, which is defined as follows:

```
LONG PhoneMakeCall(PHONEMAKECALLINFO *ppmci);
```

The only parameter that the function takes is a pointer to a `PHONEMAKECALLINFO` structure. This structure contains details about the call you are going to make:

```
typedef struct tagPHONEMAKECALLINFO{
    DWORD cbSize;
    DWORD dwFlags;
    PCWSTR pszDestAddress;
    PCWSTR pszAppName;
    PCWSTR pszCalledParty;
    PCWSTR pszComment;
} PHONEMAKECALLINFO, *PPHONEMAKECALLINFO;
```

The first member, `cbSize`, should be set to the size of the `PHONEMAKECALLINFO` structure. The next member is `dwFlags`, which should be set to `PMCF_DEFAULT` or `PMCF_PROMPTBEFORECALLING`, if you want to prompt the user to confirm that a phone call should be made.

You should place the null-terminated phone number that you want to call into the `pszDestAddress` member. Note that the validity of the phone number is not checked, so be especially careful before using the `PhoneMakeCall()` function to ensure that the number is correct. The `pszCalledParty` member can optionally be set to a null-terminated string that points to the name of the person you are calling. The remaining members, `pszAppName` and `pszComment`, are not used and should be set to `NULL`.

The following code shows how to use the `PhoneMakeCall()` function to place a phone call:

```
// Make a phone call
PHONEMAKECALLINFO phoneCall;
TCHAR tchPhoneNumber[64] = TEXT("\0");

memset(&phoneCall, 0, sizeof(PHONEMAKECALLINFO));
wsprintf(tchPhoneNumber, TEXT("5555551212"));

phoneCall.cbSize = sizeof(PHONEMAKECALLINFO);
phoneCall.dwFlags = PMCF_PROMPTBEFORECALLING; // Prompt
phoneCall.pszDestAddress = tchPhoneNumber;

if((PhoneMakeCall(&phoneCall) == 0))
   MessageBox(NULL, TEXT("Success!"), TEXT("Phone call
      attempt"), MB_OK|MB_ICONINFORMATION);
else
   MessageBox(NULL, TEXT("Failure!"), TEXT("Phone call
      attempt"), MB_OK|MB_ICONERROR);
```

SIM Manager

Every phone or data device that operates on the **GSM** (**Global System for Mobile**) network contains a small, postage stamp–sized card that is known as the **Subscriber Identity Module** (**SIM**). The SIM is actually a smart card that contains both a processor and storage for contacts, messages, and data. Typical SIM cards have between 16KB and 64KB of storage, which provides you with plenty of room for hundreds of phone numbers, messages, or other information.

You can usually remove the SIM card from the phone, which enables you to move your phone numbers, contacts, and other data between devices. For example, if you remove the SIM card from your GSM phone and place it into a Pocket PC Phone Edition device, the Pocket PC will have access to all of the dialing information, messages, and even phone numbers that the old device had. In essence, the SIM card is the storage medium for all of your personal and subscription data.

Pocket PC Phone Edition provides a set of functions called the **SIM Manager** (see Figure 8.3), which enables you to interact with the SIM card currently in the device. These APIs enable you to change the status of the phone locked state, manipulate contact entries that are on the SIM card, and read messages currently stored on the card.

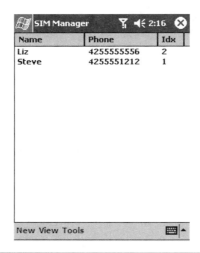

Figure 8.3 Pocket PC Phone Edition SIM Manager

In order to use the SIM Manager APIs in your applications, you need to include the `simmgr.h` header file in your project, and link with the `cellcore.lib` library.

Initialization and Notifications

Before you can access any information on the SIM card, you first must call the `SimInitialize()` function. This function actually has two purposes: One, it provides a handle to the SIM, which you will use for additional calls to get information from the card. Two, `SimInitialize()` can be used to register a callback function that will send you notifications whenever changes occur to the SIM while you have the handle open:

```
HRESULT SimInitialize(DWORD dwFlags, SIMCALLBACK
    lpfnCallBack, DWORD dwParam, LPHSIM lphSim);
```

The first parameter, `dwFlags`, specifies whether or not you want to receive notification messages from the SIM. By setting the flag to `SIM_INIT_SIMCARD_NOTIFICATIONS`, notifications will be sent to the callback function that is pointed to by the `lpfnCallback` parameter. If you do not need to receive informational messages from the SIM, you can set `dwFlags` to 0, and `lpfnCallBack` to NULL. The `dwParam` parameter is a `DWORD` value that is sent to your callback function every time a notification is sent. The last parameter, `lphSim`, is a pointer to an `HSIM` handle that you will use for making additional calls to the SIM card.

The following example initializes the SIM card for reading data without using a callback:

```
HRESULT hr = S_OK;
HSIM hSim = NULL;


// Initialize and open the SIM w/o a callback
hr = SimInitialize(0, NULL, 0, &hSim);
if(FAILED(hr)) {
   MessageBox(NULL, TEXT("Could not open the SIM"),
      TEXT("Error"), MB_OK|MB_ICONERROR);
   return FALSE;
}


// Continue with app...
```

If you decide to receive notifications from the SIM when changes occur, then you need to pass a pointer to a callback function (identified by the `lpfnCallBack` parameter). Whenever the device or another application attempts to modify the contents of the SIM card, your function will then be called. The callback function you create must have the following definition:

```
void SIMCallbackFunction(DWORD dwNotifyCode,
   const void *lpData, DWORD dwDataSize, DWORD dwParam);
```

The first parameter that will be sent to your function specifies the notification that was received from the SIM. Next, the contents of the `lpData` pointer will depend on which notification message you are receiving. For example, if you are sent a `SIM_NOTIFY_CARD_REMOVED`, then `lpData` will be `NULL`. However, if you received a `SIM_NOTIFY_PBE_DELETED` notification, `lpData` will point to a `SIMPBECHANGE` structure that provides additional information about the phonebook entry that has been modified.

Table 8.1 lists both the notification messages and the structure information sent to `lpData`.

Table 8.1 SIM Callback Notifications

Notification	lpData	Description
SIM_NOTIFY_ CARD_REMOVED	NULL	The SIM card has been removed.
SIM_NOTIFY_ FILE_REFRESH	SIMFILEREFRESH	Files on the SIM have been refreshed.
SIM_NOTIFY_ MSG_STORED	SIMMESSAGECHANGE	A message has been stored on the SIM.
SIM_NOTIFY_ MSG_DELETED	SIMMESSAGECHANGE	A message has been deleted from the SIM.
SIM_NOTIFY_ MSG_RECEIVED	SIMMESSAGECHANGE	A message was sent directly to the SIM.
SIM_NOTIFY_ PBE_STORED	SIMPBECHANGE	A phonebook entry has been stored on the SIM.
SIM_NOTIFY_ PBE_DELETED	SIMPBECHANGE	A phonebook entry has been deleted from the SIM.
SIM_NOTIFY_ RADIOOFF	NULL	The modem radio has been turned off.
SIM_NOTIFY_ RADIOON	NULL	The modem radio has been turned on.
SIM_NOTIFY_ RADIOPRESENT	DWORD	The modem radio has been installed. The DWORD value stored in lpData will indicate 0 if the radio is off, and 1 if it is on.
SIM_NOTIFY_ RADIOREMOVED	NULL	The modem radio has been removed.

The dwDataSize parameter will specify, in bytes, the size of the structure returned in lpData. The final parameter, dwParam, is the DWORD value that was previously set in your original call to the SimInitialize() function.

If any changes to the files on the SIM occur (SIM_NOTIFY_ FILE_REFRESH), your callback function will be passed a SIMFILERE FRESH structure that looks like the following:

```
typedef struct simfilerefresh_tag{
    DWORD cbSize;
    DWORD dwParams;
    DWORD dwFlags;
```

```
   DWORD dwFileCount;
   DWORD rgdwAddress[MAX_FILES];
} SIMFILEREFRESH, FAR *LPSIMFILEREFRESH;
```

The first field, cbSize, is the size, in bytes, of the SIMFILEREFRESH structure. Next, the dwParams field specifies which of the fields in the SIMFILEREFRESH structure are valid, and can be one or more of the following values:

- SIM_PARAM_FILEREFRESH_FLAGS indicates that the dwFlags field is valid.
- SIM_PARAM_FILEREFRESH_FILECOUNT indicates that the dwFileCount field is valid.
- SIM_PARAM_FILEREFRESH_FILEARRAY indicates that the rgdwAddress field is valid.
- SIM_PARAM_FILEREFRESH_ALL indicates that all the fields are valid.

The dwFlags field contains additional details about what has changed with regard to the SIM's file system, and can be one or more of the following:

- SIMFILE_FULLFILECHANGE specifies that all files have changed.
- SIMFILE_FILECHANGE specifies that only a few files have changed.
- SIMFILE_SIMINIT specifies that the SIM has been initialized.
- SIMFILE_SIMRESET specifies that the SIM has been reset.

The dwFileCount field, as the name implies, contains a DWORD value that indicates how many files have changed, and indicates the number of rgdwAddress structures in the array of files.

For example, the following code would handle a notification that some files have changed on the SIM:

```
// The SIM notification callback
void SimCallbackProc(DWORD dwNotifyCode, const void *lpData,
   DWORD dwDataSize, DWORD dwParam)
{
   // Handle a file change
   if(dwNotifyCode == SIM_NOTIFY_FILE_REFRESH) {
```

```
        SIMFILEREFRESH *pfileRefresh = (SIMFILEREFRESH *)lpData;
        TCHAR tchNotifyMessage[1024] = TEXT("\0");

        if(!pfileRefresh)
           return;

        // Handle the file change notification
        if(pfileRefresh->dwParams & SIM_PARAM_FILEREFRESH_FILECOUNT) {
           wsprintf(tchNotifyMessage, TEXT("%d files have
           changed"), pfileRefresh->dwFileCount);
           MessageBox(NULL, tchNotifyMessage, TEXT("SIM File
              Change"), MB_OK);
        }

        // Get the DWORD address of the SIM files that have changed
        // if(pfileRefresh->dwParams &
           SIM_PARAM_FILEREFRESH_FILEARRAY) {
           DWORD dwFiles = 0;
           for(dwFiles; dwFiles < pfileRefresh->dwFileCount;
              dwFiles++) {
              wsprintf(tchNotifyMessage, TEXT("File change
                 #%d. File address: %d"), dwFiles,
                 pfileRefresh->rgdwAddress[dwFiles]);
              MessageBox(NULL, tchNotifyMessage, TEXT("SIM
                 Files Change"), MB_OK);
           }
        }
     }
     return;
}


// Initialize the SIM
BOOL InitializeSIM(HSIM *phSim)
{
   HRESULT hr = S_OK;

   // Initialize and open the SIM w/ a callback
   hr = SimInitialize(SIM_INIT_SIMCARD_NOTIFICATIONS,
      (SIMCALLBACK)SimCallbackProc, 0, phSim);
```

```
    if(FAILED(hr)) {
       MessageBox(NULL, TEXT("Could not open the SIM"),
          TEXT("Error"), MB_OK|MB_ICONERROR);
       return FALSE;
    }


    return TRUE;
}
```

If the SIM detects any changes to a message located on the card (SIM_NOTIFY_MSG_STORED, SIM_NOTIFY_MSG_DELETED, or SIM_NOTIFY_MSG_RECIEVED), the callback function is passed a SIMMESSAGECHANGE structure, which is defined as follows:

```
typedef struct simmessagechange_tag{
    DWORD dwEntry;
    DWORD dwStorage;
} SIMMESSAGECHANGE, FAR *LPSIMMESSAGECHANGE;
```

This structure has only two fields: the index to the entry that has changed and its storage location. The dwStorage field will be set to the SIM_SMSSTORAGE_BROADCAST location if its storage location is with system broadcast messages; otherwise, it will be set to SIM_SMSSTORAGE_SIM.

Finally, the last type of notification you can receive deals with entries in SIM's phonebook (SIM_NOTIFY_PBE_STORED, SIM_NOTIFY_PBE_DELETED), and uses the SIMPBECHANGE structure:

```
typedef struct simpbechange_tag{
    DWORD dwEntry;
    DWORD dwStorage;
} SIMPBECHANGE, FAR *LPSIMPBECHANGE;
```

The first field is the index to the phonebook entry that has changed. The dwStorage field specifies the phonebook in which the entry is located, and can be one of the following values:

- SIM_PBSTORAGE_EMERGENCY, if the entry is located in the Emergency dial list
- SIM_PBSTORAGE_FIXEDDIALING, if the entry is in the SIM fixed dialing list

- SIM_PBSTORAGE_LASTDIALING, if the entry is in the SIM last dialing list
- SIM_PBSTORAGE_OWNNUMBERS, if the entry is in the SIM own-numbers list
- SIM_PBSTORAGE_SIM, if the entry is in the general SIM storage

The following code shows how to handle a notification message that indicates a change to one of the phonebook entries:

```
// The SIM notification callback
void SimCallbackProc(DWORD dwNotifyCode, const void *lpData,
    DWORD dwDataSize, DWORD dwParam)
{
    // Handle a phonebook change
    if(dwNotifyCode == SIM_NOTIFY_PBE_STORED ||
        dwNotifyCode == SIM_NOTIFY_PBE_DELETED) {
        SIMPBECHANGE *pPBNotify = (SIMPBECHANGE *)lpData;
        TCHAR tchNotifyMessage[1024] = TEXT("\0");
        TCHAR tchPhonebook[256] = TEXT("\0");

        if(!pPBNotify)
            return;

        switch(pPBNotify->dwStorage) {
            case SIM_PBSTORAGE_EMERGENCY:
                wsprintf(tchPhonebook, TEXT("Emergency Number List"));
                break;
            case SIM_PBSTORAGE_FIXEDDIALING:
                wsprintf(tchPhonebook, TEXT("Fixed Dialing List"));
                break;
            case SIM_PBSTORAGE_LASTDIALING:
                wsprintf(tchPhonebook, TEXT("Last Numbered
                    Dialed List"));
                break;
            case SIM_PBSTORAGE_OWNNUMBERS:
                wsprintf(tchPhonebook, TEXT("Own Number List"));
                break;
            case SIM_PBSTORAGE_SIM:
                wsprintf(tchPhonebook, TEXT("General List"));
                break;
```

```
        default:
            wsprintf(tchPhonebook, TEXT("Unknown List"));
            break;
    }

    // Build a message
    wsprintf(tchNotifyMessage, TEXT("A phonebook entry in
        the %s at index %d has been "), tchPhonebook,
        pPBNotify->dwEntry);

    // Type of notification
    if(dwNotifyCode == SIM_NOTIFY_PBE_DELETED)
        _tcscat(tchNotifyMessage, TEXT("deleted."));
    else if(dwNotifyCode == SIM_NOTIFY_PBE_STORED)
        _tcscat(tchNotifyMessage, TEXT("modified."));
    }

    return;
}
```

When you are finished working with information on the SIM, you can simply call the `SimDeinitialize()` function, which is defined as follows:

```
HRESULT SimDeinitialize(HSIM hSim);
```

The only parameter that the function needs is a handle to the SIM module that was previously returned by the original call to `SimInitialize()`.

The following code sample shows how to properly release the handle to the SIM module:

```
// Close the SIM handle
if(hSim)
    SimDeinitialize(hSim);
```

SIM Details

To get more information about what functionality the SIM supports, you can use the following function:

```
HRESULT SimGetDevCaps(HSIM hSim, DWORD dwCapsType, LPSIMCAPS
    lpSimCaps);
```

This function can be used to query specific capabilities of the SIM by functional area, or to return information about the phonebook or locking passwords. To use it, you need to pass the handle to the SIM that was returned from a previous call to `SimInitialize()` in the `hSim` parameter. The `dwCapsType` parameter can be used to set which capabilities you are interested in, and can be one or more of the following values:

- `SIM_CAPSTYPE_PBENTRYLENGTH`, to query phonebook entry lengths
- `SIM_CAPSTYPE_PBSTORELOCATIONS`, to query phonebook storage locations
- `SIM_CAPSTYPE_LOCKFACILITIES`, to query the available Lock facilities
- `SIM_CAPSTYPE_PBINDEXRANGE`, to query valid phonebook entry indexes
- `SIM_CAPSTYPE_LOCKINGPWDLENGTHS`, to query the Locking password lengths
- `SIM_CAPSTYPE_MSGMEMORYLOCATIONS`, to query Message memory locations
- `SIM_CAPSTYPE_ALL`, to query all of the SIM capabilities

The last parameter, `lpSimCaps`, should point to a `SIMCAPS` structure that will receive the capabilities specified in the `dwCapsType` parameter. The structure is defined as follows:

```
typedef struct simcaps_tag{
    DWORD cbSize;
    DWORD dwParams;
    DWORD dwPBStorages;
    DWORD dwMinPBIndex;
    DWORD dwMaxPBIndex;
    DWORD dwMaxPBEAddressLength;
    DWORD dwMaxPBETextLength;
    DWORD dwLockFacilities;
    DWORD dwReadMsgStorages;
    DWORD dwWriteMsgStorages;
    DWORD dwNumLockingPwdLengths;
    SIMLOCKINGPWDLENGTH rgLockingPwdLengths[SIM_NUMLOCKFACILITIES];
} SIMCAPS, FAR *LPSIMCAPS;
```

The `cbSize` field must be set to the size of the `SIMCAPS` structure before calling the `SimGetDevCaps()` function. The `dwParams` field indicates what other fields in the structure contain data, and can be set to one or more of the values described in Table 8.2.

Table 8.2 SIM Device Capabilities Parameters

Value	Valid Fields
SIM_PARAM_CAPS_PBSTORAGES	`dwPBStorages` is valid.
SIM_PARAM_CAPS_PBEMAXADDRESSLENGTH	`dwMaxPBEAddressLength` is valid.
SIM_PARAM_CAPS_PBEMAXTEXTLENGTH	`dwMaxPBETextLength` is valid.
SIM_PARAM_CAPS_PBEMININDEX	`dwMinPBIndex` is valid.
SIM_PARAM_CAPS_PBEMAXINDEX	`dwMaxPBIndex` is valid.
SIM_PARAM_CAPS_LOCKFACILITIES	`dwLockFacilities` is valid.
SIM_PARAM_CAPS_LOCKINGPWDLENGTH	`dwNumLockingPwdLengths` and `rgLockingPwdLengths` are valid.
SIM_PARAM_CAPS_READMSGSTORAGES	`dwReadMsgStorages` is valid.
SIM_PARAM_CAPS_WRITEMSGSTORAGES	`dwWriteMsgStorages` is valid.
SIM_PARAM_CAPS_ALL	All fields are valid.

The `dwPBStorages`, `dwMinPBIndex`, and `dwMaxPBIndex` fields contain the total number (as well as the minimum and maximum number) of entries that are available for the SIM card's phonebook. The maximum length of an address is stored in the `dwMaxPBEAddressLength` field; and `dwMaxPBETextLength` will contain the maximum length for any text string in an entry.

The `dwReadMsgStorages` and `dwWriteMsgStorages` fields pertain to the total number of read and write storage areas that are available on the SIM, respectively.

The last set of available fields deals with the locking capabilities of the SIM card. The `dwLockFacilities` field contains the total number of supported locking facilities that are available on the SIM. Each of these is described in the array of `SIMLOCKINGPWDLENGTH` structures specified by the `rgLockingPwdLengths` field. The `SIMLOCKING PWDLENGTH` structure contains information about the locking facility index and its maximum password length, and has the following prototype:

```
typedef struct simlockingpwdlength{
    DWORD dwFacility;
```

```
      DWORD dwPasswordLength;
} SIMLOCKINGPWDLENGTH, FAR *LPSIMLOCKINGPWDLENGTH;
```

The following example queries the available capabilities of a SIM card:

```
// Get the SIM capabilities
SIMCAPS simInfo;

memset(&simInfo, 0, sizeof(SIMCAPS));
simInfo.cbSize = sizeof(SIMCAPS);

hr = SimGetDevCaps(hSim, SIM_CAPSTYPE_ALL, &simInfo);
if(FAILED(hr)) {
   SimDeinitialize(hSim);
   MessageBox(NULL, TEXT("Could not query the SIM module"),
      TEXT("Error"), MB_OK|MB_ICONERROR);
   return FALSE;
}
```

To get the status of an SMS storage location, you can call the following function:

```
HRESULT SimGetSmsStorageStatus(HSIM hSim, DWORD dwStorage,
   LPDWORD lpdwUsed, LPDWORD lpdwTotal);
```

The first parameter is the previously opened handle to the SIM card, and is followed by dwStorage, which should indicate which storage location on the SIM to query. This can be set to either the SIM_SMSSTORAGE_BROADCAST location for the broadcast message location or SIM_SMSSTORAGE_SIM, for the general storage location.

The lpdwUsed parameter should point to a DWORD value that will receive the number of locations that are used, and lpdwTotal is the total number of locations available.

The following example shows how you can use SimGetSms StorageStatus() to query the storage locations on the SIM:

```
// Get the SIM general storage usage
DWORD dwUsed = 0, dwTotal = 0;
TCHAR tchStorage[1024] = TEXT("\0");

hr = SimGetSmsStorageStatus(hSim, SIM_SMSSTORAGE_SIM,
  &dwUsed, &dwTotal);
```

```
if(FAILED(hr))
   MessageBox(NULL, TEXT("Could not get general storage
      information"), TEXT("Error"), MB_OK|MB_ICONERROR);
else {
   wsprintf(tchStorage, TEXT("General SIM Storage:\r\n%d
      Used\r\n%d Free\r\n%d Total"), dwUsed, dwTotal-dwUsed,
      dwTotal);
   MessageBox(NULL, tchStorage, TEXT("SIM Usage"),
      MB_OK|MB_ICONINFORMATION);
}

// Get the SIM broadcast storage usage
dwUsed = dwTotal = 0;
hr = SimGetSmsStorageStatus(hSim, SIM_SMSSTORAGE_BROADCAST,
   &dwUsed, &dwTotal);

if(FAILED(hr))
   MessageBox(NULL, TEXT("Could not get broadcast storage
      information"), TEXT("Error"), MB_OK|MB_ICONERROR);
else {
   wsprintf(tchStorage, TEXT("General SIM Storage:\r\n%d
      Used\r\n%d Free\r\n%d Total"), dwUsed, dwTotal-dwUsed,
      dwTotal);
   MessageBox(NULL, tchStorage, TEXT("SIM Broadcast Usage"),
      MB_OK|MB_ICONINFORMATION);
}
```

The SIM Phonebook

Before you start reading and writing entries to the SIM phonebooks, let's first examine how to obtain the number of entries in a particular phonebook location (such as the Emergency dial list). To do so, you can call the following function:

```
HRESULT SimGetPhonebookStatus(HSIM hSim, DWORD dwLocation,
   LPDWORD lpdwUsed, LPDWORD lpdwTotal);
```

The first parameter is the previously opened handle to the SIM card, and is followed by dwLocation, which indicates what phonebook on the SIM to query. This should be set to one of the following: SIM_PBSTORAGE_EMERGENCY, SIM_PBSTORAGE_FIXEDDIALING,

SIM_PBSTORAGE_LASTDIALING, SIM_PBSTORAGE_OWNNUMBERS, or SIM_PBSTORAGE_SIM.

The lpdwUsed parameter should point to a DWORD value that will receive the number of entries used in the specified phonebook. The last parameter, lpdwTotal, is the total number of entry "slots" that are available for the phonebook.

The following example shows how you can use SimGetPhone bookStatus() to retrieve the number of entries in the Emergency phonebook:

```
// Get phonebook status
DWORD dwUsed = 0, dwTotal = 0;
TCHAR tchPhonebook[1024] = TEXT("\0");
hr = SimGetPhonebookStatus(hSim, SIM_PBSTORAGE_EMERGENCY,
   &dwUsed, &dwTotal);

if(FAILED(hr))
   MessageBox(NULL, TEXT("Could not get Emergency Phonebook
      information"), TEXT("Error"), MB_OK|MB_ICONERROR);
else {
   wsprintf(tchPhonebook, TEXT("Phonebook Usage:\r\n%d
      Used\r\n%d Free\r\n%d Total"), dwUsed, dwTotal-dwUsed,
      dwTotal);
   MessageBox(NULL, tchPhonebook, TEXT("SIM Emergency Phonebook"),
      MB_OK|MB_ICONINFORMATION);
}
```

To read and write entries from the SIM phonebook, you use the following two functions:

```
HRESULT SimReadPhonebookEntry(HSIM hSim, DWORD dwLocation,
   DWORD dwIndex, LPSIMPHONEBOOKENTRY lpPhonebookEntry);
```

and

```
HRESULT SimWritePhonebookEntry(HSIM hSim, DWORD dwLocation,
   DWORD dwIndex, LPSIMPHONEBOOKENTRY lpPhonebookEntry);
```

Both functions take the same four parameters: the hSim parameter should be the handle to the device's SIM card, dwLocation should be set to one of the phonebook locations (such as SIM_PBSTORAGE_ EMERGENCY), and the dwIndex parameter should be the index of the entry to write or read.

The lpPhonebookEntry parameter points to a SIMPHONE BOOKENTRY structure that contains information about the phonebook entry. If you are using the SimWritePhonebookEntry() function, the entry will be saved to the location specified by the dwLocation parameter. When reading an entry, the structure will be filled with the data from the SIM.

The structure used for a phonebook entry is defined as follows:

```
typedef struct simphonebookentry_tag{
    DWORD cbSize;
    DWORD dwParams;
    TCHAR lpszAddress[MAX_LENGTH_ADDRESS];
    DWORD dwAddressType;
    DWORD dwNumPlan;
    TCHAR lpszText[MAX_LENGTH_PHONEBOOKENTRYTEXT];
} SIMPHONEBOOKENTRY, *LPSIMPHONEBOOKENTRY;
```

The first field, cbSize, should be set to the size of the SIMPHONE BOOKENTRY structure before calling either the SimReadPhone bookEntry() or SimWritePhonebookEntry() functions. The dwParams field will indicate which of the fields in the structure contain valid data, and can be one or more of the values in Table 8.3.

Table 8.3 SIM Phonebook Entry Flags

Value	Valid Fields
SIM_PARAM_PBE_ADDRESS	The lpszAddress field is valid.
SIM_PARAM_PBE_ADDRESS_TYPE	The dwAddressType field is valid.
SIM_PARAM_PBE_NUMPLAN	The dwNumPlan field is valid.
SIM_PARAM_PBE_TEXT	The lpszText field is valid.
SIM_PARAM_PBE_ALL	All fields are valid.

The entry's phone number is stored as a null-terminated string in the lpszAddress field. Details about what type of number the entry is will be indicated by using one of the flags in Table 8.4 in the dwAddressType field.

Table 8.4 SIM Phonebook Address Types

Value	Description
SIM_ADDRTYPE_UNKNOWN	Unknown address type.
SIM_ADDRTYPE_INTERNATIONAL	International number. Note that numbers stored as international should be prefixed with a plus (+) sign before being displayed to the user.
SIM_ADDRTYPE_NATIONAL	National number.
SIM_ADDRTYPE_NETWKSPECIFIC	Network-specific number.
SIM_ADDRTYPE_SUBSCRIBER	Protocol-specific subscriber number.
SIM_ADDRTYPE_ALPHANUM	Alphanumeric number.
SIM_ADDRTYPE_ABBREV	Abbreviated number.

If the entry is a SIM_ADDRTYPE_UNKNOWN, SIM_ADDRTYPE_INTERNATIONAL, or SIM_ADDRTYPE_NATIONAL address type, the dwNumPlan field will provide additional information about the numbering plan (i.e., the format) used for the address. It can be one of the following:

- SIM_NUMPLAN_UNKNOWN specifies that the numbering plan is unknown.
- SIM_NUMPLAN_TELEPHONE specifies that a standard telephone or ISDN numbering plan (E.164/E.163) is used.
- SIM_NUMPLAN_DATA specifies an X.121 data numbering plan.
- SIM_NUMPLAN_TELEX specifies a Telex numbering plan.
- SIM_NUMPLAN_NATIONAL specifies a national numbering plan.
- SIM_NUMPLAN_PRIVATE specifies a private numbering plan.
- SIM_NUMPLAN_ERMES specifies that an ERMES (ETSI DE/PS 3 01-3) numbering plan is used.

Finally, the lpszText field contains a null-terminated string that contains any text associated with this entry.

The following code reads the first phonebook entry from the general SIM phonebook:

```
SIMPHONEBOOKENTRY simPhoneEntry;
memset(&simPhoneEntry, 0, sizeof(SIMPHONEBOOKENTRY));
```

```
simPhoneEntry.cbSize = sizeof(SIMPHONEBOOKENTRY);
hr = SimReadPhonebookEntry(hSim, SIM_PBSTORAGE_SIM, 1,
   &simPhoneEntry);

if(FAILED(hr)) {
   MessageBox(NULL, TEXT("Could not read phonebook entry"),
      TEXT("Error"), MB_OK|MB_ICONERROR);
   return FALSE;
}

// Process entry here
```

If you need to write an entry to the phonebook, you can use the following:

```
// Write a phonebook entry to the SIM
SIMPHONEBOOKENTRY simPhoneEntry;
memset(&simPhoneEntry, 0, sizeof(SIMPHONEBOOKENTRY));

simPhoneEntry.cbSize = sizeof(SIMPHONEBOOKENTRY);
simPhoneEntry.dwParams = SIM_PARAM_PBE_ALL;
simPhoneEntry.dwAddressType = SIM_ADDRTYPE_NATIONAL;
simPhoneEntry.dwNumPlan = SIM_NUMPLAN_TELEPHONE;
wsprintf(simPhoneEntry.lpszAddress, TEXT("5555551212"));
wsprintf(simPhoneEntry.lpszText, TEXT("Jeremy"));

hr = SimWritePhonebookEntry(hSim, SIM_PBSTORAGE_SIM, 3,
   &simPhoneEntry);

if(FAILED(hr))
   MessageBox(NULL, TEXT("Could not write new phonebook
      entry"), TEXT("Error"), MB_OK|MB_ICONERROR);
else
   MessageBox(NULL, TEXT("New entry added successfully"),
      TEXT("SIM Write"), MB_OK);
```

Finally, to delete a phonebook entry from the SIM card, you can use the `SimDeletePhonebookEntry()` function, which is defined as follows:

```
HRESULT SimDeletePhonebookEntry(HSIM hSim, DWORD dwLocation,
   DWORD dwIndex);
```

The only parameters that the function needs are the handle to the SIM card, the phonebook location, and the index to the entry to delete.

The following short code sample shows how you can delete a SIM phonebook entry:

```
hr = SimDeletePhonebookEntry(hSim, SIM_PBSTORAGE_SIM, 3);
if(FAILED(hr))
    MessageBox(NULL, TEXT("Could not delete entry"),
        TEXT("Error"), MB_OK|MB_ICONERROR);
else
    MessageBox(NULL, TEXT("Entry deleted."), TEXT("SIM
        Delete"), MB_OK);
```

Working with SIM-Based Messages

To read or write a Short Message Service text message in a specific storage location on the SIM, you can call the following two functions:

```
HRESULT SimReadMessage(HSIM hSim, DWORD dwStorage, DWORD
    dwIndex, LPSIMMESSAGE lpSimMessage);
```

and

```
HRESULT SimWriteMessage(HSIM hSim, DWORD dwStorage, LPDWORD
    lpdwIndex, LPSIMMESSAGE lpSimMessage);
```

Both of these functions need an open handle to the SIM card, as well as a storage location (either SIM_SMSSTORAGE_BROADCAST or SIM_SMSSTORAGE_SIM) as the first two parameters. When you are reading a message from the SIM, the third parameter, dwIndex, should be set to the index of the message you want to read. If you are writing a message, lpdwIndex will point to a DWORD value that receives the index of the message that was written when you called SimWriteMessage().

The last parameter is a pointer to a SIMMESSAGE structure. When reading a message, this structure's fields will be filled in with the contents of the message you specify with the dwIndex parameter. If you are writing a message, you should fill in the structure with the details of the message you want to save.

The SIMMESSAGE structure is defined as follows:

```
typedef struct simmessage_tag{
    DWORD cbSize;
    DWORD dwParams;
    TCHAR lpszAddress[MAX_LENGTH_ADDRESS];
    DWORD dwAddressType;
    DWORD dwNumPlan;
    SYSTEMTIME stReceiveTime;
    DWORD cbHdrLength;
    BYTE rgbHeader[MAX_LENGTH_HEADER];
    TCHAR lpszMessage[MAX_LENGTH_MESSAGE];
} SIMMESSAGE, FAR *LPSIMMESSAGE;
```

The first field, cbSize, should be set to the size of the SIMMESSAGE structure before calling either the SimReadMessage() or SimWrite Message() functions. The dwParams field will indicate which of the fields in the structure contain valid data, and can be set to one or more of the values in Table 8.5.

Table 8.5 SIM Message Parameters

Value	Valid Fields
SIM_PARAM_MSG_ADDRESS	The lpszAddress field is valid.
SIM_PARAM_MSG_ADDRESS_TYPE	The lpszAddressType field is valid.
SIM_PARAM_MSG_NUMPLAN	The dwNumPlan field is valid.
SIM_PARAM_MSG_RECEIVE_TIME	The stReceiveTime field is valid.
SIM_PARAM_MSG_HEADER	The rgbHeader field is valid.
SIM_PARAM_MSG_HEADER_LENGTH	The cbHdrLength field is valid.
SIM_PARAM_MSG_MESSAGE	The lpszMessage field is valid.
SIM_PARAM_PBE_ALL	All fields are valid.

The incoming message address and numbering plan information fields are similar to those described for SIM phonebook entries.

The stReceiveTime field will contain a SYSTEMTIME structure that contains the timestamp for the incoming message. The message header is stored in rgbHeader, and its length is specified by the cbHdrLength field.

The actual message body is stored in lpszMessage.

To delete a message from the SIM, you can use the `SimDelete Message()` function. This function needs a handle to the open a SIM card, a storage location (either `SIM_SMSSTORAGE_BROADCAST` or `SIM_SMSSTORAGE_SIM`), and the index of the message to delete. The function is defined as follows:

```
HRESULT SimDeleteMessage(HSIM hSim, DWORD dwStorage, DWORD
  dwIndex);
```

The SIM File System

Recall that the Subscriber Identity Module (SIM) card not only contains your phonebook and text messages, but is actually a smart card containing a processor and a file system. The file system that a SIM card uses is based on the ISO-7816 standard for smart card devices, and is fully specified by the GSM 11.11 standard (more information about both standards can be downloaded from http://www.etsi.org).

Although the file system on the SIM card is analogous to that of a file system on the desktop or Pocket PC device (you can read, write, or delete files), there are a few subtle differences:

- The root level of the file system is known as the **Master file**.
- Directories are known as **Dedicated files** and are of a fixed size.
- Individual records (or files) are known as **Elementary files**.
- All files are identified as an address (a `DWORD` value), rather than a filename.
- Before you can read from or write to a particular file in the SIM file system, you must first get information about the record.

Figure 8.4 shows the basic tree structure of the SIM file system.

The most noticeable difference between a regular file system (typically found on a PC) and the SIM file system (besides basic terminology) is that each file in the latter has a four-byte file identifier that uniquely identifies it, rather than a filename.

File identifiers are constructed in the following manner on a GSM SIM card. The first two bytes are used to identify the type of file:

- 3F Master file (file system root)
- 7F Dedicated file (a directory)
- 2F Elementary file underneath the Master file
- 6F Elementary file underneath the Dedicated file

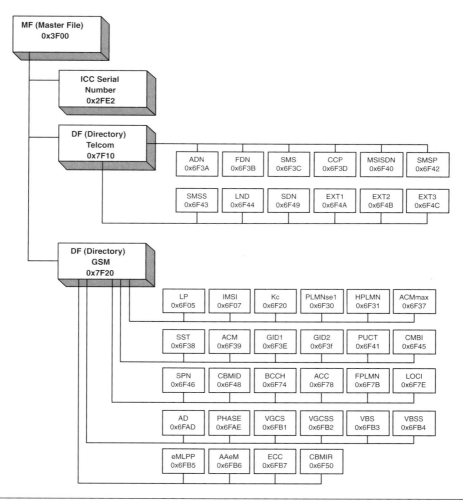

Figure 8.4 SIM card file system structure

The second two bytes are a unique identifier for the file, and are subject to the following rules:

- The file ID is created at the time of file creation.
- No two files can have the same identifier under the same parent.
- A child and a parent shall never have the same identifier.

Table 8.6 describes the different record types that the SIM card file system can store.

Table 8.6 SIM File Types

File Type	Description
Transparent	A random access file that can contain any type of data.
Linear Fixed File	A fixed-length record that can be navigated through by using next, first, last, and so on. The SIM phonebook is an example of records that are Linear Fixed.
Cyclic	A fixed-length set of records that will loop to the first entry after the last entry is read; they are stored in chronological order. The "last number dialed" list is an example of records that are Cyclic.
Variable-length records	Not supported.
Incremental	A single-byte record that can be incremented or decremented by one.

Every SIM card that is provisioned with a Pocket PC Phone Edition device already contains several required files that are needed in order to maintain compatibility with the GSM protocol. Although most of these records are marked as read-only by your wireless carrier, they contain a lot of useful information that can be used in your own applications.

Table 8.7 describes the files located in the GSM SIM file system (more detailed information about each file can also be found in the GSM 11.11 specification).

Table 8.7 The GSM File System

Name	Address (ID)	Level	Type	Description
ICC-ID	0x2FE2	Master	Transparent	ICC card serial number
GSM	0x7F20	N/A	N/A	Directory for GSM files
LP	0x6F05	Application	Transparent	Language preference
IMSI	0x6F07	Application	Transparent	International Mobile Subscriber Identity (IMSI)
KC	0x6F20	Application	Transparent	Ciphering key
PLMN	0x6F30	Application	Transparent	PLMN Selector
HPLMN	0x6F31	Application	Transparent	HPLMN search interval time
ACMMAX	0x6F37	Application	Transparent	Accumulated call meter maximum
SST	0x6F38	Application	Transparent	SIM service table
ACM	0x6F39	Application	Cyclic	Accumulated call meter
GID1	0x6F3E	Application	Transparent	Group Identifier Level 1
GID2	0x6F3F	Application	Transparent	Group Identifier Level 2

Name	Address (ID)	Level	Type	Description
SPN	0x6F46	Application	Transparent	Service provider name
PUCT	0x6F41	Application	Transparent	Price per unit and currency table
CBMI	0x6F45	Application	Transparent	Cell Broadcast Message Identifier selection
CBMID	0x6F48	Application	Transparent	Cell Broadcast Message Identifier for Data Download
CBMIR	0x6F50	Application	Transparent	Cell Broadcast Message Identifier
BCCH	0x6F74	Application	Transparent	Broadcast control channels
ACC	0x6F78	Application	Transparent	Access control class
FPLMN	0x6F7B	Application	Transparent	Forbidden PLMNs
LOCI	0x6F7E	Application	Transparent	Location information
AD	0x6FAD	Application	Transparent	Administrative data
PHASE	0x6FAE	Application	Transparent	Phase identification
VGCS	0x6FB1	Application	Transparent	Voice Group Call Service
VGCSS	0x6FB2	Application	Transparent	Voice Group Call Service status
VBS	0x6FB3	Application	Transparent	Voice Broadcast Service
VBSS	0x6FB4	Application	Transparent	Voice Broadcast Service Status
eMLPP	0x6FB5	Application	Transparent	Enhanced Multi-Level Preemption and Priority
AAeM	0x6FB6	Application	Transparent	Automatic Answer for eMLPP Service
ECC	0x6FB7	Application	Transparent	Emergency Call Codes
Telcom	0x7F10	N/A	N/A	Directory for Telcom files
ADN	0x6F3A	Telcom	Linear Fixed	Abbreviated dialing numbers
FDN	0x6F3B	Telcom	Linear Fixed	Fixed dialing numbers
SMS	0x6F3C	Telcom	Linear Fixed	Short messages
CCP	0x6F3D	Telcom	Linear Fixed	Capability configuration parameters
MSISDN	0x6F40	Telcom	Linear Fixed	MSISDN
SMSP	0x6F42	Telcom	Linear Fixed	Short message service parameters
SMSS	0x6F43	Telcom	Transparent	Short message service status
LND	0x6F44	Telcom	Cyclic	Last number dialed
SDN	0x6F49	Telcom	Linear Fixed	Service Dialing Numbers
EXT1	0x6F4A	Telcom	Linear Fixed	Extension 1
EXT2	0x6F4B	Telcom	Linear Fixed	Extension 2
EXT3	0x6F4C	Telcom	Linear Fixed	Extension 3

Reading and Writing Records

Now that you have a general idea about how the SIM file system is laid out, you can examine what is required to read and write records.

Before you can read the contents of an actual record, you must first get information from the SIM about the record—such as the type of file it is, the buffer length you need to allocate, and so on. To do so, you can use the `SimGetRecordInfo()` function, which is defined as follows:

```
HRESULT SimGetRecordInfo(HSIM hSim, DWORD dwAddress,
    LPSIMRECORDINFO lpSimRecordInfo);
```

The first parameter for this function is the handle to the open SIM card that you previously received from your call to `SimInitialize()`. The `dwAddress` parameter is the file identifier of the record you want to open (in Table 8.7, for example, the SIM card serial number would have the file address of 0x2FE2).

The last parameter should point to a `SIMRECORDINFO` structure. After the function returns, the structure will contain information about the record that will enable you to read the record's contents.

The `SIMRECORDINFO` structure looks like the following:

```
typedef struct simrecordinfo_tag{
    DWORD cbSize;
    DWORD dwParams;
    DWORD dwRecordType;
    DWORD dwItemCount;
    DWORD dwSize;
} SIMRECORDINFO, FAR *LPSIMRECORDINFO;
```

The first field, `cbSize`, should be set to the size of a `SIMRECORDINFO` structure before calling the `SimGetRecordInfo()` function. The `dwParams` field will indicate which of the remaining fields of the structure contain valid data, as described in Table 8.8.

Table 8.8 SIM Record Parameters

Value	Valid Fields
SIM_PARAM_RECORDINFO_RECORDTYPE	The `dwRecordType` field is valid.
SIM_PARAM_RECORDINFO_ITEMCOUNT	The `dwItemCount` field is valid.
SIM_PARAM_RECORDINFO_SIZE	The `dwSize` field is valid.
SIM_PARAM_RECORDINFO_ALL	All fields are valid.

The dwRecordType field indicates the type of record for which you are requesting information, and can be one of the following values:

- SIM_RECORDTYPE_UNKNOWN, if the record is an unknown file type
- SIM_RECORDTYPE_TRANSPARENT, if the record is a single-variable-length record set
- SIM_RECORDTYPE_CYCLIC, if the record is a Cyclic set of records, each of the same length
- SIM_RECORDTYPE_LINEAR, if the record is a Linear set of records, each of the same length
- SIM_RECORDTYPE_MASTER, if the record is the Master record (root) of the file system
- SIM_RECORDTYPE_DEDICATED, if the record is a parent of other records (a directory)

The dwItemCount field specifies the number of items in the record, and is typically used with records that are either SIM_RECORDTYPE_CYCLIC or SIM_RECORDTYPE_LINEAR. The last field, dwSize, is the size, in bytes, of each item.

The following example reads the record information for the IMSI (or subscriber identity 0x6F07) from the SIM:

```
// Read from the SIM file system
SIMRECORDINFO srecordInfo;
DWORD dwIMSIAddress = 0x6f07;

memset(&srecordInfo, 0, sizeof(SIMRECORDINFO));
srecordInfo.cbSize = sizeof(SIMRECORDINFO);

hr = SimGetRecordInfo(hSim, dwIMSIAddress, &srecordInfo);
if(FAILED(hr))
   MessageBox(NULL, TEXT("Could not read from SIM file
      system"), TEXT("Error"), MB_OK|MB_ICONERROR);

// Continue to read record...
```

Now that you have the record information for the file you are interested in, you can read the actual contents of the record. You can read the contents of a SIM file by calling the SimReadRecord() function, which is defined as follows:

```
HRESULT SimReadRecord(HSIM hSim, DWORD dwAddress, DWORD
   dwRecordType, DWORD dwIndex, LPBYTE lpData, DWORD dwBufferSize,
   LPDWORD lpdwBytesRead);
```

The first parameter is the handle to the open SIM, and is followed by `dwAddress`, which should specify the unique file identifier for the record you are interested in reading. The next parameter, `dwRecord Type`, specifies the type of record that you are reading, which was returned from your previous call to `SimGetRecordInfo()`. The `dwIndex` parameter is used when you have either a `SIM_RECORD TYPE_CYCLIC` or `SIM_RECORDTYPE_LINEAR` type of record, and should specify which index within the record to read.

The actual contents of the record are returned to the buffer specified by the `lpData` parameter. The size of the buffer should be set in the `dwBufferSize` parameter, and the actual number of bytes that are returned to you will be placed in the pointer specified by the `lpdw BytesRead` parameter.

Reading a record is fairly straightforward, as shown by the following sample code that reads in the IMSI information from the SIM:

```
// Continue to read record...
LPBYTE lpIMSIBuffer = NULL;
DWORD dwBytesRead = 0;

// Allocate a buffer to read in the IMSI
lpIMSIBuffer = (LPBYTE)LocalAlloc(LPTR, srecordInfo.dwSize);
if(!lpIMSIBuffer) {
   OutputDebugString(TEXT("Could not allocate buffer for
      IMSI."));
   return FALSE;
}

hr = SimReadRecord(hSim, dwIMSIAddress, srecordInfo.dwRecordType, 0,
   lpIMSIBuffer, srecordInfo.dwSize, &dwBytesRead);
if(FAILED(hr))
   MessageBox(NULL, TEXT("Could not read IMSI number"),
      TEXT("Error"), MB_OK|MB_ICONERROR);

// Do something here with the IMSI number...
```

```
// Free up used buffer
LocalFree(lpIMSIBuffer);
```

You can store information on the SIM card by calling the following function:

```
HRESULT SimWriteRecord(HSIM hSim, DWORD dwAddress, DWORD
    dwRecordType, DWORD dwIndex, LPBYTE lpData, DWORD dwByteCount);
```

The parameters for writing a SIM file are similar to those for the `SimReadRecord()` function. The first parameter is the handle to the SIM card, `dwAddress` is the file identifier for the record you want to write, and `dwRecordType` is the type of SIM file record. The `dwIndex` parameter is used with records that are either `SIM_RECORDTYPE_CYCLIC` or `SIM_RECORDTYPE_LINEAR` and specifies which index within the record to write.

The data to be written to the SIM card is specified by the `lpData` parameter, and the `dwByteCount` parameter should contain the number of bytes to write to the SIM.

SIM Locking

SIM cards have built-in security features that enable you to lock the card so that unauthorized calls cannot be made using your phone account. If the SIM itself is locked, the PIN number you specify will need to be entered before you can place a call, regardless of the device or phone in which the SIM is placed.

WARNING: You should use the SIM locking facilities with caution. If you forget your password or PIN, the SIM card will be in a locked state and you will need to contact your carrier to unlock the SIM card.

You can check the current status of the SIM by calling the following function:

```
HRESULT SimGetLockingStatus(HSIM hSim, DWORD dwLockingFacility,
    LPTSTR lpszPassword, BOOL *pfEnabled);
```

The first parameter is the open handle to the SIM card. The second parameter specifies a locking mechanism for the SIM, and can be one of the values described in Table 8.9.

Table 8.9 SIM Locking Facilities

Value	Description
SIM_LOCKFACILITY_CNTRL	Lock control surface (keyboard lock)
SIM_LOCKFACILITY_PH_SIM	Lock phone to SIM card (device will request password when anything other than current SIM is inserted)
SIM_LOCKFACILITY_PH_FSIM	Lock phone to first SIM card (device will be locked to the first SIM card that is inserted)
SIM_LOCKFACILITY_SIM	Lock SIM card (device will request password when SIM is powered up)
SIM_LOCKFACILITY_SIM_PIN2	Lock SIM card
SIM_LOCKFACILITY_SIM_FIXEDDIALING	SIM fixed dialing memory (device will dial numbers on the SIM only)
SIM_LOCKFACILITY_NETWORKPERS	Network personalization
SIM_LOCKFACILITY_NETWORKSUBPERS	Network subset personalization
SIM_LOCKFACILITY_SERVICEPROVPERS	Service provider personalization
SIM_LOCKFACILITY_CORPPERS	Corporate provider personalization

The `lpszPassword` parameter should point to a null-terminated string that contains the facility's password. The last parameter, `pfEnabled`, should point to a Boolean value that will be filled in when the function returns with a TRUE value if the particular password facility is enabled.

The following example determines whether the SIM card is locked:

```
// Get the locking status...
BOOL fLock = FALSE;

hr = SimGetLockingStatus(hSim, SIM_LOCKFACILITY_SIM,
  TEXT(""), &fLock);
if(FAILED(hr))
```

```
      MessageBox(NULL, TEXT("Could not get the Locking status
         from the SIM!"), TEXT("Error"), MB_OK|MB_ICONERROR);

if(fLock)
   MessageBox(NULL, TEXT("SIM is currently locked"),
      TEXT("SIM Password"), MB_OK|MB_ICONINFORMATION);
else
   MessageBox(NULL, TEXT("SIM is currently unlocked"),
      TEXT("SIM Password"), MB_OK|MB_ICONINFORMATION);
```

To set the locking status (again, use with caution!), you can use the `SimSetLockingStatus()` function:

```
HRESULT SimSetLockingStatus(HSIM hSim, DWORD
   dwLockingFacility, LPTSTR lpszPassword, BOOL fEnabled);
```

The first parameter is the handle to the SIM card, and is followed by the locking facility you want to enable. The `lpszPassword` parameter is a null-terminated string containing the password you want to set. The last parameter, `fEnabled`, should be set to `TRUE` to enable locking. To unlock a particular facility, you would also call `SimSetLocking Status()` with the `fEnabled` parameter set to `FALSE`.

To change the password for a specific locking facility, you can call the following function:

```
HRESULT SimChangeLockingPassword(HSIM hSim, DWORD dwLockingFacility,
   LPTSTR lpszOldPassword, LPTSTR lpszNewPassword);
```

As with all of the other SIM functions, the first parameter is an open handle to the SIM card. The second parameter, `dwLockingFacility`, is the locking mechanism for which you want to change the password. The last two parameters are null-terminated strings that should specify both the old and new passwords, respectively.

To see if the SIM is currently waiting for a password to be entered, you can simply call the `SimGetPhoneLockedState()` function. The function requires an open handle to the SIM card, and will return a

SIM_LOCKEDSTATE value in the `lpdwLockedState` pointer when it returns. The function is defined as follows:

```
HRESULT SimGetPhoneLockedState(HSIM hSim, LPDWORD lpdwLockedState);
```

The possible locked states for a SIM card are listed in Table 8.10.

Table 8.10 SIM Locked States

Value	Locked State
SIM_LOCKEDSTATE_UNKNOWN	Unknown
SIM_LOCKEDSTATE_READY	Unlocked (Ready)
SIM_LOCKEDSTATE_SIM_PIN	Waiting for SIM PIN
SIM_LOCKEDSTATE_SIM_PUK	Waiting for SIM PUK (Pin Unblocking Key)
SIM_LOCKEDSTATE_PH_SIM_PIN	Waiting for SIM Personalization PIN
SIM_LOCKEDSTATE_PH_FSIM_PIN	Waiting for first SIM Personalization PIN
SIM_LOCKEDSTATE_PH_FSIM_PUK	Waiting for first SIM Personalization PUK
SIM_LOCKEDSTATE_SIM_PIN2	Waiting for SIM PIN2
SIM_LOCKEDSTATE_SIM_PUK2	Waiting for SIM PUK2
SIM_LOCKEDSTATE_PH_NET_PIN	Waiting for Network Personalization PIN
SIM_LOCKEDSTATE_PH_NET_PUK	Waiting for Network Personalization PUK
SIM_LOCKEDSTATE_PH_NETSUB_PIN	Waiting for Network Subset Personalization PIN
SIM_LOCKEDSTATE_PH_NETSUB_PUK	Waiting for Network Subset Personalization PUK
SIM_LOCKEDSTATE_PH_SP_PIN	Waiting for Service Provider Personalization PIN
SIM_LOCKEDSTATE_PH_SP_PUK	Waiting for Service Provider Personalization PUK
SIM_LOCKEDSTATE_PH_CORP_PIN	Waiting for Corporate Personalization PIN
SIM_LOCKEDSTATE_PH_CORP_PUK	Waiting for Corporate Personalization PUK

You can use the following code fragment to find out the current locked state for a SIM:

```
// Get the current locked state
DWORD dwLockedState = 0;
TCHAR tchLocked[256] = TEXT("\0");
hr = SimGetPhoneLockedState(hSim, &dwLockedState);
```

```
if(FAILED(hr))
    MessageBox(NULL, TEXT("Could not get the current SIM
locked state!"), TEXT("Error"), MB_OK|MB_ICONERROR);


switch(dwLockedState) {
    case SIM_LOCKEDSTATE_READY:
        wsprintf(tchLocked, TEXT("SIM Ready (Unlocked)"));
        break;
    case SIM_LOCKEDSTATE_SIM_PIN:
        wsprintf(tchLocked, TEXT("Waiting for the SIM PIN"));
        break;
    case SIM_LOCKEDSTATE_SIM_PUK:
        wsprintf(tchLocked, TEXT("Waiting for the SIM Unblock
            key"));
        break;
    case SIM_LOCKEDSTATE_PH_SIM_PIN:
        wsprintf(tchLocked, TEXT("Waiting for the SIM
            Personalization PIN"));
        break;
    case SIM_LOCKEDSTATE_PH_FSIM_PIN:
        wsprintf(tchLocked, TEXT("Waiting for the first SIM
            Personalization PIN"));
        break;
    case SIM_LOCKEDSTATE_PH_FSIM_PUK:
        wsprintf(tchLocked, TEXT("Waiting for the first SIM
            Unblock Key"));
        break;
    case SIM_LOCKEDSTATE_SIM_PIN2:
        wsprintf(tchLocked, TEXT("Waiting for the SIM PIN2"));
        break;
    case SIM_LOCKEDSTATE_SIM_PUK2:
        wsprintf(tchLocked, TEXT("Waiting for the SIM Unblock
            Key 2"));
        break;
    case SIM_LOCKEDSTATE_PH_NET_PIN:
        wsprintf(tchLocked, TEXT("Waiting for Network
            Personalization Pin"));
        break;
    case SIM_LOCKEDSTATE_PH_NET_PUK:
        wsprintf(tchLocked, TEXT("Waiting for Network
            Personalization Unblock Key"));
        break;
```

```
        case SIM_LOCKEDSTATE_PH_NETSUB_PIN:
            wsprintf(tchLocked, TEXT("Waiting for Network Subset
                Personalization Pin"));
            break;
        case SIM_LOCKEDSTATE_PH_NETSUB_PUK:
            wsprintf(tchLocked, TEXT("Waiting for Network Subset
                Personalization Unblock Key"));
            break;
        case SIM_LOCKEDSTATE_PH_SP_PIN:
            wsprintf(tchLocked, TEXT("Waiting for Service Provider
                Personalization PIN"));
            break;
        case SIM_LOCKEDSTATE_PH_SP_PUK:
            wsprintf(tchLocked, TEXT("Waiting for Service Provider
                Personalization Unblock Key"));
            break;
        case SIM_LOCKEDSTATE_PH_CORP_PIN:
            wsprintf(tchLocked, TEXT("Waiting for Corporate
                Pin"));
            break;
        case SIM_LOCKEDSTATE_PH_CORP_PUK:
            wsprintf(tchLocked, TEXT("Waiting for Corporate
                Unblock Key"));
            break;
default:
    wsprintf(tchLocked, TEXT("Unknown"));
}

MessageBox(NULL, tchLocked, TEXT("SIM Locked State"),
    MB_OK|MB_ICONINFORMATION);
```

Finally, to have your application send a password to unlock a phone, you can simply use the following function:

```
HRESULT SimUnlockPhone(HSIM hSim, LPTSTR lpszPassword,
    LPTSTR lpszNewPin);
```

The first parameter should point to a valid handle for the SIM. The `lpszPassword` parameter should be a null-terminated string that specifies the password to unlock the device. The last parameter, `lpszNewPin`, is an optional second password string, and can be set to `NULL` if it is not required.

Short Message Service (SMS)

The **Short Message Service** (**SMS**) enables a Pocket PC Phone Edition device (or any other mobile device, for that matter) to instantly send and receive small messages through a **Short Message Service Center** (**SMSC**) to another mobile device on the network. Each message can be up to 160 alphanumeric characters long (140 bytes), and may be separated into multipart messages if necessary. SMS, with the introduction of the **Enhanced Messaging Service** (**EMS**) and the **Multimedia Messaging Service** (**MMS**), also has support for small binary nontext messages.

Once a message is sent to the SMSC for delivery, it is the messaging center's responsibility to forward the message to the appropriate destination mobile device. If the destination address of the device is not immediately available, the SMSC will usually store the message and continue to attempt to send it until it receives a notification that the target device has successfully received the message. SMS Messaging is based on the GSM 3.40 specification ("Technical Realization of the Short Messaging Service"), which can be downloaded from http://www.etsi.org.

One of the main differences between SMS Messaging and sending regular e-mail is that you can send SMS messages instantaneously, similar in fashion to a pager (however, SMS does not guarantee a delivery time or a confirmation) and without connecting to the Internet and a mail server. While the Pocket PC Phone Edition has seamlessly integrated SMS messaging functionality into the Inbox (see Figure 8.5), using the SMS APIs will enable you to send and receive SMS messages from within your own applications.

In order to create applications that can send and receive messages over SMS, you should include the `sms.h` header file, and link with the `sms.lib` library.

SMS Addresses

All of the SMS API functions use the `SMS_ADDRESS` structure to define the device address to which messages can be sent, and from which

Figure 8.5 SMS and the Pocket PC Inbox

messages are received. The structure defines both the type of address and the actual phone number used in conjunction with the message. The SMS_ADDRESS structure is defined as follows:

```
typedef struct sms_address_tag{
    SMS_ADDRESS_TYPE smsatAddressType;
    TCHAR ptsAddress[SMS_MAX_ADDRESS_LENGTH];
} SMS_ADDRESS, *LPSMS_ADDRESS;
```

The smsatAddressType field is used to define the type of address, and can be one of the values listed in Table 8.11.

Table 8.11 SMS Message Address Types

Value	Address Type
SMSAT_UNKNOWN	Unknown phone number type
SMSAT_INTERNATIONAL	An international phone number
SMSAT_NATIONAL	A national phone number
SMSAT_NETWORKSPECIFIC	A network-specific phone number
SMSAT_SUBSCRIBER	A subscriber phone number
SMSAT_ALPHANUMERIC	An alphanumeric phone number
SMSAT_ABBREVIATED	An abbreviated phone number

The `ptsAddress` field contains a null-terminated string that contains the address, which can be up to 255 characters long.

SMS Service Center (SMSC)

An SMS Service Center (or SMSC) is the server that performs the delivery of an SMS message. When a new message is sent from a device, the SMSC is responsible for the storing, forwarding, and relaying of the message to its appropriate destination address.

The process for delivering an SMS message from one device to another works as follows:

1. A device sends the new SMS message to the SMSC.
2. When the SMSC receives a new message, it sends an SMS request to the home location register (HLR). This is used to find out the routing information for the destination address.
3. The HLR sends a notification back to the SMSC with the status of the subscriber address. The notification indicates whether the address is inactive or active, and whether or not the address is roaming.
4. If the HLR response indicates that the subscriber is *inactive*, then the SMSC will hold the message for a period of time. Once the device address comes online on the network, the HLR sends a notification to the SMSC that the device is *active*.
5. If the HLR response is active (or the SMSC receives an active notification), the SMSC will then transfer the message to the target device address using the **Short Message Delivery Point to Point** (**SMPP**) protocol. In essence, the SMSC pages the device with the message contents.
6. Once the SMSC receives a notification from the destination device that the message has been delivered and verified, the SMSC marks the message as *sent*, and does not attempt to continue delivery.

NOTE: Every device must be configured with an SMSC phone number (or address) before it can send or receive text messages.

To get the SMS address for the current SMSC for the device, you can use the `SmsGetSMSC()` function, which is defined as follows:

```
HRESULT SmsGetSMSC(SMS_ADDRESS* const psmsaSMSCAddress);
```

As you might expect, the only parameter that the function needs is a pointer to an SMS_ADDRESS structure that will be filled in with the current SMSC information.

For example, if you wanted to get the address information for the current SMSC, your call to SmsGetSMSC() would look like the following:

```
// Get the current SMS Service Center
HRESULT hr = S_OK;
SMS_ADDRESS smscAddress;
TCHAR tchSMSC[1024] = TEXT("\0");

memset(&smscAddress, 0, sizeof(SMS_ADDRESS));
hr = SmsGetSMSC(&smscAddress);

if(FAILED(hr)) {
   OutputDebugString(TEXT("Could not get service center
      address."));
   return FALSE;
}

wsprintf(tchSMSC, TEXT("Current SMSC: %s"),
  smscAddress.ptsAddress);
MessageBox(NULL, tchSMSC, TEXT("SMSC"),
  MB_OK|MB_ICONINFORMATION);
```

To change the SMSC, you can pass an SMS_ADDRESS structure containing the new service center address to the following function:

```
HRESULT SmsSetSMSC(const SMS_ADDRESS* const
  psmsaSMSCAddress);
```

The following code fragment shows how to set a new SMSC address:

```
// Set a new SMS Service Center
SMS_ADDRESS smscNewAddress;

memset(&smscNewAddress, 0, sizeof(SMS_ADDRESS));
smscNewAddress.smsatAddressType = SMSAT_INTERNATIONAL;
wsprintf(smscNewAddress.ptsAddress,TEXT("18005555555"));

hr = SmsSetSMSC(&smscNewAddress);
```

```
if(FAILED(hr)) {
   OutputDebugString(TEXT("Could not set service center
      address."));
   return FALSE;
}
```

Opening the SMS Service

In order to either send or receive messages over the SMS service, you must first obtain a handle that you will use for subsequent messaging calls. Be aware that although you may have multiple handles open simultaneously for *sending* a message over a particular SMS protocol, you can open only one handle at a time for *receiving* messages (the Pocket PC Inbox, \Windows\tmail.exe, will typically have the receive handle already open).

To get an SMS handle, call the SmsOpen() function:

```
HRESULT SmsOpen(const LPCTSTR ptsMessageProtocol,
   const DWORD dwMessageModes,
   SMS_HANDLE* const psmshHandle, HANDLE* const
   phMessageAvailableEvent);
```

The first parameter, ptsMessageProtocol, is a null-terminated string that specifies which SMS protocol to use. There are several predefined SMS provider types, each with its own set of structures that make up different types of messages. The SMS protocols that Pocket PC Phone Edition supports are listed in Table 8.12.

The dwMessageModes parameter sets the transfer mode of the open handle. This can be set to SMS_MODE_RECEIVE if you want to receive messages, and/or SMS_MODE_SEND if you want to send messages. Note that certain SMS protocols can support only receive mode, and SmsOpen() will return an error if you try to open the protocol with the send option.

The pshmshHandle should point to the address of a variable that will receive an SMS_HANDLE when the function returns. The last parameter, phMessageAvailableEvent, is a pointer to a Windows event handle that will be signaled when a new message arrives. Although you can use this handle for wait event functions such as WaitForSingle Object(), you should *not* use any other event APIs on the handle. Calling functions such as SetEvent() and ResetEvent() will confuse the SMS engine, and unpredictable results can occur. In addition, you do not

Table 8.12 SMS Message Protocol Types

SMS Protocol Type	Send/Receive	Description
SMS_MSGTYPE_TEXT	Both	Text SMS Protocol. Uses the TEXT_PROVIDER_SPECIFIC_ DATA structure.
SMS_MSGTYPE_ NOTIFICATION	Receive only	Notification SMS Protocol. Uses the NOTIFICATION_PROVIDER_ SPECIFIC_DATA structure.
SMS_MSGTYPE_WDP	Both	WDP SMS Message. Uses the WDP_PROVIDER_SPECIFIC_ DATA structure.
SMS_MSGTYPE_WCMP	Both	WCMP SMS Message. Uses the WCMP_PROVIDER_SPECIFIC_ DATA structure.
SMS_MSGTYPE_STATUS	Receive only	Status message SMS Protocol. Uses the STATUS_PROVIDER_ SPECIFIC_DATA structure.
SMS_MSGTYPE_ BROADCAST	Receive only	Broadcast Message SMS Protocol. Uses the BROADCAST_PROVIDER_ SPECIFIC_DATA structure.
SMS_MSGTYPE_RAW	Receive only	Raw SMS Protocol. Uses the RAW_PROVIDER_SPECIFIC_ DATA structure.

need to call `CloseHandle()` on the handle returned to `pshmsh Handle`, as the SMS engine will close it when you call `SmsClose()` to shut down SMS.

Using the `SmsOpen()` function to initiate a SMS messaging session is fairly straightforward, as shown by the following example:

```
SMS_HANDLE hSms = NULL;
HANDLE hSmsEvent = NULL;
HRESULT hr = S_OK;

// Open up an SMS handle for the text provider
// Remember, tmail.exe will typically have the receive
// handle already open, and needs to be shut down before opening.
hr = SmsOpen(SMS_MSGTYPE_TEXT,
    SMS_MODE_RECEIVE|SMS_MODE_SEND, &hSms, &hSmsEvent);
```

```
if(FAILED(hr)) {
    OutputDebugString(TEXT("Could not open a handle to the
        SMS text message service."));
    return FALSE;
}
```

SMS Message Protocols

Several different SMS protocols can be used when sending a message from one device to another. Each protocol, also known as an **SMS provider**, has its own specific data structure, which makes up the message associated with it. The Pocket PC Phone Edition supports the short messaging protocols described in Table 8.12. Note that some of the protocols can be used only to receive messages, not to send them.

Complete details about SMS provider functionality and terminology can be found in the GSM 3.40 specification (found at http://www.etsi.org).

Text SMS Messages

The text SMS provider is the most commonly used protocol for sending and receiving messages. As the name implies, the content of a text message is just that—a string up to 160 characters long. When working with text SMS messages, you use the TEXT_PROVIDER_SPECIFIC_DATA structure for any additional protocol information. The structure is defined as follows:

```
typedef struct text_provider_specific_data_tag {
    DWORD dwMessageOptions;
    PROVIDER_SPECIFIC_MESSAGE_CLASS psMessageClass;
    PROVIDER_SPECIFIC_REPLACE_OPTION psReplaceOption;
} TEXT_PROVIDER_SPECIFIC_DATA;
```

The dwMessageOptions field specifies any options that can be used with the provider. It can be set to one or more of the following:

- PS_MESSAGE_OPTION_NONE indicates that no options are being used.
- PS_MESSAGE_OPTION_REPLYPATH indicates that the TP-Reply-Path bit should be set when sending a message (GSM 3.40 specification).
- PS_MESSAGE_OPTION_STATUSREPORT indicates that the TP-Status-Report-Request bit should be set when sending a message (GSM 3.40 specification).

- PS_MESSAGE_OPTION_DISCARD indicates that the TP-User-Data-Header bit should set to discard when sending a message (GSM 3.40 specification).

The psMessageClass field specifies how a message should interact with the SMS Service Center when it is received by its destination. It should be set to one of the following options:

- PS_MESSAGE_CLASS0 indicates that the message should be displayed immediately and not stored in the SIM. This is typical for an alert message, and should always send an acknowledgment back to the SMSC.
- PS_MESSAGE_CLASS1 indicates that the message should be stored in the SIM, and an acknowledgment should be sent to the SMSC once it has been received.
- PS_MESSAGE_CLASS2 indicates that the message should be stored in the SIM, and an acknowledgment should be sent to the SMSC once it has been stored. If the message cannot be stored in the SIM and other memory is available, then an "unspecified protocol error" will be returned. If there is no memory to store the message, a "memory capacity exceeded" error will be sent to the SMSC.
- PS_MESSAGE_CLASS3 indicates that an acknowledgment should be sent to the SMSC when the message has reached its target address.

The psReplaceOption field specifies how a message should be replaced for a previously received notification. It can be one of the following values:

- PSRO_NONE indicates that no earlier notifications should be replaced, and that the message should be acknowledged.
- PSRO_REPLACE_TYPE1 indicates that Replace Short Message Type 1 notifications should be replaced if the originating address and parameter values match.
- PSRO_REPLACE_TYPE2 indicates that Replace Short Message Type 2 notifications should be replaced if the originating address and parameter values match.
- PSRO_REPLACE_TYPE3 indicates that Replace Short Message Type 3 notifications should be replaced if the originating address and parameter values match.

- `PSRO_REPLACE_TYPE4` indicates that Replace Short Message Type 4 notifications should be replaced if the originating address and parameter values match.
- `PSRO_REPLACE_TYPE5` indicates that Replace Short Message Type 5 notifications should be replaced if the originating address and parameter values match.
- `PSRO_REPLACE_TYPE6` indicates that Replace Short Message Type 6 notifications should be replaced if the originating address and parameter values match.
- `PSRO_REPLACE_TYPE7` indicates that Replace Short Message Type 7 notifications should be replaced if the originating address and parameter values match.
- `PSRO_RETURN_CALL` indicates that the originating device address can accept a return call.
- `PSRO_DEPERSONALIZATION` indicates that the message contains code to depersonalize the device, and should not be displayed to the user.

Notification SMS Messages

The notification message protocol is used only when receiving messages that are **message waiting** alerts, such as a new voice mail.

Notification messages use the `NOTIFICATION_PROVIDER_SPECIFIC_DATA` structure, which is defined as follows:

```
typedef struct notification_provider_specific_data_tag {
    DWORD dwMessageOptions;
    PROVIDER_SPECIFIC_MESSAGE_CLASS psMessageClass;
    PROVIDER_SPECIFIC_REPLACE_OPTION psReplaceOption;
    NOTIFICATION_PROVIDER_SPECIFIC_MSG_WAITING_TYPE
        npsMsgWaitingType;
    int iNumberOfMessagesWaiting;
    NOTIFICATION_PROVIDER_SPECIFIC_INDICATOR_TYPE
        npsIndicatorType;
} NOTIFICATION_PROVIDER_SPECIFIC_DATA;
```

The `dwMessageOptions`, `psMessageClass`, and `psReplace Options` fields specify any additional information about the message, and are identical to those found in the `TEXT_PROVIDER_SPECIFIC_DATA` structure.

The `npsMsgWaitingType` field specifies the type of notification that was received. Pocket PC Phone Edition supports the following notification types:

- `NOTIFICATIONPSMWT_NONE`, if no message is waiting
- `NOTIFICATIONPSMWT_GENERIC`, if the waiting message is generic
- `NOTIFICATIONPSMWT_VOICEMAIL`, if the waiting message is a voice mail message
- `NOTIFICATIONPSMWT_FAX`, if the waiting message is a fax
- `NOTIFICATIONPSMWT_EMAIL`, if the waiting message is an e-mail message
- `NOTIFICATIONPSMWT_OTHER`, if the waiting message is of an unknown type

The `iNumberofMessagesWaiting` field contains the number of messages that are waiting. The last field, `npsIndicatorType`, will specify the phone line that the notification is for, and can be set to `NOTIFICATIONPSIT_NONE`, `NOTIFICATIONPSIT_LINE1`, or `NOTIFICATIONPSIT_LINE2`.

WDP SMS Messages

The **Wireless Datagram Protocol** (**WDP**) is used to send and receive packets of binary data (similar to UDP) from one wireless device to another over the SMS service, and is part of the **Wireless Application Protocol** (**WAP**) stack. More information on WDP can be found in the WAP-202-WCMP specification, which is downloadable from http://www.etsi.org.

WDP messages use the `WDP_PROVIDER_SPECIFIC_DATA` structure, which is defined as follows:

```
typedef struct wdp_provider_specific_data_tag {
    WDP_PROVIDER_SPECIFIC_PORT_ADDRESSING wdppsPortAddressing;
    WORD wDestinationPort;
    WORD wOriginatorPort;
} WDP_PROVIDER_SPECIFIC_DATA;
```

The first field, `wdppsPortAddressing`, specifies how the port numbers in the remaining fields should be addressed. This can be set to

WDPPSA_8_BIT_PORT_NUMBERS for 8-bit addressing or WDPPSPA_16_BIT_PORT_NUMBERS for 16-bit values.

The wDestinationPort and wOriginatorPort fields specify which ports should be used for the delivery and reception of WDP packets, respectively.

WCMP SMS Messages

The **Wireless Control Message Protocol** (**WCMP**) is used to send status messages and report errors that occur while using the Wireless Datagram Protocol. It is similar in functionality to TCP/IP's ICMP protocol for handling echo requests and responses. In addition, WCMP messages can be used for diagnostic and informational purposes.

WCMP messages use the WCMP_PROVIDER_SPECIFIC_DATA structure, which has the following prototype:

```
typedef struct wcmp_provider_specific_data_tag {
    WCMP_PROVIDER_SPECIFIC_MESSAGE_TYPE wcmppsMessageType;
    WORD wParam1;
    WORD wParam2;
    WORD wParam3;
    SMS_ADDRESS smsaAddress;
} WCMP_PROVIDER_SPECIFIC_DATA;
```

The wcmppsMessageType field indicates the type of WCMP message that the structure represents. It can be any of the following:

- WCMPPSMT_UNSUPPORTED, if there is no way to route the message to the destination address
- WCMPPSMT_PORT_UNREACHABLE, if the destination port is unreachable
- WCMPPSMT_MESSAGE_TOO_BIG, if the message is larger than the destination's buffer size
- WCMPPSMT_ECHO_REQUEST, if the message is an echo request
- WCMPPSMT_ECHO_REPLY, if the message is an echo response

The type of WCMP message that was sent or received (see Table 8.13) determines the value of the other fields in the structure.

Table 8.13 WCMP Message Types

Message Type	wParam1	wParam2	wParam3	smsaAddress
UNSUPPORTED	None	None	None	None
PORT_ UNREACHABLE	Destination port	Source port	None	Destination address of original datagram
MESSAGE_ TOO_BIG	Destination port	Source port	Maximum size	Destination address of original datagram
ECHO_REQUEST	Identifier	Sequence number	None	None
ECHO_REPLY	Identifier	Sequence number	None	None

Status SMS Messages

If an SMS message (such as a text or notification message) requested status information by setting the PS_MESSAGE_OPTION_STATUSREPORT value, then a status SMS message will be sent to the device.

When a status message is received, it uses the STATUS_ PROVIDER_SPECIFIC_DATA structure to report any information. The structure is defined as follows:

```
typedef struct status_provider_specific_data_tag {
    SMS_STATUS_INFORMATION smssiStatusInformation;
} STATUS_PROVIDER_SPECIFIC_DATA;
```

The only information that the structure provides is an SMS_ STATUS_INFORMATION structure. SMS_STATUS_INFORMATION will be filled in with the actual details of the status message:

```
typedef struct sms_status_information_tag {
    SMS_MESSAGE_ID smsmidMessageID;
    DWORD dwMessageStatus0;
    DWORD dwMessageStatus1;
    SMS_ADDRESS smsaRecipientAddress;
    SYSTEMTIME stServiceCenterTimeStamp;
    SYSTEMTIME stDischargeTime;
} SMS_STATUS_INFORMATION, *LPSMS_STATUS_INFORMATION;
```

The `smsmidMessageID` field is the identifier of the message for which the status message was sent, and is the same as the identifier that you are returned from calling `SmsSendMessage()`.

The `dwMessageStatus0` and `dwMessageStatus1` fields are two `DWORD` values that indicate the status message. Note that both fields must have the `MESSAGE_STATUS_UNKNOWN` flag set if the message status is truly undefined.

`dwMessageStatus0` can be one of the values described in Table 8.14.

Table 8.14 SMS Message Status

SMS Message Status	Delivered?	Description
MESSAGE_STATUS_ UNKNOWN	N/A	Unknown status message
MESSAGE_STATUS_0_ RECEIVEDBYSME	Yes	Message was received by destination
MESSAGE_STATUS_0_ FORWARDEDTOSME	Yes	Message was forwarded to destination
MESSAGE_STATUS_0_ REPLACEDBYSC	Yes	Message was replaced by SMSC
MESSAGE_STATUS_0_ CONGESTION_TRYING	No	Network congestion; continuing to try
MESSAGE_STATUS_0_ SMEBUSY_TRYING	No	Busy signal; continuing to try
MESSAGE_STATUS_0_ SMENOTRESPONDING_ TRYING	No	No response from destination; continuing to try
MESSAGE_STATUS_0_ SVCREJECTED_TRYING	No	Service rejected; continuing to try
MESSAGE_STATUS_0_ QUALITYUNAVAIL_ TRYING	No	Quality unavailable; continuing to try
MESSAGE_STATUS_0_ SMEERROR_TRYING	No	Destination error
MESSAGE_STATUS_0_ CONGESTION	No	Temporary network congestion
MESSAGE_STATUS_0_ SMEBUSY	No	Temporary busy signal at destination
MESSAGE_STATUS_0_ SMENOTRESPONDING	No	Destination is not responding temporarily

(continued)

Table 8.14 SMS Message Status (*continued*)

SMS Message Status	Delivered?	Description
MESSAGE_STATUS_0_ SVCREJECTED	No	Service has been rejected by destination temporarily
MESSAGE_STATUS_0_ QUALITYUNAVAIL_TEMP	No	Quality is temporarily unavailable
MESSAGE_STATUS_0_ SMEERROR	No	Temporary destination error
MESSAGE_STATUS_0_ REMOTEPROCERROR	No	Permanent failure
MESSAGE_STATUS_0_ INCOMPATIBLEDEST	No	Permanent failure due to destination incompatibility
MESSAGE_STATUS_0_ CONNECTIONREJECTED	No	Permanent failure due to rejection of the connection
MESSAGE_STATUS_0_ NOTOBTAINABLE	No	Permanent failure due to destination being unattainable
MESSAGE_STATUS_0_ NOINTERNETWORKING	No	Permanent failure due to internetworking being unavailable
MESSAGE_STATUS_0_ VPEXPIRED	No	Permanent failure due to validity period expiring
MESSAGE_STATUS_0_ DELETEDBYORIGSME	No	Permanent failure due to message being deleted by originator
MESSAGE_STATUS_0_ DELETEDBYSC	No	Permanent failure due to message being deleted by service center
MESSAGE_STATUS_0_ NOLONGEREXISTS	No	Permanent failure due to the message no longer existing
MESSAGE_STATUS_0_ QUALITYUNAVAIL	No	Permanent failure due to quality not existing
MESSAGE_STATUS_0_ RESERVED_COMPLETED	No	Message has been successfully reserved
MESSAGE_STATUS_0_ RESERVED_TRYING	No	Message has been reserved and is trying to be sent
MESSAGE_STATUS_0_ RESERVED_ERROR	No	Permanent failure due to a reserve error
MESSAGE_STATUS_0_ RESERVED_TMPERROR	No	Temporary error due to reserve on message
MESSAGE_STATUS_0_ SCSPECIFIC_COMPLETED	Yes	Message is destined for the SMSC and has been delivered
MESSAGE_STATUS_0_ SCSPECIFIC_TRYING	No	Continuing to try to send message to SMSC
MESSAGE_STATUS_0_ SCSPECIFIC_ERROR	No	Permanent failure due to SMSC error

The `smsaRecipientAddress` field contains the destination address for the message.

The last two fields, `stServiceCenterTimeStamp` and `stDischargeTime`, are both `SYSTEMTIME` values that are set at different stages of the messaging delivery process. The `stService CenterTimeStamp` is set when SMSC received the message, and `stDischargeTime` may or may not be stamped, depending on the `dwMessageStatus` value.

Broadcast SMS Messages

A message received over the Cell Broadcast Service is generally sent to multiple recipients from a broadcast center over a geographical area from a service provider. A broadcast message may be up to 93 characters long, and may consist of multiple messages (or pages) that need to be concatenated to form the entire message. You can find more information about the Cell Broadcast Service in the GSM 3.41 specification, which is downloadable from http://www.etsi.org.

Broadcast SMS messages use the `BROADCAST_PROVIDER_ SPECIFIC_DATA` structure, which has the following prototype:

```
typedef struct broadcast_provider_specific_data_tag {
   WORD wMessageID;
   WORD wMessageCode;
   BROADCAST_PROVIDER_SPECIFIC_GEOGRAPHICAL_SCOPE
      bpsgsGeographicalScope;
   WORD wUpdateNumber;
} BROADCAST_PROVIDER_SPECIFIC_DATA;
```

The `wMessageID` field identifies the particular type of broadcast message, and is defined by the Cell Broadcast Service center that sent the message.

The `wMessageCode` field enables you to differentiate between multiple broadcast messages that contain the same `wMessageID`. For example, if the message identifier indicated that the message was a traffic report; different codes would be used for different traffic incidents.

The `bpsgsGeographicalScope` field indicates the location for which the message is valid, as well as the display mode. It will be one of the following values:

- `BPSGS_UNKNOWN` indicates that the message type is unknown.
- `BPSGS_CELL_DISPLAY_IMMEDIATE` indicates that the message is cell-wide and should be displayed immediately.
- `BPSGS_CELL` indicates that the message is valid for the current cell.
- `BPSGS_PLMN` indicates that the message code must be different for additional messages with the same message ID for the cell.
- `BPSGS_LOCATION_AREA` indicates that the message is location-based.

Lastly, the `wUpdateNumber` field indicates a change of message content. For example, if a message has the same `wMessageID`, `wMessageCode`, and `bpsgsGeopgraphicalScope`, the update number can be used to determine old and new messages. This value is a four-bit number, and when it is eight or less higher (mod 16) than the last received message, it should be considered more recent.

Raw SMS Messages

The raw SMS message provider is used when an SMS message is received and none of the other provider types is appropriate for it.

If you receive a raw SMS message, you should use the `RAW_PROVIDER_SPECIFIC_DATA` structure:

```
typedef struct raw_provider_specific_data_tag {
    DWORD dwHeaderDataSize;
    BYTE pbHeaderData[SMS_DATAGRAM_SIZE];
} RAW_PROVIDER_SPECIFIC_DATA;
```

The `dwHeaderDataSize` field has the number of bytes that are returned in the `pbHeaderData` field, and `pbHeaderData` stores the raw user header from the incoming message.

Sending a Message

You can send a message over a specific SMS provider by using the following function:

```
HRESULT SmsSendMessage(const SMS_HANDLE smshHandle,
    const SMS_ADDRESS* psmsaSMSCAddress,
    const SMS_ADDRESS* psmsaDestinationAddress,
    const SYSTEMTIME* pstValidityPeriod,
    const BYTE* pbData, const DWORD dwDataSize,
    const BYTE* pbProviderSpecificData,
    const DWORD dwProviderSpecificDataSize,
    const SMS_DATA_ENCODING smsdeDataEncoding,
    const DWORD dwOptions, SMS_MESSAGE_ID* psmsmidMessageID);
```

As you can see, numerous parameters are needed to send a message over SMS. The first one is the handle to an open SMS provider that was returned from a previous call to SmsOpen. The next parameter, psmsaSMSCAddress, points to the SMS Service Center through which you want to route your message. If you want to use the default SMSC address that was specified by the SmsSetSMSC() function, then you can set this to NULL, as it is an optional parameter. The psmsaDestinationAddress parameter should be set to the address of the device to which the message is sent.

The **validity period** of a message tells the SMSC how long a message is valid for. It begins when the SMSC receives the message. Once the period has expired, the message is automatically deleted. The pstValidityPeriod parameter is optional and can be set to NULL.

The next two parameters contain the SMS message body. The pbData parameter should point to the contents of the message, and the dwDataSize parameter should specify the size, in bytes, of the buffer pointed to by pbData. If there is no message, then you can set pbData to NULL, and dwDataSize to 0.

The pbProviderSpecificData and dwProviderSpecificDataSize parameters contain additional information for whichever SMS protocol you are using to send your message. For example, to send a text message (using SMS_MSGTYPE_TEXT), you would need to fill out a TEXT_PROVIDER_SPECIFIC_DATA structure. A pointer to this structure would then be passed in for the pbProviderSpecificData parameter, and its size (in bytes) would be passed in for the dwProviderSpecificDataSize parameter.

The smsdeDataEncoding parameter specifies the text encoding method for the message, and can be set to one of the following options:

- SMSDE_OPTIMAL will use the best data encoding scheme that results in the least amount of space. This is the recommended option to use.

- SMSDE_GSM specifies that standard GSM-7 encoding should be used.
- SMSDE_UCS2 specifies that standard Unicode UCS2 encoding should be used.

The dwOptions flag can be set to either of the following:

- SMS_OPTION_DELIVERY_NONE, for no special options
- SMS_OPTION_DELIVERY_NO_RETRY, if you do not want the SMSC to retry sending a message if it is undeliverable

The last parameter, psmsmidMessageID, will receive a message ID once the function returns; it can be used for additional informational messages regarding the status of a sent message. This parameter is optional.

The following example shows how to send an SMS message:

```
// Send an SMS message through default SMSC
SMS_ADDRESS smsDestination;
SMS_MESSAGE_ID smsMsgId = 0;

// Set the destination address for the message
memset(&smsDestination, 0, sizeof(SMS_ADDRESS));
smsDestination.smsatAddressType = SMSAT_INTERNATIONAL;
_tcsncpy(smsDestination.ptsAddress,
   TEXT("15555555555"), SMS_MAX_ADDRESS_LENGTH);

// Create the message
DWORD dwMessageLength = 0;
TCHAR tchMessage[140] = TEXT("\0");
wsprintf(tchMessage, TEXT("This is a test text
  message\r\n"));

dwMessageLength = lstrlen(tchMessage)*sizeof(TCHAR);

// Configure the text provider
TEXT_PROVIDER_SPECIFIC_DATA txtProviderData;
DWORD dwProviderLength = 0;

memset(&txtProviderData, 0, sizeof(TEXT_PROVIDER_SPECIFIC_DATA));
txtProviderData.dwMessageOptions = PS_MESSAGE_OPTION_NONE;
txtProviderData.psMessageClass = PS_MESSAGE_CLASS0;
```

```
txtProviderData.psReplaceOption = PSRO_NONE;
dwProviderLength = sizeof(TEXT_PROVIDER_SPECIFIC_DATA);

// Send the message
hr = SmsSendMessage(hSms, NULL, &smsDestination, NULL,
    (BYTE *)tchMessage, dwMessageLength, (LPBYTE)&txtProviderData,
    dwProviderLength, SMSDE_OPTIMAL, SMS_OPTION_DELIVERY_NONE,
    &smsMsgId);

if(FAILED(hr))
    OutputDebugString(TEXT("Could not send SMS Text
        Message."));
else
    OutputDebugString(TEXT("Message Sent."));
```

If at any time you need to get the status information for a message that you have sent, you can call the SmsGetMessageStatus() function:

```
HRESULT SmsGetMessageStatus(const SMS_HANDLE smshHandle,
    SMS_MESSAGE_ID smsmidMessageID,
    SMS_STATUS_INFORMATION* const psmssiStatusInformation,
    const DWORD dwTimeout);
```

The first parameter is an SMS handle and is followed by the message ID for which you want to get status information. The message ID was returned to you when you originally called the SmsSendMessage() function. The psmssiStatusInformation parameter should point to an SMS_STATUS_INFORMATION structure that will be filled in with the message's status when the function returns (information on the SMS_STATUS_INFORMATION structure can be found in the section "Status SMS Messages"). The last parameter, dwTimeout, specifies the time to wait (in milliseconds) for the status message to be received.

The following code fragment shows how to get the status of an SMS message (notice how you change the txtProviderData. dwMessageOptions flag from the previous sample to indicate you want a status report):

```
txtProviderData.dwMessageOptions = PS_MESSAGE_OPTION_STATUSREPORT;
txtProviderData.psMessageClass = PS_MESSAGE_CLASS0;
txtProviderData.psReplaceOption = PSRO_NONE;
dwProviderLength = sizeof(TEXT_PROVIDER_SPECIFIC_DATA);
```

```
// Send the message
hr = SmsSendMessage(hSms, NULL, &smsDestination, NULL,
    (BYTE *)tchMessage, dwMessageLength, (LPBYTE)&txtProviderData,
    dwProviderLength, SMSDE_OPTIMAL, SMS_OPTION_DELIVERY_NONE,
    &smsMsgId);

if(FAILED(hr))
    OutputDebugString(TEXT("Could not send SMS Text
        Message."));
else
    OutputDebugString(TEXT("Message Sent."));

// Get message status (wait 2 seconds)
SMS_STATUS_INFORMATION smsStatus;
memset(&smsStatus, 0, sizeof(SMS_STATUS_INFORMATION));

hr = SmsGetMessageStatus(hSms, smsMsgId, &smsStatus, 2000);

if(FAILED(hr))
    OutputDebugString(TEXT("Could not get SMS message
        status"));
else {
    if(smsStatus.dwMessageStatus0 ==
        MESSAGE_STATUS_0_RECEIVEDBYSME)
        OutputDebugString(TEXT("Message has been received"));
}
```

Reading a Message

By using the event handle that was returned when you called
SmsOpen(), you can also wait for a new message to be received by your
device. Once that event handle has been signaled, reading the contents
of a message is a two-step process.

First, you need to find out how large the message is by calling the
following function:

```
HRESULT SmsGetMessageSize(const SMS_HANDLE smshHandle,
    DWORD* const pdwDataSize);
```

The function takes only two parameters: an open SMS handle and a
pointer to a DWORD value that will receive the size, in bytes, of the message.

Once you have the size of the incoming message, you can retrieve the message contents by using the `SmsReadMessage()` function. It is defined as follows:

```
HRESULT SmsReadMessage(const SMS_HANDLE smshHandle,
    SMS_ADDRESS* const psmsaSMSCAddress,
    SMS_ADDRESS* const psmsaSourceAddress,
    SYSTEMTIME* const pstReceiveTime,
    BYTE* const pbBuffer, DWORD dwBufferSize,
    BYTE* const pbProviderSpecificBuffer,
    DWORD dwProviderSpecificDataBuffer, DWORD* pdwBytesRead);
```

The first parameter, `smshHandle`, is an open SMS handle for the provider from which you are going to receive a message.

The next two parameters, `psmsaSMSCAddress` and `psmsa SourceAddress`, point to variables that will be filled in with the SMSC that delivered the message, as well as the address from which it originated. Both of these are optional and can be set to `NULL`.

The `pstReceiveTime` parameter points to a `SYSTEMTIME` structure that will be filled in with the time the message was received. The `pstReceiveTime` parameter is also optional and can be set to `NULL`.

The `pbBuffer` and `dwBufferSize` parameters are used to store the message contents. The buffer that `pbBuffer` points to should be at least the size that was returned from the call to `SmsGetMessage Size()`. The `dwBufferSize` parameter should be set to the size of `pbBuffer`.

The `pbProviderSpecificBuffer` and `dwProviderSpecific DataBuffer` parameters contain a provider-specific data structure and its size. For example, if the received message was a WDP SMS message (using the `SMS_MSGTYPE_WDP` protocol type), the `pbProvider SpecificBuffer` would then point to a `WDP_PROVIDER_SPECIFIC_ DATA` structure.

The `pdwBytesRead` parameter should point to a `DWORD` variable that will be filled in with the actual number of bytes that were put into the `pbBuffer` buffer when the function returns.

The following code example illustrates a function that is waiting for a new SMS text message to arrive. Once the SMS event is signaled, you get the size of the incoming message, allocate a buffer that is large enough for it, and finally retrieve the message:

```
// Wait for an incoming message
DWORD dwReturn = 0;
dwReturn = WaitForSingleObject(hSmsEvent, INFINITE);
```

```
// SMS event has become signaled
if(dwReturn == WAIT_ABANDONED || dwReturn == WAIT_TIMEOUT) {
   OutputDebugString(TEXT("No longer waiting for a
   message"));
   SmsClose(hSms);
   return FALSE;
}

// Receive a message. First, get the size
DWORD dwMessageSize = 0;
hr = SmsGetMessageSize(hSms, &dwMessageSize);
if(FAILED(hr)) {
   OutputDebugString(TEXT("Could not get message size"));
   SmsClose(hSms);
   return FALSE;
}

// Set up to receive the message
SMS_ADDRESS smscAddress;
SMS_ADDRESS inAddress;
SYSTEMTIME rcvTime;
TEXT_PROVIDER_SPECIFIC_DATA txtProviderData;
DWORD dwProviderLength = 0;

dwProviderLength = sizeof(TEXT_PROVIDER_SPECIFIC_DATA);
memset(&txtProviderData, 0, dwProviderLength);

memset(&smscAddress, 0, sizeof(SMS_ADDRESS));
memset(&inAddress, 0, sizeof(SMS_ADDRESS));
memset(&rcvTime, 0, sizeof(SYSTEMTIME));

// Create a buffer to get the message
TCHAR *tchMsgBuffer = NULL;
tchMsgBuffer = (TCHAR *)LocalAlloc(LPTR,
  dwMessageSize*sizeof(TCHAR));
if(!tchMsgBuffer) {
   OutputDebugString(TEXT("Could not allocate a buffer for
   the message"));
   SmsClose(hSms);
   return FALSE;
}

// Read the message
DWORD dwBytesRead = 0;
```

```
hr = SmsReadMessage(hSms, &smscAddress, &inAddress,
   &rcvTime, (LPBYTE)tchMsgBuffer, dwMessageSize,
   (LPBYTE)&txtProviderData, dwProviderLength, &dwBytesRead);
if(FAILED(hr)) {
   OutputDebugString(TEXT("There was an error reading the
   message"));
   LocalFree(tchMsgBuffer);
   SmsClose(hSms);
   return FALSE;
}


// Display the message to the user
TCHAR tchDisplayMsg[1024] = TEXT("\0");

wsprintf(tchDisplayMsg, TEXT("New
   Message!\r\nFrom:%s\r\n\r\n%s"), inAddress.ptsAddress,
   tchMsgBuffer);
MessageBox(NULL, tchDisplayMsg, TEXT("New SMS Message"),
   MB_OK|MB_ICONEXCLAMATION);
LocalFree(tchMsgBuffer);
```

Closing the SMS Handle

When you have finished working with SMS, you need to close the
handle to the SMS provider to ensure that the messaging component
is shut down properly. You can do this by using the following function call:

```
HRESULT SmsClose(const SMS_HANDLE smshHandle);
```

The only parameter that the function needs is a handle to an open
SMS session. When SmsClose() is called, both the handle specified by
the smshHandle parameter and the Windows event handle that was
returned from your call to SmsOpen() are closed.

Using the SmsClose() function is straightforward:

```
// Close the SMS handle
if(hSms) {
   SmsClose(hSms);
   hSms = NULL;
}
```

Broadcast Message Range

The SMS Messaging protocol specifies that GRPS devices should have the ability to receive messages from a Cell Broadcast Service. These messages are typically sent from a broadcast center and are transmitted over a geographic area, and may provide regional information such as traffic reports.

A Pocket PC Phone Edition device fully supports receiving broadcast messages, and provides you with functions to both read and set the accepted range of location IDs for incoming broadcast messages. These two functions are as follows:

```
HRESULT SmsSetBroadcastMsgRanges(
    const SMS_BROADCAST_RANGES* const psmsbrBroadcastRanges);
```

and

```
HRESULT SmsGetBroadcastMsgRanges(
    SMS_BROADCAST_RANGES* const psmsbrBroadcastRanges);
```

Both `SmsSetBroadcastMsgRanges()` and `SmsGetBroadcast MsgRanges()` take one parameter: a pointer to an `SMS_BROADCAST_ RANGES` structure, which defines the specifics about the accepted broadcast ranges. The structure is defined as follows:

```
typedef struct sms_broadcast_ranges_tag {
    DWORD cbSize;
    DWORD dwParams;
    DWORD dwNumRanges;
    DWORD dwBroadcastMsgLangs;
    BOOL bAccept;
    SMS_RANGE smsrBroadcastRanges[];
} SMS_BROADCAST_RANGES, *LPSMS_BROADCAST_RANGES;
```

The first field, `cbSize`, needs to be set to the size of the `SMS_BROADCAST_RANGES` structure before calling either `SmsSet BroadcastMsgRanges()` or `SmsGetBroadcastMsgRanges()`.

The `dwParams` field indicates which of the remaining fields of the structure contain valid data, and can be one or more of the following options:

- `SMS_PARAM_SBR_BROADCASTMSGIDS` indicates that the `dwNum Ranges` and `smsrBroadcastRanges` fields are valid.

- ■ SMS_PARAM_SBR_BROADCASTMSGLANGS indicates that the dwBroadcastMsgLangs field is valid.
- ■ SMS_PARAM_SBR_ACCEPTIDS indicates that the bAccept field is valid.

The dwNumRanges field specifies how many items are in the smsr BroadcastRanges array. This array is comprised of several SMS_ARRAY structures, each specifying a minimum and maximum number of mobile IDs to listen to. The SMS_ARRAY structure is defined as follows:

```
typedef struct sms_range_tag {
    DWORD dwMinimum;
    DWORD dwMaximum;
} SMS_RANGE, *LPSMS_RANGE;
```

The dwBroadcastMsgLangs field specifies which languages are supported by the Pocket PC device, and can be one or more of the languages listed in Table 8.15.

Table 8.15 Broadcast Message Languages

Broadcast Languages	
SMS_DCSLANG_UNKNOWN	SMS_DCSLANG_NORWEGIAN
SMS_DCSLANG_GERMAN	SMS_DCSLANG_GREEK
SMS_DCSLANG_ENGLISH	SMS_DCSLANG_TURKISH
SMS_DCSLANG_ITALIAN	SMS_DCSLANG_HUNGARIAN
SMS_DCSLANG_FRENCH	SMS_DCSLANG_POLISH
SMS_DCSLANG_SPANISH	SMS_DCSLANG_CZECH
SMS_DCSLANG_DUTCH	SMS_DCSLANG_PORTUGUESE
SMS_DCSLANG_SWEDISH	SMS_DCSLANG_FINNISH
SMS_DCSLANG_DANISH	SMS_DCSLANG_ALL

The last field, bAccept, is used to indicate whether or not the message IDs defined by dwBroadcastMsgLangs and smsrBroadcast Ranges are accepted or not. If bAccept is set to TRUE, then the device will accept message from the specified identifiers.

SMS Notifications

Pocket PC Phone Edition provides your application with the capability to receive SMS messages even if it is not currently running. The function

SmsSetMessageNotification() can be used to configure an application that should be started when a message from a specific SMS protocol arrives. The function is defined as follows:

```
HRESULT SmsSetMessageNotification(
    const SMSREGISTRATIONDATA* psmsrd);
```

The only parameter that SmsSetMessageNotification() uses is a pointer to an SMSREGISTRATIONDATA structure, which looks like the following:

```
typedef struct smsregistrationdata_tag {
    DWORD cbSize;
    TCHAR tszAppName[SMS_MAX_APPNAME_LENGTH];
    TCHAR tszParams[SMS_MAX_PARAMS_LENGTH];
    TCHAR tszProtocolName[SMS_MAX_PROTOCOLNAME_LENGTH];
} SMSREGISTRATIONDATA, *LPSMSREGISTRATIONDATA;
```

The first field should be set to the size of the SMSREGISTRATION DATA structure. The second field, tszAppName, specifies the application name and path that should be run when a new message arrives. When the application is run, the command-line parameters that are set in the tszParams field will be passed to it.

The last field, tszProtocolName, indicates the message provider (protocol) for which the notification is being set, and can be one of the following:

- SMS_MSGTYPE_TEXT, for messages using the Microsoft Text SMS Protocol
- SMS_MSGTYPE_NOTIFICATION, for messages using the Microsoft Notification SMS Protocol
- SMS_MSGTYPE_WDP, for messages using the Microsoft WDP SMS Protocol
- SMS_MSGTYPE_WCMP, for messages using the Microsoft WCMP SMS Protocol
- SMS_MSGTYPE_STATUS, for messages using the Microsoft Status Message Protocol
- SMS_MSGTYPE_RAW, for messages using the Microsoft Raw SMS Protocol

Be aware that when you set a new notification for a specific SMS protocol, you will overwrite any existing notifications for the provider.

To cancel notification messages from an SMS provider, simply call the following:

```
HRESULT SmsClearMessageNotification(
    const LPCTSTR tszProtocolName);
```

The only parameter the function takes is the name of the protocol for which you want to remove notification messages. This should be the same as the provider name that was passed into the SMSREGISTRATIONDATA structure's tszProtocolName field when setting up the notification.

Getting Additional Information from the SIM

The SMS service on the Pocket PC Phone Edition supports two additional functions that enable you to get more information about the device from the SMS service.

To get the SMS address of the device you are using, you can use the following function:

```
HRESULT SmsGetPhoneNumber(SMS_ADDRESS* const psmsaAddress);
```

The only parameter that SmsGetPhoneNumber() needs is a pointer to an SMS_ADDRESS structure, which will be filled in with the device's phone number when the function returns, as shown in the following example:

```
// Device phone number
SMS_ADDRESS mySmsAddress;

memset(&mySmsAddress, 0, sizeof(SMS_ADDRESS));
hr = SmsGetPhoneNumber(&mySmsAddress);

if(FAILED(hr)) {
    OutputDebugString(TEXT("Could not open a handle to the
        SMS text message service."));
    return FALSE;
}

MessageBox(NULL, mySmsAddress.ptsAddress, TEXT("Device Phone
    Number"), MB_ICONINFORMATION|MB_OK);
```

To get an estimate of the current time, you can call the SmsGet Time() function. This function will try to figure out the time by using the last status report message that was sent to the device from the SMS Service Center. The function is defined as follows:

```
HRESULT SmsGetTime(SYSTEMTIME* const ptsCurrentTime,
   DWORD* const pdwErrorMargin);
```

The first parameter, `ptsCurrentTime`, is a pointer to a SYSTEM TIME structure that will be filled in with the estimate of the current time. The time that is returned to you will be in Universal Coordinated Time (UTC) format and should be converted to a local format before being used.

The `pdwErrorMargin` parameter is the maximum amount of time, in seconds, that the returned time could be off by. If SMS cannot determine the error margin, this will be set to 0xFFFFFFFF.

The following example shows how you can get the current estimated time from SMS and properly convert it:

```
// Estimate current time from SMS
SYSTEMTIME estTime;
DWORD dwErrorMargin = 0;

memset(&estTime, 0, sizeof(SYSTEMTIME));

hr = SmsGetTime(&estTime, &dwErrorMargin);
if(FAILED(hr)) {
   OutputDebugString(TEXT("Could not get estimated time
      from SMSC."));
   return FALSE;
}

// Since the time information is a UTC value, we will need
// to convert it.
FILETIME estFileTime;
FILETIME localFileTime;

SystemTimeToFileTime(&estTime, &estFileTime);
FileTimeToLocalFileTime(&estFileTime, &localFileTime);

// Convert it back
SYSTEMTIME estLocalSysTime;
memset(&estLocalSysTime, 0, sizeof(SYSTEMTIME));

FileTimeToSystemTime(&localFileTime, &estLocalSysTime);

// Use estLocalSysTime to set clock, etc....
```

CHAPTER 9

Desktop Synchronization

That's okay, I don't know what synchronize means anyway.

—*Gonzo*, Muppet Babies

Up until this point, we have discussed the various communication technologies that are available to you when developing applications that run directly on a Pocket PC device. Although the Pocket PC can be used as a great stand-alone mobile device, it was actually designed to be a portable companion to your desktop computer. By establishing a partnership with your desktop using **ActiveSync** (which every device comes with), you can enable your Pocket PC to replicate and synchronize files, e-mail messages, appointments, and contacts, convert files between device and desktop formats, and even execute functions from the PC that will run remotely on your Pocket PC.

This chapter describes how ActiveSync controls and manages the synchronization process between data on the desktop and a partnered device. It covers several different topics that deal with specific aspects of a desktop-device partnership, including the following:

- How the **Remote API** (**RAPI**) enables a desktop application to execute a function on a connected Pocket PC device (this is similar to a remote procedure call). RAPI is typically used when a desktop application needs to manage or get information from a connected device, such as a listing of its files.
- How device profiles are managed using the **CEUtil** functions. CEUtil is a set of APIs that enables a desktop application to query the ActiveSync Manager for device information, such as specific synchronization settings or platform information for a previously established partner device.
- How to create **file filters**. File filters are components that plug into the desktop side of ActiveSync, and are used to convert files as

they are sent back and forth between the desktop and a Pocket PC device.

■ How to write ActiveSync **Synchronization Service Providers** (**SSPs**). SSPs are custom components residing on both the desktop and a Pocket PC device that handle data synchronization, replication, and conflict management for specific data objects.

■ How both the Pocket PC and the desktop use **notifications** to alert an application when a connection has been established or when the synchronization process has either started or finished.

Before we dive deeper into developing synchronization components and using the various replication APIs, let's first take a look at how the ActiveSync Manager coordinates and manages all of the connectivity services, service providers, and helper DLLs that are used in the synchronization process.

The ActiveSync Manager

The **ActiveSync Manager** (or just **ActiveSync**) is an application that runs on both your desktop and Pocket PC device, and is responsible for maintaining the partnerships between them (see Figure 9.1). It also

Figure 9.1 The desktop ActiveSync Manager

handles the connection (over USB, Network, and so on), synchronization, and the replication of data between a device and its desktop counterpart.

There are two main components to ActiveSync: the **Service Manager** and **Service Providers**.

The **Service Manager** is responsible for comparing data on the Pocket PC device with that on the desktop. Once it has looked at the data on both for a particular application (and based on synchronization rules the user has configured), it will update them with the most recent information. Think of it as the *synchronization engine* for your data (see Figure 9.2). The ActiveSync Manager is the application that an end user works with to configure service providers and their configuration options. In addition, ActiveSync is also responsible for connectivity services, either locally or remotely, that can be established over a serial, infrared, Ethernet, or wireless connection.

The other half of ActiveSync is the **Service Providers**. A service provider is a COM component that is registered within the Service Manager and provides specific synchronization functionality for a particular

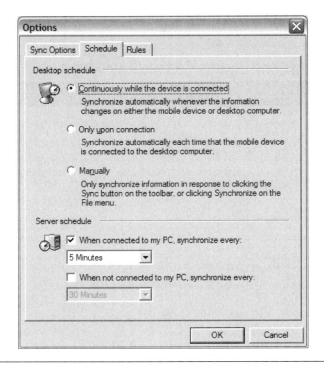

Figure 9.2 ActiveSync synchronization options

application. For example, applications such as Pocket Outlook, Inbox, Pocket Word, and Pocket Excel all have ActiveSync Service Providers. A typical service provider will consist of two modules: one that runs on the desktop and one that runs on a Pocket PC device.

Another type of service provider that ActiveSync will also use is File Filters. File Filters run on the desktop and are used to handle the conversion of a particular file type when copied between a device and a desktop computer. File Filters are also registered with the Service Manager.

Using the ActiveSync Manager

The ActiveSync Manager is typically launched when a connection is established to a Pocket PC device. If you need to manually execute it, the safest way to find out where it is located is by looking in the desktop's registry. You will need to examine the registry key `HKEY_LOCAL_ MACHINE\SOFTWARE\Microsoft\Windows CE Services` and look at the `InstalledDir` subkey value. This will contain the path that ActiveSync was installed in. You can then run the `wcesmgr.exe` executable to start the Service Manager.

When starting ActiveSync, you can run it with any of the command-line options described in Table 9.1.

Table 9.1 ActiveSync Manager Command-Line Options

Parameter	Description
	No command-line parameter. This will just run ActiveSync without displaying the status window.
/quit	Shuts down ActiveSync while keeping a connection active.
/show	Starts ActiveSync and makes the status window visible.
/syncmgr	Starts ActiveSync and displays the Options dialog box.
/syncnow	Starts ActiveSync and immediately synchronizes data with the connected device.

Let's take a look at how you can use the `CreateProcess()` function to start ActiveSync on your desktop:

```
// Open the registry
HKEY hKey = NULL;
TCHAR tchPath[MAX_PATH+1] = TEXT("\0");
TCHAR tchActiveSyncInsPath[MAX_PATH+1] = TEXT("\0");
DWORD dwSize = MAX_PATH;
```

```
wsprintf(tchPath, TEXT("SOFTWARE\\Microsoft\\Windows CE
   Services"));
if(RegOpenKeyEx(HKEY_LOCAL_MACHINE, tchPath, 0, KEY_READ,
   &hKey) != ERROR_SUCCESS)
   return FALSE;

// Get the path to where ActiveSync is installed
if(RegQueryValueEx(hKey, TEXT("InstalledDir"), NULL, NULL,
     (LPBYTE)&tchActiveSyncInsPath, &dwSize) !=
     ERROR_SUCCESS) {
   RegCloseKey(hKey);
   return FALSE;
}

if(hKey)
   RegCloseKey(hKey);

// Launch it
STARTUPINFO si;
PROCESS_INFORMATION pi;
_tcsncat(tchActiveSyncInsPath, TEXT("\\wcesmgr.exe"),
   MAX_PATH);

memset(&si, 0, sizeof(STARTUPINFO));
memset(&pi, 0, sizeof(PROCESS_INFORMATION));

si.cb = sizeof(STARTUPINFO);
CreateProcess(tchActiveSyncInsPath, NULL, NULL, NULL, FALSE,
   NORMAL_PRIORITY_CLASS, NULL, NULL, &si, &pi);
```

Note that ActiveSync uses a proprietary protocol known as **Direct Cable Connect Manager** (**DCCM**) to send commands, replicate information, and communicate with a connected device. In order for ActiveSync to work properly, you need to ensure that the TCP/IP ports 990, 999, 5678, and 5679 are available for it to use.

More information about configuring a system to use DCCM can be found in the Microsoft Knowledge Base article Q259369, located at http://support.microsoft.com/default.aspx?scid=kb;en-us;259369.

Remote API (RAPI)

The **Remote API** (**RAPI**) provides a set of helper functions that enable a desktop-based application to execute code on a connected Pocket PC device. Once a function has returned, the results are sent back to the PC. In essence, RAPI is a type of one-way **Remote Procedure Call** (**RPC**)—the client (your desktop application) makes a request to the server (a connected Pocket PC device) to execute some functionality, and returns the results to it.

RAPI was originally designed as a way to manage a Pocket PC device from the desktop. It includes functions that enable an application to query the file system, registry, and device databases, as well as get information about the Pocket PC's system configuration. You can even create your own functions, which can be run over the RAPI APIs.

You will quickly notice that most of the functions in RAPI look similar to the functions in the standard Pocket PC and Windows 32 API. In fact, they typically have the same definition and number of parameters, as well as the same return values, as a standard desktop function call. The only difference is that they all are prefixed with the letters **Ce**. For example, the RAPI function CeFindFirstFile() is the same as the desktop FindFirst File() API, except that it will enumerate the files on a connected Pocket PC device, rather than those on the desktop. This being the case, I will not provide a detailed description of each function available via the RAPI API.

Because RAPI is run on the desktop, you must ensure that the computer running your application has the latest version of ActiveSync installed on it. This will ensure that rapi.dll (which is required for your application to work) is present on the desktop, as you may not distribute rapi.dll on your own. You can call RAPI from console applications, window applications, and even a .NET assembly.

In order to use the Remote API within your applications, you need to include the rapi.h header file in your project, as well as link with the rapi.lib library (note that because this is a desktop library, it is located in the .\wce300\Pocket PC 2002\support\ActiveSync\ lib directory in the folder where you have installed Embedded Visual C++).

Using RAPI

Before you can use any of the RAPI functions, you must first initialize Windows CE's remote services and establish a communications link with a connected device by calling either the `CeRapiInit()` or `CeRapi InitEx()` functions.

The simplest way to start RAPI is by calling the synchronous (i.e., blocking) function `CeRapiInit()`, which is defined as follows:

```
HRESULT CeRapiInit();
```

Once the function is called, it will immediately attempt to establish a connection to a Pocket PC device, and *will not* return control to your application until either a connection has been made or the function fails. `CeRapiInit()` will return `E_SUCCESS` if a successful connection can be made and RAPI has initialized without a problem; otherwise, you will be returned `E_FAIL`. If RAPI has already been initialized, you will receive `CERAPI_E_ALREADYINITIALIZED` as the return value.

The following short code sample shows you how to use the `CeRapi Init()` function:

```
HRESULT hr = S_OK;
hr = CeRapiInit();

if(FAILED(hr)) {
    if(hr == CERAPI_E_ALREADYINITIALIZED)
      OutputDebugString(TEXT("RAPI has already been
          initalized"));
    return FALSE;
}
```

Although using the `CeRapiInitEx()` function is a bit more involved, you will find that it provides you with a greater amount of control because it is asynchronous (the function will return to you immediately). This means, of course, that you will have to periodically check the RAPI event handle you are returned in order to find out when it has become signaled.

The `CeRapiInitEx()` function is defined as follows:

```
HRESULT CeRapiInitEx(RAPIINIT *pRapiInit);
```

The only parameter that the function takes is a pointer to a `RAPIINIT` structure, which contains information about the RAPI event handle and its status. The structure is defined as follows:

```
typedef struct _RAPIINIT {
    DWORD cbSize;
```

```
    HANDLE heRapiInit;
    HRESULT hrRapiInit;
} RAPIINIT;
```

The first field, `cbSize`, should be set before calling `CeRapiInit Ex()` with the size of the `RAPIINIT` structure. This is followed by `heRapiInit`, which will be filled in with the event handle that you can use to check on the status of your RAPI connection. The last field, `hrRapiInit`, will be filled in with the return code from `CeRapi InitEx()` once `heRapiInit` becomes signaled.

The following code snippet shows how you can use the `CeRapi InitEx()` function to initialize your RAPI connection by using the `WaitForSingleObject()` function to monitor the RAPI event handle:

```
HRESULT hr = S_OK;
RAPIINIT rapiInit;

memset(&rapiInit, 0, sizeof(RAPIINIT));
rapiInit.cbSize = sizeof(RAPIINIT);

hr = CeRapiInitEx(&rapiInit);
if(FAILED(hr)) {
    if(hr == CERAPI_E_ALREADYINITIALIZED)
        OutputDebugString(TEXT("RAPI has already been
        initalized"));
    return FALSE;
}

// Wait for RAPI to be signaled
DWORD dwResult = 0;
dwResult = WaitForSingleObject(rapiInit.heRapiInit, 5000);
if(dwResult == WAIT_TIMEOUT || dwResult == WAIT_ABANDONED) {
    // RAPI has failed or timed out. Proceed with cleanup
    CeRapiUninit();
    return FALSE;
}

if(dwResult == WAIT_OBJECT_0 && SUCCEEDED(rapiInit.hrRapiInit)) {
    // RAPI has succeeded.
    OutputDebugString(TEXT("RAPI Initialized."));

    // Do something here
}
```

When working with applications that use RAPI, it is important to remember that you are relying on a network connection between the desktop and a device. When a function fails, an error can occur in either the RAPI layer or the function itself. You can determine where the error has actually occurred by calling into the `CeRapiGetError()` function, which is defined as follows:

```
HRESULT CeRapiGetError(void);
```

The function takes no parameters, and will return a value other than 0 if RAPI itself was responsible for the function failing. If `CeRapiGetError()` returns 0, however, you know that the error occurred in the actual remote function, and you can use the `CeGet LastError()` function to determine the error code, as shown in the following example:

```
DWORD dwError = CeRapiGetError();

if(dwError == 0) {
   // The error did not occur in RAPI, find out what the
   // remote function returned
   dwError = CeGetLastError();
}
```

A few functions (`CeFindAllDatabases()`, `CeFindAllFiles()`, and `CeReadRecordProps()`) will allocate memory on the desktop when they are called. In order to properly free this memory, you can use the following function:

```
HRESULT CeRapiFreeBuffer(LPVOID);
```

The only parameter you need to pass in is a pointer to the buffer that was allocated. If the function succeeds, then you will be returned a value of `S_OK`.

When you have finished using RAPI, you must also make sure that you properly shut down the remote connection services. To do so, you can simply use the following function:

```
HRESULT CeRapiUninit();
```

The function takes no parameters, and will return a value of `E_FAIL` if RAPI has not been previously initialized.

File System RAPI Functions

Table 9.2 lists the Remote API functions for working with the Pocket PC file system.

Table 9.2 RAPI File System Functions

Remote File System Functions

```
BOOL CeCloseHandle(HANDLE);
BOOL CeCopyFile(LPCWSTR, LPCWSTR, BOOL);
BOOL CeCreateDirectory(LPCWSTR, LPSECURITY_ATTRIBUTES);
BOOL CeDeleteFile(LPCWSTR);
BOOL CeFindAllFiles(LPCWSTR, DWORD, LPDWORD,
  LPLPCE_FIND_DATA);
BOOL CeFindClose(HANDLE);
BOOL CeFindNextFile(HANDLE, LPCE_FIND_DATA);
BOOL CeGetFileSize(HANDLE, LPDWORD);
BOOL CeGetFileTime(HANDLE, LPFILETIME, LPFILETIME,
  LPFILETIME);
BOOL CeMoveFile(LPCWSTR, LPCWSTR);
BOOL CeReadFile(HANDLE, LPVOID, DWORD, LPDWORD,
  LPOVERLAPPED);
BOOL CeRemoveDirectory(LPCWSTR);
BOOL CeSetEndOfFile(HANDLE);
BOOL CeSetFileAttributes(LPCWSTR, DWORD);
BOOL CeSetFileTime(HANDLE, LPFILETIME, LPFILETIME,
  LPFILETIME);
BOOL CeWriteFile(HANDLE, LPCVOID, DWORD, LPDWORD,
  LPOVERLAPPED);
DWORD CeGetFileAttributes(LPCWSTR);
DWORD CeSetFilePointer(HANDLE, LONG, PLONG, DWORD);
HANDLE CeCreateFile(LPCWSTR, DWORD, DWORD,
  LPSECURITY_ATTRIBUTES, DWORD, DWORD, HANDLE);
HANDLE CeFindFirstFile(LPCWSTR, LPCE_FIND_DATA);
```

The following example shows how you can use the Remote API's `CeFindAllFiles()` (as well as `CeRapiFreeBuffer()`) function on the desktop to easily retrieve a list of the wave files that are located on the device:

```
LPVOID lpvFindData = NULL;
DWORD dwFileCount = 0;

// Get a list of the WAV files in the \Windows folder
if(CeFindAllFiles(TEXT("\\Windows\\*.wav"),
   FAF_NO_HIDDEN_SYS_ROMMODULES|FAF_NAME, &dwFileCount,
   (LPLPCE_FIND_DATA)&lpvFindData) == FALSE) {

   DWORD dwError = CeRapiGetError();
   TCHAR tchError[128] = TEXT("\0");

   if(dwError == 0)
      dwError = CeGetLastError();

   wsprintf(tchError, TEXT("Error: %d"), dwError);
   OutputDebugString(tchError);
   return FALSE;
}

// Walk through the files
LPCE_FIND_DATA pFindData = (LPCE_FIND_DATA)lpvFindData;

for(DWORD dwCount = 0; dwCount<dwFileCount; dwCount++) {
   TCHAR tchFile[MAX_PATH+1] = TEXT("\0");

   wsprintf(tchFile, TEXT("Remote File:%s\r\n"),
      pFindData[dwCount].cFileName);
   OutputDebugString(tchFile);
}

// Clean up the buffer
if(lpvFindData)
   CeRapiFreeBuffer(lpvFindData);
```

Registry RAPI Functions

Table 9.3 lists the Remote API functions that are available for manipulating the Pocket PC registry from the desktop host.

Table 9.3 RAPI Registry Functions

Remote Registry Functions

```
LONG CeRegCloseKey(HKEY);
LONG CeRegCreateKeyEx(HKEY, LPCWSTR, DWORD, LPWSTR, DWORD,
  REGSAM, LPSECURITY_ATTRIBUTES, PHKEY, LPDWORD);
LONG CeRegDeleteKey(HKEY, LPCWSTR);
LONG CeRegDeleteValue(HKEY, LPCWSTR);
LONG CeRegEnumKeyEx(HKEY, DWORD, LPWSTR, LPDWORD, LPDWORD,
  LPWSTR, LPDWORD, PFILETIME);
LONG CeRegEnumValue(HKEY, DWORD, LPWSTR, LPDWORD, LPDWORD,
  LPDWORD, LPBYTE, LPDWORD);
LONG CeRegOpenKeyEx(HKEY, LPCWSTR, DWORD, REGSAM, PHKEY);
LONG CeRegQueryInfoKey(HKEY, LPWSTR, LPDWORD, LPDWORD,
  LPDWORD, LPDWORD, LPDWORD, LPDWORD, LPDWORD, LPDWORD,
  LPDWORD, PFILETIME);
LONG CeRegQueryValueEx(HKEY, LPCWSTR, LPDWORD, LPDWORD,
  LPBYTE, LPDWORD);
LONG CeRegSetValueEx(HKEY, LPCWSTR, DWORD, DWORD, LPBYTE,
  DWORD);
```

Database RAPI Functions

Table 9.4 lists the Remote API functions for working with Pocket PC databases.

Table 9.4 RAPI Database Functions

Remote Database Functions

```
BOOL CeDeleteDatabase(CEOID);
BOOL CeDeleteDatabaseEx(PCEGUID, CEOID);
BOOL CeDeleteRecord(HANDLE, CEOID);
BOOL CeEnumDBVolumes(PCEGUID, LPWSTR, DWORD);
BOOL CeFindAllDatabases(DWORD, WORD, LPWORD,
  LPLPCEDB_FIND_DATA);
BOOL CeFlushDBVol(PCEGUID);
BOOL CeMountDBVol(PCEGUID, LPWSTR, DWORD);
BOOL CeOidGetInfo(CEOID, CEOIDINFO*);
BOOL CeOidGetInfoEx(PCEGUID, CEOID, CEOIDINFO*);
BOOL CeSetDatabaseInfo(CEOID, CEDBASEINFO*);
BOOL CeSetDatabaseInfoEx(PCEGUID, CEOID, CEDBASEINFO*);
```

Remote Database Functions

```
BOOL CeUnmountDBVol(PCEGUID);
CEOID CeCreateDatabase(LPWSTR, DWORD, WORD, SORTORDERSPEC*);
CEOID CeFindNextDatabase(HANDLE);
CEOID CeCreateDatabaseEx(PCEGUID, CEDBASEINFO*);
CEOID CeFindNextDatabaseEx(HANDLE, PCEGUID);
CEOID CeReadRecordProps(HANDLE, DWORD, LPWORD, CEPROPID*,
  LPBYTE*, LPDWORD);
CEOID CeReadRecordPropsEx(HANDLE, DWORD, LPWORD, CEPROPID*,
  LPBYTE*, LPDWORD, HANDLE);
CEOID CeSeekDatabase(HANDLE, DWORD, DWORD, LPDWORD);
CEOID CeWriteRecordProps(HANDLE, CEOID, WORD, CEPROPVAL*);
CEOID CeWriteRecordProps(HANDLE, CEOID, WORD, CEPROPVAL*);
HANDLE CeFindFirstDatabase(DWORD);
HANDLE CeFindFirstDatabaseEx(PCEGUID, DWORD);
HANDLE CeOpenDatabase(PCEOID, LPWSTR, CEPROPID, DWORD, HWND);
HANDLE CeOpenDatabaseEx(PCEGUID, PCEOID, LPWSTR, CEPROPID,
  DWORD, CENOTIFYREQUEST *);
```

System Configuration and Information RAPI Functions

Table 9.5 lists the Remote API functions for retrieving Pocket PC configuration and system information.

Table 9.5 RAPI System Information Functions

Remote System Configuration and Information Functions

```
BOOL CeCheckPassword(LPWSTR);
BOOL CeCreateProcess(LPCWSTR, LPCWSTR, LPSECURITY_ATTRIBUTES,
  LPSECURITY_ATTRIBUTES, BOOL, DWORD, LPVOID, LPWSTR,
  LPSTARTUPINFO, LPPROCESS_INFORMATION);
BOOL CeGetStoreInformation(LPSTORE_INFORMATION);
BOOL CeGetSystemPowerStatusEx(PSYSTEM_POWER_STATUS_EX, BOOL);
BOOL CeGetVersionEx(LPCEOSVERSIONINFO);
DWORD CeGetLastError(void);
int CeGetDesktopDeviceCaps(int);
int CeGetSystemMetrics(int);
VOID CeGetSystemInfo(LPSYSTEM_INFO);
VOID CeGlobalMemoryStatus(LPMEMORYSTATUS);
```

Shell RAPI Functions

Table 9.6 lists the Remote API shell management functions.

Table 9.6 RAPI Shell Management Functions

Remote Shell Functions
| ```
BOOL CeSHGetShortcutTarget(LPWSTR, LPWSTR, int);
DWORD CeGetSpecialFolderPath(int, DWORD, LPWSTR);
DWORD CeGetTempPath(DWORD, LPWSTR);
DWORD CeSHCreateShortcut(LPWSTR, LPWSTR);
``` |

Window RAPI Functions

Table 9.7 lists the Remote API window management functions.

Table 9.7 RAPI Window Management Functions

Remote Window Functions
| ```
HWND CeGetWindow(HWND, UINT);
int CeGetClassName(HWND, LPWSTR, int);
int CeGetWindowText(HWND, LPWSTR, int);
LONG CeGetWindowLong(HWND, int);
``` |

Creating Your Own RAPI Functions

While the Remote API provides a wide breadth of functions that cover most of the basic information you need about your Pocket PC device, there are certainly going to be times when you will need to communicate with your device in a way that isn't supported by the supplied functions. Fortunately, RAPI also provides you with an API that gives you the capability to create and execute your own functions on the Pocket PC.

You can use two different methods to call your own RAPI functions:

1. **Block mode**. When you call a remote function through RAPI in block (or *synchronous*) mode, your desktop application will not be returned control until the function has completed. RAPI will send the command to the device, load the specified DLL into

memory, call the function you want to execute, and return any data through RAPI when it is finished.

2. **Stream mode**. When calling a remote function in stream (or *asynchronous*) mode, your application is returned control immediately after making the call. You then need to use an **IRAPIStream** COM interface (based on IStream) to send data back and forth between the desktop and the remote device. Using stream mode typically provides faster communications with a remote device than block mode.

Both block mode and stream mode use the same function, CeRapi Invoke(), to execute your own user-defined function, and is defined as follows:

```
HRESULT CeRapiInvoke(LPCWSTR pDllPath, LPCWSTR
    pFunctionName, DWORD cbInput, BYTE *pInput, DWORD *pcbOutput,
    BYTE **ppOutput, IRAPIStream **ppIRAPIStream, DWORD dwReserved);
```

The first parameter, pDllPath, should point to a null-terminated string that contains the full name and path of the DLL (in Unicode) on the Pocket PC that contains the function you are calling. The next parameter, pFunctionName, is the name of the function that you want RAPI to execute.

The next two parameters are used to set up the data you are going to send to the remote function. The cbInput parameter should specify the number of bytes that are located in the data buffer, which is specified by the pointer to which you set the pInput parameter. Be aware that the buffer you pass in the pInput parameter will be freed by the function you are calling into, so you should make sure that you allocate it by using the LocalAlloc() function.

The pcbOutput and ppOutput parameters are used to receive data from the remote function. The pcbOutput parameter is a pointer to a DWORD value that will be filled in with the number of bytes that are contained in the data buffer to which ppOutput points. Because the remote function (and RAPI) has allocated memory on the desktop for the returned data buffer, you need to remember to call the LocalFree() function to free the memory that is being used by the ppOutput buffer when you are finished using it.

The `ppIRAPIStream` parameter will determine whether you are using stream mode or block mode to call the remote function. To call your function using block mode, you can simply set this to `NULL`. To use stream mode, you need to set this parameter to a pointer of an `IRAPIStream` interface.

The last parameter is reserved, and should be set to 0.

Although you can name your remote function anything you like, you have to make sure that it matches the following prototype:

```
STDAPI RAPIFunctionName(DWORD cbInput, BYTE *pInput, DWORD
    *pcbOutput, BYTE **ppOutput, IRAPIStream *pIRAPIStream);
```

The first two parameters, `cbInput` and `pInput`, specify the size and data buffer parameters, respectively, that are passed from the desktop call to `CeRapiInvoke()`. Because RAPI has automatically allocated data for `pInput`, your function needs to call `LocalFree()` on the buffer that is being passed in so that memory can be properly managed.

The next two parameters, `pcbOutput` and `ppOutput`, are used to allocate a buffer, set the size of it, and return data to the desktop. The desktop application calling your remote function is responsible for freeing any data you allocate for the output buffer.

The last parameter, `pIRAPIStream`, will point to an `IRAPIStream` object that RAPI has allocated if you are communicating with your desktop counterpart in stream mode.

Now that you know how to call your own remote functions using `CeRapiInvoke()`, let's take a look at what's actually involved with writing a remote function that returns information from the Subscriber Identity Module (SIM) phonebook on a Pocket PC Phone Edition device (see Chapter 8 for more information about using the SIM Manager APIs).

Using Block Mode

Calling your own functions using RAPI's block mode interface is extremely straightforward. All you need to do is create a DLL for the Pocket PC device that contains the functions you need (following the prototype shown above). A desktop application can then use `CeRapi Invoke()` to call your function (be sure to pass in `NULL` for the `ppIRAPIStream` parameter). Essentially, this operates in the same fashion as all of the standard RAPI function calls.

Let's take a look at how you can create a RAPI function to read a specific phonebook entry by using the `SimReadPhonebookEntry()` function on a Pocket PC Phone Edition device.

The code for the DLL that you will be putting on your Pocket PC Phone Edition device would look like the following:

```
#include <windows.h>
#include <Simmgr.h>

// Exported function prototypes
#ifdef __cplusplus
extern "C" {
#endif
__declspec(dllexport) INT MyCeGetPhonebookEntry(DWORD,
   BYTE *, DWORD *, BYTE **, PVOID);
#ifdef __cplusplus
}
#endif

// Standard DLL entry point
BOOL WINAPI DllMain(HANDLE hinstDLL, DWORD dwReason,
   LPVOID lpvReserved)
{
   return TRUE;
}

// Remote Block Function
int MyCeGetPhonebookEntry(DWORD cbInput, BYTE *pInput,
   DWORD *pcbOutput, BYTE **ppOutput, PVOID *pVoid)
{
   // Check to see if we have an input buffer
   if(!pInput || sizeof(cbInput)>4)
      return -1;

   // Get the phone entry that was requested
   DWORD dwEntry = 0;
   memcpy(&dwEntry, pInput, cbInput);

   // Free up the buffer that was passed in
   LocalFree(pInput);
```

```
// Initialize the SIM
HRESULT hr = S_OK;
HSIM hSim = NULL;

if(FAILED(SimInitialize(0, NULL, 0, &hSim)))
    return -1;

// Get the data from the SIM
SIMPHONEBOOKENTRY simEntry;

memset(&simEntry, 0, sizeof(SIMPHONEBOOKENTRY));
simEntry.cbSize = sizeof(SIMPHONEBOOKENTRY);

hr = SimReadPhonebookEntry(hSim, SIM_PBSTORAGE_SIM,
    dwEntry, &simEntry);

SimDeinitialize(hSim);

// If the read failed, just exit
if(FAILED(hr))
    return -1;

// Allocate the return buffer
DWORD dwBufferLength =
    (MAX_LENGTH_PHONEBOOKENTRYTEXT+MAX_LENGTH_ADDRESS+1);
TCHAR tchBuffer[MAX_LENGTH_PHONEBOOKENTRYTEXT+MAX_
    LENGTH_ADDRESS+1];
BYTE *pOutputBuffer = NULL;

pOutputBuffer = (BYTE*)LocalAlloc(LPTR, dwBufferLength);

if(!pOutputBuffer)
    return -1;

// Copy the name and phone to the buffer
wsprintf(tchBuffer, TEXT("%s %s"), simEntry.lpszText,
    simEntry.lpszAddress);

// Convert it to non-unicode
wcstombs((char *)pOutputBuffer, tchBuffer,
    dwBufferLength);

// Set up for the return
*ppOutput = (BYTE *)pOutputBuffer;
```

```
   *pcbOutput = dwBufferLength;
   return 1;
}
```

Your code on the desktop for calling the remote function, `MyCeGet
PhonebookEntry()`, in block mode is as follows:

```
#include <windows.h>
#include <stdio.h>
#include <tchar.h>
#include <rapi.h>

// Entry point for a console app on the desktop
int wmain()
{
   HRESULT hr = S_OK;

   // Initalize RAPI
   hr = CeRapiInit();
   if(FAILED(hr)) {
      printf("Could not initialize RAPI\r\n");
      return -1;
   }

   // Set up stuff to send over
   DWORD dwSIMEntry = 1;
   DWORD dwSize = sizeof(dwSIMEntry);
   DWORD dwOutputSize = 0;
   BYTE *pOutput = NULL;
   BYTE *pInput = NULL;

   pInput = (BYTE *)LocalAlloc(LPTR, dwSize);
   memcpy(pInput, &dwSIMEntry, dwSize);

   // Call into the Remote API function
   hr = CeRapiInvoke(TEXT("myrapice"),
      TEXT("MyCeGetPhonebookEntry"), dwSize,
      pInput, &dwOutputSize, &pOutput, NULL, 0);

   if(FAILED(hr)) {
      printf("Could not get SIM information!\r\n");
      CeRapiUninit();
      return -1;
   }
```

```
    if(pOutput) {
       printf((char *)pOutput);
       LocalFree(pOutput);
    }

    CeRapiUninit();
    return 0;
}
```

In order to call this function in block mode from the desktop, you need to first allocate a buffer that will be used to pass information to the remote function. In this case, you want to pass in an argument that indicates which entry number from the SIM phonebook you are interested in. Once you have allocated a DWORD, you set it with the entry number you would like, and call the CeRapiInvoke() function. When the call returns, the output buffer will be filled in with a null-terminated string that contains the name and phone number of the entry. You must remember to call LocalFree() on the returned buffer in order to properly free the allocated memory.

Using Stream Mode

Although using the Remote API's stream mode to communicate with a device might seem a bit more complicated because it uses a COM object to send and receive data, using it is actually fairly straightforward, and the benefits outweigh the additional code. Not only will you have control returned to your application immediately after calling CeRapiInvoke(), using stream mode also enables you to more precisely control the flow of data between the desktop and a device.

To use stream mode, all you need to do is call the CeRapiInvoke() function and pass in a pointer to an IRAPIStream object that has been initialized and set to NULL for the ppIRAPIStream parameter, as shown in the following example:

```
IRAPIStream *pIRAPIStream = NULL;
DWORD dwOutputSize = 0;
BYTE *pOutput = NULL;

// Initalize the RAPI Stream interface
CoInitialize(NULL);
```

```
// Call into the Remote API function
hr = CeRapiInvoke(TEXT("myrapice"), TEXT("MyCeSimDir"),
    0, NULL, &dwOutputSize, &pOutput, &pIRAPIStream, 0);
```

As you can see, what makes using stream mode easy is that RAPI itself implements the `IRAPIStream` object—you only need to talk to the object to send and receive data.

The `IRAPIStream` interface is based on the standard `IStream`, which generically supports sending and receiving data from other stream objects. Only two additional methods have been added to the `IRAPIStream` interface, and they enable you to get and set timeout values for your communications stream. They are defined as follows:

```
HRESULT SetRapiStat(RAPISTREAMFLAG Flag, DWORD dwValue);
HRESULT GetRapiStat(RAPISTREAMFLAG Flag, DWORD *pdwValue);
```

For both setting and getting the timeout value, the first parameter must be set to `STREAM_TIMEOUT_READ`. If you are setting the timeout value, you should set `dwValue` to the amount of time you want to elapse before the communications stream times out. If you are getting the value, then you need to pass in only a pointer to a `DWORD` variable that will receive the set timeout.

When calling a remote function using stream mode, you can still use `CeRapiInvoke()` to pass in some initial data using its `cbInput` and `pInput` parameters. However, once the initial call has been made, it is recommended that you use the stream object's `Read()` and `Write()` methods to pass data back and forth.

Let's take a look at what would be involved if you wanted to use RAPI's stream mode to get a directory of phonebook entries from the SIM card on a Pocket PC Phone Edition device.

The code for the DLL that contains the `MyCeSimDir()` command you will be putting on your Pocket PC Phone Edition device would look like the following:

```
#include <windows.h>
#include <Simmgr.h>
#include <rapi.h>

#ifdef __cplusplus
extern "C" {
#endif
```

```
__declspec(dllexport) INT MyCeSimDir(DWORD, BYTE *, DWORD *,
   BYTE **, IRAPIStream *);
#ifdef __cplusplus
}
#endif

BOOL WINAPI DllMain(HANDLE hinstDLL, DWORD dwReason,
   LPVOID lpvReserved)
{
   return TRUE;
}

int MyCeSimDir(DWORD cbInput, BYTE *pInput,
   DWORD *pcbOutput, BYTE **ppOutput, IRAPIStream *pIRAPIStream)
{
   // This sample will return all entries, so ignore the
   // buffer that was passed in
   if(pInput)
      LocalFree(pInput);

   // Make sure that the IRAPIStream is valid
   if(!pIRAPIStream)
      return -1;

   // Initialize the SIM
   HRESULT hr = S_OK;
   HSIM hSim = NULL;

   if(FAILED(SimInitialize(0, NULL, 0, &hSim)))
      return -1;

   // Get the total number of entries
   DWORD dwUsed = 0, dwTotal = 0;

   hr = SimGetPhonebookStatus(hSim, SIM_PBSTORAGE_SIM,
      &dwUsed, &dwTotal);

   if(FAILED(hr)) {
      SimDeinitialize(hSim);
      return -1;
   }
```

```
   // Make sure there's something to return
   if(dwUsed == 0) {
      SimDeinitialize(hSim);
      return -1;
   }


   // Get each entry
   // We'll pass them back as a Name [Phonenumber] string.
   SIMPHONEBOOKENTRY simEntry;
   TCHAR tchEntry[MAX_LENGTH_PHONEBOOKENTRYTEXT+
      MAX_LENGTH_ADDRESS+1];
   DWORD dwLength = 0, dwBytesWritten = 0;

   for(DWORD dwEntry = 0; dwEntry<dwUsed; dwEntry++) {
      memset(&simEntry, 0, sizeof(SIMPHONEBOOKENTRY));
      simEntry.cbSize = sizeof(SIMPHONEBOOKENTRY);

      hr = SimReadPhonebookEntry(hSim, SIM_PBSTORAGE_SIM,
         dwEntry, &simEntry);
      if(FAILED(hr))
         break;

      // Build the string
      memset(tchEntry, 0,
         MAX_LENGTH_PHONEBOOKENTRYTEXT+MAX_LENGTH_ADDRESS+1);
      wsprintf(tchEntry, TEXT("%s [%s]"), simEntry.lpszText,
         simEntry.lpszAddress);

      // Write it to the stream
      // First, send the length
      dwLength = (lstrlen(tchEntry)+1)*sizeof(TCHAR);
      hr = pIRAPIStream->Write(&dwLength, sizeof(dwLength),
         &dwBytesWritten);

      // Next, send the buffer
      hr = pIRAPIStream->Write(tchEntry, dwLength,
         &dwBytesWritten);
      if(FAILED(hr))
         break;
   }

   // Clean up
   SimDeinitialize(hSim);
```

```
   // Send that there's "No more data"
   DWORD dwFinished = 0xFFFFFFFF;
   hr = pIRAPIStream->Write(&dwFinished, sizeof(dwFinished),
      &dwBytesWritten);

   // Release the stream interface
   pIRAPIStream->Release();
   return 0;
}
```

On the desktop side, you can create a simple console application that will call into your remote function using stream mode to output the contents of the SIM phonebook:

```
#include <windows.h>
#include <stdio.h>
#include <tchar.h>
#include <rapi.h>

#define BUFFER_SIZE 1024

// Entry point for a console app on the desktop
int wmain()
{
   HRESULT hr = S_OK;

   // Initalize RAPI
   hr = CeRapiInit();
   if(FAILED(hr)) {
      printf("Could not initialize RAPI\r\n");
      return -1;
   }

   // Set up stuff to send over
   IRAPIStream *pIRAPIStream = NULL;
   DWORD dwOutputSize = 0;
   BYTE *pOutput = NULL;

   // Initalize the RAPI Stream interface
   CoInitialize(NULL);

   // Call into the Remote API function
   hr = CeRapiInvoke(TEXT("myrapice"), TEXT("MyCeSimDir"),
      0, NULL, &dwOutputSize, &pOutput, &pIRAPIStream, 0);
```

```
    if(FAILED(hr)) {
        DWORD dwError = CeRapiGetError();
        if(dwError == 0)
            dwError = CeGetLastError();

        printf("Could not get SIM information! Error: %u\r\n",
            dwError);
        CeRapiUninit();
        return -1;
    }

    // Read from the remote stream
    TCHAR tchEntry[BUFFER_SIZE+1];
    DWORD dwSize = BUFFER_SIZE;
    DWORD dwBytesRead = 0;
    DWORD dwLength = 0;

    do {
        // Get the length. If it is 0xFFFFFFFF, we're done.
        hr = pIRAPIStream->Read(&dwLength, sizeof(dwLength),
            &dwBytesRead);

        if(FAILED(hr) || dwLength == 0xFFFFFFFF)
            break;

        // Ok, read the buffer
        hr = pIRAPIStream->Read(tchEntry, dwLength,
            &dwBytesRead);

        // Do something with the output here
        // ....

        // Clean up for next entry
        dwSize = BUFFER_SIZE;
        memset(tchEntry, 0, BUFFER_SIZE+1);
        dwBytesRead = 0;
    } while(1);

    // Clean up
    pIRAPIStream->Release();
    CeRapiUninit();
    return 0;
}
```

CEUtil Helper APIs

When a partnership exists between a desktop computer and a Pocket PC device, ActiveSync makes extensive use of the registry to store information about that device, such as its partnership settings, synchronization objects, and other device-specific configuration information. In addition, the registry on the desktop is used to configure global ActiveSync items, such as new synchronization service providers and file filters that are installed.

This information is stored in two locations in the desktop's registry:

- **HKEY_LOCAL_MACHINE\SOFTWARE\Microsoft\ Windows CE Services** is used to store general ActiveSync configuration information. This key is used to configure connection notifications, add new synchronization objects, set up defaults for installed file filters, and even add additional menu items for your own extensions to the ActiveSync application.
- **HKEY_CURRENT_USER\Software\Microsoft\Windows CE Services** is used to store information about both the individual settings and the defaults for a device partnership. This includes how a synchronization provider works with a particular device, what file filters are enabled on it, as well as other general device configuration information for connected devices.

While you can design your desktop-side ActiveSync applications to directly manipulate information based on the current registry locations, the CEUtil helper functions facilitate development by wrapping all of the functionality that is required to navigate through the registry (i.e., it internally uses functions such as RegOpenKeyEx(), RegQueryValue Ex(), etc.). Another advantage to using the CEUtil APIs is that you are guaranteed that your application will still work properly even if future versions of ActiveSync change the location in the registry where information is stored.

Note that the CEUtil helper library works only with partnerships that are already established on the local desktop PC. While it does not perform any direct communications with a Pocket PC device, applications will typically use the CEUtil library in conjunction with other APIs, such as the Remote API, to find out specific information about a device. This enables you to get to information even when a device is not currently connected to ActiveSync.

In order to use the CEUtil helper APIs in your applications, you need to include the `ceutil.h` header file in your project, as well as link with the `ceutil.lib` library (because this is a desktop library, it is located in the `.\wce300\Pocket PC 2002\support\ActiveSync\lib` directory in the folder where you have installed Embedded Visual C++).

Finding Partnered Devices

Every device that has a partnership with a desktop has a unique identifier known to ActiveSync as its *device ID*. As you may have guessed, before you can use any of the functions in the CEUtil helper library, you must first determine the device ID for the partnered device with which you want to work.

To determine the identifier of the device that currently has an established connection to ActiveSync, you can simply call the following function:

```
DEVICEID CeGetDeviceId(void);
```

This will return a DEVICEID (which is just a DWORD value) of the currently connected device, or zero if no device is connected. If you receive a value of 0xFFFFFFFF, the connected device is a *guest device*.

Therefore, to find out the ID of a device that is currently connected, you can do the following:

```
// Get the connected device ID
DEVICEID devId = 0;
devId = CeGetDeviceId();

if(devId == 0xFFFFFFFF) {
   OutputDebugString(TEXT("Guest device connected."));
   return 0;
} else
   printf("The connected device id is: 0x%x", devId);
```

To retrieve the ID of the device that is currently selected for display in ActiveSync, you can use the `CeGetSelectedDeviceId()` function, which is prototyped as follows:

```
DEVICEID CeGetSelectedDeviceId(void);
```

This will have the same return values as `CeGetDeviceId()`.

Finally, you can use the `CeSvcEnumProfiles()` function to enumerate all of the devices that currently have partnerships established with the desktop PC. The function is defined as follows:

```
HRESULT CeSvcEnumProfiles(PHCESVC phSvc, DWORD
    lProfileIndex, PDWORD plProfile);
```

The first parameter, `phSvc`, is a pointer to an enumeration handle that will be used in additional calls to `CeSvcEnumProfiles()`. In order to use the function properly, you must set the variable that `phSvr` points to with a `NULL` value the first time that you use it. When `CeSvc EnumProfiles()` returns successfully, you will have a valid handle for future enumeration calls.

The next parameter, `lProfileIndex`, is the index value for the enumeration and should be set to 0 the first time the function is called. This value should be incremented every time you call `CeSvcEnum Profiles()`.

Finally, the `plProfile` parameter is a pointer to a `DWORD` value that will receive the device ID when the function returns a value of `NOERROR`. This is the ID that can be used for making additional calls into the CEUtil helper functions.

If `CeSvcEnumProfiles()` returns a value of `ERROR_NO_MORE_ ITEMS`, then you have reached the end of the partnered device profile enumeration.

There are two ways to properly close and release the enumeration handle that you are using: You can continue to call `CeSvcEnum Profiles()` until you receive an `ERROR_NO_MORE_ITEMS` error, or you can use the `CeSvcClose()` function (which is described in the next section) to close the handle. Either way, you want to make sure that the function properly closes the handle and frees the memory associated with the enumeration.

The following code shows how you can use the `CeSvcEnum Profiles()` function to enumerate through all of the partnerships that have been established with the desktop:

```
HCESVC hCeDevices = NULL;
LONG lDeviceProfile = 0;
DEVICEID dwDeviceId = 0;
HRESULT hr = S_OK;
```

```
do {
   hr = CeSvcEnumProfiles(&hCeDevices, lDeviceProfile,
      &dwDeviceId);
   if(FAILED(hr))
      break;

   // Ok, we have the device ID, do something
   // ...

   // Increment the profile ID for enumeration
   lDeviceProfile++;
   dwDeviceId = 0;
} while(1);
```

Working with a Partnered Device's Configuration Information

Now that you have determined the device ID that you want to work with, you can go ahead and open the registry key associated with the device by using the CeSvcOpen() function, which is defined as follows:

```
HRESULT CeSvcOpen(UINT uSvc, LPTSTR pszPath, BOOL fCreate,
   PHCESVC phSvc);
```

The first parameter, uSvc, specifies the registry key that you are interested in. Table 9.8 describes the pre-defined values that can be used.

What you pass in for the uSvc flag will determine what you should use for the second parameter, pszPath. If you have passed in the CESVC_DEVICEX flag, pszPath should point to a DWORD value that specifies the device ID for which you are interested in opening the registry. This is the same device ID that you were returned from a previous call to CeGetSelectedDeviceId() or CeSvcEnumProfiles().

If you use any of the other flags, then the pszPath parameter will expect a pointer to a null-terminated string that contains that path to a registry subkey value under the root that was specified by the uSvc flag.

The next parameter, fCreate, should be set to TRUE if you want CeSvcOpen() to create the subkey you have specified if it does not already exist in the desktop registry. If this is set to FALSE, the function will fail if it cannot open the key.

The phSvc parameter should point to a CESVC (which is actually an HKEY registry handle) value that will receive a handle to the opened

Table 9.8 Device Configuration Registry Flags

uSvc Flag	Registry Key Root	Description
CESVC_ROOT_MACHINE	HKLM\Software\Microsoft\ Windows CE Services	ActiveSync root
CESVC_FILTERS	HKLM\Software\Microsoft\ Windows CE Services\Filters	Filters root
CESVC_CUSTOM_MENUS	HKLM\Software\Microsoft\ Windows CE Services\ Custom Menus	Custom Menu root
CESVC_SERVICES_COMMON	HKLM\Software\Microsoft\ Windows CE Services\Services	Services root
CESVC_SYNC_COMMON	HKLM\Software\Microsoft\ Windows CE Services\ Services\Synchronization	Synchronization Provider root
CESVC_ROOT_USER	HKCU\Software\Microsoft\ Windows CE Services\	ActiveSync root for current user
CESVC_DEVICES	HKCU\Software\Microsoft\ Windows CE Services\Partners	Device registration root
CESVC_DEVICEX	HKCU\Software\Microsoft\ Windows CE Services\Partners\ (device ID)\	Root key for a specific device
CESVC_DEVICE_SELECTED	HKCU\Software\Microsoft\ Windows CE Services\Partners\ (selected device ID)	Root key for the selected device
CESVC_SERVICES_USER	HKCU\Software\Microsoft\ Windows CE Services\Partners\ (device ID)\Services	Root key for services on a specific device
CESVC_SYNC	HKCU\Software\Microsoft\ Windows CE Services\ Partners\(device id)\Services\ Synchronization	Root key for synchronization settings for a specific device

registry key. This handle should be used for further function calls to the CEUtil helper APIs, and should be closed by using the `CeSvcClose()` function to free any resources associated with it.

The following example gets a handle for the currently selected device:

```
DEVICEID devId = 0;
HRESULT hr = S_OK;
HCESVC hSvcRoot = NULL;
```

```
devId = CeGetSelectedDeviceId();
if(devId == 0)
   return 0;

hr = CeSvcOpen(CESVC_DEVICEX, (LPTSTR)devId, FALSE,
   &hSvcRoot);
if(FAILED(hr))
   return 0;

// Do something here with the handle
// ...

CeSvcClose(hSvcRoot);
```

Once you have an open handle to the device partnership registry, you can open any additional subkeys by using the CeSvcOpenEx() function:

```
HRESULT CeSvcOpenEx(HCESVC hSvcRoot, LPTSTR pszPath, BOOL
   fCreate, PHCESVC phSvc);
```

The first parameter is the handle to the root key that was opened by your previous call to the CeSvcOpen() function. This is followed by pszPath, which should point to a null-terminated string of the sub-key that you are interested in opening. The next parameter, fCreate, should be set to TRUE if you want the function to create the key if it does not already exist. Finally, the open handle to the registry sub-key will be returned in the variable to which the phSvc parameter points.

To open a registry sub-key value, you could do the following:

```
HCESVC hSvcKey = NULL;
hr = CeSvcOpenEx(hSvcRoot, TEXT("Filters"), FALSE,
   &hSvcKey);
if(FAILED(hr)) {
   CeSvcClose(hSvcRoot);
   return 0;
}

// Do something with the Filters sub-key
// ...

CeSvcClose(hSvcKey);
CeSvcClose(hSvcRoot);
```

Remember that the handles returned by `CeSvcOpen()` and `CeSvc OpenEx()` are standard registry key handles, and need to be closed properly in order to free any memory or resources that are allocated to the handle.

To close the handle and free any resources that are allocated, you can use the following function:

```
HRESULT CeSvcClose(HCESVC hSvc);
```

The only parameter that `CeSvcClose()` takes is a handle to the registry entry that was opened from your call to `CeSvcOpen()` or `CeSvcOpenEx()`.

Getting and Setting Values

Six functions are provided in the CEUtil helper library to read and write values in the registry. All of the functions take the same first two parameters: `hSvc` and `pszValName`. The `hSvc` parameter is the handle to the registry sub-key that was opened with `CeSvcOpen()` or `CeSvc OpenEx()` and is followed by the `pszValName` parameter. This should point to a null-terminated string specifying the name of the value that you are interested in.

String values are handled with the following functions:

```
HRESULT CeSvcGetString(HCESVC hSvc, LPCTSTR pszValName,
    LPTSTR pszVal, DWORD cbVal);
HRESULT CeSvcSetString(HCESVC hSvc, LPCTSTR pszValName,
    LPCTSTR pszVal);
```

When reading string values, the `pszVal` parameter should point to a buffer that will receive the registry data. The `cbVal` parameter specifies the size of the buffer to which `pszVal` points.

Setting string values requires only the `pszVal` parameter, which points to a null-terminated value that contains the string data. `DWORD` values are handled with the following:

```
HRESULT CeSvcGetDword(HCESVC hSvc, LPCTSTR pszValName,
    LPDWORD pdwVal);
HRESULT CeSvcSetDword(HCESVC hSvc, LPCTSTR pszValName,
    DWORD dwVal);
```

To get a DWORD value, the pdwVal parameter should point to a DWORD variable that will receive the registry data. Setting a DWORD value only requires you to pass in a DWORD via the dwVal parameter.

Finally, binary registry values are read and set by using the following:

```
HRESULT CeSvcGetBinary(HCESVC hSvc, LPCTSTR pszValName,
    LPBYTE lpData, LPDWORD pcbVal);
HRESULT CeSvcSetBinary(HCESVC hSvc, LPCTSTR pszValName,
    LPBYTE pszVal, DWORD cbVal);
```

Reading binary data from the registry requires a buffer, lpData. The size of the buffer should be set with the variable to which pcbVal points. When the function returns, pcbVal will be set with the actual number of bytes that were copied to the lpData buffer.

To set a binary value, lpData should point to a buffer containing the data to be written to the registry, with the size of the buffer, in bytes, specified by the cbVal parameter.

To delete a value from the registry, you can use the CeSvcDelete Val() function, which is defined as follows:

```
HRESULT CeSvcDeleteVal(HCESVC hSvc, LPCTSTR pszValName);
```

The only parameters that the function requires are a handle to the registry sub-key and the value name to delete.

Adding a Custom Menu Item to ActiveSync

If you have developed an application on the desktop that communicates with a Pocket PC device through the Remote API, a good way to integrate it with CE Services is by adding an additional menu option to the ActiveSync Tools menu (see Figure 9.3).

To add additional menu items to ActiveSync, you need to add a new sub-key value for your menu option under the registry key HKEY_ LOCAL_MACHINE\SOFTWARE\Microsoft\Windows CE Services\ CustomMenus. You also need to set several additional values for your applications. Table 9.9 describes the values that you need to configure.

Figure 9.3 Extending the ActiveSync Tools menu

Table 9.9 Registry Values for Extending the ActiveSync Manager

Name	Type	Description
DisplayName	String	The name that will be displayed as the menu option. You can use an ampersand (&) to specify a menu hotkey (e.g., "&Backup").
Command	String	The full path and executable name of the application to launch when the command is selected.
CommandArguments	String	Any command-line arguments that you want to have passed to your application.
StatusHelp	String	The text that will be displayed on the status bar when the item is selected in the menu.
Version	DWORD	Application version. This value should be set to 0x00020000.

The following code sample shows how you can add your own menu items to ActiveSync by using the CEUtil helper functions:

```
// Add a Custom Menu entry
DEVICEID devId = 0;
HRESULT hr = S_OK;
HCESVC hCustomMenu = NULL;
```

```
// Open/create the new key
hr = CeSvcOpen(CESVC_CUSTOM_MENUS, TEXT("MyMenuItem"), TRUE,
  &hCustomMenu);
if(FAILED(hr))
    return 0;

// Add the details
DWORD dwVersion = 0x00020000;
CeSvcSetString(hCustomMenu, TEXT("DisplayName"), TEXT("&My
  Custom Menu"));
CeSvcSetString(hCustomMenu, TEXT("Command"),
    TEXT("c:\\program files\\myapp\\myexe.exe"));
CeSvcSetString(hCustomMenu, TEXT("CommandArguments"),
    TEXT("-dSomeArguments"));
CeSvcSetString(hCustomMenu, TEXT("StatusHelp"),
    TEXT("This is the details for my custom menu"));
CeSvcSetDword(hCustomMenu, TEXT("Version"), dwVersion);

// Clean up
CeSvcClose(hCustomMenu);
```

File Conversion (File Filters)

File Filters are COM-based objects that reside on the desktop and that ActiveSync uses when converting files between a PC and mobile file format. When a file is copied to or from a connected Pocket PC device via the Mobile Device folder, ActiveSync checks whether a file filter is available for the type of file that is being transferred. If one exists, ActiveSync will then load the filter into memory and call into its methods for converting the file. For example, if you copy an Excel spreadsheet from the desktop to a device, ActiveSync will load in the Excel file filter and convert it to the Pocket Excel format, which can be read by a Pocket PC device. Likewise, if you copy a Pocket PC Excel file from a device to the desktop, it will be converted to the standard desktop Excel format.

Note that only files copied through ActiveSync will use the File Filters and be converted. A file filter lives on the desktop, so if your device downloads a file directly from a Web site or FTP server, it will not go through ActiveSync and thus will not be converted.

The interfaces that you use to create your own filter objects are defined in the replfilt.h header file.

Registering a File Filter

You need to configure your file filter in several locations in the desktop registry in order for ActiveSync to be able to use it when copying files to or from a device.

First, you need to register the file extension by adding an entry in the `HKEY_CLASSES_ROOT\{New File Extension}` key. The key only needs to have its default value set to the class name for the extension, as shown in Table 9.10.

Table 9.10 Registry Settings for a File Filter Extension

Key\Value Name	Description
Default	{Extension Class Name}

Under the `HKEY_CLASSES_ROOT\{Extension Class Name}` key, set the values shown in Table. 9.11.

Table 9.11 Registry Settings for a File Filter Type

Key\Value Name	Description
Default	Description of the file type that will be displayed in the Type column in Windows Explorer
DefaultIcon	Filename or index of the icon for this file type

Second, you have to register the COM object that implements your file filter, under the `HKEY_CLASSES_ROOT\CLSID\{GUID}` key. The object needs to have the keys and values shown in Table 9.12 set.

Table 9.12 Registry Settings for the File Filter COM Object

Key\Value Name	Description
`Default`	Description of the file type. This will be displayed in the Type column of Windows Explorer.
`DefaultIcon`	Filename or index of the icon for this file type.
`InProcServer32`	Full filename and path to the DLL that the object is in.
`InProcServer32\ThreadingModel`	Should be set to "Apartment".
`PegasusFilter\Description`	String to be displayed when the conversion dialog box is shown.
`PegasusFilter\NewExtension`	Extension for the newly converted file.
`PegasusFilter\Import`	If it exists, then the conversion type is for importing from computer to device; otherwise, assume export.
`PegasusFilter\HasOptions`	If it exists, then the `ICeFileFilter::FilterOption()` method is supported.

Figure 9.4 shows the registry settings for a COM file filter.

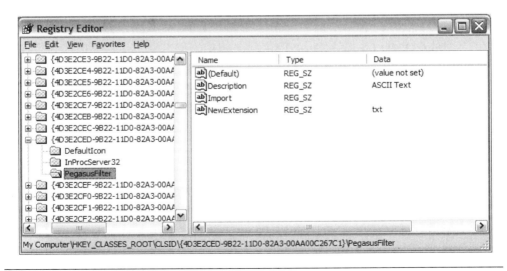

Figure 9.4 Registry settings for a file filter COM object

Now that you have registered the COM object for your file filter, you need to let ActiveSync know about it. To do so, you will have to create a new entry under the `HKEY_LOCAL_MACHINE\SOFTWARE\Microsoft\ Windows CE Services\Filters\{New File Extension}` key. Table 9.13 describes the values that need to be configured.

Table 9.13 File Filter Registry Settings

Key\Value Name	Description
DefaultImport	{GUID} or "Binary Copy"
DefaultExport	{GUID} or "Binary Copy"
InstalledFilters\{GUID}	One or more GUIDs for various filters for the file type

The `DefaultImport` and `DefaultExport` values are used to determine which objects are used when copying a file to or from the device. These values can be set either to the GUID of the COM object that implements the conversion interface, or to the string "Binary Copy". Setting either one to perform a "Binary Copy" tells ActiveSync that no conversion is necessary when a file of this type is copied. For example, a text (.txt) file will use "Binary Copy" for both its import and export modes because no conversion is necessary.

Because a file (such as a Word document) can have one or more filters associated with it, you can use the `InstalledFilters` key to specify the GUID for each filter that is installed.

Finally, you can register a file filter with an individual device by setting the `HKEY_CURRENT_USER\Software\Microsoft\Windows CE Services\Partners\{Partner ID}\Filters\{New File Extension}` key. The device partnership registry setting takes the same entries as the global key, as defined in Table 9.14.

Table 9.14 Registry Settings for a File Filter on a Specific Partner ID

Key\Value Name	Description
DefaultImport	{GUID} or "Binary Copy"
DefaultExport	{GUID} or "Binary Copy"
InstalledFilters\{GUID}	One or more GUIDs for various filters for the file type

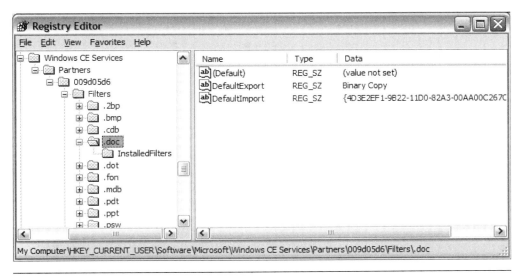

Figure 9.5 Registry settings for a file filter for a partnered device

Figure 9.5 shows the registry values for a file filter.

To get a better idea of all of the settings that are required for a file filter, let's take a look at an export of the keys required for the Pocket Word filter:

```
// Registry entries for the file type
//
[HKEY_CLASSES_ROOT\.pwd]
@="pwdfile"

[HKEY_CLASSES_ROOT\pwdfile]
@="Pocket Word Document-H/PC"
[HKEY_CLASSES_ROOT\pwdfile\DefaultIcon]
@="C:\\Program Files\\Microsoft ActiveSync\\minshell.dll,-
    2004"
[HKEY_CLASSES_ROOT\pwdfile\Shell\Open\command]
@="\"D:\\OfficeXP\\Office10\\WINWORD.EXE\" /n /dde \"%1\""

//
// Registry entries for the COM object
//
[HKEY_CLASSES_ROOT\CLSID\
    {4D3E2CF9-9B22-11D0-82A3-00AA00C267C1}]
@="Word 97/2000"
```

```
[HKEY_CLASSES_ROOT\CLSID\
    {4D3E2CF9-9B22-11D0-82A3-00AA00C267C1}\DefaultIcon]
@="C:\\Program Files\\Microsoft ActiveSync\\pwdcnv.dll,0"
[HKEY_CLASSES_ROOT\CLSID\
    {4D3E2CF9-9B22-11D0-82A3-00AA00C267C1}\InProcServer32]
@="C:\\Program Files\\Microsoft ActiveSync\\pwdcnv.dll"
"ThreadingModel"="Apartment"
[HKEY_CLASSES_ROOT\CLSID\
    {4D3E2CF9-9B22-11D0-82A3-00AA00C267C1}\PegasusFilter]
"Description"="Word 97/2000 Document"
"NewExtension"="doc"

//
// Registry entries for the File Filter
//
[HKEY_LOCAL_MACHINE\SOFTWARE\Microsoft\Windows CE
    Services\Filters\.pwd]
"DefaultImport"="Binary Copy"
"DefaultExport"="{4D3E2CF9-9B22-11D0-82A3-00AA00C267C1}"

[HKEY_LOCAL_MACHINE\SOFTWARE\Microsoft\Windows CE
    Services\Filters\.pwd\InstalledFilters]
"{4D3E2CF9-9B22-11D0-82A3-
    00AA00C267C1}"="Software\\Microsoft\\Windows CE
    Services\\Filters\\PWordData\\Export"
"{4D3E2CFA-9B22-11D0-82A3-
    00AA00C267C1}"="Software\\Microsoft\\Windows CE
    Services\\Filters\\PWordData\\Export"
"{4D3E2CFB-9B22-11D0-82A3-00AA00C267C1}"=""
"{4D3E2CFC-9B22-11D0-82A3-00AA00C267C1}"=""

//
// Registry entries for a Partnered Device
//
[HKEY_CURRENT_USER\Software\Microsoft\Windows CE
    Services\Partners\11111111\Filters\.pwd]
"DefaultImport"="Binary Copy"
"DefaultExport"="{4D3E2CF9-9B22-11D0-82A3-00AA00C267C1}"

[HKEY_CURRENT_USER\Software\Microsoft\Windows
    CEServices\Partners\11111111\
    Filters\.pwd\InstalledFilters]
```

```
"{4D3E2CF9-9B22-11D0-82A3-00AA00C267C1}"="
   Software\\Microsoft\\Windows CE
   Services\\Filters\\PWordData\\Export"
"{4D3E2CFA-9B22-11D0-82A3-00AA00C267C1}"="
   Software\\Microsoft\\Windows CE
   Services\\Filters\\PWordData\\Export"
"{4D3E2CFB-9B22-11D0-82A3-00AA00C267C1}"=""
"{4D3E2CFC-9B22-11D0-82A3-00AA00C267C1}"=""
```

As you can see, a lot of information needs to be set up in the registry before your filter can be used by ActiveSync. Fortunately, you can also use the CEUtil helper APIs (discussed in the previous section) to help register a custom filter.

Using the CEUtil Helper APIs to Register a File Filter

To help you register your file filter using the CEUtil library functions, you can do the following:

```
// Register a custom filter
DEVICEID devId = 0;
HRESULT hr = S_OK;
HCESVC hCustomFilter = NULL, hInsFilters = NULL,
   hCeDevices = NULL, hDevRoot = NULL, hCustomFilterRoot = NULL;

// Set up the new filter information
TCHAR tchExtension[32] = TEXT("\0");
TCHAR tchFilterGUID[128] = TEXT("\0");
wsprintf(tchExtension, TEXT(".txl"));
wsprintf(tchFilterGUID,
   TEXT("{85A31804-3251-4d13-9405-AA4C86F1C58A}"));

// Open/create the new filter key
// First, create the generic ActiveSync keys
hr = CeSvcOpen(CESVC_FILTERS, tchExtension, TRUE,
  &hCustomFilter);
if(FAILED(hr))
   return 0;

// Set up the entry values
CeSvcSetString(hCustomFilter, TEXT("DefaultImport"),
  tchFilterGUID);
```

```
CeSvcSetString(hCustomFilter, TEXT("DefaultExport"),
   TEXT("Binary Copy"));

hr = CeSvcOpenEx(hCustomFilter, TEXT("InstalledFilters"),
   TRUE, &hInsFilters);
if(FAILED(hr)) {
   CeSvcClose(hCustomFilter);
   return -1;
}

CeSvcSetString(hInsFilters, tchFilterGUID, TEXT(""));
CeSvcClose(hInsFilters);
CeSvcClose(hCustomFilter);

// Next, add it to each partnered device
LONG lDeviceProfile = 0;
DEVICEID dwDeviceId = 0;

do {
   hr = CeSvcEnumProfiles(&hCeDevices, lDeviceProfile,
     &dwDeviceId);
   if(FAILED(hr))
     break;

   // Ok, we have the device ID, register the filter for it
   // Start by opening up the device key
   hr = CeSvcOpen(CESVC_DEVICEX, (LPTSTR)dwDeviceId, FALSE,
     &hDevRoot);
   if(FAILED(hr))
   break;

   // Next, get the handle to the Filters key
   hr = CeSvcOpenEx(hDevRoot, TEXT("Filters"), FALSE,
     &hCustomFilterRoot);
   if(FAILED(hr)) {
      CeSvcClose(hDevRoot);
      break;
   }

   // Create the new key
   hr = CeSvcOpenEx(hCustomFilterRoot, tchExtension, TRUE,
     &hCustomFilter);
   if(FAILED(hr)) {
      CeSvcClose(hCustomFilterRoot);
```

```
        CeSvcClose(hDevRoot);
        break;
    }

    // Set up the entry values
    CeSvcSetString(hCustomFilter, TEXT("DefaultImport"),
        tchFilterGUID);
    CeSvcSetString(hCustomFilter, TEXT("DefaultExport"),
        TEXT("Binary Copy"));

    hr = CeSvcOpenEx(hCustomFilter, TEXT("InstalledFilters"),
        TRUE, &hInsFilters);
    if(FAILED(hr)) {
        CeSvcClose(hCustomFilter);
        CeSvcClose(hCustomFilterRoot);
        CeSvcClose(hDevRoot);
        return -1;
    }

    CeSvcSetString(hInsFilters, tchFilterGUID, TEXT(""));

    // Close the handles
    CeSvcClose(hInsFilters);
    CeSvcClose(hCustomFilter);
    CeSvcClose(hCustomFilterRoot);
    CeSvcClose(hDevRoot);

    // Increment the profile ID for enumeration
    lDeviceProfile++;
    dwDeviceId = 0;
} while(1);
```

File Filter Interfaces Overview

Now that you've seen how a file filter is configured on the desktop, let's see what is required to build your own custom filter. ActiveSync uses three COM interfaces when performing a conversion of a file between a desktop and a device:

- The **ICeFileFilter** interface is used to perform the actual file conversion. It is the only interface that you are *required* to implement.
- The **ICeFileFilterOptions** interface is an optional interface that is used to set additional filter options.

- A pointer to an **ICeFileFilterSite** interface will be passed to you when the `ICeFileFilter::NextConvertFile()` method is called. This interface is already implemented by ActiveSync, and contains functions to open and close the files involved with the conversion, as well as to send status information back to ActiveSync.

Implementing *ICeFileFilter*

The `ICeFileFilter` interface is the only interface you are required to implement in order for ActiveSync to call into your object when converting a file from one format to another. `ICeFileFilter` has three methods (outside of the standard `IUnknown` methods), described in Table 9.15.

Table 9.15 `ICEFileFilter` Methods

Method	Description
`FilterOptions()`	Used to display a dialog box for any filter-specific conversion options.
`FormatMessage()`	Formats a message from an error code.
`NextConvertFile()`	This is where the bulk of the conversion work is done. This method is called whenever ActiveSync needs to convert a file.

The `NextConvertFile()` method performs the actual file conversion when your filter is called by ActiveSync. Note that it will be called repeatedly (so that you can create multiple destination files) until you return a value of ERROR_NO_MORE_ITEMS. The function is defined as follows:

```
HRESULT ICeFileFilter::NextConvertFile(int nConversion,
    CFF_CONVERTINFO *pci, CFF_SOURCEFILE *psf,
    CFF_DESTINATIONFILE *pdf, BOOL *pbCancel, CF_ERROR *perr);
```

The first parameter, nConversion, is incremented every time the function is called for the same source file, enabling you to create multiple destination files. `ICeFileFilter::NextConvertFile()` will continue to be called with the same source file until you return the ERROR_NO_MORE_VALUES return code.

Next, the `pci` parameter is a pointer to a `CFF_CONVERTINFO` structure that you can use to get some general information about the conversion. The structure also contains the pointer to an `ICeFileFilterSite` object that you will use to open and close the source and destination files involved in the conversion, as well as pass information back to ActiveSync.

The `CFF_CONVERTINFO` structure looks like the following:

```
typedef struct tagCFF_CONVERTINFO {
    BOOL bImport;
    HWND hwndParent;
    BOOL bYesToAll;
    ICeFileFilterSite *pffs;
} CFF_CONVERTINFO;
```

The `bImport` field specifies the direction of the file conversion. If this is set to `TRUE`, then you are converting a file from the desktop to the Pocket PC device. If `FALSE`, then you are exporting a file from the device to the PC. The `hwndParent` field is a handle to a parent window that you can use for any dialog boxes or messages that need to be displayed during the conversion process. The `bYesToAll` field is used in conjunction with the ActiveSync dialog box that is presented to an end user when overwriting files; if it is set to `TRUE`, then the Yes To All button will be included on the warning dialog box that is displayed. The last field, `pffs`, points to the `ICeFileFilterSite` interface, which you can use to open and close files.

The next parameter, `psf`, points to a `CFF_SOURCEFILE` structure that contains information about the source file being used for the conversion. It contains details about the file's source path, file size, creation time, and so on, and is defined as follows:

```
typedef struct tagCFF_SOURCEFILE {
    TCHAR szFullpath[_MAX_PATH];
    TCHAR szPath[_MAX_PATH];
    TCHAR szFilename[_MAX_FNAME];
    TCHAR szExtension[_MAX_EXT];
    DWORD cbSize;
    FILETIME ftCreated;
    FILETIME ftModified;
} CFF_SOURCEFILE;
```

The `pdf` parameter points to a `CFF_DESTINATIONFILE` structure, which contains details about the file you are converting to. The `CFF_DESTINATIONFILE` structure is defined as follows:

```
typedef struct tagCFF_DESTINATIONFILE {
    TCHAR szFullpath[_MAX_PATH];
    TCHAR szPath[_MAX_PATH];
    TCHAR szFilename[_MAX_FNAME];
    TCHAR szExtension[_MAX_EXT];
} CFF_DESTINATIONFILE;
```

Next, `pbCancel` will be set to `TRUE` if the user presses the Cancel button at any time while the conversion process is taking place. Because this value can be changed by another thread while a file conversion is in progress, you need to check the value regularly to determine whether the user has canceled out. If `pbCancel` is set to `TRUE`, then you need to return the `ERROR_CANCELLED` return code from the function.

The last parameter, `perr`, should be set with an error code if something goes wrong during the conversion. This error will then be sent to the `ICeFileFilter::FormatMessage()` function for processing. If you do use `perr`, you should set the return value to `E_FAIL`.

NOTE: If you need to call any of the Remote API (RAPI) functions while performing a conversion, you do not need to call the `CeRapiInit()` or `CeRapiInitEx()` functions, as a connection to the device is already established when `ICeFileFilter::NextConvertFile()` is called. Calling either of the RAPI initialization functions from `NextConvertFile()` will result in an error.

The `ICeFileFilter::FilterOptions()` method provides you with a handle to the parent window, which you can use for a dialog box when the Options button is pressed in ActiveSync. The function has the following prototype:

```
HRESULT ICeFileFilter::FilterOptions(HWND hwndParent);
```

The only parameter is the handle to the ActiveSync parent window. Remember that the Options button is enabled in ActiveSync only if the `HasOptions` value has been set in the `HKEY_CLASSES_ROOT\CLSID\{GUID}\PegasusFilter` registry key.

The last method that you need to implement in `ICeFileFilter` is the `FormatMessage()` function. `FormatMessage()` is used to convert an error code to a string that ActiveSync can display. It is defined as follows:

```
HRESULT ICeFileFilter::FormatMessage(DWORD dwFlags, DWORD
    dwMessageId, DWORD dwLanguageId, LPTSTR lpBuffer, DWORD nSize,
    va_list *Arguments, DWORD *pcb);
```

The parameters that `ICeFileFilter::FormatMessage()` uses are almost exactly the same as what the standard WinCE API's `Format Message()` function takes. In fact, unless you are specifying some user-defined errors, you can use this function to process the request, as shown in the following example:

```
STDMETHODIMP CTextFileFilter::FormatMessage(DWORD dwFlags,
    DWORD dwMessageId, DWORD dwLanguageId, LPTSTR lpBuffer,
    DWORD nSize, va_list *Arguments, DWORD *pcb)
{
    DWORD dwMsgLength = 0;

    dwMsgLength = ::FormatMessage(dwFlags, 0, dwMessageId,
        dwLanguageId, lpBuffer, nSize, Arguments);
    if(dwMsgLength)
        *pcb = dwMsgLength;
    else
        return E_FAIL;

    return S_OK;
}
```

The only additional parameter you need to worry about is `pcb`, which should be set to the length of the string that you are returning from the function.

382 Chapter 9 Desktop Synchronization

Implementing *ICeFileFilterOptions*

The `ICeFileFilterOptions` interface is optional, i.e., its implementation is not required in order for a filter to function properly. The only method that is currently supported is the `SetFilterOptions()` function, which is defined as follows:

```
HRESULT ICeFileFilterOptions::SetFilterOptions
  (CFF_CONVERTOPTIONS *pco);
```

The only parameter that the function takes is `pco`, which is a pointer to a `CFF_CONVERTOPTIONS` structure. The structure defines whether or not ActiveSync should prevent any modal user interface interaction during the conversion process. The structure is defined as follows:

```
typedef struct tagCFF_CONVERTOPTIONS {
   ULONG cbSize;
   BOOL bNoModalUI;
} CFF_CONVERTOPTIONS;
```

The `cbSize` field should be set to the size of `CFF_CONVERT OPTIONS`, and `bNoModalUI` should be set to `TRUE` if you want to prevent modal interaction.

The *ICeFileFilterSite* Interface

The `ICeFileFilterSite` interface is used to open and close files and communicate the status of a file conversion back to ActiveSync. A pointer to the interface is passed when the `ICeFileFilter::NextConvert File()` method is called. Table 9.16 lists the methods that are implemented in the `ICeFileFilterSite` object.

Let's take a look at the available functions you can call in `ICeFileFilterSite` during the conversion process in more detail.

To open a source file for conversion, you can use the `OpenSource File()` function, which is defined as follows:

```
HRESULT ICeFileFilterSite::OpenSourceFile(int
  nHowToOpenFile, LPVOID *ppObj);
```

The first parameter, `nHowToOpenFile`, must be set to the constant `CF_OPENFLAT`. After calling the function, the `ppObj` parameter will receive a pointer to an `IStream` COM object that can be used to read

Table 9.16 `ICeFileFilterSite` Methods

Method	Description
`CloseDestinationFile()`	Closes the destination file used for conversion
`CloseSourceFile()`	Closes the source file used for conversion
`OpenDestinationFile()`	Opens a destination file for conversion
`OpenSourceFile()`	Opens a source file for conversion
`ReportLoss()`	Reports any information about discarded data during the conversion
`ReportProgress()`	Reports the progress of a file conversion to ActiveSync

from the source file. You must remember to call the `ICeFileFilter Site::CloseSourceFile()` function when you are finished reading information from the stream in order to release it properly.

The `ICeFileFilterSite::OpenDestinationFile()` function is defined as follows:

```
HRESULT ICeFileFilterSite::OpenDestinationFile(int nHowToOpenFile,
    LPCTSTR pszFullpath, LPVOID *ppObj);
```

The first parameter, `nHowToOpenFile`, must be set with the constant `CF_OPENFLAT`. Next, `pszFullPath` should point to a null-terminated string that should be used for the full name and path of the destination file. This parameter is optional, and can be set to `NULL` to use the default destination name. The last parameter, `ppObj`, will point to an `IStream` object for the destination file once the function returns successfully. You can then use this object to output the converted file data. Remember that you must call the `ICeFileFilterSite::CloseDestinationFile()` function to properly close the file when you are finished converting it.

To close the source file, you can call the following:

```
HRESULT ICeFileFilterSite::CloseSourceFile(LPUNKNOWN pObj);
```

The only parameter the function requires is the pointer to the `IStream` interface that you received from your call to `ICeFile FilterSite::OpenSourceFile()`.

To close the destination file, you can use the following function:

```
HRESULT ICeFileFilterSite::CloseDestinationFile(BOOL bKeepFile,
    LPUNKNOWN pObj);
```

The first parameter, `bKeepFile`, determines whether or not ActiveSync should delete the destination file. If this is set to `TRUE`, then the file that you have been writing to will be saved when it is closed. You should set this to `FALSE` when an error occurs during the conversion process and you do not want to keep the file you have been writing to. The `pObj` parameter should point to the `IStream` object that was returned from your original call to `ICeFileFileter::Open DestinationFile()`.

The `ICeFileFilterSite::ReportProgress()` function is used to send the ActiveSync window a message regarding how much of the conversion process has been completed. The function is defined as follows:

```
HRESULT ICeFileFilterSite::ReportProgress(UINT nPercent);
```

The only parameter that the function takes is an unsigned-integer value that specifies the percentage of the file that has been converted. This value is then displayed on the progress bar in the ActiveSync window as the conversion occurs.

If you have intentionally decided to discard any data during a file conversion (for example, removing comments from a text file), you can call the `ICeFileFilterSite::ReportLoss()` function to explain the data loss to the end user:

```
HRESULT ICeFileFilterSite::ReportLoss(DWORD dw, LPCTSTR psz,
  va_list args);
```

The first parameter, `dw`, specifies a `DWORD` value that will be passed to the `ICeFileFilter::FormatMessage()` method and should contain an error code to be formatted by the function. If you would rather set the description immediately, use the `psz` parameter to point to a null-terminated string that describes the error. You cannot, however, use both the `dw` and `psz` parameters at the same time. If you set one, the other should be set to a `NULL` value. The last parameter, `args`, can be used as a pointer to an array of values that will be inserted into the formatted string.

Writing a Custom File Filter

Now that we've examined the interfaces that are involved with the file conversion process, let's examine how the conversion process works, and how you can actually build your own file filter.

Whenever a file is dragged into or from the Mobile Device folder, ActiveSync checks the registry for the file type based on its extension. If a filter is properly registered for the file type, ActiveSync will then call into your COM object using the `IUnknown::QueryInterface()` function to get a pointer to your `ICeFileFilterOptions` and `ICeFile Filter` objects. If `ICeFileFilterOptions` exists, it will then call into the `ICeFileFilterOptions::SetFilterOptions()` function to set the modality of the conversion operation.

The conversion process begins when ActiveSync starts to call into your `ICeFileFilter::NextConvertFile()` method for each file you are working with.

The following example builds a simple file filter that converts a text file in lowercase into a text file in uppercase. Your lowercase text file will have a .txl extension, and your destination uppercase file will have the extension .txu.

For this example, let's put the code for registering your filter (including using the CEUtil helper library) into the `DllRegister Server()` function that you export from your DLL (as well as the code to remove it in `DllUnregisterServer()`). As with any COM object, these functions are called whenever `regsvr32.exe` is used to register a COM server object. After the filter has registered, the registry will look as follows:

```
// Registry entries for file type
[HKEY_CLASSES_ROOT\.txl]
@="textlower"

[HKEY_CLASSES_ROOT\textlower]
@="Lowercase text file"


//
// COM object registry settings
//
[HKEY_CLASSES_ROOT\CLSID\
  {087CCBD5-BAB3-46c0-9AE6-E8CC68397FB8}]
@="Lowercase text file"
```

```
[HKEY_CLASSES_ROOT\CLSID\
  {087CCBD5-BAB3-46c0-9AE6-E8CC68397FB8}\DefaultIcon]
@="MyTextFilter.dll, 0"

[HKEY_CLASSES_ROOT\CLSID\
  {087CCBD5-BAB3-46c0-9AE6-E8CC68397FB8}\InProcServer32]
@="MyTextFilter.dll"
"ThreadingModel"="Apartment"

[HKEY_CLASSES_ROOT\CLSID\
  {087CCBD5-BAB3-46c0-9AE6-E8CC68397FB8}\PegasusFilter]
"Description"="Lowercase text file"
"NewExtension"="txu"
"Import"=""
"HasOptions"=""

//
// Registry entries for the file filter
//
[HKEY_LOCAL_MACHINE\SOFTWARE\Microsoft\Windows CE
  Services\Filters\.txl]
"DefaultImport"="{087CCBD5-BAB3-46c0-9AE6-E8CC68397FB8}"

[HKEY_LOCAL_MACHINE\SOFTWARE\Microsoft\Windows CE
  Services\Filters\.txl\InstalledFilters]
"{087CCBD5-BAB3-46c0-9AE6-E8CC68397FB8}"=""

//
// Registry entries for a partnered device
//
[HKEY_CURRENT_USER\Software\Microsoft\Windows CE
  Services\Partners\009d05d6\Filters\.txl]
"DefaultImport"="{087CCBD5-BAB3-46c0-9AE6-E8CC68397FB8}"

[HKEY_CURRENT_USER\Software\Microsoft\Windows CE
  Services\Partners\009d05d6\Filters\.txl\InstalledFilters]
"{087CCBD5-BAB3-46c0-9AE6-E8CC68397FB8}"=""
```

Besides handling all of the standard COM "goo" (I use the term *goo* to specify all of the code for your class factory and IUnknown interface),

you need to implement the ICeFileFilter methods. The most interesting part of your object is how you handle the ICeFileFilter::
NextConvertFile() function:

```
STDMETHODIMP CTextFileFilter::NextConvertFile(int nConversion,
    CFF_CONVERTINFO *pci, CFF_SOURCEFILE *psf,
    CFF_DESTINATIONFILE *pdf,
    volatile BOOL *pbCancel, CF_ERROR *perr)
{
    ICeFileFilterSite *pFilterSite = NULL;
    IStream *pSourceStream = NULL;
    IStream *pDestStream = NULL;
    HRESULT hr = S_OK;

    // We need to do only one conversion
    if(nConversion != 0)
        return HRESULT_FROM_WIN32(ERROR_NO_MORE_ITEMS);

    // Since this is an import filter, make sure we're
    // copying from the desktop to device
    if(!pci->bImport)
        return HRESULT_FROM_WIN32(ERROR_INVALID_PARAMETER);

    pFilterSite = pci->pffs;
    if(!pFilterSite)
        return E_FAIL;

    // Create buffers to use to read in
    LPBYTE lpBuffer = NULL;
    lpBuffer = (LPBYTE)LocalAlloc(LPTR, BUFFER_SIZE+1);
    if(!lpBuffer)
        return E_OUTOFMEMORY;

    // Open the source file
    hr = pFilterSite->OpenSourceFile(PF_OPENFLAT,
        (LPVOID*)&pSourceStream);
    if(FAILED(hr)) {
        LocalFree(lpBuffer);
        return E_FAIL;
    }

    // Open the destination file
    hr = pFilterSite->OpenDestinationFile(PF_OPENFLAT, NULL,
```

```
            (LPVOID *)&pDestStream);
    if(FAILED(hr)) {
       LocalFree(lpBuffer);
       pFilterSite->CloseSourceFile(pSourceStream);
       return E_FAIL;
    }

    // Read in a chunk from the source
    ULONG ulBytesRead = 0, ulBytesWritten = 0,
       ulTotalBytes = 0;
    pSourceStream->Read(lpBuffer, BUFFER_SIZE, &ulBytesRead);

    while(ulBytesRead > 0) {
       // Check to see if it was cancelled
       if(*pbCancel == TRUE) {
          LocalFree(lpBuffer);
          pFilterSite->CloseSourceFile(pSourceStream);
          pFilterSite->CloseDestinationFile(FALSE,
              pDestStream);
          return HRESULT_FROM_WIN32 (ERROR_CANCELLED);
       }

       // Convert it
       _strupr((char *)lpBuffer);

       // Write it
       pDestStream->Write(lpBuffer, ulBytesRead,
          &ulBytesWritten);
       ulTotalBytes += ulBytesWritten;

       // Update progress
       pFilterSite->ReportProgress(ulTotalBytes/psf->cbSize
          * 100);

       // Clean up
       ulBytesRead = 0;
       ulBytesWritten = 0;
       memset(lpBuffer, 0, BUFFER_SIZE+1);

       // Read next blob
       hr = pSourceStream->Read(lpBuffer, BUFFER_SIZE,
          &ulBytesRead);
       if(FAILED(hr))
```

```
            break;
      }

      // Close files and clean up
      pFilterSite->CloseSourceFile(pSourceStream);
      pFilterSite->CloseDestinationFile(TRUE, pDestStream);
      LocalFree(lpBuffer);
      return NOERROR;
}
```

To complete your filter, you also need to implement the `ICeFileFilter::FormatMessage()` and `ICeFileFilter::FilterOptions()` functions:

```
STDMETHODIMP CTextFileFilter::FilterOptions
      (HWND hwndParent) {
   MessageBox(hwndParent, TEXT("Filter Options go here"),
      TEXT("Filter Options"), MB_OK|MB_ICONINFORMATION);
   return S_OK;
}


STDMETHODIMP CTextFileFilter::FormatMessage(DWORD dwFlags,
  DWORD dwMessageId, DWORD dwLanguageId, LPTSTR lpBuffer, DWORD
  nSize, va_list *Arguments, DWORD *pcb)
{
   DWORD dwMsgLength = 0;

   dwMsgLength = ::FormatMessage(dwFlags, 0, dwMessageId,
      dwLanguageId, lpBuffer, nSize, Arguments);
   if(dwMsgLength)
      *pcb = dwMsgLength;
   else
      return E_FAIL;

   return S_OK;
}
```

Synchronization Service Providers

When a Pocket PC device establishes a connection with ActiveSync, the desktop will use **Synchronization Service Providers** (**SSPs**) to handle the replication and synchronization of data between the device and the desktop. ActiveSync hosts the Service Manager, which handles the basic overhead of establishing connections, mapping data, handling conflicts, and transferring objects to the device. In addition, the Service Manager also controls any SSPs that are installed and active for the current device partnership whenever it needs to work with specific application data (see Figure 9.6).

An individual SSP will handle the details of synchronizing data for a particular application, and is comprised of two COM objects: one that is installed and registered on the desktop, and another for the device. Each provider will be "plugged" into ActiveSync so it can receive instructions on the data that it is working with, and will be able to send information

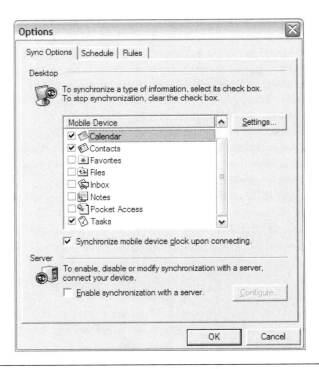

Figure 9.6 ActiveSync and Its Synchronization Service Providers

back to ActiveSync regarding status, synchronization settings, or any other user interface updates.

The process for synchronizing information on the device to the desktop is relatively straightforward—when a partnership is established, the Service Manager on the desktop communicates with the Service Manager on the device, each initializing its own respective SSPs for the application data that is being synchronized. Each SSP will then compare individual objects of data between the desktop and the device. Once ActiveSync has been notified that a comparison is complete, it updates both the desktop and the device with the most recent data.

When designing a synchronization provider for your application, it is important to spend some time thinking about how you want to handle your data so that ActiveSync can compare it as efficiently as possible. It is recommended that providers be able to divide data into the following components:

- An individual "blob" of data, such as a contact, should be considered an **object**.
- A grouping of similar objects requires a named **object type**, such as *contacts*.
- Each object must have a unique **object identifier**. An object identifier is a 32-bit value that cannot be changed or used by another object, and must represent a sort order so that you can tell which objects come first.
- A group of objects require a **data store**, which is used to hold the objects, and can be a file, database, or some other custom file format. The "contacts database" is an example of a synchronization store for contact objects.
- Each service provider must provide its own **method for comparing objects**.

The interfaces that you will use to create both the desktop and device service provider modules are defined in the `cesync.h` header file.

Writing a Desktop Synchronization Provider Module

Most of the work that goes into building a synchronization provider is done on the desktop side of the connection. Three COM interfaces will interest you when developing a desktop synchronization provider:

- The **IReplNotify** interface is implemented by the ActiveSync Manager. The interface provides a synchronization object with the ability to send notification messages to the main ActiveSync window.
- The **IReplStore** interface must be implemented by the synchronization provider. It is used by the ActiveSync Manager when enumerating, comparing, and resolving conflicts with objects.
- The **IReplObjHandler** interface also must be implemented by the synchronization provider. It provides the methods that are needed to exchange object data between the desktop and the device, as well as delete objects.

Before examining each of the interfaces that you will be working with, let's take a quick look at how a new desktop module needs to be configured in the registry.

NOTE: Throughout the rest of this section, which covers Service Providers, I will be referencing parts of an example that synchronizes all of the files in a particular directory on the desktop with the device.

Registering a Desktop Provider

In order for ActiveSync to be able to use your synchronization provider, you need to ensure it is registered properly in the desktop system registry.

The first thing you need to set up is the standard COM settings for an InProc COM server module. This means adding an entry to the `HKEY_CLASSES_ROOT\CLSID\{New Class ID}` key, which contains the values described in Table 9.17.

Table 9.17 Class ID Registry Settings for a Desktop Provider COM Object

Key\Value Name	Description
Default	Description of the desktop provider
InProcServer32\Default	Full path to the desktop module COM object that implements the `IReplStore` interface
ProgID\Default	Name of the program identifier `{ProgID}` for the desktop provider module

In addition, COM needs to have the `HKEY_CLASSES_ROOT\` `{ProgID}` key, which contains the values described in Table 9.18.

Table 9.18 Program ID Registry Settings for a Desktop Provider COM Object

Key\Value Name	Description
`Default`	Description of the desktop provider
`DisplayName`	Name of the service provider to be displayed in ActiveSync
`Version`	DWORD value indicating the version of the provider
`CLSID\Default`	The {New Class ID} for the service provider

ActiveSync must have the provider itself registered in order for it to be used in synchronization operations. This can be done by placing a new entry in the following location:

```
HKEY_LOCAL_MACHINE\SOFTWARE\Microsoft\Windows CE Services\
    Services\Synchronization\All\{ProgID}
```

This key will require the entries described in Table 9.19.

Table 9.19 Registry Settings Describing a Desktop Synchronization Provider

Key\Value Name	Description
`Default`	Description of the service provider.
`{New Object Type}\Default`	Description of the object type.
`{New Object Type}\DefaultIcon`	Filename or index of the icon for this object type.
`{New Object Type}\DisplayName`	Name of the object type to be displayed in ActiveSync.
`{New Object Type}\Plural Name`	Name of two or more objects of this type to be displayed in ActiveSync.
`{New Object Type}\Store`	The {ProgID} of the COM object that implements the `IReplStore` and `IReplObjHandler` interfaces.
`{New Object Type}\Disabled`	If set to 1, the object type is automatically disabled when ActiveSync creates a new partnership. If set to 0 or removed, ActiveSync will mark it as enabled.

To understand all of the settings that are required for a file filter, let's take a look at an export of the keys that are used for Pocket Inbox:

```
//
// Registry entries for the Inproc COM Server
//
[HKEY_CLASSES_ROOT\MS.WinCE.OutLook\CLSID]
@="{A585E741-1D36-11d0-8B9B-00A0C90D064A}"

[HKEY_CLASSES_ROOT\CLSID\{A585E741-1D36-11d0-8B9B-
   00A0C90D064A}]
@="Microsoft OutLook Store"

[HKEY_CLASSES_ROOT\CLSID\
    {A585E741-1D36-11d0-8B9B-00A0C90D064A}\InprocServer32]
@="C:\\Program Files\\Microsoft ActiveSync\\outstore.dll"

[HKEY_CLASSES_ROOT\CLSID\
   {A585E741-1D36-11d0-8B9B-00A0C90D064A}\ProgID]
@="MS.WinCE.OutLook"

[HKEY_CLASSES_ROOT\MS.WinCE.OutLook]
@="Microsoft OutLook Store"
"Display Name"="Microsoft Outlook"
"Version"=dword:00030000

[HKEY_CLASSES_ROOT\MS.WinCE.OutLook\CLSID]
@="{A585E741-1D36-11d0-8B9B-00A0C90D064A}"

//
// Registry entries for the service provider
//
[HKEY_LOCAL_MACHINE\SOFTWARE\Microsoft\Windows CE
   Services\Services\Synchronization\All\MS.WinCE.OutLook]
@="Microsoft Windows CE Outlook Synchronization"

//
// Registry entries for the particular object type in the
// service provider
//
[HKEY_LOCAL_MACHINE\SOFTWARE\Microsoft\Windows CE
   Services\Services\Synchronization\All\MS.WinCE.OutLook\Inbox]
```

```
@="Windows Messaging Client"
"Store"="MS.WinCE.Outlook"
"Display Name"="Inbox"
"Plural Name"="E-mail messages"
"Disabled"=dword:00000001
"DefaultIcon"="C:\\Program Files\\Microsoft
ActiveSync\\outstore.dll,-154"
"EmailAttach"=dword:ffffffff
"EmailLines"=dword:00000064
"EmailOpt"=dword:00000132
```

The *IReplStore* Interface

The main interface that you need to implement on the desktop side of a service provider is encapsulated by the IReplStore interface. IRepl Store provides the methods that enable ActiveSync to examine application data that you are synchronizing. This includes functions that enumerate objects in the data store, check for changes in object data, copy data between objects, and even handle the user interface for setting up synchronization options. Everything that ActiveSync needs in order to get information about your data from your application is handled here.

The IReplStore interface is composed of the methods described in Table 9.20.

Table 9.20 IReplStore Methods

Method	Description
ActivateDialog()	Pops up a provider-specific dialog box
BytesToObject()	Converts an array of bytes to a folder handle or object
CompareItem()	Compares two synchronization objects
CompareStoreIDs()	Compares two store identifiers
CopyObject()	Copies a synchronization object to another synchronization object.
FindFirstItem()	Returns the handle to the first object found in a synchronization folder
FindItemClose()	Closes the handle to the Find operation started with IReplStore::FindFirstItem()
FindNextItem()	Returns the handle to the next object found in a synchronization folder
FreeObject()	Frees a specified synchronization object handle
GetConflictInfo()	Gets details about two objects that are in conflict

(continued)

Table 9.20 `IReplStore` Methods *(continued)*

Method	Description
`GetFolderInfo()`	Gets a handle to a folder containing specified object types
`GetObjTypeUIData()`	Gets user interface data (such as an object icon) that will be used by the ActiveSync Manager
`GetStoreInfo()`	Gets information about an object data store
`Initialize()`	Initializes the service provider
`IsFolderChanged()`	Checks whether any object has changed in the specified folder
`IsItemChanged()`	Checks whether an object has changed
`IsItemReplicated()`	Checks whether an object should be replicated
`IsValidObject()`	Checks whether an object is valid
`ObjectToBytes()`	Coverts the handle of a folder or object to an array of bytes
`RemoveDuplicates()`	Finds and removes duplicate objects from the store
`ReportStatus()`	Used by ActiveSync to get status information about the synchronization process
`UpdateItem()`	Updates information about a particular synchronization object

Almost every aspect of working with your data objects is handled by the `IReplStore` interface. Let's take a more detailed look at how ActiveSync uses the methods that you have implemented when synchronizing information between the desktop and the device.

How a Desktop Provider Is Initialized

When a connection occurs between a device and the desktop, ActiveSync must initialize the Service Providers that are enabled for the particular device. Every SSP will be called in the same manner from ActiveSync.

A service provider is initialized by receiving a call into the `IReplStore::Initalize()` function:

```
HRESULT IReplStore::Initialize(IReplNotify *pNotify,
    UINT uFlags);
```

The first parameter will point to the `IReplNotify` interface that is implemented by the ActiveSync Manager. As you will see later in this chapter, the `IReplNotify` interface can be used to send a status message back to the ActiveSync window. This is followed by `uFlags`, which can be set to `ISF_SELECTED_DEVICE` if the store has already been already initialized, or `ISF_REMOTE_CONNECTED` if the store is used via a remote connection. A few words of caution: If a device is connected remotely, you should take special care to not use any blocking API functions, display any type of user interface, or automatically take any default actions, because a user might not be able to respond right away.

The `IReplStore::Initialize()` function can be used to perform any general initialization routines for your service provider, as shown in the following example:

```
STDMETHODIMP CMyReplStore::Initialize(IReplNotify *pNotify,
  UINT uFlags)
{
   // Initialize the service provider. The way our store
   // works is as follows:
   // A single folder, m_hFolder, is used to store the OPML
   // files that we are syncronizing. Each file is an HREPLITEM.
   if(!pNotify)
      return E_FAIL;

   // Store the pointer to ActiveSync
   m_pNotify = pNotify;
   m_fInitialized = TRUE;
   return NOERROR;
}
```

Once the service provider has been initialized, ActiveSync will perform a check to determine whether any of the data on the desktop store has changed since the last synchronization. The first step to this process is for the Service Manager to call into the `IReplStore::Get StoreInfo()` function to get the **store identifier** and then pass it to `IReplStore::CompareStoreIDs()` to see if it has changed since the last synchronization. By using a store identifier, ActiveSync can tell if a partnership is using the same data store as before, or if a new mapping needs to be established.

The `IReplStore::GetStoreInfo()` function has the following prototype:

```
HRESULT IReplStore::GetStoreInfo(PSTOREINFO pStoreInfo);
```

The only parameter that is passed to you is a pointer to a STOREINFO structure, which you need to fill in with information about the data store for the provider. The structure is defined as follows:

```
typedef struct tagStoreInfo {
   UINT cbStruct;
   UINT uFlags;
   TCHAR szProgId[256];
   TCHAR szStoreDesc[200];
   UINT uTimerRes;
   UINT cbMaxStoreId;
   UINT cbStoreId;
   LPBYTE lpbStoreId;
 } STOREINFO, *PSTOREINFO;
```

The first field, cbStruct, specifies the size of the STOREINFO structure that is being passed in. Next, uFlags can be set to the following options:

- SCF_SINGLE_THREAD, if the provider does not support multi-threaded access to the data in the store. If this is set, the ActiveSync Manager will serialize calls to the service provider.
- SCF_SIMULATE_RTS, if the provider supports real-time changes to the store data

The szProgId field is used to specify the null-terminated string of the programmatic identifier (such as "MS.WinCE.Outlook" for the Inbox) for the service provider, and is followed by szStoreDesc, which can be used to set a description of the data store.

The uTimerRes field should be set only if the SCF_SIMULATE_RTS flag is set in uFlags. This will determine the frequency with which the data store is checked for changes, and is specified in microseconds. If the flag is not set, you should set this to 0.

The last three parameters involve the store identifier. The maximum value that the Service Manager can accept for a store ID is passed in via the cbMaxStoreId field. You can then use the cbStoreId and lpbStoreId fields to set the identifier and its size, in bytes.

Once ActiveSync has retrieved the store identifier, it will immediately call into the IReplStore::CompareIDs() function. This enables you to determine if the store that the Service Manager is using matches the one with which it was last synchronized.

The function is defined as follows:

```
HRESULT IReplStore::CompareStoreIDs(LPBYTE lpbID1, UINT
  cbID1, LPBYTE lpbID2, UINT cbID2);
```

The first two parameters passed to the function, `lpbID1` and `cbID1`, specify the size, in bytes of the buffer, and a long pointer to the buffer of the first store identifier. `lpbID2` and `cbID2` pass in the same information for the second ID.

It is the function's responsibility to determine whether the two identifiers that are passed in represent the same store. You need to perform whatever logic is needed in order to make the determination. If the two stores match, you must return a value of 0 for the function. Otherwise, return a value of -1 if the first store is smaller than the second or 1 if the first store is larger than the second one.

The following example shows how you can handle the request to get store information and the comparison of store identifiers:

```
STDMETHODIMP CMyReplStore::GetStoreInfo(PSTOREINFO
  pStoreInfo)
{
  // Get the store identifier
  if(!pStoreInfo)
    return E_POINTER;

  if(pStoreInfo->cbStruct != sizeof(STOREINFO))
    return E_INVALIDARG;

  // Set up the STOREINFO structure with the basic store
  // info
  pStoreInfo->uFlags = SCF_SINGLE_THREAD;
  wsprintf(pStoreInfo->szProgId, TEXT("OPML.Sync"));
  wsprintf(pStoreInfo->szStoreDesc, TEXT("OPML File
    Sync"));

  // If the object has not been initialized, just exist
  if(!m_fInitialized)
    return NOERROR;

  // Set up the unique store ID. For this example, let's just
  // hard-code the ID to "OpmlSyncFiles" since we are not worried
  // about different stores.
```

```
      TCHAR tchStoreID[32] = TEXT("\0");
      DWORD dwNumBytes = 0;
      wsprintf(tchStoreID, TEXT("OpmlSyncFiles"));

      dwNumBytes = (lstrlen(tchStoreID)+sizeof(TCHAR))*sizeof(TCHAR);
      if(pStoreInfo->cbMaxStoreId < dwNumBytes)
         return E_OUTOFMEMORY;
      if(!pStoreInfo->lpbStoreId)
         return E_POINTER;

      // Copy the store ID over
      pStoreInfo->cbStoreId = dwNumBytes;
      memcpy(pStoreInfo->lpbStoreId, tchStoreID, dwNumBytes);
      return NOERROR;
}


STDMETHODIMP_(INT) CMyReplStore::CompareStoreIDs(LPBYTE
   lpbID1, UINT cbID1, LPBYTE lpbID2, UINT cbID2)
{
      // Make sure that we're using the same store ID as the
      // last time
      // if(!lpbID1 || !lpbID2)
         return 0;

      if(cbID1 < cbID2)
         return -1;
      if(cbID1 > cbID2)
         return 1;

      return memcmp(lpbID1, lpbID2, cbID1);
}
```

If the Service Manager receives a response from `IReplStore::CompareStoreIDs()` indicating that the two stores are different, then ActiveSync will remove any mapping information it already has for the provider, and prompt the end user if they want to combine the data on the device or merge them.

Once ActiveSync has determined that the data store it is using matches the one that was used the last time the device was synchronized, it will attempt to enumerate the desktop objects to see if any data has changed.

ActiveSync Data Object Types

Before we dive into how a service provider works with the data from your application, you should understand the two data types that ActiveSync uses to perform synchronization.

In order to uniquely identify objects, ActiveSync makes use of a generic handle type known as HREPLITEM, which represents a handle to a single data object. This handle is a 32-bit value that a service provider will need in order to get access to a particular piece of data. Whenever ActiveSync needs to work with a particular object, it uses the HREPLITEM handle as the parameter. Note that the IRepl Store::FindFirstItem() and IReplStore::FindNextItem() functions are the only two methods that are called to create new HREPLITEM handles.

For example, when the Service Manager requires you to compare data between two objects (which it will quite frequently), it will call the IReplStore::CompareItem() function that you have implemented, passing in two HREPLITEM handles for the objects to compare:

```
HRESULT IReplStore::CompareItem(HREPLITEM hItem1, HREPLITEM
   hItem2);
```

Both parameters are object handles for data that was returned from a previous call into the IReplStore::FindFirstItem() or IRepl Store::FindNextItem() function. You should return a value of 0 if they match, 1 if hItem1 is larger than the second, or -1 if hItem1 is smaller than the second.

The other data type that ActiveSync uses is HREPLFLD, which represents a unique 32-bit handle to a folder of objects. As with HREPLITEM, the actual value of an HREPLFLD handle has no particular meaning to the Service Manager; it merely represents a way to access a container object that contains a bunch of HREPLITEMs.

When ActiveSync needs to get the folder handle, it will call into the IReplStore::GetFolderInfo() function, which has the following prototype:

```
HRESULT IReplStore::GetFolderInfo(LPSTR lpszObjType,
   HREPLFLD *phFld, IUnknown **ppObjHandler);
```

The first parameter is a null-terminated string that contains the name of the object for which it is requesting the folder handle. Once you have created an internal data structure with the folder, you can return the handle in the `phFld` parameter. The last parameter should point to the `IReplObjHandler` interface that is used to serialize items in the folder.

The following example shows how you can implement the creation of a new folder handle:

```
STDMETHODIMP CMyReplStore::GetFolderInfo(LPSTR lpszObjType,
  HREPLFLD *phFld, IUnknown **ppunk)
{
   // Get the folder handle. We will have only one folder,
   // the directory for OPML files
   SYNCOBJ *pSyncFolder = (SYNCOBJ *)*phFld;

   if(!pSyncFolder) {
      pSyncFolder = new SYNCOBJ;
      memset(pSyncFolder, 0, sizeof(SYNCOBJ));
      pSyncFolder->bType = ID_FOLDER;
      wsprintf(pSyncFolder->tchName, TEXT("C:\\DesktopSync\\OPML"),
         MAX_PATH);
      *phFld = (HREPLFLD)pSyncFolder;
   }

   // Make sure the data handler is hooked up
   *ppunk = (IUnknown *)m_pObjHandler;
   return NOERROR;
}
```

During the synchronization process, ActiveSync also needs to occasionally check whether a data object represented by either a `HREPLITEM` or `HREPLFLD` handle is still valid. When the check needs to occur, your service provider will receive a call into the `IReplStore::IsValid Object()` function, which is defined as follows:

```
HRESULT IReplStore::IsValidObject(HREPLFLD hFld, HREPLITEM
  hObject, UINT uFlags);
```

The first two parameters, `hFld` and `hObject`, can specify either the handle to the folder or the handle to the object that the service provider should check for validity. The last parameter, `uFlags`, is not used.

The function should return a value of `NOERROR` if the object or folder still exists, as shown in the following example:

```
STDMETHODIMP CMyReplStore::IsValidObject(HREPLFLD hFld,
  HREPLITEM hObject, UINT uFlags)
{
   SYNCOBJ *pSyncObjectFld = (SYNCOBJ *)hFld;
   SYNCOBJ *pSyncObject = (SYNCOBJ *)hObject;

   // Check the folder
   if(pSyncObjectFld) {
      if(pSyncObjectFld->bType != ID_FOLDER)
         return RERR_CORRUPT;
   }

   // Check the object
   if(pSyncObject) {
      if(pSyncObject->bType != ID_OBJECT)
         return RERR_CORRUPT;
   }
   return NOERROR;
}
```

When ActiveSync needs to copy either a folder handle or a data object, it will call the appropriately named `IReplStore::Copy Object()` function:

```
HRESULT IReplStore::CopyObject(HREPLOBJ hObjSrc,
  HREPLOBJ hObjDest);
```

The only parameters you are passed here are the handles to the source and destination objects. If the copy is successful, you should return TRUE.

The following example shows how you can handle a request to copy an object:

```
STDMETHODIMP_(BOOL) CMyReplStore::CopyObject(HREPLOBJ
  hObjSrc, HREPLOBJ hObjDest)
{
```

```
      // Copy the object
      SYNCOBJ *pSyncObjectSrc = (SYNCOBJ *)hObjSrc;
      SYNCOBJ *pSyncObjectDst = (SYNCOBJ *)hObjDest;

      // If it's the folder, just return
      if(pSyncObjectSrc->bType == ID_FOLDER)
         return TRUE;

      // Copy the object
      _tcscpy(pSyncObjectDst->tchName,
         pSyncObjectSrc->tchName);
      pSyncObjectDst->bType = ID_OBJECT;
      memcpy(&pSyncObjectDst->ftModified,
         &pSyncObjectSrc->ftModified,
         sizeof(FILETIME));
      return TRUE;
}
```

Finally, when ActiveSync requires that the memory that an object has allocated needs to be released, it will call into your `IRepl Store::FreeObject()` function, which has the following prototype:

```
HRESULT IReplStore::FreeObject(HREPLOBJ hObject);
```

ActiveSync and Object Enumeration

Now that we've taken a quick look at how ActiveSync works with data objects and folders, let's see what happens when the Service Manager needs to enumerate the items in a desktop store in order to perform synchronization. After a device provider has been initialized and the Service Manager has determined that the data store is the same as it was after the last synchronization process, ActiveSync will check all of the object data folders to see if anything has changed.

As the first step of the enumeration process, the Service Manager checks whether a folder has been modified since the last time it was called:

```
HRESULT IReplStore::IsFolderChanged(HREPLFLD hFld,
  BOOL *pfChanged);
```

The first parameter is a handle to a data object folder. It is followed by `pfChanged`, which you should set to TRUE if the folder has changed since the last time the function was called. If this is the first time the function is called from the service provider (or you're not using real-time synchronization), set it to TRUE so that ActiveSync will proceed to scan the application's data objects. The Service Manager will typically call this function every time it needs to determine whether the store has been changed when your provider object is using real-time synchronization (which is turned on by the `IReplStore::GetStoreInfo()` function), instead of scanning the entire data store.

The next function that is called in the data enumeration process is `IReplStore::FindFirstItem()`. This begins the actual process of walking through each item in the data store. You also use this function to assign the handles that you will be using for your data objects.

The function has the following prototype:

```
HRESULT IReplStore::FindFirstItem(HREPLFLD hFld,
  HREPLITEM *phItem, BOOL *pfExist);
```

The first parameter, `hFld`, will indicate the handle to the folder that contains the objects for enumeration. The `phItem` pointer should be set to the handle of the first object that you find in the folder. Finally, if there are no objects in the folder, set `pfExist` to FALSE.

When ActiveSync is ready for the next HREPLITEM handle, it will call into the following:

```
HRESULT IReplStore::FindNextItem(HREPLFLD hFld,
  HREPLITEM *phItem, BOOL *pfExist);
```

The first parameter is the handle to the folder you are enumerating. Next, the pointer that is passed in by the `phItem` parameter should be set to the next HREPLFLD handle in the enumeration. The last parameter, `pfExist`, should be set to FALSE if there are no objects left in the folder to enumerate.

When the enumeration process is complete (when either `IRepl Store::FindFirstItem()` or `IReplStore::FindNextItem()` sets the `pfExist` flag to FALSE), the ActiveSync Manager will call into the `IReplStore::FindItemClose()` function. This function should be used to clean up any temporary variables or to free memory that was allocated to perform the enumeration:

```
HRESULT IReplStore::FindItemClose(HREPLFLD hFld);
```

The only parameter that is passed is the handle to the folder that was being enumerated.

The following example shows how you can implement the functions in a service provider to handle object enumeration:

```
STDMETHODIMP CMyReplStore::FindFirstItem(HREPLFLD hFld,
  HREPLITEM *phItem, BOOL *pfExist)
{
  // Start the enumeration of items. This will be a list of
  // each OPML file that is in the folder. Each item will get a
  // SYNCOBJ created for it.
  SYNCOBJ *pSyncFolder = (SYNCOBJ *)hFld;
  SYNCOBJ *pSyncObject = NULL;
  TCHAR tchOPMLFilePath[MAX_PATH+1] = TEXT("\0");
  WIN32_FIND_DATA w32Find;

  if(m_hFileEnum != NULL)
     return E_UNEXPECTED;

  memset(&w32Find, 0, sizeof(WIN32_FIND_DATA));

  wsprintf(tchOPMLFilePath, TEXT("%s\\*.opml"),
      pSyncFolder->tchName);
  m_hFileEnum = FindFirstFile(tchOPMLFilePath, &w32Find);

  if(m_hFileEnum == INVALID_HANDLE_VALUE)
     return E_OUTOFMEMORY;

  pSyncObject = new SYNCOBJ;
  memset(pSyncObject, 0, sizeof(SYNCOBJ));
  pSyncObject->bType = ID_OBJECT;
  pSyncObject->ftModified = w32Find.ftLastWriteTime;
  _tcscpy(pSyncObject->tchName, w32Find.cFileName);

  *pfExist = TRUE;
  *phItem = (HREPLITEM)pSyncObject;
  return NOERROR;
}

STDMETHODIMP CMyReplStore::FindNextItem(HREPLFLD hFld,
  HREPLITEM *phItem, BOOL *pfExist)
{
```

```
   SYNCOBJ *pSyncObject = NULL;
   WIN32_FIND_DATA w32Find;

   if(pfExist)
      *pfExist = FALSE;
   if(!m_hFileEnum)
      return E_FAIL;

   // Get the next item, return an HREPLITEM for it
   if(FindNextFile(m_hFileEnum, &w32Find) == 0)
      return E_FAIL;

   // Got an additional file, so get the info
   pSyncObject = new SYNCOBJ;
   memset(pSyncObject, 0, sizeof(SYNCOBJ));
   pSyncObject->bType = ID_OBJECT;
   pSyncObject->ftModified = w32Find.ftLastWriteTime;
   _tcscpy(pSyncObject->tchName, w32Find.cFileName);

   *pfExist = TRUE;
   *phItem = (HREPLITEM)pSyncObject;

   return NOERROR;
}

STDMETHODIMP CMyReplStore::FindItemClose(HREPLFLD hFld)
{
   if(!m_hFileEnum)
      return E_FAIL;

   // Close up the find function
   FindClose(m_hFileEnum);
   m_hFileEnum = NULL;
   return NOERROR;
}
```

Object Storage

The ActiveSync Service Manager uses its own persistent file for storing information about an object type that is currently marked for synchronization. This file, which is transparent to the service provider, is used by ActiveSync to map objects to their store IDs, and store information about the last synchronization, as well as some additional overhead information.

When ActiveSync needs to save data to this file, it calls into the `IReplStore::ObjectToBytes()` function. This function is used to convert the handle for an `HREPLITEM` or `HREPLFLD` object into an array of bytes that the Service Manager will save:

The `IReplStore::ObjectToBytes()` function has the following prototype:

```
HRESULT IReplStore::ObjectToBytes(HREPLOBJ hObject,
  LPBYTE lpb);
```

The first parameter is the handle for either an `HREPLITEM` or `HREPLFLD` object. The `lpb` parameter points to the buffer that should be used to store the array that the handle represents. After you have copied your data to the buffer, you should use the number of bytes that are stored in the buffer as the return value.

The first time that the Service Manager calls into the `IRepl Store::ObjectToBytes()` function, the `lpb` pointer will be set to `NULL`. Simply return the number of bytes that you require for storing the object, and ActiveSync will automatically provide a correctly sized buffer on future calls.

The reverse operation, which converts a series of bytes into an object, is done by the following function:

```
HRESULT IReplStore::BytesToObject(LPBYTE lpb, UINT cb);
```

The first parameter is the array of bytes for the object, and is followed by `cb`, which indicates the size of the buffer. You should convert the buffer to an appropriate object, and return the new `HREPLITEM` or `HREPLFLD` for it.

The following example shows how you can implement the object conversion functions:

```
STDMETHODIMP_(UINT) CMyReplStore::ObjectToBytes(HREPLOBJ
  hObject, LPBYTE lpb)
{
   // Convert an SYNCOBJ to an array of bytes. Our object
   // array will have the following structure:
   // VERSION TYPE BYTES_NAME NAME FTMODIFIED
   // Also, here's some constant information:
   // VERSION_INFO = 1, ID_FOLDER = 0, ID_OBJECT = 1
   DWORD dwBytes = 0;
```

```
BOOL fCopyToBytes = TRUE;
SYNCOBJ *pSyncObject = (SYNCOBJ *)hObject;
DWORD dwBufferLength = 0;


// If we receive a NULL buffer, then we just return the
// number of bytes needed
if(!lpb)
   fCopyToBytes = FALSE;


// Copy the object to bytes (or just the size)
// Version:
if(fCopyToBytes) {
   *lpb = VERSION_INFO;
   lpb++;
}
dwBytes++;


// Object type
if(fCopyToBytes) {
   *lpb = pSyncObject->bType;
   lpb++;
}
dwBytes++;


/////////////////////////////////////
// Copy the URL
dwBufferLength = lstrlen(pSyncObject->tchName)
*sizeof(TCHAR);
if(fCopyToBytes) {
   // URL Length
   memcpy(lpb, &dwBufferLength, sizeof(DWORD));
   lpb += sizeof(DWORD);

   // URL
   memcpy(lpb, pSyncObject->tchName, dwBufferLength);
   lpb += dwBufferLength;
}

dwBytes += sizeof(DWORD) + dwBufferLength;


// Copy the date modified
if(fCopyToBytes) {
```

```
        memcpy(lpb, &pSyncObject->ftModified,
              sizeof(FILETIME));
        lpb += sizeof(FILETIME);;
    }
    dwBytes += sizeof(FILETIME);

    // Return the number of bytes
    return dwBytes;
}

STDMETHODIMP_(HREPLOBJ) CMyReplStore::BytesToObject(LPBYTE
  lpb, UINT cb)
{
    // Convert the byte stream to an object.
    // VERSION TYPE BYTES_NAME NAME FTMODIFIED
    // Also, here's some constant information:
    // VERSION_INFO = 1, ID_FOLDER = 0, ID_OBJECT = 1

    if(!lpb)
        return NULL;

    BYTE bVersion = *lpb++;
    BYTE bType = *lpb++;
    DWORD dwBufferLength = 0;
    SYNCOBJ *pSyncObject = new SYNCOBJ;

    memset(pSyncObject, 0, sizeof(SYNCOBJ));

    // Check to see if we have a folder
    if(bType == ID_FOLDER)
        pSyncObject->bType = ID_FOLDER;
    else
        pSyncObject->bType = ID_OBJECT;

    // We have a file object, copy the info to it.
    // Get the file name
    memcpy(&dwBufferLength, lpb, sizeof(DWORD));
    lpb += sizeof(DWORD);

    memcpy(pSyncObject->tchName, lpb, dwBufferLength);
    lpb += dwBufferLength;

    // Get the last modified date
    memcpy(&pSyncObject->ftModified, lpb, sizeof(FILETIME));
    lpb += dwBufferLength;
```

```
    // Return the handle
    return (HREPLOBJ)pSyncObject;
}
```

The ActiveSync Synchronization Process (Desktop Side)

Now that we've looked at how ActiveSync initializes the desktop provider, stores its data internally, and enumerates desktop data objects, let's examine the actual synchronization process.

After the Service Manager determines that the store identifier returned by the service provider matches the one that was stored in the ActiveSync Manager's persistent data file, it will begin synchronization. ActiveSync accomplishes this by looking at the list of handles with each enumeration of the data store, and then it makes a determination about data objects that have changed or been deleted.

When enumeration begins, ActiveSync marks each handle in its internal table, which was loaded from the persistent data store. After getting the folder information and calling into the desktop provider's `IReplStore::FindFirstFile()` and `IReplStore::FindNext File()` functions, ActiveSync looks for a handle that matches the object that has already been stored. If no match is found, it simply creates the new object. If the handle matches, then ActiveSync removes the mark on the handle and calls into the `IReplStore::IsItemChanged()` method that your provider has implemented to determine whether anything has been modified.

The function that you need to implement has the following prototype:

```
HRESULT IReplStore::IsItemChanged(HREPLFLD hFld, HREPLITEM
  hItem, HREPLITEM hItemComp);
```

The first parameter will be the handle to the folder that contains the object. Next, `hItem` will specify the handle to the item. The last parameter, `hItemComp`, is the handle to the object that should be compared. If `hItemComp` is NULL, you should check the item by opening the object that `hItem` specifies to see if anything has changed since the last synchronization. Returning TRUE for this function signifies that the object has changed.

If the item has changed, the Service Manager will call into `IRepl Store::CopyObject()`, updating the internal data store with the new object's information. After that has completed, ActiveSync will call into

`IReplStore::IsItemReplicated()` to determine whether or not the change should be copied to the device:

```
HRESULT IReplStore::IsItemReplicated(HREPLFLD hFld,
  HREPLITEM hItem);
```

The function is passed two handles: the handle to the folder for the object and the handle to the data object itself. If the `hItem` parameter is a `NULL` value, then the service provider will have to determine whether or not the folder itself should be replicated. Return a value of `TRUE` to specify that the object should be copied to the device.

The following example shows how to implement the functions in `IReplStore` that are used to determine whether an object has changed:

```
STDMETHODIMP_(BOOL) CMyReplStore::IsItemChanged(HREPLFLD
  hFld, HREPLITEM hItem, HREPLITEM hItemComp)
{
    SYNCOBJ *pSyncFolder = (SYNCOBJ *)hFld;
    SYNCOBJ *pSyncObject = (SYNCOBJ *)hItem;
    SYNCOBJ *pSyncObjectComp = (SYNCOBJ *)hItemComp;
    SYNCOBJ pTempObj;
    BOOL fChanged = FALSE;

    // If there's nothing to compare to, then find the object
    if(!pSyncObjectComp) {
        // Find the object in the node list
        if(!FindObject(pSyncFolder->tchName,
                pSyncObject->tchName, &pTempObj))
            return FALSE;

        pSyncObjectComp = &pTempObj;
    }

    // Check to make sure that the last modified time is
    // the same
    if(CompareFileTime(&pSyncObject->ftModified,
        &pSyncObjectComp->ftModified) != 0)
        fChanged = TRUE;

    return fChanged;
}
```

```
STDMETHODIMP_(BOOL) CMyReplStore::IsItemReplicated(HREPLFLD
  hFld, HREPLITEM hItem)
{
    // Replicate all objects.
    return TRUE;
}
```

This process continues until all of the items in the data store have been enumerated.

After the first successful synchronization occurs, the ActiveSync Service Manager calls into the `IReplStore::RemoveDuplicates()` function. It is typical to have duplicate items in the data store, especially after data has been combined.

The function is defined as follows:

```
HRESULT IReplStore::RemoveDuplicates(LPSTR lpszObjType,
  UINT uFlags);
```

The first parameter is the null-terminated string specifying the type of object that you will check for duplicate entries. The `uFlags` parameter is unused.

Updating ActiveSync

While the synchronization process is in progress, the ActiveSync Service Manager continuously calls the `IReplStore::ReportStatus()` method to send information on the current status:

```
HRESULT IReplStore::ReportStatus(HREPLFLD hFld, HREPLITEM
  hItem, UINT uStatus, UINT uParam );
```

The first two parameters, `hFld` and `hItem`, specify the handles for the folder and data object that the notification is for (and will be `NULL` if the status message doesn't apply to a particular folder or object). The last two parameters, `uStatus` and `uParam`, contain the message details. A status message can be one of the message types described in Table 9.21.

Table 9.21 Synchronization Status Messages

uStatus Value	Description
RSC_BEGIN_SYNC	Synchronization is about to begin. `uParam` will be set to `BSF_AUTO_SYNC` or `BSF_REMOTE_SYNC`.
RSC_END_SYNC	Synchronization is complete.
RSC_BEGIN_CHECK	ActiveSync is about to call into `IReplStore::FindFirstItem()` or `IReplStore::FindNextItem()`.
RSC_END_CHECK	Enumeration has completed and is about to call into `IReplStore::FindCloseItem()`.
RSC_DATE_CHANGED	The system date has changed.
RSC_RELEASE	ActiveSync is about to call into `IReplStore::Release()`.
RSC_REMOTE_SYNC	Remote synchronization is about to start if the `uParam` value is set to `TRUE`. If `uParam` is `FALSE`, then remote synchronization is complete.
RSC_INTERRUPT	ActiveSync is about to interrupt the synchronization process.
RSC_BEGIN_SYNC_OBJ	Synchronization is about to start for a particular object type.
RSC_END_SYNC_OBJ	Synchronization has completed for a particular object type.
RSC_OBJ_TYPE_ENABLED	A specific object type is enabled for synchronization.
RSC_OBJ_TYPE_DISABLED	A specific object type is disabled for synchronization.
RSC_BEGIN_BATCH_WRITE	The `IReplObjHandler::SetPackets()` function is about to be called.
RSC_END_BATCH_WRITE	The service provider should commit the packet transfer.
RSC_CONNECTION_CHG	The status of the connection has changed. The `uParam` value will be set to `TRUE` if it has been established; otherwise, it will be set to `FALSE`.
RSC_WRITE_OBJ_FAILED	An error occurred while writing information to the device.
RSC_DELETE_OBJ_FAILED	An error occurred while deleting an object on the device.
RSC_WRITE_OBJ_SUCCESS	An object was successfully written to the device.
RSC_DELETE_OBJ_SUCCESS	An object was successfully deleted from the device.
RSC_READ_OBJ_FAILED	An error occurred while reading an object from the device.
RSC_TIME_CHANGED	The system time has changed.
RSC_BEGIN_BACKUP	The backup process is about to begin.

uStatus Value	Description
RSC_END_BACKUP	The backup process has completed.
RSC_BEGIN_RESTORE	The restore process is about to begin.
RSC_END_RESTORE	The restore process has completed.
RSC_PREPARE_SYNC_FLD	Synchronization is about to begin on a specific folder.

Whenever the ActiveSync Service Manager needs to write the data for an object to the persistent store, it will call into the `IReplStore::UpdateItem()` method:

```
HRESULT IReplStore::UpdateItem(HREPLFLD hFld, HREPLITEM
   hItemDst, HREPLITEM hItemSrc);
```

The parameters that the functions receive specify the folder as well as the source and destination object data handles.

ActiveSync and User Interface Elements

ActiveSync will also call into your desktop service provider when the user wants to change any synchronization options. The desktop provider is required to implement its own dialog boxes for configuring the data that will be transferred to a device.

When the user selects the Settings button in ActiveSync, your provider will have the following function called:

```
HRESULT IReplStore::ActivateDialog(UINT uidDialog,
   HWND hwndParent, HREPLFLD hFld, IEnumReplItem *penumItem);
```

The first parameter, `uidDialog`, specifies the dialog box that ActiveSync is requesting to activate. At this time, only the `OPTIONS_DIALOG` flag is supported. This is followed by the handle to the parent window, `hwndParent`. The last two parameters contain information about the object folder and a pointer to an `IEnumReplItem` interface, which contains an enumeration of `HREPLITEM` objects for the folder.

After you have shown the dialog box, you should set the return value based on how the user closed the dialog box.

The following is a list of return codes for `IReplStore::Activate Dialog()`:

- `NOERROR` should be returned if the user pressed OK to save the changes.
- `RERR_CANCEL` should be returned to ignore any changes.
- `RERR_SHUT_DOWN` should be returned if the user pressed OK, and ActiveSync needs to be restarted due to the changes.
- `RERR_UNLOAD` should be returned if the user pressed OK, and ActiveSync needs to reload the synchronization provider for the change to be enabled.
- `E_NOTIMPL` should be returned if you do not support any synchronization options.

The ActiveSync Service Manager will also contact your provider when it needs information about user interface elements for your object types, using the following function:

```
HRESULT IReplStore::GetObjTypeUIData(HREPLFLD hFld,
   POBJUIDATA pData);
```

The `hFld` parameter is the handle to the folder that contains the objects. The next parameter, `pData`, points to an `OBJUIDATA` structure that you will need to fill in. The structure is defined as follows:

```
typedef struct tagObjUIData {
    UINT cbStruct;
    HICON hIconLarge;
    HICON hIconSmall;
    char szName[MAX_PATH];
    char szSyncText[MAX_PATH];
    char szTypeText[80];
    char szPlTypeText[80];
} OBJUIDATA, *POBJUIDATA;
```

The first field, `cbStruct`, specifies the size of the structure. Next, the handles for the large and small icons for your data object should be set in the `hIconLarge` and `hIconSmall` fields. The rest of the fields deal with the null-terminated strings that are displayed: `szName` is used for the Name column, `szSyncText` for the Sync Copy In column, `szTypeText` for the object type, and `szPlTypeText` for the plural version of `szTypeText`.

Handling Conflicts

When data on both the device and the desktop has changed since the last time they were synchronized, a *conflict* occurs. When the Service Manager detects a conflict, it automatically pulls the conflicting data from the device (by using the `IReplObjHandler` interface, which is discussed later in this chapter), and creates a temporary desktop object. ActiveSync then calls into the `IReplStore::GetConflictInfo()` function, enabling you to examine both objects. The function requires you to fill in some information in the structure that it is passed, so ActiveSync can display a Conflict Resolution dialog box to the user. The function is defined as follows:

```
HRESULT IReplStore::GetConflictInfo(PCONFINFO pConfInfo);
```

The function receives a single parameter, which is a pointer to a `CONFINFO` structure. This structure provides detailed information about the conflicting data:

```
typedef struct tagConfInfo {
    UINT cbStruct;
    HREPLFLD hFolder;
    HREPLITEM hLocalItem;
    HREPLITEM hRemoteItem;
    OBJTYPENAME szLocalName;
    TCHAR szLocalDesc[512];
    OBJTYPENAME szRemoteName;
    TCHAR szRemoteDesc[ 512 ];
} CONFINFO, *PCONFINFO;
```

The first field, `cbStruct`, contains the size, in bytes, of the `CONFINFO` structure. The `hFolder` field contains the handle to the folder for the conflicting object, and is followed by handles for both the local object and the temporary object that was created.

The rest of the fields are used by the ActiveSync Service Manager to fill in information in the Conflict Resolution dialog box. The local object name and description should be filled in the `szLocalName` and `szLocalDesc` fields, respectively; `szRemoteName` and `szRemote Desc` should be used for the temporary object.

Returning a value of `NOERROR` forces ActiveSync to prompt the user with a dialog box to handle the conflict. The automatic handling of a data conflict (which you should do for remote users), is determined by the return value:

- RERR_IGNORE should be returned if you want ActiveSync to just ignore the conflict.
- RERR_DISCARD should be returned if you want ActiveSync to delete the object on the device.
- RERR_DISCARD_LOCAL should be returned if you want ActiveSync to delete the object on the desktop.

For example, to handle a conflict, you could do the following:

```
STDMETHODIMP CMyReplStore::GetConflictInfo(PCONFINFO
  pConfInfo)
{
   if(pConfInfo->cbStruct != sizeof(CONFINFO))
      return E_INVALIDARG;

   _tcscpy(pConfInfo->szLocalName, TEXT("OPML File"));
   _tcscpy(pConfInfo->szRemoteName, pConfInfo->szLocalName);

   // Compare local and remote
   SYNCOBJ *pSyncObjectLocal =
      (SYNCOBJ *)pConfInfo->hLocalItem;
   SYNCOBJ *pSyncObjectRemote =
      (SYNCOBJ *)pConfInfo->hRemoteItem;

   // Check to see if identical
   if(pSyncObjectLocal && pSyncObjectRemote) {
      if(!_tcscmp(pSyncObjectLocal->tchName,
            pSyncObjectRemote->tchName))
         return RERR_IGNORE;
   }

   // No? Put information in the dialog
   SYSTEMTIME sysTime;

   if(pSyncObjectLocal) {
      FileTimeToSystemTime(&pSyncObjectLocal->ftModified,
         &sysTime);
      wsprintf(pConfInfo->szLocalDesc, TEXT("Name:
         %s\r\nModified: %d-%d-%d"),
         pSyncObjectLocal->tchName, sysTime.wDay,
         sysTime.wMonth,sysTime.wYear);
   }
```

```
        if(pSyncObjectRemote) {
            FileTimeToSystemTime(&pSyncObjectRemote->ftModified,
                &sysTime);
            wsprintf(pConfInfo->szRemoteDesc,
                TEXT("Name: %s\r\nModified: %d-%d-%d"),
                pSyncObjectRemote->tchName,
                sysTime.wDay, sysTime.wMonth, sysTime.wYear);
        }

        return NOERROR;
}
```

Implementing IReplObjHandler

You must implement the `IReplObjHandler` interface inside your desktop service provider, which enables the ActiveSync Service Manager to convert a data object (either a folder or object) into a series of bytes to transfer to the connected device. This process is known as *serializing*. Converting the data from a series of bytes into an object is called *deserializing*.

Table 9.22 describes the methods that must be implemented by the `IReplObjHandler` interface.

Now let's look at how ActiveSync uses these functions to send and receive data.

Table 9.22 `IReplObjHandler` Methods

Method	Description
DeleteObj()	Deletes an object from the data store.
GetPacket()	Deserializes an object. This function is called when a data object needs to be converted into one or more packets of data.
Reset()	Resets the service provider and frees used resources.
SetPacket()	Serializes a data packet. This function is called when one or more packets of data need to be converted back into an object.
Setup()	Configures the service provider so it can begin serializing and deserializing data.

How ActiveSync Sends and Receives Objects

The first function that ActiveSync will call into when it needs to serialize or deserialize data is the `IReplObjHandler::Setup()` function, which is called for every object it needs to convert. The function has the following prototype:

```
HRESULT IReplObjHandler::Setup(PREPLSETUP pSetup);
```

The only parameter that the method is passed is a pointer to a `REPLSETUP` structure, which contains information about the object:

```
typedef struct _tagReplSetup {
    UINT cbStruct;
    BOOL fRead;
    DWORD dwFlags;
    HRESULT hr;
    OBJTYPENAME szObjType;
    IReplNotify *pNotify;
    DWORD oid;
    DWORD oidNew;
    IReplStore *pStore;
    HREPLFLD hFolder;
    HREPLITEM hItem;
} REPLSETUP, *PREPLSETUP;
```

The first field, `cbStruct`, specifies the size of the `REPLSETUP` structure. If the `fRead` field is set to `TRUE`, you are setting up for the serialization of data. If set to `FALSE`, you are getting ready to deserialize the object. The `dwFlags` and `hr` fields are reserved.

The next several fields provide you with information about the object that you are going to either serialize or deserialize. The `szObjType` field is a null-terminated string that contains the name of the object type you are working with. The `oid` and `oidNew` fields provide object identifiers that are used by ActiveSync. You can access the particular object by using the `pStore`, `hFolder`, and `hItem` fields, which will pass you the interface handle to the object's `IReplStore` interface as well as the folder and object handles.

The `pNotify` field points to the ActiveSync Service Manager's `IReplNotify` interface pointer.

The following code shows what is involved when implementing the `IReplObjHandler::Setup()` function:

```
STDMETHODIMP CMyRplObjHandler::Setup(PREPLSETUP pSetup)
{
   if(pSetup->cbStruct != sizeof(REPLSETUP))
      return E_INVALIDARG;

   // Since reading/writing can occur at the same time,
   // must set up for both
   if(pSetup->fRead)
      m_pReadSetup = pSetup;
   else
      m_pWriteSetup = pSetup;

   return NOERROR;
}
```

Whether the object needs to be serialized or deserialized determines the next function into which the ActiveSync Manager calls. If the object requires serialization, then it will call into the `IReplObjHandler::` `GetPacket()` function:

```
HRESULT IReplObjHandler::GetPacket(LPBYTE *lppbData,
  DWORD *pcbData, DWORD cbRecommend);
```

The first parameter is a pointer to the data buffer of the outgoing packet, which can be used to copy your data into. The size of the buffer is specified by the `pcbData` parameter. It is necessary for the desktop provider to allocate and de-allocate the buffer used for the data packet.

The last parameter, `cbRecommend`, is the maximum recommended size of each packet.

The `IReplObjHandler::GetPacket()` will be called continuously for the object it is trying to send until you return a value of `RWRN_LAST_OBJECT`.

The following code serializes an object into a packet:

```
STDMETHODIMP CMyRplObjHandler::GetPacket(LPBYTE *lppbData,
  DWORD *pcbData, DWORD cbRecommend)
{
   // Make sure we have the setup information for the read
   if(!m_bPacket)
      return E_UNEXPECTED;
```

```
// We'll need to build a packet based on the object
// (i.e., a file)
// m_pReadSetup will be used.
SYNCOBJ *pSyncObject = (SYNCOBJ *)m_pReadSetup->hItem;
SYNCOBJ *pSyncObjectFld =
    (SYNCOBJ *)m_pReadSetup->hFolder;
TCHAR tchFilePath[MAX_PATH+1] = TEXT("\0");
HANDLE hFile = NULL;
DWORD dwBytesRead = 0;

wsprintf(tchFilePath, TEXT("%s\\%s"),
    pSyncObjectFld->tchName, pSyncObject->tchName);
hFile = CreateFile(tchFilePath, GENERIC_READ,
    FILE_SHARE_READ, NULL, OPEN_EXISTING, 0, NULL);
if(hFile == INVALID_HANDLE_VALUE)
    return HRESULT_FROM_WIN32(ERROR_FILE_NOT_FOUND);

memset(m_bPacket, 0, PACKET_SIZE);

if(!ReadFile(hFile, m_bPacket, PACKET_SIZE, &dwBytesRead,
    NULL)) {
    CloseHandle(hFile);
    return RERR_BAD_OBJECT;
}

CloseHandle(hFile);

*lppbData = (LPBYTE)m_bPacket;
*pcbData = dwBytesRead;
return RWRN_LAST_PACKET;
}
```

If ActiveSync needs to deserialize the object, the `IReplObj Handler::SetPacket()` function will be called:

```
HRESULT IReplObjHandler::SetPacket(LPBYTE lpbData, DWORD
  cbData);
```

The function is passed a pointer to the incoming packet of data, as well as its size.

The following code shows how to deserialize an object:

```
STDMETHODIMP CMyRplObjHandler::SetPacket(LPBYTE lpbData,
  DWORD cbData)
{
   // Create a SYNCOBJ from the packet
   if(!m_pWriteSetup)
      return E_UNEXPECTED;

   SYNCOBJ *pSyncObject = (SYNCOBJ *)m_pWriteSetup->hItem;
   SYNCOBJ *pSyncObjectFld =
      (SYNCOBJ *)m_pWriteSetup->hFolder;
   TCHAR tchFilePath[MAX_PATH+1] = TEXT("\0");
   HANDLE hFile = NULL;
   DWORD dwBytesWritten = 0;

   wsprintf(tchFilePath, TEXT("%s\\%s"),
      pSyncObjectFld->tchName, pSyncObject->tchName);
   hFile = CreateFile(tchFilePath,
      GENERIC_READ|GENERIC_WRITE, 0, NULL,
      CREATE_ALWAYS, FILE_ATTRIBUTE_NORMAL, NULL);
   if(hFile == INVALID_HANDLE_VALUE)
      return HRESULT_FROM_WIN32(ERROR_FILE_NOT_FOUND);

   // Write to the file
   WriteFile(hFile, lpbData, cbData, &dwBytesWritten, NULL);
   CloseHandle(hFile);

   // Create the new SYNCOBJ
   SYNCOBJ *pNewSyncObj = new SYNCOBJ;
   SYSTEMTIME sysTime;
   FILETIME ft;

   memset(pNewSyncObj, 0, sizeof(SYNCOBJ));
   pNewSyncObj->bType = ID_OBJECT;
   _tcscpy(pNewSyncObj->tchName, pSyncObject->tchName);

   GetSystemTime(&sysTime);
   SystemTimeToFileTime(&sysTime, &ft);
   FileTimeToLocalFileTime(&ft, &pSyncObject->ftModified);

   m_pWriteSetup->hItem = (HREPLITEM)pSyncObject;
   return NOERROR;
}
```

Note that the packets you receive from `IReplObjHandler::SetPacket()` are guaranteed to be in the same number and order as they were when sent from `IReplObjHandler::GetPacket()`.

Once all of the objects have been serialized or deserialized, the ActiveSync Service Manager makes a final call into `IReplObj Handler::Reset()`. The method has the following prototype:

```
HRESULT IReplObjHandler::Reset(PREPLSETUP pSetup);
```

The only parameter is a handle to a `REPLSETUP` structure: `IReplObjHandler::Reset()` will be called once per object, and can be used to free any memory that was used when converting your data.

The last function called by the ActiveSync Service Manager is `IReplObjHandler::DeleteObj()`. This method is used whenever an object needs to be deleted during conflict resolution or synchronization:

```
HRESULT IReplObjHandler::DeleteObj(PREPLSETUP pSetup);
```

The only parameter that is received is a pointer to a `REPLSETUP` structure.

Calling ActiveSync from Your Provider (Using `IReplNotify`)

Both the `IReplObjHandler` and `IReplStore` interfaces receive a pointer to an `IReplNotify` object that can be used to retrieve some basic information from the ActiveSync Service Manager. In addition, you can use this interface to notify ActiveSync when a change has occurred in an object's data so that real-time synchronization can occur. The interface is already implemented by ActiveSync, and supports the methods described in Table 9.23.

Table 9.23 `ReplNotify` Methods

Method	Description
GetWindow()	Gets the handle to the ActiveSync window. This handle should be used as the parent handle for any dialog box that the service provider creates.
OnItemNotify()	Notifies ActiveSync when a data object has been created, deleted, or modified.
QueryDevice()	Requests information about a device from ActiveSync, such as the name or type of device.

To get the handle to the ActiveSync window to use as a parent, you can call into the following function:

```
HRESULT IReplNotify::GetWindow(UINT uFlags);
```

The uFlags parameter is not currently used, and should be set to 0.

To get information about the connected device, use the IRepl Notify::QueryDevice() function:

```
HRESULT IReplNotify::QueryDevice(UINT uCode,
  LPVOID *ppvData);
```

The first parameter, uCode, should be used to specify what information you want to receive from the Service Manager about a device. The value you set determines the buffer to which ppvData should point.

The uCode parameter can be set to the following:

- QDC_SEL_DEVICE should be used to get information about the selected device. The ppvData pointer should point to a DEVINFO structure.
- QDC_CON_DEVICE should be used to get information about the connected device. The ppvData pointer should point to a DEVINFO structure.
- QDC_SYNC_DATA should be used to get custom device synchronization information. See the SyncData() function on the device service provider for more information. The ppvData pointer should point to an SDREQUEST structure.
- QDC_SEL_DEVICE_KEY should be used to get the registry key that can be used to store specific information for the selected device. The ppvData pointer should point to an HKEY.
- QDC_CON_DEVICE_KEY should be used to get the registry key that can be used to store information about the connected device. The ppvData pointer should point to an HKEY.

The DEVINFO structure is defined as follows:

```
typedef struct tagDevInfo {
    DWORD pid;
    char szName[MAX_PATH];
    char szType[80];
    char szPath[MAX_PATH];
} DEVINFO, *PDEVINFO;
```

The structure's fields contain the device ID, and its name, type, and path.

The last function that you will use to send messages back to ActiveSync is the `IReplNotify::OnItemNotify()` method. This method is extremely useful when performing real-time synchronization, as it lets ActiveSync know that an object has been changed, added, or deleted:

```
HRESULT IReplNotify::OnItemNotify(UINT uCode, LPSTR
  lpszProgId, LPSTR lpszName, HREPLITEM hItem, ULONG ulFlags);
```

The first parameter lets ActiveSync know what has happened to the data object. It can be set to any of the following: `RNC_CREATED` indicates that a new object has been created, `RNC_MODIFIED` indicates that an object has been changed, `RNC_DELETED` indicates that an object has been deleted, and `RNC_SHUTDOWN` indicates whether the store has been terminated and ActiveSync should unload the synchronization provider.

The next parameter, `lpszProgId`, is the programmatic identifier of the data store, and is followed by `lpszName`, which should point to a null-terminated string specifying the object type. The `hItem` parameter is the handle to the object you are notifying ActiveSync about. The last parameter, `ulFlags`, is unused.

Writing the Device Provider Module

The other half of a custom synchronization component is the device-side provider module, which will consist of the following items:

- The device provider must implement the same **IReplObjHandler** interface as the desktop, to ensure that data packets are serialized and deserialized properly.
- Three functions must be exported from the device provider DLL: **GetObjTypeInfo()**, **InitObjType()**, and **ObjectNotify()**. In addition, there are three optional functions: **FindObjects()**, **ReportStatus()**, and **SyncData()**.

Before taking a more detailed look at the device provider, let's see how a new device provider module needs to be properly configured in the registry.

Registering the Device Provider

Registering the device side of a synchronization provider is much less complicated than its desktop counterpart. To register the synchronization component, you need to place a new key in the following location:

```
HKEY_LOCAL_MACHINE\SOFTWARE\Windows CE
    Services\Synchronization\Objects\{New Object Name}
```

This key requires the values described in Table 9.24.

Table 9.24 Registry Settings for a Device-Side Synchronization Provider

Key\Value Name	Description
Store	Full path to the library that exports the device's provider functions
DisplayName	Name to be used in the device's ActiveSync Service Manager

Let's take a look at the registry keys that are used for the device side of the Pocket Inbox synchronization provider:

```
//
// Registry entries for the object used by the device service
// provider
//
[HKEY_LOCAL_MACHINE\Windows CE
    Services\synchronization\objects\Merlin Mail]
"Store"="cemailsync.dll"
```

Implementing IReplObjHandler on the Device

The implementation of IReplObjHandler that you need to create for the device side of a synchronization provider should be the same as the desktop implementation. This ensures that packets sent to the desktop are in the correct format, and that packets that are received can be turned into objects properly.

In addition to IReplObjHandler, you need to have your synchronization provider export the functions described in Table 9.25.

Table 9.25 `IReplObjHandler` Methods

Key\Value Name	Description
`GetObjTypeInfo()`	Gets the type of object specified.
`InitObjType()`	Initializes and returns a pointer to the device provider's `IReplObjHandler` interface.
`ObjectNotify()`	Notifies the device-side ActiveSync Service Manager when an object is added, changed, or deleted.
`ReportStatus()`	Optional. Gets the status for synchronization objects.
`FindObjects()`	Optional. Used to synchronize database volumes.
`SyncData()`	Optional. Used to provide the desktop provider with a simple way to send and receive data to and from the device.

Let's take a look at how the device's ActiveSync Service Manager uses your provider to perform synchronization tasks.

NOTE: There is currently no way to debug a device-side ActiveSync provider. I recommend creating some functions that will write output to a log file to help debug your device-side SSP.

Initializing a Device Provider

When the ActiveSync Manager on the device needs to initialize or terminate the device provider, it will call into the `InitObjType()` function for each object type that it supports. The function has the following prototype:

```
BOOL InitObjType(LPWSTR lpszObjType,
  IReplObjHandler **ppObjHandler, UINT uPartnerBit);
```

The first parameter, `lpszObjType`, is a null-terminated string that provides you with the object type that ActiveSync is trying to initialize. As part of the initialization process, you need to instantiate the `IReplObj Handler` interface for the object type it is requesting, and return the pointer to it in the `ppObjHandler` parameter. The last parameter, `uPartnerBit`, specifies which partner desktop it is connecting with, either partner 1 or partner 2.

If the `lpszObjType` value is `NULL`, then ActiveSync is unloading your service provider, and you should do whatever cleanup is necessary.

The following example initializes the device provider:

```
DllExport BOOL InitObjType(LPWSTR lpszObjType,
  IReplObjHandler **ppObjHandler, UINT uPartnerBit)
{
   // Initialize/uninitialize
   if(!lpszObjType) {
      // Uninit'ing, so cleanup here
      WriteToLog(TEXT("InitObjType: Close\r\n"));
      if(hLogFile)
         CloseHandle(hLogFile);
      return TRUE;
   }

   // Take care of the log
   hLogFile = CreateFile(TEXT("\\synclog.txt"),
      GENERIC_WRITE|GENERIC_READ,
      FILE_SHARE_READ, NULL, CREATE_ALWAYS,
      FILE_ATTRIBUTE_NORMAL, NULL);
   WriteToLog(TEXT("InitObjType: Open\r\n"));

   // Set up the handler
   *ppObjHandler = new CMyRplObjHandler();
   return TRUE;
}
```

Device Object Enumeration

The bulk of the work on the client side is done through object enumeration, but it is significantly different from what was implemented in the `IReplStore::FindFirstItem()` and `IReplStore::FindNext Item()` functions on the desktop provider.

When a device partnership has been established, ActiveSync enumerates every file system object and call into each service provider's `ObjectNotify()` function. It is the responsibility of `Object Notify()` to determine whether or not a change to the data should be synchronized.

The function has the following prototype:

```
BOOL ObjectNofity(POBJNOTIFY pon);
```

The only parameter you are passed is a pointer to an OBJNOTIFY structure, which is defined as follows:

```
typedef struct tagObjNotify {
    UINT cbStruct;
    OBJTYPENAME szObjType;
    UINT uFlags;
    UINT uPartnerBit;
    CEOID oidObject;
    CEOIDINFO oidInfo;
    UINT cOidChg;
    UINT cOidDel;
    UINT *poid;
    LPBYTE lpbVolumeID;
    UINT cbVolumeID;
} OBJNOTIFY, *POBJNOTIFY;
```

The first field, cbStruct, provides the size of the OBJNOTIFY structure that is being pass in, and is followed by a null-terminated string that holds the object type. The uFlags field specifies the type of object that the structure is for, and can be one or more of the objects described in Table 9.26.

Table 9.26 ObjectNotify() Flags

uFlag Value	Description
ONF_FILE	The object type is a file.
ONF_DIRECTORY	The object type is a folder.
ONF_DATABASE	The object type is a database.
ONF_RECORD	The object type is a database record.
ONF_CHANGED	The object has changed.
ONF_DELETED	The object has been deleted.
ONF_CLEAR_CHANGE	The object is a synchronized object identifier, and should be marked as up-to-date.
ONF_CALL_BACK	Requests ActiveSync to try again in two seconds.
ONF_CALLING_BACK	ActiveSync sets this in response to a ONF_CALL_BACK request.

Next, the uPartnerBit field will specify the desktop partner, either 1 or 2, with which the device is connected.

The remaining fields of the structure are used to provide object identifier (OID) information about the data object(s) that have changed. The `oidObject` field is the OID for the file system object, database, or database record to which you are being passed information by the structure. If an object has been modified, then you need to set the `oidInfo` field with a completed `OIDINFO` structure regarding the updated object. The flags that are set in the `uFlag` field determine the value of the next two items. When `uFlag` has the `ONF_CHANGED` flag set, the `cOidChg` field should be set to the number of OIDs that have changed and require synchronization; otherwise, set it to 0. When `uFlag` has the `ONF_DELETED` flag set, `cOidDel` should be set to the number of OIDs that have been deleted.

The last field, `poid`, is a pointer to an array of object identifiers. The number of objects required in the array is specified by the number of changed or deleted items, `cOidChg` or `cOidDel`, respectively.

You should return a value of `TRUE` if you want to specify that the changed object should be synchronized.

The following example shows how you can handle a call into the `ObjectNotify()` function:

```
DllExport BOOL ObjectNotify(POBJNOTIFY pNotify)
{
   WriteToLog(TEXT("Start ObjectNotify\r\n"));

   if(pNotify->cbStruct != sizeof(OBJNOTIFY))
   return FALSE;

   /* Log File */
   TCHAR tchLogBuffer[MAX_PATH] = TEXT("\0");

   wsprintf(tchLogBuffer, TEXT("\tObj Name: %s\r\n\tOID:
      %u\r\n"), pNotify->szObjType, pNotify->oidObject);
   WriteToLog(tchLogBuffer);

   CEOIDINFO *pOidInfo = &pNotify->oidInfo;
   if(pOidInfo) {
      if(pOidInfo->wObjType == OBJTYPE_FILE)
         wsprintf(tchLogBuffer, TEXT("\tFile Object: %s,
            Length: %d\r\n"), pOidInfo->infFile.szFileName,
            pOidInfo->infFile.dwLength);
      else
         wsprintf(tchLogBuffer, TEXT("\tNo file
               object\r\n"));
```

```
        WriteToLog(tchLogBuffer);
    }
    /* End Log File */

    // Handle the object notify
    if(_tcsicmp(pNotify->szObjType, TEXT("OPML Files"))
        != 0) {
        WriteToLog(TEXT("\tObjectNotify: Invalid Object
            Type\r\n"));
        return FALSE;
    }

    // Handle the notifications we're interested in
    BOOL fReturn = FALSE;

    if(pNotify->uFlags & ONF_FILE) {
        if(pNotify->oidInfo.wObjType == OBJTYPE_FILE) {
            // Interested in DELETE and CHANGE notifications
            if(pNotify->uFlags & ONF_DELETED) {
                WriteToLog(TEXT("\tObjectNotify: Deleted\r\n"));
                pNotify->cOidDel = 1;
                fReturn = TRUE;
            }
            if(pNotify->uFlags & ONF_CHANGED) {
                WriteToLog(TEXT("\tObjectNotify: Changed\r\n"));
                pNotify->cOidChg = 1;
                fReturn = TRUE;
            }
        }
    }

    if(fReturn)
        WriteToLog(TEXT("\tObjectNotify: TRUE\r\n"));
    else
        WriteToLog(TEXT("\tObjectNotify: FALSE\r\n"));

    pNotify->poid = (UINT *)&pNotify->oidObject;
    return fReturn;
}
```

Whenever the ActiveSync Service Manager needs more information about an object type, it calls into the GetObjTypeInfo() function:

```
BOOL GetObjTypeInfo(POBJTYPEINFO poti);
```

The only parameter you are passed is a pointer to an OBJTYPEINFO structure, which you will need to fill in. The structure is defined as follows:

```
typedef struct tagObjTypeInfo {
    UINT cbStruct;
    OBJTYPENAMEW szObjType;
    UINT uFlags;
    WCHAR szName[80];
    UINT cObjects;
    UINT cbAllObj;
    FILETIME ftLastModified;
} OBJTYPEINFO, *POBJTYPEINFO;
```

The first field specifies the size of the structure, in bytes; and is followed by szObjType, a null-terminated string that contains the name of the object type. The uFlags field is reserved, and set to 0.

You should set the rest of the OBJTYPEINFO structure's fields with the information about the type. The szName field should be set to a string that contains the name of the file system object that stores them; cObjects should be set to the number of objects; cbAllObj should be set to the total number of bytes; and ftLastModified should be set to the FILETIME that specifies the last time that any of the objects were modified.

You can handle a request to the GetObjTypeInfo() function as follows:

```
DllExport BOOL GetObjTypeInfo(POBJTYPEINFO pInfo)
{
    WriteToLog(TEXT("Start GetObjTypeInfo\r\n"));

    if(pInfo->cbStruct < sizeof(OBJTYPEINFO))
        return FALSE;

    /* Log File */
    TCHAR tchLogBuffer[MAX_PATH] = TEXT("\0");

    wsprintf(tchLogBuffer, TEXT("\tObj Type Name: %s\r\n"),
        pInfo->szObjType);
    WriteToLog(tchLogBuffer);
    /* End Log File */

    // Set up the information about the device object that will
    // store the OPML items
    wsprintf(pInfo->szName, TEXT("OPML Files"));
```

```
    // Find out how many items
    WIN32_FIND_DATA w32Find;
    HANDLE hFileEnum = 0;
    memset(&w32Find, 0, sizeof(WIN32_FIND_DATA ));

    pInfo->cObjects = 0;
    pInfo->cbAllObj = 0;

    WriteToLog(TEXT("Starting Enum\r\n"));
    hFileEnum = FindFirstFile(TEXT("\\*.opml"), &w32Find);
    do {
       pInfo->cObjects++;
       pInfo->cbAllObj =+ w32Find.nFileSizeLow;
       pInfo->ftLastModified = w32Find.ftLastWriteTime;

       WriteToLog(TEXT("Found in Enum: "));
       WriteToLog(w32Find.cFileName);
       WriteToLog(TEXT("\r\n"));
       if(FindNextFile(hFileEnum, &w32Find) == FALSE)
          break;
    } while(hFileEnum != NULL);

    if(hFileEnum) {
       WriteToLog(TEXT("Closing Enum\r\n"));
       FindClose(hFileEnum);
    }

    return TRUE;
}
```

If you have exported the `FindObjects()` function, ActiveSync will also use it to help speed up database synchronization. It is used to enumerate all the objects that are to be synchronized in a database and return the list of OIDs to ActiveSync.

The function is defined as follows:

```
HRESULT FindObjects(PFINDOBJINFO pfoi);
```

`FindObjects()` has only a single parameter, which is a pointer to a `FINDOBJINFO` structure. The structure has the following prototype:

```
typedef struct tagFindObjInfo {
   UINT uFlags;
   OBJTYPENAME szObjType;
```

```
    UINT *poid;
    UINT cUnChg;
    UINT cChg;
    LPBYTE lpbVolumeID;
    UINT cbVolumeID;
    LPVOID lpvUser;
} FINDOBJINFO, *PFINDOBJINFO;
```

The first field, uFlags, indicates whether ActiveSync is starting or finishing an enumeration. The first time ActiveSync calls into Find Objects(), uFlags will be set to 0. This indicates that you should enumerate all of the objects with which the device provider synchronizes. You should set uFlags to FO_MORE_VOLUME if there are more objects to be returned. The uFlags field will be set to FO_DONE_ONE_VOL by the ActiveSync Service Manager if it is finished with the OIDs you have sent to it.

The next field, szObjType, will contain the null-terminated string of the object type that needs enumeration. The poid field should point to an array of OIDs for the objects that are synchronized by the provider. You need to ensure that the first items in the list are those that haven't changed, followed by the OIDs for modified objects. The cUnChg field specifies the number of unchanged objects in poid, and cChg specifies the number of changed objects.

The lpbVolumeID field is the ID of the database volume. If the database is in the local object store, then you can set this to NULL. The size of the volume that you are enumerating should be set in the cbVolumeID field. A few cautionary words: If a synchronized database is stored on more than one volume, you must return one list per volume (and use the FO_MORE_VOLUME flag). The last field, lpvUser, is an empty data pointer that you can use to save any additional information you'd like.

Device-Side Status Reporting

When the ActiveSync Manager on the device has additional information about a synchronization process in progress, it will call into the Report Status() function if you have exported it from your device provider. The function is defined as follows:

```
BOOL ReportStatus(LPWSTR lpszObjType, UINT uCode, UINT
    uParam);
```

The first parameter is a null-terminated string that contains the name of the object type. The uCode and uParam parameters are the same as for the desktop IReplStore::ReportStatus() function.

Custom Synchronization Information

ActiveSync also provides a way for your desktop synchronization provider to make a direct request to the device-side provider. This is done by having the desktop call into the IReplNotify::QueryDevice() function using the QDC_SYNC_DATA flag. This request is immediately processed, and the device-side provider receives a call into the optional SyncData() function:

```
HRESULT SyncData(PSDREQUEST psd);
```

The only parameter that the function receives is a pointer to a SDREQUEST structure, which is defined as follows:

```
typedef struct SDREQUEST {
    OBJTYPENAME szObjType;
    BOOL fSet;
    UINT uCode;
    LPBYTE lpbData;
    UINT cbData;
} SDREQUEST, *PSDREQUEST;
```

The first field, szObjType, is a null-terminated string that specifies the object type. The fSet field should be set to TRUE if data is being sent to the device from the desktop. This field should be set to FALSE if you are returning data from the device. The uCode field is a user-defined code that is used when getting data from the device. This value must be lower than 8.

The last two fields are used to specify the data buffer and the size. The first time ActiveSync calls into the function, the lpbData field will be set to NULL. At this time, you should set the cbData field with the size of the buffer that you will require. The next time SyncData() is called, the buffer will be properly allocated.

Desktop Connection Notifications

The ActiveSync Manager provides the desktop with two different ways of receiving notifications when a Pocket PC device is either connected or disconnected from it:

1. **The desktop registry.** You can use the registry on a desktop machine that has ActiveSync installed on it to set up which applications are to be run when a device is connected or disconnected.
2. **COM-based notification.** You can implement a COM object that can be registered with ActiveSync; it will receive notifications when various device connection events occur.

Although using the registry to launch an application is the easiest way to handle a connection notification, no other information about the connection event is provided to you. You should create a COM object notification if more details are required.

Using the Desktop Registry for Connection Notifications

To have an application launch when a connection is made with the desktop, you need to create a new string value underneath the following registry entry:

```
HKEY_LOCAL_MACHINE\SOFTWARE\Microsoft\Windows CE Services\
   AutoStartOnConnect
```

It is recommended that the key name for the new string value should uniquely represent the application you are launching, along with the company name. The data value should point to the full path and name, and include any command-line arguments for the application you want to launch. If you include any arguments, you must also wrap the full path in double quotes.

For example, to launch the application devicebackup.exe when a connection is established, the registry will look like the following:

```
[HKEY_LOCAL_MACHINE\SOFTWARE\Microsoft\Windows CE
   Services\AutoStartOnConnect]
   "BionicFrogDeviceBackup"="\"C:\\Program
   Files\\BionicFrog\\devicebackup.exe\""
```

To have an application launch when a device is disconnected from the desktop, you can place a new registry string value underneath the following key:

```
HKEY_LOCAL_MACHINE\SOFTWARE\Microsoft\Windows CE Services\
    AutoStartOnDisconnect
```

Like the `AutoStartOnConnect` key, the disconnect registry key also takes a string value with the application path in order to run.

COM Desktop Notifications

Two interfaces are used to perform notification of connection events when using COM:

1. The **IDccMan** interface is already implemented by ActiveSync, and is used to register your IDccManSink object. It provides your application with some control of the communication aspects of ActiveSync.
2. The **IDccManSink** interface is what you are required to implement in order to receive notifications from IDccMan. The object's functions are called by ActiveSync whenever connection events occur.

The interfaces that you will use to work with the notification objects are prototyped in the `dccole.h` header file.

Implementing IDccManSink

The IDccManSink interface is the only interface that your application needs to implement in order to receive notifications from the ActiveSync Manager. Table 9.27 describes the methods supported by IDccManSink that are called during the various states of a device's connection to the desktop.

All of the methods that IDccManSink supports are pretty self-explanatory—each is called by IDccMan whenever a particular event takes place. The only method that has any useful additional information is the IDccManSink::OnLogIpAddr(DWORD dwIpAddr) method, which will pass you the connecting device's IP address when a communications link has been established.

Table 9.27 `IDccManSink` Methods

Method	Description
OnLogActive()	Notification when a connection is established between a device and ActiveSync
OnLogAnswered()	Notification when ActiveSync has detected a device
OnLogDisconnection()	Notification when a connection has been terminated between the device and ActiveSync
OnLogError()	Notification when ActiveSync has failed to start communications between the desktop and the device
OnLogInActive()	Notification when ActiveSync is in a disconnected state
OnLogIpAddr()	Notification when an IP address has been established for communications between the device and the desktop
OnLogListen()	Notification that a connection is waiting to be established
OnLogTerminated()	Notification when ActiveSync has been shut down

The IDccMan Object

The `IDccMan` interface is implemented by the ActiveSync Manager, and enables you to register your own `IDccManSink` interface to receive notifications from it. Table 9.28 describes the methods that are implemented by the `IDccMan` object.

Table 9.28 `IDccMan` Methods

Method	Description
Advise()	Registers an IDccManSink object for notification messages
ShowCommSettings()	Shows the ActiveSync Communications Settings dialog box
Unadvise()	Prevents an IDccManSink object from receiving any further notification messages

To register a new notification object with ActiveSync, you must pass a pointer to the `IDccManSink` interface that you implemented to the `IDccMan::Advise()` function. It is defined as follows:

```
HRESULT IDccMan::Advise(IDccManSink *pDccSink,
  DWORD *pdwContext);
```

The first parameter is a pointer to the notification object that will be used by `IDccMan` to send notifications to. The `pdwContext` parameter will be filled in with a `DWORD` value that uniquely identifies the object you passed into `pDccSink`. The value that you are returned must be used to call the `IDccMan::Unadvise()` function when you are finished receiving notifications.

You can also tell ActiveSync to display the Communication Configuration dialog box by using the following function:

```
HRESULT IDccMan::ShowCommSettings();
```

The only other function that `IDccMan` provides is what you use to let ActiveSync know you are no longer interested in receiving notification. The `IDccMan::Unadvise()` function takes a single parameter, which is the context value that was returned from your call to `IDccMan::Advise()`. The function is defined as follows:

```
HRESULT IDccMan::Unadvise(DWORD dwContext);
```

Using COM-Based Notifications

The process for using COM-based notification is relatively simple. Your application needs to first call `CoInitializeEx()` and `CoCreate Instance()` in order to get a pointer to the `IDccMan` object that ActiveSync has implemented.

The code for getting the `IDccMan` interface pointer is as follows:

```
// Get the IDccMan Interface
IDccMan *pDccMan = NULL;
HRESULT hr = S_OK;

hr = CoCreateInstance(CLSID_DccMan, NULL, CLSCTX_SERVER,
  IID_IDccMan, (LPVOID *)&pDccMan);
if(FAILED(hr))
    return 0;
```

Once you have received the pointer, you can call into the `IDcc Man::Advise()` function to register the `IDccManSink` you have implemented in your application.

For example, you can register your object for notification as follows:

```
// Hook up the notification
DWORD dwContext = 0;
hr = pDccMan->Advise(pDccManSink, &dwContext);
```

Once the application is ready to stop receiving notifications, remember to call the `IDccMan::UnAdvise()` function, as well as clean up the other COM objects you used:

```
// Clean up
if(pDccMan) {
   pDccMan->Unadvise(dwContext);
   pDccMan->Release();
}
```

The implementation for a basic `IDccManSink` interface is shown in the following example code:

```
// CeNotify.h
#include <windows.h>
#include <initguid.h>
#include <dccole.h>
#include "resource.h"

INT_PTR CALLBACK DlgProc(HWND hwndDlg, UINT uMsg, WPARAM
  wParam, LPARAM lParam);

// IDccManSink
class CDccSink:public IDccManSink {
private:
   long m_lRef;
public:
   CDccSink();
   ~CDccSink();

   // IUnknown
   STDMETHODIMP QueryInterface(REFIID riid, LPVOID *ppv);
   STDMETHODIMP_(ULONG) AddRef();
   STDMETHODIMP_(ULONG) Release();
```

```
      // IDccManSink
      STDMETHODIMP OnLogIpAddr(DWORD dwIpAddr);
      STDMETHODIMP OnLogTerminated();
      STDMETHODIMP OnLogActive();
      STDMETHODIMP OnLogInactive();
      STDMETHODIMP OnLogAnswered();
      STDMETHODIMP OnLogListen();
      STDMETHODIMP OnLogDisconnection();
      STDMETHODIMP OnLogError();
};


//////////////////////////////////////////////////
// CeNotify.cpp
#include "cenotify.h"

int WINAPI WinMain(HINSTANCE hInstance, HINSTANCE
  hPrevInstance, LPSTR lpCmdLine, int nShowCmd)
{
   // Initalize COM
   CoInitialize(NULL);

   // Get the IDccMan interface
   IDccMan *pDccMan = NULL;
   HRESULT hr = S_OK;

   hr = CoCreateInstance(CLSID_DccMan, NULL, CLSCTX_SERVER,
      IID_IDccMan, (LPVOID *)&pDccMan);
   if(FAILED(hr))
      return 0;

   // Get an instance of our IDccManSink
   CDccSink *pDccSink = new CDccSink();
   IDccManSink *pDccManSink = NULL;
   hr = pDccSink->QueryInterface(IID_IDccManSink,
      (void **)&pDccManSink);
   if(FAILED(hr)) {
      pDccMan->Release();
      return 0;
   }

   // Hook up the notification
   DWORD dwContext = 0;
   hr = pDccMan->Advise(pDccManSink, &dwContext);
```

```
      // Do something while getting notifications
      DialogBox(hInstance, MAKEINTRESOURCE(IDD_DIALOG), NULL,
         (DLGPROC)DlgProc);

      // Clean up
      if(pDccMan) {
         pDccMan->Unadvise(dwContext);
         pDccMan->Release();
      }

      return 0;
}

INT_PTR CALLBACK DlgProc(HWND hwndDlg, UINT uMsg, WPARAM
   wParam, LPARAM lParam)
{
   switch (uMsg) {
      case WM_COMMAND:
      switch (LOWORD(wParam)) {
         case IDOK:
         case IDCANCEL:
            EndDialog(hwndDlg, wParam);
         return TRUE;
         }
      }
   return FALSE;
}

// DccSink object
CDccSink::CDccSink() {
   m_lRef = 1;
   return;
}

CDccSink::~CDccSink() {
   return;
}

// IDccManSink's IUnknown interface
STDMETHODIMP CDccSink::QueryInterface(REFIID riid,
   LPVOID *ppv) {
   if(IsEqualIID(riid, IID_IUnknown) || IsEqualIID(riid,
      IID_IDccManSink)) {
```

```
      *ppv = (IDccManSink *)this;
      AddRef();
      return NO_ERROR;
   }

   *ppv = NULL;
   return E_NOINTERFACE;
}


STDMETHODIMP_(ULONG) CDccSink::AddRef() {
   return (ULONG)InterlockedIncrement(&m_lRef);
}


STDMETHODIMP_(ULONG) CDccSink::Release() {
   ULONG ulCount = (ULONG)InterlockedDecrement(&m_lRef);
   if(ulCount == 0)
      delete this;

   return ulCount;
}


// IDccManSink implementation
STDMETHODIMP CDccSink::OnLogIpAddr(DWORD dwIpAddr) {
   OutputDebugString(TEXT("Received a new IP Address\r\n"));
   return NO_ERROR;
}


STDMETHODIMP CDccSink::OnLogTerminated() {
   OutputDebugString(TEXT("On Log Terminated\r\n"));
   return NO_ERROR;
}


STDMETHODIMP CDccSink::OnLogActive() {
   OutputDebugString(TEXT("On Log Active\r\n"));
   return NO_ERROR;
}


STDMETHODIMP CDccSink::OnLogInactive() {
   OutputDebugString(TEXT("On Log InActive\r\n"));
   return NO_ERROR;
}


STDMETHODIMP CDccSink::OnLogAnswered() {
   OutputDebugString(TEXT("On Log Answered\r\n"));
```

```
     return NO_ERROR;
}

STDMETHODIMP CDccSink::OnLogListen() {
   OutputDebugString(TEXT("On Log Listen\r\n"));
   return NO_ERROR;
}

STDMETHODIMP CDccSink::OnLogDisconnection() {
   OutputDebugString(TEXT("On Log Disconnection\r\n"));
   return NO_ERROR;
}

STDMETHODIMP CDccSink::OnLogError() {
   OutputDebugString(TEXT("On Log Error\r\n"));
   return NO_ERROR;
```

CHAPTER 10

Pocket Outlook Object Model

Your contact, while interesting in the context of science fiction, was, at least in my memory, recounting a poorly veiled synopsis of an episode of Rocky and Bullwinkle.

—*Dana Scully,* The X-Files

Managing the nitty-gritty details of your day-to-day life is one of the most common uses of a PDA. On the Pocket PC devices, the application that is used for managing your contacts, appointments, and tasks is Pocket Outlook. As you might have guessed from the name, Pocket Outlook is the mobile companion to the desktop Outlook application that ships with Microsoft Office. Figure 10.1 shows Pocket Outlook's Calendar feature.

One of the most interesting things about Pocket Outlook is that it supports a set of COM objects, known as the **Pocket Outlook Object Model** (**POOM**), that provide application developers with easy access to the data stored in the Pocket Outlook applications. In addition, you can also use POOM to add new contacts, schedule appointments, and provide task tracking in your own applications. You can even add menu items (or *plug-ins*) to the Tasks, Contacts, and Appointment applications.

In this chapter, you learn how to use the POOM interfaces, and how to integrate Outlook data in your own applications. If you are writing any application that will need contact information, scheduling, or task completion, it is a good idea to integrate it with Pocket Outlook. By doing so, you will provide the end user of your product with a way to seamlessly use the data that is already stored on the device, rather than replicating functionality. For example, suppose you are writing a project management application. By using POOM, you can integrate project completion dates with the Tasks on the device, assign tasks based on contact data, etc.

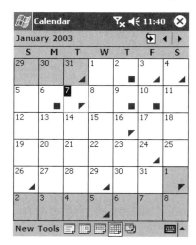

Figure 10.1 Pocket Outlook's Calendar

To use the Pocket Outlook Object Model interfaces within your applications, you need to include the `pimstore.h` header file, and define the `INITGUID` constant, as shown in the following example:

```
#define INITGUID
#include <windows.h>
#include <pimstore.h>
```

The Pocket Outlook Object Model

Before you can begin developing applications that integrate with Pocket Outlook, let's first examine the object model that POOM uses to expose the contact, appointment, and task data that has been stored on the device. Figure 10.2 illustrates the relationships among the objects in Pocket Outlook.

The Pocket Outlook Object Model consists of the following interfaces:

- The main interface of POOM is `IPOutlookApp`. This is the interface with which you log on to Outlook, and the one from which you derive all other interfaces.
- Information about various time zones can be accessed through the `ITimeZone` interface.

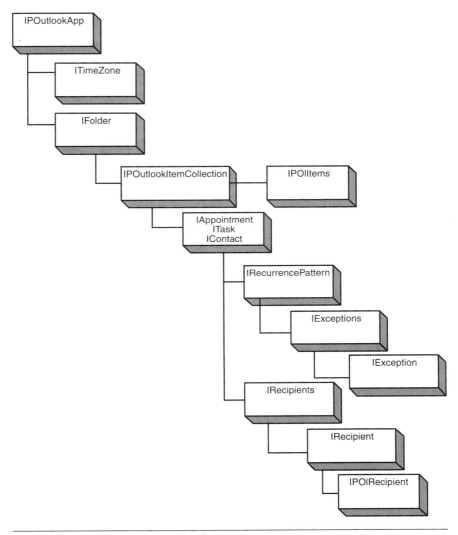

Figure 10.2 Pocket Outlook's Data Object Model

- Each Outlook application is contained within its own `IFolder` interface. There is one for Contacts, Appointments, and Tasks, each of which essentially "wraps" its respective database. In addition, there is a special folder for handling the sending and receiving of infrared data.
- Enumeration of the items in a folder is handled through the `IPOutlookItemCollection` and `IPOlItems` interfaces.

- `IContact` is the interface for working with an individual contact entry.
- `IAppointment` is the interface for working with an individual appointment.
- The `IRecipients`, `IRecipient`, and `IPOlRecipient` interfaces are used to specify recipients of an appointment (which is considered a *meeting request*).
- `ITask` is the interface for working with an individual task.
- The `IRecurrencePattern`, `IExceptions`, and `IException` interfaces are used for setting up recurring appointments and tasks.

NOTE: In previous versions of Windows CE, POOM also supported additional information about various cities using the `ICity` interface. As of Pocket PC 2002, this city data has been removed, and calling `IPOutlookApp::GetDefaultFolder()` to return a City folder will return an E_NOTIMPL error code.

The data that was previously used for the interface is now provided by a comma-separated value file that is located in the `.\wce300\Pocket PC 2002\citylist\citylist.csv` directory. This file contains information such as city names, longitude and latitude, airport codes, and area codes.

A Word about Object Identifiers (OIDs)

Every item stored within any of the Pocket Outlook applications contains a unique `DWORD` value that can be used to identify it. This is also known as an item's **object identifier** (**OID**). As you will see, each of the interfaces in the Pocket Outlook Object Model provides a property value that you can use to retrieve an object's OID. While you can use an object's identifier to quickly get access to an item and its interface (by using the `IPOutlookApp::GetItemfromOid()` method), it is typically *not* a good idea to store this value in a permanent form. Because of the design of the Windows CE object store, object identifiers are changed whenever a user does a backup and restore of the device, thus making the previous OID invalid.

The IPOutlookApp Interface

The IPOutlookApp interface is the main object that is used to gain access to all of the POOM data on a device. It is the only object that can be created by calling the CoCreateInstance() function, and is used to gain access to both folder and time zone information. The interface supports the methods described in Table 10.1.

Table 10.1 IPOutlookApp Methods

Method	Description
GetDefaultFolder()	Gets an IFolder interface for Calendar, Tasks, Contacts, or Infrared
GetItemFromOid()	Gets the interface for an item based on its OID
GetTimeZoneFromIndex()	Gets an ITimeZone from the index
GetTimeZoneInformationFromIndex()	Gets time zone information
Logoff()	Logs off from Pocket Outlook
Logon()	Logs on to Pocket Outlook
ReceiveFromInfrared()	Receives an Outlook item over infrared

Table 10.2 describes the properties supported by the IPOutlookApp interface.

Table 10.2 IPOutlookApp Properties

Property	Get/Put	Description
Application	Get	Returns a pointer to the IPOutlookApp interface
OutlookCompatible	Get	Returns TRUE if synchronized with Outlook; FALSE, if with Schedule+
Version	Get	Returns the current version information for Pocket Outlook

The first thing you need to do to get access to Pocket Outlook's data is create a new instance of the IPOutlookApp interface, which is done by calling the CoCreateInstance() function:

```
HRESULT hr = S_OK;
IPOutlookApp *pOlApp = NULL;

if(FAILED(CoInitializeEx(NULL, 0)))
   return FALSE;

// Get a pointer to the IPOutlookApp interface
hr = CoCreateInstance(CLSID_Application, NULL,
  CLSCTX_INPROC_SERVER, IID_IPOutlookApp, (LPVOID *)&pOlApp);
if (FAILED(hr))
   return FALSE;
```

Once you have successfully created a new instance of the IPOutlookApp interface, you need to "log in" to the Pocket Outlook session before you can call any of the other POOM functions. This can be done by using the IPOutlookApp::Logon() function, which has the following prototype:

```
HRESULT IPOutlookApp::Logon(long hWnd);
```

The only parameter the function uses is an optional handle to a window, which can be set to NULL. This handle is used by POOM as the parent window whenever any of the Outlook items (such as Tasks, Contacts, etc.) receive a call into their own ::Display() method. In addition, the Infrared Transfer dialog box uses this handle as its parent.

Once you have logged into Pocket Outlook, you can continue to make additional calls into the object. When you have completed whatever operations you needed to use POOM with, be sure to log off of Pocket Outlook using the following function:

```
HRESULT IPOutlookApp::Logoff();
```

The following code sample shows how easily you can log in and out of the POOM interfaces:

```
#define INITGUID
#include <windows.h>
#include <pimstore.h>
```

```
int WINAPI WinMain(HINSTANCE hInstance, HINSTANCE
  hPrevInstance, LPWSTR lpCmdLine, int nShowCmd)
{
  HRESULT hr = S_OK;
  IPOutlookApp *pOlApp = NULL;

  if(FAILED(CoInitializeEx(NULL, 0)))
    return FALSE;

  // Get a pointer to the IPOutlookApp interface
  hr = CoCreateInstance(CLSID_Application, NULL,
    CLSCTX_INPROC_SERVER, IID_IPOutlookApp, (LPVOID *)&pOlApp);
  if(FAILED(hr))
    return FALSE;

  // Log into Pocket Outlook
  hr = pOlApp->Logon(NULL);
  if(FAILED(hr))
    return FALSE;

  // Do whatever we want with POOM
  // ...

  // Log off and clean up
  pOlApp->Logoff();
  pOlApp->Release();
  return 0;
}
```

You may also need to get information about the version of Pocket Outlook that is running on the device:

```
HRESULT IPOutlookApp::get_Version(BSTR *pbstrVersion);
```

The only parameter that this property takes is a pointer to a BSTR value that will be filled in with the version information. Remember that whenever POOM allocates a string, you must call the SysFree String() function to properly free the memory that it uses, as shown in the following example:

```
// Get the current POOM version
BSTR bstrVersion;
```

```
hr = pOlApp->get_Version(&bstrVersion);
if(FAILED(hr))
    OutputDebugString(TEXT("Could not get POOM version"));

// Do something with it ...

// When finished, free it
SysFreeString(bstrVersion);
```

Accessing Pocket Outlook Folders

Each of the data objects (an individual task, contact, or appointment is considered an individual object) used within Pocket Outlook is contained within its own folder object, and is handled through its own `IFolder` interface. Essentially, each folder is a wrapper to the internal database that Outlook will use for each item type.

To get the pointer for a particular folder, you use the `IPOutlook App::GetDefaultFolder()` function, which is prototyped as follows:

```
HRESULT IPOutlookApp::GetDefaultFolder(int olFolder,
    IFolder **ppIFolder);
```

The first parameter, `olFolder`, specifies which folder to get, and can be one of the following options:

- Use the `olFolderCalendar` flag to get the Calendar folder. Items in this folder are represented by the `IAppointment` interface.
- Use the `olFolderTasks` flag to get the Tasks folder. Items in this folder are represented by the `ITasks` interface.
- Use the `olFolderContacts` flag to get the Contacts folder. Items in this folder are represented by the `IContact` interface.
- Use the `olFolderInfrared` flag to get the Infrared folder. This folder is used to send and receive Outlook data over the infrared port.

The last parameter, `ppIFolder`, should be a pointer to a pointer of an `IFolder` interface, which is filled in with the proper folder object when the function returns. Remember that folders cannot be created, changed, or deleted in Pocket Outlook.

As you can see by the following code sample, getting the pointer to the folder containing calendar items is fairly straightforward:

```
// At this point, we should already be logged into IPOutlookApp
IFolder *pIFolder = NULL;
hr = pOlApp->GetDefaultFolder(olFolderCalendar, &pIFolder);
if(FAILED(hr))
   OutputDebugString(TEXT("Could not get the calendar
      folder"));
else {
   // Do something here...
}


// Clean up
if(pIFolder)
   pIFolder->Release();
```

Working with Time Zones

In addition to providing access to the various Outlook folder objects, the IPOutlookApp interface has two support functions that are used for handling time zone information. The first function, IPOutlookApp:: GetTimeZoneInformationFromIndex(), uses the standard Windows CE TIME_ZONE_INFORMATION structure to retrieve time zone information. The function is defined as follows:

```
HRESULT IPOutlookApp::GetTimeZoneInformationFromIndex(int
   cTimezone, TIME_ZONE_INFORMATION *ptzInfo);
```

The Pocket Outlook Object Model also provides the ITimeZone interface, which is used for retrieving information about daylight savings time for a particular time zone. To get a pointer to the ITimeZone object, you can use the following function:

```
HRESULT IPOutlookApp::GetTimeZoneFromIndex(int cTimezone,
   ITimeZone **ppTz);
```

The first parameter is the index to the time zone that you are interested in, and is followed by a pointer to a pointer value that will be filled in with the ITimeZone interface.

Table 10.3 describes the properties supported by the ITimeZone interface.

Table 10.3 ITimeZone pPoperties

Property	Get/Put	Description
Application	Get	Returns a pointer to the IPOutlookApp interface.
Bias	Get	Gets the current bias, in minutes, for the local time translations (UTC = Local Time + Bias).
DaylightBias	Get	Gets the offset, in minutes, when a time zone is in daylight savings time.
DaylightDate	Get	Gets the date when the time returns to daylight savings time.
DaylightDayOfWeekMask	Get	Gets the day of the week on which daylight savings time begins.
DaylightInstance	Get	Gets the week of the month in which daylight savings time begins.
DaylightMonthOfYear	Get	Gets the month of the year in which daylight savings time begins.
DaylightName	Get	Gets the name of the time zone when in daylight savings time.
IsDaylightAbsoluteDate	Get	Indicates whether the daylight date is the absolute or relative date. Returns TRUE if it is the standard date, FALSE if it is relative.
IsStandardAbsoluteDate	Get	Indicates whether the standard date is the absolute or relative date. Returns TRUE if it is the standard date, FALSE if it is relative.
StandardBias	Get	Gets the offset, in minutes, when a time zone is in standard time.
StandardDate	Get	Indicates when the date returns to a standard time.
StandardDayOfWeekMask	Get	Gets the day of the week on which standard time returns from daylight savings time.
StandardInstance	Get	Gets the week of the month (from 1 to 5) in which standard time begins.
StandardMonthOfYear	Get	Gets the month of the year in which standard time begins.
StandardName	Get	Gets the name of the time zone when in standard time.
SupportsDST	Get	Indicates whether the time zone supports daylight savings time.

The following short code example shows how you can get time zone information for Pacific Standard Time:

```
// Get the time zone information for PST
ITimeZone *pTimeZone = NULL;
hr = pOlApp->GetTimeZoneFromIndex(4, &pTimeZone);
if(FAILED(hr))
   OutputDebugString(TEXT("Could not get the calendar
      folder"));
else {
   TCHAR tchDaylightStart[256] = TEXT("\0");
   TCHAR tchStandardStart[256] = TEXT("\0");

   // Figure out daylight savings time
   BSTR bstrName = NULL;
   SYSTEMTIME stDaylight;
   VARIANT_BOOL vbDate;

   hr = pTimeZone->get_DaylightName(&bstrName);
   if(FAILED(hr))
      return FALSE;

   // PST uses a relative date, but let's just make sure
   pTimeZone->get_IsDaylightAbsoluteDate(&vbDate);
   if(vbDate == VARIANT_FALSE) {
      DATE pDaylight = NULL;
      LONG lDayOfWeek = 0, lMonth = 0, lDayInstance = 0;

      // Get the date
      if(FAILED(pTimeZone->get_DaylightDayOfWeekMask
            (&lDayOfWeek)))
         return FALSE;
      if(FAILED(pTimeZone->get_DaylightInstance
            (&lDayInstance)))
         return FALSE;
      if(FAILED(pTimeZone->get_DaylightMonthOfYear(&lMonth)))
         return FALSE;

      // Get the time
      if(FAILED(pTimeZone->get_DaylightDate(&pDaylight)))
         return FALSE;

      // Fill out the structure:
      memset(&stDaylight, 0, sizeof(SYSTEMTIME));
      VariantTimeToSystemTime(pDaylight, &stDaylight);
```

```
        wsprintf(tchDaylightStart,
            TEXT("%s\r\nDaylight Savings Time will
            begin:\r\nWeek: %d\r\nDay of
            Week: %d\r\nMonth: %d\r\nat %d:%d"), bstrName,
            lDayOfWeek, lDayInstance, lMonth, stDaylight.wHour,
            stDaylight.wMinute);
    } else {
        // Place absolute date handler stuff here
    }

    // MessageBox
    MessageBox(NULL, tchDaylightStart, TEXT("Daylight"),
        MB_OK);

    // Free resources
    SysFreeString(bstrName);
}

if(pTimeZone)
    pTimeZone->Release();
```

Pocket Outlook Folders

A Pocket Outlook folder defined by the `IFolder` interface contains a collection of objects that are specific to the folder type. For example, the Tasks folder contains only `ITask` items. To get the pointer for an `IFolder` interface, you use the `IPOutlookApp::GetDefault Folder()` function.

Once you have the pointer to a particular `IFolder` interface, you can then access, modify, and delete Pocket Outlook items. Table 10.4 describes the method supported by each `IFolder` interface (for Contacts, Calendar, and Tasks).

Table 10.4 `IFolder` Method

Method	Description
ReceiveFromInfrared()	Starts to receive items over infrared

Table 10.5 describes the properties supported by the `IFolder` interface.

Table 10.5 `IFolder` Properties

Property	Get/Put	Description
Application	Get	Returns a pointer to the `IPOutlookApp` interface
DefaultItemType	Get	Returns the folder type (except for the infrared folder)
Items	Get	Returns an `IPOutlookItemCollection` interface for the items in the folder

The most common use for a folder is to get access to the collection object for the items that it is storing. To do so, use the following function:

```
HRESULT IFolder::get_Items(IPOutlookItemCollection
   **ppolItems);
```

The only parameter that the function takes is a pointer to an `IPOutlookItemCollection` interface pointer. Once this pointer has been returned, you can begin to sort and access individual Outlook data items.

You can get the collection of Outlook items in the following manner:

```
// Get the calendar items
IPOutlookItemCollection *pICalItems = NULL;
hr = pIFolder->get_Items(&pICalItems);
if(FAILED(hr)) {
   pIFolder->Release();
   return FALSE;
}

// Do something with the items
TCHAR tchMsg[1024] = TEXT("\0");
int nCount = 0;

pICalItems->get_Count(&nCount);
wsprintf(tchMsg, TEXT("There are %d items"), nCount);
MessageBox(NULL, tchMsg, TEXT("Calendar"), MB_OK);
```

```
// Clean up
if(pICalItems)
   pICalItems->Release();
```

Sending and Receiving Items over Infrared

In addition to the three standard folders—Contacts, Tasks, and Calendar—there is a special fourth folder that doesn't contain any actual Outlook items. The Infrared folder is used for sending items over the IR port to another Pocket PC device. You can get a pointer to the Infrared folder just as you do for other folders, by using the `IPOutlookApp::Get DefaultFolder()` function, as shown in the following example:

```
// Infrared
IFolder *pIRFolder = NULL;
hr = pOlApp->GetDefaultFolder(olFolderInfrared, &pIRFolder);
if(FAILED(hr)) {
   OutputDebugString(TEXT("Could not get the infrared
      folder"));
   return FALSE;
}

if(pIRFolder)
   pIRFolder->Release();
```

Table 10.6 describes the additional methods supported by the `IFolder` interface, which are used when working with the Infrared folder.

Table 10.6 `IFolder` Methods for the Infrared Folder

Method	Description
`AddItemToInfraredFolder()`	Adds a list of items to be sent over infrared
`SendToInfrared()`	Sends the items in the folder to the IR port

You can add any type of item that is supported by Pocket Outlook to the folder by calling into the `IFolder::AddItemToInfrared Folder()` method, which is defined as follows:

```
HRESULT IFolder::AddItemToInfraredFolder(int olItem,
   IDispatch *polItem);
```

The first parameter should specify the type of item that is being added, and can be set to olAppointmentItem, olContactItem or olTaskItem. The polItem parameter should point to the actual item that is being added.

After you have added all of the contacts, appointments, and tasks that you want to send, you can simply instruct the folder to transmit them by calling the following function:

```
HRESULT IFolder::SendToInfrared();
```

The following example shows how to use these functions to send a Pocket Outlook appointment item over infrared:

```
// Get the calendar items
IPOutlookItemCollection *pICalItems = NULL;
hr = pIFolder->get_Items(&pICalItems);
if(FAILED(hr)) {
   pIFolder->Release();
   return FALSE;
}


// Get an item
IAppointment *pICalEntry = NULL;
hr = pICalItems->Item(1, (IDispatch **)&pICalEntry);
// Send it to IR
if(SUCCEEDED(hr)) {
   pIRFolder->AddItemToInfraredFolder(olAppointmentItem,
      pICalEntry);
   pIRFolder->SendToInfrared();
}
```

When you want to receive Outlook data over the infrared port, there are two different methods that you can use:

1. The IPOutlookApp::ReceiveFromInfrared() method handles any type of Outlook item and places it in the correct folder when it is received.
2. The IFolder::ReceiveFromInfrared() method handles only receiving items of the correct folder type. For example, if you called this function from the Contacts folder, any Task items sent would be rejected.

To set up your application to receive data over the infrared port, you can do the following:

```
// Infrared
IFolder *pIRFolder = NULL;
hr = pOlApp->GetDefaultFolder(olFolderInfrared, &pIRFolder);
if(FAILED(hr)) {
    OutputDebugString(TEXT("Could not get the infrared
        folder"));
    return FALSE;
}

// Receive
pIRFolder->ReceiveFromInfrared();

if(pIRFolder)
    pIRFolder->Release();
```

Outlook Data Collections

In Pocket Outlook, the IPOutlookItemCollection object is used to represent all of the contacts, tasks, and appointments in a folder. Once you have the pointer to a collection object, you can use it to add or delete items, find an individual object, and filter Outlook items based on their content.

Table 10.7 describes the methods supported by the IPOutlook ItemCollection interface.

Table 10.7 IPOutlookItemCollection Methods

Method	Description
Add()	Creates a new item in the collection
Find()	Finds the first item in the collection that matches the search criteria
FindNext()	Finds the next item in the collection that matches the search criteria
Item()	Gets a specified item in the collection
Remove()	Deletes an item from the collection
Restrict()	Creates a new collection based on search criteria
Sort()	Sorts the items in the collection

Table 10.8 describes the properties supported by the `IPOutlook ItemCollection` interface.

Table 10.8 `IPOutlookItemCollection` Properties

Property	Get/Put	Description
Application	Get	Returns a pointer to the `IPOutlookApp` interface
Count	Get	Gets the number of items in the collection
IncludeRecurrences	Get/put	Indicates whether recurrences should be included in the collection

To get the pointer for an `IPOutlookItemCollection` object that represents the contents of an individual folder, you can use the `IFolder::get_Items()` function. Once you have the pointer to a valid collection interface for a particular Outlook folder, getting an item is as simple as calling the `IPOutlookItemCollection::Item()` method, which is defined as follows:

```
HRESULT IPOutlookItemCollection::Item(int iIndex,
   IDispatch **ppolItem);
```

The first parameter is the index (which starts at one) of the item from the collection that you are interested in looking at. The second parameter, ppolItem, is a pointer to a pointer that will be filled in with the appropriate Outlook Item, as shown in the following example:

```
// Get the calendar items
IPOutlookItemCollection *pICalItems = NULL;
hr = pIFolder->get_Items(&pICalItems);
if(FAILED(hr)) {
   pIFolder->Release();
   return FALSE;
}

// Get an item
IAppointment *pICalEntry = NULL;
hr = pICalItems->Item(1, (IDispatch **)&pICalEntry);
if(SUCCEEDED(hr)) {
   // Do something with it

   // Clean up
   if(pICalEntry)
```

```
      pICalEntry->Release();
}


// Clean up
if(pICalItems)
   pICalItems->Release();
```

Adding and Deleting Folder Items

To create a new item in an Outlook collection for a particular folder, you can call the IPOutlookItemCollection::Add() method:

```
HRESULT IPOutlookItemCollection::Add(IDispatch **ppolItem);
```

The only parameter the method needs is a pointer to a pointer for the new object that you wish to add to the collection. If you attempt to add an invalid object type for the folder (for example, if you attempt to add a task to the Contacts folder) an error will be returned. When adding a new Outlook item, you must also remember to call the ::Save() method of the object you are adding in order for it to be saved in the object store. If you do not, the new item will exist only in memory and will be destroyed when the collection is destroyed.

The following example shows how to create a new Contact item and add it to the Contact collection:

```
// Folder
IFolder *pIFolder = NULL;
hr = pOlApp->GetDefaultFolder(olFolderContacts, &pIFolder);
if(FAILED(hr)) {
   OutputDebugString(TEXT("Could not get the contacts
       folder"));
   return FALSE;
}


// Add a new contact
IPOutlookItemCollection *pIContactItems = NULL;
hr = pIFolder->get_Items(&pIContactItems);
if(FAILED(hr)) {
   pIFolder->Release();
   return FALSE;
}
```

```
// Get an item
IContact *pNewContact = NULL;
hr = pIContactItems->Add((IDispatch **)&pNewContact);
if(FAILED(hr))
   return FALSE;

// Configure the contact
pNewContact->put_FirstName(TEXT("Randy"));
pNewContact->put_LastName(TEXT("Rants"));
pNewContact->put_WebPage(TEXT("http://www.randyrants.com"));

// Save it
hr = pNewContact->Save();

if(FAILED(hr)) {
   pNewContact->Release();
   return FALSE;
}

if(pNewContact)
   pNewContact->Release();
```

To remove an item from the collection, you call the `IPOutlook ItemCollection::Remove()` method, which requires only the index of the object to remove. The index is based on the current sort order of the collection. The function is defined as follows:

```
HRESULT IPOutlookItemCollection::Remove(int iIndex);
```

Sorting Items

You can sort the data in a collection using the following function:

```
HRESULT IPOutlookItemCollection::Sort(BSTR pwszProperty,
   VARIANT_BOOL fDescending);
```

The first parameter is the property that you want to sort the collection of items on. This can be any property that the items contained in the collection support, except for the `Categories`, `BodyInk`, `Reminder Time`, or `Recipients` properties. You must also remember to enclose the property string you are using in brackets (i.e., [ ]).The next property determines the sort order, which should be set to `TRUE` for descending, or `FALSE` for ascending.

For example, the following code sorts a collection of contacts by first name:

```
IPOutlookItemCollection *pIContactItems = NULL;
hr = pIFolder->get_Items(&pIContactItems);
if(FAILED(hr)) {
   pIFolder->Release();
   return FALSE;
}

// Sort by first name
hr = pIContactItems->Sort(TEXT("[FirstName]"), TRUE);
if(FAILED(hr)) {
   pIContactItems->Release();
   pIFolder->Release();
   return FALSE;
}
```

Finding and Filtering Outlook Items

There are two different ways to find items (or an individual item) located within an Outlook collection:

1. The IPOutlookItemCollection::Find() and IPOutlook ItemCollection::FindNext() methods can be used to enumerate items that match a search string in an existing collection.
2. The IPOutlookItemCollection::Restrict() method can be used to create a new collection object based on your search criteria.

Regardless of which method you use to find items within a collection, both require you to specify a **restriction string**. A restriction string is a Boolean expression that returns either TRUE or FALSE for a particular item. The IPOutlookItemCollection::Find(), IPOutlookItem Collection::FindNext(), and IPOutlookItemCollection:: Restrict() methods return only those items that evaluate to TRUE.

Remember a few things about restriction strings:

■ Property names should be enclosed in brackets.
■ Expressions can be combined using AND or OR.

- Restrictions cannot be made on the `BodyInk`, `ReminderTime`, and `Recipients` properties.
- Comparisons can be made using the `<`, `<=`, `>`, `>=`, `=`, or `<>` operators.

For example, the following restriction string would return only those contacts that have `Kirk` as the first name:

```
[FirstName] = "Kirk"
```

To enumerate through the items in the current collection for a particular restriction string, you can use the following method:

```
HRESULT IPOutlookItemCollection::Find(BSTR pwszRestriction,
   IDispatch **ppItem);
```

The first parameter, `pwszRestriction`, should be the string you want to use to find the items that match, and `ppItem` points to a pointer to the first item found by the function. If `ppItem` is NULL, then no matches were found.

To find the next item that matches the restriction, you use the `IPOutlookItemCollection::FindNext()` method:

```
HRESULT IPOutlookItemCollection::FindNext(IDispatch
  **ppItem);
```

The method takes a single parameter, which is a pointer to a pointer for the next item that matches the restriction pattern. You can keep calling the `IPOutlookItemCollection::FindNext()` method until `ppItem` returns NULL, which indicates that no more items match.

The following code shows how you can enumerate a list of contacts located in the state of Washington:

```
// Find contacts
IPOutlookItemCollection *pIContactItems = NULL;
hr = pIFolder->get_Items(&pIContactItems);
if(FAILED(hr)) {
   pIFolder->Release();
   return FALSE;
}
```

```
IContact *pContact = NULL;
hr = pIContactItems->Find(TEXT("[HomeAddressState] =
  \"WA\""), (IDispatch **)&pContact);
if(FAILED(hr)) {
   OutputDebugString(TEXT("No entries found"));
   return FALSE;
}

// Walk though the entries
while(pContact != NULL) {
   // Do something with the contact
   BSTR bstrFirstName = NULL, bstrLastName = NULL;

   pContact->get_FirstName(&bstrFirstName);
   pContact->get_LastName(&bstrLastName);

   TCHAR tchName[64] = TEXT("\0");
   wsprintf(tchName, TEXT("%s %s"), bstrFirstName,
       bstrLastName);
   MessageBox(NULL, tchName, TEXT("Contacts"), MB_OK);

   // Clean up
   if(bstrFirstName)
      SysFreeString(bstrFirstName);
   if(bstrLastName)
      SysFreeString(bstrLastName);

   pContact->Release();

   // Get the next one
   hr = pIContactItems->FindNext((IDispatch **)&pContact);
   if(FAILED(hr))
      break;
};
```

When you have a large number of results that match a restriction string, it is sometimes easier to just create a new IPOutlookItem Collection interface based on the restriction string. You can do so by using the following method:

```
HRESULT IPOutlookItemCollection::Restrict(BSTR
  pwszRestriction, IPOutlookItemCollection **ppolItems);
```

The first parameter is the restriction string you want to use to evaluate items for your new collection. The `ppolItems` parameter points to a pointer that will receive the new collection interface pointer.

The `IPOlItems` Interface

When working with the Contacts folder, you can use an additional interface to speed up the generation of a collection of Contact items. By using the `IPOlItems` interface, you can specify a list of the properties that you are interested in, rather then retrieving all of them (there are 55+ properties for a Contact item). This can be extremely useful when you want to examine a few fields in a large number of contacts quickly.

Note that when you use the `IPOlItems` interface to specify the columns to be returned for the objects, all of the other item's properties will be automatically set to NULL. Therefore, when you use the `IPOutlookItemCollection::Item()` method to get a particular item, it will have only the properties that you specified set. This being the case, you cannot modify contacts that were found with the `IPOlItems` interface.

Table 10.9 describes the method supported by the `IPOlItems` interface.

Table 10.9 `IPOlItems` Method

Method	Description
`SetColumns()`	Limits the columns that are returned, to enhance performance

To specify the columns that are to be returned in a Contact's item collection list, you can use the `IPOlItems::SetColumns()` method:

```
HRESULT IPOlItems::SetColumns(BSTR Columns);
```

The only parameter that the method takes is a string that specifies the columns to be returned. Each column name should be separated by a comma.

The following example shows how you can get a list of contacts containing only the Company Name, First Name, and Last Name columns:

```
IPOutlookItemCollection *pIContactItems = NULL;
hr = pIFolder->get_Items(&pIContactItems);
```

```
if(FAILED(hr)) {
   pIFolder->Release();
   return FALSE;
}

IPOlItems *pFastContacts = NULL;
hr = pIContactItems->QueryInterface(IID_IPOlItems,
   (LPVOID *)&pFastContacts);

if(FAILED(hr)) {
   pIContactItems->Release();
   pIFolder->Release();
   return FALSE;
}

hr = pFastContacts->SetColumns(TEXT("CompanyName, FirstName,
   LastName"));
if(FAILED(hr)) {
   pFastContacts->Release();
   pIContactItems->Release();
   pIFolder->Release();
   return FALSE;
}

// The contacts now only have the Company Name, First Name,
// and Last Name
// Do something that's read-only...

// Cleanup below...
if(pFastContacts)
   pFastContacts->Release();
```

Because the `IPOutlookItemCollection` interface returned with `IPOlItems` is considered read-only, you can get access to the full item by using the `IPOutlookApp::GetItemFromOid()` method.

Outlook Items

Every individual contact, appointment, and task stored within Pocket Outlook is considered its own object. Each has its own unique identifier, as well as a set of properties and methods that are appropriate for the object type.

All of the item interfaces (`IContact`, `ITask`, and `IAppointment`) expose the methods described in Table 10.10, which are used for adding, deleting, and modifying the object.

Table 10.10 Base Methods for the Outlook Item Interfaces

Method	Description
`Copy()`	Copies the object
`Delete()`	Deletes the object
`Display()`	Displays the object
`Save()`	Saves the object

Using the base methods of an object is fairly straightforward. For example, let's look at what is involved in using the `IContact::Display()` method to show a contact:

```
// Get an item
IContact *pNewContact = NULL;
hr = pIContactItems->Add((IDispatch **)&pNewContact);
if(FAILED(hr))
   return FALSE;

// Configure the contact
pNewContact->put_FirstName(TEXT("Randy"));
pNewContact->put_LastName(TEXT("Rants"));
pNewContact->put_WebPage(TEXT("http://www.randyrants.com"));

// Save it, then display it
hr = pNewContact->Save();
hr = pNewContact->Display();
```

Figure 10.3 illustrates the contact that is shown when calling the `IContact::Display()` method.

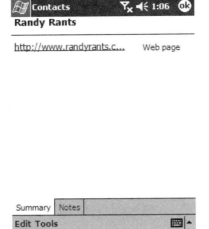

Figure 10.3 The IContact::Display() method in action

The IContact Interface

The IContact interface is used to represent an individual contact entry in the Contacts folder. The interface implements the common Outlook item methods—Save(), Delete(), Copy(), and Display()—and supports the properties described in Table 10.11.

Table 10.11 IContact Properties

Property	Get/Put	Description
Anniversary	Get/put	Gets or sets the anniversary date
Application	Get	Returns a pointer to the IPOutlookApp interface
AssistantName	Get/put	Gets or sets the name of the contact's assistant
AssistantTelephoneNumber	Get/put	Gets or sets the telephone number of the contact's assistant
Birthday	Get/put	Gets or sets the birthday
Body	Get/put	Gets or sets any notes for the contact (up to 60KB)

20

Property	Get/Put	Description
BodyInk	Get/put	Gets or sets an InkNote BLOB (Binary Large Object) for the contact. Both the `IContact::Body` and `IContact::BodyInk` properties access the same note; however, `IContact::Body` returns only the text, whereas `IContact::BodyInk` returns the entire ink object.
Business2TelephoneNumber	Get/put	Gets or sets the second business telephone number
BusinessAddressCity	Get/put	Gets or sets the business city
BusinessAddressCountry	Get/put	Gets or sets the business country
BusinessAddressPostalCode	Get/put	Gets or sets the business zip code
BusinessAddressState	Get/put	Gets or sets the business state
BusinessAddressStreet	Get/put	Gets or sets the business street
BusinessFaxNumber	Get/put	Gets or sets the business fax number
BusinessTelephoneNumber	Get/put	Gets or sets the business telephone number
CarTelephoneNumber	Get/put	Gets or sets the car phone number
Categories	Get/put	Gets or sets the categories for the contact (up to 1,023 characters)
Children	Get/put	Gets or sets the number of children
CompanyName	Get/put	Gets or sets the company name
Department	Get/put	Gets or sets the department
Email1Address	Get/put	Gets or sets the first e-mail address
Email2Address	Get/put	Gets or sets the second e-mail address
Email3Address	Get/put	Gets or sets the third e-mail address

(continued)

Table 10.11 IContact Properties (*continued*)

Property	Get/Put	Description
FileAs	Get/put	Gets or sets the filing string for the contact
FirstName	Get/put	Gets or sets the first name
Home2TelephoneNumber	Get/put	Gets or sets the second home telephone number
HomeAddressCity	Get/put	Gets or sets the home city
HomeAddressCountry	Get/put	Gets or sets the home country
HomeAddressPostalCode	Get/put	Gets or sets the home zip code
HomeAddressState	Get/put	Gets or sets the home state
HomeAddressStreet	Get/put	Gets or sets the home street address
HomeFaxNumber	Get/put	Gets or sets the home fax number
HomeTelephoneNumber	Get/put	Gets or sets the home telephone number
JobTitle	Get/put	Gets or sets the contact's job title
LastName	Get/put	Gets or sets the last name
MiddleName	Get/put	Gets or sets the middle name
MobileTelephoneNumber	Get/put	Gets or sets the mobile phone number
OfficeLocation	Get/put	Gets or sets the office location for the contact
Oid	Get	Gets the object identifier
OtherAddressCity	Get/put	Gets or sets the other address city
OtherAddressCountry	Get/put	Gets or sets the other address country
OtherAddressPostalCode	Get/put	Gets or sets the other address zip code
OtherAddressState	Get/put	Gets or sets the other address state
OtherAddressStreet	Get/put	Gets or sets the other address street
PagerNumber	Get/put	Gets or sets the pager number
RadioTelephoneNumber	Get/put	Gets or sets the radio telephone number
Spouse	Get/put	Gets or sets the spouse's name
Suffix	Get/put	Gets or sets the suffix for the contact's name

Property	Get/Put	Description
Title	Get/put	Gets or sets the contact's title
WebPage	Get/put	Gets or sets the Web page for the contact
YomiCompanyName	Get/put	Gets or sets the Japanese phonetic rendering of the contact's company name
YomiFirstName	Get/put	Gets or sets the Japanese phonetic rendering of the contact's first name
YomiLastName	Get/put	Gets or sets the Japanese phonetic rendering of the contact's last name

To add a new contact to Pocket Outlook's database, you can create a new `IContact` item by using the `IPOutlookItemCollection` interface to get a pointer and add it to the Contacts folder. Once you have modified the properties for the contact, use the `IContact::Save()` method to save it to the object store.

In addition to storing the basic properties for a contact, Pocket Outlook also supports the capability to store an **InkNote** with each item (see Figure 10.4). An InkNote is a **Binary Large Object** (**BLOB**) that

Figure 10.4 An InkNote attached to a contact

contains data. They are drawn on the screen (attached to the item), and are used with the Rich Ink control.

To work with an InkNote that is attached to an Outlook contact (or any other Outlook item), you can use the `Body` and `BodyInk` parameters. The `Body` parameter is used to extract a text string from the hand-drawn note.

The `IAppointment` Interface

The `IAppointment` interface is used to represent an object in the Calendar folder, and can specify an appointment, meeting, or recurring event (such as a weekly meeting). In addition to the common Outlook item methods—`Save()`, `Delete()`, `Copy()`, and `Display()`—the `IAppointment` interface also supports the methods described in Table 10.12.

Table 10.12 `IAppointment` Methods

Method	Description
`Cancel()`	Sends a cancellation request for the appointment
`ClearRecurrencePattern()`	Clears the recurrence pattern for the appointment
`GetRecurrencePattern()`	Gets the `IRecurrencePattern` interface for the appointment
`Send()`	Sends the appointment (meeting request) to all recipients

The `IAppointment` interface supports the properties described in Table 10.13.

You can create, modify, and delete Pocket Outlook appointments just as you would any other Pocket Outlook object. After getting a pointer to the `IPOutlookItemCollection` interface for the Calendar database, you can perform any action you want on it.

Table 10.13 IAppointment Properties

Property	Get/Put	Description
AllDayEvent	Get/put	Indicates whether the appointment is an all-day appointment
Application	Get	Returns a pointer to the IPOutlookApp interface
Body	Get/put	Gets or sets the note attached to the appointment (up to 20KB)
BodyInk	Get/put	Gets or sets an InkNote BLOB for the appointment. Both the IAppointment::Body and IAppointment::BodyInk properties access the same note; however, IAppointment::Body returns only the text, whereas IAppointment::BodyInk returns the entire ink object.
BusyStatus	Get/put	Gets or sets the status when a meeting is occurring; options include Busy, Free, Out of Office, or Tentative
Categories	Get/put	Gets or sets the categories assigned
Duration	Get/put	Gets or sets the length of the appointment, in minutes
End	Get/put	Gets or sets the end date and time of the appointment. This must be later than or equal to the start time.
isRecurring	Get	Indicates whether the appointment is recurring
Location	Get/put	Gets or sets the location
MeetingStatus	Get	Indicates whether the appointment is a meeting request or not. An appointment is considered a meeting if it has recipients.
Oid	Get	Gets the object identifier
Recipients	Get	Gets the IRecipients interface for the appointment

(continued)

Table 10.13 IAppointment Properties *(continued)*

Property	Get/Put	Description
ReminderMinutesBeforeStart	Get/put	Gets or sets the number of minutes before the start of the appointment that the reminder should be launched
ReminderOptions	Get/put	Gets or sets the reminder options for the appointment
ReminderSet	Get/put	Indicates whether the user should be reminded of the appointment
ReminderSoundFile	Get/put	Gets or sets the path and filename of the sound file to be used for the reminder. The IAppointment::Reminder Set property should be set to TRUE, and the IAppointment::Reminder Options should have the olSound option turned on.
Sensitivity	Get/put	Indicates the sensitivity of the appointment: normal or private
Start	Get/put	Gets or sets the start date and time of the appointment. This must be earlier or equal to the end time.
Subject	Get/put	Gets or sets the subject of the appointment (up to 4,096 characters)

For example, if you wanted to add a new appointment, you could do the following:

```
// Calendar folder
IFolder *pIFolder = NULL;
hr = pOlApp->GetDefaultFolder(olFolderCalendar, &pIFolder);
if(FAILED(hr)) {
   OutputDebugString(TEXT("Could not get the calendar
        folder"));
   return FALSE;
}
```

```
// Get the collection
IPOutlookItemCollection *pIAppItems = NULL;
hr = pIFolder->get_Items(&pIAppItems);
if(FAILED(hr)) {
   pIFolder->Release();
   return FALSE;
}

// Add a new appointment
IAppointment *pIAppoint = NULL;
hr = pIAppItems->Add((IDispatch **)&pIAppoint);
if(FAILED(hr)) {
   pIAppItems->Release();
   pIFolder->Release();
   return FALSE;
}

// Set up my appointment details
SYSTEMTIME sysTime;
DATE dtAppoint;

memset(&sysTime, 0, sizeof(SYSTEMTIME));
sysTime.wMonth = 8;
sysTime.wDay = 30;
sysTime.wYear = 2003;

SystemTimeToVariantTime(&sysTime, &dtAppoint);

pIAppoint->put_Subject(TEXT("Mike's Birthday"));
pIAppoint->put_Start(dtAppoint);
pIAppoint->put_AllDayEvent(VARIANT_TRUE);

// Save it
pIAppoint->Save();

// Clean up
if(pIAppoint)
   pIAppoint->Release();
if(pIAppItems)
   pIAppItems->Release();
if(pIFolder)
   pIFolder->Release();
```

Two additional interfaces can be used in conjunction with the `IAppointment` interface to provide more robust appointments:

1. The `IRecurrencePattern` interface is used to set up appointments and meetings that occur on more than one occasion.
2. The `IRecipients` interface is used to change an appointment into a meeting request.

The methods `IAppointment::ClearRecurrencePattern()` and `IAppointment::GetRecurrencePattern()` are used with the `IRecurrencePattern` interface, and are covered later in this chapter (both the `ITask` and `IAppointment` interfaces can support recurrence patterns).

When you create a new appointment, you generally need to include other individuals besides yourself. This is where the `IRecipients` interface is used; it changes an appointment into what is called a *meeting request*. The methods `IAppointment::Cancel()` and `IAppointment::Send()` are used for canceling and sending these types of requests to other people.

To get the pointer to the `IRecipients` interface that will be used for an appointment, you can use the `IAppointment::get_Recipients()` property, which is defined as follows:

```
HRESULT IAppointment::get_Recipients(IRecipients **pRecipients);
```

This property returns a pointer to an `IRecipient` interface that you can use to add, modify, or delete people from the recipients list.

Appointment Recipients

The `IRecipients` interface is a collection of recipients for an appointment. The interface supports the methods described in Table 10.14.

Table 10.14 `IRecipients` Methods

Method	Description
Add()	Adds a recipient to the meeting request
Item()	Gets the `IRecipient` interface for the specified item
Remove()	Removes a recipient

The `IRecipients` interface also supports the properties described in Table 10.15.

Table 10.15 `IRecipients` Properties

Property	Get/Put	Description
Application	Get	Returns a pointer to the `IPOutlookApp` interface
Count	Get	Gets the number of recipients in the list

Each individual recipient in the collection is represented by an `IRecipient` interface, which supports the properties described in Table 10.16.

Table 10.16 `IRecipient` Properties

Property	Get/Put	Description
Address	Get/put	Gets or sets the e-mail address of the recipient. This property cannot be set to `NULL`.
Application	Get	Returns a pointer to the `IPOutlookApp` interface
Name	Get	Gets the display name of the recipient

To either add or delete individuals from a meeting request, you first must get the appointment's specific `IRecipients` interface by calling the `IAppointment::get_Recipients()` property. For example, if you wanted to add a few individuals to a meeting request, you could do the following:

```
// Get the collection
IPOutlookItemCollection *pIAppItems = NULL;
hr = pIFolder->get_Items(&pIAppItems);
if(FAILED(hr)) {
   pIFolder->Release();
   return FALSE;
}

// Get an appointment
IAppointment *pIAppoint = NULL;
hr = pIAppItems->Item(1, (IDispatch **)&pIAppoint);
```

```
if(FAILED(hr)) {
   pIAppItems->Release();
   pIFolder->Release();
   return FALSE;
}

// Get the recipient list
IRecipients *pIRecip = NULL;
hr = pIAppoint->get_Recipients(&pIRecip);
if(FAILED(hr)) {
   pIAppoint->Release();
   pIAppItems->Release();
   pIFolder->Release();
   return FALSE;
}

// Add recipients
IRecipient *pINewRecipient = NULL, *pINewRecipient2 = NULL;
pIRecip->Add(TEXT("Barry"), &pINewRecipient);
pIRecip->Add(TEXT("Jennifer"), &pINewRecipient2);

// Remember to save appointment
pIAppoint->Save();
```

Verifying a Recipient

After you have used the `IRecipients::Add()` method to add new people to a recipient list for an appointment (or you have modified the list), it is a good practice to verify that the names you have added are actually valid. This task is simplified by using the `IPOlRecipient` interface. The interface has a single method, described in Table 10.17.

Table 10.17 `IPOlRecipient` Method

Method	Description
Resolve()	Resolves the name of a recipient with the Contacts database

To get a valid pointer for the `IPOlRecipient` interface, you need to call the `QueryInterface()` function on the `IRecipient` object that you want to validate:

```
// Resolve
IPOlRecipient *pResolvRecip = NULL;
```

```
hr = pINewRecipient->QueryInterface(IID_IPOlRecipient,
    (LPVOID *)&pResolvRecip);
```

After you have the pointer to the interface, you can call the `IPOl Recipient::Resolve()` method. This will validate the name of the `IRecipient` object by searching the Contacts database for a matching first and last name. The method has the following prototype:

```
HRESULT IPOlRecipient::Resolve(VARIANT_BOOL fShowDialog,
    VARIANT_BOOL *pfResolved);
```

The first parameter, `fShowDialog`, should be set to `TRUE` if you want the method to display a dialog box that lists all of the matching e-mail addresses. If it is set to `FALSE`, then the function will fail if more than one contact matches. The `pfResolved` parameter will return `TRUE` or `FALSE`, depending on whether the function has successfully resolved an address or not.

The `ITask` Interface

The `ITask` interface is used to represent an individual task that is located in the Tasks folder. In addition to the common Outlook item methods—`Save()`, `Delete()`, `Copy()`, and `Display()`—the `ITask` interface also supports the methods described in Table 10.18.

The `ITask` interface supports the properties described in Table 10.19.

Table 10.18 `ITask` Methods

Method	Description
`ClearRecurrencePattern()`	Clears the recurrence pattern for the task
`GetRecurrencePattern()`	Gets the `IRecurrencePattern` interface for the task
`SkipRecurrence()`	Moves the recurrence pattern forward one recurrence

Table 10.19 `ITask` Properties

Property	Get/Put	Description
Application	Get	Returns a pointer to the `IPOutlookApp` interface
Body	Get/put	Gets or sets the note attached to the task (up to 60KB)
BodyInk	Get/put	Gets or sets an InkNote BLOB for the task. Both the `ITask::Body` and `ITask::BodyInk` properties access the same note; however, `ITask::Body` returns only the text, whereas `ITask::BodyInk` returns the entire ink object.
Categories	Get/put	Gets or sets the categories for the task
Complete	Get/put	Indicates whether the task has been completed
DateCompleted	Get	Gets the date and time when the task was completed, depending on whether the `ITask::Complete` property is set to `TRUE`
DueDate	Get/put	Gets or sets the date the task is due
Importance	Get/put	Gets or sets the importance level of the task (Low, Normal, or High)
IsRecurring	Get	Indicates whether the task is recurring
Oid	Get	Gets the object identifier
ReminderOptions	Get/put	Gets or sets the reminder options for the task
ReminderSet	Get/put	Indicates whether the user should be reminded of the task
ReminderSoundFile	Get/put	Gets or sets the path and filename of the sound file to be used for the reminder. The `ITask::ReminderSet` property should be set to `TRUE`, and the `ITask::ReminderOptions` should have the `olSound` option turned on.
ReminderTime	Get/put	Gets or sets when the reminder will occur
Sensitivity	Get/put	Gets or sets the sensitivity of the task to either Normal or Private
StartDate	Get/put	Gets or sets the start date for the task
Subject	Get/put	Gets or sets the subject for the task (up to 4,095 characters)
TeamTask	Get/put	Indicates whether the task is a team task or not

Using Recurrence Patterns in Appointments and Tasks

Both the `IAppointment` and `ITask` interfaces enable you to set up a recurrence pattern for a particular Outlook item by using the `IRecurrencePattern` interface. The interface supports the method described in Table 10.20.

Table 10.20 `IRecurrencePattern` Method

Method	Description
GetOccurrence()	Gets a specific `IAppointment` interface occurring on the specified date and at the specified time

The `IRecurrencePattern` interface supports the properties described in Table 10.21.

Table 10.21 `IRecurrencePattern` Properties

Property	Get/Put	Type	Valid For	Description
Application	Get	All	Both	Returns a pointer to the `IPOutlookApp` interface
DayOfMonth	Get/put	Monthly, Yearly	Both	Gets or sets the days in a month on which the recurrence occurs (from 1 to 31)
DayOfWeekMask	Get/put	MonthNth, Weekly, YearNth	Both	Gets or sets the days of the week on which the recurrence occurs (from `olSunday` through `olSaturday`)

(continued)

Table 10.21 `IRecurrencePattern` Properties (*continued*)

Property	Get/Put	Type	Valid For	Description
Duration	Get/put	All	IAppointment	Gets or sets the duration of the recurring task or appointment. This value is ignored if both IRecurrence Pattern::Start Time and IRecurrence Pattern:: EndTime are set.
EndTime	Get/put	All	IAppointment	Gets or sets the time when a recurring task or appointment ends
Exceptions	Get	All	IAppointment	Gets the list of appointments that cause an exception to the recurrence pattern. Returns a pointer to the IException interface.
Instance	Get/put	MonthNth, YearNth	Both	Gets or sets the week of the month on which the recurrence occurs (from 1 to 5)
Interval	Get/put	Daily, Monthly, MonthNth, Weekly	Both	Gets or sets the number of units between occurrences (from 1 to 999)
MonthOfYear	Get/put	Yearly, YearNth	Both	Gets or sets the month in which a recurrence occurs (from 1 to 12)

Property	Get/Put	Type	Valid For	Description
NoEndDate	Get/put	All	Both	Indicates whether the pattern has an end date
Occurrences	Get/put	All	Both	Gets or sets the number of occurrences
PatternEndDate	Get/put	All	Both	Gets or sets the end date of the recurrence. You must set IRecurrence Pattern:: NoEndDate to TRUE.
PatternStartDate	Get/put	All	Both	Gets or sets the start date of the recurrence
RecurrenceType	Get/put	All	Both	Gets or sets the recurrence type (Daily, Weekly, Monthly, Every Nth Month, Yearly, or Every Nth Years)
StartTime	Get/put	All	IAppointment	Gets or sets the start time for recurring tasks or appointments

To create a new recurring appointment or task, you first need to get the `IRecurrencePattern` interface for the `IAppointment` or `ITask` object by calling the `::GetRecurrencePattern()` method on the object.

You should initially configure how often the recurrence will occur by using the `IRecurrencePattern::RecurrenceType()` property. A recurrence pattern's frequency can be set with one of the following values:

- Use the `olRecursDaily` constant to have the task or appointment repeat every day.

- Use the `olRecursWeekly` constant to have the task or appointment repeat every week.
- Use the `olRecursMonthly` constant to have the task or appointment repeat every month.
- Use the `olRecursMonthNth` constant to have the task or appointment repeat every Nth month.
- Use the `olRecursYearly` constant to have the task or appointment repeat every year.
- Use the `olRecursYearNth` constant to have the task or appointment repeat every Nth year.

Once you have set the `IRecurrencePattern::Recurrence Type()` property, you can proceed to configure the start time and date for the pattern.

The following example creates a new task that has a recurrence pattern:

```
// Create a new task
IFolder *pIFolder = NULL;
hr = pOlApp->GetDefaultFolder(olFolderTasks, &pIFolder);
if(FAILED(hr)) {
   OutputDebugString(TEXT("Could not get the tasks
       folder"));
   return FALSE;
}


// Get the collection
IPOutlookItemCollection *pITaskItems = NULL;
hr = pIFolder->get_Items(&pITaskItems);
if(FAILED(hr)) {
   pIFolder->Release();
   return FALSE;
}


// Create a new task
ITask *pITask = NULL;
hr = pITaskItems->Add((IDispatch **)&pITask);
if(FAILED(hr)) {
   pITaskItems->Release();
   pIFolder->Release();
   return FALSE;
}
```

```
// Add some info
pITask->put_Subject(TEXT("Check morning news"));

// Get the recurrence pattern
IRecurrencePattern *pIRecur = NULL;
hr = pITask->GetRecurrencePattern(&pIRecur);
if(FAILED(hr)) {
   pITask->Release();
   pITaskItems->Release();
   pIFolder->Release();
   return FALSE;
}

// Set it to fire daily starting tommorow
SYSTEMTIME sysTime;
DATE dtAppoint;

GetSystemTime(&sysTime);
sysTime.wDay++;
SystemTimeToVariantTime(&sysTime, &dtAppoint);

pIRecur->put_RecurrenceType(olRecursDaily);
pIRecur->put_NoEndDate(VARIANT_TRUE);
pIRecur->put_StartTime(dtAppoint);

// Save it
pITask->Save();

// Clean up
pIRecur->Release();
pITask->Release();
pITaskItems->Release();
pIFolder->Release();
```

Recurrence Exceptions

Whenever an appointment that already has a recurrence pattern assigned
to it is modified, Pocket Outlook will automatically create an **exception**
for it. To get a list of exceptions for a recurring appointment, you can use
the `IRecurrencePattern::get_Exceptions()` property, as shown
in the following example:

```
IExceptions *pIExcepts = NULL;
hr = pIRecur->get_Exceptions(&pIExcepts);
```

```
if(FAILED(hr)) {
   pIRecur->Release();
   pITask->Release();
   pITaskItems->Release();
   pIFolder->Release();
   return FALSE;
}


// Do something with the exceptions...
```

The `IExceptions` interface that is returned is a read-only collection of exceptions for the appointment. The interface supports the single method shown in Table 10.22.

Table 10.22 `IExceptions` Method

Method	Description
Item()	Gets a specific `IException` item

The `IExceptions` interface supports the properties described in Table 10.23.

Table 10.23 `IExceptions` Properties

Property	Get/Put	Description
Application	Get	Returns a pointer to the `IPOutlookApp` interface
Count	Get	Gets the number of `IException` items from the collection

To retrieve a specific exception, you should use the `IExceptions::Item()` method, which is defined as follows:

```
HRESULT IExceptions::Item(int iIndex,
   IException **ppExcept);
```

The first parameter is the index for the exception you are interested in, and is followed by a pointer to a value that will be filled in with the pointer to the specific `IException` interface.

The `IException` interface supports the properties described in Table 10.24.

Table 10.24 `IException` Properties

Property	Get/Put	Description
Application	Get	Returns a pointer to the `IPOutlookApp` interface
AppointmentItem	Get	Gets the `IAppointment` interface for the item causing the exception
Deleted	Get	Returns `TRUE` if the exception is caused because the appointment is being deleted
OriginalDate	Get	Gets the date on which the exception originally occurred

Creating Pocket Outlook Plug-ins

All of the Pocket Outlook applications (Calendar, Tasks, and Contacts) enable you to add your own menu items to their individual Tools menu. Adding a new menu item is as simple as creating a DLL that exports your function, and setting up the registry with information about the plug-in (see Figure 10.5). When the user selects your menu item, the Pocket Outlook application will load your DLL and call into the function that you have specified. Pocket Outlook will also pass information about the selected items to your function.

To add an additional menu item to a Pocket Outlook application, you need to add a new sub-key value for your menu option under the registry key:

```
HKEY_LOCAL_MACHINE\Software\Microsoft\PimApps\PimExtension\
    PIMAPP\AddIns
```

Replace the *PIMAPP* constant with the name of the application to which you want to add a menu item. This can be set to `Contacts`, `Tasks`, or `Calendar`.

Table 10.25 describes the values that need to be configured for your new menu item.

Figure 10.5 A Pocket Outlook plug-in

Table 10.25 Pocket Outlook Plug-in Registry Settings

Name	Type	Description
DLL	String	The full path and name of the DLL that contains your exported plug-in module
Menu	String	The text that will be displayed in the Tools menu

To implement your plug-in, you need to create a DLL that exports the `CePimCommand()` function, which has the following prototype:

```
void CePimCommand(HWND hWnd, PIMTYPE ptData, UINT
  uDataCount, HANDLE *rghData, void *pReserved);
```

The first parameter that is passed to you is the window handle of the parent Pocket Outlook application. It is followed by `ptData`, which specifies the application that called into the function. This will be set to `PT_CALENDAR`, `PT_TASKS`, or `PT_CONTACT`.

The `uDataCount` and `rghData` parameters refer to the items that are currently selected in the calling Pocket Outlook application. A pointer to an array of Pocket Outlook object identifiers is passed to you in the `rghData` parameter, and the number of items in the array is specified by `uDataCount`.

Once you have a specific OID, you can use the `IPOutlookApp::GetItemFromOid()` method to get the interface for that item.

Let's look at some code for developing a Pocket Outlook plug-in that displays a calendar item. The registry for your new item would look like the following:

```
// Registry settings
[HKEY_LOCAL_MACHINE\SOFTWARE\Microsoft\PimApps\PimExtensions
  \Calendar\AddIns\MyPlugin]
"Menu"="My Outlook Plugin"
"dll"="myplugin.dll"
```

Finally, let's look at the actual code to display the subject of the selected appointment:

```
#define INITGUID
#include <windows.h>
#include <pimstore.h>

typedef enum tagPIMTYPE {
    PT_CONTACT = 0,
    PT_CALENDAR,
    PT_TASKS
} PIMTYPE;


HINSTANCE hInstance = NULL;

BOOL WINAPI DllMain(HANDLE hInstDll, DWORD dwReason, LPVOID
  lpvReserved){
    hInstance = (HINSTANCE)hInstDll;
    return TRUE;
}


void CePimCommand(HWND hWnd, PIMTYPE ptData, UINT
  uDataCount, HANDLE *rghData, void *pReserved)
{
    // Abort if not in the calendar
    if(ptData != PT_CALENDAR)
        return;
```

```
// Abort if no items are selected
if(uDataCount == 0)
   MessageBox(hWnd, TEXT("Nothing selected!"), TEXT("My
      Plugin"), MB_OK);

// Ok, let's get the first item
CEOID calItemOid = (CEOID)rghData[0];

// Start up and log into poom
HRESULT hr = S_OK;
IPOutlookApp *pOlApp = NULL;

if(FAILED(CoInitializeEx(NULL, 0))) {
   MessageBox(hWnd, TEXT("Couldnt start COM"), TEXT("My
      Plugin"), MB_OK);
   return;
}

// Get a pointer to the IPOutlookApp interface
hr = CoCreateInstance(CLSID_Application, NULL,
   CLSCTX_INPROC_SERVER, IID_IPOutlookApp, (LPVOID *)&pOlApp);
if(FAILED(hr)) {
   MessageBox(hWnd, TEXT("Couldnt get the IPOutlookApp
      Interface"), TEXT("My Plugin"), MB_OK);
   return;
}

// Log into Pocket Outlook
hr = pOlApp->Logon((long)hWnd);
if(FAILED(hr)) {
   MessageBox(hWnd, TEXT("Couldnt log into POOM"),
      TEXT("My Plugin"), MB_OK);
   return;
}

// Get the item that was passed in
IAppointment *pIAppoint = NULL;
hr = pOlApp->GetItemFromOid(calItemOid,
   (IDispatch **)&pIAppoint);
if(FAILED(hr)) {
```

```
        MessageBox(hWnd, TEXT("Couldnt get object"), TEXT("My
            Plugin"), MB_OK);
        pOlApp->Logoff();
        pOlApp->Release();
        return;
    }

    // Got it, now display it
    BSTR bstrSubject;

    pIAppoint->get_Subject(&bstrSubject);
    MessageBox(hWnd, bstrSubject, TEXT("My Plugin"), MB_OK);

    // Clean up
    SysFreeString(bstrSubject);
    pIAppoint->Release();
    pOlApp->Logoff();
    pOlApp->Release();
    return;
}
```

CHAPTER 11

E-mail

Because the mail never stops. Every day it keeps coming in, and the faster it goes out, the faster it comes in. And the stacks grow higher and higher. And then the bar code reader breaks, and it's Publisher's Clearing House day!

—Newman, Seinfeld

In the last several years, nothing has changed the way that companies do business and people communicate more than e-mail and the World Wide Web. The capability to send electronic mail instantaneously from one place to another has quietly integrated itself into everyday life. Combine e-mail with a Personal Digital Assistant such as a Pocket PC device, and your applications can provide your users with a popular and pervasive way to communicate with others (for example, your scheduling application can e-mail status reports).

As you have already seen in previous chapters, Pocket PC provides a variety of ways to have its software talk over a wired or wireless Internet connection. Back in Chapter 1, you learned how to use the socket interface, or Winsock, to develop applications that use TCP/IP to enable two devices to communicate with each other. Although you could certainly use sockets to write an e-mail application, developing a mail application from the ground up is not only time-consuming, it can also be extremely proprietary in the way it stores messages. Fortunately, Pocket PC already provides a robust set of programming libraries for working with all aspects of e-mail.

It is recommended that any application that will interact with electronic mail on a Pocket PC device use the built-in **Mail API**, or **MAPI**. The MAPI library provides developers with several COM objects that are used to handle a variety of e-mail protocols, as well as a standard way to work with message attachments and the storage of e-mail messages. In addition, by using MAPI, you will be working with a *centralized message*

Figure 11.1 Pocket Inbox

store. This not only enables your application to leverage mail transports and message storage that other developers have built, but gives other applications access to a mail transport that you have written or to messages that you have placed in the message store.

Every standard Pocket PC device includes the Inbox application (see Figure 11.1) for sending and receiving messages.

To use the Mail API (as well as the COM e-mail interfaces that are supported on Pocket PC) within your application, you need to include the `cemapi.h` header file, and link with the `cemapi.lib` library.

MAPI Overview

The Mail API on Pocket PC provides you with a set of COM interfaces that are used primarily to work with the data associated with e-mail. This includes the capability to create new messages, manipulate e-mail folders, read existing messages and attachments, and receive notifications when e-mail activity occurs. In order to send and receive messages, most applications use an existing **e-mail transport**, an interface that enables communication from a device to a server; and an existing e-mail application (such as Inbox) for general communication needs. How an application uses MAPI depends on what it is trying to accomplish with e-mail.

Three basic categories of applications use MAPI:

1. **Generic applications that require e-mail integration**. These applications use MAPI to send and read messages. For example, the Pocket Outlook Calendar uses MAPI to send e-mail messages for a meeting request.
2. **MAPI Transports**. Another type of MAPI object is a *mail transport,* which provides the communications functionality to connect a device with a server. Applications such as an e-mail client (e.g., Pocket Inbox) directly use MAPI transports to synchronize with a mail server. An example of a MAPI transport that ships with Pocket PC is POP3.
3. **E-mail clients**. E-mail clients use MAPI transports along with the other MAPI interfaces to create e-mail messages, synchronize with a server, and so on. The Pocket Inbox is an e-mail client application.

As a developer, you might have already begun to recognize the MAPI acronym. The Mail API that is available on a Pocket PC device is a "slimmed down" version of the MAPI found on a normal Windows desktop machine. If you are already familiar with the MAPI objects and interfaces in Windows XP, then be forewarned: Many of the objects and interfaces found on the desktop are not present or implemented on Pocket PC.

NOTE: The MAPI interfaces are new to Pocket PC 2002. Previous versions of Windows CE and Pocket PC use the CE Message Store APIs, which are no longer supported on Pocket PC.

Figure 11.2 illustrates the object model that MAPI uses to expose e-mail that has been stored on the device.

Figure 11.3 illustrates how the MAPI component object architecture relates to the Pocket PC Inbox:

The Mail API Object Model consists of the following interfaces:

- The parent object that you use when writing software that uses MAPI is the `IMAPISession` interface. This is used to initialize MAPI, and enables you to log on to a message store.
- The `IMsgStore` interface is used to provide access to the file storage associated with a specific e-mail transport.

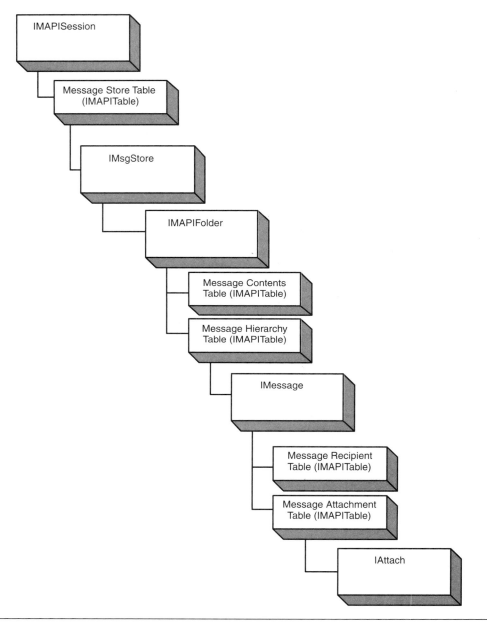

Figure 11.2 Pocket PC Mail API Object Model

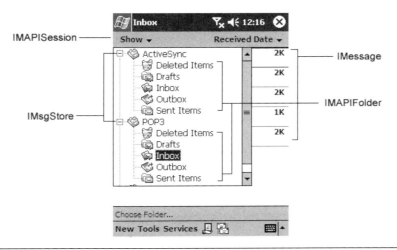

Figure 11.3 Breakdown of the Pocket PC Inbox

- The `IMAPIFolder` interface is used to access messages and sub-folders contained within a message store.
- The `IMAPIContainer` interface is a parent interface that is used to handle operations on container objects such as folders. The `IMAPIFolder` interface is derived from `IMAPIContainer`.
- The `IMAPITable` interface is used to view collections of MAPI objects. For example, a MAPI folder will contain a table of messages.
- The `IMAPIProp` interface is used to set and retrieve MAPI object properties.
- The `IMAPIAdviceSink` interface is used for handling MAPI notification messages.
- The `IMessage` interface is used to handle individual e-mail messages.
- The `IAttach` interface is used to handle e-mail message attachments.

In addition, MAPI provides you with several functions and macros to simplify the use of the various MAPI data types. Other functions enable you to log on to a MAPI session, and perform memory management on data objects that MAPI returns to you.

Before learning how to write MAPI applications, let's take a quick look at two additional support interfaces that MAPI uses: `IMailSync Handler` and `IMailSyncCallback`.

A Word about MAPI Transports

You can use several MAPI transports that ship with Pocket PC to send and receive e-mail messages:

- The ActiveSync transport synchronizes e-mail data with a desktop version of Outlook.
- The POP3/SMTP transport receives e-mail over the Post Office Protocol (see RFC 1225) and sends e-mail over the Simple Mail Transfer Protocol (see RFC 821).
- The SMS transport is used on Pocket PC Phone Edition devices to send and receive e-mail over the Short Message Service.
- The IMAP4 transport is used to send and receive messages over the Internet Message Access Protocol version 4 (see RFC 2060).

Each e-mail transport implements the `IMailSyncHandler` interface. This interface is used by e-mail client applications to directly communicate with the transport for performing synchronization with a server. Although developing new mail transports is beyond the scope of this chapter, I have included a list of the methods that it supports.

Table 11.1 describes the methods supported by the `IMailSync Handler` interface.

Table 11.1 `IMailSyncHandler` Methods

Method	Description
`Connect()`	Requests the transport to connect to a server
`DecodeEvent()`	Decodes a logged event to a string
`Disconnect()`	Requests the transport to disconnect from a server
`DoProperties()`	Reserved
`FolderOptions()`	Enumeration used by `IMailSyncHandler::` `SetFolderOptions` to set various folder options
`GetCapability()`	Gets the setting for a specific transport capability
`GetFolderHierarchy()`	Queries the transport for the folder hierarchy
`Initialize()`	Initializes the transport
`Install()`	Configures the transport
`SetCapability()`	Sets a specific transport capability setting
`SetFolderOptions()`	Sets an option on a specific transport folder
`Shutdown()`	Shuts down the transport
`Synchronize()`	Places a synchronization request with the transport
`UnInstall()`	Removes the transport

Before a transport can be used by a mail application, it needs to be properly registered in the Pocket PC registry in the following location:

```
HKEY_LOCAL_MACHINE\Software\Microsoft\Inbox\Svc\Transport Name
```

Each transport name represents an installed mail transport. Table 11.2 describes the values that need to be configured for each transport.

Table 11.2 Registry Settings for a Mail Transport

Name	Type	Description
DLL	String	Name and path to the transport DLL
Name	String	Name to be displayed for the transport
Port	DWORD	Server port to connect with

The following example shows how you can enumerate the e-mail transports that are installed on a Pocket PC device:

```
// Enumerate installed e-mail transports
// Step 1. Open a handle to the transports in the registry
HKEY hKey = NULL;
DWORD dwValType = 0, dwSize = sizeof(DWORD);
if(RegOpenKeyEx(HKEY_LOCAL_MACHINE, TEXT("Software\\
  Microsoft\\Inbox\\Svc"), 0, 0, &hKey) != ERROR_SUCCESS)
    return FALSE;

// Step 2. Enumerate the keys - each will represent a
// transport
TCHAR tchTransName[256] = TEXT("\0");
DWORD dwNameSize = 255;
int nIndex = 0;
long lResult;

do {
    lResult = RegEnumKeyEx(hKey, nIndex, tchTransName,
      &dwNameSize, NULL, NULL, NULL, NULL);

    if(lResult == ERROR_NO_MORE_ITEMS)
      break;

    // Got the transport name, do something with it. For this
    // example, we'll just print out the installed transports.
```

```
    MessageBox(NULL, tchTransName, TEXT("Installed
    Transports"), MB_OK);

    nIndex++;
    dwNameSize = 255;
    memset(tchTransName, 0, 256*sizeof(TCHAR));
} while(1);

// Step 3. Close up the registry
if(hKey)
    RegCloseKey(hKey);
```

Building E-mail Client Applications

Another topic that should be briefly covered is the building of new client e-mail applications. This section does not provide detailed information, however, because the Pocket PC Logo Certification Guidelines specify that although application developers should use MAPI for working with the universal e-mail stores, they should not replicate the functionality of Pocket Inbox. However, for the sake of completeness, let's take a quick look at the `IMailSyncCallback` interface.

The `IMailSyncCallback` interface needs to be implemented by an e-mail client application in order to enable a mail transport to communicate with it. The interface needs to expose the methods described in Table 11.3.

Table 11.3 `IMailSyncCallback` Methods

Method	Description
`AllocateMem()`	Allocates memory for the calling message transport
`DisplayMessageBox()`	Reserved
`FreeMem()`	Frees memory that has been allocated by a call to the `IMailSyncCallback::AllocateMem()` function
`GetGlobalSetting()`	Gets the value for a setting from the e-mail application that has implemented the `IMailSyncCallback` interface
`LogEvent()`	Logs an error event
`Progress()`	Progress notification for synchronization events in the transport
`RequestCredentials()`	Request from the transport about user credentials
`RequestSync()`	Reserved

Working with MAPI Objects and Data Types

In order to become familiar with how MAPI works, it is important to first understand some MAPI-specific data types and interfaces that are consistently used when working with an e-mail message store. This section focuses on MAPI entry identifiers, MAPI tables, MAPI object properties, and MAPI memory allocation. Regardless of what you do with MAPI, understanding how data is stored and accessed is the key to writing a good, e-mail-friendly application.

Entry Identifiers

As you might have already guessed by its name, a MAPI entry ID is a unique identifier assigned by a message store to identify an individual object. Almost every item in MAPI has a unique identifier associated with it, and is specified by using the ENTRYID structure. Some objects that have an entry identifier include message stores, folders, messages, attachments, and distribution lists.

The ENTRYID structure, which will typically be read-only for a client application, is defined as follows:

```
typedef struct {
   BYTE abFlags[4];
   BYTE ab[MAPI_DIM];
} ENTRYID, FAR *LPENTRYID;
```

The first field, abFlags, is a four-byte flag that is used to describe the type of entry identifier. The first byte, abFlags[0], can be set to one of the following values:

- MAPI_NOTRECIP indicates that the entry cannot be used as a recipient of a message.
- MAPI_NOTRESERVED indicates that the entry identifier can be reused by other sessions.
- MAPI_NOW indicates that the entry identifier can be used only now.
- MAPI_SHORTTERM indicates that the entry identifier is guaranteed to be unique only during the current session.
- MAPI_THISSESSION indicates that the entry identifier cannot be used by other sessions.

The remaining three bytes of the `abFlags` field are reserved. The other field, `ab`, is an array of binary data that represents the unique ID for the entry.

As you will see in the section "Accessing MAPI Objects," you use the `ENTRYID` structure to reference particular entries in a message store. For example, it is used as a parameter to the `::OpenEntry()` method that many of the MAPI objects implement, enabling you to get a pointer to the interface for the particular object to which the `ENTRYID` refers.

Remember that the binary data inside an `ENTRYID` structure is used only internally by a message store, and should be considered only a reference to an object (the data has no meaning outside the message store). This being the case, you cannot determine if two `ENTRYID` structures represent the same object just by simply comparing the binary data—you need to use the `IMAPISession::CompareEntryIDs()` function, described later in this chapter.

Table 11.4 describes the macros that MAPI provides to help you more efficiently work with the `ENTRYID` structure.

Table 11.4 `ENTRYID` Macro Functions

Macro	Description
`CbNewENTRYID(_cb)`	Calculates the number of bytes for a new `ENTRYID` of a specified size
`SizedENTRYID(_cb, _name)`	Creates a new `ENTRYID` of a specified size

MAPI Object Properties

Almost every object found within MAPI uses a set of attributes that describe the object and provide more information about it (such as the subject of a message, or an object identifier). These attributes are also known as **properties**.

Every property has a unique *property tag* that can be used to identify it (for example, the `PR_ENTRYID` tag is used for the entry identifier of an object). A property tag is a 32-bit number that consists of two parts: a *property type* and a *property identifier*. Every property tag is prefixed with the letters `PR_`. As you will see in the next section, properties are also used by MAPI tables to represent individual columns of data.

The property type is specified in the lower 16 bits of the property tag, and is used to identify the data type of the property. Table 11.5 describes the valid property types.

Table 11.5 MAPI Property Data Types

Property Type	Description
PR_BOOLEAN	16-bit Boolean
PR_LONG | PT_I4	Signed 32-bit value
PR_OBJECT	Embedded object in a property
PT_APPTIME	Application time value
PT_BINARY	Counted byte array
PT_CLSID	GUID
PT_CURRENCY	Signed 64-bit integer value
PT_DOUBLE | PT_R8	Floating point value
PT_ERROR	32-bit error value
PT_FLOAT | PT_R4	4-byte floating point value
PT_LONGLONG | PT_I8	8-byte signed integer value
PT_NULL	NULL value
PT_SHORT | PT_I2	Signed 16-bit value
PT_STRING8	8-bit character string
PT_SYSTIME	FILETIME 64-bit integer
PT_TSTRING | PT_UNICODE	Unicode string
PT_UNSPECIFIED	Reserved

The remaining 16 bits of a property tag are used for the property identifier, and fall within the range of `0x0001-0xFFFF`.

Table 11.6 describes the macros that MAPI provides to help you efficiently work with object properties.

Table 11.6 Property Macro Functions

Macro	Description
PROP_ID(ulPropTag)	Gets the property identifier for a property tag
PROP_TAG(ulPropType, ulPropID)	Gets the property tag for a specific property identifier and type
PROP_TYPE(ulPropTag)	Gets the property type for a property tag

For example, if you wanted to retrieve the property identifier and type for a value that was returned from `SRowSet` (more on `SRowSet` later in this chapter), you could do the following:

```
TCHAR tchProperties[10] = TEXT("\0");
DWORD dwType = 0, dwID = 0;

dwType = PROP_TYPE (pRowSet->aRow[0].lpProps[nVal].
   ulPropTag);
dwID = PROP_ID(pRowSet->aRow[0].lpProps[nVal].ulPropTag);
wsprintf(tchProperties, TEXT("0x%08x Type:%04x ID:%04x\r\n"),
   pRowSet->aRow[0].lpProps[nVal].ulPropTag, dwType, dwID);
OutputDebugString(tchProperties);
```

Accessing Object Properties

On Pocket PC, the `IAttach`, `IMAPIContainer`, `IMessage`, and `IMsgStore` interfaces are derived from the `IMAPIProp` interface. The `IMAPIProp` interface provides the implementation details for getting and setting property values, as well as deleting them. It supports the methods described in Table 11.7.

Table 11.7 `IMAPIProp` Methods

Method	Description
DeleteProps()	Deletes one or more properties
GetIDsFromNames()	Gets the property identifiers for specific property names
GetProps()	Gets specific property values
OpenProperty()	Gets a pointer to an interface to access property values, instead of using the `IMAPIProp::GetProps()` and `IMAPIProp::SetProps()` interfaces
SetProps()	Sets specific property values

Two functions are used to retrieve property values from an object. To simply return one or more property values from a MAPI object to your application, you can use the `IMAPIProp::GetProps()` function:

```
HRESULT IMAPIProp::GetProps(LPSPropTagArray lpPropTagArray,
   ULONG ulFlags, ULONG *lpcValues, LPSPropValue
   *lppPropArray);
```

The first parameter, `lpPropTagArray`, is a pointer to an `SPropTagArray` structure that contains an array of property tags that you are interested in retrieving from the object. This is followed by `ulFlags`, which should be set to the `MAPI_UNICODE` flag. The `lpcValues` parameter should point to a `ULONG` value that will be filled in with the number of properties returned. Finally, the lppPropArray parameter points to an SPropValue array that contains the returned property values. Note that property values are returned in the same order that is specified in the lpPropTagArray structure.

The SPropTagArray structure that is used to list the properties you are interested in is defined as follows:

```
typedef struct _SPropTagArray {
    ULONG cValues;
    ULONG aulPropTag[MAPI_DIM];
} SPropTagArray, FAR *LPSPropTagArray;
```

The structure contains only two fields: an array of property tags specified by the aulPropTag field, and the number of items in the array, which should be specified by the cValues member.

The SPropValue structure that is filled in with the property values is defined as follows:

```
typedef struct _SPropValue {
    ULONG ulPropTag;
    ULONG dwAlignPad;
    union _PV Value;
} SPropValue, FAR *LPSPropValue;
```

The first field, ulPropTag, specifies the property tag for the property. The Value field is filled in with the specific value based on the data type for the property. The dwAlignPad field is used by MAPI to ensure that the structure has proper memory alignment, and should not be tampered with.

Table 11.8 describes the macros that MAPI provides to help you build SPropTagArray structures.

Table 11.8 SPropTagArray Macro Functions

Macro	Description
CbNewSPropTagArray(_ctag)	Calculates the number of bytes for a new SPropTagArray structure
CbSPropTagArray(_lparray)	Calculates the number of bytes of an existing SPropTagArray structure
SizedSPropTagArray(_ctag, _name)	Creates a named SPropTagArray structure for a specific number of property tags

The following example shows how you can use the `IMAPIProp::GetProps()` function to return the `ENTRYID` and `OBJECT_TYPE` properties for a MAPI folder:

```
LPSPropValue rgprops = NULL;
LPSPropValue lppPropArray = NULL;
ULONG cValues = 0;
IMAPIFolder *pPOPInboxFolder = NULL;
SizedSPropTagArray(2, rgTags) =
    {2,{PR_CE_IPM_INBOX_ENTRYID,PR_OBJECT_TYPE}};

// Now get the Inbox folder
hr = pPop3Store->GetProps((LPSPropTagArray)&rgTags,
    MAPI_UNICODE, &cValues, &rgprops);
```

If you require the capability to open a large property, such as a message attachment or message body, you need to use the `IMAPIProp::OpenProperty()` method to access it. This function opens a property value and uses an `IStream` interface for reading the property data in large blocks.

```
HRESULT IMAPIProp::OpenProperty(ULONG ulPropTag, LPCIID
    lpiid, ULONG ulInterfaceOptions, ULONG ulFlags, LPUNKNOWN
    *lppUnk);
```

The first parameter, `ulPropTag`, should specify the property tag that you are interested in. The `lpiid` and `ulInterfaceOptions` parameters are not supported on Pocket PC, and are ignored. The `ulFlags` parameter determines the access mode of the property value you are opening. The default value opens as read-only. If you need to open it for reading or writing, you should use the `MAPI_MODIFY` flag. The last parameter, `lppUnk`, receives a pointer to the interface for the `IStream` object when the function returns.

Modifying and Deleting Property Values

To delete a property value, you can call the `IMAPIProp::DeleteProps()` function:

```
HRESULT IMAPIProp::DeleteProps(LPSPropTagArray
   lpPropTagArray, LPSPropProblemArray *lppProblems);
```

The first parameter should point to an SPropTagArray that specifies the property tags you want to delete. The lppProblems parameter, which is optional, can point to an SPropProblemArray, which will provide you with detailed information regarding any errors that occur when the function returns. If you are not interested in the problem list, set this value to NULL.

The SPropProblemArray structure contains an array of SPropProblem structures. It is defined as follows:

```
typedef struct _SPropProblemArray {
   ULONG cProblem;
   SPropProblem aProblem[MAPI_DIM];
} SPropProblemArray, FAR *LPSPropProblemArray;
```

The cProblem field contains the number of SPropProblem structures that are in the array specified by the aProblem field.

An SPropProblem structure contains information about a specific problem that occurred. The structure has the following definition:

```
typedef struct _SPropProblem {
   ULONG ulIndex;
   ULONG ulPropTag;
   SCODE scode;
} SPropProblem, FAR *LPSPropProblem;
```

The first field, ulIndex, indicates the index of the item in the lpPropTagArray that was passed into the IMAPIProp::Delete Props() or IMAPIProp::SetProps() function containing the error. The ulPropTag field indicates the property tag that caused the error, and the scode field indicates the error value.

Table 11.9 describes the macros that MAPI provides to help you work with SPropProblemArray structures.

Table 11.9 SPropProblemArray Macro Functions

Macro	Description
CbNewSPropProblemArray (_cprob)	Calculates the number of bytes for a new SPropProblemArray structure
CbSPropProblemArray (_lparray)	Calculates the number of bytes of an existing SPropProblemArray structure
SizedSPropProblemArray (_cprob, _name)	Creates a named SPropProblemArray struc- ture for a specific number of SPropProblem structures

Use the following to change or set a property value:

```
HRESULT IMAPIProp::SetProps(ULONG cValues, LPSPropValue
    lpPropArray, LPSPropProblemArray *lppProblems);
```

The first parameter, cValues, is the number of property values in lpPropArray (and cannot be 0). The lpPropArray parameter should point to an array of SPropValue structures that contain the new or modified property values. Finally, lppProblems can optionally point to an SPropProblemArray structure if you are interested in more detailed error reporting, as shown in the following example:

```
SPropValue sMsgProps[2];
SPropProblemArray *psPropProblems = NULL;
TCHAR tchSubject[128] = TEXT("\0");

memset(&sMsgProps, 0, sizeof(sMsgProps));
wsprintf(tchSubject, TEXT("Test Message Subject"));

sMsgProps[0].ulPropTag = PR_MESSAGE_FLAGS;
sMsgProps[0].Value.ul = MSGFLAG_UNSENT;
sMsgProps[1].ulPropTag = PR_SUBJECT;
sMsgProps[1].Value.lpszW = tchSubject;

hr = pNewMessage->SetProps(2, sMsgProps, psPropProblems);
```

One last note: If a property value you are writing to is too large, you will usually receive the MAPI_E_NOT_ENOUGH_MEMORY error. In order to handle a large property value (such as the body of an e-mail message), you need to use the `IMAPIProp::OpenProp()` function and write to the `IStream` interface directly, instead of using the `IMAPIProp::SetProps()` function.

MAPI Tables

One interface that MAPI makes extensive use of is the `IMapiTable` object. The main use of a MAPI table is to provide you with a read-only view of a collection of properties that are owned by a parent MAPI object. For example, the MAPI Session object (`IMAPISession`) owns a table of the `ENTRYID`s of the message stores currently installed and in use on the device. Each message store, in turn, has another collection of MAPI object properties that are represented by a different table, and that specify the folders that the individual store contains.

An easy way to visualize a MAPI table is to think of a spreadsheet. Each row in the table represents a different object that is contained by the parent object. Every column represents a different property of the object. Every object in a MAPI table contains at least a column for its unique `ENTRYID`, which is specified by the `PR_ENTRYID` property.

Figure 11.4 shows how a collection of MAPI message store objects would be represented by a MAPI table.

Table 11.10 describes the different types of tables that you use with MAPI.

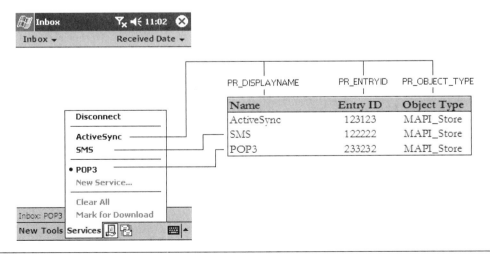

Figure 11.4 Layout of a MAPI table

Table 11.10 MAPI Table Types

MAPI Table	Parent Object	Description
Attachment	IMessage	A list of attachments for a message
Folder	IMsgStore	A list of root folders in a message store
Hierarchy	IFolder	A list of child folders in a folder
Message Stores	IMAPISession	A list of message store providers that are available to the MAPI session
Message	IFolder	A list of messages in a folder
Recipient	IMessage	A list of message recipients

You can access the data within a table through the IMAPITable interface. Getting a pointer to a specific table ultimately depends on the parent interface (for example, to get the table of message store providers, you would call the IMAPISession::GetMsgStoresTable() function).

The IMAPITable interface supports the methods described in Table 11.11.

Table 11.11 IMAPITable Methods

Method	Description
QueryPosition()	Returns the current table row position of the cursor. Also returns the cursor's relative position to the end of the table.
QueryRows()	Returns row data.
Restrict()	Restrictions are not implemented on Pocket PC.
SeekRow()	Moves the cursor row position.
SetColumns()	Sets the properties and column order for returned data rows.
SortTable()	Sorting is not implemented on Pocket PC.

Just by looking at the methods that are supported with the IMAPITable interface, you can probably already tell that it is similar to using a database table. There are functions to sort table data, apply filter criteria for restrictive results, query a table for an arbitrary amount of data, and even keep track of your current position in a table by using a cursor.

Table Structures and Macros

Whenever a called method accesses the table and returns data, MAPI represents an individual row (or object) by using the SRow structure. It is defined as follows:

```
typedef struct _SRow {
   ULONG ulAdrEntryPad;
   ULONG cValues;
   LPSPropValue lpProps;
} SRow, FAR *LPSRow;
```

The first field, ulAdrEntryPad, is a set of bytes that are used to properly align the structure in memory. This field is reserved, and should not be tampered with.

The other fields are used to describe the individual properties (or columns) for the entry. The cValues field contains the number of items that are in the array of SPropValue structures to which lpProps points. Each entry in the array represents a column in the table.

When you make a typical query on a table for a set of objects, you receive more than one row back. For this, MAPI provides the SRowSet structure, which is defined as follows:

```
typedef struct _SRowSet {
   ULONG cRows;
   SRow aRow[MAPI_DIM];
} SRowSet, FAR *LPSRowSet;
```

The structure simply represents an array of SRow structures that are specified by the aRow member. The number of SRow structures in the array can be found in the cRows field.

Remember that whenever you are returned an SRow or SRowSet structure, you also need to call the FreeProws() and MAPIFree Buffer() functions accordingly to properly free any memory that has been allocated. More information about MAPI memory allocation can be found later in this section.

Table 11.12 describes the macros that MAPI provides to help you efficiently work with the SRowSet structure.

Table 11.12 SRowSet Macro Functions

Macro	Description
CbNewSRowSet(_crow)	Calculates the number of bytes for a new SRowSet structure
CbSRowSet(_lprowset)	Calculates the number of bytes of an existing SRowSet structure
SizedSRowSet(_crow, _name)	Creates a named SRowSet structure for a specific number of rows

Getting Data from a Table

To retrieve information about the objects that are contained in a table, you use the IMAPITable::QueryRows() function. The function is defined as follows:

```
HRESULT IMAPITable::QueryRows(LONG lRowCount, ULONG ulFlags,
   LPSRowSet *lppRows);
```

The first parameter, lRowCount, is the number of rows that you want to return from the table, starting at the current cursor position. This can be set to a maximum of 10 rows at a time, and must be a positive number (you cannot retrieve retral rows). The next parameter, ulFlags, is not supported, and can be set to 0. The lppRows parameter will point to an SRowSet structure that contains the row data.

As you will soon learn, you can also filter and sort the data returned to you in the lppRows structure by using the IMAPITable::Restrict(), IMAPITable::SortTable(), and IMAPITable::SetColumns() functions.

The following example shows how you can use the IMAPITable::QueryRows() function to return all of the rows in the message store table:

```
IMAPITable *pIMapiStoresTable = NULL;
hr = pIMapi->GetMsgStoresTable(0, &pIMapiStoresTable);
while(1) {
   SRowSet *pRowSet = NULL;

   hr = pIMapiStoresTable->QueryRows(1, 0, &pRowSet);
   if(pRowSet->cRows != 1)
      break;

   // Do something with the entry
```

```
   // Free up the row memory
   MAPIFreeBuffer(pRowSet->aRow);
   MAPIFreeBuffer(pRowSet);
   break;
}
```

When making a query to a MAPI table, you will be returned the default properties (columns) appropriate for the table type. If you want to specify any additional columns, or apply a specific sort order to them, you can call the `IMAPITable::SetColumns()` function before calling `IMAPITable::QueryRows()`. The function is defined as follows:

```
HRESULT IMAPITable::SetColumns(LPSPropTagArray
  lpPropTagArray, ULONG ulFlags);
```

The first parameter is a pointer to an array of the property tags (columns) that you want to return when you call into `IMAPITable::QueryRows()`, and cannot be set to a `NULL` value. The order of the properties that you are returned in `SRowSet` will reflect the order specified in `lpPropTagArray`.

The `ulFlags` parameter is not used and must be set to 0.

For example, if you wanted to retrieve both the display name and the entry identifier columns from the message store table, you would do the following:

```
IMAPITable *pIMapiStoresTable = NULL;
hr = pIMapi->GetMsgStoresTable(0, &pIMapiStoresTable);
while(1) {
   SRowSet *pRowSet = NULL;
   SizedSPropTagArray(2, tblColumns) = {2,
       {PR_DISPLAY_NAME,PR_ENTRYID}};
   pIMapiStoresTable->SetColumns((LPSPropTagArray)
       &tblColumns, 0);

   hr = pIMapiStoresTable->QueryRows(1, 0, &pRowSet);
   if(pRowSet->cRows != 1)
      break;

   // Do something with the entry (such as print out the
   // name)
   OutputDebugString
      (pRowSet->aRow[0].lpProps[0].Value.lpszW);
```

```
    // Free up the row memory
    MAPIFreeBuffer(pRowSet->aRow);
    MAPIFreeBuffer(pRowSet);
    break;
}
```

Table Cursor Position

As previously mentioned, MAPI tables use a *cursor* to track the current position within a table. To determine your current location in the table at any given time, you can use the `IMAPITable::QueryPosition()` function:

```
HRESULT IMAPITable::QueryPosition(ULONG *lpulRow, ULONG
    *lpulNumerator, ULONG *lpulDenominator);
```

The first parameter, `lpulRow`, points to the number of the current row (tables begin at 0). The `lpulNumerator` and `lpulDenominator` parameters are used to calculate a fractional position in the table that can be used to set scroll bar positions. For example, if the `lpulNumerator` parameter returns a value of 5 and the `lpulDenominator` parameter returns a value of 25, you know you are 5/25ths or one-fifth of the way through the table.

To move the cursor to a specific location in the table, you can use the `IMAPITable::SeekRow()` function, which is defined as follows:

```
HRESULT IMAPITable::SeekRow(BOOKMARK bkOrigin, LONG
    lRowCount, LONG *lplRowsSought);
```

The first parameter, `bkOrigin`, must be set to `BOOKMARK_BEGINNING`, which will start moving the cursor from the beginning of the table. The `lRowCount` parameter specifies the number of rows to move the cursor ahead. The last parameter, `lplRowsSought`, is unused and should be set to 0.

MAPI Object Memory Allocation

When writing applications that use MAPI, it is important to use some new memory functions that MAPI provides to allocate and free memory that is used by MAPI and your application. The primary reason that

MAPI provides new memory allocation functions is to eliminate the issue of "who" releases memory—the client application or the MAPI session. For example, when you request an `SRowSet` from a MAPI Table, MAPI automatically allocates the necessary memory to hold the row data. To free it properly, the client needs to call the `MAPIFreeBuffer()` function. If you are passing data to MAPI, if it has been allocated by using the `MAPIAllocateBuffer()` function, MAPI can automatically allocate more memory or release it when it is finished using it.

Use the following to allocate a buffer that MAPI can use:

```
SCODE MAPIAllocateBuffer(ULONG cbSize, LPVOID *lppBuffer);
```

The first parameter, `cbSize`, specifies the size of the memory allocation. The `lppBuffer` parameter will point to a newly allocated buffer when the function returns.

To free a memory buffer that was allocated by MAPI (by a call to `MAPIAllocateBuffer()`), you can use the following function:

```
ULONG MAPIFreeBuffer(LPVOID lpBuffer);
```

The only parameter the function requires is a pointer to the buffer to be freed.

If a buffer is not large enough, and you need to allocate additional memory, you can use the `MAPIAllocateMore()` function. It has the following prototype:

```
SCODE MAPIAllocateMore(ULONG cbSize, LPVOID lpObject,
    LPVOID *lppBuffer);
```

The first parameter, `cbSize`, specifies the size, in bytes, of the new buffer. The `lpObject` parameter should point to a buffer that was previously allocated by the `MAPIAllocateBuffer()` function. Finally, the `lppBuffer` parameter will point to a newly allocated buffer when the function returns.

When freeing the memory for an object that has used the `MAPIAllocateMore()` function, you should use the pointer that was passed into the `lpObject` parameter when calling `MAPIFreeBuffer()`, as the buffers are automatically linked together by MAPI.

Finally, when working with MAPI tables, you can use the `FreeProws()` function to free the memory that was allocated for an `SRowSet` structure. Because MAPI will internally use `MAPIAllocateBuffer()`

for each `SRow` structure, the `FreeProws()` structure will automatically walk through each `SRow` and call `MAPIFreeBuffer()` on it:

```
void FreeProws(LPSRowSet prows);
```

The only parameter the function takes is a pointer to an `SRowSet` structure.

MAPI Session Handling

Before you can access any of the MAPI objects or any part of the messaging subsystem, you first need to establish a MAPI **session**, which is a managed link between a client application and the rest of the MAPI components. After you have initialized and logged into MAPI, you are returned a pointer to an object that implements the `IMAPISession` interface, which can then be used to access messages, folders, and other objects in the MAPI message stores. You also need to use the `IMAPISession` interface to log out of MAPI when you have finished using it.

The `IMAPISession` interface implements the methods described in Table 11.13.

Table 11.13 `IMapiSession` Methods

Method	Description
`Advise()`	Sets up an `IMAPIAdviseSink` interface that will receive notification events for the session.
`CompareEntryIDs()`	Compares two `ENTRYID` structures to see if they are the same.
`GetMsgStoresTable()`	Returns an `IMAPITable` interface for the table. This interface lists the message stores that are installed on the device.
`Logoff()`	Ends a MAPI session.
`OpenEntry()`	Returns an interface for a specific MAPI object based on its `ENTRYID`.
`OpenMsgStore()`	Returns an `IMsgStore` interface for a specific message store.
`Unadvise()`	Cancels a notification event sink that was set up with a previous call to `IMAPISession::Advise()`.

To get the pointer to the `IMAPISession` interface, you cannot simply call into the `CoCreateInstance()` function to instantiate a new session object. Instead, you must properly initialize MAPI by first calling into the `MAPIInitialize()` function:

```
HRESULT MAPIInitialize(LPVOID lpMapiInit);
```

The `lpMapiInit` parameter is ignored on the Pocket PC.

After MAPI has been initialized, you need to log on to the messaging subsystem by calling into the `MAPILogonEx()` function. This will return to you a pointer to the MAPI session interface that you then use to access the rest of the MAPI objects:

```
HRESULT MAPILogonEx(ULONG ulUIParam, LPTSTR lpszProfileName,
   LPTSTR lpszPassword, FLAGS flFlags,
   LPMAPISESSION FAR *lppSession);
```

All of the parameters for `MAPILogonEx()` are unused, except for the `lppSession` parameter, which points to the `IMAPISession` interface pointer when the function returns.

The following code shows how you use `MAPILogonEx()` to get the pointer to an `IMAPISession` object:

```
HRESULT hr = S_OK;

// Initialize COM
if(FAILED(CoInitializeEx(NULL, 0)))
   return FALSE;

// Initialize and log on to MAPI
IMAPISession *pIMapi = NULL;

if(MAPIInitialize(NULL) != S_OK)
   return FALSE;

if(MAPILogonEx(0, NULL, NULL, 0, &pIMapi) != S_OK) {
   MAPIUninitialize();
   return FALSE;
}

// MAPI is ready, now do something with it...
```

When you are finished using MAPI, it is important to remember to properly close the MAPI session in order for the e-mail subsystem to clean up memory and free up any resources that it is using. Before you log off the current session, you should make sure that any MAPI objects that have been instantiated have already called into their IUnknown:: Release() method. In addition, any memory allocations made with the MAPIAllocateBuffer() function should be freed by calling into MAPIFreeBuffer().

After you are sure that all of the MAPI objects have been properly cleaned up, you can use the IMAPISession::Logoff() function, which has the following prototype:

```
HRESULT IMAPISession::Logoff(ULONG ulUIParam, ULONG ulFlags,
    ULONG ulReserved);
```

On Pocket PC, all of the parameters should be set to 0.

Finally, to free any additional resources, use the MAPI Uninitialize() function to end your MAPI session:

```
HRESULT MAPIUninitialize();
```

Cleaning up from a MAPI session is relatively straightforward:

```
// Cleanup
if(pIMapi) {
   pIMapi->Logoff(0, 0, 0);
   pIMapi->Release();
   pIMapi = NULL;
}

MAPIUninitialize();
return TRUE;
```

Accessing MAPI Objects

Now that you have successfully logged into a MAPI session, you can start working with the various objects in the messaging subsystem. Let's take a quick look at how you can get the interface pointer to a few of the MAPI objects that are described in the remainder of this chapter.

To get the MAPI table of the message stores that have been installed and are available on the device, you can use the following function:

```
HRESULT IMAPISession::GetMsgStoresTable(ULONG ulFlags,
    LPMAPITABLE *lppTable);
```

The first parameter, `ulFlags`, is unused and should be set to 0. The `lppTable` parameter will point to an `IMAPITable` interface that contains the list of available message stores.

If you already have the `ENTRYID` for a particular message store that you want to open, use the `IMAPISession::OpenMsgStore()` function:

```
HRESULT IMAPISession::OpenMsgStore(ULONG ulUIParam, ULONG
  cbEntryID, LPENTRYID lpEntryID, LPCIID lpInterface, ULONG
  ulFlags, LPMDB *lppMDB);
```

The `ulUIParam`, `lpInterface`, and `ulFlags` parameters are ignored and should be set to 0. The `ENTRYID` of the message store that you want to open should be set by the `lpEntryID` parameter, and the `cbEntryID` parameter is used to set its size. Finally, the `lppMDB` parameter will point to the `IMsgStore` interface when the function returns. If you set the `lpEntryID` parameter to `NULL`, the default store (ActiveSync) will be opened.

Finally, to get the interface pointer for any MAPI object that has an `ENTRYID`, use the `IMAPISession::OpenEntry()` function:

```
HRESULT IMAPISession::OpenEntry(ULONG cbEntryID, LPENTRYID
  lpEntryID, LPCIID lpInterface, ULONG ulFlags, ULONG
  *lpulObjType, LPUNKNOWN *lppUnk);
```

The first parameter, `cbEntryID`, should specify the number of bytes of the `ENTRYID`. The `lpEntryID` parameter points to the actual `ENTRYID` that you want to open. The `lpInterface` parameter is used to point to an interface identifier for the interface that you are trying to open. If this is set to `NULL`, you will be returned the default interface for the object type (for example, opening a MAPI message object will return an `IMessage` interface pointer).

When the function returns, the `lpUlObjType` parameter will point to the object type that was opened. Because this is an optional parameter, it can also be set to `NULL` if you are not interested in the type information. The last parameter, `lppUnk`, gets the interface pointer for the `ENTRYID` that was specified in `lpEntryID`.

Remember that you need to call into the object's `IUnknown::Release()` method when you have completed using it.

Working with Message Stores

A message store is the "root" object that will be used by MAPI for a specific mail transport instance. Pocket PC contains a default message store that is used by ActiveSync when you synchronize with a connected desktop, and additional message stores are created automatically whenever a new MAPI transport is configured on the device. For example, when you create a new connection to a POP3 mail server, a new message store is created to handle the MAPI objects related to that connection.

Each message store provides the storage mechanism as well as the hierarchy model for objects contained within it. This includes all of the tables, messages, folders, and attachments for a specific mail configuration.

The MAPI message store object is implemented by the `IMsgStore` interface, and supports the methods described in Table 11.14.

Table 11.14 `IMsgStore` Methods

Method	Description
Advise()	Sets up an IMAPIAdviseSink interface that receives notification events for the message store
GetReceiveFolder()	Returns the ENTRYID for the folder that was specified to receive incoming messages
OpenEntry()	Returns an interface for a specific MAPI object based on its ENTRYID
Unadvise()	Cancels a notification event sink that was set up with a previous call to IMsgStore::Advise()

The `IMsgStore` interface is derived from `IMAPIProp`, and supports the properties described in Table 11.15 for each message store.

Table 11.15 `IMsgStore` Properties

Property Tag	Property Type	Description
PR_CE_IPM_DRAFTS_ENTRYID	PT_BINARY	The entry identifier for the Drafts folder
PR_CE_IPM_INBOX_ENTRYID	PT_BINARY	The entry identifier for the Inbox folder

Property Tag	Property Type	Description
PR_DISPLAYNAME	PT_TSTRING	The display name of the object
PR_ENTRYID	PT_BINARY	The object's entry identifier
PR_IPM_OUTBOX_ENTRYID	PT_BINARY	The entry identifier for the Outbox folder of the store
PR_IPM_SENTMAIL_ENTRYID	PT_BINARY	The entry identifier for the Sent Items folder of the store
PR_IPM_SUBTREE_ENTRYID	PT_BINARY	The entry identifier for the root folder of the store
PR_IPM_WASTEBASKET_ENTRYID	PT_BINARY	The entry identifier for the Deleted Items folder of the store
PR_LAST_MODIFICATION_TIME	PT_SYSTIME	The last date and time the object was modified
PR_NULL	PT_NULL	A NULL value
PR_OBJECT_TYPE	PT_LONG	The type of object

To open a specific message store, you need to use the IMAPI Session::OpenMsgStore() function and provide it with the ENTRYID of the store you want to use. Because the ENTRYID might not be persistent (depending on the message store), you will usually have to get the table of message stores from the current MAPI session first, and look for the entry you are interested in. This can be accomplished by using the IMAPISession::GetMsgStoresTable() function.

The following example shows how you can open a message store that has the name POP3. This requires you to perform several actions to find the proper ENTRYID for the message store you are interested in:

```
// Open up the POP3 inbox by getting a list of message
// Stores
IMAPITable *pIMapiStoresTable = NULL;

hr = pIMapi->GetMsgStoresTable(0, &pIMapiStoresTable);
if(FAILED(hr))
    return FALSE;

// Query the table. We need the ENTRY_ID and DISPLAY_NAME
// for the store
IMsgStore *pPop3Store = NULL;
```

```
while(1) {
    SRowSet *pRowSet = NULL;

    SizedSPropTagArray(2, tblColumns) = {2,{PR_DISPLAY_NAME,
        PR_ENTRYID}};
    pIMapiStoresTable->SetColumns((LPSPropTagArray)
        &tblColumns, 0);
    hr = pIMapiStoresTable->QueryRows(1, 0, &pRowSet);

    if(pRowSet->cRows != 1)
        break;

    // Compare the name with "POP3"
    if(_tcscmp(TEXT("POP3"),
        pRowSet->aRow[0].lpProps[0].Value.lpszW) == 0) {
        ENTRYID *pEntry = (ENTRYID *)pRowSet->aRow[0].
            lpProps[1].Value.bin.lpb;
        ULONG ulStoreBytes = pRowSet->aRow[0].lpProps[1].
            Value.bin.cb;

        hr = pIMapi->OpenMsgStore(NULL, ulStoreBytes, pEntry,
            NULL, NULL, &pPop3Store);

        MAPIFreeBuffer(pRowSet->aRow);
        MAPIFreeBuffer(pRowSet);
        break;
    }

    // Free buffers allocated by MAPI
    MAPIFreeBuffer(pRowSet->aRow);
    MAPIFreeBuffer(pRowSet);
};

// Did it open?
if(!pIMapi)
    return FALSE;

// Open the Inbox folder
LPSPropValue rgprops = NULL;
LPSPropValue lppPropArray = NULL;
ULONG cValues = 0;
IMAPIFolder *pPOPInboxFolder = NULL;
SizedSPropTagArray(2, rgTags) =
    {2,{PR_CE_IPM_INBOX_ENTRYID,PR_OBJECT_TYPE}};
```

```
// Now get the Inbox folder.
hr = pPop3Store->GetProps((LPSPropTagArray)&rgTags,
  MAPI_UNICODE, &cValues, &rgprops);
if(FAILED(hr)) {
   // Remember to clean up
   return FALSE;
}

hr = pPop3Store->OpenEntry(rgprops[0].Value.bin.cb,
   (LPENTRYID)rgprops[0].Value.bin.lpb, NULL, MAPI_MODIFY,
   NULL, (LPUNKNOWN*)&pPOPInboxFolder);

// pPOPInboxFolder should now point to the inbox..
```

As you can see from the example, after you have logged into a MAPI session, you call into the `IMAPISession::GetMsgStoresTable()` function to get the list of available stores on the device. Because you are interested only in the store name and its entry identifier, you set the columns that you need by using the `IMAPITable::SetColumns()` function to return only the PR_DISPLAY_NAME and PR_ENTRYID properties. Next, you use the `IMAPITable::QueryRows()` function on the returned message store table to return a single object at a time.

After the object data has been returned to you, you can check the entry to see if it is the POP3 message store. Once you find it, you can use the ENTRYID to open the proper message store by using either the `IMsgStore::OpenEntry()` or `IMAPISession::OpenEntry()` functions.

MAPI Folders

The MAPI folder object is used to organize both messages and subfolders in a message store. Each message store will typically contain at least five folders that are commonly used: Deleted Items, Drafts, Inbox, Outbox, and Sent Items. Every folder in the message store implements the `IMAPIFolder` interface, which can be used to create new messages, as well as copy and delete them. In addition, you can use `IMAPIFolder` to manage any subfolders.

Because a MAPI folder can contain objects that have multiple sub-folders, or hierarchy, management of the tables supported in the folder object is handled by the `IMAPIContainer` interface, from which all `IMAPIFolder` objects are derived.

The `IMAPIContainer` interface supports the methods described in Table 11.16.

Table 11.16 `IMAPIContainer` Methods

Method	Description
GetContentsTable()	Returns an `IMAPITable` interface for a table that lists the contents of the container
GetHierarchyTable()	Returns an `IMAPITable` interface for a table that lists the container's hierarchy table
OpenEntry()	Returns an interface for a specific MAPI object based on its `ENTRYID`

As you can see, two different types of tables are available to a client application from the `IMAPIContainer` interface. **Contents tables** are used to return data about the objects contained within the current folder, and **hierarchy tables** are used only to return data about child objects within the current folder.

More specifically, if you wanted to get a table of the messages in a folder, you would use the `IMAPIContainer::GetContentsTable()` function. To get a list of subfolders for the current folder, you would use `IMAPIContainer::GetHierarchyTable()` instead.

The `IMAPIContainer` object is also derived from `IMAPIProp`, and supports the properties described in Table 11.17.

Table 11.17 `IMAPIContainer` Properties

Property Tag	Property Type	Description
PR_DISPLAYNAME	PT_TSTRING	The display name of the object
PR_ENTRYID	PT_BINARY	The object's entry identifier
PR_LAST_MODIFICATION_ TIME	PT_SYSTIME	The last date and time the object was modified
PR_NULL	PT_NULL	A NULL value
PR_OBJECT_TYPE	PT_LONG	The type of object
PR_PARENT_ENTRYID	PT_BINARY	The parent object's entry identifier

The `IMAPIFolder` interface supports the methods described in Table 11.18.

Table 11.18 `IMAPIFolder` Methods

Method	Description
CopyFolder()	Copies or moves a folder
CopyMessages()	Copies or moves messages
CreateFolder()	Creates a new subfolder and returns a new `IMAPIFolder` interface
CreateMessage()	Creates a new message and returns a new `IMessage` interface
DeleteFolder()	Deletes a subfolder
DeleteMessages()	Deletes a message

In order to get the interface pointer for a specific MAPI folder object, you need to determine the `ENTRYID` for the folder to be used with the `IMsgStore::OpenEntry()` function.

One way to get the table of the folders in a message store is to use the `IMAPIProp::GetProps()` function on the message store to get the `ENTRYID` for the root object (using the `PR_IPM_SUBTREE_ENTRYID` property):

```
// After we have the pointer to the store we are interested
// in (pPop3Store) get the PR_IPM_SUBTREE_ENTRYID to get the
// entry identifer for the root folder.
LPSPropValue rgStoreProps = NULL;
ULONG cStoreValues = 0;
IMAPIFolder *pPOPRootFolder = NULL;
SizedSPropTagArray(2, rgStoreTags) = {2,{PR_IPM_SUBTREE_
  ENTRYID, PR_OBJECT_TYPE}};

// Now get the root folder.
hr = pPop3Store->GetProps((LPSPropTagArray)&rgStoreTags,
  MAPI_UNICODE, &cStoreValues, &rgStoreProps);
if(FAILED(hr))
   return FALSE;
```

```
hr = pPop3Store->OpenEntry(rgStoreProps[0].Value.bin.cb,
   (LPENTRYID)rgStoreProps[0].Value.bin.lpb, NULL,
       MAPI_MODIFY, NULL, (LPUNKNOWN*)&pPOPRootFolder);
if(FAILED(hr))
   return FALSE;

// Get the hierarchy table to get the entry identifier and
// name of each folder.
IMAPITable *pIFoldersTable = NULL;
hr = pPOPRootFolder->GetHierarchyTable(0, &pIFoldersTable);

while(1) {
   SRowSet *pRowSet = NULL;

   SizedSPropTagArray(2, tblColumns) = {2,{PR_DISPLAY_NAME,
       PR_ENTRYID}};
   pIFoldersTable->SetColumns((LPSPropTagArray)&tblColumns, 0);
   hr = pIFoldersTable->QueryRows(1, 0, &pRowSet);

   if(pRowSet->cRows != 1)
      break;

   // Do something, such as display the name
   OutputDebugString(pRowSet->aRow[0].lpProps[0].Value.lpszW);

   // Free buffers allocated by MAPI
   FreeProws(pRowSet);
};
```

The message store object on Pocket PC also supports properties that can be used to specify any of the following standard folders:

- PM_IPM_OUTBOX_ENTRYID, for the Outbox folder
- PM_IPM_SENTMAIL_ENTRYID, for the Sent Items folder
- PM_IPM_WASTEBASKET_ENTRYID, for the Deleted Items folder
- PM_CE_IPM_DRAFTS_ENTRYID, for the Drafts folder
- PM_CE_IPM_INBOX_ENTRYID, for the Inbox folder

Once you have the pointer to the IMAPIFolder interface that you are interested in, you can then perform any operations on the folder, such as creating a new message, copying a message, or even creating a new subfolder.

To get a list of the subfolders for a particular folder object, you can use the `IMAPIContainer::GetHierarchyTable()` function:

```
HRESULT IMAPIContainer::GetHierarchyTable(ULONG ulFlags,
    LPMAPITABLE *lppTable);
```

The first parameter is ignored and can be set to 0. The `lppTable` parameter will point to a new `IMAPITable` interface when the function returns.

Messages

MAPI Message objects are contained in folders that are part of a message store, each representing an individual e-mail message. The messaging system provides you with complete functionality to create, send, read, move, and delete messages. In addition to the actual message body, an e-mail message can have one or more attachments associated with it. An attachment is a *blob* of binary data, such as a picture or sound file that is transmitted as part of the message.

Messages in MAPI are represented by the `IMessage` interface, which supports the methods described in Table 11.19.

Table 11.19 `IMessage` Methods

Method	Description
`CreateAttach()`	Creates a new message attachment and returns a new `IAttach` interface
`DeleteAttach()`	Deletes a message attachment
`GetAttachmentTable()`	Returns an `IMAPITable` interface that represents the message attachments
`GetRecipientTable()`	Returns an `IMAPITable` interface that represents the message recipients
`ModifyRecipients()`	Replaces the message recipient address list with a new one
`OpenAttach()`	Opens a message attachment and returns its `IAttach` interface
`SubmitMessage()`	Saves all changes and marks the message to be sent by the message transport

The `IMessage` interface is also derived from the `IMAPIProp` interface and supports the properties described in Table 11.20.

Table 11.20   `IMessage` Properties

Property Tag	Property Type	Description
PR_ADDRTYPE	PT_TSTRING	The e-mail address type. SMTP is currently the only address type supported on Pocket PC.
PR_BODY	PT_TSTRING	The body of the e-mail message.
PR_CE_XHEADERS	PT_TSTRING	The entire string of the message x-headers.
PR_CONTENT_LENGTH_EX	PT_LONG	The full size of the message on the server.
PR_EMAIL_ADDRESS	PT_TSTRING	The actual e-mail address.
PR_ENTRYID	PT_BINARY	The object's entry identifier.
PR_HASATTACH	PT_BOOLEAN	Specifies whether the e-mail message has an attachment table.
PR_LAST_ MODIFICATION_TIME	PT_SYSTIME	The last date and time the object was modified.
PR_MESSAGE_CLASS	PT_TSTRING	The type of message.
PR_MESSAGE_DELIVERY_ TIME	PT_SYSTIME	The date and time that the message was delivered.
PR_MESSAGE_FLAGS	PT_LONG	Flags for the message. Can be set to MSGFLAG_READ to mark the message as read, or MSGFLAG_UNSENT to specify that the message is being written.
PR_MESSAGE_SIZE	PT_LONG	The size of the entire message, including headers and attachments.
PR_NULL	PT_NULL	A null value.
PR_OBJECT_TYPE	PT_LONG	The type of object.
PR_PARENT_ENTRYID	PT_BINARY	The parent object's entry identifier.
PR_SENDER_EMAIL_ ADDRESS	PT_TSTRING	E-mail address of the sender of the message.
PR_SENDER_NAME	PT_TSTRING	Name of the sender of the message.
PR_SUBJECT	PT_TSTRING	Subject of the message.
PR_SUBJECT_PREFIX	PT_TSTRING	Prefix of the message subject, such as Re: for a reply, or Fw: for a forwarded e-mail message.

To retrieve a list of messages stored in a particular folder, get the folder's content table using the `IMAPIContainer::GetContents Table()` function, which is defined as follows:

```
HRESULT IMAPIContainer::GetContentsTable(ULONG ulFlags,
    LPMAPITABLE *lppTable);
```

The first parameter is ignored and should be set to 0. The `lppTable` parameter will point to the MAPI table interface for the list of messages.

As with any other MAPI object, you can get the interface pointer to an individual message by using the `IMAPIContainer::OpenEntry()` function once you have its `ENTRYID` property.

Message Address Lists

Every e-mail message, whether incoming or outgoing, needs a list of recipients for whom the message is intended. This includes both new messages that you are creating (using the `IMAPIFolder::Create Message()` function) and messages that already exist (by getting the pointer to the `IMessage` interface using the `IMAPIContainer::Open Entry()` function). Either way, once you have the pointer to an `IMessage` interface, you can use the `IMessage::ModifyRecipients()` and `IMessage::GetRecipientTable()` functions to add or manipulate message recipients.

Message recipients are stored in MAPI using the `ADRLIST` structure, which contains an array of `ADRENTRY` structures. It is defined as follows:

```
typedef struct _ADRLIST {
    ULONG cEntries;
    ADRENTRY aEntries[MAPI_DIM];
} ADRLIST, FAR *LPADRLIST;
```

The `cEntries` field contains the number of `ADRENTRY` structures in the array, specified by the `aEntries` field.

An `ADRENTRY` structure contains a list of properties that belong to a recipient. Typically, when creating an e-mail recipient, you need to configure only the `PR_ADDRTYPE` and `PR_EMAIL_ADDRESS` properties. The structure has the following definition:

```
typedef struct _ADRENTRY {
    ULONG ulReserved1;
    ULONG cValues;
    LPSPropValue rgPropVals;
} ADRENTRY, FAR *LPADRENTRY;
```

The first field, `ulReserved1`, is not used and must be set to 0. The `cValues` field contains the number of property values that are specified in `rgPropVals`. The `rgPropVals` field points to an `SPropValue` array that contains the property values for the specific recipient.

Table 11.21 describes the macros that MAPI provides to help you efficiently work with the `ADRLIST` structure.

Table 11.21 `ADRLIST` Macro Functions

Macro	Description
`CbADRLIST(_lpadrlist)`	Calculates the number of bytes of an existing `ADRLIST` structure
`CbNewADRLIST (_centries)`	Calculates the number of bytes for a new `ADRLIST` structure
`SizedADRLIST(_centries, _name)`	Creates a named `ADRLIST` structure for a specific number of `ADRENTRY` structures

Common Tasks with MAPI

Now that you have looked at all of the basic interfaces for working with the various MAPI objects, let's take a more detailed look at how you can use them to perform specific tasks with e-mail.

Opening a Message Store

1. Initialize and log into a MAPI session.
2. Get the pointer to the table of message stores from the MAPI session object.
3. Search the table based on the display name matching the store you want to open.
4. Open the message store.

The following sample shows how to open a message store:

```
HRESULT hr = S_OK;

/////////////////////////////////////////////
// Step 1 - Initialize COM/MAPI, and log on
IMAPISession *pIMapi = NULL;
if(FAILED(CoInitializeEx(NULL, 0)))
    return FALSE;
```

```
if(MAPIInitialize(NULL) != S_OK)
   return FALSE;

if(MAPILogonEx(0, NULL, NULL, 0, &pIMapi) != S_OK) {
   MAPIUninitialize();
   return FALSE;
}

//////////////////////////////////////////////////
// Step 2 - Get the pointer to the Message Store Table
IMAPITable *pIMapiStoresTable = NULL;
hr = pIMapi->GetMsgStoresTable(0, &pIMapiStoresTable);
if(FAILED(hr)) {
   pIMapi->Logoff(0, 0, 0);
   pIMapi->Release();
   pIMapi = NULL;
   MAPIUninitialize();
   return FALSE;
}

/////////////////////////////////////////////////////////
// Step 3 - Query the table for the entry that matches the
// name of the store we are interested in.
IMsgStore *pPop3Store = NULL;
while(1) {
   SRowSet *pRowSet = NULL;

   SizedSPropTagArray(2, tblColumns) = {2,{PR_DISPLAY_NAME,
      PR_ENTRYID}};
   pIMapiStoresTable->SetColumns((LPSPropTagArray)
      &tblColumns, 0);
   hr = pIMapiStoresTable->QueryRows(1, 0, &pRowSet);
   if(FAILED(hr))
      break;

   if(pRowSet->cRows != 1)
      break;

/////////////////////////////////////////////////////////
// Step 4 - Compare the name with "POP3". If it's a
// match, open it
if(_tcscmp(TEXT("POP3"), pRowSet->aRow[0].lpProps[0].
  Value.lpszW) == 0) {ENTRYID *pEntry =
      (ENTRYID *) pRowSet->aRow[0].lpProps[1].Value.bin.lpb;
```

```
        ULONG ulStoreBytes =
            pRowSet->aRow[0].lpProps[1].Value.bin.cb;

        pIMapi->OpenMsgStore(NULL, ulStoreBytes, pEntry, NULL,
            NULL, &pPop3Store);
        FreeProws(pRowSet);
        break;
    }

    // Free buffers allocated by MAPI
    FreeProws(pRowSet);
};

// Clean up the store table
pIMapiStoresTable->Release();

// Make sure we opened the store
if(!pPop3Store) {
    pIMapi->Logoff(0, 0, 0);
    pIMapi->Release();
    pIMapi = NULL;

    MAPIUninitialize();
    return FALSE;
}

// Do something now..
```

Creating a New Message

1. Open a MAPI message store that will be used to contain the new message. See "Opening a Message Store" for details.
2. Open the Drafts folder.
3. Create a new message using the `IMAPIFolder::Create Message()` function.
4. Add the subject and the message flags to the message using the `IMessage::SetProps()` function.
5. Add the message body by using the `IMessage::Open Property()` function to get the `IStream` interface that you can write the message to.

6. Create a recipient list.

7. Call `IMessage::SubmitMessage()` to move the message from the Drafts folder to the Outbox. The next time the message store is synchronized, the message will be sent.

The following sample shows how to create a new message:

```
/////////////////////////////////////
// Step 2 - Open up the Pop3 Drafts folder
LPSPropValue rgprops = NULL;
LPSPropValue lppPropArray = NULL;
ULONG cValues = 0;
IMAPIFolder *pPOPDraftsFolder = NULL;
SizedSPropTagArray(2, rgTags) =
    {2,{PR_CE_IPM_DRAFTS_ENTRYID,PR_OBJECT_TYPE}};

// Now get the Drafts folder
hr = pPop3Store->GetProps((LPSPropTagArray)&rgTags,
  MAPI_UNICODE, &cValues, &rgprops);
if(FAILED(hr))
   return FALSE;

hr = pPop3Store->OpenEntry(rgprops[0].Value.bin.cb,
    (LPENTRYID)rgprops[0].Value.bin.lpb, NULL, MAPI_MODIFY,
    NULL, (LPUNKNOWN*)&pPOPDraftsFolder);
if(FAILED(hr))
   return FALSE;

/////////////////////////////////////
// Step 3 - Create a new message object
IMessage *pNewMessage = NULL;

hr = pPOPDraftsFolder->CreateMessage(NULL, 0, &pNewMessage);
if(FAILED(hr))
   return FALSE;

/////////////////////////////////////
// Step 4 - Add a subject and message flags
SPropValue sMsgProps[2];
TCHAR tchSubject[128] = TEXT("\0");

memset(&sMsgProps, 0, sizeof(sMsgProps));
```

```
wsprintf(tchSubject, TEXT("Test Message Subject"));

sMsgProps[0].ulPropTag = PR_MESSAGE_FLAGS;
sMsgProps[0].Value.ul = MSGFLAG_UNSENT;
sMsgProps[1].ulPropTag = PR_SUBJECT;
sMsgProps[1].Value.lpszW = tchSubject;

hr = pNewMessage->SetProps(2, sMsgProps, NULL);
if(FAILED(hr)) {
   pNewMessage->Release();
   return FALSE;
}

//////////////////////////////////////
// Step 5 - Stream the message body
IStream *pStream = NULL;
TCHAR tchBody[255] = TEXT("\0");

wsprintf(tchBody, TEXT("This is a test of the message body"));

hr = pNewMessage->OpenProperty(PR_BODY, NULL, 0,
   MAPI_CREATE|MAPI_MODIFY, (IUnknown **)&pStream);
if(FAILED(hr)) {
   pNewMessage->Release();
   return FALSE;
}

// Copy the body into the stream
DWORD dwLength = (lstrlen(tchBody)+1)*sizeof(TCHAR);
pStream->Write(tchBody, dwLength, NULL);
pStream->Release();

//////////////////////////////////////
// Step 6 - Create a recipient list
SizedADRLIST(1, msgAdrList);

// Allocate a buffer for the entry
SPropValue rgMsgProps[3];

memset(&rgMsgProps, 0, sizeof(rgMsgProps));

rgMsgProps[0].ulPropTag = PR_ADDRTYPE;
rgMsgProps[0].Value.lpszW = TEXT("SMTP");
```

```
rgMsgProps[1].ulPropTag = PR_EMAIL_ADDRESS;
rgMsgProps[1].Value.lpszW =
    TEXT("emailname@emailaddress.com");

rgMsgProps[2].ulPropTag = PR_RECIPIENT_TYPE;
rgMsgProps[2].Value.ul = MAPI_TO;

msgAdrList.cEntries = 1;
msgAdrList.aEntries->cValues = 3;
msgAdrList.aEntries->rgPropVals = rgMsgProps;

// Add the list to the message
hr = pNewMessage->ModifyRecipients(MODRECIP_ADD,
    (LPADRLIST)&msgAdrList);

// Free the buffer
MAPIFreeBuffer((LPADRLIST)&msgAdrList);

////////////////////////////////////////
// Step 7 - Submit the message
hr = pNewMessage->SubmitMessage(0);
if(FAILED(hr))
    return FALSE;

// Clean up
pNewMessage->Release();
pPOPDraftsFolder->Release();
pPop3Store->Release();
```

Reading a Message

1. Open a MAPI message store that contains the message you want to read. See "Opening a Message Store" for details.
2. Open the Inbox folder.
3. Get the table of messages in the Inbox folder.
4. Open the first message by using the `IMsgStore::OpenEntry()` function with the `ENTRYID` of the message you want to open.
5. Open the message and retrieve its properties for display.

To read the contents of a message, you would do the following:

```
////////////////////////////////////////
// Step 2 - Open up the Pop3 Inbox folder
LPSPropValue rgprops = NULL;
```

```
ULONG cValues = 0;
IMAPIFolder *pPOPInboxFolder = NULL;
SizedSPropTagArray(2, rgTags) =
    {2,{PR_CE_IPM_INBOX_ENTRYID,PR_OBJECT_TYPE}};

// Now get the Inbox folder
hr = pPop3Store->GetProps((LPSPropTagArray)&rgTags,
  MAPI_UNICODE, &cValues, &rgprops);
if(FAILED(hr))
   return FALSE;

hr = pPop3Store->OpenEntry(rgprops[0].Value.bin.cb,
    (LPENTRYID)rgprops[0].Value.bin.lpb, NULL, MAPI_MODIFY,
    NULL, (LPUNKNOWN*)&pPOPInboxFolder);
if(FAILED(hr))
   return FALSE;

/////////////////////////////////////////////////////////////
// Step 3 - Get the list of messages in the folder and their
// ENTRY IDs
IMAPITable *pIInboxTable = NULL;
IMessage *pMsg = NULL;
hr = pPOPInboxFolder->GetContentsTable(0, &pIInboxTable);

if(FAILED(hr)) {
   pPOPInboxFolder->Release();
   return FALSE;
}

while(1) {
   SRowSet *pRowSet = NULL;

   // Get the From, Subject and ID fields
   SizedSPropTagArray(3, tblMessages) =
       {3,{PR_SENDER_NAME,PR_SUBJECT,PR_ENTRYID}};
   pIInboxTable->SetColumns((LPSPropTagArray)&tblMessages, 0);
   hr = pIInboxTable->QueryRows(1, 0, &pRowSet);

   if(pRowSet->cRows != 1)
      break;
```

```
for(int nVal = 0; nVal < pRowSet->aRow[0].cValues;
    nVal++) {
  TCHAR tchProperties[10] = TEXT("\0");
  DWORD dwType = 0, dwID = 0;

  dwType =
    PROP_TYPE(pRowSet->aRow[0].lpProps[nVal].ulPropTag);
  dwID =
    PROP_ID(pRowSet->aRow[0].lpProps[nVal].ulPropTag);
  wsprintf(tchProperties, TEXT("0x%08x Type:%04x
    ID:%04x\r\n"),
    pRowSet->aRow[0].lpProps[nVal].ulPropTag, dwType,
    dwID);

  // Do something, such as show the messages in a list?
  OutputDebugString(tchProperties);
}

/////////////////////////////////////////////////////////
// Step 4 - Open the message. For the sake of this example,
// let's open the first message and break out
hr = pPop3Store->OpenEntry
  (pRowSet->aRow[0].lpProps[2].Value.bin.cb, (LPENTRYID)
  pRowSet->aRow[0].lpProps[2].Value.bin.lpb, NULL,
  MAPI_MODIFY, NULL, (LPUNKNOWN*)&pMsg);

  FreeProws(pRowSet);
  break;
}

/////////////////////////////////////////////////////////
// Step 5 - Do something w/ the message
if(pMsg) {
  // Get the from and subject
  LPSPropValue rgMsgprops = NULL;
  ULONG cMsgValues = 0;
  SizedSPropTagArray(2, rgMsgTags) = {2,{PR_SENDER_NAME,
    PR_SUBJECT}};

  hr = pMsg->GetProps((LPSPropTagArray)&rgMsgTags,
    MAPI_UNICODE, &cMsgValues, &rgMsgprops);
```

```
// Get the body
IStream *pStream = NULL;
TCHAR tchBody[255] = TEXT("\0");

hr = pMsg->OpenProperty(PR_BODY, NULL, 0, 0,
    (IUnknown **)&pStream);
if(FAILED(hr)) {
   pMsg->Release();
   pIInboxTable->Release();
   pPOPInboxFolder->Release();
   return FALSE;
}

// Read from the stream into the tchBody
hr = pStream->Read(tchBody, 254, NULL);
pStream->Release();

// Do something with it:
TCHAR tchMsg[1024] = TEXT("\0");
wsprintf(tchMsg, TEXT("From: %s\r\nSubject: %s\r\nMsg:
   %s"), rgMsgprops[0].Value.lpszW,rgMsgprops[1].
   Value.lpszW, tchBody); MessageBox(NULL, tchMsg,
   TEXT("New Message!"), MB_OK|MB_ICONINFORMATION);

// Msg cleanup
MAPIFreeBuffer(rgMsgprops);
pMsg->Release();
}

// Cleanup
pIInboxTable->Release();
pPOPInboxFolder->Release();
```

Working with Message Attachments

Message attachments are used to send one or more additional "blobs" of data, such as a picture or sound file, along with an e-mail message. Each individual attachment to a message is supported by the IAttach interface.

Although the `IAttach` interface has no unique methods, it is derived from the `IMAPIProp` interface. Table 11.22 describes the properties that are used to configure an attachment.

Table 11.22 `IAttach` Properties

Property Tag	Property Type	Description
PR_ATTACH_DATA_BIN	PT_BINARY	`IStream` interface that can be used to access the attachment
PR_ATTACH_FILENAME	PT_TSTRING	Display name for the attachment
PR_ATTACH_METHOD	PT_LONG	Must be set to PR_ATTACH_BY_VALUE
PR_ATTACH_NUM	PT_LONG	Number that uniquely identifies the attachment within the message
PR_ATTACH_SIZE	PT_LONG	The size, in bytes, of the attachment and all of the attachment properties
PR_ENTRYID	PT_BINARY	The object's entry identifier
PR_LAST_MODIFICATION_TIME	PT_SYSTIME	The last date and time the object was modified
PR_NULL	PT_NULL	A NULL value
PR_OBJECT_TYPE	PT_LONG	The type of object
PR_PARENT_ENTRYID	PT_BINARY	The parent object's entry identifier

Creating an Attachment

1. Create a new message that will have an attachment. See the section "Creating a New Message" for details.
2. After you have completed setting up the message subject, body, and recipient list, use the `IMessage::CreateAttach()` method to get the interface pointer for a new `IAttach` object.
3. Set up the properties for the attachment. You need to configure the `PR_ATTACH_METHOD`, `PR_ATTACH_DATA_BIN`, and `PR_ATTACH_FILENAME` property tags.
4. Stream in the binary data for the file. This is accomplished by using the `IAttach::OpenProperty()` method to get the `IStream` interface for the data property. You can then use the `IStream::Write()` method to stream the data to the attachment.

5. Submit the message to the Outbox using `IMessage::Submit Message()`. This will set up the message to be sent the next time the store is synchronized.

The following example creates a message with an attachment:

```
// This is at the point where our message has been created,
// and we are about to send it. Before we do, let's attach
// a sound file to the message.

////////////////////////////////////////
// Step 2 - Attach a file to the message
IAttach *pAttach = NULL;
ULONG ulAttachNo = 0;
hr = pNewMessage->CreateAttach(NULL, 0, &ulAttachNo,
  &pAttach);

if(FAILED(hr))
   return FALSE;

//////////////////////////////////////////////////
// Step 3 - Set up the properties for the attachment
SPropValue rgAttachProps[3];
TCHAR tchFileName[MAX_PATH] = TEXT("\0");
TCHAR tchFilePath[MAX_PATH] = TEXT("\0");

wsprintf(tchFileName, TEXT("Alarm1.wav"));
wsprintf(tchFilePath, TEXT("\\Windows\\Alarm1.wav"));
memset(&rgAttachProps, 0, sizeof(rgAttachProps));

rgAttachProps[0].ulPropTag = PR_ATTACH_METHOD;
rgAttachProps[0].Value.ul = ATTACH_BY_VALUE;

// Specify that we are attaching binary data. We'll stream
// in the data using IStream below.
rgAttachProps[1].ulPropTag = PR_ATTACH_DATA_BIN;

rgAttachProps[2].ulPropTag = PR_ATTACH_FILENAME;
rgAttachProps[2].Value.lpszW = tchFileName;

hr = pAttach->SetProps(3, rgAttachProps, NULL);

//////////////////////////////////////////////////
// Step 4 - Using IStream, let's stream in the attachment data
```

```
// from the file
HANDLE hAttachFile = NULL;
IStream *pAttachStream = NULL;

// Get the pointer to the property stream
hr = pAttach->OpenProperty(PR_ATTACH_DATA_BIN, NULL, 0,
   MAPI_CREATE|MAPI_MODIFY, (IUnknown **)&pAttachStream);

// Open up the file
hAttachFile = CreateFile(tchFilePath, GENERIC_READ,
  FILE_SHARE_READ, NULL, OPEN_EXISTING, FILE_ATTRIBUTE_
     NORMAL, 0);
if(hAttachFile == INVALID_HANDLE_VALUE) {
   pAttach->Release();
   pNewMessage->Release();
   pPOPDraftsFolder->Release();
   pPop3Store->Release();
   return FALSE;
}

// Read from the file, and write it to the stream
DWORD dwRead = 0, dwWritten = 0;
LPVOID lpBuffer = NULL;

lpBuffer = (LPVOID)LocalAlloc(LPTR, 4096);
do {
   ReadFile(hAttachFile, lpBuffer, 4096, &dwRead, NULL);
   if(dwRead > 0) {
      hr = pAttachStream->Write(lpBuffer, dwRead,
         &dwWritten);
      if(FAILED(hr))
         break;
   }
}while(dwRead > 0);

CloseHandle(hAttachFile);
LocalFree(lpBuffer);

pAttachStream->Commit(STGC_DEFAULT);
pAttachStream->Release();

///////////////////////////////////////
// Step 5 - Submit the message
hr = pNewMessage->SubmitMessage(0);
```

```
if(FAILED(hr))
   return FALSE;

// Clean up
pAttach->Release();
pNewMessage->Release();
pPOPDraftsFolder->Release();
pPop3Store->Release();
```

Opening an Attachment

1. Open an IMessage interface pointer for the message that contains attachments. See "Reading a Message" for details.

2. Get the attachment table for the message using IMessage::GetAttachmentTable().

3. Query the table for the PR_ATTACH_NUM for the attachment you are interested in opening.

4. Get the properties from the table entry that you will use to open the attachment stream.

5. Using the IMessage::OpenAttach() method with the attachment number you found in the query, you can get the IAttach interface pointer.

6. Get the IStream pointer for the PR_ATTACH_DATA_BIN property. In addition, create a new file handle for the output of the data stream.

7. Read from the stream and output to the file.

The following example shows how to open a message attachment:

```
/////////////////////////////////////////////////////////
// Step 2 - Already have a message that is opened
// so, let's go ahead and get the message's attachment by
// first getting the attachment table for the message
if(!pMsg)
   return FALSE;

IMAPITable *pAttachTable = NULL;
hr = pMsg->GetAttachmentTable(0, &pAttachTable);

/////////////////////////////////////////////////////////
// Step 3 - Get the properties from the table for the
// attachments for the first attachment. We'll only extract
// the first one in this example.
```

```
SRowSet *pAttachRowSet = NULL;
SizedSPropTagArray(3, tblAttachColumns) =
   {3,{PR_ATTACH_NUM,PR_ATTACH_SIZE,PR_ATTACH_FILENAME}};

pAttachTable->SetColumns((LPSPropTagArray)&tblAttachColumns, 0);
hr = pAttachTable->QueryRows(1, 0, &pAttachRowSet);
if(pAttachRowSet->cRows != 1)
   return FALSE;

//////////////////////////////////////////////////////////
// Step 4 - Grab the properties that we'll use
long lAttachNum = 0;
DWORD dwAttachSize = 0;
TCHAR tchAttachName[MAX_PATH] = TEXT("\0");

lAttachNum = pAttachRowSet->aRow[0].lpProps[0].Value.l;
dwAttachSize = pAttachRowSet->aRow[0].lpProps[1].Value.ul;
_tcscpy(tchAttachName, pAttachRowSet->aRow[0].lpProps[2].
  Value.lpszW);

FreeProws(pAttachRowSet);

//////////////////////////////////////////////////////////
// Step 5 - Get the IAttach interface for the attachment
IAttach *pAttach = NULL;

hr = pMsg->OpenAttach(lAttachNum, 0, 0, &pAttach);
if(FAILED(hr))
   return FALSE;

//////////////////////////////////////////////////////////
// Step 6 - Get the IStream interface to stream the PR_ATTACH_
// DATA_BIN property out. Also, set up a file to write to.
IStream *pAttachStream = NULL;
HANDLE hAttachFile = NULL;
TCHAR tchFilePath[MAX_PATH] = TEXT("\0");

wsprintf(tchFilePath, TEXT("\\%s"), tchAttachName);
hAttachFile = CreateFile(tchFilePath, GENERIC_WRITE, 0, NULL,
  CREATE_ALWAYS, FILE_ATTRIBUTE_NORMAL, 0);
hr = pAttach->OpenProperty(PR_ATTACH_DATA_BIN, NULL, 0, 0,
   (IUnknown **)&pAttachStream);
```

```
if(hAttachFile == INVALID_HANDLE_VALUE || FAILED(hr)) {
   pAttachStream->Release();
   pAttach->Release();
   pAttachTable->Release();
   pMsg->Release();
   pIInboxTable->Release();
   pPOPInboxFolder->Release();
   return FALSE;
}

//////////////////////////////////////////////////////////
// Step 7 - Read from the stream, write to the file.
LPVOID lpBuffer = NULL;
DWORD dwRead = 0, dwWritten = 0;
lpBuffer = (LPVOID)LocalAlloc(LPTR, 4096);

do {
   memset(lpBuffer, 0, 4096);
   pAttachStream->Read(lpBuffer, 4096, &dwRead);
   if(dwRead > 0)
      WriteFile(hAttachFile, lpBuffer, dwRead, &dwWritten,
   NULL);
} while(dwRead > 0);

CloseHandle(hAttachFile);
LocalFree(lpBuffer);

// Done. Clean up
pAttachStream->Release();
pAttach->Release();
pAttachTable->Release();
pMsg->Release();
pIInboxTable->Release();
pPOPInboxFolder->Release();
```

MAPI Notifications

MAPI notifications are used as a communication method by a MAPI
object and your application. Whenever a specific change has occurred
within either a message store or a message session object, you will receive
a notification **event** that provides you with the details of what has
changed. For example, if a new message is received by a message store,

you will receive a notification that a message has arrived. MAPI notifications can also be used when an error occurs within either one of the MAPI objects.

NOTE: Pocket PC supports notification events only on MAPI objects within your own process space. This means you can register to receive notifications for actions that occur in your application, but *cannot* be informed when another application, such as the Inbox, has done something with the message store.

In order for your application to receive notifications from MAPI, you must implement the `IMAPIAdviseSink` interface. The interface supports the single method described in Table 11.23.

Table 11.23 `IMAPIAdviseSink` Method

Method	Description
OnNotify()	A notification event has occurred.

Notifications are enabled once your client application has registered itself with a particular MAPI object as an **advise sink**. Both the `IMsg Store` and `IMAPISession` interfaces can be used as *advise sources* for your notification object, and you will use them to manage the connection between the two.

To register your `IMAPIAdviseSink` interface with the MAPI session, you use the `IMAPISession::Advise()` function. Registering with the session object provides you with notification events regarding any errors that occur during the MAPI session. The function is defined as follows:

```
HRESULT IMAPISession::Advise(ULONG cbEntryID, LPENTRYID
    lpEntryID, ULONG ulEventMask, LPMAPIADVISESINK
    lpAdviseSink, ULONG *lpulConnection);
```

The first two parameters are unused and should be set to 0. Because the session object supports only error notifications, you can also set the `ulEventMask` parameter to `NULL`. The `lpAdviseSink` parameter should point to the `IMAPIAdviseSink` interface that you want to use for receiving notifications. The last parameter, `lpulConnection`, will point to a connection identifier after the function has returned. This will be used later by the `::Unadvise()` function to stop receiving notifications.

Registering your notification sink with a message store will provide you with much more detailed events from MAPI. For example, you can receive notifications when new mail arrives, when objects are modified or deleted, and even when an object is moved. To register for notifications with a message store object, you can call the `IMsgStore::Advise()` function:

```
HRESULT IMsgStore::Advise(ULONG cbEntryID, LPENTRYID
  lpEntryID, ULONG ulEventMask, LPMAPIADVISESINK
  lpAdviseSink, ULONG *lpulConnection);
```

The first two parameters are used to specify a particular MAPI object for which you want to receive events. To monitor a specific folder or message, set the `lpEntryID` parameter to point to the entry identifier, and set the `cbEntryID` parameter to the size the `ENTRYID` of the object. You can also set the `lpEntryID` parameter to `NULL` if you want to receive notifications for all objects in the message store.

The `ulEventMask` parameter is used to specify what notification events you want to receive. It can be set to one or more of the following:

- Use the `fnevObjectCreated` flag for receiving notifications when a new object is created.
- Use the `fnevObjectCopied` flag for receiving notifications when an object is copied.
- Use the `fnevObjectDeleted` flag for receiving notifications when an object is deleted.
- Use the `fnevObjectModified` flag for receiving notifications when an object is modified.
- Use the `fnevObjectMoved` flag for receiving notifications when an object is moved.

The `lpAdviseSink` parameter should point to the `IMAPIAdvise Sink` interface that you want to use for receiving notification events. The last parameter, `lpulConnection`, will point to a connection identifier after the function has returned. This will be used later by the `::Unadvise()` function to stop receiving notifications.

When your application does not want to receive any more notifications, you must cancel your notification registration with the object from which you are receiving events. To do so, use the following function:

```
HRESULT ::Unadvise(ULONG ulConnection);
```

The only parameter that you need to provide is the connection identifier that was returned to you from your previous call to the IMsg Store::Advise() or IMAPISession::Advise() functions.

The following example shows how you can set up a program that is registered to receive notification events on the POP3 message store:

```
/////////////////////////////////////
// MAPINOTIFY.H

// Remember to link with cemapi.lib, ole32.lib,
// oleaut32.lib, and uuid.lib
#include <objbase.h>
#include <initguid.h>

#define INITGUID
#define USES_IID_IMAPIAdviseSink

#include <windows.h>
#include <cemapi.h>
#include <mapiutil.h>

class CMAPIAdviseSink:public IMAPIAdviseSink {
private:
    long m_lRef;
public:
    CMAPIAdviseSink();
    ~CMAPIAdviseSink();

    // IUnknown
    STDMETHODIMP QueryInterface(REFIID riid, LPVOID *ppv);
    STDMETHODIMP_(ULONG) AddRef();
    STDMETHODIMP_(ULONG) Release();

    // IMAPIAdviseSink
    STDMETHODIMP_(ULONG) OnNotify(ULONG cNotif,
        LPNOTIFICATION lpNotifications);
};
```

```
//////////////////////////////////
// MAPINOTIFY.CPP
#include "mapinotify.h"

int WINAPI WinMain(HINSTANCE hInstance, HINSTANCE
  hPrevInstance, LPTSTR lpCmdLine, int nShowCmd)
{
   HRESULT hr = S_OK;

   // Initalize COM
   if(FAILED(CoInitializeEx(NULL, 0)))
      return FALSE;

   // Get an instance of our IMAPIAdviseSink
   CMAPIAdviseSink *pMapiNotifySink = new CMAPIAdviseSink();
   IMAPIAdviseSink *pMapiSink = NULL;
   hr = pMapiNotifySink->QueryInterface(IID_IMAPIAdviseSink,
      (void **)&pMapiSink);
   if(FAILED(hr)) {
      pMapiNotifySink->Release();
      return 0;
   }

   // Initialize MAPI and hook up the notification
   IMAPISession *pIMapi = NULL;

   if(MAPIInitialize(NULL) != S_OK)
      return FALSE;

   if(MAPILogonEx(0, NULL, NULL, 0, &pIMapi) != S_OK) {
      MAPIUninitialize();
      return FALSE;
   }

   // Open up the POP3 Message Store
   IMAPITable *pIMapiStoresTable = NULL;
   hr = pIMapi->GetMsgStoresTable(0, &pIMapiStoresTable);
   if(FAILED(hr)) {
      pIMapi->Logoff(0, 0, 0);
      pIMapi->Release();
      pIMapi = NULL;
      MAPIUninitialize();
      return FALSE;
   }
```

```
// Query the store table. We need to get the ENTRYID and
// Display name to find the POP3 store
IMsgStore *pPop3Store = NULL;
while(1) {
   SRowSet *pRowSet = NULL;

   SizedSPropTagArray(2, tblColumns) = {2,
      {PR_DISPLAY_NAME,PR_ENTRYID}};
   pIMapiStoresTable->SetColumns((LPSPropTagArray)
      &tblColumns, 0);
   hr = pIMapiStoresTable->QueryRows(1, 0, &pRowSet);

   if(pRowSet->cRows != 1)
      break;

   // Compare the name with "POP3". If it's a match, open
   // the msg store
   if(_tcscmp(TEXT("POP3"), pRowSet->aRow[0].lpProps[0].
      Value.lpszW) == 0)
   {
      ENTRYID *pEntry =
         (ENTRYID *)pRowSet->aRow[0].lpProps[1].Value.
            bin.lpb;
      ULONG ulStoreBytes = pRowSet->aRow[0].lpProps[1].
            Value.bin.cb;

      pIMapi->OpenMsgStore(NULL, ulStoreBytes, pEntry,
         NULL, NULL, &pPop3Store);
      FreeProws(pRowSet);
      break;
   }

   // Free buffers allocated by MAPI
   FreeProws(pRowSet);
};

// Create a new message.
// Start by opening the Drafts folder
LPSPropValue rgprops = NULL;
LPSPropValue lppPropArray = NULL;
ULONG cValues = 0;
IMAPIFolder *pPOPDraftsFolder = NULL;
SizedSPropTagArray(2, rgTags) =
   {2,{PR_CE_IPM_DRAFTS_ENTRYID,PR_OBJECT_TYPE}};
```

```
// Now get the Drafts folder.
hr = pPop3Store->GetProps((LPSPropTagArray)&rgTags,
   MAPI_UNICODE, &cValues, &rgprops);
if(FAILED(hr))
   return FALSE;

hr = pPop3Store->OpenEntry(rgprops[0].Value.bin.cb,
   (LPENTRYID)rgprops[0].Value.bin.lpb, NULL,
   MAPI_MODIFY, NULL, (LPUNKNOWN*)&pPOPDraftsFolder);
if(FAILED(hr))
   return FALSE;

// Now that the folder is open, establish a notification
// sink on the POP3 Store
ULONG ulConnNum = 0;
hr = pPop3Store->Advise(0, NULL,
   fnevObjectCreated|fnevObjectMoved|
   fnevObjectCopied|fnevObject Deleted|fnevObjectModified,
   pMapiSink, &ulConnNum);

if(FAILED(hr))
   return FALSE;

// DO SOMETHING HERE, such as create a new message,
// etc...

// Now we are finished, so clean up
pIMapiStoresTable->Release();

// Disconnect the advise sink
if(pMapiSink) {
   pPop3Store->Unadvise(ulConnNum);
   pMapiSink->Release();
   delete pMapiNotifySink;
}

pPop3Store->Release();
pIMapi->Logoff(0, 0, 0);
```

```
      pIMapi->Release();
      pIMapi = NULL;
      MAPIUninitialize();

      return 0;
}

// CMAPIAdviseSink object
CMAPIAdviseSink::CMAPIAdviseSink() {
   m_lRef = 1;
   return;
}

CMAPIAdviseSink::~CMAPIAdviseSink() {
   return;
}

// IMAPIAdviseSink's IUnknown interface
STDMETHODIMP CMAPIAdviseSink::QueryInterface(REFIID riid,
   LPVOID *ppv) {
      if(IsEqualIID(riid, IID_IUnknown) || IsEqualIID(riid,
         IID_IMAPIAdviseSink)){
         *ppv = (IMAPIAdviseSink *)this;
         AddRef();
         return NO_ERROR;
      }

      *ppv = NULL;
      return E_NOINTERFACE;
}

STDMETHODIMP_(ULONG) CMAPIAdviseSink::AddRef() {
   return (ULONG)InterlockedIncrement(&m_lRef);
}

STDMETHODIMP_(ULONG) CMAPIAdviseSink::Release() {
   ULONG ulCount = (ULONG)InterlockedDecrement(&m_lRef);
   if(ulCount == 0)
      delete this;

   return ulCount;
}
```

```
STDMETHODIMP_(ULONG) CMAPIAdviseSink::OnNotify(ULONG cNotif,
   LPNOTIFICATION lpNotifications)
{
   switch(lpNotifications->ulEventType) {
      case fnevCriticalError:
         OutputDebugString(TEXT("Critical Error\r\n"));
         break;
      case fnevNewMail:
         OutputDebugString(TEXT("New Mail\r\n"));
         break;
      case fnevObjectCreated:
         OutputDebugString(TEXT("Object Created\r\n"));
         break;
      case fnevObjectDeleted:
         OutputDebugString(TEXT("Object Deleted\r\n"));
         break;
      case fnevObjectModified:
         OutputDebugString(TEXT("Object Modified\r\n"));
         break;
      case fnevObjectMoved:
         OutputDebugString(TEXT("Object Moved\r\n"));
         break;
      case fnevObjectCopied:
         OutputDebugString(TEXT("Object Copied\r\n"));
         break;
      case fnevTableModified:
         OutputDebugString(TEXT("Table Modified\r\n"));
         break;
   }
   return NO_ERROR;
}
```

Receiving Notifications

When an event occurs, the IMAPIAdviseSink object that was registered receives a call into the IMAPIAdviseSink::OnNotify() function. This function is defined as follows:

```
ULONG IMAPIAdviseSink::OnNotify(ULONG cNotif,
   LPNOTIFICATION lpNotifications);
```

The cNotif parameter specifies the number of NOTIFICATION
structures in the array pointed to by the lpNotifications parameter.

Each notification that is received is specified by an individual NOTIFICATION structure. It is defined as follows:

```
typedef struct {
   ULONG ulEventType;
   union {
      ERROR_NOTIFICATION            err;
      NEWMAIL_NOTIFICATION          newmail;
      OBJECT_NOTIFICATION           obj;
      TABLE_NOTIFICATION            tab;
      EXTENDED_NOTIFICATION         ext;
      STATUS_OBJECT_NOTIFICATION statobj;
   } info;
} NOTIFICATION, FAR *LPNOTIFICATION;
```

The first field, ulEventType, specifies the notification type for the current event. The info field will be filled in with the appropriate structure for the event you have received.

CHAPTER 12

The .NET Compact Framework

The human subconscious is a fascinating place—malleable, permeable, fallible.

—*Harvey,* Farscape

The introduction of the .NET Framework made the last year or so an extremely exciting time for software developers. Not only does .NET provide an entirely new platform for creating software, it also introduces an extremely rich (and quite large) set of class libraries for building managed applications, as well as a new type-safe object-oriented programming language known as C#.

The .NET Compact Framework is a version of .NET specifically designed for small form factor devices, such as Pocket PC. The class library provided with the Compact Framework is extremely similar to its desktop counterpart, except that certain functionality has been "slimmed down" (or entirely eliminated) to better support the limited memory, storage space, and performance of a mobile device.

Because covering the entire Compact Framework would be a book in itself, this chapter provides you with information about using some of the .NET classes that are of particular interest to Pocket PC application developers. We first take a look at performing Winsock communications (see Chapter 1) between devices using the Sockets class library that is provided by the Compact Framework. This is followed by an explanation of how to write applications that request data using standard Internet protocols, such as HTTP (see Chapter 2).

This chapter also describes how you can consume Web Services, probably one of the most intriguing concepts for a mobile developer. A Web Service is a standardized way to access distributed program logic by using "off-the-shelf" Internet protocols. For example, suppose you had an application running on a Pocket PC device that kept an itinerary of your travel plans. You could use one Web Service to get information about flight delays, another to get the weather report at your destination, and another to pull gate information, tying all of the information together within your application. What makes Web Services unique is that any communications with the server hosting the Web Service are done through a standardized XML format. By using Web Services, you can easily create robust mobile applications that pull data from a variety of sources on the Internet.

Finally, we'll take a look at using some of the APIs that are native to the Pocket PC, such as the Connection Manager (see Chapter 7) and SMS Messaging (see Chapter 8), from applications written in C#.

Unlike writing standard C++ applications for a Pocket PC device using Embedded Visual C++ 3.0, you use Visual Studio 2003.NET for developing C# and VB.NET applications. At this time, you cannot use C++ to develop .NET applications for the Compact Framework.

Networking with the Compact Framework

When developing applications that communicate over a network using .NET, most of the classes that you will need to familiarize yourself with are part of the **System.Net** namespace. It contains classes for handling Internet communications with objects that support proxy servers, IP addresses, DNS name resolution, network data streams, and specific classes for handling *pluggable protocols* such as the Hypertext Transfer Protocol (HTTP).

Table 12.1 describes the objects contained in the System.Net namespace.

Table 12.1 The `System.Net` Namespace

Name	Object Type	Description
AuthenticationManager	Class	Manages authentication models
Authorization	Class	Handles authorization messages to a sever
Dns	Class	Handles domain name resolution
EndPoint	Class	Abstract class for identifying a network address
GlobalProxySelection	Class	Handles the default proxy for HTTP requests
HttpContinueDelegate	Delegate	Callback used for HTTP requests
HttpStatusCode	Enumeration	Status codes used for HTTP requests
HttpVersion	Class	Handles version numbers supported by HTTP requests
HttpWebRequest	Class	Handles an HTTP request
HttpWebResponse	Class	Handles the response of an HTTP request
IAuthenticationModule	Interface	Interface used for Web authentication
ICertificatePolicy	Interface	Interface that validates a server's certificate
ICredentials	Interface	Interface for handling Web client authentication
IPAddress	Class	Handles IP addressing
IPEndPoint	Class	Handles an IP address and port number
IPHostEntry	Class	Handles Internet host address information
IrDAEndPoint	Class	Handles an infrared connection to another device
IWebProxy	Interface	Interface to handle a proxy request
IWebRequestCreate	Interface	Interface to handle new `WebRequest` instances

(continued)

Table 12.1 The System.Net Namespace (*continued*)

Name	Object Type	Description
`NetworkCredential`	Class	Handles network usernames and passwords
`ProtocolViolationException`	Class	Exception used when a network protocol error occurs
`ServicePoint`	Class	Handles connection management for HTTP
`ServicePointManager`	Class	Handles a collection of `ServicePoint` classes
`SocketAddress`	Class	Stores information from `EndPoint` classes
`WebException`	Class	Exception used when an error occurs accessing the network
`WebExceptionStatus`	Enumeration	Status codes used with the `WebException` class
`WebHeaderCollection`	Class	Handles protocol headers for a network request or response
`WebProxy`	Class	Handles HTTP proxy settings
`WebRequest`	Class	Handles a request to a URI
`WebResponse`	Class	Handles a response to a URI

TCP/IP Addresses

In Chapter 1, you learned about the Internet Protocol version 4 (or IPv4) address scheme on Pocket PC. You may remember that an IPv4 address is used by a device to specify its unique host and subnet address, which it uses to communicate over a TCP/IP network. All of the methods and properties that are needed to manage an Internet address within the Compact Framework are handled by the `System.Net.IPAddress` class.

The `IPAddress` constructor is defined as follows:

```
public IPAddress(long newAddress);
```

The only parameter needed is the 32-bit value of the IP address. The class also contains the methods and properties described in Table 12.2.

Table 12.2 `IPAddress` Class Methods and Properties

Method	Description
`HostToNetworkOrder()`	Converts from host byte order to network byte order
`IsLoopback()`	Returns TRUE if the network address is the loopback adapter
`NetworkToHostOrder()`	Converts from network byte order to host byte order
`Parse()`	Converts a string to an `IPAddress` class

Property	Get/Set/Read-Only	Description
`Address`	Get/set	Value of the IP address
`Any`	Read-only field	Indicates that the IP address is used for all network adapters
`Broadcast`	Read-only field	Returns the IP broadcast address
`Loopback`	Read-only field	Returns the IP loopback address
`None`	Read-only field	Indicates that the IP address is not used for any network adapter

One of the most useful methods in the `IPAddress` class is the `Parse()` method. You can use this to easily construct a new IP Address object using the standard dotted-notation Internet address, as shown in the following example:

```
System.Net.IPAddress localIPAddress =
    System.Net.IPAddress.Parse("127.0.0.1");
```

Although the `IPAddress` class by itself is useful for managing an Internet address, most of the networking functions in the Compact Framework use the `System.Net.IPEndPoint` class to specify another machine on the network. An `IPEndPoint` not only specifies the IP address of the remote connection, but also contains information about the port that will be used to connect with the service running on the remote device (for more information about Internet ports, see Chapter 1).

There are two ways to construct a new `IPEndPoint` class. The first method takes the 32-bit value of the IP address and a port:

```
public IPEndPoint(long address, int port);
```

You can also create a new `IPEndPoint` by passing in a previously created `IPAddress` object:

```
public IPEndPoint(IPAddress address, int port);
```

The following code shows how you can create an `IPEndPoint` that represents a connection to the local machine on port 80:

```
System.Net.IPAddress localIPAddress =
System.Net.IPAddress.Parse("127.0.0.1");

System.Net.IPEndPoint localIPEndpoint = new
    System.Net.IPEndPoint(localIPAddress, 80);
```

The `IPEndPoint` class consists of the methods and properties described in Table 12.3.

Table 12.3 `IPEndPoint` Class Methods and Properties

Method	Description
Create() Serialize()	Creates an `IPEndPoint` based on an IP address and port Serializes `IPEndPoint` information into a `SocketAddress` instance

Property	Get/Set/Read-Only	Description
Address	Get/set	Value of the IP address
AddressFamily	Get	Gets the address family for the IP address
Port	Get/set	Value of the port
MaxPort	Read-only field	Specifies the maximum value for the port
MinPort	Read-only field	Specifies the minimum value for the port

Name Resolution

The resolution of a domain name (such as www.furrygoat.com) or IP address is handled by the `System.Net.Dns` class. It contains the methods described in Table 12.4.

Table 12.4 Dns Class Methods

Method	Description
BeginGetHostByName()	Starts an asynchronous GetHostByName() request
BeginResolve()	Starts an asynchronous Resolve() request
EndGetHostByName()	Ends an asynchronous GetHostByName() request
EndResolve()	Ends an asynchronous Resolve() request
GetHostByAddress()	Gets host information based on the IP address
GetHostByName()	Gets host information based on the name
Resolve()	Resolves a host name or IP address to an IPHostEntry() class

After the DNS resolution process has completed, information about the domain is stored in a new instance of the System.Net.IPHost Entry class. The class has the properties described in Table 12.5.

Table 12.5 IPHostEntry Class Properties

Property	Get/Set/Read-Only	Description
AddressList	Get/set	Gets or sets a list of IPAddress objects associated with the host
Aliases	Get/set	Gets or sets a list of aliases associated with the host
HostName	Get/set	Gets or sets the DNS host name

The following code shows how you can create an IPEndPoint that is associated with the Microsoft Web Server by using the System. Net.Dns class to first resolve the IP address:

```
// Resolve the MS Web Server IP address
System.Net.IPHostEntry microsoftHost =
   System.Net.Dns.GetHostByName("www.microsoft.com");

// Copy the resolved IP address to a string
String msIP = microsoftHost.AddressList[0].ToString();

// Create the endpoint
System.Net.IPEndPoint microsoftEndPoint = new
   System.Net.IPEndPoint(microsoftHost.AddressList[0], 80);
```

Winsock and .NET

The `System.Net.Sockets` namespace provides all of the classes that are needed to communicate over the Winsock interface (see Chapter 1 for more information about general Winsock programming) when using the Compact Framework. The namespace provides the classes and enumerations described in Table 12.6.

Table 12.6 The `System.Net.Sockets` Namespace

Name	Object Type	Description
AddressFamily	Enumeration	Address scheme for a `Socket` class
IrDACharacterSet	Enumeration	Character sets supported for infrared transfers
IrDAClient	Class	Handles the client in an infrared transfer
IrDADeviceInfo	Class	Provides information about infrared connections and servers
IrDAHints	Enumeration	Infrared device types
IrDAListener	Class	Handles the server in an infrared transfer
LingerOption	Class	Handles the socket linger options
MulticastOption	Class	Handles multicast address groups
NetworkStream	Class	Handles a stream over a network connection
ProtocolFamily	Enumeration	Socket protocol types that are available
ProtocolType	Enumeration	Socket protocols
SelectMode	Enumeration	Socket polling modes
Socket	Class	Class to handle socket communications
SocketException	Class	Exception that is used when an error occurs in a `Socket` class
SocketFlags	Enumeration	Socket constants
SocketOptionLevel	Enumeration	Socket level option constant values
SocketOptionName	Enumeration	Socket names option constant values
SocketShutdown	Enumeration	Socket shutdown constants
SocketType	Enumeration	Type of socket
TcpClient	Class	Class to handle TCP socket connections to a server
TcpListener	Class	Class to handle TCP socket connections as a server
UdpClient	Class	Class to handle UDP socket connections for both client and server

The namespace provides four classes that you will use primarily when working with Winsock connections:

1. The `System.Net.Sockets.Socket` class is essentially a full wrapper around a traditional `SOCKET` handle. It provides all of the functionality for both connectionless and connection-based TCP and UDP communications.
2. The `System.Net.Sockets.TcpClient` class provides all of the methods and properties for the client side of a TCP connection to a server.
3. The `System.Net.Sockets.TcpListener` class provides all of the methods and properties for the server side of a TCP connection that will listen for incoming connections on a specific port.
4. The `System.Net.Sockets.UdpClient` class provides all of the methods and properties for sending and receiving connectionless datagrams.

The Generic Socket Class

The `System.Net.Sockets.Socket` class is used to perform basic Winsock functionality in a manner similar to using a standard `SOCKET` handle. To create a new `Socket` object, you use the following constructor:

```
public Socket(AddressFamily addressFamily, SocketType
  socketType, ProtocolType protocolType);
```

All of the parameters that you use are standard enumerations that are part of the `System.Net.Sockets` namespace. The first parameter, `addressFamily`, should specify the addressing scheme for the socket, such as `AddressFamily.InterNetwork` for an IPv4 socket. This is followed by the type of socket you are creating, which is followed by the protocol that the socket should use.

The following example creates a standard IPv4 socket for communicating over a TCP connection using the IP protocol:

```
using System;
using System.Data;
using System.Net.Sockets;

namespace PocketPCNetworkProgramming {
  class SocketTestClass {
```

```
static void Main(string[] args) {
    // Create a new socket
    System.Net.Sockets.Socket newSocket = new Socket(
        AddressFamily.InterNetwork,
        SocketType.Stream,
        ProtocolType.IP);

    // Do something with the new socket
    }
  }
}
```

The `System.Net.Sockets.Socket` class supports the methods and properties described in Table 12.7.

Table 12.7 `Socket` Class Methods and Properties

Method	Description
`Accept()`	Creates a new `System.Net.Sockets.Socket` for the incoming connection
`BeginAccept()`	Begins asynchronous `Accept()` operation
`BeginConnect()`	Begins asynchronous `Connect()` operation
`BeginReceive()`	Begins asynchronous `Receive()` operation
`BeginReceiveFrom()`	Begins asynchronous `Receive()` operation from a specific remote `EndPoint`
`BeginSend()`	Begins asynchronous `Send()` operation
`BeginSendTo()`	Begins asynchronous `Send()` operation to a specific remote `EndPoint`
`Bind()`	Associates the socket with a local `EndPoint`
`Close()`	Closes the socket
`Connect()`	Establishes a connection with another host
`EndAccept()`	Asynchronously accepts an incoming connection
`EndConnect()`	Ends asynchronous `Connect()` operation
`EndReceive()`	Ends asynchronous `Receive()` operation
`EndReceiveFrom()`	Ends asynchronous `Receive()` operation from a specific remote `EndPoint`
`EndSend()`	Ends asynchronous `Send()` operation
`EndSendTo()`	Ends asynchronous `Send()` operation to a specific remote `EndPoint`
`GetSocketOption()`	Returns the value of the socket options
`IOControl()`	Sets low-level socket options
`Listen()`	Listens for an incoming socket connection

Method	Description
Poll()	Returns the status of the socket
Receive()	Receives data over a socket
ReceiveFrom()	Receives data over a socket from a specific remote EndPoint
Select()	Returns the status of one or more sockets
Send()	Sends data over a socket
SendTo()	Sends data over a socket to a specific remote EndPoint
SetSocketOption()	Sets the value of the socket options
Shutdown()	Stops communications over a socket

Property	Get/Set	Description
AddressFamily	Get	Gets the addressing scheme used for the socket
Available	Get	Gets the amount of data on the socket that is ready to be read
Blocking	Get/set	Gets or sets whether the socket is in blocking mode
Connected	Get	Returns TRUE if the socket is connected
Handle	Get	Gets the socket handle
LocalEndPoint	Get	Gets the local EndPoint for the socket
ProtocolType	Get	Gets the protocol type for the socket
RemoteEndPoint	Get	Gets the remote EndPoint for the socket
SocketType	Get	Gets the type of socket

Once you have created your Socket class, communicating over the Internet is relatively straightforward. The class supports methods such as Send() and Receive(), which are almost identical to the standard Winsock functions:

```
// Create a new socket
System.Net.Sockets.Socket webSocket = new
   Socket(AddressFamily.InterNetwork, SocketType.Stream,
   ProtocolType.IP);

// Make a request from a Web server
// Resolve the IP address for the server, and get the
//   IPEndPoint for it on port 80
```

```
System.Net.IPHostEntry webServerHost =
   System.Net.Dns.GetHostByName("www.furrygoat.com");
System.Net.IPEndPoint webServerEndPt = new
   System.Net.IPEndPoint(webServerHost.AddressList[0], 80);

// Set up the HTTP request string to get the main index page
byte[] httpRequestBytes =
   System.Text.Encoding.ASCII.GetBytes("GET /
   HTTP/1.0\r\n\r\n");

// Connect the socket to the server
webSocket.Connect(webServerEndPt);

// Send the request synchronously
int bytesSent = webSocket.Send(httpRequestBytes,
  httpRequestBytes.Length, SocketFlags.None);

// Get the response from the request. We will continue to request
// 4096 bytes from the response stream and concat the string into
// the strReponse variable
byte[] httpResponseBytes = new byte[4096];
int bytesRecv = webSocket.Receive(httpResponseBytes,
  httpResponseBytes.Length, SocketFlags.None);

strResponse = System.Text.Encoding.ASCII.GetString
  (httpResponseBytes, 0, bytesRecv);

while(bytesRecv > 0) {
   bytesRecv = webSocket.Receive(httpResponseBytes,
   httpResponseBytes.Length, SocketFlags.None);

   strResponse = strResponse +
     System.Text.Encoding.ASCII.GetString(
     httpResponseBytes, 0, bytesRecv);
}

// At this point, the strResponse string has the Web page.
// Do something with it
// ...
```

```
// Clean up the socket
webSocket.Shutdown(SocketShutdown.Both);
webSocket.Close();
```

Although using the `Socket` class provides you with a robust set of methods to handle almost any type of connection, you are more likely to use one of the more specific connection classes, such as `TcpClient` or `TcpListener`, to handle your protocol-specific network communications.

TCP Connections

As described in Chapter 1, a TCP (or streaming) socket provides you with an error-free data pipe (between a client and server) that is used to send and receive data over a communications session. The format of the data sent over the connection is typically up to you, but several well-known Internet protocols, such as HTTP and FTP, use this type of connection.

The .NET Compact Framework provides you with two separate classes that can be used to handle TCP communications. The `System.Net.Sockets.TcpListener` class is used to create a socket that can accept an incoming connection request. This is also known as a *server*.

To create a TCP client, you use the `System.Net.Sockets.TcpClient` class. The methods provide functionality to connect to a server that is listening on a specific port.

TCP Servers

To create a new `TcpListener` object, you can use one of the following constructors:

```
public TcpListener(int port);
public TcpListener(IPAddress localaddr, int port);
public TcpListener(IPEndPoint localEP);
```

All three constructors basically do the same thing. The first one needs only the port number on which you want the object to listen. The second requires an `IPAddress` class that represents the local IP address of the device, and is followed by the port. The final constructor takes an `IPEndPoint` class, which should represent the local IP address and port on which to listen.

The following example shows how you can use each one of the constructors to initialize a new `TcpListener` class:

```
// Method 1 - Listen on the local IP address, port 80.
System.Net.Sockets.TcpListener tcpServerSocket = new
  TcpListener(80);

// Method 2 - Listen on the local IP address, port 80.
System.Net.IPAddress localIPAddr =
  System.Net.IPAddress.Parse("127.0.0.1");
System.Net.Sockets.TcpListener tcpServerSocket2 = new
  TcpListener(localIPAddr, 80);

// Method 3 - Listen on the local IP address by creating an
// endpoint
System.Net.IPEndPoint localIpEndPoint = new
  System.Net.IPEndPoint(localIPAddr, 80);
System.Net.Sockets.TcpListener tcpServerSocket3 = new
  TcpListener(localIpEndPoint);
```

The `TcpListener` object provides the methods and property described in Table 12.8.

Table 12.8 `TCPListener` Class Methods and Properties

Method	Description
AcceptSocket()	Accepts an incoming TCP connection request and returns a `Socket` class
AcceptTcpClient()	Accepts an incoming TCP connection request and returns a `TcpClient` class
Pending()	Determines whether any incoming connection requests are waiting
Start()	Starts listening for incoming requests
Stop()	Stops listening for incoming requests

Property	Get/Set	Description
LocalEndpoint	Get	Gets the local `EndPoint` to which the `TcpListener` is bound

Once you have constructed a `TcpListener` object, you can have it start listening on the port that you passed in by calling the `Start()` method. Now that you have a `TcpListener` socket that is awaiting a connection, let's take a brief look at network streams.

Using Network Streams

The `System.Net.Sockets.NetworkStream` class is used for both sending and receiving data over a TCP socket. To create a `Network Stream` object, use one of the following constructors:

```
public NetworkStream(Socket socket);
public NetworkStream(Socket socket, bool ownsSocket);
public NetworkStream(Socket socket, FileAccess access);
public NetworkStream(Socket socket, FileAccess access, bool
  ownsSocket);
```

Each constructor specifies a `Socket` class with which the new stream object should be associated. The `ownsSocket` parameter should be set to `TRUE` if you want the `Stream` object to assume ownership of the socket. The `access` parameter can be used to specify any `FileAccess` values for determining access to the stream (such as `Read`, `Write`, or `ReadWrite`).

In addition, you can use the `TcpClient.GetStream()` method (as you will see in the next section) to get the `NetworkStream` for the active connection.

The `NetworkStream` class supports the methods and properties described in Table 12.9.

The following example shows how you can use the `NetworkStream` class to send data to a client that is connected to a `TcpListener` object:

```
// Create a socket that is listening for incoming connections on
// port 8080
string hostName = System.Net.Dns.GetHostName();
System.Net.IPAddress localIPAddress =
   System.Net.Dns.Resolve(hostName).AddressList[0];
System.Net.Sockets.TcpListener tcpServer = new
   TcpListener(localIPAddress, 8080);

// Start listening synchronously
tcpServer.Start();
```

Table 12.9 `NetworkStream` Class Methods and Properties

Method	Description
`BeginRead()`	Begins an asynchronous `Read()` operation
`BeginWrite()`	Begins an asynchronous `Write()` operation
`Close()`	Closes the `NetworkStream`
`CreateWaitHandle()`	Creates a `WaitHandle` object for handling asynchronous operation blocking events
`Dispose()`	Releases resources used by the `NetworkStream` object
`EndRead()`	Ends asynchronous `Read()` operation
`EndWrite()`	Ends asynchronous `Write()` operation
`Read()`	Reads from the `NetworkStream`
`ReadByte()`	Reads a byte from the `NetworkStream`
`Write()`	Writes to the `NetworkStream`
`WriteByte()`	Writes a byte to the `NetworkStream`

Property	Get/Set	Description
`CanRead`	Get	Returns TRUE if the `NetworkStream` supports reading
`CanWrite`	Get	Returns TRUE if the `NetworkStream` supports write operations
`DataAvailable`	Get	Returns TRUE if the `NetworkStream` has data to be read
`Length`	Get	Returns the amount of data waiting to be read on the stream

```
// Get the client socket when a request comes in
Socket tcpClient = tcpServer.AcceptSocket();

// Make sure the client is connected
if(tcpClient.Connected == false)
    return;

// Create a network stream to send data to the client
NetworkStream clientStream = new NetworkStream(tcpClient);

// Write some data to the stream
byte[] serverBytes = System.Text.Encoding.ASCII.GetBytes(
    "Howdy. You've connected!\r\n");
clientStream.Write(serverBytes, 0, serverBytes.Length);
```

```
// Immediately disconnect the client
tcpClient.Shutdown(SocketShutdown.Both);
tcpClient.Close();
```

TCP Clients

To establish a connection with a TCP server listening on a specific port, you use the `System.Net.Sockets.TcpClient` class. Its constructor is defined as follows:

```
public TcpClient();
public TcpClient(IPEndPoint localEP);
public TcpClient(string hostname, int port);
```

The `TcpClient` class has the methods and properties described in Table 12.10.

Table 12.10 `TcpClient` Class Methods and Properties

Method	Description
Close()	Closes the `TcpClient` socket
Connect()	Connects to a remote host
GetStream()	Gets the `NetworkStream` object to send and receive data

Property	Get/Set	Description
LingerState	Get/set	Gets or sets the socket linger time
NoDelay	Get/set	Set to TRUE to disable the delay on a socket when the receive buffer is not full
ReceiveBufferSize	Get/set	Gets or sets the receive buffer size
SendBufferSize	Get/set	Gets or sets the send buffer size

Now that you have looked at both of the TCP client and server classes, let's examine how you could use the `TcpListener` class to write a small (and extremely simple) Web server that runs on the Pocket PC:

```
using System;
using System.Data;
using System.Net.Sockets;
```

```
namespace TCPServer {
   class WebServer {
      static void Main(string[] args) {
         // Create a socket that is listening for incoming
         // connections on port 80.
         string hostName = System.Net.Dns.GetHostName();
         System.Net.IPAddress localIPAddress =
            System.Net.Dns.Resolve(hostName).AddressList[0];
         System.Net.Sockets.TcpListener tcpServer = new
            TcpListener(localIPAddress, 80);

         // Start listening synchronously and wait for an
         // incoming socket
         tcpServer.Start();
         Socket tcpClient = tcpServer.AcceptSocket();

         // Make sure the client is connected
         if(tcpClient.Connected == false)
            return;

         // Create a network stream that we will use to send
         // and receive data.
         NetworkStream clientStream = new NetworkStream
            (tcpClient);

         // Get a basic request.
         byte[] requestString = new byte[1024];
         clientStream.Read(requestString, 0, 1024);

         // Do something with the client request here.
         // Typically, you'll need to parse the request, open the
         // file and send the contents back. For this example,
         // we'll just write out a simple HTTP response to the
         // stream.
         byte[] responseString =
            System.Text.Encoding.ASCII.GetBytes("HTTP/1.0
            200 OK\r\n\r\nTest Reponse\r\n\r\n");
         clientStream.Write(responseString, 0,
            responseString.Length);
```

```
        // Disconnect the client
        tcpClient.Shutdown(SocketShutdown.Both);
        tcpClient.Close();
    }
  }
}
```

Let's also take a look at the code for a small client that requests a Web page from the server:

```
using System;
using System.Data;
using System.Net.Sockets;

namespace TCPWebClientTest {
  class WebClientTest {
    static void Main(string[] args) {
      // Create a socket that will grab a Web page
      System.Net.Sockets.TcpClient tcpWebClient = new
        TcpClient();

      // Set up the HTTP request string to get the main
      // index page
      byte[] httpRequestBytes = System.Text.Encoding.
        ASCII.GetBytes("GET / HTTP/1.0\r\n\r\n");

      // Connect the socket to the server
      tcpWebClient.Connect("www.microsoft.com", 80);

      // Make sure we are connected
      if(tcpWebClient == null)
        return;

      // Create a network stream that we will use to send
      // and receive data.
      NetworkStream webClientStream = tcpWebClient.
        GetStream();

      // Send the request synchronously
      webClientStream.Write(httpRequestBytes, 0,
        httpRequestBytes.Length);
```

```
// Get the response from the request. We will continuously
// request 4096 bytes from the response stream and concat
// the string into the strReponse variable.
string strResponse = "";
byte[] httpResponseBytes = new byte[4096];
int bytesRecv = webClientStream.Read
    (httpResponseBytes, 0, httpResponseBytes.Length);

strResponse = System.Text.Encoding.ASCII.
    GetString(httpResponseBytes, 0, bytesRecv);

while(bytesRecv > 0) {
    bytesRecv = webClientStream.Read
        (httpResponseBytes, 0, httpResponseBytes.Length);
    strResponse = strResponse + System.Text.Encoding.
        ASCII.GetString(httpResponseBytes, 0, bytesRecv);
}

// At this point, the strResponse string has the
// Web page. Do something with it

// Clean up the socket
tcpWebClient.Close();
        }
    }
}
```

Sending and Receiving Data over UDP

Both the sending and receiving of a datagram (or packet) over a connectionless socket is handled by the `System.Net.Sockets.UdpClient`
class. A new `UdpClient` object is created by using one of the following
constructors:

```
public UdpClient();
public UdpClient(int port);
```

```
public UdpClient(IPEndPoint localEP);
public UdpClient(string hostname, int port);
```

The `UdpClient` class supports the methods and properties described in Table 12.11.

Table 12.11 `UdpClient` Class Methods and Properties

Method	Description
Close()	Closes the UDP socket
Connect()	Connects to a remote host
DropMulticastGroup()	Leaves a multicast group
JoinMulticastGroup()	Joins a multicast group
Receive()	Receives a UDP datagram from a remote host
Send()	Sends a UDP datagram to a remote host

Property	Get/Set	Description
Active	Get/set	Indicates whether a connection has been made to a remote host
Client	Get/set	Gets or sets the socket handle

The following code shows how you can create a socket that sends a UDP datagram to a specific host and port:

```
using System;
using System.Data;
using System.Net;
using System.Net.Sockets;

namespace udpTest {
   class UdpTestSend {
      static void Main(string[] args) {
         // Setup the target device address. For this sample, we
         // are assuming it is a machine at 192.168.123.199, and on
         // port  40040.
         System.Net.IPEndPoint ipTarget = new
            IPEndPoint(System.Net.IPAddress.Parse
            ("192.168.123.199"), 40040);
```

```
            System.Net.Sockets.UdpClient udpSend = new
               UdpClient(ipTarget);

            // Send a datagram to the target device
            byte[] sendBytes = System.Text.Encoding.ASCII.
               GetBytes("Testing a datagram buffer");

            udpSend.Send(sendBytes, sendBytes.Length);
        }
    }
}
```

The code for receiving the datagram would look like the following:

```
using System;
using System.Data;
using System.Net;
using System.Net.Sockets;

namespace udpTest {
    class UdpTestListen {
        static void Main(string[] args) {
            // Listen for datagrams on port 40040
            System.Net.Sockets.UdpClient udpListener = new
               UdpClient();

            if(udpListener == null)
                return;

            // Create an endpoint for the incoming datagram
            IPEndPoint remoteEndPoint = new IPEndPoint
               (IPAddress.Any, 40040);

            // Get the datagram
            byte[] recvBytes = udpListener.Receive(ref
               remoteEndPoint);
            string returnData = System.Text.Encoding.ASCII.
               GetString(recvBytes, 0, recvBytes.Length);

            // Do something with the data....
        }
    }
}
```

Internet Protocols and the .NET Pluggable Protocol Model

When requesting data over the Internet using a standardized protocol such as HTTP (the protocol for the Web), you use a Uniform Resource Identifier (URI) to specify the protocol, server, and name of the resource that you are attempting to access. The .NET Compact Framework provides two abstract classes for handling any Internet resource request and response: `System.Net.WebRequest` and `System.Net.Web Response`.

Client applications use the `WebRequest` class to make the request for a specific URI from an Internet location over a specific protocol (such as HTTP or FTP). Instead of calling a constructor for the `WebRequest` class, you initialize a new request by calling the `WebRequest. Create()` method. This automatically instantiates a new request object based on the protocol that you used for the request. For example, if you are trying to access a resource on the Web using the HTTP protocol, you are returned an `HttpWebRequest` object for which you can set properties and receive a response stream.

Once your request has been configured, you can call the `Web Request.GetResponse()` method to get a `Stream` class that is used to receive the data from the request.

The `WebRequest` object is an abstract class that contains the methods and properties described in Table 12.12.

Table 12.12 `WebRequest` Class Methods and Properties

Method	Description
`Abort()`	Cancels an asynchronous request to an Internet resource
`BeginGetRequestStream()`	Begins an asynchronous `GetRequestStream()` operation
`BeginGetResponse()`	Begins an asynchronous `GetResponse()` operation
`Create()`	Creates a new `WebRequest` object
`EndGetRequestStream()`	Ends an asynchronous `GetRequestStream()` operation
`EndGetResponse()`	Ends an asynchronous `GetResponse()` operation *(continued)*

Table 12.12 `WebRequest` Class Methods and Properties (*continued*)

Method	Description
`GetRequestStream()`	Gets a `Stream` class for writing data to the Internet resource
`GetResponse()`	Gets a `WebResponse` object that returns the response to an Internet request
`RegisterPrefix()`	Registers a new URI type

Property	Get/Set	Description
`ConnectionGroupName`	Get/set	Abstract property used to get or set the connection group name in descendant classes
`ContentLength`	Get/set	Abstract property used to get or set the length of the request data
`ContentType`	Get/set	Abstract property used to get or set the content type of the request
`Credentials`	Get/set	Abstract property used to get or set the credentials for the request
`Headers`	Get/set	Abstract property used to get or set the headers and values for the request
`Method`	Get/set	Abstract property used to get or set the method used for the request
`PreAuthenticate`	Get/set	Abstract property used to determine whether the request should be pre-authenticated
`Proxy`	Get/set	Abstract property used to get or set the proxy to be used for the request
`RequestUri`	Get/set	Abstract property used to get or set the URI for the request
`Timeout`	Get/set	Abstract property used to get or set the length of time before the request times out

The `WebResponse` object is also abstract, and contains the methods and properties described in Table 12.13.

Table 12.13 WebResponse Class Methods and Properties

Method	Description
Close()	Closes the response stream
GetResponseStream()	Gets the Stream for reading the response

Property	Get/Set	Description
ContentLength	Get/set	Abstract property used to get or set the length of the data being received
ContentType	Get/set	Abstract property used to get or set the content type for the data being received
Headers	Get/set	Abstract property used to get or set the headers and values of the request
RequestUri	Get/set	Abstract property used to get or set the URI for the resource requested

Both the WebRequest and WebResponse abstract classes form the basis for what is known as **pluggable protocols**. The concept of pluggable protocols is fairly straightforward—a client application can make a request for any Internet resource using a URI and not have to worry about the underlying details of the network protocol being used. When a request is made using the WebRequest.Create() method, the appropriate protocol-specific class is automatically instantiated and returned to the client application.

Consider the following request for a Web resource:

```
// Set up the URI
System.Uri urlRequest = new System.Uri("http://www.furrygoat.com/");

// Make the request
HttpWebRequest httpReq = (HttpWebRequest)WebRequest.
  Create(urlRequest);

// Get the response
HttpWebResponse webResponse = (HttpWebResponse)httpReq.
  GetResponse();
```

This request will return a new object that is based on the `Http WebRequest` class. The `HttpWebRequest` class is actually derived from `WebRequest`, but adds all of the protocol specifics surrounding HTTP.

What makes the pluggable protocol model extremely useful is that you can also use it to *create your own classes* for handling new protocols that are not native to the .NET Compact Framework.

Creating a Pluggable Protocol

Any new class that is designed to be used as a pluggable protocol is always derived from `WebRequest` and `WebResponse`. All new pluggable protocol classes must also be registered with the base `WebRequest` object in order for the `WebRequest.Create()` method to appropriately instantiate the correct object for the protocol.

To register a new protocol with the `WebRequest` class, you can use the following function:

```
public static bool WebRequest.RegisterPrefix(string prefix,
    IWebRequestCreate creator);
```

The first parameter, `prefix`, is a string that represents the protocol that will be used in URI requests for the new object. For example, if you were creating a new protocol that handled requests for resources over the File Transfer Protocol (such as `ftp://ftp.microsoft.com/ dir/filename.txt`), you could simply use `ftp` for the prefix value. The `creator` parameter should be set to an object that implements the `IWebRequestCreate` interface, which is used to create the new `WebRequest` class.

The following code shows the basic layout for creating a new protocol-specific class that can be used by the `WebRequest.Create()` method:

```
/// <summary>Ftp request protocol handler</summary>
class FtpWebRequest: WebRequest {
    // Private internal variables.
    private NetworkCredential reqCredentials;
    private WebHeaderCollection reqHeaders;
    private WebProxy reqProxy;
    private System.Uri reqUri;
    private string reqConnGroup;
    private long reqContentLength;
    private string reqContentType;
    private string reqMethod;
```

```csharp
    private bool reqPreAuthen;
    private int reqTimeout;

    // Constructor
    public FtpWebRequest(System.Uri uri) {
        reqHeaders = new WebHeaderCollection();
        reqUri = uri;
    }

    // Properties
    public override string ConnectionGroupName {
        get { return reqConnGroup; }
        set { reqConnGroup = value; }
    }
    public override long ContentLength {
        get { return reqContentLength; }
        set { reqContentLength = value; }
    }
    public override string ContentType {
        get { return reqContentType; }
        set { reqContentType = value; }
    }
    public override ICredentials Credentials {
        get { return reqCredentials; }
        set { reqCredentials = (System.Net.NetworkCredential)
            value; }
    }
    public override WebHeaderCollection Headers {
        get { return reqHeaders; }
        set { reqHeaders = value; }
    }
    public override string Method {
        get { return reqMethod; }
        set { reqMethod = value; }
    }
    public override bool PreAuthenticate {
        get { return reqPreAuthen; }
        set { reqPreAuthen = value; }
    }
    public override IWebProxy Proxy {
        get { return reqProxy; }
        set { reqProxy = (System.Net.WebProxy)value; }
    }
    public override Uri RequestUri {
```

```
            get { return reqUri; }
    }
    public override int Timeout {
        get { return reqTimeout; }
        set { reqTimeout = value; }
    }


    // Methods. These are just stubbed in here for this example.
    // In an actual FTP client, you would need to implement these by
    // using p/Invoke to call into the WinInet FTP functions.
    public override void Abort() {
        base.Abort();
    }
    public override IAsyncResult BeginGetRequestStream
        (AsyncCallback callback, object state) {
        return base.BeginGetRequestStream (callback, state);
    }
    public override IAsyncResult BeginGetResponse
        (AsyncCallback callback, object state) {
        return base.BeginGetResponse (callback, state);
    }
    public override Stream EndGetRequestStream(IAsyncResult
        asyncResult) {
        return base.EndGetRequestStream (asyncResult);
    }
    public override WebResponse EndGetResponse(IAsyncResult
        asyncResult) {
        return base.EndGetResponse (asyncResult);
    }
    public override Stream GetRequestStream() {
        return base.GetRequestStream ();
    }
    public override WebResponse GetResponse() {
        return base.GetResponse();
    }
}


/// <summary>Ftp request registration interface</summary>
class FtpWebRequestCreate: IWebRequestCreate {
    public System.Net.WebRequest Create(System.Uri uri) {
```

```
      System.Net.WebRequest request = new FtpWebRequest
         (uri);
      return request;
   }
}


/// <summary>Ftp request response handler</summary>
class FtpWebResponse: WebResponse {
   // Private internal variables.
   private WebHeaderCollection respHeaders;
   private System.Uri respUri;
   private long respContentLength;
   private string respContentType;

   // Properties
   public override long ContentLength {
      get { return respContentLength; }
      set { respContentLength = value; }
   }
   public override string ContentType {
      get { return respContentType; }
      set { respContentType = value; }
   }
   public override WebHeaderCollection Headers {
      get { return respHeaders; }
      set { respHeaders = value; }
   }
   public override Uri ResponseUri {
      get { return reqUri; }
   }


   // Methods. These are just stubbed in here for this example.
   // In an actual FTP client, you would need to implement these by
   // using p/Invoke to call into the WinInet FTP functions.
   public override void Close() {
      base.Close ();
   }
   public override Stream GetResponseStream() {
      return base.GetResponseStream ();
   }
}
```

Remember that you also need to register the protocol with the `WebRequest` class in order for it to be properly instantiated:

```
class FtpTest {
    static void Main(string[] args) {
        // Create a pluggable protocol
        System.Uri urlRequest = new
            System.Uri("ftp://ftp.microsoft.com/developr/
                readme.txt");

        // Register it
        WebRequest.RegisterPrefix("ftp", new
            FtpWebRequestCreate());

        // Make the request
        FtpWebRequest ftpClient = (FtpWebRequest)WebRequest.
            Create(urlRequest);

        // Get the response
        FtpWebResponse ftpResponse = (FtpWebResponse)
            ftpClient.GetResponse();

        // Use a StreamReader class to read in the response
        StreamReader responseStream = new
            StreamReader(ftpResponse.GetResponseStream(),
            System.Text.Encoding.ASCII);

        // Since FTP can be binary or ASCII, you would want
        // to copy it in chunks to the destination file...

        // Close the stream
        responseStream.Close();
    }
}
```

Accessing Content on the Web

One of the built-in pluggable protocols available in the .NET Compact Framework for handling HTTP and HTTPS requests to the Internet is the `HttpWebRequest` class. As with any other protocol-specific class, it has been derived from the `WebRequest` class and can be created by using the `WebRequest.Create()` method:

```
HttpWebRequest httpReq =
    (HttpWebRequest)WebRequest.Create("http://www.
    furrygoat.com");
```

The `HttpWebRequest` class contains the methods and properties described in Table 12.14.

Table 12.14 `HttpWebRequest` Class Methods and Properties

Method	Description
`Abort()`	Cancels an asynchronous request to an Internet resource
`AddRange()`	Adds a Range header to the request
`BeginGetRequestStream()`	Begins an asynchronous `GetRequestStream()` operation
`BeginGetResponse()`	Begins an asynchronous `GetResponse()` operation
`EndGetRequestStream()`	Ends an asynchronous `GetRequestStream()` operation
`EndGetResponse()`	Ends an asynchronous `GetResponse()` operation
`GetRequestStream()`	Gets a `Stream` class for writing data to the Internet resource
`GetResponse()`	Gets a `WebResponse` object that returns the response to an Internet request
`RegisterPrefix()`	Registers a new URI type

Property	Get/Set	Description
`Accept`	Get/set	Gets or sets the HTTP Accept header
`Address`	Get	Gets the URI of the resource that responded to the request
`AllowAutoRedirect`	Get/set	Indicates whether the request should follow a redirect
`AllowWriteStreamBuffering`	Get/set	Indicates whether to buffer the data sent to the resource
`Connection`	Get/set	Gets or sets the HTTP Connection header
`ConnectionGroupName`	Get/set	Gets or sets the name of the connection group

(continued)

Table 12.14 `HttpWebRequest` Class Methods and Properties (*continued*)

Property	Get/Set	Description
ContentLength	Get/set	Gets or sets the HTTP Content-Length header
ContentType	Get/set	Gets or sets the HTTP Content-Type header
ContinueDelegate	Get/set	Gets or sets the delegate for HTTP requests
Credentials	Get/set	Gets or sets credentials for the request
Expect	Get/set	Gets or sets the HTTP Expect header
Headers	Get	Gets the collection of HTTP headers for the request
IfModifiedSince	Get/set	Gets or sets the HTTP If-Modified-Since header
KeepAlive	Get/set	Indicates whether or not the HTTP request should use a persistent connection
MaximumAutomatic Redirections	Get/set	Gets or sets the number of HTTP redirects the request will comply with
MediaType	Get/set	Gets or sets the media type of the request
Method	Get/set	Gets or sets the HTTP method used with the request
Pipelined	Get/set	Indicates whether the request is pipelined
PreAuthenticate	Get/set	Indicates whether to pre-authenticate a request
ProtocolVersion	Get/set	Gets or sets the HTTP version to use with the request
Proxy	Get/set	Gets or sets proxy information
Referer	Get/set	Gets or sets the HTTP Referer header
RequestUri	Get	Gets the original request URI
SendChunked	Get/set	Indicates whether to send the data in segments
ServicePoint	Get	Gets the service point for the request
Timeout	Get/set	Gets or sets the time-out value
TransferEncoding	Get/set	Gets or sets the HTTP Transfer-Encoding header
UserAgent	Get/set	Gets or sets the HTTP User-Agent header

To get the results for the request that was made by the `HttpWeb Request` object, you can use the `GetResponse()` method:

```
HttpWebResponse webResponse =
    (HttpWebResponse)httpReq.GetResponse();
```

The `HttpWebResponse` class supports the methods and properties described in Table 12.15.

Table 12.15 `HttpWebResponse` Class Methods and Properties

Method	Description
Close()	Closes the response stream
GetResponseHeader()	Gets the header that was returned for the response
GetResponseStream()	Gets the `Stream` for reading the response

Property	Get/Set	Description
CharacterSet	Get	Gets the character set for the response
ContentEncoding	Get	Gets the encoding scheme used for the response
ContentLength	Get	Gets the length of the response
ContentType	Get	Gets the type of the response
Headers	Get	Gets the headers associated with the response
LastModified	Get	Gets the last modified time of the response
Method	Get	Gets the method used to return the response
ProtocolVersion	Get	Gets the HTTP version used for the response
ResponseUri	Get	Gets the URI of the resource that responded to the request
Server	Get	Gets the name of the server that sent the response
StatusCode	Get	Gets the HTTP status code for the response
StatusDescription	Get	Gets the HTTP status description for the response

The following code shows how to create a new request for a Web resource, using the `StreamReader` class to read in the response that you receive from the Web server:

```
using System;
using System.Data;
```

```
using System.Net;
using System.IO;

namespace WebSample {
    class WebTest {
        static void Main(string[] args) {
            // Make a new WebRequest object
            System.Uri urlRequest = new
                System.Uri("http://www.furrygoat.com/");
            HttpWebRequest webClient = (HttpWebRequest)
                WebRequest.Create(urlRequest);

            // Get the response
            HttpWebResponse webResponse = (HttpWebResponse)
                webClient.GetResponse();

            // Use a StreamReader class to read in the response
            StreamReader responseStream = new StreamReader(
                webResponse.GetResponseStream(),
                System.Text.Encoding.ASCII);

            // Copy the stream to a string, do something with it
            // string strResponse = responseStream.ReadToEnd();

            // Close the stream
            responseStream.Close();
        }
    }
}
```

The response stream, `strResponse`, contains the HTML code that was downloaded from the Web site:

```
<HTML>
<title>The Furrygoat Experience</title>
<body>
<p><b><font face="Arial">This is the Furrygoat homepage!
  </font></b></p>
</body>
</HTML>
```

Consuming Web Services

.NET Web Services is a form of distributed computing that enables your application to use the logic of a remote component over the Internet using standard protocols. Web Services is one of the most exciting aspects of using the Compact Framework on a mobile device such as Pocket PC, because it enables you to create rich applications that can access Web Service data from one or many sources without being tethered to a desktop.

For example, consider a Pocket PC device that has a GPS unit attached to it over the serial port (you may someday even be able to use a Pocket PC Phone Edition device to request your current position based on the nearest cellular tower). You could hypothetically use a Web Service to request a map of you current surroundings based on the longitude and latitude that the GPS provides. You could then access another Web Service to get a list of the ATMs or restaurants in your local area. By using Web Services, your applications can focus on tying remote data together into a useful program, rather than concentrate on how to get the data to your device, or replicate functionality that has already been developed elsewhere.

The .NET Compact Framework supports the following functionality regarding Web Services on a Pocket PC device:

- All Web Services must be based on the HTTP protocol. Other protocols, such as SMTP, are not supported.
- Data is transmitted using the Simple Object Access Protocol (SOAP) XML format.
- The Compact Framework supports consuming Web Services by client applications only, and does not natively support hosting them. If you need to support hosting a Web Service using the Compact Framework, you can manually build an HTTP listener (using the `TcpListener` class) and manually handle incoming SOAP requests.

TIP: A great Web site for finding Web Services that are publicly available on the Internet is www.xmethods.com. There you can find Web Services for everything from currency conversion to stock quotes.

In the next section, you will learn what is involved on the client side to consume a Web Service on the Pocket PC.

The Microsoft TerraServer Web Service

The Microsoft TerraServer, located at http://terraserver.microsoft.com, is a massive database (about 3.3 terabytes) of both satellite images and topographic maps for much of the United States. By using TerraServer's search engine, you can zoom in on aerial images for almost any street in the U.S., as well as obtain data about surrounding landmarks. Terra-Server fortunately also provides a Web Service that you can use to perform queries and get maps from the database (which is rather nice, as it would be rather difficult to store all 3.3 terabytes on a Pocket PC).

In this section, we will use the TerraServer Web Services (also called TerraService) as an example of how you can use and consume .NET Web Services on a Pocket PC device using the .NET Compact Framework. More information about the Web Service API that TerraServer provides is available at http://terraserver.homeadvisor.msn.com/webservices.aspx.

The first thing you need to do to consume a Web Service is create a new project. To do this, select the Smart Device Application project type under the Visual C# Project tree. For this example, let's call the new project TerraServiceTest.

After the project has been created, you need to add a new reference for the Web Service you are planning to use in your class. All you need to do is right-click on References in the Solution Explorer and select Add Web Reference (see Figure 12.1).

The Add Web Reference dialog box will appear (see Figure 12.2). In it, you specify the URL for the WSDL or ASMX file that describes the Web Service. The TerraServer Web Service description is located at http://terraserver.homeadvisor.msn.com/TerraService.asmx.

After you have entered the URL, click the Add Reference button. This will cause Visual Studio to generate a proxy class that will be used by

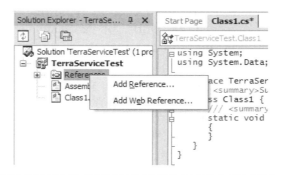

Figure 12.1 Adding a Web reference

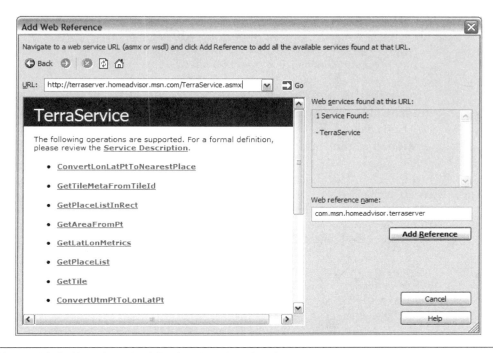

Figure 12.2 Entering the URL for the Web Service

your project to access the Web Service. Once this has completed, you will notice that the reference to the Web Service is now in your project (see Figure 12.3).

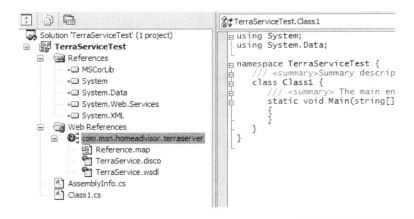

Figure 12.3 The Web reference is added to the project.

Now, all you need to do to use the TerraServer Web Service is add the namespace to your current project as follows:

```
using TerraServiceTest.com.msn.homeadvisor.terraserver;
```

That's it! Your C# program can now use the APIs and structures that are part of the Web Service just as if the component were on the device.

Let's take a look at some sample code that uses TerraService to download a "tile" of satellite image data for the Redmond, Washington, area:

```csharp
using System;
using System.Data;
using System.IO;
using TerraServiceTest.com.msn.homeadvisor.terraserver;

namespace TerraServiceTest {
    /// <summary>Summary description for Class1. </summary>
    class Class1 {
        /// <summary> The main entry point for the
        /// application. </summary>
        static void Main(string[] args) {
            // Create a new TerraService object
            TerraService ts = new TerraService();

            // Build a place to request tile information on
            Place pl = new Place();
            pl.City = "Redmond";
            pl.State = "WA";
            pl.Country = "USA";
            PlaceFacts pf = ts.GetPlaceFacts(pl);

            // Get the bounding box for the area
            AreaBoundingBox abb = ts.GetAreaFromPt(pf.Center,
                Theme.Photo, Scale.Scale16m, 640, 480);

            // Grab the center tile
            Byte[] imageBytes = ts.GetTile(abb.Center.
                TileMeta.Id);

            // Create a new file and dump the buffer to it
            FileStream outputFileStream = new FileStream
                ("\\map.jpg", FileMode.CreateNew);
```

```
BinaryWriter outputBinaryWriter = new BinaryWriter
    (outputFileStream);

// Write
outputBinaryWriter.Write(imageBytes, 0, imageBytes.
    Length);

// Clean up
outputBinaryWriter.Close();
outputFileStream.Close();
    }
  }
}
```

After the class has completed, you can view the downloaded map by launching Pocket Internet Explorer (see Figure 12.4).

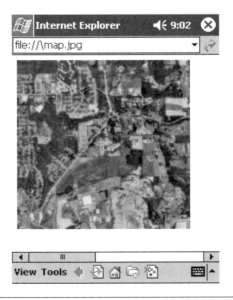

Figure 12.4 Satellite map of the Redmond, WA, area downloaded via TerraServer

Pocket PC and P/Invoke

The last topic we are going to cover regarding the .NET Compact Framework is its ability to call into unmanaged code using **Platform Invoke** (**P/Invoke**). As you have seen throughout this book, most of the APIs that are supported on a Pocket PC platform are exported by using dynamic link libraries (DLLs) that your application imports. By using the P/Invoke service, you can also access the same API functions from within a .NET application. This enables you to integrate much of the functionality that is native to the Pocket PC, and not natively supported by the Compact Framework. For example, the Pocket PC Phone Edition supports the capability to send and receive SMS messages (see Chapter 8). Although the Compact Framework does not come with any classes to support this, you can use P/Invoke to enable your managed code to call into the unmanaged SMS API found in the `cellcore.dll` library.

To declare within your application a method that will use P/Invoke, you need to use the `DllImport` attribute, which supports the fields described in Table 12.16.

Table 12.16 `DllImport` Attributes

Field	Description
EntryPoint	The function name that you want to call into
CharSet	Specifies how the string arguments should be marshaled
CallingConvention	Specifies the calling convention to use when passing arguments
SetLastError	Set this value to TRUE to enable calling the `Marshal.GetLastWin32Error` method to check if an error occurred when invoking this method

For example, the following code shows how you can use the `MessageBox()` function from a managed application by using P/Invoke:

```
using System;
using System.Data;
using System.Runtime.InteropServices;

namespace invokeTest {
   class Class1 {
```

```
    // Hook up Windows API methods
    [DllImport("coredll.dll", EntryPoint="MessageBox",
        CharSet=CharSet.Unicode, SetLastError=true)]
    static extern Int32 MessageBox(Int32 hWnd, string
        stText,
        string stCaption, Int32 mbType);

    static void Main(string[] args) {
        // Call into the MessageBox function
        MessageBox(0, "MessageText", "MessageCaption", 0);
    }
  }
}
```

Once a function has been declared with the DllImport attribute, you can then call it in the same manner as any other managed function.

Note a few minor differences regarding P/Invoke on the .NET Compact Framework when comparing it to its desktop counterpart:

- There is no Unicode-to-ANSI string conversion. All string pointers are passed to an unmanaged function as a Unicode string.
- There is no marshaling of objects contained within structures.
- If a function returns a pointer to a structure, it is not marshaled to a managed structure. You need to create a wrapper function that handles simple data types.
- Platform Invoke services does not support COM interoperability with the Compact Framework. If you wish to call into COM objects, you need to create a wrapper DLL that exports non-COM-based functions.
- The DllImport attribute supports only the CharSet.Unicode and CharSet.Auto character sets.
- The DllImport attribute supports only the CallingConvention.Winapi calling convention.

Sending an SMS Message from .NET

The following example shows a slightly more complicated way of using the Platform Invoke services. Because the Compact Framework does not support the marshaling of objects that are contained within a structure, you need to create a C++ "wrapper" library in order to call the Pocket PC Phone Edition's SMS API functions (see Chapter 8).

First, create the wrapper library using Embedded Visual C++ 3.0.
The code for the library will look as follows:

```
// First is the definition file for the DLL
// smsinvoke.def
LIBRARY    SMSINVOKE
EXPORTS
   SendSMSInvokeMsg    @1


// Here is the wrapper DLL
// smsinvoke.cpp
#include <windows.h>
#include <sms.h>


#ifdef __cplusplus
extern "C" {
#endif
__declspec(dllexport) BOOL SendSMSInvokeMsg(TCHAR
  *tchPhoneNumber, TCHAR *tchMessage);
#ifdef __cplusplus
}
#endif


BOOL WINAPI DllMain(HANDLE hinstDLL, DWORD dwReason,
  LPVOID lpvReserved)
{
   return TRUE;
}


BOOL SendSMSInvokeMsg(TCHAR *tchPhoneNumber, TCHAR
  *tchMessage)
{
   SMS_HANDLE hSms = NULL;
   HANDLE hSmsEvent = NULL;
   HRESULT hr = S_OK;
   BOOL fReturn = FALSE;

   // Make sure we have a number and a message
   if(!tchPhoneNumber || !tchMessage)
      return fReturn;
```

```
// Open up SMS
hr = SmsOpen(SMS_MSGTYPE_TEXT, SMS_MODE_SEND, &hSms,
   &hSmsEvent);

if(FAILED(hr)) {
   OutputDebugString(TEXT("Could not open a handle to
      the SMS text message service."));
   return fReturn;
}

// Wait for SMS to become signaled as ready
DWORD dwReturn = 0;
dwReturn = WaitForSingleObject(hSmsEvent, INFINITE);

// SMS Event has become signaled
if(dwReturn == WAIT_ABANDONED || dwReturn ==
   WAIT_TIMEOUT) {OutputDebugString(TEXT("No longer waiting for
   a message"));
   SmsClose(hSms);
   return fReturn;
}

// Send an SMS Message through default SMSC
SMS_ADDRESS smsDestination;
SMS_MESSAGE_ID smsMsgId = 0;

// Set the destination address for the message
memset(&smsDestination, 0, sizeof(SMS_ADDRESS));
smsDestination.smsatAddressType = SMSAT_INTERNATIONAL;
_tcsncpy(smsDestination.ptsAddress, tchPhoneNumber,
   SMS_MAX_ADDRESS_LENGTH);

// Create the message
DWORD dwMessageLength = 0;
dwMessageLength = lstrlen(tchMessage)*sizeof(TCHAR);

// Configure the Text Provider
TEXT_PROVIDER_SPECIFIC_DATA txtProviderData;
DWORD dwProviderLength = 0;

memset(&txtProviderData, 0, sizeof(TEXT_PROVIDER_
   SPECIFIC_DATA));
```

```
txtProviderData.dwMessageOptions =
   PS_MESSAGE_OPTION_STATUSREPORT;
txtProviderData.psMessageClass = PS_MESSAGE_CLASS0;
txtProviderData.psReplaceOption = PSRO_NONE;
dwProviderLength = sizeof(TEXT_PROVIDER_SPECIFIC_DATA);

// Send the message
hr = SmsSendMessage(hSms, NULL, &smsDestination, NULL,
   (BYTE *)tchMessage, dwMessageLength, (LPBYTE)&txtProviderData,
   dwProviderLength, SMSDE_OPTIMAL, SMS_OPTION_DELIVERY_NONE,
   &smsMsgId);

if(FAILED(hr))
   OutputDebugString(TEXT("Could not send SMS Text
      Message."));
else {
   OutputDebugString(TEXT("Message has been sent."));
   fReturn = TRUE;
}

SmsClose(hSms);
return fReturn;
}
```

Second, use P/Invoke from C# to send an SMS by calling into the wrapper function, as follows:

```
using System;
using System.Data;
using System.Runtime.InteropServices;

namespace SmsInvokeTest {
   class Class1 {
      // Hook up to wrapper function
      [DllImport("smsinvoke.dll", EntryPoint=
         "SendSMSInvokeMsg", CharSet=CharSet.Unicode,
         SetLastError=true)]

      static extern Int32 SendSmsMessage(string
         stPhoneNumber, string stMessage);

      static void Main(string[] args) {
         // Create a message, and send it via SMS
```

```
        string stPhone = "4254432273";
        string stMessage = "Hi there from the Compact
            Framework!";
        int nResult = 0;

        nResult = SendSmsMessage(stPhone, stMessage);
    }
  }
}
```

Index

Register
Your Book
at www.awprofessional.com/register

You may be eligible to receive:

- Advance notice of forthcoming editions of the book
- Related book recommendations
- Chapter excerpts and supplements of forthcoming titles
- Information about special contests and promotions throughout the year
- Notices and reminders about author appearances, tradeshows, and online chats with special guests

Contact us

If you are interested in writing a book or reviewing manuscripts prior to publication, please write to us at:

Editorial Department
Addison-Wesley Professional
75 Arlington Street, Suite 300
Boston, MA 02116 USA
Email: AWPro@aw.com

Visit us on the Web: http://www.awprofessional.com